The
HUMAN
RECORD
Volume II

The HUMAN RECORD

SOURCES OF GLOBAL HISTORY

FIFTH EDITION / Volume II: Since 1500

Alfred J. Andrea

Emeritus Professor of History, University of Vermont

James H. Overfield

Professor of History, University of Vermont

HOUGHTON MIFFLIN COMPANY   BOSTON NEW YORK

Editor-in-Chief: Jean L. Woy
Senior Sponsoring Editor: Nancy Blaine
Senior Development Editor: Julie Dunn
Editorial Associate: Annette Fantasia
Senior Project Editor: Margaret Park Bridges
Manufacturing Coordinator: Carrie Wagner
Senior Marketing Manager: Sandra McGuire

Cover image: The Newark Museum/Art Resource, NY

Source credits appear on pages 539–543, which constitute an extension of the copyright page.

Printed in the U.S.A.

Library of Congress Control Number: 2003110176

ISBN: 0-618-37041-2

123456789-MV-08 07 06 05 04

As always, our love and thanks to
Juanita B. Andrea and Susan L. Overfield

Contents

Geographic Contents

Topical Contents

Religion

Western Expansion and Colonialism

Preface

The fifth edition of *The Human Record: Sources of Global History* follows the principles that guided the first four editions. Foremost is our commitment to the proposition that all students of history must meet the challenge of analyzing primary sources, thereby becoming active inquirers into the past. Working with primary-source evidence enables students to see that historical scholarship is an intellectual process that involves drawing inferences and discovering patterns from clues yielded by the past, not of memorizing someone else's judgments. Furthermore, such analysis motivates students to learn by stimulating curiosity and imagination, and it helps them develop into critical thinkers who are equipped to deal with the complex intellectual challenges of life.

Themes and Structure

We have compiled a source collection that traces the course of human history from the rise of the earliest civilizations to the present. Volume I follows the evolution of cultures that most significantly influenced the history of the world from around 3500 B.C.E. to 1700 C.E., with emphasis on the development of the major social, religious, intellectual, and political traditions of the societies that flourished in Africa and Eurasia. Although our focus in Volume I is on the Eastern Hemisphere, we do not neglect the Americas. Volume I concurrently develops the theme of the growing links and increasingly important exchanges among the world's cultures down to the early modern era. Volume II picks up this theme of growing human interconnectedness by tracing the gradual establishment of Western global hegemony; the simultaneous historical developments in other civilizations and societies around the world; the anti-Western, anticolonial movements of the twentieth century; and the emergence of the twenty-first century's integrated but still often bitterly divided world.

To address these themes in the depth and breadth they deserve, we have chosen primary sources that present an overview of global history in mosaic form. Each source serves two functions: It presents an intimate glimpse into some meaningful aspect of the human past and simultaneously contributes to the creation of a single large picture — an integrated history of the world. With this dual purpose in mind, we have tried to avoid isolated sources that provide a taste of some culture or age but, by their dissociation, shed no light on patterns of cultural creation, continuity, change, and interchange — the essential components of world history.

In selecting and arranging the various pieces of our mosaic, we have sought to create a balanced picture of human history that reflects many different perspectives and experiences. Believing that the study of history properly concerns every aspect of past human activity and thought, we have chosen sources that mirror the practices and concerns of as wide a variety of representative persons and groups as availability and space allow.

Our pursuit of historical balance has also led us into the arena of artifactual evidence. Although most historians center their research on documents, the discipline of history requires us to consider all of the clues surrendered by the past, and these include its artifacts. Moreover, we have discovered that students enjoy analyzing artifacts and seem to remember vividly the insights they draw from them. For these reasons, we have included works of art and other artifacts that users of this book can and should analyze as historical sources.

New to This Edition

We have been gratified with the positive response by colleagues and especially students to the first four editions of *The Human Record*. Many have taken the trouble to write or otherwise contact us to express their satisfaction. No textbook is perfect, however, and these correspondents have been equally generous in sharing their perceptions of how we might improve our book and meet more fully the needs of its readers. Such suggestions, when combined with continuing advances in historical scholarship and our own deeper reflections on a variety of issues, have mandated periodic revisions. In the current revision, as was true in the previous three, our intent has been to make the book as interesting and useful as possible to students and professors alike.

As difficult as it is to let go of sources that have proved valuable and important for us and our students (and our classroom has always been the laboratory in which we test and refine *The Human Record*), we are always searching for sources that enable us and our students to explore more fully and deeply the rich heritage of world history. For this reason, almost one-third of the sources that appear in the fifth edition are new.

In Volume I we added eight new sources relating to the Silk Road and the peoples of Central Asia, scattering them among three chapters. The United States' heightened interest and involvement in the lands and cultures of that region was one factor that led to this decision, but equally important were the voices of many users of the text who asked for more material on the pastoral peoples of Inner Asia and the manner in which they related to their neighbors. Now students can study *The Old Tang History*'s account of how an eighth-century Chinese emperor used an imperial marriage alliance to gain the help of the Uighurs in putting down a civil war. Among the other new Silk Road sources, there is the biography of the nun An Lingshou, which illustrates how Buddhism infiltrated into China from Central Asia during the fifth century; a seventh-century Chinese description of Nalanda, India's premier Buddhist monastery and a magnet for wandering saints and scholars from lands as distant as Persia and Sumatra; and the Spaniard Ruy Gonzalez de Clavijo's description of how Samarqand became the most prosperous city in Central Asia during the Age of Tamerlane.

In response to an avalanche of recent interest in the Sufi poetry of Jalaluddin al-Rumi, Chapter 8 of Volume I contains several of this thirteenth-century mystic's poems and a short excerpt from Ahmed al-Aflaki's biography of al-Rumi, *The Virtues of Those Who Know*. Several other sources also offer the special insight that poetry provides. New selections from the poetry of Du Fu provide, better than ever before, a privileged view of China's turbulent history in the mid eighth century. To illustrate the vivacity of Egypt's New Kingdom, we have included several love songs probably composed by an upper-class woman. Love is also a key element in the *Pillow Book* of Sei Shonagon, an eleventh-century Japanese court lady, whose frank and, at times, scandalous ruminations force us to rethink stereotypical images of East Asian women and their place in society.

American Indian civilizations also get a new look, thanks to three Mayan sculptures and Diego Durán's *Book of the Gods and Rites,* which reveals the confluence of commercial vitality and religion in the Aztec marketplace. Religion and tragic drama existed side by side in the theaters of Classical Greece, and nowhere is this better illustrated than in Euripides' *The Bacchae.* Complementing this masterpiece are three new Hellenic works of art, including the provocative *Meanad,* or female Bacchic devotee.

Among the many other new sources in Volume I, several have received new translations by A. J. Andrea that are improvements on flawed or antiquated available translations. These include works by two first-century Roman authors: Pliny the Elder's description of Roman trade with India and other lands to its east and Tacitus's two accounts of the rebellion of Queen Boudica in first-century Britain. They also include several Roman sources relating to the persecution of Christians and an early-fourteenth-century description of China by the Italian missionary Odoric of Pordenone.

A number of sources carried over from the fourth edition have been reconfigured and revised. In Volume I these include excerpts from China's *Book of Songs,* the *Analects of Confucius,* the *Quran,* Charlemagne's *Capitularies,* excerpts from the writings of Maimonides, as well as the already-mentioned poems of Du Fu.

Longtime users of Volume II of *The Human Record* will note that its organization in the fifth edition has been changed in subtle but significant ways. First, the chapter order of Part One has been recast. Ever since the second edition, this part has begun with a chapter on Europe, with those on Africa and the Americas, South and Southwest Asia, and East and Southeast Asia following. This arrangement sent the unintended message to some of our students that Europe came first because it was more important, more advanced, and more powerful than other regions of the world. Putting Europe first for such reasons might be defensible for later periods in world history, but certainly not for the years covered in these initial chapters, when in most fields of human endeavor — art, literature, technology, government, military power, agriculture, commerce, and manufacturing — Europe lagged behind the older civilizations of the Middle East, India, and East Asia. Now European material is covered in Chapter 3, which follows chapters on East and Southeast Asia and the Islamic heartland and precedes the material on Africa and the Americas, the two regions most affected by Europe's overseas expansion.

The other organizational change in Volume II is that material on the world since 1945 has been broken down into two chapters, meaning that for the first time in its publishing history Volume II of *The Human Record* will have fourteen, not thirteen, chapters. The reason for the change is simple: Time marches on and history expands. Ever since the first edition of *The Human Record* Chapter 13 has been entitled "The Global Community since 1945." In the first edition this meant it covered forty-five years of recent history, already a formidable task. For the fifth edition the number of years to be covered increased almost 33 percent to almost sixty years. In these additional years the Cold War ended, the Soviet Union collapsed, the Internet revolution took place, globalization became a hot topic, new pandemics swept the world, and world terrorism emerged as a major threat. In this edition Chapter 13 covers the period from 1945 to the mid 1980s, while Chapter 14 covers the last two decades.

Of the approximately forty new sources in Volume II, four are in Chapter 14. Two sources are devoted to the debate on the role of free trade and open markets in the new global economy, with Ralph Nader's 1993 anti-NAFTA essay representing free trade's critics and the excerpt from Brookings Institution scholars' 1998 book *Globaphobia* presenting the views of free trade's defenders. Chapter 14 also includes a section on terrorism, with focus on the events of September 11, 2001. The subsection consists of two sources: first, excerpts from Osama bin Laden's 1996 "Declaration of Jihad against Americans," and second, excerpts from "The Last Night," the list of instructions drawn up by the chief planner of the September 11 suicide missions, Mohammed Atta, that was to be read by the participants on the evening of September 10.

The other new sources for Volume II fall into two main categories. First, a number of sources that appeared in one or more of the first three editions of the book and disappeared in later editions reappear in the fifth edition. Every source we drop from one edition of the book to the next is someone's favorite, and we usually hear about it via e-mail, phone calls, letters, or conversations at professional meetings. It appears that quite a few people favored some of the sources dropped from the fourth edition, such as Darwin's writings on evolution, Voltaire's moving defense of religious toleration, Anna Bijn's spirited poem "Unyoked Is Best," the "Declaration of the Rights of Man and of the Citizen," and the encomienda records from Nestalpa, Mexico. All of these have been reinstated.

Totally new sources make up the second category. They have been introduced to the fifth edition because we believe they will be more effective and useful for classroom teaching than those they replaced. Several new sources on women have been introduced to strengthen what has been an emphasis in *The Human Record* since it first appeared. They include excerpts from Leon Battista Alberti's *On the Family,* a book that provides instructive insights into upper-class Florentine male attitudes toward wives and daughters. It has the further advantage of adding a source on the Italian Renaissance. Chapter 2 includes a new source consisting of legal opinions and judgments by the seventeenth-century Islamic jurist Khayr al-Din Ramli pertaining to marriage, divorce, and sexual abuse in the region of Syria-Palestine in the Ottoman Empire. It is a fascinating source, with much more potential for classroom use than the short section on divorce from Ogier de Busbecq's *Turkish Letters* that had to suffice in previous editions.

Other new sources in Volume II include three documents in Chapter 3 on the motives behind Europe's overseas expansion (excerpts from Azurara's *Chronicle of Guinea*; the 1492 agreement between Columbus and the Spanish monarchs; and Hakluyt's *A Discourse on Western Planting*). Chapter 5 now includes a series of political cartoons that illustrates the loss of privilege on the part of the clergy and nobility in the early years of the French Revolution. A soldier's memoir has been added to Chapter 11 to convey the horrors and futility of trench warfare in World War I. It replaces poems by Wilfred Owen and two artworks, which our students found moving but did not spark much in the way of class discussion. Excerpts from Theodor Herzl's *The Jews' State* have been added to the section on European nationalism in Chapter 8, and sources on sixteenth-century Chinese commerce, German reaction to the Treaty of Versailles, and pre–World War II Japanese nationalism also appear for the first time.

We also have an obligation to reflect in our work the most up-to-date scholarly discoveries and controversies. With that in mind, we have revised many of our introductions and commentaries. More than one-third of the pages dedicated to editorial commentary and notes have been rewritten.

Learning Aids

Source analysis can be a daunting challenge for any student. With this in mind, we have labored to make these sources as accessible as possible by providing the student-user with a variety of aids. First there is the *Prologue,* in which we explain, initially in a theoretical manner and then through concrete examples, how a historian interprets written and artifactual sources. Next we offer *part, chapter, sub-chapter,* and *individual source introductions* — all to help the reader place each selection into a meaningful context and understand each source's significance. Because we consider *The Human Record* to be an interpretive overview of global history and therefore a survey of the major patterns of global history that stands on its own as a text, our introductions are significantly fuller than what one normally encounters in a book of sources.

Suggested *Questions for Analysis* precede each source; their purpose is to help the student make sense of each piece of evidence and wrest from it as much insight as possible. The questions are presented in a three-tiered format designed to resemble the historian's approach to source analysis and to help students make historical comparisons on a global scale. The first several questions are usually quite specific and ask the reader to pick out important pieces of information. These initial questions require the student to address two issues: What does this document or artifact say, and what meaningful facts can I garner from it? Addressing concrete questions of this sort prepares the student researcher for the next, more significant, level of critical thinking and analysis: drawing inferences. Questions that demand inferential conclusions follow the fact-oriented questions. Finally, whenever possible, we offer a third tier of questions that challenge the student to compare the individual or society that produced a particular source with an individual, group, or culture encountered earlier in the volume. We believe such comparisons help students fix more firmly in their minds the distinguishing cultural characteristics of the various societies they encounter in their survey of world history. Beyond that, it underscores the fact that global history is, at least on one level, comparative history.

Another form of help we offer is to *gloss the sources,* explaining fully words and allusions that first-year college students cannot reasonably be expected to know. To facilitate reading and to encourage reference, the notes appear at the bottom of the page on which they are cited. A few documents also contain *interlinear notes* that serve as transitions or provide needed information.

Some instructors might use *The Human Record* as their sole textbook. Most will probably use it as a supplement to a standard narrative textbook, and many of these might decide not to require their students to analyze every entry. To assist instructors (and students) in selecting sources that best suit their interests and needs, we have prepared *two analytical tables of contents* for each volume. The first lists readings and artifacts by geographic and cultural area, the second by topic. The two tables suggest to professor and student alike the rich variety of material available within these pages, particularly for essays in comparative history.

In summary, our goal in crafting *The Human Record* has been to do our best to prepare the student-reader for success — *success* being defined as comfort with historical analysis, proficiency in critical thinking, learning to view history on a global scale, and a deepened awareness of the rich cultural varieties, as well as shared characteristics, of the human family.

Using The Human Record: *Suggestions from the Editors*

Specific suggestions for assignments and classroom activities appear in the manual *Using* The Human Record: *Suggestions from the Editors*. In it we explain why we have chosen the sources that appear in this book and what insights we believe students should be capable of drawing from them. We also describe classroom exercises for encouraging student thought and discussion on the various sources. The advice we present is the fruit of our own use of these sources in the classroom.

Feedback

As already suggested, we want to receive comments and suggestions from professors and students who are using this book. Comments on the Prologue and Volume I should be addressed to A. J. Andrea, whose e-mail address is <Alfred.Andrea@uvm.edu>; comments on Volume II should be addressed to J. H. Overfield at <James.Overfield@uvm.edu>.

Acknowledgments

We are in debt to the many professionals who offered their expert advice and assistance during the various incarnations of *The Human Record*. Scholars and friends at The University of Vermont who generously shared their expertise with us over the years as we crafted these five editions include Abbas Alnasrawi, Doris Bergen, Robert V. Daniels, Carolyn Elliott, Bogac Ergene, Shirley Gedeon, Erik Gilbert, William Haviland, Walter Hawthorn, Richard Horowitz, William Mierse, George Moyser, Kristin M. Peterson-Ishaq, Abubaker Saad, Wolfe W. Schmokel, Peter Seybolt, John W. Seyller, Sean Stilwell, Marshall True, Diane Villemaire, Janet Whatley, and Denise Youngblood. Additionally, Ms. Tara Coram of the Arthur M. Sackler Gallery and Freer Gallery of Art of the Smithsonian Institution deserves special thanks for the assistance she rendered A. J. Andrea in his exploration of the Asian art holdings of the two museums.

We wish also to acknowledge the following instructors whose comments on the fourth edition helped guide our revision: Timothy Connell, Laurel School; Moshe Gershovich, University of Nebraska at Omaha; Erik Gilbert, Arkansas State University; Randee Brenner Goodstadt, Asheville-Buncombe Technical Community College; Richard S. Horowitz, California State University, Northridge; Cynthia Kosso, Northern Arizona University; Scott C. Levi, University of Louisville; Yihong Pan, Miami University; James A. Polk, College of Charleston; Harold M. Tanner, University of North Texas; and Ronald Young, Georgia Southern University.

Finally, our debt to our spouses is beyond payment, but the dedication to them of each edition of this book reflects in some small way how deeply we appreciate their constant support and good-humored tolerance.

A. J. A.
J. H. O.

The
HUMAN
RECORD
Volume II

Prologue

Primary Sources and How to Read Them

Imagine a course in chemistry in which students never set foot in a laboratory; or a literature course in which they read commentaries on Shakespeare's plays but none of the plays; or a course on the history of jazz in which they never listen to a note of music. Most students would consider such courses strange and deficient, and many would soon be beating a path to the door of their academic advisor or college dean with complaints about flawed teaching methods and wasted tuition payments. No one can understand chemistry without doing experiments. No one can understand literature without reading plays, poetry, and fiction. No one can understand music without listening to performances.

In much the same way, no one can understand history without reading and analyzing *primary sources*. Although we shall see an exception to the rule when we look at oral traditions, in most instances, *primary sources are historical records produced at the same time the event or period that is being studied took place or soon thereafter.* They are distinct from *secondary sources* — books, articles, television documentaries, and even historical films — produced well after the events they describe and interpret. Secondary sources — *histories* in the conventional sense of the term — organize the jumble of past events into understandable narratives. They also provide interpretations, make comparisons, and discuss motive and causation. When done well, they provide pleasure and insight to their readers and viewers. But such works, no matter how well done, are still secondary, in that they are written well after the fact and, more important, derive their evidence and information from primary sources.

History is an ambitious discipline that deals with all aspects of past human activity and belief. This means that the primary sources historians use to recreate the past are equally wide-ranging and diverse. Most of the primary sources they use are written sources — government records, law codes, private correspondence, literary works, religious texts, merchants' account books, memoirs, and the list goes on almost endlessly. So important are written records to the study of history that societies and cultures that had or have no system of writing are called *prehistoric* — not because they lack a history but because there is no way to construct a detailed narrative of their histories due to the lack of written records. Of course, even so-called prehistoric societies leave behind evidence of their experiences, creativity, and belief systems in their *oral traditions* and their *artifacts*.

Let us look first at oral traditions — the remembered past passed down by word of mouth. The difficulty of working with such evidence is significant. You are aware of how stories change as they are transmitted from person to person. Imagine how difficult it is to use such stories as historical evidence. Yet, despite the challenge they offer us, these sources cannot be overlooked. Although the oral traditions of ancient societies were often written down long after they were first articulated, they are often the only recorded evidence that we have of a far-distant society or event. So, the farther back in history we go, the more we see the inadequacy of the definition of primary sources that we offered above ("historical records produced at the same time the event or period that is being studied took place or soon thereafter"). The early chapters of Volume I contain quite a few primary sources based on oral traditions. We will inform you when this is the case and offer you sufficient information and suggestions as to which questions you can validly ask of them to enable you to use them effectively.

Artifacts can help us place oral traditions into a clearer context by producing tangible evidence that supports or calls into question legends. Artifacts can also tell us something about prehistoric societies whose oral traditions are lost to us. They even serve as primary sources for historians who study literate cultures. Written records, no matter how extensive and diverse, never allow us to draw a complete picture of the past, and we can fill at least some of those gaps by studying what human hands have fashioned. Everyday objects, such as fabrics, tools, kitchen implements, weapons, farm equipment, jewelry, pieces of furniture, and family photographs, provide windows into the ways that common people lived. Grander cultural products — paintings, sculpture, buildings, musical compositions, and, more recently, film — are equally important because they also reflect the values, attitudes, and styles of living of their creators and those for whom they were created.

To be a historian is to work with primary sources. But to do so effectively is not an easy task. Each source provides only one glimpse of reality, and no single source by itself gives us the whole picture of past events and developments. Many sources are difficult to understand, and can be interpreted only after the precise meaning of their words have been deciphered and their backgrounds thoroughly investigated. Many sources contain distortions and errors that can be discovered only by rigorous internal analysis and comparison with evidence from other sources. Only after all these source-related difficulties have been overcome can a historian hope to achieve a coherent and reasonably accurate understanding of the past.

To illustrate some of the challenges of working with primary sources, let us imagine a time in the mid twenty-first century when a historian decides to write a history of your college class in connection with its fiftieth reunion. Since no one has written a book or article about your class, our historian has no secondary sources to consult, and must rely entirely on primary sources. What primary sources might he or she use? The list would be a long one: the school catalogue, class lists, academic transcripts, yearbooks, college rules and regulations, and similar official documents; lecture notes, syllabi, examinations, term papers, and textbooks; diaries and private letters; articles from the campus newspaper and programs for sporting events, concerts, and plays; posters and handbills; recollections written down or otherwise recorded by some of your classmates long after they graduated. With a bit of thought you could add other items to the list, among them some artifacts, such as souvenirs sold in the campus store, and other unwritten sources, such as recordings of music popular at the time and photographs and videotapes of student life and activity.

Even with this imposing list of sources our future historian will only have an incomplete record of the events that made up your class's experiences. Many of those moments — telephone conversations, meetings with professors, and gossip exchanged at the student union — never made it into any written record. Also consider the fact that all the sources available to our future historian will be fortunate survivors. They will represent only a small percentage of the material generated by you, your classmates, professors, and administrators over a two- or four-year period. Wastebaskets and recycling bins will have claimed much written material; the "delete" key and inevitable changes in computer technology might make it impossible to retrieve basic sources, such as your college's website, e-mail, and a vast amount of other online materials. It is also probable that it will be difficult to find information about certain groups within your class, such as part-time students, nontraditional students, and commuters. The past always has its so-called silent or near-silent groups of people. Of course, they were never truly silent, but often nobody was listening to them. It is the historian's task to find whatever evidence exists that gives them a voice, but often that evidence is tantalizingly slim.

For these reasons, the evidence available to our future historian will be fragmentary at best. This is always the case when doing historical research. The records of the past cannot be retained in their totality, not even those that pertain to the recent past.

How will our future historian use the many individual pieces of surviving documentary evidence about your class? As he or she reviews the list, it will quickly become apparent that no single primary source provides a complete or unbiased picture. Each source has its own perspective, value, and limitations. Imagine that the personal essays submitted by applicants for admission were a historian's only sources of information about the student body. On reading them, our researcher might draw the false conclusion that the school attracted only the most gifted, talented, interesting, and intellectually committed students imaginable.

Despite their flaws, however, essays composed by applicants for admission can still be important pieces of historical evidence. They certainly reflect the would-be students' perceptions of the school's cultural values and the types of people it hopes to attract, and usually the applicants are right on the mark because they have read the school's catalogue and the brochures prepared for prospective students by the admissions office. Admissions materials and, to a degree, even the catalogue, are forms of creative advertising, and both present an idealized picture of campus life. But such publications have value for the careful researcher because they reflect the values of the faculty and administrators who composed them. The catalogue also provides useful information regarding rules and regulations, courses, instructors, school organizations, and similar items. Such factual information, however, is the raw material of history, not history itself, and certainly it does not reflect anything close to the full historical reality of your class's collective experience.

What is true of the catalogue is equally true of the student newspaper and every other piece of evidence pertinent to your class. Each primary source is a part of a larger whole, but as we have already seen, we do not have all the pieces. Think of historical evidence in terms of a jigsaw puzzle. Many of the pieces are missing, but it is possible to put most, though probably not all, of the remaining pieces together in a fashion to form a fairly accurate and coherent picture. The picture that emerges will not be complete, but it can still be useful and valid. The keys to fitting these pieces together are hard work and imagination. Each is absolutely necessary.

Examining Primary Sources

Hard work speaks for itself, but students are often unaware that historians also need imagination to reconstruct the past. After all, many students ask, doesn't history consist of strictly defined and irrefutable dates, names, and facts? Where does imagination enter into the process of learning these facts? Again, let us consider your class's history and its documentary sources. Many of those documents provide factual data — dates, names, grades, statistics. While these data are important, individually and collectively they have no historical meaning until they have been *interpreted*. Your college class is more than a collection of statistics and facts. It is a group of individuals who, despite their differences, shared and helped mold a collective experience. It was and is a community evolving within a particular time and place. Any valid or useful history must reach beyond dates, names, and facts and interpret the historical characteristics and role of your class. What were its values? How did it change and why? What impact did it have? These are some of the important questions a historian asks of the evidence.

To arrive at answers, the historian must examine each and every piece of relevant evidence in its full context and wring from that evidence as many *inferences* as possible. *An inference is a logical conclusion drawn from evidence, and it is the heart and soul of historical inquiry.* Facts are the raw materials of history, but inferences are its finished products.

Every American schoolchild learns at an early age that "in fourteen hundred and ninety-two, Columbus sailed the ocean blue." In subsequent history classes, he or she might learn other facts about the famous explorer: that he was born in Genoa in 1451; that he made three other transatlantic voyages in 1493, 1497, and 1503; that he died in Spain in 1506. Knowing these facts is of little value, however, unless it contributes to our understanding of the motives, causes, and significance of Columbus's voyages. Why did Columbus sail west? Why did Spain support such enterprises? Why were Europeans willing and able to exploit, as they did, the so-called New World? What were the short- and long-term consequences of the European presence in the Americas? Finding answers to questions such as these are the historian's ultimate goal, and these answers can only be found in primary sources.

One noted historian, Robin Winks, has written a book entitled *The Historian as Detective,* and the image is appropriate although inexact. Like a detective, the historian examines evidence to reconstruct events. Like a detective, the historian is interested in discovering "what happened, who did it, and why." Like a detective interrogating witnesses, *the historian also must carefully examine the testimony of sources.*

First and foremost, the historian must evaluate the *validity* of the source. Is it what it purports to be? Artful forgeries have misled many historians. Even authentic sources still can be misleading if the author lied or deliberately misrepresented reality. In addition, the historian can easily be led astray by not fully understanding the *perspective* reflected in the document. As is soon learned by any detective who has examined eyewitnesses to an event, witnesses' accounts often differ widely. The detective has the opportunity to re-examine witnesses and offer them the opportunity to change their testimony in the light of new evidence and deeper reflection. The historian is not so fortunate. Even when the historian compares a piece of documentary evidence with other evidence in order to uncover its flaws, there is no way to cross-examine its author. Given this fact, it is absolutely necessary for the historian to understand as fully as possible the source's perspective. Thus, the historian must ask several key questions — all of which share the letter W.

- *What* kind of document is it?
- *Who* wrote it?
- For *whom* and *why*?
- *Where* was it composed and *when*?

What is important because understanding the nature of a source gives the historian an idea of what kind of information he or she can expect to find in it. Many sources simply do not address the questions a historian would like to ask of them, and knowing this can save a great deal of frustration. Your class's historian would be foolish to try to learn much about the academic quality of your school's courses from a study of the registrar's class lists and grade sheets. Student and faculty class notes, copies of syllabi, examinations, student papers, and textbooks would be far more useful.

Who, for whom, and *why* are equally important questions. The school catalogue and publicity materials prepared by the admissions office undoubtedly address some issues pertaining to student social life. But should documents like these — designed to attract potential students and to place the school in the best possible light — be read and accepted uncritically? Obviously not. They must be tested against student testimony discovered in such sources as private letters, memoirs, posters, the student newspaper, and the yearbook.

Where and *when* are also important questions to ask of any primary source. As a rule, distance from an event in space and time colors perceptions and can diminish the reliability of a source. Recollections of a person celebrating a twenty-fifth class reunion could be an insightful and valuable source of information for your class's historian. Conceivably this graduate would have a perspective and information that he or she lacked a quarter of a century earlier. Just as conceivably, that person's memory of what college was like might have faded to the point where his recollections have little value.

You and the Sources

This book will actively involve you in the work of historical inquiry by asking you to draw inferences based on your analysis of primary source evidence. This might prove difficult at first, but it is well within your capability.

You will analyze two types of evidence: documents and artifacts. Each source will be authentic, so you do not have to worry about validating it. Editorial material in this book also supplies you with the information necessary to place each piece of evidence into its proper context and will suggest questions you legitimately can and should ask of each source.

It is important to keep in mind that historians approach each source they consider with questions, even though they might be vaguely formulated. Like detectives, historians want to discover some particular truth or shed light on a particular issue. This requires asking specific questions of the witnesses or, in the historian's case, of the evidence. These questions should not be prejudgments. One of the worst errors a historian can make is setting out to prove a point or to defend an ideological position. Questions are essential, but they are starting points, nothing else. Therefore, as you approach a source, have your question or questions fixed in your mind and constantly remind yourself as you work your way through a source what issue or issues you are investigating. Each source in this anthology is preceded by a number of suggested *Questions for Analysis.* You or your professor might want to ask other questions. Whatever the case, keep focused on your questions and issues, and take notes as you read a source. Never rely on unaided memory; it will almost inevitably lead you astray.

Above all else, you must be honest and thorough as you study a source. Read each explanatory footnote carefully to avoid misunderstanding a word or an allusion. Try to understand exactly what the source is saying and what its author's perspective is. Be careful not to wrench items, words, or ideas out of context, thereby distorting them. Be sure to read the entire source so that you understand as fully as possible what it says and does not say.

This is not as difficult as it sounds. But it does take concentration and work. And do not let the word "work" mislead you. True, primary source analysis demands attention to detail and some hard thought, but it is also rewarding. There is great satisfaction in developing a deeper and truer understanding of the past based on a careful exploration of the evidence.

Analyzing Two Sample Sources

To illustrate how you should go about this task and what is expected of you, we will now take you through a sample exercise, in which we analyze two sources:

a document from the pen of Christopher Columbus and an early-sixteenth-century woodcut. We present each source as it would appear in this book: first an introduction, then suggested Questions for Analysis, and finally the source itself, with explanatory notes. Because we want to give you a full introduction to the art of documentary source analysis, this excerpt is longer than any other document in the book. Also, in order to help you refer back to the letter as we analyze it, we have numbered each fifth line. No other source in this book will have numbered lines. Our notes that comment on the text are probably fuller than necessary, but we prefer to err on the side of providing too much information and help rather than too little. But do not let the length of the document or its many notes intimidate you. Once you get into the source, you should find it fairly easy going.

"With the Royal Standard Unfurled"
▼▼▼

▼ *Christopher Columbus,*
A LETTER CONCERNING RECENTLY DISCOVERED ISLANDS

Sixteenth-century Spain's emergence as the dominant power in the Americas is forever associated with the name of a single mariner — Christopher Columbus (1451–1506). Sponsored by King Ferdinand II of Aragon and Queen Isabella I of Castile, this Genoese sea captain sailed west into the Atlantic seeking a new route to the empires of East Asia described by John Mandeville, Marco Polo, and other travel writers he had avidly read. On October 12, 1492, his fleet of three ships dropped anchor at a small Bahamian island, which Columbus claimed for Spain, naming it San Salvador. The fleet then sailed to two larger islands, which he named Juana and Española (today known as Cuba and Hispaniola).

After exploring these two islands and establishing on Española the fort of Navidad del Señor, Columbus departed for Spain in January 1493. On his way home, the admiral prepared a preliminary account of his expedition to the "Indies" for Luis de Santángel, a counselor to King Ferdinand and one of Columbus's enthusiastic supporters. In composing the letter, Columbus borrowed heavily from his official ship's log, often lifting passages verbatim. When he landed in Lisbon in early March, Columbus dispatched the letter overland, expecting it to precede him to the Spanish royal court in faraway Barcelona, where Santángel would communicate its contents to the two monarchs. The admiral was not disappointed. His triumphal reception at the court in April was proof that the letter had served its purpose.

QUESTIONS FOR ANALYSIS

1. What does Columbus's description of the physical attributes of the islands suggest about the motives for his voyage?
2. Often the eyes only see what the mind prepares them to see. Is there any evidence that Columbus saw what he wanted to see and discovered what he expected to discover?
3. Is there any evidence that Columbus's letter was a carefully crafted piece of self-promotion by a person determined to prove he had reached the Indies?
4. Is there any evidence that Columbus attempted to present an objective and fairly accurate account of what he had seen and experienced?
5. In light of your answers to questions 2–4, to what extent, if at all, can we trust Columbus's account?
6. What do the admiral's admitted actions regarding the natives and the ways in which he describes these people allow us to conclude about his attitudes toward these "Indians" and his plans for them?
7. What does this letter tell us about the culture of the Tainos on the eve of European expansion into their world? Is there anything that Columbus tells us about these people that does not seem to ring totally true?
8. How, if at all, does this letter illustrate that a single historical source read in isolation can mislead the researcher?

1 Sir, as I know that you will be pleased at the great victory with which Our Lord has crowned my voyage, I write this to you, from which you will learn how in thirty-three days, I passed from the 5 Canary Islands to the Indies[1] with the fleet which the most illustrious king and queen, our sovereigns, gave to me. And there I found very many islands filled with people[2] innumerable, and of them all I have taken possession for their high- 10 nesses, by proclamation made and with the royal standard unfurled, and no opposition was offered to me. To the first island which I found, I gave the name *San Salvador,*[3] in remembrance of the Divine Majesty, Who has marvelously bestowed 15 all this; the Indians call it "Guanahani." To the second, I gave the name *Isla de Santa Maria de Concepción;*[4] to the third, *Fernandina;* to the fourth, *Isabella;* to the fifth, *Isla Juana,*[5] and so to each one I gave a new name.

When I reached Juana, I followed its coast to 20 the westward, and I found it to be so extensive that I thought that it must be the mainland, the province of Catayo.[6] And since there were neither towns nor villages on the seashore, but only small hamlets, with the people of which I could not 25 have speech, because they all fled immediately, I went forward on the same course, thinking that I should not fail to find great cities and towns. And, at the end of many leagues,[7] seeing that there was no change and that the coast was bear- 30 ing me northwards, which I wished to avoid, since winter was already beginning, . . . [I] retraced my path as far as a certain harbor known to me. And from that point, I sent two men inland

---

[1]A term that referred to the entire area of the Indian Ocean and East Asia.
[2]The Tainos, a tribal branch of the Arawak language family. Arawak speakers inhabited an area from the Amazon River to the Caribbean.
[3]"Holy Savior," Jesus Christ.
[4]"The Island of Holy Mary of the Immaculate Conception." Catholics believe that Mary, the mother of Jesus, was abso-

lutely sinless, to the point that she was conceived without the stain of Original Sin (the sin of Adam and Eve) on her soul.
[5]Named for Prince Juan, heir apparent of Castile.
[6]The Spanish term for *Cathay* — technically northern China. Columbus, however, meant by it the entire Chinese Empire of the Great Khan (see note 23).
[7]A league is about three miles.

35 to learn if there were a king or great cities. They traveled three days' journey and found an infinity of small hamlets and people without number, but nothing of importance. For this reason, they returned.

40 I understood sufficiently from other Indians, whom I had already taken,[8] that this land was nothing but an island. And therefore I followed its coast eastwards for one hundred and seven leagues to the point where it ended. And from 45 that cape, I saw another island . . . to which I at once gave the name "Española." And I went there and followed its northern coast. . . . This island and all the others are very fertile to a limitless degree, and this island is extremely so. In it there 50 are many harbors on the coast of the sea, beyond comparison with others which I know in Christendom, and many rivers, good and large, which is marvelous. Its lands are high, and there are in it very many sierras and very lofty mountains, be-55 yond comparison with the island of Teneriffe.[9] All are most beautiful, of a thousand shapes, and all are accessible and filled with trees of a thousand kinds and tall, and they seem to touch the sky. And I am told that they never lose their foliage, as 60 I can understand, for I saw them as green and as lovely as they are in Spain in May, and some of them were flowering, some bearing fruit, and some in another stage, according to their nature. And the nightingale was singing and other birds 65 of a thousand kinds in the month of November there where I went. There are six or eight kinds of palm, which are a wonder to behold on account of their beautiful variety, but so are the other trees and fruits and plants. In it are marvelous pine 70 groves, and there are very large tracts of cultivatable lands, and there is honey, and there are birds of many kinds and fruits in great diversity. In the interior are mines of metals, and the population is without number. Española is a marvel.

The sierras and mountains, the plains and 75 arable lands and pastures, are so lovely and rich for planting and sowing, for breeding cattle of every kind, for building towns and villages. The harbors of the sea here are such as cannot be believed to exist unless they have been seen, and so 80 with the rivers, many and great, and good waters, the majority of which contain gold.[10] In the trees and fruits and plants, there is a great difference from those of Juana. In this island, there are many spices and great mines of gold and of other 85 metals.

The people of this island, and of all the other islands which I have found and of which I have information, all go naked, men and women, as their mothers bore them,[11] although some 90 women cover a single place with the leaf of a plant or with a net of cotton which they make for the purpose. They have no iron or steel or weapons, nor are they fitted to use them, not because they are not well built men and of hand-95 some stature, but because they are very marvelously timorous. They have no other arms than weapons made of canes, cut in seeding time, to the ends of which they fix a small sharpened 100 stick. And they do not dare to make use of these, for many times it has happened that I have sent ashore two or three men to some town to have speech, and countless people have come out to them, and as soon as they have seen my men ap-105 proaching they have fled, even a father not waiting for his son. And this, not because ill has been done to anyone; on the contrary, at every point where I have been and have been able to have speech, I have given to them of all that I had, 110 such as cloth and many other things, without receiving anything for it; but so they are, incurably timid. It is true that, after they have been reassured and have lost their fear, they are so guileless and so generous with all they possess, that no one 115

---

[8]Columbus took seven Tainos on board at San Salvador to instruct them in Spanish and use them as guides and interpreters.

[9]One of the Canary Islands.

[10]Although Columbus obtained items of gold and received plenty of reports of nearby gold mines, the metal was rare in the islands.

[11]Marco Polo described a number of islanders in South Asia who went naked. Compare also Columbus's description of this nudity with John Mandeville's account of the people of Sumatra in Volume I, Chapter 12, source 98.

120 would believe it who has not seen it. They never refuse anything which they possess, if it be asked of them; on the contrary, they invite anyone to share it, and display as much love as if they would give their hearts, and whether the thing be of
125 value or whether it be of small price, at once with whatever trifle of whatever kind it may be that is given to them, with that they are content.[12] I forbade that they should be given things so worthless as fragments of broken crockery and scraps of
130 broken glass, and ends of straps, although when they were able to get them, they fancied that they possessed the best jewel in the world. So it was found that a sailor for a strap received gold to the weight of two and a half *castellanos,*[13] and others
135 much more for other things which were worth much less. As for new *blancas,*[14] for them they would give everything which they had, although it might be two or three *castellanos'* weight of gold or an *arroba*[15] or two of spun cotton. . . .
140 They took even the pieces of the broken hoops of the wine barrels and, like savages, gave what they had, so that it seemed to me to be wrong and I forbade it. And I gave a thousand handsome good things, which I had brought, in order that they
145 might conceive affection, and more than that, might become Christians and be inclined to the love and service of their highnesses and of the whole Castilian nation, and strive to aid us and to give us of the things which they have in abun-
150 dance and which are necessary to us. And they do not know any creed and are not idolaters;[16] only they all believe that power and good are in the heavens, and they are very firmly convinced that I, with these ships and men, came from the heav-
155 ens, and in this belief they everywhere received

me, after they had overcome their fear. And this does not come because they are ignorant; on the contrary, they are of a very acute intelligence and are men who navigate all those seas, so that it is amazing how good an account they give of every- 160 thing, but it is because they have never seen people clothed or ships of such a kind.

And as soon as I arrived in the Indies, in the first island which I found, I took by force some of them, in order that they might learn and give me 165 information of that which there is in those parts, and so it was that they soon understood us, and we them, either by speech or signs, and they have been very serviceable. I still take them with me, and they are always assured that I come from 170 Heaven, for all the intercourse which they have had with me; and they were the first to announce this wherever I went, and the others went running from house to house and to the neighboring towns, with loud cries of, "Come! Come to see 175 the people from Heaven!" So all, men and women alike, when their minds were set at rest concerning us, came, so that not one, great or small, remained behind, and all brought something to eat and drink, which they gave with ex- 180 traordinary affection. In all the island, they have very many canoes, like rowing *fustas,*[17] some larger, some smaller, and some are larger than a *fusta* of eighteen benches. They are not so broad, because they are made of a single log of wood, but a 185 *fusta* would not keep up with them in rowing, since their speed is a thing incredible. And in these they navigate among all those islands, which are innumerable, and carry their goods. One of these canoes I have seen with seventy and 190 eighty men in her, and each one with his oar.

---

[12]Compare this with Mandeville's description of the people of Sumatra's attitude toward possessions (see note 11).

[13]A gold coin of considerable value that bore the seal of Castile.

[14]The smallest and least valuable Spanish coin, it was worth about one-sixtieth of a castellano. It had a whitish hue, hence the name *blanca,* or white.

[15]The equivalent of about sixteen skeins, or balls, of spun textile.

[16]Normally *idolater* means someone who worships idols, or sacred statues, but it is unclear exactly what Columbus

means here. The Tainos worshiped a variety of deities and spirits known as *cemis,* whom they represented in stone statues and other images, also known as cemis. It is hard to imagine Columbus's not having seen carved cemis, which filled the Tainos' villages. To compound the problem of what Columbus meant by their not being idolaters, consider lines 289–291 of this letter, where he refers to idolaters who will be enslaved.

[17]A small oared boat, often having one or two masts.

In all these islands, I saw no great diversity in the appearance of the people or in their manners and language. On the contrary, they all under-
195 stand one another,[18] which is a very curious thing, on account of which I hope that their highnesses will determine upon their conversion to our holy faith, towards which they are very in-clined. . . .

200 I can say that [Juana] is larger than England and Scotland together,[19] for . . . there remain to the westward two provinces to which I have not gone. One of these provinces they call "Avan,"[20] and there the people are born with tails;[21] . . . as I
205 could understand from those Indians whom I have and who know all the islands.

The other, Española, has a circumference greater than all Spain.[22] . . . It is a land to be de-sired and, seen, it is never to be left. And . . . I
210 have taken possession for their highnesses . . . this Española, in [a] situation most convenient and in the best position for the mines of gold and for all intercourse as well with the mainland . . . belonging to the Grand Khan,[23] where will be
215 great trade and gain. I have taken possession of a large town, to which I gave the name *Villa de Navidad*,[24] and in it I have made fortifications and a fort, which now will by this time be entire-ly finished, and I have left in it sufficient men for such a purpose with arms and artillery and provi- 220 sions for more than a year, and a *fusta*, and one, a master of all seacraft, to build others, and great friendship with the king of that land, so much so, that he was proud to call me, and to treat me as a brother. And even if he were to change his atti- 225 tude to one of hostility towards these men, he and his do not know what arms are and they go naked, as I have already said, and are the most timorous people that there are in the world, so that the men whom I have left there alone would 230 suffice to destroy all that land, and the island is without danger for their persons, if they know how to govern themselves.[25]

In all these islands, it seems to me that all men are content with one woman, and to their chief or 235 king they give as many as twenty.[26] It appears to me that the women work more than the men. And I have not been able to learn if they hold pri-vate property; what seemed to me to appear was that, in that which one had, all took a share, es- 240 pecially of eatable things.[27]

In these islands I have so far found no human monstrosities, as many expected,[28] but on the contrary the whole population is very well-formed, nor are they negroes as in Guinea,[29] but 245

---

[18]This is not totally accurate. Columbus's Taino interpreters knew only a little of the language of the Ciguayos whom the admiral encountered on Española in January 1493 (note 30).
[19]Not so.
[20]Which the Spaniards transformed into La Habana, or Havana.
[21]Marco Polo reported the existence of tailed humans in the islands of Southeast Asia. In his description of the various fantastic people who supposedly inhabited the islands of Southeast Asia, John Mandeville listed hairy persons who walked on all fours and climbed trees.
[22]Not so.
[23]The Mongol emperor of Cathay (Volume I, Chapter 12, source 103). Columbus did not know that the Mongol khans had been expelled from power in China in 1368.
[24]"Village of the Nativity" (of the Lord). The destruction of the *Santa Maria* off the coast of Española on Christmas Day (Navidad del Señor) forced Columbus to leave behind thirty-nine sailors at the village garrison, which he named after the day of the incident.
[25]When Columbus returned in November 1493, he discov-ered the fortification burned to the ground and all thirty-nine men dead. Almost as soon as Columbus had sailed away, the Spaniards began fighting among themselves and split into factions, with only eleven remaining to garrison the fort. The widely scattered groups of Spaniards were wiped out by Tainos led by a chief named Caonabó. Gua-canagarí, the king to whom Columbus refers, apparently was wounded trying to defend the Spaniards.
[26]Generally only chiefs could afford large numbers of wives because of the substantial bride prices that were paid, in goods or services, to the families of the women. Notwith-standing, many commoners could and did have two or three wives.
[27]See note 12.
[28]Based on the Greek, Roman, and Arab geographies avail-able to them, Europeans were prepared to find various races of monstrous humans and semihumans in the Indies. Ac-cepted accounts of the wonders of the East, such as the trav-elogue of John Mandeville, told of dog-headed people and a species of individuals who, lacking heads, had an eye on each shoulder.
[29]Sub-Saharan West Africa (see Volume I, Chapter 12, source 108).

their hair is flowing, and they are not born where there is intense force in the rays of the sun; it is true that the sun has there great power. . . .

As I have found no monsters, so I have had no report of any, except in an island "Quaris," the second at the coming into the Indies, which is inhabited by a people who are regarded in all the islands as very fierce and who eat human flesh. They have many canoes with which they range through all the islands of India and pillage and take as much as they can.[30] They are no more malformed than the others, except that they have the custom of wearing their hair long like women, and they use bows and arrows of the same cane stems, with a small piece of wood at the end, owing to lack of iron which they do not possess. They are ferocious among these other people who are cowardly to an excessive degree, but I make no more account of them than of the rest. These are those who have intercourse with the women of "Matinino," which is the first island met on the way from Spain to the Indies, in which there is not a man. The women engage in no feminine occupation, but use bows and arrows of cane, like those already mentioned, and they

arm and protect themselves with plates of copper, of which they have much.[31]

In another island, which they assure me is larger than Española, the people have no hair.[32] In it, there is gold incalculable, and from it and from the other islands, I bring with me Indians as evidence.[33]

In conclusion, to speak only of that which has been accomplished on this voyage, which was so hasty, their highnesses can see that I will give them as much gold as they may need, if their highnesses will render me very slight assistance; moreover, spice and cotton,[34] as much as their highnesses shall command; and mastic,[35] as much as they shall order to be shipped and which, up to now, has been found only in Greece, in the island of Chios,[36] and the Seignory[37] sells it for what it pleases; and aloe wood, as much as they shall order to be shipped, and slaves, as many as they shall order to be shipped and who will be from the idolaters.[38] And I believe that I have found rhubarb and cinnamon,[39] and I shall find a thousand other things of value, which the people whom I have left there will have discovered, for I have not delayed at any point, so far as

---

[30]These were the Caribs, who shortly before the arrival of Columbus began to displace the Arawak peoples of the Lesser Antilles, the archipelago to the east and south of Hispaniola. Sixteenth-century Spanish writers unanimously agreed that the Caribs were fierce warriors and cannibalistic. On January 13, 1493, Columbus and his men had a short skirmish on Española (Hispaniola) with some previously unknown natives, whom the admiral incorrectly assumed were Caribs. They were actually Ciguayos, who were less peaceful than the Tainos.

[31]The same account appears in Columbus's log. Father Ramón Pane, who composed an ethnographic study of Taino culture during Columbus's second voyage of 1493–1494, also related in great detail the legend of the island of Matinino, where only women resided. The story, as reported by Pane, however, contains no hint that they were war-like women. Apparently Columbus took this Taino legend and combined it with the Greco-Roman myth of the warrior Amazons. Mandeville wrote of the land of Amazonia, populated totally by warrior women, and Marco Polo described two Asian islands, one inhabited solely by women and another exclusively by men. There is no evidence that this female society reported by Columbus and Pane ever existed in the Caribbean. The Tainos, however, who were essentially a stone-age people, did import from South America an alloy of copper and gold, which they used for ornaments.

[32]John Mandeville described people with little body hair, and Marco Polo told of Buddhist monks whose heads and faces were shaved.

[33]Columbus brought seven Tainos back to Spain, where they were baptized, with King Ferdinand and Prince Juan acting as godparents. One remained at the Spanish court, where he died, and the others returned with Columbus on his second voyage of 1493.

[34]The only indigenous spice was the chili pepper; the wild cotton was excellent but not plentiful.

[35]Columbus and his men wrongly identified a native gumbo-limbo tree, which contains an aromatic resin, with the rare mastic tree, whose costly resin was a profitable trade item for Genoa (note 37).

[36]An island in the eastern Mediterranean.

[37]The ruling body of Genoa, Columbus's native Italian city-state. Chios was a possession of Genoa, whose merchants controlled the mastic trade.

[38]Church law forbade the enslavement of Christians, except in the most exceptional circumstances.

[39]Actually, when members of the crew showed Columbus what they thought were aloe, mastic, and cinnamon, the admiral accepted the aloe and mastic as genuine but rejected the supposed cinnamon. One of his lieutenants reported seeing rhubarb while on a scouting expedition.

the wind allowed me to sail, except in the town of Navidad, in order to leave it secured and well established, and in truth, I should have done much more, if the ships had served me, as reason 300 demanded.

This is enough . . . and the eternal God, our Lord, Who gives to all those who walk in His way triumph over things which appear to be impossible, and this was notably one; for, although 305 men have talked or have written of these lands, all was conjectural, without suggestion of ocular evidence, but amounted only to this, that those who heard for the most part listened and judged it to be rather a fable than as having any vestige 310 of truth. So that, since Our Redeemer[40] has given this victory to our most illustrious king and queen, and to their renowned kingdoms, in so great a matter, for this all Christendom ought to feel delight and make great feasts and give solemn thanks to the Holy Trinity[41] with many 315 solemn prayers for the great exaltation which they shall have, in the turning of so many people to our holy faith, and afterwards for temporal benefits,[42] for not only Spain but all Christians will have hence refreshment and gain. 320

This in accordance with that which has been accomplished, thus briefly.

Done in the caravel,[43] off the Canary Islands, on the fifteenth of February, in the year one thousand four hundred and ninety-three. 325

At your orders.   El Almirante.[44]

---

[40]Jesus Christ.
[41]The Christian belief of three divine persons — Father, Son, and Holy Spirit — contained in a single divine essence.
[42]Benefits that are of this world and last only for a time, as opposed to eternal, or heavenly, rewards.
[43]A Spanish ocean-going ship.
[44]The Admiral.

Interpreting Columbus's Letter

As already noted, a historian always has to evaluate the worth of each source, which means understanding its point of view and reliability. So let us concentrate on those two issues. By so doing, we will address questions 1–5 and 8.

In this letter several things are obvious. Columbus believed he had reached Asian islands (lines 5–23). Marco Polo, John Mandeville, and other writers had provided a number of reference points by which to recognize the Orient (notes 11, 12, 21, 28, 31, and 32), and Columbus believed he had found many of them. It is equally obvious that Columbus tried to present his discoveries in the best light possible. He sent this letter ahead to the court of Ferdinand and Isabella to ensure that when he arrived he would be received with due honor.

There is plenty of exaggeration, self-puffery, error, coverup, and even some deliberate distortion in this account. He overestimated the size of several islands (lines 200–201 and 207–208) and, except for chilies, the spices he claimed to have discovered (lines 85, 283, and 292) were not there. The admiral also failed to mention that the *Santa Maria* had been lost (note 24). Columbus could not escape informing his royal patrons of this unhappy incident, but presumably he wanted to wait until he was at the court, where he could put his own spin on the facts surrounding the incident. Also not mentioned is a skirmish that he and his men had on January 13, 1493, with some hostile strangers, whom he incorrectly assumed were Caribs (note 30). That incident, if reported without explanation, probably would have weakened the admiral's implied claim that Spain could easily subjugate these timid Indians (lines 93–113 and 225–233). Indeed, his statement that the crew members he left behind at Navidad del Señor were in no danger "if they know how to govern themselves" (lines 232–233) suggests that he chose not to mention that some ugly incidents had already taken place, possibly rape of island women, and he feared the Tainos would not tolerate further outrages. And this proved to be the case as note 25 informs us.

Generally, however, despite Columbus's enthusiasm and understandable tendency to exaggerate, to neglect mentioning anything negative, and to see what he wanted to see, the admiral *seems* to have wanted to present an essentially factual account. Well, that certainly sounds like a strange conclusion, given all of the flaws that we just pointed out or alluded to.

One feature of the letter that leads us to this position is how Columbus described the people of the islands. His reading of popular travel accounts had prepared him to encounter every sort of human monstrosity (note 28), and undoubtedly he would have enjoyed reporting such contacts. But he honestly reported that all the natives he encountered were quite unmonstrous in appearance and temperament (lines 242–245). Of course, he reported stories of people with tails, cannibals, and warlike women who lived apart from men (lines 204–206 and 249–272), but it is unlikely that the admiral was deliberately misleading anyone on this issue. The Carib cannibals were real enough. Rumors of tailed people and latter-day Amazons conceivably were nothing more than the natives' effort to please Columbus or simply the result of poor communication. It is not difficult to imagine that when the admiral inquired after the locations of the various human curiosities whom Mandeville, Polo, and others had placed in the islands of the Indian Ocean, the Tainos, not knowing what he was asking, agreeably pointed across the waters to other islands.

This raises one issue that has long vexed historians and goes straight to the heart of the question of this source's overall reliability. *How well was Columbus able to communicate with these people?* Columbus insisted that through gestures and learned words the Spaniards and Tainos were able to communicate with one another (lines 163–169), and he certainly learned enough of the Tainos' language to report that they called the island on which he initially landed *Guanahani* (line 15). Nevertheless, we suspect that, despite Columbus's use of captive interpreters, only the most primitive forms of communication were possible between the Europeans and the Tainos in 1492–1493. We should, therefore, have a healthy skepticism about anything that Columbus reports about the Tainos' beliefs and cosmological perspectives (for example, lines 150–156 and 170–176).

All things considered, it seems reasonable to conclude that Columbus's letter can be accepted as a somewhat honest but far from accurate account of his discoveries and experiences. Put another way, Columbus was a "spin doctor," very much like some modern politicians who think they are speaking the truth, but their version of the truth is colored by their hopes, dreams, ambitions, and promises made. Columbus's honesty, compromised by an understandable enthusiasm to present his accomplishments positively, comes through in his attempt to describe the islands' physical qualities and the people he encountered. The picture that emerges tells us a lot about the complex motives that underlay his great adventure.

We notice that Columbus had taken possession of the lands in the names of the Spanish monarchs and even renamed the islands, without once giving thought to the claims of anyone else (lines 7–19). He also thought nothing of seizing some natives as soon as he arrived (lines 40–41 and 164–169) and of carrying several Indians back to Spain (lines 276–277). Moreover, he noted toward the end of his letter that the monarchs of Spain could obtain as many *slaves* as they desired from among the islands' *idolaters* (lines 289–291). At the same time (and this might strike the modern student as curious), Columbus claimed that he had acted generously and protectively toward the native people (lines 107–112 and 140–145), and he conveys in his letter a tone of admiration and even affection for the people whom he had encountered. Indeed, the admiral expressed a deep interest in winning over the native people in an avowed hope that they might become Catholic Christians and loyal subjects of Ferdinand and Isabella (lines 143–150), and he even claimed that they were strongly inclined toward religious conversion (lines 197–199). Yet the very qualities that Columbus implied made the Tainos prime candidates for conversion — intelligence, timidity, naiveté, generosity, ignorance, technological backwardness, lack of an articulated religious creed, an ability to communicate freely among themselves, and a sense of wonder at the Europeans — also made them ripe for subjugation.

The tone of this letter suggests that Columbus was concerned with these people as humans and was genuinely interested in helping them achieve salvation through conversion. It is equally clear, however, Columbus believed that he and Catholic Spain had a right and duty to subjugate and exploit these same people. Such tension continued throughout the Spanish colonial experience in the Americas.

Subjugation of the Indians and their lands involved more than just a sense of divine mission and Christian altruism — as real as those motives were. Columbus, his royal patrons, and most others who joined overseas adventures expected to gain in earthly wealth as well (see especially lines 278–295). Even a superficial reading of his letter reveals the admiral's preoccupation with the riches of the islands — riches that he appears to have exaggerated and even misrepresented (note 39). Gold, spices, cotton, aromatic mastic, and, of course, slaves were the material rewards that awaited Christian Europeans, and Columbus was fully interested in them and wanted Ferdinand and Isabella to underwrite future trips so that he could discover them in abundance. So exaggeration can be found in this account, but it seems to be largely exaggeration based on conviction.

Was Columbus being cynical, hypocritical, or deliberately ironic when in his closing words he claimed that Jesus Christ had provided this great victory to the Spanish monarchs (and indeed to all Christendom) and from that victory would flow the dual benefits of the conversion of so many people and worldly riches (lines 310–320)? Cynicism, hypocrisy, and conscious irony are not likely explanations. It seems more likely that these closing remarks reveal the mind of a man who saw no contradiction between spreading the faith and benefiting materially from that action, even if doing so meant exploiting the converts.

Perhaps you disagree with our conclusion that Columbus's letter is basically an honest and valuable source, despite its shortcomings. Well, if you do, you are in excellent company. Two eminent historians — William D. Phillips Jr. and Carla Rahn Phillips, in their book *The Worlds of Christopher Columbus* — characterize this letter as "a tissue of exaggerations, misconceptions, and outright lies." Although we acknowledge the letter's exaggerations, misconceptions, and prevarications (a somewhat less damning form of falsehood), we disagree as to the degree, nature, and extent of the letter's misstatements. Well, no historian is infallible, and certainly we do not claim that distinction. Moreover, no source is so clear in all respects that it lacks areas of potential disagreement for historians. That, in fact, is one of the exciting aspects of historical research. Despite all the facts and conclusions that historians generally agree on, there are numerous areas in which they carry on spirited debate. *The very nature of history's fragmentary, flawed evidence makes debate inevitable.*

What is more, no historian can possibly see everything there is to be seen in every source. What this means, so far as you are concerned, is that *there is plenty of latitude in the sources that appear in this book for you to arrive at valid insights that are unique to you.* In so doing, however, you must at all times attempt to divorce yourself of present-mindedness and to enter imaginatively into the world of the author whose work you are analyzing.

We can ask many other questions of Columbus's letter and garner other insights from it. Certainly it tells us a lot about Taino culture. Despite his cultural blinders, his naiveté, his tendency to see what he wanted to see, and his probably exaggerated belief in his ability to communicate with these people, Columbus seems to be a reasonably accurate and perceptive observer. Thus anyone interested in Caribbean cultures before the Europeans had much of a chance to influence them must necessarily look to this and similar accounts of first contacts. In fact, it would be good practice for you, right now, to try to answer question 7, which we have deliberately left unanswered. You will be surprised at how much you can learn about the Tainos from this brief description. As you do this exercise, however, do not forget to ask yourself constantly: How reliable does Columbus appear to be on this specific point, and what is the basis for my conclusion?

After you have tested your own powers of historical analysis in this exercise, it would be wise to put the letter aside for the present. We trust that by now you have a good idea of how to examine and mine a documentary source. Now let us consider an artifact and proceed to interpret it.

The Family Dinner

▼▼▼

▼ *AN ANONYMOUS WOODCUT OF 1511*

Columbus arrived in Barcelona in April 1493 to learn not only had his letter arrived, but it had already been published and publicly circulated. Within months the letter was translated into several languages; the Latin translation alone went through nine editions, several of which were lavishly illustrated, before the end of 1494. Printers discovered that educated Europeans had an almost insatiable desire to learn about the peoples and lands Columbus and other explorers were discovering, and they catered to that interest. Their clientele wanted not only to read about the fascinating peoples, plants, and animals of these lands — they wanted also to see them. Consequently, as books on the new explorations proliferated, so did the number of printed illustrations. Many are fanciful and tell us more about the Europeans who created them than the peoples and regions they supposedly portrayed. The woodcut print we have chosen appeared in a popular English pamphlet of 1511.

QUESTIONS FOR ANALYSIS

1. What scene has the artist set? What has the artist placed to the immediate right of the standing man, and what function does it have in this scene?
2. What do each person's actions, dress, and demeanor tell us about her or him?
3. What does this illustration tell us about popular European notions concerning the natives of the New World?

Interpreting the Woodcut

What a charming, even idyllic domestic scene! An attractive mother nurses an infant at her breast while amusing an older child with a feather. A well-muscled, equally attractive, and proud father stands nearby, holding the tools of his trade while next to him the family's dinner is slowly cooking. Dinner, of course, may strike us as macabre, as these are cannibals, and it looks like roast human is on the menu. The tools of the father's trade are weapons. Both children are naked, and the parents are virtually nude, save for what appear to be leaves that cover their loins, decorative necklaces, armbands and anklets of some indeterminate material, and feathers in their long and unkempt hair.

What is the message? What we have is a reprise of the image provided by Columbus in his letter of 1493: the *noble savage.* These are fully human beings with human bonds and affections. Yet they are still savages, as their clothing (or lack of it), decorations, hair styles, weapons, and choice of food would have suggested to most sixteenth-century Europeans. Here, as Columbus and many of those who followed agreed, were a people who could become Christians but who also, by virtue of their backwardness, were to be subjugated. There is something appealing about their innocent savagery, but what of that poor fellow whose severed leg and head are slowly roasting?

Have we read too much into the woodcut? It is arguable that we may have. The historian always faces this problem when trying to analyze an isolated piece of evidence, particularly an artifactual source. Yet this artifact is not completely isolated, for we brought to its analysis insight gained from documentary evidence — Columbus's letter. That is how we generally read the artifacts of historical cultures. We attempt to place them in the context of what we have already learned or inferred from documentary sources. Documents illuminate artifacts, and artifacts make more vivid and tangible the often shadowy world of words.

As you attempt to interpret the unwritten sources in this book, keep in mind what you have learned from the documents you have already read, your textbook, and class lectures. Remember that we have chosen these artifacts to illustrate broad themes and general trends. You should not find their messages overly subtle. As with the documents, always try to place each piece of artifactual evidence into its proper context, and in that regard, read the introductions and Questions for Analysis very carefully. We will do our best to provide you with all the information and clues you need.

Good luck and have fun!

Part One

▼▼▼

A New Era of Human Interconnectedness: The Fifteenth through Seventeenth Centuries

Change is a word that can be used to describe each and every era in world history. Wars are won and lost; dynasties come and go; new ideas are discovered, and old ones discarded. In some eras, however, change occurs more rapidly, affects more human beings, and alters basic human relationships. The three centuries from the 1400s to the 1600s were just such an era.

What changes took place? In politics the 1400s saw the consolidation of authority by the Ming Dynasty in China (1368–1644) and the establishment of new empires by the Ottoman Turks in the Middle East, the Aztecs in Central Mexico, and the Incas in South America. More political changes took place in the 1500s and early 1600s, when the Songhai Empire in West Africa, the Safavid Empire in Persia, and the Mughal Empire in India emerged, the Tokugawa clan ended decades of civil war in Japan, and the princes of Muscovy established a unified Russian state. Europe remained politically divided among hundreds of political entities that ranged from small city-states to large sprawling monarchies. Here too important political changes took place, notably the winning of independence from Spain by the Netherlands, the establishment of Spanish dominance in Italy, and the strengthening of centralized monarchies in Spain, England, and France.

Significant religious developments also occurred. In Europe the emergence of Protestantism broke the hold of Roman Catholicism on religious life, bringing with it sectarian conflict and religious war. In India, Nanak (1469–1539) drew on Hindu and Islamic traditions to develop a unique religious perspective that became the basis for Sikhism, a religion that today commands the allegiance of millions. Also in India, Bhakti Hinduism, with its emphasis on divine love and devotion to a single god, gained new adherents. In the world of Islam, Sufism, which emphasizes the ability of humans to achieve personal union with God, and Shiism, whose unique doctrines became the state religion in Persia, both added followers.

Innovation also took place in other areas. Intellectuals in Europe, for example, broke with ancient Greek science and achieved new insights into mathematics, astronomy, and physics. In China and Japan, Confucian studies flourished under government patronage, as did painting and poetry in the Mughal and Ottoman empires. New technologies took root. In Europe printed

1

books (which had appeared in China and Korea centuries earlier) proliferated after the development of printing by movable type by Gutenberg in the 1450s. Across Eurasia gunpowder weapons, first developed in China around 1200, came into widespread use. For the world at large, average annual temperatures gradually rose beginning in the late 1400s, resulting in greater agricultural yields. International trade and manufacturing both increased, and world population grew from approximately 350 million in 1400 to approximately 550 million in 1600, despite catastrophic population losses in the Americas.

As significant as these developments were, they are not, either singly or collectively, the reason the period from the fifteenth through seventeenth centuries is considered a turning point in history. Rather, the reason lies in the dramatic increase in human interaction and interconnectedness that took place in these years. Interaction among human societies was of course nothing new. As foragers and hunters, our first human ancestors were continually on the move in search of game and edible plants, and their movements inevitably brought them into contact with other human bands. After the spread of agriculture between 8500 and 3500 B.C.E., economic diversification, urbanization, and the appearance of organized states encouraged further interaction through military conquest and trade. In later centuries, the emergence of Buddhism, Christianity, and Islam, three religions committed to converting nonbelievers, inspired missionaries to travel to other lands seeking converts. During the postclassical age (approximately 500 C.E. to 1400 C.E.), economic, political, and cultural interaction among the peoples of Africa and Eurasia was further stimulated by the growth of regional trading systems centered in northwestern Europe, the Mediterranean basin, the Middle East, the Arabian Sea, the Bay of Bengal, and the South China Sea. These regional trading systems came to be loosely linked together by long-distance trade in the Indian Ocean basin and across a series of roads known as the Silk Road that stretched from China to Syria.

Nonetheless, the world in 1400 was far from being one world. It consisted of many worlds — the worlds of China, India, the Middle East, sub-Saharan Africa, and Europe, and two worlds that no one in Africa-Eurasia knew existed, Oceania and the Americas. No matter where they lived people ate locally grown foods and wore clothes made of locally produced materials. They had distinctive religions and cultures. Military threats and political interference from outside their worlds were rare or nonexistent, and as a result their histories followed trajectories that seldom intersected.

By the mid seventeenth century, however, the world had changed. By then the capture of a Spanish treasure ship by pirates in the Caribbean affected the price of silk in Japan and China; the growing taste for sweets in Europe meant that millions of Africans became slaves on sugar plantations in Brazil and the West Indies; the collapse of the Ming Dynasty in China stimulated the porcelain industry in the Netherlands and England; policies adopted by Japanese shoguns and Chinese emperors drew the attention of papal officials in Rome; wealthy Europeans warmed themselves by wearing fur coats and hats made from the hides of animals that had been trapped in North America or Siberia; many Chinese peasants paid their taxes with silver mined in Mexico or Peru.

In explaining how and why the world became more integrated between the 1400s and 1600s, historians emphasize the role of Europe, specifically Europe's voyages of exploration, which began in the fifteenth century when the Portuguese first sent ships down Africa's Atlantic coast seeking gold, trade, and ways to hurt their Muslim rivals. By the 1450s they added another goal, to gain access to the Indian Ocean by sailing around Africa's southern tip. The Portuguese mariner Vasco da Gama did just this in 1498, six years after the Italian mariner in the service of Spain, Christopher Columbus, discovered the Americas while seeking Asia. During the sixteenth century Europe's worldwide expansion continued. The Portuguese pushed on from bases in East Africa and India to establish a series of fortified trading posts in key locations in the East Indies, China, and Japan. Spain established its authority in much of the Americas. Northern European merchants, mariners, and rulers soon joined the competition for overseas territory and markets. The French, Dutch, English, Danes, and Swedes struck claims to lands in the Americas and the Caribbean, and the French, Dutch, and English challenged the Portuguese in Asia.

The consequences of Europe's expansion were momentous. Millions of Native Americans died from Old World diseases. Survivors immediately or gradually lost their lands and independence, and many were converted to Christianity. The New World became a major grower of tobacco and sugar, and to meet demand, by the mid seventeenth century millions of African slaves had been imported to the Americas to do the work. The world's money supply received a major infusion from American gold and silver, and this resulted in widespread inflation, increased investment, and growth in international commerce. The integration of the Americas into the world market also had biological consequences. Horses, cattle, swine, and chickens as well as wheat, oats, barley, and fruit trees were introduced to the Americas, while American crops such as potatoes, tomatoes, peppers, and cassava came to be grown in Africa and Eurasia.

As important as it was, Europe's expansion must be kept in perspective. The first great upsurge in global interaction took place earlier, in the thirteenth century, when the Mongols conquered a vast Eurasian empire in which merchants, travelers, and ideas moved freely. Some historians would push the first example of global integration back even further, to the Arab-dominated Abbasid Empire, which in its heyday included the Middle East, northern Africa, and the Iberian Peninsula in Europe.

It is also important to note that Europe's global expansion did not mean that Europe had become the world's leading power. Europeans achieved dominance only in the Americas, the Philippines, and the Atlantic islands off Africa's west coast, where political disunity, epidemics, and unsophisticated technology gave them a military advantage. In Asia and Africa, Europeans conquered and held a few coastal cities such as Goa in India and Melaka on the Malay Peninsula, but otherwise they carried on commerce from a relatively small number of trading posts which they held at the pleasure of local rulers. Although Europe had become a new presence in world markets, Europe's overall economic output was dwarfed by that of India, the world's leading exporter of textiles, and of China, which produced high-quality silks and porcelain in demand throughout Eurasia and parts of Africa. Europeans neither grew nor manufactured any products that interested Asian buyers, meaning they paid for their purchases in Asia with silver from the Americas. Without that silver, Europeans' participation in world trade would have been negligible.

By the mid seventeenth century, Europeans had changed the world in many ways. But it still was not Europe's world. This would be the case 250 years later, but only after the world had undergone further transformations.

Chapter 1

▼▼▼

Continuity and Change in East and Southeast Asia

Important changes took place in East and Southeast Asia from the fifteenth through the seventeenth centuries but in a political and cultural context that remained what it had been for more than a millennium. In terms of size, wealth, population, technology, and military might, China overshadowed the smaller states and nomadic societies that surrounded it. With some justification the Chinese considered their state the "central kingdom" and viewed all other peoples as barbarians. Three neighboring states — Japan, Korea, and Vietnam — were strongly influenced by Chinese thought and institutions, and at times Korea and Vietnam had been conquered by China and actually incorporated into the Chinese empire. All three, however, maintained their cultural distinctiveness.

Southeast Asia, which includes both the Asian mainland east of India and south of China and also the thousands of islands that today comprise Indonesia and the Philippines, remained an area of political and cultural diversity. Small kingdoms, chiefdoms, and independent cities rather than large territorial states dominated the region, and Hinduism, Buddhism, and Islam all had substantial followings.

The arid region to the north of China had fewer people, no large cities, and no centralized states. It was populated by various peoples — Turks, Khitan, Jurchen, and Mongols — who supported themselves through pastoralism and, where feasible, agriculture. Their raids on agricultural lands to the south were a constant threat to China and sometimes developed into full-blown invasions. No less than four Chinese dynasties, the Liao, Jin, Yuan, and Qing, originated among these so-called barbarian peoples of the steppe.

As it had for centuries, in the 1400s East and Southeast Asia played a key role in the world economy. With approximately 20 million inhabitants and half a dozen cities with populations over 100,000, Southeast Asia was one of the world's richest regions. Its geography made it a commercial crossroads linking the Chinese and Japanese markets to the north with India, Southwest Asia, Europe, and Africa to the west. It was also an important source of regionally traded goods, such as cotton, rice, salt fish, forest products, copper, lead, and other items that were exchanged for Indian textiles and Chinese silks, ceramics, copper and brass wares, medicines, paper, and tea. More significantly, the islands of Southeast Asia grew the spices that were so highly prized throughout the Afro-Eurasian world. Pepper was produced in Sumatra, Java, and Borneo, while nutmeg, cloves, and mace were grown in the island groups known as the Moluccas and the Bandas. When Europeans sought direct ocean routes to Asia, their most coveted prize was access to the spices of Southeast Asia.

Although important, Southeast Asia's economy could not rival the size and significance of China's. Although estimates vary, China's population in 1500 was probably between 100 and 125 million, in either case larger than the population of Europe. Its two largest cities, Beijing and Nanjing, with populations around 700,000, were slightly smaller than Istanbul, the world's most populous city, but were six times larger than Europe's biggest city, Paris, which in 1500 numbered approximately 125,000. Much Chinese economic activity was devoted to supplying this vast domestic market with foodstuffs, mostly rice and vegetables, and with manufactured goods ranging from clothes, shoes, tools, and household goods to medicines, firecrackers, paper, wine, incense, candles, and special paper money to be burned in sacrifices. China also played a major role in international trade. Large Chinese merchant communities existed in Japan, Korea, and Southeast Asia, and thousands of foreign merchants resided in Chinese coastal cities. China's major exports were silks, satins, and brocades, whose lustrous textures and colorful designs were unmatched, and ceramics, the quality of which was recognized throughout Eurasia and Africa. Although the Chinese imported spices from Southeast Asia and cotton textiles from India, they were interested in little else that was produced abroad except gold and silver currency. This meant that year after year and century after century, China had a favorable balance of trade that made it the "ultimate sink" for much of the world's gold and especially silver.

Until the sixteenth century direct contact between East and Southeast Asia and Europe had been exceptionally rare, even during the thirteenth century, when the Mongol Empire made the journey across Eurasia somewhat less dangerous and arduous. Trade between the two regions had existed for centuries, but the goods exchanged — silver from Europe to Asia and spices, silks, and porcelain from Asia to Europe — had always been carried by Arab, Indian, and central Asian intermediaries.

Then in the early 1500s, the Portuguese arrived in the region's coastal cities seeking direct access to spice markets, trade, and converts to Christianity. The Spanish, Dutch, and English soon followed, and in time these and other Westerners would have immense impact on the region. In the sixteenth and seventeenth centuries, however, the arrival of Europeans had little effect on the unfolding of events. The exception was Southeast Asia, where the Portuguese captured the strategically located port city of Melaka in 1511, and the Spaniards gradually subjugated the Philippines beginning in the 1560s. Although the Spaniards turned Manila into a major port, the Portuguese had only partial success in their attempt to gain a stranglehold on the region's spice trade. Both the Portuguese and the Spanish sent Roman Catholic missionaries to the region, but except in the Philippines, converts were few. Greater changes came to the region in the early 1600s when the aggressive, profit-driven Dutch became the dominant European power. Bent on establishing a monopoly on the cultivation and sale of nutmeg, cloves, and pepper, the Dutch took over the island of Java, expelled the Portuguese from Melaka in 1641, and took control of key ports and regions in Sumatra, the Moluccas, and the Malay Peninsula. An example of their ruthlessness was their conduct in the nutmeg-producing Banda islands, where the Dutch killed, starved, or enslaved all 15,000 people who lived there. Despite resistance from native peoples and continuing competition from the Spanish and English, the Dutch maintained their hold on the East Indies until after World War II.

Elsewhere, the arrival of Europeans was a minor event. In Japan, the most significant development was its political recovery in the late 1500s after decades of civil war. Building on the achievements of Toyotomi Hideyoshi (1535–1598), a general who had brought unity to Japan in 1590, the Tokugawa family seized power after Hideyoshi's death and installed Tokugawa Ieyasu as shogun, or military ruler, in 1603. This was the beginning of the Tokugawa Shogunate, which brought more than two centuries of stability to Japan before it was overthrown in 1867. As part of their campaign to bring order to Japan, the Tokugawa rulers took steps to limit the activities of European missionaries, who had converted several hundred thousand Japanese to Catholicism, and of European merchants, who had sold firearms to rebellious aristocrats in the 1500s. By the 1640s Catholic missionaries had been expelled, Christianity outlawed, and trade with Europeans limited to one Dutch ship a year, which was required to unload its cargo under close government inspection on Deshima Island, in Nagasaki harbor.

In China and Korea, the Europeans' arrival had even less effect. Both countries had been conquered by the Mongols, and both countries needed to rebuild after Mongol power collapsed in the late 1300s. In Korea the Yi Dynasty (1392–1910) did so effectively, but having been weakened by a Japanese invasion in the 1590s, it was conquered in 1636 by the Manchus and forced to become a vassal state of the people who conquered China a few years later. In China the Ming Dynasty, on taking power in 1368, revived the civil service examinations, supported commercial expansion, and carried on ambitious economic reconstruction projects. In the late 1500s, however, Ming rule deteriorated, and the Chinese experienced rising taxes, bureaucratic factionalism, neglect of public works, peasant rebellion, and foreign invasion — indications throughout Chinese history of a dynasty in decline. The last Ming emperor, Sizong, paid the price when a peasant rebellion ended his rule in 1644 and led to the founding of a new foreign dynasty under the invading Manchus. Through all these years, the Chinese permitted the Portuguese to carry on limited trade in a single port, Macao, and allowed a small number of Jesuit missionaries to reside at the imperial court in Beijing. Here they impressed the Chinese elite with their mechanical clocks and astronomical knowledge but had little effect on Chinese politics or culture.

▼▼▼

Confucianism in China and Japan

No philosopher has influenced the values and behavior of more human beings than the Chinese thinker Kong Fuzi (ca. 551–479 B.C.E.), known in the West by his Latinized name Confucius. Like many other thinkers of his day, Confucius was distressed by the political fragmentation and turbulence that plagued China during the Eastern Zhou Era (771–256 B.C.E.). A scholar intent on pursuing a career in public service, he turned to teaching only after his efforts to achieve a position as a ruler's trusted advisor had failed. He proved to be a gifted teacher, one who is reputed to have had more than 3,000 students, some of whom collected his sayings in a book entitled *Lun-yu,* or *Analects.*

Confucius taught that China's troubles were rooted in the failure of its people and leaders to understand and act according to the rules of proper conduct. Proper conduct meant actions conforming to the standards of an idealized Chinese past, when all of China was structured along lines of behavior and authority paralleling those of a harmonious family. Confucius taught that just as fathers, wives, sons, and daughters have specific roles and obligations within families, individuals have roles and obligations in society that depend on age, gender, marital status, ancestry, and social standing. Subjects owed rulers obedience, and rulers were expected to be models of virtue and benevolence. Children owed parents love and reverence, and parents, especially fathers, were expected to be kind and just. Children learned from parents, and subjects from rulers. Confucius also taught that whatever one's status, one must live according to the principles of *jen,* which means humaneness, benevolence, and love, and *li,* a term that encompasses the concepts of ceremony, propriety, and good manners. Because the wisdom and practices of ancient sages were central to his teaching, Confucius taught that his disciples could achieve virtue by studying the literature, history, and rituals of the past. Education in traditional values and behavior was the path to sagehood, the quality of knowing what is proper and good and acting accordingly.

Although Confucius' philosophy competed with many other schools of thought in his own time, during the Han Dynasty (206 B.C.E.–220 C.E.) it became the official program of studies for anyone seeking an office in the imperial administration. Mastery of the Confucian Classics and their commentaries was the only path to success on the civil service examinations by which China chose its officials. Although the examination system was abolished by China's Mongol rulers during the Yuan Era (1264–1368), it was revived under the Ming (1368–1644) and continued in use until 1905. For almost 2,000 years, China was administered by a literary elite devoted to Confucianism.

Confucianism's influence was not limited to China. Although it had to compete with Buddhism and other indigenous religions, Confucianism deeply affected the thought, politics, and everyday life of Korea, Vietnam, and Japan.

"Doing Good" in Seventeenth-Century China
▼▼▼
1 ▼ *MERITORIOUS DEEDS AT NO COST*

During the sixteenth and seventeenth centuries, interpretations of Confucianism drew mainly on the work of scholars from the Song Era (960–1279 C.E.). Known as Neo-Confucianists, these scholars had brought new energy and rigor to the Confucian tradition after several centuries of stagnation and declining influence. The greatest Neo-Confucianist was Zhu Xi (1130–1200), who presided over a huge project of historical research and wrote detailed commentaries on most of the Confucian Classics. His commentaries came to be viewed as the orthodox version of Confucianism and the official interpretation for evaluating performance on the civil service examinations during the Ming and Qing eras.

Confucian scholarship in the 1500s and 1600s, however, was more than simply rehashing and refining Neo-Confucian ideas and formulas. With generous support from the emperor and high officials, Ming scholars completed vast research projects on history, medicine, ethics, and literature. In reinterpreting Confucianism, they sought to apply the Sage's wisdom to a China experiencing population growth, commercialization, urbanization, and ultimately dynastic decline and foreign conquest. Many endeavored to make Confucianism less elitist and more "popular."

Traditional Confucianism had taught that the erudition and virtue necessary for true sagehood were theoretically attainable by anyone, but that in reality they could be achieved only by a small number of privileged males who had the wealth and leisure for years of study and self-cultivation. Women, artisans, peasants, and even merchants were capable of understanding and internalizing aspects of Confucian teaching by observing the words and deeds of their superiors, but serious scholarship, true morality, and sagehood were beyond them. At the beginning of the sixteenth century such ideas were challenged by Wang Yangming (1472–1529), a widely published scholar who taught that everyone, regardless of his or her station, was capable of practicing exemplary morality and achieving sagehood. An official as well as a scholar, Wang was also convinced that a healthy Chinese polity depended on teaching sound moral principles to all classes of people.

Wang's ideas were well received in a China where urbanization, increased literacy, and growing wealth were creating a burgeoning demand for books, many of which brought Confucian ideas to the broad reading public. These included summaries of the Confucian Classics, editions of the Classics themselves, manuals to prepare candidates for the civil service examinations, and what were termed "morality books." Morality books, which first appeared in the Song and Yuan eras, discussed good and bad behavior not just for the learned elite but for all classes of people, irrespective of social status, wealth, gender, and formal education. People read these books avidly. With titles such as *A Record of the Practice of Good Deeds* and *Establishing One's Own Destiny,* morality books taught that good deeds would be rewarded by worldly success, robust health, many sons, and a long life.

Among the most popular morality books was the anonymous *Meritorious Deeds at No Cost,* which appeared in the mid seventeenth century. Unlike other such books, which recommended costly good deeds such as paying for proper family rituals in connection with marriage, coming of age, funerals, and ancestral rites, *Meritorious Deeds at No Cost* discussed laudable acts that required little or no outlay of money. It lists actions considered good for "people in general," but mainly concentrates on good deeds appropriate to specific groups ranging from local gentry and scholars to soldiers and household servants. Its prescriptions provide insights into basic Confucian values and contemporary Chinese views of class, family, and gender.

Meritorious Deeds at No Cost begins with the "local gentry," a term that refers to individuals who have the rank and status of government officials, but who reside at home and may not have any specific political responsibilities. The next group, "scholars," refers to individuals at various stages of preparing for the civil service examinations. As educated individuals and potential officials, their status placed them below the gentry but above the common people. The recommended meritorious deeds for this group reveal that many "scholars" were also teachers.

QUESTIONS FOR ANALYSIS

1. In what ways do the responsibilities of the various groups differ from one another? In what ways do they reflect certain underlying assumptions about what makes a good society?
2. According to this document, what should be the attitude of the upper classes (gentry and scholars) to those below them? Conversely, how should peasants, merchants, and artisans view their social superiors?
3. What views of women and sexuality are stated or implied in this treatise?
4. What views of money and moneymaking are stated or implied in this treatise?
5. According to this treatise, what specific kinds of behaviors and attitudes are components of filial piety?
6. Taking the document as a whole, what conclusions can be drawn about the ultimate purpose or highest good the author hopes to achieve through the various kinds of behaviors he describes?

LOCAL GENTRY

Take the lead in charitable donations.

Rectify your own conduct and transform the common people.

Make a sincere effort to inform the authorities of what would be beneficial to the people of your locality. . . .

If people have suffered a grave injustice, expose and correct it.

Settle disputes among your neighbors fairly.

When villagers commit misdeeds, admonish them boldly and persuade them to desist.

Do not let yourself be blinded by emotion and personal prejudices.

Be tolerant of the mistakes of others.

Be willing to listen to that which is displeasing to your ears.

Do not make remarks about women's sexiness.

Do not harbor resentment when you are censured.

Protect virtuous people.

Hold up for public admiration women who are faithful to their husbands and children who are obedient to their parents.

Restrain those who are stubborn and unfilial.[1]

Prevent plotting and intrigue.

Endeavor to improve manners and customs. . . .

Prevent the younger members of your family from oppressing others by taking advantage of your position. . . .

Do not be arrogant, because of your own power and wealth, toward relatives who are poor or of low status. . . .

Do not ignore your own relatives and treat others as if they were your kin.

[1] Being disobedient or disrespectful to one's parents.

Influence other families to cherish good deeds. . . .

Do not disport yourself with lewd friends. . . .

Do not allow yourself to be overcome by personal feelings and therefore treat others unjustly. . . .

Restrain others from arranging lewd theater performances. . . .

Instruct your children, grandchildren, and nephews to be humane and compassionate toward all and to avoid anger and self-indulgence.

Do not deceive or oppress younger brothers or cousins.

Encourage others to read and study without minding the difficulties.

Urge others to esteem charity and disdain personal gain.

Do not underestimate the value of others [or underpay them]. . . .

Persuade others to settle lawsuits through conciliation.

Try to settle complaints and grievances among others. . . .

Curb the strong and protect the weak.

Show respect to the aged and compassion for the poor.

Do not keep too many concubines.

Do not keep catamites.[2] . . .

SCHOLARS

Be loyal to the emperor and filial to your parents.

Honor your elder brothers and be faithful to your friends. . . .

Instruct the common people in the virtues of loyalty and filial piety. . . .

Be wholehearted in inspiring your students to study. . . .

Try to improve your speech and behavior.

Teach your students also to be mindful of their speech and behavior. . . . *to better themselves*

Be patient in educating the younger members of poor families.

If you find yourself with smart boys, teach them sincerity; and with children of the rich and noble, teach them decorum and duty. . . .

Do not expose the private affairs of others or harbor evil suspicions about them.

Do not write or post notices which defame other people.

Do not write petitions or accusations to higher authorities. . . .

Do not encourage the spread of immoral and lewd novels [by writing, reprinting, expanding, etc.]. . . .

Do not attack or vilify commoners; do not oppress ignorant villagers. . . .

Do not ridicule other people's handwriting. . . .

Make others desist from unfiliality toward their parents or unkindness toward relatives and friends.

Educate the ignorant to show respect to their ancestors and live in harmony with their families. . . .

PEASANTS

Do not miss the proper time for farm work. . . .

Do not obstruct or cut off paths. Fill up holes that might give trouble to passersby. . . .

Do not steal and sell your master's grain in connivance with his servants.

Do not damage crops in your neighbors' fields by leaving animals to roam at large, relying on your landlord's power and influence to protect you.

Do not encroach [on others' property] beyond the boundaries of your own fields and watercourses, thinking to ingratiate yourself with your landlord. . . .

---

[2]Boys kept by men for sexual purposes.

In plowing, do not infringe on graves or make them hard to find. . . .

Do not damage the crops in neighboring fields out of envy because they are so flourishing. . . .

Do not through negligence in your work do damage to the fields of others.

Do not become lazy and cease being conscientious because you think your landlord does not provide enough food and wine or fails to pay you enough.

Fill up holes in graves.

Take good care of others' carts and tools. . . .

Keep carts and cattle from trampling down others' crops.

CRAFTSMEN

. . . Whenever you make something, try to make it strong and durable.

Do not be resentful toward your master if he fails to provide enough food and drink. . . .

When making things, do not leave them unfinished or rough. . . .

Do not reveal and spread abroad the secrets of your master's house.

Do not make crude imitations.

Finish your work without delay.

In your trade with others, do not practice deceit through forgery.

Do not mix damaged articles with good.

Do not break or damage finished goods.

Do not recklessly indulge in licentiousness.

Do not spoil the clothes of others.

Do not steal the materials of others.

Do not use the materials of others carelessly. . . .

MERCHANTS

Do not deceive ignorant villagers when fixing the price of goods.

Do not raise the price of fuel and rice too high.

When the poor buy rice, do not give them short measure.

Sell only genuine articles. . . .

When sick people have urgent need of something, do not raise the price unreasonably.

Do not deceitfully serve unclean dishes or leftover food to customers who are unaware of the fact.

Do not dispossess or deprive others of their business by devious means.

Do not envy the prosperity of others' business and speak ill of them wherever you go.

Be fair in your dealings.

Treat the young and the aged on the same terms as the able-bodied.

When people come in the middle of the night with an urgent need to buy something, do not refuse them on the ground that it is too cold [for you to get up and serve them].

Pawnshops should lend money at low interest.

Give fair value when you exchange silver for copper coins. Especially when changing money for the poor, be generous to them.

When a debtor owes you a small sum but is short of money, have mercy and forget about the difference. Do not bring him to bankruptcy and hatred by refusing to come to terms.

When the poor want to buy such things as mosquito nets, clothing, and quilts, have pity on them and reduce the price. Do not refuse to come to terms.

PEOPLE IN GENERAL

Do not show anger or worry in your parents' sight.

Accept meekly the reproaches and anger of your parents.

Persuade your parents to correct their mistakes and return to the right path.

Do not divulge your parents' faults to others.

Do not let your parents do heavy work.

Do not be disgusted with your parents' behavior when they are old and sick.

Do not yell at your parents or give them angry looks.

Love your brothers. . . .

Be attentive and obedient to the principles of Heaven and the laws of the ruler. . . .

If you are poor, do not entertain thoughts of harming the rich.

If you are rich, do not deceive and cheat the poor. . . .

Do not speak of others' humble ancestry.

Do not talk about the private [women's] quarters of others. [Commentary: When others bring up such things, if they are of the younger generation, reprimand them with straight talk, and if they are older or of the same generation as you, change the subject.] . . .

Respect women's chastity. . . .

Do not instigate quarrels. . . .

Do not stir up your mind with lewd and wanton thoughts.

Do not besmirch others' honor or chastity.

Do not intimidate others to satisfy your own ambition.

Do not assert your own superiority by bringing humiliation upon others. . . .

Do not dwell on others' faults while dilating [expounding at length] on your own virtues.

Try to promote friendly relations among neighbors and relatives. . . .

Do not gossip about others' wrongdoing. . . .

Do not be avaricious. . . .

When you hear someone speaking about the failings of others, make him stop.

When you hear a man praising the goodness of others, help him to do so. . . .

When you see a man about to go whoring or gambling, try to dissuade him. . . .

Do not say sharp or cruel things. . . .

Do not deceive cripples, fools, old men, the young, or the sick. . . .

Make peace between husbands and wives who are about to separate.

Do not forget the kindness of others; do not remember the wrongdoing of others. . . .

Show the way to those who have become lost.

Help the blind and disabled to pass over dangerous bridges and roads. . . .

Cut down thorns by the roadside to keep them from tearing people's clothes. . . .

Put stones in muddy places [to make them passable].

Lay wooden boards where the road is broken off.

At night, light a lamp for others.

Lend rainwear to others in case of rain. . . .

Do not listen to your wife or concubines if they should encourage you to neglect or abandon your parents. . . .

Do not humiliate or ridicule the aged, the young, or the crippled. . . .

Do not say words which are harmful to morals and customs.

Do not stealthily peep at others' womenfolk when they are exposed by a fire in their home. . . .

Do not be impudent toward your superiors. . . .

Do not sell faithful dogs to dog butchers. . . .

Even if you see that the good sometimes suffer bad fortune and you yourself experience poverty, do not let it discourage you from doing good.

Even if you see bad men prosper, do not lose faith in ultimate recompense.[3]

Never fail to give rice cakes or drugs first of all to your parents and only after that to your children and grandchildren. . . .

In all undertakings, think of others.

---

[3]The idea that one is rewarded for good or bad actions.

Teaching the Young in Tokugawa Japan
▼▼▼

2 ▼ *Kaibara and Token Ekiken,* COMMON SENSE TEACHINGS FOR JAPANESE CHILDREN *and* GREATER LEARNING FOR WOMEN

Although Chinese Neo-Confucianism had been brought to Japan by Zen Buddhist monks during the fourteenth and fifteenth centuries, it had little influence on Japan's aristocratic ruling class until the Tokugawa Era, when the early shoguns actively supported it. The shoguns were attracted to Confucianism because it emphasized the need for social hierarchy and obedience to the ruler of a centralized state. Hayashi Razan (1583–1657), a leading Confucian scholar, was an advisor of Tokugawa Ieyasu, and the school founded by the Hayashi family at Edo in 1630 with shogunal financial support became the center of Confucian scholarship and education in Japan. Many provincial lords founded similar academies in their domains, and the education samurai received in these schools and from private tutors helped transform Japan's warrior aristocracy into a literate bureaucratic ruling class committed to Confucian ethical values.

Among the Confucian scholars of the early Tokugawa period, few matched the literary output and popularity of Kaibara Ekiken (1630–1714). After studying in Kyoto and Edo, he served the Kuroda lords of the Fukuoka domain in southwestern Japan as physician, tutor, and scholar-in-residence. He wrote more than 100 works on medicine, botany, philosophy, and education.

This selection draws on material from two of Ekiken's works. The first part is excerpted from his *Common Sense Teachings for Japanese Children,* a manual for tutors of children in aristocratic households. The second part is taken from *Greater Learning for Women,* a discussion of moral precepts for girls. It is thought that this treatise was written in collaboration with Token, Ekiken's wife.

QUESTIONS FOR ANALYSIS

1. According to *Common Sense Teachings for Japanese Children,* what moral qualities should be inculcated in students?
2. What attitudes toward the lower classes are expressed in these two treatises?
3. How do the goals and purposes of education differ for Japanese boys and girls? How are they similar?
4. What do these treatises say about Japanese marriage customs and family life?
5. What is there in Ekiken's educational treatises that would have furthered the Tokugawa shoguns' ambition to provide Japan with stable and peaceful government?

COMMON SENSE TEACHINGS FOR JAPANESE CHILDREN

In January when children reach the age of six, teach them numbers one through ten, and the names given to designate 100, 1,000, 10,000 and 100,000,000. Let them know the four directions, East, West, North and South. Assess their native intelligence and differentiate between quick and slow learners. Teach them Japanese pronunciation from the age of six or seven, and let them learn how to write. . . . From this time on, teach them to respect their elders, and let them know the distinctions between the upper and lower classes and between the young and old. Let them learn to use the correct expressions.

When the children reach the age of seven, do not let the boys and girls sit together, nor must you allow them to dine together. . . .

For the eighth year. This is the age when the ancients began studying the book *Little Learning*.[1] Beginning at this time, teach the youngsters etiquette befitting their age, and caution them not to commit an act of impoliteness. Among those which must be taught are: daily deportment, the manners set for appearing before one's senior and withdrawing from his presence, how to speak or respond to one's senior or guest, how to place a serving tray or replace it for one's senior, how to present a wine cup and pour rice wine and to serve side dishes to accompany it, and how to serve tea. Children must also learn how to behave while taking their meals.

Children must be taught by those who are close to them the virtues of filial piety and obedience. To serve the parents well is called filial piety, and to serve one's seniors well is called obedience. The one who lives close to the children and who is able to teach must instruct the children in the early years of their life that the first obligation of a human being is to revere the parents and serve them well. Then comes the next lesson which includes respect for one's seniors, listening to their commands and not holding them in contempt. One's seniors include elder brothers, elder sisters, uncles, aunts, and cousins who are older and worthy of respect. . . . As the children grow older, teach them to love their younger brothers and to be compassionate to the employees and servants. Teach them also the respect due the teachers and the behavior codes governing friends. The etiquette governing each movement toward important guests — such as standing, sitting, advancing forward, and retiring from their presence — and the language to be employed must be taught. Teach them how to pay respect to others according to the social positions held by them. Gradually the ways of filial piety and obedience, loyalty and trustworthiness, right deportment and decorum, and sense of shame must be inculcated in the children's minds and they must know how to implement them. Caution them not to desire the possessions of others, or to stoop below one's dignity in consuming excessive amounts of food and drink. . . .

Once reaching the age of eight, children must follow and never lead their elders when entering a gate, sitting, or eating and drinking. From this time on they must be taught how to become humble and yield to others. Do not permit the children to behave as they please. It is important to caution them against "doing their own things."

At the age of ten, let the children be placed under the guidance of a teacher, and tell them about the general meaning of the five constant virtues and let them understand the way of the five human relationships.[2] Let them read books by the Sage[3] and the wise men of old and cultivate the desire for learning. . . . When not engaged in reading, teach them the literary and military arts. . . .

---

[1]The *Little Learning* was written in 1187 by the Song scholar Liu Zucheng, a disciple of Zhu Xi. A book of instruction for young children, it contains rules of behavior and excerpts from the Classics and other works.
[2]The *five virtues* are human heartedness, righteousness, propriety, wisdom, and good faith. The *five relationships* are ruler–subject, father–son, husband–wife, older brother–younger brother, and friend–friend.
[3]The term *Sage* refers to Confucius.

Fifteen is the age when the ancients began the study of the *Great Learning*.[4] From this time on, concentrate on the learning of a sense of justice and duty. The students must also learn to cultivate their personalities and investigate the way of governing people. . . .

Those who are born in the high-ranking families have the heavy obligations of becoming leaders of the people, of having people entrusted to their care, and of governing them. Therefore, without fail, a teacher must be selected for them when they are still young. They must be taught how to read and be informed of the ways of old, of cultivating their personalities, and of the way of governing people. If they do not learn the way of governing people, they may injure the many people who are entrusted to their care by the Way of Heaven. That will be a serious disaster. . . .

GREATER LEARNING FOR WOMEN

Seeing that it is a girl's destiny, on reaching womanhood, to go to a new home, and live in submission to her father-in-law, it is even more incumbent upon her than it is on a boy to receive with all reverence her parents' instructions. Should her parents, through their tenderness, allow her to grow up self-willed, she will infallibly show herself capricious in her husband's house, and thus alienate his affection; while, if her father-in-law be a man of correct principles, the girl will find the yoke of these principles intolerable. She will hate and decry her father-in-law, and the end of those domestic dissensions will be her dismissal from her husband's house and the covering of herself with ignominy. Her parents, forgetting the faulty education they gave her, may indeed lay all the blame on the father-in-law. But they will be in error; for the whole disaster should rightly be attributed to the faulty education the girl received from her parents.

▼ ▼ ▼

More precious in a woman is a virtuous heart than a face of beauty. The vicious woman's heart is ever excited; she glares wildly around her, she vents her anger on others, her words are harsh and her accent vulgar. When she speaks, it is to set herself above others, to upbraid others, to envy others, to be puffed up with individual pride, to jeer at others, to outdo others — all things at variance with the way in which a woman should walk. The only qualities that befit a woman are gentle obedience, chastity, mercy, and quietness.

▼ ▼ ▼

From her earliest youth a girl should observe the line of demarcation separating women from men. The customs of antiquity did not allow men and women to sit in the same apartment, to keep their wearing apparel in the same place, to bathe in the same place, or to transmit to each other anything directly from hand to hand. A woman . . . must observe a certain distance in her relations even with her husband and with her brothers. In our days the women of lower classes, ignoring all rules of this nature, behave disorderly; they contaminate their reputations, bring down reproach upon the head of their parents and brothers, and spend their whole lives in an unprofitable manner. Is not this truly lamentable?

▼ ▼ ▼

It is the chief duty of a girl living in the parental house to practice filial piety towards her father and mother. But after marriage her duty is to honor her father-in-law and mother-in-law, to honor them beyond her father and mother, to love and reverence them with all ardor, and to tend them with practice of every filial piety. . . . Even if your father-in-law and mother-in-law are inclined to hate and vilify you, do not be angry with them, and murmur not. If you carry piety

---

[4]The *Great Learning*, a chapter taken from the *Record of Rituals,* is one of the four relatively short works that came to be known within the Confucian Classics as the Four Books.

towards them to its utmost limits, and minister to them in all sincerity, it cannot be but that they will end by becoming friendly to you.

▼▼▼

The great lifelong duty of a woman is obedience. . . . When the husband issues his instructions, the wife must never disobey them. In a doubtful case, she should inquire of her husband and obediently follow his commands. . . .

Should her husband be roused at any time to anger, she must obey him with fear and trembling, and not set herself up against him in anger and forwardness. A woman should look upon her husband as if he were Heaven itself, and never weary of thinking how she may yield to her husband and thus escape celestial castigation.

▼▼▼

Her treatment of her servant girls will require circumspection. Those low-born girls have had no proper education; they are stupid, obstinate, and vulgar in their speech. . . . Again, in her dealings with those lowly people, a woman will find many things to disapprove of. But if she be always reproving and scolding, and spend her time in hustle and anger, her household will be in a continual state of disturbance. When there is real wrongdoing, she should occasionally notice it, and point out the path of amendment, while lesser faults should be quietly endured without anger. . . .

Commerce in a Confucian World
▼▼▼

3 ▼ *Zhang Han,*
"ON STRANGE TALES" and
"ON MERCHANTS"

The Confucian tradition considered merchants as necessary evils at best. Farmers were the backbone of a healthy society, but merchants, according to many Confucians, were unproductive, uncultured, and obsessed with profit rather than the good of society. Their travels kept them away from the ancestral hearth and prevented them from performing their duties to parents and ancestral spirits. Until 775 C.E., merchants were not permitted to take the civil service examinations, and both their consumption habits and business activities were closely regulated by generally unsympathetic government officials. Despite merchants' low status, commerce flourished in most periods of Chinese history, and during the Ming Era, in which population grew and trade expanded, the merchant's calling came to be viewed more favorably. Sons and daughters of merchants married more frequently into the families of officials and great landowners, and more sons of merchants became government officials after passing the civil service examinations. Some Confucian thinkers praised commerce as necessary for the well-being of society, and others even advanced the argument that successful merchants were equal to or just slightly below the status of officials and gentry.

Zhang Han (1511–1593) is an example of a Ming official who came from a family of successful merchants but was educated to enter government service rather than the family textile business. After passing his civil service examinations in the 1530s, he had a successful government carreer, including appointments as governor-general of Guangdong and Guangxi provinces and important postings in Nanjing and Beijing. After retiring in 1577, he devoted himself to painting and writing. Before his death he wrote numerous essays, including the autobiographical "Yiwen Ji" ("On Strange Tales") and "Shanggu Ji" ("On Merchants"). In these essays he shows a certain ambiguity about the merchant's calling. Although he repeats many of the traditional Confucian criticisms of merchants, he also shows an appreciation of their social importance.

QUESTIONS FOR ANALYSIS

1. On the basis of the information conveyed in Zhang's essays, what conclusions can you draw about the strength of the profit motive in Ming China? To what extent might one characterize the attitudes he describes as capitalistic?
2. Zhang's attitude toward merchants has been described as ambivalent. To what extent do these excerpts affirm such a description?
3. On the basis of the overview provided by Zhang, how would you characterize the Chinese government's policy toward merchants? What was the government's motivation for its policies?
4. What changes does Zhang recommend in the commercial policies of the Ming government? What would his proposed changes accomplish?
5. How important is foreign trade in the overall commercial activity of China?

"ON STRANGE TALES"

Ancestor Yian was of a humble family and made liquor as his profession, In the years of Chenghua (1465–1487) there was a flood. At that time my great-grandfather was living beside a river, and when the water flooded it entered the building. All the liquor he was making was completely spoiled. For several evenings he went out to look at his spoiled liquor and inundated jugs. One evening as he was returning home, someone suddenly called him from behind. My great-grandfather turned to greet him, and was handed something warm. Suddenly the person was not to be seen. When he got home he lit the lamp and shone it on what turned out to be a small ingot of silver. With this he gave up making liquor and bought a loom. He wove ramie and silk of several colours, and achieved a very high level of craftsmanship. Every time a roll of fabric came off the loom, people competed to buy it. He calculated his profit at 20%. After saving for twenty years he bought another loom. Later he increased his looms to over twenty. The mer-

chants who dealt in textiles constantly thronged the house inside and out, and still he couldn't meet their orders. Hereafter, the family profession brought great wealth. The next four ancestors carried on the profession, each gaining wealth in the tens of thousands. The story of his receiving silver late that night is very strange, yet . . . it has been passed down. How is it that it should have started with a spirit's gift?

"ON MERCHANTS"

How important to people are wealth and profit! Human disposition is such that people pursue what is profitable to them, and with this profit in mind they will even face harm. They gallup in pursuit of it day and night, never satisfied with what they have, though it wears down their spirits and exhausts them physically. Profit is what people covet. Since all covet it, they rush after it like torrents pouring into a valley: they come and go without end, never resting day or night, never reaching the point at which the raging floods within them subside such that they finally come to rest. . . . They use up all their energy chasing after the most negligible profits, and become forgetful of their diurnal [daily] exhaustion. How is this any different from thinking the hair's tip big and the mountain small? . . . It is as though they were being led on by the nose and pushed from behind.

Thus it has come to be that the children of merchants may take pleasure in their food and and clothing. Their ornamented stallions are harnessed into teams, their carriages stretch on one after the other like bolts of cloth across the land or like ripples across a river; . . . Crafty, clever men latch on to their wealth and power, flattering them and scurrying about at their disposal. The young women . . . and the girls . . . play on string and reed instruments, perform on zithers, dangle long sleeves and trip about in pointed slippers, vying for beauty and currying favor.

The merchants boast that their knowledge and ability are sufficient to get them anything they want. They set their minds on monopolizing the operations of change in the natural world and scheme to exploit the natural transformations of man and and animal. They shift with the times; when they offer their goods for sale, they control the prices. Tallying it all up, they do not let a hundredth part slip by. Yet they are unembarrassed by the pettiness of this knowledge and ability.

▼ ▼ ▼

In ancient times the sage kings[1] . . . valued agriculture and depreciated commerce. Hence the commercial taxes were double the agricultural taxes. From the time that Emperor Wu of the Han adopted Sang Hongyang's[2] policies, monopolizing all commodities in the empire, and selling them when they were dear and buying them when were cheap, merchants had no way to realize profits and the prices of goods remained stable. . . . He further decreed that merchants could not wear silk, ride in carriages, serve at court, or become officials. He increased their taxes and duties, and thereby disgraced them with misfortune. From this time on, those who pursued this profession saw their possessions exhausted because of this severity. . . .

At the beginning of the Tang dynasty [618–907 C.E.] . . . legal structure became rather lax. The government forced down the prices on merchants' goods, which was purchasing in name but confiscation in fact.

The Song dynasty [960–1279 C.E.] forestalled the corrupt practices of the Tang. The Office of Miscellaneous Purchasing was established, engaging capital officials and eunuchs to run it jointly. . . . When the state storehouses were sufficiently provided for, they were ordered to discontinue purchasing. The rich and powerful merchants were all suspicious and uneasy, watching this but not daring to act, and so the whole point of trading was gone. . . .

Ming dynasty [1368–1644 C.E.] . . . has been more meticulous than previous dynasties. Transport is supervised by the Customs Houses under the jurisdiction of the Ministry of Revenue. Wood products are supervised by the Office of Produce Levies under the jurisdiction of the Ministry of Works. The salt taxation system has both Distribution Commissions and Distribution Superintendancies; as well, there are censors to review it. The administration of the tea tax is also handled in this way. The rest is controlled by the Ministry of Revenue. Thus the laws for exactions on merchants are precise and comprehensive.

▼ ▼ ▼

In the capital[3] the merchants' task is heavy. It is flat land, facing mountains. The area offers rich profits in millet, grain, donkeys, horses, fruits and vegetables. As well, goods from all over the country collect in the markets of the larger cities and then are brought here on carts or carried on shoulders. What is displayed and bartered here goes beyond just the fruits of the land or the

---

[1]China's "sage kings" were mythical rulers whose reigns preceded the appearance of China's first dynasties.
[2]A high official who lived from 150 to 82 B.C.E. He favored a policy of state monopolies and state supervision of the economy.
[3]Beijing.

necessities of clothing. The larger objects clutter up rooms and the precious curios fill trunks, and all are costly in the extreme. Tibetan jade, Hainan pearls, Yunnanese gold, Annamese feathers[4] — all the treasures of the mountains and seas — are what the central kingdom lacks. So men from strange and distant lands do not shirk the dangers of expeditions, and converge here in wave after wave. . . .

South of the capital, Henan takes its place in the center of the empire, with Kaifeng as its capital. One can go north down the Wei and Zhang Rivers right to the edge of the national capital, or follow east along the Bian and Si Rivers to the Han and the Yangzi. Land communications extend in all directions, and merchants delight in gathering here. The region is rich in lacquer, fine hemp fiber, nettle hemp fiber, ramie,[5] cotton thread, cotton wadding, tin, wax, and leather. . . .

To the west of the Yellow River is the old territory of Yong, today called Shaanxi. Being closed in on all four sides by mountains and rivers, it was once called "the fort of heaven.". . . The region is abundant in donkeys, horses, cattle, sheep, felt, fur, meat, and bones. . . .

South of the Yangzi is Iguang. The profit in fish and grain here in the upper reaches extends throughout the empire. . . .

Further down the Yangzi is Nanjing, the place where the first Ming emperor founded his dynasty. . . . From all directions people come like spokes to a hub, from all places in the world they pour into this region. The eunuchs of the Office of the Emperor's Wardrobe value the clothes and shoes here. From the north and the south of the empire, merchants clamor to come. . . . To the east are Songjiang and Changshu, and in the middle is Suzhou. The wealth which the people derive through fish and rice is extreme, and the superb and ornate objects of the artisans are enough to dazzle the people's minds. Those who

are set on wealthy extravagance rush in after them. . . .

Guangdong and Guangxi are between the mountains and the sea. . . . The capital of Guangdong is Guangzhou. . . . Various foreigners come and go along the seacoast between Leizhou and Qiongzhou: they are intent on trade and not on pillaging the border. . . .

Pearls, rhinoceros horn, drugs, tortoise shell, gold, and feathers mostly come by the foreigners' ships, and so merchants gather in Guangdong. . . .

▾ ▾ ▾

As for the border markets in the northwest and the maritime markets in the southeast, we should compare their profits and losses, and their advantages and disadvantages. . . . The markets on the border began by dealing in silks adulterated with ramie, but today they deal in brocades.[6] Horses are all that the tribal chieftains trade in return. I think that if China exchanged adulterated silk for broken horses, the profit is still on our side. They carry it off and no harm comes of it. Today however we sell our brocaded silk. Once they take the gold thread and go, they never return it. When the tribesmen get the silk worn in China for useless hacks, doesn't that go against common sense? . . .

In the southeast, the various foreigners gain profits from our Chinese goods, and China also gains profits from the foreigners' goods. Trading what we have for what we lack is China's intention in trade. . . . Why shrink from doing so? You might say, "The foreigners frequently invade; the situation is such that we cannot do business with them." But you don't understand that the foreigners will not do without their profits from China, just as we cannot do without our profits from them. Prohibit this, keep them from contact, and how can you avoid their turning to piracy?[7] I maintain that once the mar-

---

[4]Hainan is an island off China's coast in the South China Sea; Yunnan is a southern Chinese province; Annam is the eastern coastal region of Indochina, today a part of Vietnam.
[5]Ramie is a plant in the nettle family whose fibrous stem is used to make rope and coarse fabrics.

[6]Brocade is a lustrous textile interwoven with silk, gold, or silver thread.

itime markets are opened, the aggressors will cease of their own accord. . . . What is paid out through the border markets is entirely the precious reserves of the state or the wealth of the rich. What is traded in the maritime market is entirely goods produced among the people, of no consequence to the finances of the state. The border markets operate at a loss and no gain results, whereas the maritime markets could operate at a profit and no harm would ensue. Why don't the government planners think of this?

▼ ▼ ▼

As for taxes on China's merchants, even though they do contribute to the government's revenue,

they are exacted through too many channels. This must be stopped. At every point where a merchant passes a customs house or a ford, the officials there either insist on unloading the carts or docking the boats and checking through the sacks and crates, or just overestimate the value and collect excessive payment. What has passed the customs house or ford has already been taxed, yet the markets then tax it again. One piece of merchandise should be subject to one taxing. There are the institutionalized surtax and the regular tax. The merchants cannot bear the interference caused by the further demands of constables and the exactions of sub-officials. How can merchants who have to pay double what they should not feel heavily afflicted?

---

[7]A major problem of late Ming China was pirate raids on the southeast coast. Most of the pirates were Japanese.

▼ ▼ ▼

Political Decline and Recovery in China and Japan

Eighteenth-century China and Japan were models of well-governed, prosperous states with enlightened rulers and obedient subjects. This had seemed highly unlikely a century and a half earlier, when both societies faced severe political problems. Japan, in the midst of a devastating civil war, seemed on the brink of disintegrating into dozens of small feuding states. China, meanwhile, was suffering from the incompetent rule of a declining Ming Dynasty.

The incessant civil strife of sixteenth-century Japan was rooted in long-standing tensions inherent in Japan's feudal society. In the 1300s power had begun to shift away from the shogun, a military commander who since the late twelfth century had ruled Japan through his armed retainers in the name of the emperor, to local military families who controlled districts and provinces. With a weakened central government, local wars and feuds became endemic among the *daimyo,* the emerging provincial lords, who enlisted both commoners and *samurai,* lesser members of the nobility, to fight in their armies. The warfare intensified between 1467 and 1568, a period sometimes called the Warring States era.

This ruinous feudal anarchy ended as a result of the efforts of three strong military leaders bent on unifying Japan. Oda Nobunaga (1534–1582) brought approximately half of Japan under his rule before a traitorous vassal assassinated him. His successor, Toyotomi Hideyoshi (1536–1598), continued the work of consolidation. It was completed by Tokugawa Ieyasu (1542–1616), who conquered his rivals and had himself declared shogun in 1603. Ieyasu and his successors stabilized Japan by imposing a sociopolitical order that lasted until 1867.

China's political problems under the late Ming had multiple causes, ranging from foreign military threats to fluctuations in the value of silver to a series of poor harvests after the weather turned cold and wet in the early 1600s. Just as these problems began to mount, the quality and effectiveness of Ming rulers plummeted, especially during the interminable reign of Emperor Wanli (1573–1620). Disgusted with his bickering and quarrelsome advisors, Wanli withdrew from politics, ceased to meet with his high officials, and failed to fill vacancies in the administration. Paralyzed by a feud between court eunuchs and Confucian officials, the imperial government drifted as China's problems worsened. Factional strife, oppressive taxation, corruption, unchecked banditry, famine, and bankruptcy led to rebellion, the dynasty's collapse, and foreign conquest. In 1644 a rebel leader, Li Zicheng (1605–1645) captured Beijing, and in despair the last Ming emperor hanged himself. Within months, however, Li was driven from the city by the Manchus, northern invaders from the region of the Amur River. In the following decades the Manchus extended their authority over all of China, established China's last dynasty, the Qing, and breathed new life into the imperial system.

Symptoms of Ming Decline

▼▼▼

4 ▼ *Yang Lien,*
MEMORIAL TO EMPEROR MING XIZONG
CONCERNING EUNUCH WEI ZHONGXIAN

Governing China had always been a formidable task. Expenditures had to be kept in line with revenues; borders needed to be defended; bridges, roads, and dams had to be maintained; countless daily decisions were required of the emperor and his top officials. In the late sixteenth century governing China became even harder. Mongol military pressure grew in the north, pirates continued to raid southern coastal cities, and in the 1590s the Japanese invaded China's ally, Korea. Peasant discontent boiled over into peasant rebellion as rural misery deepened as a result of a series of poor harvests, worsening banditry, and rising taxes, made even more burdensome by fluctuations in the value of silver currency. From the 1580s onward, however, emperors ignored or were distracted from dealing with both their mundane tasks and their extraordinary new challenges. They paid a price for their indifference. Rebellion overwhelmed the government and brought about the fall of the Ming in 1644.

The following selection, a memorial (memorandum) directed to the Xizong emperor by a high official, Yang Lien, highlights another problem of late Ming government, namely the venomous conflict between court eunuchs and Confucian scholar-officials. Eunuchs, castrated males whose theoretical purpose was to manage the day-to-day business of the imperial palace, assumed a greater importance in government when the Wanli emperor secluded himself in the palace and eunuchs became the only intermediary between the emperor and his officials. Eunuch influence was opposed by Confucian officials, especially elite members of the Donglin Society, a group of scholar-officials and former officeholders connected with the Donglin Academy at Wusih on the lower Yangzi River.

The conflict between court eunuchs and the scholar-officials came to a head in the 1620s when the eunuch Wei Zhongxian rose to power during the reign of Emperor Xizong (1568–1627). Wei, who had served as a butler for the emperor's mother and was a close friend of the emperor's former wet nurse, with the backing of spies and a small eunuch army in the palace purged his enemies, levied new taxes, and flouted rules and procedures.

In 1624, Yang Lien, a member of the Donglin Society, took the bold step of denouncing Wei in a memorandum to the emperor. He was carrying out his duties as a member of the Board of Censors, a branch of the administration that served as the "eyes and ears" of the emperor by investigating officals' conduct, hearing subjects' complaints, and reporting problems to the emperor. Emperor Xizong ignored the memorandum, and in 1625 Yang was accused of treason, tortured, and executed on orders of Wei. Wei fell from power in 1627 when the new emperor Chongzhen (r. 1627–1644) exiled him to Anhui province, where Wei hanged himself rather than face an official inquiry. But the Ming government had suffered another wound, and in less than two decades would no longer exist.

QUESTIONS FOR ANALYSIS

1. According to Yang, what motivated him to write this memorandum to the emperor?
2. This excerpt contains only a few of Wei's twenty-four alleged "crimes." How many of them can you find in the excerpt?
3. What is it about Wei's actions that particularly violate the Confucian sensibilities of Yang?
4. What does the memorandum reveal about the basis of Wei's authority and political strength?
5. What does the memorandum tell us about the qualities of the Emperor Ming Xizong?

A treacherous eunuch has taken advantage of his position to act as emperor. He has seized control and disrupted the government, deceived the ruler, and flouted the law. He recognizes no higher authority, turns his back on the favors the emperor has conferred on him, and interferes with the inherited institutions. I beg Your Majesty to order an investigation so that the dynasty can be saved.

When Emperor Hongwu[1] first established the laws and institutions, eunuchs were not allowed to interfere in any affairs outside the palace; even

---

[1]The first Ming emperor, who ruled from 1368 to 1398.

within it they did nothing more than clean up. Anyone who violated these rules was punished without chance of amnesty, so the eunuchs prudently were cautious and obedient. The succeeding emperors never changed these laws. . . .

How would anyone have expected that, with a wise ruler like Your Majesty on the throne, there would be a chief eunuch like Wei Zhongxian, a man totally uninhibited, who destroys court precedents, ignores the ruler to pursue his selfish ends, corrupts good people, ruins the emperor's reputation as a Yao or Shun,[2] and brews unimaginable disasters? The entire court has been intimidated. No one dares denounce him by name. My responsibility really is painful. But when I was supervising secretary of the office of scrutiny for war, the previous emperor personally ordered me to help Your Majesty become a ruler like Yao and Shun. I can still hear his words. If today out of fear I also do not speak out, I will be abandoning my determination to be loyal and my responsibility to serve the state. I would also be turning my back on your kindness in bringing me back to office after retirement and would not be able to face the former emperor in Heaven.

I shall list for Your Majesty Zhongxian's twenty-four most heinous crimes. Zhongxian was originally an ordinary, unreliable sort. He had himself castrated in middle age in order to enter the palace. He is illiterate. . . . Your Majesty was impressed by his minor acts of service and plucked him out of obscurity to confer honors on him. . . .

Our dynastic institutions require that rescripts[3] be delegated to the grand secretaries. This not only allows for calm deliberation and protects from interference, but it assures that someone takes the responsibility seriously. Since Zhongxian usurped power, he issues the imperial edicts. If he accurately conveys your orders, it is bad enough. If he falsifies them, who can argue with him? Recently, men have been forming groups of three or five to push their ideas in the

halls of government, making it as clamorous as a noisy market. Some even go directly into the inner quarters without formal permission. It is possible for a scrap of paper in the middle of the night to kill a person without Your Majesty or the grand secretaries knowing anything of it. The harm this causes is huge. The grand secretaries are so depressed that they ask to quit. Thus Wei Zhongxian destroys the political institutions that had lasted over two hundred years. . . .

One of your concubines, of virtuous and pure character, had gained your favor. Zhongxian was afraid she would expose his illegal behavior, so conspired with his cronies. They said she had a sudden illness to cover up his murdering her. Thus Your Majesty is not able to protect the concubines you favor. . . .

During the forty years that your father the former emperor was heir apparent, Wang An[4] was unique in worrying about all the dangers he faced, protecting him from harm, never giving in to intimidation or temptation. Didn't he deserve some of the credit for your father's getting to the throne? When he died and Your Majesty succeeded, Wang An protected you, so he cannot be called disloyal. Even if he had committed some offense, Your Majesty should have explained what he had done wrong publicly for all to see. Instead Zhongxian, because of his personal hatreds, forged an imperial order and had him killed in Nanhai park. His head and body were separated, his flesh given to the dogs and pigs. This not only revealed his enmity toward Wang An, but his enmity toward all the former emperor's old servants, even his old dogs and horses. It showed him to be without the slightest fear. From that time on, which of the eunuchs was willing to be loyal or principled? I do not know how many thousands or hundreds of the rest of the eunuchs, important and unimportant alike, were slaughtered or driven away for no crime. . . .

Doesn't Your Majesty remember the time when Zhongxian, against all rules, rode his horse

---

[2]Legendary emperors from China's prehistoric past, famous for their virtue and wisdom.
[3]Official decrees and edicts.

[4]The eunuch Wang An was a supporter of the Donglin party and a bitter opponent of Wei Zhongxian. He was killed on Wei's orders in 1621.

in the palace grounds? Those who are favored too much become arrogant; those who receive too many favors grow resentful. I heard that this spring when he rode a horse in front of Your Majesty, you shot and killed the horse, but forgave Zhongxian. Despite your generosity, Zhongxian did not beg to die for his offense, but rather acted more arrogantly in Your Majesty's presence and spoke resentfully of Your Majesty when away. He is on guard morning and night, missing nothing. His trusted followers keep guard all the time. In the past traitors and bandits have struggled to wreak havoc and take over. This is in fact what Your Majesty now faces. How can you release a tiger right by your elbow? Even if Zhongxian were cut into mincemeat, it would not atone for his sins. . . .

There is adequate evidence of his crimes. They are widely known and have been widely witnessed; they are not a matter of gossip. Zhongxian, guilty of these twenty-four great crimes, kills or replaces any eunuch he fears will expose his treachery. Thus those close at hand are terrified and keep silent. He expels or imprisons any of the officials he fears will expose his villainy, so the officials also all look the other way and keep silent. There are even ignorant spineless fellows eager to get rich and powerful who attach themselves to him or hang around his gate. They praise whatever he likes and criticize whatever he hates, doing whatever is needed. Thus whatever he inside wants they do outside, whatever they outside say he responds to inside. Disaster or good luck can depend on slight movements. And if per chance the evil deeds of the inner court are revealed, there is still Lady Ke[5] to make excuses or cover up.

As a consequence, everyone in the palace recognizes the existence of Zhongxian but not of Your Majesty; everyone in the capital recognizes the existence of Zhongxian but not of Your Majesty. Even the major and minor officials and workers, by turning toward the sources of power, unconsciously show that they do not recognize the existence of Your Majesty, only of Zhongxian. Whenever they see that some matter needs urgent attention or an appointment needs to be made, they always say, "It must be discussed with the eunuch." When a matter cannot be handled or a person appointed, they just explain that the eunuch is not willing. All matters, large and small, in both the palace and the government offices, are decided by Zhongxian alone. . . .

In the tenth year of the first emperor of the dynasty [1377], there was a eunuch who had been in service a long time but carelessly mentioned a governmental matter. The emperor dismissed him that very day and told his officials, "Even though we attribute the fall of the Han and Tang[6] dynasties to the eunuchs, it was the rulers who made it possible by trusting and loving them. If in the past eunuchs had not commanded troops or participated in politics, they would not have been able to cause disorder no matter what they wanted. This eunuch has admittedly served me a long time, but I cannot overlook his mistake. Getting rid of him decisively will serve as a warning to those to come." How brilliant! A eunuch who mentioned a governmental matter became a warning for the future. What about Zhongxian who deceives his ruler, recognizes no one above him, and piles up crimes? How can he be left unpunished?

I beg Your Majesty to take courage and thunder forth. Take Zhongxian to the ancestral temple in fetters. Assemble the military and civil officials of all ranks and have the judicial officials interrogate him. Check all the precedents from previous reigns on eunuchs having contacts with the outside, usurping imperial authority, breaking dynastic laws, disrupting court business, alienating the people, and violating the trust of

---

[5]Lady Ke, who had been the emperor's wet nurse, was instrumental in Wei's rise to power and reputedly his lover.

[6]The Han Dynasty ruled China from 206 B.C.E. to 220 C.E.; the Tang, from 618 to 907.

the ruler. Sentence him in a way that will please the gods and satisfy public indignation. . . .

If all this is done and yet Heaven does not show its pleasure, the people do not rejoice, and there is not a new era of peace within the country and at its borders, then I ask that you behead me as an offering to Zhongxian. I am well aware that once my words become known, Zhongxian's clique will detest me, but I am not afraid. If I could get rid of the one person Zhongxian and

save Your Majesty's reputation as a Yao and Shun, I would fulfill the command of the former emperor and could face the spirits of all ten of the former [Ming] emperors. My lifetime goal has been to serve loyally. I would not regret having to die as a way of paying back the extraordinary favors I have received during two reigns. I hope Your Majesty recognizes my passion and takes prompt action.

The Tokugawa Formula for Japan
▼▼▼

5 ▼ *Tokugawa Hidetada,*
LAWS GOVERNING THE
MILITARY HOUSEHOLDS

In 1605, two years after defeating his enemies among the daimyo and becoming shogun, Tokugawa Ieyasu resigned the shogunate and conferred the office on his son, Hidetada, to ensure an orderly succession. Ieyasu, however, continued as de facto ruler until his death in 1616. In 1615 he issued under his son's name the following code for Japan's warrior aristocrats. Drawn up with the aid of Confucian scholars, it is a succinct statement of the Tokugawa formula for ending the social and political ills that had caused Japan's disintegration in the sixteenth century.

QUESTIONS FOR ANALYSIS

1. What provisions of this edict are meant to ensure the shogun's control of the daimyo?
2. Even though the independence of the daimyo was limited by Tokugawa policies, the daimyo still retained certain political powers. How many can be identified in this document?
3. How does the code define the ideal samurai?
4. What sort of social order does the code envision?
5. Where in this document is it possible to detect the influence of Confucian principles?

1. The study of literature and the practice of the military arts, archery and horsemanship, must be cultivated diligently. . . .

From of old the rule has been to practice "the arts of peace on the left hand, and the arts of war on the right"; both must be mastered. Archery and horsemanship are indispensable to military men. Though arms are called instruments of evil, there are times when they must be resorted to. In peacetime we should not be oblivious to the danger of war. Should we not, then, prepare ourselves for it?

2. Drinking parties and wanton revelry should be avoided. *more things that could with it*

In the codes that have come down to us this kind of dissipation has been severely proscribed. Sexual indulgence and habitual gambling lead to the downfall of a state.

3. Offenders against the law should not be harbored or hidden in any domain.

Law is the basis of social order. Reason may be violated in the name of the law, but law may not be violated in the name of reason. Those who break the law deserve heavy punishment.

4. Great lords [daimyo], the lesser lords, and officials should immediately expel from their domains any among their retainers or henchmen who have been charged with treason or murder.

Wild and wicked men may become weapons for overturning the state and destroying the people. How can they be allowed to go free?

5. Henceforth no outsider, none but the inhabitants of a particular domain, shall be permitted to reside in that domain.

Each domain has its own ways. If a man discloses the secrets of one's own country to another domain or if the secrets of the other domain are disclosed to one's own, that will sow the seeds of deceit. . . .

6. Whenever it is intended to make repairs on a castle of one of the feudal domains, the [shogunate] should be notified. The construction of any new castles is to be halted and stringently prohibited.

"Big castles are a danger to the state."[1] Walls and moats are the cause of great disorders.

7. Immediate report should be made of innovations which are being planned or of factional conspiracies being formed in neighboring domains.

Men all incline toward partisanship; few are wise and impartial. There are some who refuse to obey their masters, and others who feud with their neighbors.[2] Why, instead of abiding by the established order, do they wantonly embark upon new schemes?

8. Do not enter into marriage privately [i.e., without notifying the shogunate authorities].

Marriage follows the principle of harmony between yin and yang,[3] and must not be entered into lightly. In the *Book of Changes*,[4] . . . it says, "Marriage should not be contracted out of enmity (against another). Marriages intended to effect an alliance with enemies [of the state] will turn out badly." The Peach Blossom ode in *The Book of Poetry* also says that "When men and women are proper in their relationships and marriage is arranged at the correct time; then throughout the land there will be no loose women." To form an alliance by marriage is the root of treason.

9. Visits of the daimyo to the capital are to be in accordance with regulations.

---

[1]The quotation is a paraphrase from *The Tradition of Tso,* a commentary on *The Spring and Autumn Annals.*

[2]From the Seventeen Article Constitution of Prince Shotuku (573–621). While serving as regent for his aunt, Empress Suiko, the prince drew up seventeen principles of government designed to strengthen central authority and end disorder. He drew heavily on Confucian principles.

[3]*Yin* and *yang* are the two fundamental forces, tendencies, or elements in Chinese philosophy that since ancient times have been used to explain change in natural processes of all sorts. Yin suggests qualities that are female, weak, dark, cold, and connected with the moon; yang suggests qualities that are male, strong, warm, bright, and connected with the sun. Every being and substance contains both elements in varying proportions. As one of the elements increases within a being or substance, the other decreases but is never eliminated.

[4]*The Book of Changes,* a treatise on divination, and *The Book of Poetry,* a collection of songs, are among the oldest Confucian texts.

The *Chronicles of Japan, continued*[5] contains a regulation that "Clansmen should not gather together whenever they please, but only when they have to conduct some public business; and also that the number of horsemen serving as an escort in the capital should be limited to twenty. . . ." Daimyo should not be accompanied by a large number of soldiers. Twenty horsemen shall be the maximum escort for daimyo with an income of from one million to two hundred thousand *koku* of rice.[6] For those with an income of one hundred thousand koku or less, the escort should be proportionate to their income. On official missions, however, they may be accompanied by an escort proportionate to their rank.

10. Restrictions on the type and quality of dress to be worn should not be transgressed.

Lord and vassal, superior and inferior, should observe what is proper to their station in life. [Then follows an injunction against the wearing of fine white damask or purple silk by retainers without authorization.]   *privilege*

11. Persons without rank shall not ride in palanquins.[7]

From of old there have been certain families entitled to ride in palanquins without special permission, and others who have received such permission. Recently, however, even the ordinary retainers and henchmen of some families have taken to riding about in palanquins, which is truly the worst sort of presumption. Henceforth permission shall be granted only to the lords of the various domains, their close relatives and ranking officials, medical men and astrologers, those over sixty years of age, and those ill or infirm. In the cases of ordinary household retainers or henchmen who willfully ride in palanquins, their masters shall be held accountable.

Exceptions to this law are the court families, Buddhist prelates, and the clergy in general.

12. The samurai of the various domains shall lead a frugal and simple life.

When the rich make a display of their wealth, the poor are humiliated and envious. Nothing engenders corruption so much as this, and therefore it must be strictly curbed.

13. The lords of the domains should select officials with a capacity for public administration.

Good government depends on getting the right men. Due attention should be given to their merits and faults; rewards and punishments must be properly meted out. If a domain has able men, it flourishes; if it lacks able men it is doomed to perish. This is the clear admonition of the wise men of old.

---

[5]*Nihongi, The Chronicles of Japan,* written in 720, is the oldest official history of Japan, covering the mythical age of the gods up to the time of the Empress Jito, who reigned from 686 to 697. This quotation comes from a sequel to *The Chronicles* called the *Shoku nihongi.*

[6]One *koku* equals about five bushels; a person's rank was determined by the amount of rice his lands produced.
[7]Enclosed carriages, usually for one person, borne on the shoulders of carriers by means of poles.

▼▼▼

Europeans in East and Southeast Asia

The Europeans' early impact on East and Southeast Asia varied from their conquest of the Philippines to their expulsion from Japan. In the Philippines after several false starts the Spaniards subjugated the major islands between 1565 and

1571, established a regime modeled on New Spain in the Americas, and undertook the conversion of Filipinos to Catholicism. This was far different from the Europeans' experience in Japan, where their century-long presence as traders and missionaries ended in the 1630s when the shogun expelled all Europeans and decreed that only one Dutch ship a year would be permitted to trade with Japan. The shogun's seriousness was underscored by the experience of two Portuguese envoys who came to Japan in 1640 to petition for the reopening of trade and were promptly executed.

The rest of the region had experiences that fell somewhere between those of Japan and the Philippines. The Chinese treated the newly arrived Europeans like all other foreigners who sought trade and diplomatic relations with the Central Kingdom. Europeans would have to recognize China's superiority and realize that trade with China could take place only at the pleasure of the emperor and according to his rules. The Portuguese at first had trouble abiding by these rules, so the Chinese expelled them in 1522 and allowed them back only after restricting their commercial activity to the small peninsula of Macao, some seventy miles from Guongzhou. European trade with China continued but did not grow appreciably until the eighteenth century.

A small number of Chinese showed an interest in European culture and Christianity. Jesuit fathers, with their knowledge of European mathematics and science, were welcomed to the emperor's court as long as they honored Confucius, wore Chinese garb, and were subservient to the emperor. With their presence tolerated by the emperors, Catholic missionaries managed to convert several hundred thousand Chinese to Christianity by the late 1600s. In the eighteenth century, however, emperors and their officials took umbrage at the refusal of many non-Jesuit clergy to accommodate themselves to Chinese thought and practices. In the 1720s the suppression of Christianity began.

No area had more variety in its dealings with Europeans than Southeast Asia. In Burma, Cambodia, Vietnam, Thailand, and Laos, the European presence was limited to small trading posts in no more than a dozen ports and an even smaller number of religious missions. In the East Indies and Malay Peninsula, the Portuguese burst on the scene with their conquest of Melaka in 1511 and their establishment of fortified trading posts in other locations. Their thrust into the region soon stalled, however, and their dream of establishing a commercial monopoly was never realized. Their missionary efforts also foundered. Conversions were rare and, paradoxically, Portuguese aggressiveness might have even strengthened Islam, which came to be viewed as a symbol of resistance to the Europeans. The Netherlands, which became the dominant European power in the East Indies during the seventeenth century, established tighter control of the spice trade and displaced native rulers in Java and the Moluccas. But until the late 1600s, even the well-organized and single-minded Dutch were simply another new participant in the region's age-old patterns of commercial rivalry and politics.

The Seclusion of Japan
▼▼▼

6 ▼ *Tokugawa Iemitsu,*
CLOSED COUNTRY EDICT OF 1635

For close to a century Japan was a European success story in Asia. Portuguese traders and missionaries began visiting Japan regularly in the 1540s, and the Spanish, Dutch, and English soon followed. The Japanese were fascinated by European goods such as eyeglasses and clocks and were quick to appreciate the military potential of European firearms and artillery. Some even adopted European dress. Daimyo on the island of Kyushu in southwestern Japan competed for European trade by tolerating the presence of Catholic missionaries and in a few cases converting to Christianity themselves. Oda Nobunaga, the military leader who unified approximately half of Japan in the 1570s and 1580s, encouraged Catholic missionary activity to weaken his rivals, the powerful and wealthy Buddhist monasteries. His tolerance of missionary activity led to numerous conversions in the district of Kyoto, Japan's capital city. By the early seventeenth century approximately 500,000 Japanese had become Christians.

By then, however, anti-European sentiment was growing. Nobunaga's successor, Hideyoshi, became suspicious of Europeans after the Spaniards conquered the Philippines, and he began to question the loyalty of daimyo who had become Christians. In 1597 he ordered the crucifixion of nine Catholic missionaries and seventeen Japanese converts. The early Tokugawa shoguns, in their single-minded pursuit of stability and order, also feared the subversive potential of Christianity. They sought to obliterate it, while at the same time limiting commercial contacts with China, Southeast Asia, and Europe.

Japan's isolation policy was fully implemented by Tokugawa Iemitsu, Ieyasu's grandson and shogun from 1623 to 1651. His edicts largely closed Japan to all foreigners and prevented his subjects from leaving Japan. The following document, the most famous of Iemitsu's exclusion edicts, is directed to the two commissioners of Nagasaki, a port city in southern Japan and an early center of Christianity.

QUESTIONS FOR ANALYSIS

1. What steps are to be taken to suppress Christianity?
2. How are commercial dealings with foreigners to be handled before they are ended altogether?
3. In what ways did the edict affect the shogun's Japanese subjects?
4. Does trade or Christianity seem to have been the greater threat to Japan according to the edict?

1. Japanese ships are strictly forbidden to leave for foreign countries.

2. No Japanese is permitted to go abroad. If there is anyone who attempts to do so secretly, he must be executed. The ship so involved must be impounded and its owner arrested, and the matter must be reported to the higher authority.

3. If any Japanese returns from overseas after residing there, he must be put to death.

4. If there is any place where the teachings of the [Catholic] priests is practiced, the two of you must order a thorough investigation.

5. Any informer revealing the whereabouts of the followers of the priests must be rewarded accordingly. If anyone reveals the whereabouts of a high ranking priest, he must be given one hundred pieces of silver. For those of lower ranks, depending on the deed, the reward must be set accordingly.

6. If a foreign ship has an objection (to the measures adopted) and it becomes necessary to report the matter to Edo,[1] you may ask the Omura[2] domain to provide ships to guard the foreign ship. . . .

7. If there are any Southern Barbarians[3] who propagate the teachings of the priests, or otherwise commit crimes, they may be incarcerated in the prison. . . .

8. All incoming ships must be carefully searched for the followers of the priests.

9. No single trading city shall be permitted to purchase all the merchandise brought by foreign ships.

10. Samurai[4] are not permitted to purchase any goods originating from foreign ships directly from Chinese merchants in Nagasaki.

11. After a list of merchandise brought by foreign ships is sent to Edo, as before you may order that commercial dealings may take place without waiting for a reply from Edo.

12. After settling the price, all white yarns[5] brought by foreign ships shall be allocated to the five trading cities[6] and other quarters as stipulated.

13. After settling the price of white yarns, other merchandise [brought by foreign ships] may be traded freely between the [licensed] dealers. However, in view of the fact that Chinese ships are small and cannot bring large consignments, you may issue orders of sale at your discretion. Additionally, payment for goods purchased must be made within twenty days after the price is set.

14. The date of departure homeward of foreign ships shall not be later than the twentieth day of the ninth month. Any ships arriving in Japan later than usual shall depart within fifty days of their arrival. As to the departure of Chinese ships, you may use your discretion to order their departure after the departure of the Portuguese *galeota*.[7]

15. The goods brought by foreign ships which remained unsold may not be deposited or accepted for deposit.

16. The arrival in Nagasaki of representatives of the five trading cities shall not be later than the fifth day of the seventh month. Anyone arriving later than that date shall lose the quota assigned to his city.

17. Ships arriving in Hirado[8] must sell their raw silk at the price set in Nagasaki, and are not permitted to engage in business transactions until after the price is established in Nagasaki.

---

[1]Modern Tokyo, the seat of the Tokugawa government.
[2]The area around the city of Nagasaki.
[3]Westerners.
[4]Members of Japan's military aristocracy.
[5]Raw silk.

[6]The cities of Kyoto, Edo, Osaka, Sakai, and Nagasaki.
[7]A galleon, an ocean-going Portuguese ship.
[8]A small island, not far from Nagasaki.

Catholic-Confucian Tension in Late Ming China
▼▼▼
7 ▼ *Matteo Ricci, JOURNALS*

Wherever they went in Asia, the Portuguese sought more than commercial profit. They also sought to convert nonbelievers to Christianity, and to do so they enlisted the help of the Society of Jesus, or Jesuits, a new religious order founded by the Spaniard Ignatius Loyola in the 1540s. The greatest prize for European missionaries was China, where the Portuguese arrived in 1514, and after a series of misunderstandings and conflicts, were granted permission to build a permanent settlement and carry on trade in Macao, approximately thirty miles south of the major port city of Guangzhou. Macao also became the base from which the Jesuits planned and managed their missionary work in China.

Hindered by thin funding and the Chinese refusal to allow Catholic priests on the mainland, the Jesuits' missionary efforts made little progress until 1582, when officials allowed the Jesuits to establish a residence in Zhaoqing, a city some sixty miles west of Guangzhou. This was also the year in which a thirty-one-year-old Italian Jesuit, Matteo Ricci, fresh from training in Rome and Goa, took up residence in Zhaoqing. Under Ricci's leadership, the Jesuits developed a missionary strategy that differed from their tactics in Japan, where they had preached Christianity directly to the common people. In China, the Jesuits targeted intellectuals, officials, and ultimately, members of the imperial court, whom they sought to impress by learning Chinese, adopting Chinese dress, giving gifts of clocks and other mechanical instruments, and displaying their scientific and mathematical erudition. By the early 1600s, approximately two dozen Jesuit priests were active in China, with residences in several cities including the capital, Beijing, where in 1601 on the strength of his knowledge of astronomy and mathematics, Ricci was invited to establish a residence by the Wanli emperor himself. Here Ricci remained until his death in 1610, by which time the Jesuits had converted several thousand Chinese, including some members of the imperial family.

In addition to winning converts, the Jesuits also made enemies, and they could never be sure if permission granted by one official to establish a residence in a city would be withdrawn by that official's successor. An example of the difficulties they faced is the episode that took place in Nanchang in 1607, when local magistrates sought to close the Jesuit residence. The course of events is recorded in Ricci's journal, which a Jesuit colleague edited and published shortly after Ricci's death. In Ricci's account of the Nanchang incident, we can see some of the cultural barriers and attitudes that made the Jesuits' efforts to accommodate Christianity to Chinese civilization so difficult.

QUESTIONS FOR ANALYSIS

1. What aspects of Christianity most offended the Confucians who brought charges against Jesuits?

2. The Jesuits' association with Father Ricci seems to have favored them in the conflict with the Nanchang Confucians. Why? What was there about Ricci that gave his Jesuit colleagues an aura of legitimacy?
3. Why did Ricci view the outcome of the dispute as a Christian victory?
4. How do you think the Nanchang Confucians viewed the outcome of the dispute? Why?

During 1606 and the year following, the progress of Christianity in Nanchang was in no wise retarded. . . . The number of neophytes [new converts] increased by more than two hundred, all of whom manifested an extraordinary piety in their religious devotions. As a result, the reputation of the Christian religion became known throughout the length and breadth of this metropolitan city. . . .

Through the efforts of Father Emanuele Dias another and a larger house was purchased, in August of 1607, at a price of a thousand gold pieces. This change was necessary, because the house he had was too small for his needs and was situated in a flood area. Just as the community was about to change from one house to the other, a sudden uprising broke out against them. . . .

At the beginning of each month, the Magistrates hold a public assembly . . . in the temple of their great Philosopher.[1] When the rites of the new-moon were completed in the temple, and these are civil rather than religious rites,[2] one of those present took advantage of the occasion to speak on behalf of the others, and to address the highest Magistrate present. . . . "We wish to warn you," he said, "that there are certain foreign priests in this royal city, who are preaching a law [moral law], hitherto unheard of in this kingdom, and who are holding large gatherings of people in their house." Having said this, he referred them to their local Magistrate, . . . and he in turn ordered the plaintiffs to present their case in writing, assuring them that he would support it with all his authority, in an effort to have the foreign priests expelled. The complaint was written out that same day and signed with twenty-seven signatures. . . . The content of the document was somewhat as follows.

Matthew Ricci, Giovanni Soerio, Emanuele Dias, and certain other foreigners from western kingdoms, men who are guilty of high treason against the throne, are scattered amongst us, in five different provinces. They are continually communicating with each other and are here and there practicing brigandage on the rivers, collecting money, and then distributing it to the people, in order to curry favor with the multitudes. They are frequently visited by the Magistrates, by the high nobility and by the Military Prefects, with whom they have entered into a secret pact, binding unto death.

These men teach that we should pay no respect to the images of our ancestors, a doctrine which is destined to extinguish the love of future generations for their forebears. Some of them break up the idols, leaving the temples empty and the gods to be pitied, without any patronage. In the beginning they lived in small houses, but by this time they have bought up large and magnificent residences. The doctrine they teach is something infernal. It attracts the ignorant into its fraudulent meshes, and great crowds of this class are continually assembled at their houses. Their doctrine gets beyond the city walls and spreads itself through the neighboring towns and villages and into the open country, and the people become so wrapt up in its falsity, that students are not following their course, laborers are neglecting their work, farmers are not cultivating their acres, and even the women

---

[1]Confucius.
[2]Ricci and his fellow Jesuits viewed Confucian ceremonies in honor of deceased ancestors as civil, not religious, rites, therefore not in conflict with Christianity.

have no interest in their housework. The whole city has become disturbed, and, whereas in the beginning there were only a hundred or so professing their faith, now there are more than twenty thousand. These priests distribute pictures of some Tartar or Saracen,[3] who they say is God, who came down from heaven to redeem and to instruct all of humanity, and who alone, according to their doctrine, can give wealth and happiness; a doctrine by which the simple people are very easily deceived. These men are an abomination on the face of the earth, and there is just ground for fear that once they have erected their own temples, they will start a rebellion. . . . Wherefore, moved by their interest in the maintenance of the public good, in the conservation of the realm, and in the preservation, whole and entire, of their ancient laws, the petitioners are presenting this complaint and demanding, in the name of the entire province, that a rescript of it be forwarded to the King, asking that these foreigners be sentenced to death, or banished from the realm, to some deserted island in the sea. . . .

Each of the Magistrates to whom the indictment was presented asserted that the spread of Christianity should be prohibited, and that the foreign priests should be expelled from the city, if the Mayor saw fit, after hearing the case, and notifying the foreigners. . . . But the [Jesuit] Fathers, themselves, were not too greatly disturbed, placing their confidence in Divine Providence, which had always been present to assist them on other such dangerous occasions.

▷ Father Emanuele is summoned before the Chief Justice.

Father Emanuele, in his own defense, . . . gave a brief outline of the Christian doctrine. Then he

showed that according to the divine law, the first to be honored, after God, were a man's parents. But the judge had no mind to hear or to accept any of this and he made it known that he thought it was all false. After that repulse, with things going from bad to worse, it looked as if they were on the verge of desperation, so much so, indeed, that they increased their prayers, their sacrifices, and their bodily penances, in petition for a favorable solution of their difficulty. Their adversaries appeared to be triumphantly victorious. They were already wrangling about the division of the furniture of the Mission residences, and to make results doubly certain, they stirred up the flames anew with added accusations and indictments. . . .

The Mayor, who was somewhat friendly with the Fathers, realizing that there was much in the accusation that was patently false, asked the Magistrate Director of the Schools,[4] if he knew whether or not this man Emanuele was a companion of Matthew Ricci, who was so highly respected at the royal court, and who was granted a subsidy from the royal treasury, because of the gifts he had presented to the King. Did he realize that the Fathers had lived in Nanjing for twelve years, and that no true complaint had ever been entered against them for having violated the laws? Then he asked him if he had really given full consideration as to what was to be proven in the present indictment. To this the Director of the Schools replied that he wished the Mayor to make a detailed investigation of the case and then to confer with him. The Chief Justice then ordered the same thing to be done. Fortunately, it was this same Justice who was in charge of city affairs when Father Ricci first arrived in Nanchang. It was he who first gave the Fathers permission, with the authority of the Viceroy, to open a house there. . . .

After the Mayor had examined the charges of the plaintiffs and the reply of the defendants, he

---

[3]A reference to Jesus.

[4]A local Confucian official and one of the Jesuits' enemies.

subjected the quasi-literati[5] to an examination in open court, and taking the Fathers under his patronage, he took it upon himself to refute the calumnies of their accusers. He said he was fully convinced that these strangers were honest men, and that he knew that there were only two of them in their local residence and not twenty, as had been asserted. To this they replied that the Chinese were becoming their disciples. To which the Justice in turn replied: "What of it? Why should we be afraid of our own people? Perhaps you are unaware of the fact that Matthew Ricci's company is cultivated by everyone in Beijing, and that he is being subsidized by the royal treasury. How dare the Magistrates who are living outside of the royal city expel men who have permission to live at the royal court? These men here have lived peacefully in Nanjing for twelve years. I command," he added, "that they buy no more large houses, and that the people are not to follow their law." . . .

A few days later, the court decision was pronounced and written out . . . and was then posted at the city gates as a public edict. The following is a summary of their declaration. Having examined the cause of Father Emanuele and his companions, it was found that these men had come here from the West because they had heard so much about the fame of the great Chinese Empire, and that they had already been living in the realm for some years, without any display of ill-will. Father Emanuele should be permitted to practice his own religion, but it was not considered to be the right thing for the common people, who are attracted by novelties, to adore the God of Heaven. For them to go over to the religion of foreigners would indeed be most unbecoming. . . . It would therefore seem to be . . . [in] . . . the best interests of the Kingdom, to . . . [warn] . . . everyone in a public edict not to abandon the sacrifices of their ancient religion by accepting the cult of foreigners. Such a movement might, indeed, result in calling together certain gatherings, detrimental to the public welfare, and harmful also to the foreigner, himself. Wherefore, the Governor of this district, by order of the high Magistrates, admonishes the said Father Emanuele to refrain from perverting the people, by inducing them to accept a foreign religion. The man who sold him the larger house is to restore his money and Emanuele is to buy a smaller place, sufficient for his needs, and to live there peaceably, as he has done, up to the present. Emanuele, himself, has agreed to these terms and the Military Prefects of the district have been ordered to make a search of the houses there and to confiscate the pictures of the God they speak of, wherever they find them. It is not permitted for any of the native people to go over to the religion of the foreigners, nor is it permitted to gather together for prayer meetings. Whoever does contrary to these prescriptions will be severely punished, and if the Military Prefects are remiss in enforcing them, they will be held to be guilty of the same crimes. To his part of the edict, the Director of the Schools added, that the common people were forbidden to accept the law of the foreigners, and that a sign should be posted above the door of the Father's residence, notifying the public that these men were forbidden to have frequent contact with the people.

The Fathers were not too disturbed by this pronouncement, because they were afraid that it was going to be much worse. In fact, everyone thought it was rather favorable, and that the injunction launched against the spread of the faith was a perfunctory order to make it appear that the literati were not wholly overlooked, since the Fathers were not banished from the city, as the literati had demanded. Moreover it was not considered a grave misdemeanor for the Chinese to change their religion, and it was not customary to inflict a serious punishment on those violating such an order. The neophytes, themselves, proved this when they continued, as formerly, to attend Mass.

---

[5]Ricci's term for the Jesuits' opponents in Nanchang. These were scholars who by passing the first and most basic of the three Chinese civil service examinations earned recognition as competent students, but were not eligible for appointments to posts in the imperial administration. By calling them "quasi-literati," Ricci is making the point that they had not yet gained the status of true scholars.

Siamese-Dutch Tensions in the Seventeenth Century

▼▼▼

8 ▾ *LETTER TO THE DUTCH EAST INDIA COMPANY BOARD OF DIRECTORS*

The Dutch, having won their political independence from Spain at the close of the sixteenth century, immediately and aggressively entered the competition for profits in Asia. This weakened the commercial empire of Portugal, which lacked the wealth and organization to maintain its position against the Dutch East India Company, a joint stock company founded in 1602 and backed by the Dutch government, which had ample capital, military muscle, and a board of directors in Amsterdam (known as "the Seventeen") that controlled its operations. The fall of Melaka to the Dutch in 1641 ended the Portuguese empire in Southeast Asia except on the island of Timor, which the Portuguese held until the twentieth century. The Dutch also took political control of Java and the Moluccas and defeated or weakened regional challengers such as the kingdom of Acheh.

As the following document shows, however, even with their wealth and organization, the Dutch still needed to cultivate good relations with the region's rulers to be successful. This letter was written by an agent of the Dutch East India Company stationed in Jakarta to the Seventeen in 1655. He expressed his concern about a diplomatic problem with the king of Siam (modern Thailand) and its implications for Dutch trade and prestige. Siam, with its capital to the north of Bangkok in Ayutthaya, was the strongest monarchy in Southeast Asia, with leaders who were skillful in playing off one European power against another. The letter was prompted by Siamese anger over the recent Dutch blockade of Tennasserim, a city in a Siamese vassal state on the Bay of Bengal, and the refusal of the Dutch to help the Siamese king suppress a rebellion in Singgora, another vassal state on the Bay of Siam.

QUESTIONS FOR ANALYSIS

1. How would you characterize Siamese attitudes toward the Dutch?
2. How did the Dutch resident Westerwolt react when the Siamese court became antagonistic toward the Dutch? What does his behavior reveal about Dutch attitudes toward the Siamese?
3. According to the author and Westerwolt, how might the Dutch be weakened by their disfavor with the king?
4. How in the short run did the Dutch try to solve their problems with the unhappy Siamese king?
5. What does the document reveal about the competition the Dutch were facing from the English in Southeast Asia?

It appears that the merchant Hendrich Craijer Zalr had promised, so they[1] say, 20 ships, which was a very rash proceeding on his part, and thereupon they made the above-mentioned expedition, which they said, if our support did not appear, would be obliged to return unsuccessful and with shame and dishonor to the crown, as was actually the case. Moreover, it happened that a writing had come unexpectedly from the governor of Tennasserim that two Dutch ships had held the harbor there for 2 months, and had prevented the entrance and departure of foreign traders, which caused great annoyance in Siam, especially at Court, and embittered everyone against us. This gave the Companies[2] very favorable opportunity to blacken us and to make us odious to everyone, and to change the King's feeble opposition into open enmity. . . .

Wherefore the resident Westerwolt,[3] who was convinced of the contrary, since he would certainly have been informed before any such action was taken, finally found himself obliged to ask that certain persons, on the King's behalf and on his own, should be . . . sent overland to Tennasserim, in order to discover on the spot the truth of the case, which request was granted by the King, and on our behalf the junior merchant, Hugo van Crujlenburgh was sent.

Meanwhile the aforementioned resident Westerwolt had on various occasions made complaint of the bad and unreasonable treatment received [at the Siamese court], but got nothing by it but a summons to court, and before four councilors was questioned on certain points to which he had to answer forthwith, and the answer was written down word for word, to be laid before the King, who sat by and waited, and every now and then asked whether one of the questions had yet been put. So that the resident was in very great embarrassment and did not know whether

even his life was any longer safe. These questions were for the most part on the subject of the help asked for against Singgora, the Siamese professing to have gone to war with the Spanish on our account, and to have suffered much damage in the same, and that we now refused to assist his Majesty against the rebels with ships and men; whereas the beforementioned merchant, Hendrich Craijer, had definitely made him such promises. Therefore he [the king] had sent his forces to Ligor so as to cooperate with him [Craijer] on his arrival and keep his word: But instead we had sent our ships to Tennasserim and had taken possession of the place in order to keep foreigners away and to ruin their trade. In consequence of this inquiry Westerwolt was inclined to depart from Siam and so make an end of this business, as he had sometimes proposed to do, and as there were two of our ships lying ready at the bar . . . he thought he could initiate and carry his proposal into execution, but was warned that no living soul would escape the power of the King since he could kill them all and trample them under foot and that his threats [of departing] were not at all to the purpose.

For all which reasons the aforesaid resident could not answer the questions put to him without embarrassment: And nothing followed thereon, except that four or five days later a prohibition was published that, for the future, neither Siamese nor Peguers[4] were to be allowed to serve the Dutch, thus putting great contempt upon the nation. From all which contemptuous proceedings the above-mentioned Westerwolt came to the conclusion that in case the long expected help could not be sent this year we should have trouble in Siam; also that this same year the Japanese cargoes were likely to be unimportant, even if he were allowed to ship and dispatch them. This gave us no small concern, for now, in addition to the war with Portugal, we

---

[1]Refers to the Siamese royal court.
[2]The British East India Company; it is unclear why the plural is used.
[3]The resident agent of the Dutch East India Company at the Siamese royal court.

[4]A city in modern Myanmar (Burma), then a vassal state of Siam.

had come to a rupture with the new government in England,[5] and it still continued impossible for us to spare any force in ships or men for Siam, and it was also inadvisable to continue to keep the King any longer in an uncertain hope, whereby our cause could only be made worse the longer it lasted, since it was quite uncertain whether we in the near future should have the power to help him. Besides it is not the Company's function nor does it agree with its maxims to interpose itself in the wars of foreign potentates over questions and quarrels which do not concern it in the least.

Nevertheless, it was decided and considered necessary to send thither at least one good fly-boat[6] to take the cargo for Japan,[7] if it were allowed, or, in case of refusal, to sail to Taiwan, in order to return hither at its proper time with sugar. For which purpose the aforesaid *Crowned*

Charity was again employed, departing on the 21st May . . . with a letter and a handsome present to the King, also one to the Oja Zebartiban above mentioned, in answer to his [letter] written to us from Ligor: In which we have made known clearly and definitely our inability to send assistance, and that it was impossible to say when it could be sent on account of the wars referred to above. That so his Majesty should therefore no longer wait for it and that we should be freed from the vexations which would otherwise probably be renewed every year. We have also sent on the 5th September the ship *Schiedam* in order that, all being well, it should return hither at once, laden with rice, sapan wood[8] and other necessaries, or if it can get no cargo, to sail to the Moluccas and bring us thence as much pepper as it can take in. . . .

---

[5]Actually, the first Anglo–Dutch War, fought over English efforts to block Dutch ships from entering English ports, had ended in 1654, but the news seems not to have reached the author.

[6]A small sea-going vessel for carrying cargo.

[7]The Dutch were the only traders allowed in Japan after the Japanese seclusion acts of the 1630s. There was some question in the author's mind about how strictly they were being enforced.

[8]A Southeast Asian wood that yields a red dye.

Chapter 2

▼▼▼

The Islamic Heartland and India

In the early thirteenth century Mongol warriors under the legendary conqueror Chinggis Khan, his sons, and grandsons descended on Southwest Asia. After overrunning Persia, defeating the Seljuk Turks in 1243 in Asia Minor, and obliterating the enfeebled Abbasid Empire in 1258, the Mongols incorporated much of the region into their vast empire that stretched from Hungary to Korea. As Mongol political authority declined in the fourteenth century, Southwest Asia became a battleground for local dynasties, religious sects, nomad armies, and military adventurers, the most notable of whom was Timur the Lame, the Turko-Mongol conqueror whose large but short-lived empire collapsed after his death in 1405. Although India was spared the Mongol onslaught, its political history was as chaotic and turbulent as Southwest Asia's. Until 1526 northern India was nominally ruled by the sultanate of Delhi, but revolt, warfare, and a devastating raid by Timur the Lame in 1398 had sapped the regime's power long before its final demise. In the 1400s India consisted of hundreds of states of varying sizes and degrees of effectiveness.

Following these years of conquest and upheaval, three dominant empires emerged in South and Southwest Asia between the mid fifteenth and early sixteenth centuries. The first empire to take shape was that of the Ottoman Turks, a semi-nomadic people who had migrated from central Asia to Anatolia in the 1200s and almost immediately embarked on conquests that expanded their state in Anatolia and extended it into southeastern Europe. In 1453 they conquered the last remnant of the Byzantine Empire when they captured the imperial city, Constantinople, and made it the seat of their sultan's expanding state. During the 1500s the Ottomans ruled an empire that included Egypt, Anatolia, Syria, and lands in North Africa, the western coast of the Arabian Peninsula, and southeastern Europe. Meanwhile, on the Ottoman Empire's eastern flank in the early sixteenth century, Ismail I created the Safavid Empire in Persia, distinguished by its rulers' fervent devotion to Shia Islam. Finally, during the 1500s, the Mughal Empire emerged in India as a result of the conquests of Babur (1483–1530), a military adventurer originally from central Asia who won control of northwest India, and those of his grandson, Akbar (1542–1605), who extended Mughal authority to the east and south.

In addition to their leaders' common allegiance to Islam, these three empires resembled one another in several respects. Each was established through military conquest, each was ruled by an all-powerful emperor, and each was a formidable military power. In each, the arts and literature flourished. Each at first rested on a strong economic foundation, and each experienced the weakening of that foundation by inflation, high taxation, bureaucratic corruption, and broad changes in the world economy.

Differences among the three empires were most pronounced in the sphere of religion. The devotion of the Safavids to Shiism antagonized the Sunni Ottomans, and led to frequent Ottoman-Safavid wars. Furthermore, Safavid Persia was unique in that it had relatively few non-Muslim subjects. In contrast, the Ottomans' subjects in Europe were mostly Christian, and smaller numbers of Christians and Jews were scattered throughout the rest of their empire. Most of the Mughals' subjects were Hindus.

The three empires also had different experiences with Europeans. The Ottomans and Europeans were archrivals, each representing to the other a despised religion and, moreover, a threat to their territory and commerce. European and Ottoman fleets clashed in the Mediterranean, and their armies fought for control of southeastern Europe. Nonetheless, European merchants continued to trade and even reside in Ottoman cities, and European powers such as France forged military alliances with the Ottoman sultan when it suited their purposes.

Relations between Europeans and Safavid Persia, on the other hand, were more cordial. Shah Abbas I (r. 1587–1629) drew on the expertise of European military advisors and sent missions to Europe in 1599 and 1608 to explore the possibility of joint military action against the Ottoman Turks.

In India the Portuguese quickly capitalized on the success of Vasco da Gama's voyage around Africa to Calicut in 1498.

They undercut the monopoly of Arab merchants in the spice trade on the west Indian coast and established a base of operations on the island of Goa, which they forcibly annexed from the local Muslim ruler. The Dutch, English, and French became seriously involved in India only after 1600. They, too, established commercial operations on the coast, but only after having gained the permission of a local ruler or a Mughal official. Emperors Akbar and Jahangir were interested in European art and religion, but overall, Mughal rulers and their chief advisors were indifferent to the small number of European merchants who traded on the coast and stayed out of politics.

By the mid seventeenth century all three Islamic empires showed signs of deterioration. In the eighteenth century the Safavids were overthrown, and the authority of the Mughal emperors was reduced to little more than the imperial capital and its vicinity. The Ottoman Empire survived until after World War I, but its days of military prowess and economic vitality had ended long before its final demise.

▼▼▼

Rulers and Their Challenges in the Ottoman, Safavid, and Mughal Empires

Many factors — resources, wealth, technological development, social coherence, cultural unity, and military strength — contribute to the rise and fall of states. But as the histories of the Ottoman, Safavid, and Mughal empires all confirm, quality of rule is also significant, especially when authority is exercised by a single all-powerful ruler.

The early history of all three empires confirms the importance of leadership, especially on the battlefield. The Ottoman state resulted from the conquests of three men — Mehmet II (r. 1451–1481), who directed the siege of Constantinople in 1453; Selim I (r. 1512–1520), who conquered Egypt, Syria, Palestine, and parts of southern and western Arabia; and Suleiman I (r. 1520–1566), who added Hungary, the Mediterranean island of Rhodes, and some Persian territory to Ottoman domains. The Safavid Empire was forged through the exploits of Shaykh Ismail (r. 1501–1524), a charismatic leader whose original power base was Azerbaijan in northern Persia. Believed by his followers to be a descendant of the Prophet Muhammad's son-in-law, Ali, he defeated his rivals and in 1501 assumed the title *shah,* or emperor. Babur, the founder of the Mughal Empire in India, was a military adventurer of Mongol-Turkish ancestry who invaded India after having lost his original kingdom in Afghanistan. In 1526 he led an army of 12,000 troops into northern India and, with superior tactics and firepower, defeated the army of the Lodis, the Delhi sultanate's last dynasty.

The cultural achievements of these Islamic empires also depended on the interests and patronage of individual rulers. Akbar (r. 1556–1605), a brilliant military commander whose conquests expanded and consolidated Mughal authority through much of the subcontinent, patronized painters, poets, historians, and religious thinkers. Under his free-spending successors, Jahangir (r. 1605–1627) and Shah Jahan (r. 1627–1658), Mughal culture reached new heights. The Taj Mahal, one of the world's most beautiful buildings, is only one of many masterpieces they planned and paid for. Under Shah Abbas I (r. 1587–1629) the Safavid capital, Isfahan, was transformed through the construction of mosques, formal gardens, palaces, royal tombs, and public squares. Similarly, the early Ottoman sultans, following the precedent of Mehmet II, who had the magnificent Greek Orthodox church of Hagia Sophia in Constantinople converted into a mosque, all sought to leave their mark on Islamic culture by sponsoring ambitious building programs and the work of scholars, poets, and artists.

The sources in this section provide insights into the personalities and policies of three of the most renowned Islamic rulers of the sixteenth and seventeenth centuries — Suleiman I, Jahangir, and Abbas I. They allow us to analyze their styles of leadership and the strengths and weaknesses of their regimes.

A European Diplomat's Impressions of Suleiman I

▼▼▼

9 ▼ *Ogier Ghiselin de Busbecq, TURKISH LETTERS*

Suleiman I, known to Europeans as Suleiman the Magnificent, is remembered largely for his military conquests, but his accomplishments go beyond battlefield exploits. He was a patron of history and literature, oversaw the codification of Ottoman law (hence his honorific title *the Lawgiver*), and contributed to the architectural grandeur of Istanbul, the seat of Ottoman government. He was one of the outstanding rulers of the age.

The following observations of Suleiman and Ottoman society were recorded by Ogier Ghiselin de Busbecq (1522–1590), a Flemish nobleman who spent most of his life in the service of the Hapsburgs, in particular Ferdinand I, who was the archduke of Austria, king of Hungary and Bohemia, and, from 1558 to 1564, Holy Roman Emperor. In 1555 Ferdinand sent Busbecq to Suleiman's court in Istanbul to represent his interests in a dispute over the status of Transylvania, a region that had been part of Hungary and today is in Romania. After six years of discussions, the two sides agreed on a compromise by which Transylvania became an autonomous state in theory but paid an annual tribute to the sultan.

During his six years in Ottoman lands Busbecq recorded his observations and impressions and sent them in the form of four long letters to his friend Nicholas

Michault, who as a Hapsburg diplomat himself was in a position to communicate some of Busbecq's views to high-ranking Hapsburg officials. All four letters were published in Paris in 1589. Subsequently appearing in numerous Latin versions and translated into the major European languages, Busbecq's letters provide a wealth of information about Ottoman society.

The following excerpt begins with a description of Busbecq's first meeting with Suleiman I in 1555. It then goes on to comment on Ottoman military power. It concludes with a summary of an event that had taken place in 1553, the murder of Suleiman's oldest son and most likely successor, Mustafa. It is an example of the conflict and intrigue surrounding issues of succession in the Ottoman state, where one of the sons of the sultan would succeed his father, but not necessarily the eldest. As Busbecq explains, Mustafa's interests clashed with the ambitions of Roxelana, Suleiman's Russian-born wife and the mother of two sons and a daughter by Suleiman. To ensure that her son Selim would become sultan after Suleiman's death, she convinced her aging husband that Mustafa was plotting against him and must be killed.

QUESTIONS FOR ANALYSIS

1. What does Busbecq's first meeting with Suleiman reveal about the sultan's attitudes toward Europeans? What further insights into his attitudes are provided later in the excerpt?
2. What does Busbecq see as the main difference between Ottoman and European attitudes toward social privilege and inherited status? How do these attitudes affect Ottoman government?
3. What insights does Busbecq provide about Ottoman military power? What can one infer from his comments about his views of the most appropriate European response to the Ottomans?
4. What does the episode of Mustafa's assassination reveal about the power and influence of Roxelana? About Ottoman attitudes toward the imperial succession? About Suleiman's character?
5. What advantages and disadvantages were there in the Ottoman practice of not making the eldest son the automatic heir of the reigning sultan?
6. Shortly after Suleiman's reign the Ottoman Empire began to decline. What in Busbecq's account points to future problems for the Ottoman state?

FIRST IMPRESSIONS

On our arrival . . . we were taken to call on Achmet Pasha (the chief Vizier) and the other pashas[1] — for the Sultan himself was not then in the town — and commenced our negotiations with them touching the business entrusted to us by King Ferdinand. The pashas . . . told us that the whole matter depended on the Sultan's pleasure. On his arrival we were admitted to an audi-

---

[1]*Pasha* was an honorary title for a high-ranking military or government official; the *grand vizier* was the sultan's chief advisor and head of the Ottoman administration.

ence; but the manner and spirit in which he . . . listened to our address, our arguments, and our message was by no means favorable. . . .

On entering we were separately conducted into the royal presence by the chamberlains, who grasped our arms. . . . After having gone through a pretense of kissing his [Suleiman's] hand, we were conducted backwards to the wall opposite his seat, care being taken that we should never turn our backs on him. The Sultan then listened to what I had to say; but the language I used was not at all to his taste, for the demands of his Majesty[2] breathed a spirit of independence and dignity, which was by no means acceptable to one who deemed that his wish was law; and so he made no answer beyond saying in an impatient way, "Giusel, giusel," i.e. well, well. After this we were dismissed to our quarters.

The Sultan's hall was crowded with people, among whom were several officers of high rank. Besides these there were all the troopers of the Imperial guard, and a large force of Janissaries,[3] but there was not in all that great assembly a single man who owed his position to anything save his valor and his merit. No distinction is attached to birth among the Turks; the respect to be paid to a man is measured by the position he holds in the public service. There is no fighting for precedence; a man's place is marked out by the duties he discharges. . . . It is by merit that men rise in the service, a system which ensures that posts should only be assigned to the competent. . . . Those who receive the highest offices from the Sultan are for the most part the sons of shepherds or herdsmen, and so far from being ashamed of their parentage, they actually glory in it, and consider it a matter of boasting that they owe nothing to the accident of birth; for they do not believe that high qualities are either natural or hereditary, nor do they think that they can be handed down from father to

son, but that they are partly the gift of God, and partly the result of good training, great industry, and unwearied zeal. . . . Among the Turks, therefore, honors, high posts, and judgeships are the rewards of great ability and good service.

OTTOMAN MILITARY STRENGTH

Against us stands Suleiman, that foe whom his own and his ancestors' exploits have made so terrible; he tramples the soil of Hungary with 200,000 horses, he is at the very gates of Austria, threatens the rest of Germany, and brings in his train all the nations that extend from our borders to those of Persia. The army he leads is equipped with the wealth of many kingdoms. Of the three regions, into which the world is divided,[4] there is not one that does not contribute its share towards our destruction. . . .

▼ ▼ ▼

The Turkish monarch going to war takes with him over 40,000 camels and nearly as many baggage mules, of which a great part, when he is invading Persia, are loaded with rice and other kinds of grain. These mules and camels also serve to carry tents and armor, and likewise tools and munitions for the campaign. The territories, which bear the name of Persia, . . . are less fertile than our country, and even such crops as they bear are laid waste by the inhabitants in time of invasion in hopes of starving out the enemy, so that it is very dangerous for an army to invade Persia if it is not furnished with abundant supplies. . . .

▼ ▼ ▼

After dinner I practice the Turkish bow, in the use of which weapon people here are marvelously expert. From the eighth, or even the seventh, year of their age they begin to shoot at a mark, and practice archery ten or twelve years. This

---

[2]Archduke Ferdinand, Busbecq's employer.
[3]An elite military force in the service of the sultan. Its ranks were filled by highly trained soldiers who as young boys had been requisitioned from Christian families in the Balkans

and converted to Islam. They lived by a strict code of absolute obedience, austerity, religious observance, celibacy, and confinement to barracks.
[4]Asia, Europe, and Africa.

constant exercise strengthens the muscles of their arms, and gives them such skill that they can hit the smallest marks with their arrows. . . . So sure is their aim that in battle they can hit a man in the eye or in any other exposed part they choose.

▾ ▾ ▾

No nation in the world has shown greater readiness than the Turks to avail themselves of the useful inventions of foreigners, as is proved by their employment of cannons and mortars, and many other things invented by Christians. . . . The Turks are much afraid of carbines and pistols, such as are used on horseback. The same, I hear, is the case with the Persians, on which account someone advised Rustem,[5] when he was setting out with the Sultan on a campaign against them, to raise from his household servants a troop of 200 horsemen and arm them with firearms, as they would cause much alarm . . . in the ranks of the enemy. Rustem, in accordance with this advice, raised a troop of dragoons,[6] furnished them with firearms, and had them drilled. But they had not completed half the journey when their guns began to get out of order. Every day some essential part of their weapons was lost or broken, and it was not often that armorers could be found capable of repairing them. So, a large part of the firearms having been rendered unserviceable, the men took a dislike to the weapon; and this prejudice was increased by the dirt which its use entailed, the Turks being a very cleanly people; for the dragoons had their hands and clothes begrimed with gunpowder, and moreover presented such a sorry appearance, with their ugly boxes and pouches hanging about them, that their comrades laughed at them and called them apothecaries. So, . . . they gathered around Rustem and showing him their broken and useless firearms, asked what advantage he hoped to gain from

them when they met the enemy, and demanded that he should relieve them of them, and give them their old arms again. Rustem, after considering their request carefully, thought there was no reason for refusing to comply with it, and so they got permission to resume their bows and arrows.

PROBLEMS OF THE SUCCESSION

Suleiman had a son by a concubine who came from the Crimea. . . . His name was Mustafa, and at the time of which I am speaking he was young, vigorous, and of high repute as a soldier. But Suleiman had also several other children, by a Russian woman.[7] . . . To the latter he was so much attached that he placed her in the position of wife. . . .

Mustafa's high qualities and matured years marked him out to the soldiers who loved him, and the people who supported him, as the successor of his father, who was now in the decline of life. On the other hand, his step-mother [Roxelana], by throwing the claim of a lawful wife onto the balance, was doing her utmost to counterbalance his personal merits and his rights as eldest son, with a view to obtaining the throne for her own children. In this intrigue, she received the advice and assistance of Rustem, whose fortunes were inseparably linked with hers by his marriage with a daughter she had had by Suleiman. . . .

Inasmuch as Rustem was chief Vizier, . . . he had no difficulty . . . in influencing his master's mind. The Turks, accordingly, are convinced that it was by the calumnies of Rustem and the spells of Roxelana, who was in ill repute as a practitioner of sorcery, that the Sultan was so estranged from his son as to entertain the design of getting rid of him. A few believe that Mustafa, being aware of the plans, . . . decided to

---

[5]Rustem, the grand vizier, was also Suleiman's son-in-law. He married the daughter of Suleiman and Roxelana, originally a Russian slave girl in the sultan's harem.

[6]Heavily armed mounted troops.

[7]A reference to Roxelana.

anticipate them, and thus engaged in designs against his father's throne and person. The sons of Turkish Sultans are in the most wretched position in the world, for, as soon as one of them succeeds his father, the rest are doomed to certain death. The Turk can endure no rival to the throne, and, indeed, the conduct of the Janissaries renders it impossible for the new Sultan to spare his brothers; for if one of them survives, the Janissaries are forever asking generous favors. If these are refused, the cry is heard, "Long live the brother!" "God preserve the brother!" — a tolerably broad hint that they intend to place him on the throne. So that the Turkish Sultans are compelled to celebrate their succession by staining their hands with the blood of their nearest relatives. . . .

Being at war with Shah Tahmasp, Shah of the Persians, he [Suleiman] had sent Rustem against him as a commander-in-chief of his armies. Just as he was about to enter Persian territory, Rustem suddenly halted, and hurried off dispatches to Suleiman, informing him that affairs were in a very critical state; that treason was rife; . . . that the soldiers had been tampered with, and cared for no one but Mustafa; . . . and he must come at once if he wished to preserve his throne. Suleiman was seriously alarmed by these dispatches. He immediately hurried to the army, sent a letter to summon Mustafa to his presence, inviting him to clear himself of those crimes of which he was suspected. . . .

There was great uneasiness among the soldiers, when Mustafa arrived. . . . He was brought to his father's tent, and there everything betokened peace. . . . But there were in the tent certain mutes — . . . strong and sturdy fellows, who had been appointed as his executioners. As soon as he entered the inner tent, they threw themselves upon him, and endeavored to put the fatal noose around his neck. Mustafa, being a man of considerable strength, made a stout defense and fought — there being no doubt that

if he escaped . . . and threw himself among the Janissaries, the news of this outrage on their beloved prince would cause such pity and indignation, that they would not only protect him, but also proclaim him Sultan. Suleiman felt how critical the matter was, being only separated by the linen hangings of his tent from the stage on which this tragedy was being enacted. When he found that there was an unexpected delay in the execution of his scheme, he thrust out his head from the chamber of his tent, and glared on the mutes with fierce and threatening eyes; at the same time, with signs full of hideous meaning, he sternly rebuked their slackness. Hereon the mutes, gaining fresh strength from the terror he inspired, threw Mustafa down, got the bowstring round his neck, and strangled him. Shortly afterwards they laid his body on a rug in front of the tent, that the Janissaries might see the man they had desired as their Sultan. . . .

Meanwhile, Roxelana, not content with removing Mustafa from her path, . . . did not consider that she and her children were free from danger, so long as his offspring survived. Some pretext, however, she thought necessary, in order to furnish a reason for the murder, but this was not hard to find. Information was brought to Suleiman that, whenever his grandson appeared in public, the boys of Ghemlik[8] — where he was being educated — shouted out, "God save the Prince, and may he long survive his father;" and that the meaning of these cries was to point him out as his grandsire's future successor, and his father's avenger. Moreover, he was bidden to remember that the Janissaries would be sure to support the son of Mustafa, so that the father's death had in no way secured the peace of the throne and realm. . . .

Suleiman was easily convinced by these arguments to sign the death-warrant of his grandson. He commissioned Ibrahim Pasha to go to the Ghemlik with all speed, and put the innocent child to death.[9]

---

[8]A town in northwest Turkey.
[9]The assassination was carried out by a eunuch hired by Ibrahim Pasha, who had succeeded Rustem as grand vizier.

A Carmelite Friar's View of Shah Abbas I
▼▼▼

10 ▼ *Father Paul Simon, REPORT TO POPE PAUL V*

When Shah Abbas I ascended the Safavid throne in 1587 after the forced abdication of his father, he inherited an empire on the brink of disintegration. He faced a rebellion from Turkoman tribal leaders and invasions by the Ottomans from the west and the Uzbeks from the east. Within fifteen years he crushed the rebels and routed the Uzbeks and Ottomans. Subsequently, Abbas defeated the Mughals in 1621, taking Kandahar, seized the Persian Gulf island of Bahrain in 1622, and with English help expelled the Portuguese from their trading post at Ormuz in the same year. In addition to his military exploits, Abbas encouraged foreign and domestic trade, lent his support to manufacturing enterprises, and presided over a glorious era in Persian culture.

Part of Abbas's strategy to make Persia strong and prosperous was the cultivation of useful contacts with foreigners, especially Europeans. Two English brothers, Anthony and Robert Sherley, helped the shah enlarge and modernize his army and used their contacts to increase Persian trade with the English and Dutch. Abbas also sought alliances with European states against his enemy, the Ottomans. To that end he sent two embassies to Europe in 1599 and 1608 and tolerated the activities of Catholic missionaries, who were encouraged to think he might convert.

Such was the background for the negotiations between the envoys of Abbas I and Pope Clement VIII in 1600 that led to the dispatch of three Carmelite friars to Isfahan in 1604 to explore opportunities for missionary work. After an arduous journey through Poland and Russia, the three friars reached Isfahan in 1605 and remained in Persia six months. One of the three, Father Paul Simon of Jesus Mary (1576–1643), a Genoese who became a Carmelite friar in 1595, traveled extensively during his visit. After a hair-raising return journey on foot through Ottoman territory, Father Simon presented a report on Persia to the new pope, Paul V. Paul then dispatched Father Simon to Spain to discuss with King Philip III the complaints of Abbas I concerning the activities of Portuguese merchants in Ormuz, an important port city in the shah's territory, which the Portuguese (now subjects of the King of Spain) had controlled since 1507. Until his death in 1643 Father Simon held a number of administrative posts within his order.

QUESTIONS FOR ANALYSIS

1. What sort of impression does Abbas attempt to make on his subjects? What strategies does he use to make this impression?
2. What methods has Abbas used to suppress the powerful descendants of the Kizilbash who helped Ismail I (r. 1501–1524) establish the Safavid state (referred to by Father Simon as "the old nobles of Persia")?

3. What impresses Father Simon about Abbas's army? How do his comments and observations resemble Busbecq's characterization of Suleiman's troops (source 9)?
4. On the basis of Father Simon's account, what conclusions can be drawn about Abbas's religious views?
5. What factors seem to have shaped Abbas's policies toward the European Christians?
6. Despite the impressive strength of the Safavid Empire under Abbas, it quickly declined after his death. What underlying weaknesses do you see in the empire during Abbas's rule?

PERSONALITY AND POLICIES

The king . . . is sturdy and healthy, accustomed to much exercise and toil: many times he goes about on foot, and recently he had been forty days on pilgrimage, which he made on foot the whole time. He has extraordinary strength, and with his scimitar[1] can cut a man in two and a sheep with its wool on at a single blow — and the Persian sheep are of large size. . . . In his food he is frugal, as also in his dress, and this [is] to set an example to his subjects; and so in public he eats little else than rice, and that cooked in water only. His usual dress is of linen, and very plain: similarly the nobles and others in his realm follow suit, whereas formerly they used to go out dressed in brocade with jewels and other fopperies: and if he sees anyone who is over-dressed, he takes him to task, especially if it be a soldier. But in private he eats what he likes.

He is sagacious in mind, likes fame and to be esteemed: he is courteous in dealing with everyone and at the same time very serious. For he will go through the public streets, eat from what they are selling there and other things, speak at ease freely with the lower classes, cause his subjects to remain sitting while he himself is standing, or will sit down beside this man and that. He says that is how to be a king, and that the king of Spain and other Christians do not get

any pleasure out of ruling, because they are obliged to comport themselves with so much pomp and majesty. . . .

He is very strict in executing justice and pays no regard to his own favorites in this respect; but rather is the stricter with them in order to serve an example for others. So he has no private friends, nor anyone who has influence with him. . . . While we were at Court, he caused the bellies of two of his favorites to be ripped open, because they behaved improperly to an ordinary woman. . . .

He is very speedy in dispatching business: when he gives audience, which he does at the gate of his palace, . . . he finishes off all the cases that are brought to him. The parties stand present before him, the officers of justice and his own council, with whom he consults when it pleases him. The sentence which he gives is final and is immediately executed. If the guilty party deserves death, they kill him at once: to this end, when he gives audience, twelve men and twelve dogs who devour men alive, are kept ready: he keeps them in order to use the greater severity. Apart from the officials, once the sentence is given, it is not permitted to anyone to make any reply: for the person is at once driven off with blows of the sticks of some 30 to 40 royal guards, who stand ready to do this. When he wants to stop giving audience, he causes it to be pro-

---

[1]A curved steel saber.

claimed that no one, on pain of death, may bring him petitions, and, when he wants to go out of doors unaccompanied, that no one should follow him. . . .

He has to be obeyed absolutely: anyone failing in the slightest will pay for it with his head. And so he has had most of the old nobles of Persia killed off and put in their stead low-bred persons whom he has aggrandized. In the whole of Persia there are only two of the old-time governors. . . . Because of the great obedience they pay him, when he wills to have one of the nobles killed, he dispatches one of his men to fetch the noble's head: the man goes off to the grandee, and says to him: "The Shah wants your head." The noble replies: "Very well," and lets himself be decapitated — otherwise he would lose it and, with it, all his family would become extinct. But, when they [the nobles] allow themselves to be decapitated, he aggrandizes the children.

The Shah of Persia is very rich, because, besides having the treasure of his predecessors, he has seized those of the princes of Lar and of Gilan,[2] who were powerful and rich princes, and others. He has many sources of income and is master over the property of his subjects. . . .

MILITARY STRENGTH

He is very valiant and has a great liking for warfare and weapons of war, which he has constantly in his hands: we have been eye-witnesses of this because, whenever we were with him, he was adjusting scimitars, testing arquebuses,[3] etc.: and to make him a present that will give him pleasure is to give him some good pieces of arms. This is the great experience which he has obtained of warfare over so many years, that he makes it in person and from the first it has made him a fine soldier and very skilled, and his men so dexterous that they are little behind our men in Europe. He has introduced into his militia the use of and esteem for arquebuses and muskets, in which they are very practiced. Therefore it is that his realm has been so much extended on all sides. . . .

His militia is divided into three kinds of troops: one of the Georgians,[4] who will be about 25,000 and are mounted; . . . this is the old-time militia of the kings of Persia for the guarding of their persons. The present king has introduced the second force, which is made up of slaves of various races, many of them Christian renegades; their number will be as many again, and they are more esteemed than the first cited, both because they are servants of the king, and he assigns posts to them and promotes them. . . . The third body consists of soldiers whom the great governors of Persia are obliged to maintain and pay the whole year; they will be about 50,000. . . . When they [the governors] accomplish something signal in war, he gives them a governorship which produces greater revenue and sometimes the territory they capture is left to them. All the above-mentioned soldiers, who will total some 100,000, receive pay for the whole year. Then, according to the campaign and enterprise the king wishes to undertake, he enlists others, and, when it is necessary to make a great effort, he has it proclaimed throughout his country that whosoever is his well-wisher should follow him. Then everyone takes up arms.

THE SHAH'S FAMILY

The Shah has three sons: the eldest aged 22 years; . . . His mother was a Christian, and he is friendly toward Christians and not so quick-tempered as his father. The second son, 12 years old, has a temperament similar to that of his father. The third is aged 5 or 6. He has several daughters. His predecessors were wont to kill off their daughters because there were no neighbor-

---

[2]Lar was a province on the Persian Gulf; Gilan was a province in northwest Persia.
[3]A portable matchlock gun invented in the fifteenth century and usually fired from a support.

[4]A Christian people inhabiting a region between the Caspian and Black seas.

ing monarchs of equal rank to whom to marry them, and they did not like giving them in marriage to nobles of the country, for fear of the latter rebelling. In order to eliminate such cruel procedure this present Shah marries them to men of lowly position, as he did when we were there, giving one daughter to a camp commandant, the other to a captain. The eldest son born to the Shah inherits the throne even though he be by a slave woman.

HIS RELIGIOUS VIEWS

Regarding the religion of the king I think that no one knows what he believes: he does not observe the Muslim law in many things, nor is he a Christian. Six or seven years ago he displayed many signs of not being averse to our Faith. . . .

It is true that when the Augustinian Fathers[5] went to Persia the king showed himself extraordinarily affectionate with them, and gave many signs of being well disposed toward the Christian Faith and of wanting to embrace it. . . . In notifying the king [of] the objects of their mission, the Augustinian Fathers told him that they came to show him the True Faith, and to baptize him. He answered that he would discuss that at more length when he had the opportunity. Almost always he kept them near him. . . . He gave them 2,000 scudi[6] yearly for their subsistence, and entertained them several times at banquets, always making them sit near him, and he took one of them into the harem of his women, which was an exceptional mark of favor, since he did not even allow his own son to enter it; he made some of them [the women] dance. When the Fathers proposed to him [that he should adopt] our Faith, he made show to agree to everything. He gave them . . . a writing in which he promised to construct a church with bells in every town he should capture from the

Turks, to allow the Gospel to be preached, if the King of Spain kept to that which he promised him by the same Fathers, i.e. to take up arms against the Turks, and to send him artillery and engineers, which up till now has not been fulfilled. As evidence that he still had the mind to fulfil what he was promising, he said that on the following day he would go to their church — as in fact he did. . . .

> By the time Father Simon arrived in Persia in 1607, Abbas's views of European Christians, especially the Portuguese Augustinians, had changed. As Father Simon states, this change was caused by two things: the efforts of the Augustinians to turn the shah's newly conquered Armenian Christian subjects into Roman Catholics and the failure of the King of Spain, who at this point also ruled Portugal, to attack the Ottoman Empire.

In Tabriz it was told the king that the Augustinian Fathers had put up a bell in their church in Isfahan and that for this reason there were many people sick in that town. The Shah bit his finger, muttering two or three times: "Church with a bell! church with a bell!"; and gave orders that they should immediately take it down, as they did. In many other actions he demonstrated the small goodwill he had for Christians; and this increased to such an extent that, when we arrived in the city of Isfahan, he had given instructions for publication of an edict to the effect that all 'Frankish'[7] Christians and the Augustinian Fathers should quit his realm. . . .

. . . The cause of so great a change . . . God alone knows; the Augustinian Fathers say that in the beginning the king was merely pretending and that those demonstrations of affection and goodwill did not come from his heart. Other people attribute it to the many causes for annoyance the officials of his Catholic Majesty in Ormuz[8] have given him; to the Christian princes,

---

[5]Members of the Augustinian religious order, which traces its spiritual lineage to St. Augustine (354–430). The Augustinians in question were Portuguese.
[6]A gold or silver coin minted in Italy.

[7]"Frankish" was a term for European.
[8]Ormuz, a port city on the Persian Gulf, had been taken by the Portuguese in 1507; between 1580 and 1640 Portugal was ruled by the king of Spain.

His Holiness, the Emperor, the king of Spain not having kept the word they had given to various ambassadors that they would make war on the Turks, when they exhorted him himself to do the same, as he in fact has done; to many of the Franks, who had gone to his country, having committed a great many follies; and, more recently still, to the Emperor having agreed to a treaty[9] of peace between himself and the Turks, without giving him notice. . . . Certain it is that the mullahs[10] — this the name they give in their tongue to the learned men of their belief — went to the Shah, and told him to reflect on what he was doing — that he knew very well that the [Ottoman] Sultan was the head of the Muslim belief; if he should bring about the destruction of the latter in this warfare, the Christians would do the same to him, and to all of their belief. For they observed what poor sort of friends they were, when even their kings did not keep their word to him, while, the Franks who came to his country, what scant respect they paid him. It would be better to make peace with the Turkish Sultan, and then both of them together to attack the Christians. . . .

▷ All this left Father Simon at a loss about Abbas's true religious convictions.

---

[9]A reference to the Treaty of Sitvatorok, signed on November 11, 1606.
[10]A Muslim religious leader trained in law and doctrine.

In his seraglio he has many Christian Armenian, Georgian, and Circassian woman.[11] I think that he lets them live as they wish, because when I enquired what the Shah did with so many holy pictures that were presented to him as gifts and some relics of the Saints, for which he asked, the answer was that he used to give them to the women in his seraglio. Besides that he is well informed regarding the mysteries of our holy Faith and discourses on the mystery of the most holy Trinity: he knows many examples and allusions which the Saints give in order to prove it, and discourses about the other mysteries . . . if he does not discourse about the women in his seraglio or about some demon or other. On account of the many disappointments which he asserts the Christians have caused him all this fervor has cooled. With all that he does not detest them, for he converses and eats with them, he suffers us to say frankly what we believe about our Faith and his own: sometimes he asks us about this. To us he has given a house: he knows that we say Mass publicly, he allows whoever may wish among the Persians to come to it, and we can teach them freely regarding our holy Faith, whenever they make inquiries about it. . . . Till now none of them has been converted: I think they are waiting for one of the nobles or of their mullahs to break the ice. . . .

[11]Like the Georgians, the Circassians were a Christian people living between the Caspian and Black seas.

A Self-Portrait of Jahangir

▼▼▼

11 ▾ Jahangir, *MEMOIRS*

Jahangir, Mughal emperor from 1605 to 1627, modestly increased the size of the empire through conquest, snuffed out a half dozen rebellions, and on the whole continued the policies of his illustrious father, Akbar (r. 1556–1605). The lands he ruled provided him the wealth to indulge his tastes for formal gardens, entertaining, ceremony, sports, literature, and finely crafted books. In addition to subsidizing the work of hundreds of painters and writers, Jahangir himself contributed to the literature of his age by writing a memoir. Intended to glorify himself and instruct his heirs, it covered the first thirteen years of his reign, before his addiction to alcohol and opium sapped his energy and effectiveness.

QUESTIONS FOR ANALYSIS

1. Other than to glorify the person of the emperor, what political purposes might have been served by Jahangir's elaborate coronation ceremony?
2. What do the "twelve special regulations" issued at the beginning of Jahangir's reign reveal about his priorities as emperor?
3. How does Jahangir view his Hindu subjects? What are his reasons for allowing them to practice their religion?
4. What does the episode of the Afghan bandits reveal about Jahangir's view of the emperor's responsibilities?
5. What similarities and differences do you see in the authority and leadership style of Suleiman I (source 9), Abbas I (source 10), and Jahangir?

JAHANGIR'S CORONATION

On the eighth of the latter month of Jammaudy, of the year of the Hegira one thousand and fourteen,[1] in the metropolis of Agra, and in the forenoon of the day, being then at the age of thirty-eight, I became Emperor, and under the most felicitous auspices, took my seat on the throne of my wishes. . . . Hence I assumed the titles of Jahangir Padshah, and Jahangir Shah: the world-subduing emperor; the world-subduing king. I ordained that the following legend should be stamped on the coinage of the empire: "Stricken at Agra by that . . . safeguard of the world; the sovereign splendor of the faith, Jahangir, son of the imperial Akbar."

On this occasion I made use of the throne prepared by my father, and enriched at an expense without parallel, for the celebration of the festival of the new year. . . . In the fabrication of the throne a sum not far short of ten krours of ashrefies[2] was expended in jewels alone. . . .

. . . The legs and body of the throne were at the same time loaded with fifty maunds of ambergris,[3] so that wherever it might be found expedient to put it together, no further perfumes were necessary for an assemblage of whatever magnitude.

Having thus seated myself on the throne of my expectation and wishes, I caused also the imperial crown, which my father had caused to be made after the manner of that which was worn by the great kings of Persia, to be brought before me, and then, in the presence of the whole assembled Emirs,[4] having placed it on my brows, as an omen auspicious to the stability and happiness of my reign, kept it there for the space of a full . . . hour. On each of the twelve points of this crown was a single diamond . . . the whole purchased by my father with the resources of his

---

[1] October 10, 1605. Jahangir uses the Muslim calendar, dated from the Hegira, Muhammad's flight from Mecca to Medinain.

[2] A *krour* is a measurement of weight, and an *ashrefy* is a unit of money. Although it is impossible to determine the exact value of ten "krours of ashrefies," it is an enormous sum.

[3] A *maund* was a unit of weight, which could vary from as little as 10 pounds to as much as 160; *ambergris,* a waxy substance secreted by sperm whales and found floating in tropical seas, is used as a perfume.

[4] High government officials.

own government, not from anything accruing to him by inheritance from his predecessors. At the point in the center of the top part of the crown was a single pearl . . . and on different parts of the same were set altogether two hundred rubies. . . .

For forty days and forty nights I caused the . . . great imperial state drum to strike up, without ceasing, the strains of joy and triumph; and . . . around my throne, the ground was spread by my directions with the most costly brocades and gold embroidered carpets. Censers[5] of gold and silver were disposed in different directions for the purpose of burning fragrant drugs, and nearly three thousand camphorated wax lights, . . . in branches of gold and silver perfumed with ambergris, illuminated the scene from night till morning. Numbers of blooming youth, . . . clad in dresses of the most costly materials, woven in silk and gold, with . . . amulets sparkling with the lustre of the diamond, the emerald, the sapphire, and the ruby, awaited my commands, rank after rank, and in attitude most respectful. And finally, the Emirs of the empire, . . . stood round in brilliant array, also waiting for the commands of their sovereign. . . .

THE EMPEROR'S DECREES

The very first ordinance that issued from me . . . related to the chain of justice, one end of which I caused to be fastened to the battlements of the royal tower of the castle of Agra, and the other to a stone post near the bed of the river Jumnah; to the end that whenever those charged with administering the courts were slack in dispensing justice to the downtrodden, he who had suffered injustice by applying his hand to the chain would find himself in the way of obtaining speedy redress.[6] . . .

I issued twelve special regulations to be implemented and observed in all the realm.

1. I canceled the tamgha, the mirabari,[7] and all other imposts the jagirdars[8] of every province and district had imposed for their own profit.
2. I ordered that when a district lay wasted by thieves and highway bandits or was destitute of inhabitants, that towns should be built, . . . and every effort made to protect the subjects from injury. I directed the jagirdars in such deserted places to erect mosques and caravansaries, or places for the accommodation of travelers, in order to render the district once more an inhabited country, and that men might again be able to travel back and forth safely. . . .
3. Merchants travelling through the country were not to have their bales or packs opened without their consent.
4. When a person shall die and leave children, whether he is an infidel[9] or Muslim, no man was to interfere a pin's point in his property; but when he has no children or direct and unquestionable heirs his inheritance is to be spent on approved expenditures such as construction of mosques and caravansaries, repair of bridges, and the creation of water-tanks and wells.
5. No person was permitted either to make or to sell wine or any other intoxicating liquor. I undertook to institute this regulation, although it is sufficiently well known that I myself have the strongest inclination for wine, in which from the age of sixteen I have liberally indulged. . . .
6. No official was permitted to take up his abode in the house of any subject of my realm. On the contrary, when individuals

---

[5]A container for burning incense.
[6]Presumably pulling the chain would be the first step in bringing the perceived injustice to the emperor's attention.
[7]The *tamgha* and *mirabari* were both customs duties.
[8]A *jagir* was a grant of land by the emperor that entitled the

holder to the income from the land. The income was to be used mainly to finance the maintenance of troops. A *jagirdar* was the holder of a jagir.
[9]A Hindu.

serving in the state armies come to any town, and can rent a place to live, it would be commendable; otherwise they were to pitch their tents outside the town and prepare abodes for themselves.

7. No person was to suffer, for any offence, the cutting off of a nose or ear. For theft, the offender was to be scourged with thorns, or deterred from further transgressions by an oath on the Quran.[10]

8. I decreed that superintendents of royal lands and jagirdars were prohibited from seizing the lands of their subjects or cultivating the lands themselves for their own benefit. . . . On the contrary, his attention was to be wholly and exclusively devoted to the cultivation and improvement of the district allotted to him.

9. The tax collectors of royal lands and jagirdars may not intermarry with the people of the districts in which they reside without my permission.[11]

10. Governors in all the large cities were directed to establish infirmaries and hospitals with physicians appointed to treat the sick. Expenses are to be covered by income from royal lands.

11. During the month of my birth there could be no slaughter of animals in my realm. . . . In every week also, on Thursday, that being the day of my accession, and Sunday, my father's birthday, . . . and also because it is the day attributed to the sun and the day on which the creation of the world was begun. It was unjustifiable to deprive any animal of life on such a day.

12. I issued a decree confirming the dignitaries and jagirs of my father's government in all that they had enjoyed while he was living; and where I found sufficient merit, I conferred an advance of rank in various gradations. . . .

POLICY TOWARD THE HINDUS

I am here led to relate that at the city of Banaras[12] a temple had been erected [in which] . . . the principal idol . . . had on its head a tiara or cap, enriched with jewels. . . . [Also] placed in this temple, moreover, as the associates and ministering servants of the principal idol, [were] four other images of solid gold, each crowned with a tiara, in the like manner enriched with precious stones. It was the belief of these nonbelievers that a dead Hindu, provided when alive he had been a worshiper, when laid before this idol would be restored to life. As I could not possibly give credit to such a pretense, I employed a confidential person to ascertain the truth; and, as I justly supposed, the whole was detected to be an impudent fraud. . . .

On this subject I must however acknowledge, that having on one occasion asked my father the reason why he had forbidden anyone to prevent or interfere with the building of these haunts of idolatry, his reply was in the following terms: "My dear child," said he, "I find myself a powerful monarch, the shadow of God upon earth. I have seen that he bestows the blessing of his gracious providence upon all his creatures without distinction. . . . With all of the human race, with all of God's creatures, I am at peace: why then should I permit myself, under any consideration, to be the cause of molestation or aggression to any one? Besides, are not five parts in six . . . either Hindus or aliens to the faith; and were I to be governed by motives of the kind suggested in your inquiry, what alternative can I have but to put them all to death! I have thought it therefore my wisest plan to let these men alone. Neither is it to be forgotten, that the class of whom we are speaking . . . are usefully engaged, either in the pursuits of science or the arts, or of improvements for the benefit of mankind, and have in numerous instances arrived at the highest dis-

---

[10]Islam's sacred book.
[11]This was to prevent any tax collector or jagirdar from gaining a vested interest in the fortunes of a particular region or family.

[12]A city on the Ganges River.

tinctions in the state, there being, indeed, to be found in this city men of every description, and of every religion on the face of the earth." . . .

▼ ▼ ▼

In the practice of being burnt on the funeral pyre of their husbands[13] as sometimes exhibited among the widows of the Hindus, I had previously directed that no woman who was the mother of children should be thus made a sacrifice, however willing to die; and I now further ordained, that in no case was the practice to be permitted, when compulsion was in the slightest degree employed, whatever might be the opinions of the people. In other respects they were in no way to be molested in the duties of their religion, nor exposed to oppression or violence in any manner whatever. . . .

THE DUTIES OF THE EMPEROR

. . . It had been made known to me that the roads about Kandahar[14] were grievously infested by the Afghans, who by their vexatious exactions rendered the communications in that quarter extremely unsafe for travelers of every description. . . .

Lushker Khan . . . was despatched by my orders toward Kabul for the purpose of clearing the roads in that direction, which had been rendered unsafe by the outrages of licentious bandits. It so happened that when this commander had nearly reached the point for which he was destined he found opposed to him a body of mountaineers . . . , who had assembled to the number of forty thousand, horse and foot and musketeers, had shut up the approaches against him, and prevented his further advance. . . . A conflict began, which continued . . . from dawn of day until nearly sunset. The enemy were however finally defeated, with the loss of seventeen thousand killed, a number taken prisoners, and a still greater proportion escaping to their hiding-places among the mountains. The prisoners were conducted to my presence yoked together, with the heads of the seventeen thousand slain in the battle suspended from their necks. After some deliberation as to the destiny of these captives, I resolved that their lives should be spared, and that they should be employed in bringing forage for my elephants.

. . . The shedding of so much human blood must ever be extremely painful; but until some other resource is discovered, it is unavoidable. Unhappily the functions of government cannot be carried on without severity, and occasional extinction of human life: for without something of the kind, some species of coercion and chastisement, the world would soon exhibit the horrible spectacle of mankind, like wild beasts, worrying each other to death with no other motive than rapacity and revenge. God is witness that there is no repose for crowned heads. There is no pain or anxiety equal to that which attends the possession of sovereign power, for to the possessor there is not in this world a moment's rest. . . .

---

[13]A woman who burned herself in this way was known as *sati* (Sanskrit for "virtuous woman"). The word *sati* also is used to describe the burning itself.

[14]A city in Afghanistan.

Religion and Society in South and Southwest Asia

Although many major religions — Hinduism, Buddhism, Zoroastrianism, Judaism, Islam, and Christianity — originated in South and Southwest Asia, by the sixteenth century, the region was dominated by two faiths. They were Islam, ascendant everywhere except India, and Hinduism, the Indian subcontinent's ancient religion that endured despite centuries of competition from Buddhism, Jainism, and Islam.

At first glance, one is struck by the many differences between Islam — with its uncompromising monotheism, its reliance on its holy book, the Quran, and its origin in the prophecies of a single human being, Muhammad — and Hinduism — with its thousands of gods, its slow and continuous evolution, and its lack of a single creed or holy book. Yet on a deeper level, a fundamental similarity exists in the religions. Both reject any separation between the religious and secular spheres of an individual's life. Islam and Hinduism not only guide each believer's spiritual development but also define that believer's role as a parent, spouse, subject, and man or woman. Secularism as such does not exist in either religious tradition.

Islam originated in the seventh century C.E. and was based on the prophecies of Muhammad (ca. 570–632 C.E.), whose revelations from Allah (Arabic for God) were recorded in Islam's most holy book, the Quran. *Islam* in Arabic means "submission," and a Muslim is one who submits to God's will. Islam's basic creed is the statement that every follower must utter daily: "There is no God but God, and Muhammad is the Prophet of God." All Muslims are expected to accept the Quran as the word of God, perform works of charity, fast during the holy month of Ramadan, say daily prayers, and, if possible, make a pilgrimage to Mecca, the city on the Arabian Peninsula where Muhammad received Allah's revelation. Islam teaches that at death each person will be judged by Allah, with the faithful rewarded by Heaven and the unfaithful damned to an eternity in Hell.

Hinduism, which evolved over many centuries, has no single creed, set of rituals, holy book, or organized church. Unlike Judaism, Christianity, and Islam, which affirm the existence of only one God, Hinduism includes thousands of deities in its pantheon, although all are believed to be manifestations of the Divine Essence or Absolute Reality, called Brahman. Hindus believe many paths can lead to enlightenment, and Hinduism thus encompasses a wide range of beliefs and rituals.

All Hindus are part of the caste system, a religiously sanctioned order of social relationships that goes back to the beginnings of Indian civilization between 1500 and 1000 B.C.E. A person's caste, into which he or she is born for life, determines the individual's social and legal status, restricts marriage partners to other caste members, limits the individual to certain professions, and, in effect, minimizes contacts with members of other castes. The English word *caste* is derived from the

Portuguese word *casta,* meaning "pure." Hindus use two different words for caste: *varna* (color) and *jati* (birth). *Varna* refers only to the four most ancient and fundamental social-religious divisions: *Brahmins* (priests and teachers), *Kshatriyas* (warriors, nobles, and rulers), *Vaisyas* (landowners, merchants, and artisans), and *Sudras* (peasants and laborers). Outside the caste system and at the bottom of the Hindu hierarchy are the "untouchables," who are relegated to despised tasks such as gathering manure, sweeping streets, and butchering animals. Each of the four major castes is further divided into *jatis,* local hereditary occupational groups that during the 1500s and 1600s numbered around 3,000.

The caste system is related to the doctrine of the transmigration of souls, or reincarnation. This is the belief that each individual soul, or *atman,* a fragment of the Universal Soul, or Brahman, strives through successive births to reunite with Brahman and win release from the chains of material existence and the cycle of death and rebirth. Reincarnation is based on one's *karma,* the fruit of one's actions, or the soul's destiny, which is decided by how well or poorly a person has conformed to *dharma,* the duty to be performed by members of each *jati* and *varna.* If a person fulfills his or her *dharma,* in the next incarnation he or she will move up the cosmic ladder, closer to ultimate reunion with the One.

Sunni-Shia Conflict in the Early Sixteenth Century

▼▼▼

12 ▼ Sultan Selim I, *LETTER TO SHAH ISMAIL OF PERSIA*

The following letter, written by the Ottoman sultan Selim I (r. 1512–1520) to the founder of the Persian Safavid Empire, Ismail I (r. 1501–1524), is an example of the enduring bitterness between Shia and Sunni Muslims. Selim, who in the Ottoman tradition was a Sunni, was deeply disturbed by the emergence of a Shia state in Persia under Ismail. Ismail, believed by his followers to have descended from Ali, the Prophet Muhammad's son-in-law, had many supporters among the Turks of eastern Anatolia and had aided Selim's brother and rival, Ahmed, in the succession conflict following Sultan Bayezid's death in 1512. When Ismail invaded eastern Ottoman territory in 1513, war seemed inevitable. Nonetheless, Selim wrote the following letter to Ismail in early 1514 threatening to destroy him militarily unless he embraced Sunni Islam and relinquished his conquests. Ismail did neither, and later in the year, Selim's armies defeated Ismail's forces at the battle of Chaldiran, on the border of the two empires. Despite this loss, Persia remained under Ismail's control and thus committed to Shiism. The battle of Chaldiran was only the first act in a long and bitter struggle between the two Islamic empires.

QUESTIONS FOR ANALYSIS

1. Even though Selim's letter is designed to malign Shiism, not define Islam, it contains many references to essential Muslim beliefs. Which ones can you find?
2. What does Selim's letter reveal about the differences between Sunnis and Shias?
3. How does Selim perceive himself within the Islamic world?
4. Selim must have realized that the deeply religious Ismail was unlikely to abandon Shiism. Why might he have written the letter, despite the likelihood that its appeal would fall on deaf ears?

The Supreme Being who is at once the sovereign arbiter of the destinies of men and the source of all light and knowledge, declares in the holy book[1] that the true faith is that of the Muslims, and that whoever professes another religion, far from being hearkened to and saved, will on the contrary be cast out among the rejected on the great day of the Last Judgment. He says further, this God of truth, that His designs and decrees are unalterable, that all human acts are perforce reported to Him, and that he who abandons the good way will be condemned to hell-fire and eternal torments. Place yourself, O Prince, among the true believers, those who walk in the path of salvation, and who turn aside with care from vice and infidelity. . . .

I, sovereign chief of the Ottomans, master of the heroes of the age; . . . I, the exterminator of idolators, destroyer of the enemies of the true faith, the terror of the tyrants and pharaohs of the age; I, before whom proud and unjust kings have humbled themselves, and whose hand breaks the strongest sceptres; I, the great Sultan-Khan, son of Sultan Bayezid-Khan, son of Sultan Muhammad-Khan, son of Sultan Murad-Khan, I address myself graciously to you, Emir Ismail, chief of the troops of Persia, comparable in tyranny to Sohak and Afrasiab,[2] and predestined to perish . . . in order to make known to you that

the works emanating from the Almighty are not the fragile products of caprice or folly, but make up an infinity of mysteries impenetrable to the human mind. The Lord Himself says in his holy book: "We have not created the heavens and the earth in order to play a game" [Quran, 21:16]. Man, who is the noblest of the creatures and the summary of the marvels of God, is in consequence on earth the living image of the Creator. It is He who has set up Caliphs[3] on earth, because, joining faculties of soul with perfection of body, man is the only being who can comprehend the attributes of the divinity and adore its sublime beauties; but he possesses this rare intelligence, he attains this divine knowledge only in our religion and by observing the precepts of the prince of prophets . . . the right arm of the God of Mercy [Muhammad]; it is then only by practicing the true religion that man will prosper in this world and merit eternal life in the other. As to you, Emir Ismail, such a recompense will not be your lot; because you have denied the sanctity of the divine laws; because you have deserted the path of salvation and the sacred commandments; because you have impaired the purity of the dogmas of Islam; because you have dishonored, soiled, and destroyed the altars of the Lord, usurped the sceptre of the East by unlawful and tyrannical means; because coming forth from the

---

[1]The Quran.
[2]Legendary kings of central Asia.

[3]Deputies, or political successors, of the Prophet Muhammad who lead the Muslim community on earth.

dust, you have raised yourself by odious devices to a place shining with splendor and magnificence; because you have opened to Muslims the gates of tyranny and oppression; because you have joined iniquity, perjury, and blasphemy to your sectarian impiety; because under the cloak of the hypocrite, you have sowed everywhere trouble and sedition; because you have raised the standard of irreligion and heresy; because yielding to the impulse of your evil passions, and giving yourself up without rein to the most infamous disorders, you have dared to throw off the control of Muslim laws and to permit lust and rape, the massacre of the most virtuous and respectable men, the destruction of pulpits and temples, the profanation of tombs, the ill-treatment of the *ulama,* the doctors and emirs[4] descended from the Prophet, the repudiation of the Quran, the cursing of the legitimate Caliphs.[5] Now as the first duty of a Muslim and above all of a pious prince is to obey the commandment, "O, you faithful who believe, be the executors of the decrees of God!" the *ulama* and our doctors have pronounced sentence of death against you, perjurer and blasphemer, and have imposed on every Muslim the sacred obligation to arm in defense of religion and destroy heresy and impiety in your person and that of all your partisans.

Animated by the spirit of this *fatwa,*[6] conforming to the Quran, the code of divine laws, and wishing on one side to strengthen Islam, on the other to liberate the lands and peoples who writhe under your yoke, we have resolved to lay aside our imperial robes in order to put on the shield and coat of mail [armor], to raise our ever victorious banner, to assemble our invincible armies, to take up the gauntlet of the avenger, to march with our soldiers, whose sword strikes mortal blows, and whose point

will pierce the enemy even to the constellation of Sagittarius. In pursuit of this noble resolution, we have entered upon the campaign, and guided by the hand of the Almighty, we hope soon to strike down your tyrannous arm, blow away the clouds of glory and grandeur which trouble your head and cause your fatal blindness, release from your despotism your trembling subjects, smother you in the end in the very mass of flames which your infernal *jinn*[7] raises everywhere along your passage, accomplishing in this way on you the maxim which says: "He who sows discord can only reap evils and afflictions." However, anxious to conform to the spirit of the law of the Prophet, we come, before commencing war, to set out before you the words of the Quran, in place of the sword, and to exhort you to embrace the true faith; this is why we address this letter to you. . . .

We urge you to look into yourself, to renounce your errors, and to march towards the good with a firm and courageous step; we ask further that you give up possession of the territory violently seized from our state and to which you have only illegitimate pretensions, that you deliver it back into the hands of our lieutenants and officers; and if you value your safety and repose, this should be done without delay.

But if, to your misfortune, you persist in your past conduct, puffed up with the idea of your power and your foolish bravado, you wish to pursue the course of your iniquities, you will see in a few days your plains covered with our tents and inundated with our battalions. Then prodigies of valor will be done, and we shall see the decrees of the Almighty, Who is the God of Armies, and sovereign judge of the actions of men, accomplished. For the rest, victory to him who follows the path of salvation!

---

[4]Shias originally broke away from mainstream Islam over disagreements concerning the early caliphate. They believe that Ali, Muhammad's cousin and son-in-law (the fourth caliph), should have been the first. As a result, the Shias believe that the first three caliphs (all legitimate according to the Sunnis) are illegitimate.

[5]*Ulama* were bodies of religious teachers and interpreters of Muslim law; *doctors* here means teachers; *emirs* were military commanders and princes.
[6]Religious decree.
[7]Supernatural spirit.

A Muslim's Description of
Hindu Beliefs and Practices
▼▼▼

13 ▼ Abul Fazl, AKBARNAMA

As Akbar, Mughal ruler from 1556 to 1605, expanded and strengthened his empire, at his side was Abul Fazl, his close friend and advisor from 1579 until his assassination in 1602. Abul Fazl is best known as the author of the *Akbarnama,* a long laudatory history of Akbar's reign full of information about the emperor's personality and exploits. At the time of Abul Fazl's assassination, instigated by Akbar's son and future emperor Jahangir, his history had covered only the first forty-six years of Akbar's life, but that was enough to ensure his work's standing as one of the masterpieces of Mughal literature.

One reason for the lengthiness of the *Akbarnama* is that in addition to chronicling Akbar's life, it contains numerous descriptions of Indian society such as the passage on Hinduism that follows. Abul Fazl, who shared the tolerant religious views of the emperor, was interested in presenting Hinduism favorably to his Islamic readers, many of whom opposed the religious freedom Akbar offered his Hindu subjects. Even more disturbing to many Muslims was Akbar's genuine interest not just in Hinduism but also Christianity, Jainism, and Zoroastrianism, all of which he drew upon to found a new religious cult, *Din Illahi,* or Divine Faith. Abul Fazl sought to lessen the concerns of orthodox Muslims that Hindus were guilty of the two greatest sins against the majesty and oneness of God — idolatry (the worship of idols) and polytheism (a belief in many gods). He also explained the religious basis of the Hindu caste system, the rigid hierarchies of which were far removed from the Muslim belief in the equality of all believers before Allah.

QUESTIONS FOR ANALYSIS

1. How does Abul Fazl counter the charge that Hindus are polytheists? Do you find his arguments convincing? Why?
2. How does Abul Fazl address the charge that Hindus are idol worshipers?
3. In what ways do caste and karma provide Hindus a moral understanding of the universe?
4. What do the dharmas of the castes reveal about Hindu social values?
5. Where do women fit into the structure of the ladder of reincarnation? What does this suggest about their status in Hindu society?
6. Abul Fazl is attempting to make Hinduism more acceptable to Muslims, but this does not necessarily invalidate what he writes. If you accept what he says as basically true, what conclusions can you reach about the ways Hindus perceive and relate to Divine Reality?

They one and all believe in the unity of God, and as to the reverence they pay to images of stone and wood and the like, which simpletons regard as idolatry, it is not so. The writer of these has exhaustively discussed the subject with many enlightened and upright men, and it became evident that these images . . . are fashioned as aids to fix the mind and keep the thoughts from wandering, while the worship of God alone is required as indispensable. In all their ceremonial observances and usage they ever implore the favor of the world-illumining sun and regard the pure essence of the Supreme Being as transcending the idea of power in operation.

Brahma . . . they hold to be the Creator; Vishnu, the Nourisher and Preserver; and Rudra,[1] called also Mahadeva, the Destroyer. Some maintain that God who is without equal, manifested himself under these three divine forms, without thereby sullying the garment of His inviolate sanctity, as the Nazarenes hold of the Messiah.[2] Others assert that these were human creatures exalted to these dignities through perfectness of worship, probity of thought and righteousness of deed. The godliness and self-discipline of this people is such as is rarely to be found in other lands.

They hold that the world had a beginning, and some are of opinion that it will have an end. . . . They allow of no existence external to God. The world is a delusive appearance, and as a man in sleep sees fanciful shapes, and is affected by a thousand joys and sorrows, so are its seeming realities. . . .

Brahman is the Supreme Being; and is essential existence and wisdom and also bliss. . . .

Since according to their belief, the Supreme Deity can assume an elemental form without defiling the skirt of the robe of omnipotence, they first make various idols of gold and other substances to represent this ideal and gradually withdrawing the mind from this material worship, they become meditatively absorbed in the ocean of His mysterious Being. . . .

They believe that the Supreme Being in the wisdom of His counsel, assumes an elementary form of a special character[3] for the good of the creation, and many of the wisest of the Hindus accept this doctrine. . . .

CASTE

The Hindu philosophers reckon four states of auspiciousness which they term *varna*. 1. *Brahmin*. 2. *Kshatriya*. 3. *Vaisya*. 4. *Sudra*. Other than these are termed *Mlechchha*.[4] At the creation of the world the first of these classes was produced from the mouth of Brahma . . . ; the second, from his arms; the third, from his thigh and the fourth from his feet; the fifth from the cow *Kamadhenu*, the name of Mlechchha being employed to designate them.

The *Brahmins* have six recognized duties. 1. The study of the Vedas[5] and other sciences. 2. The instruction of others (in the sacred texts). 3. The performance of the *Jag*, that is oblation [a religious offering] of money and kind to the Devatas.[6] 4. Inciting others to the same. 5. Giving presents. 6. Receiving presents.

Of these six the *Kshatriya* must perform three. 1. Perusing the holy texts. 2. The performance of the Jag. 3. Giving presents. Further they must, 1. Minister to Brahmins. 2. Control the administration of worldly government and receive the reward thereof. 3. Protect religion. 4. Exact fines for delinquency and observe adequate measure

---

[1]Also known as Shiva.
[2]Abul Fazl makes two comparisons here. First he compares this Hindu trinity with the Christian Trinity (three divine and full separate persons in one God); then he points out the similarities in Christian and Hindu beliefs in incarnation, whereby God or a god becomes embodied in an earthly form. His Muslim readers would have known basic Christian beliefs.

[3]That is, the Hindu Supreme Being assumes various bodies. These incarnations are known as *avataras*.
[4]The "untouchables" or outcasts of Hindu society.
[5]The four collections of ancient poetry that are sacred texts among Hindus.
[6]Hindu deities.

therein. 5. Punish in proportion to the offense. 6. Amass wealth and duly expend it. 7. Supervise the management of elephants, horses, and cattle and the functions of ministerial subordinates. 8. Levy war on due occasion. 9. Never ask for alms. 10. Favor the meritorious and the like.

The *Vaisya* also must perform the same three duties of the Brahmin, and in addition must occupy himself in: 1. Service. 2. Agriculture. 3. Trade. 4. The care of cattle. 5. The carrying of loads. . . .

The Sudra is incapable of any other privilege than to serve these three castes, wear their cast-off garments and eat their leavings. He may be a painter, goldsmith, blacksmith, carpenter, and trade in salt, honey, milk, butter-milk, clarified butter and grain.

Those of the fifth class, are reckoned as beyond the pale of religion, like infidels, Jews, and the like.[7] By the inter-marriages of these, sixteen other classes are formed. The son of Brahmin parents is acknowledged as a Brahmin. If the mother be a Kshatriya (the father being a Brahmin), the progeny is called *Murdhavasikta.* If the mother be a Vaisya, the son is named *Ambastha,* and if a Sudra girl, *Nishada.* If the father and mother are both Kshatriya, the progeny is Kshatriya. If the mother be a Brahmin (and the father a Kshatriya), the son is called *Suta.* If the mother be a Vaisya, the son is *Mahisya.* If the mother be a Sudra, the progeny is *Ugra.* If both parents be Vaisya, the progeny is Vaisya. If the mother be a Brahmin (which is illicit), the progeny is *Vaideha* but if she be a Kshatriya, which also is regarded as improper, he is *Magadha.* From the Vaisya by a Sudra mother is produced a *Karana.* When both parents are Sudra, the progeny is Sudra. If the mother be a Brahmin, the progeny is *Chandala.* If she be a Kshatriya, it is called *Chatta.* From a Sudra by a Vaisya girl is produced the *Ayogava.*

In the same way still further ramifications are formed, each with different customs and modes

of worship and each with infinite distinctions of habitation, profession, and rank of ancestry that defy computation. . . .

KARMA

. . . This is a system of knowledge of an amazing and extraordinary character, in which the learned of Hindustan concur without dissenting opinion. It reveals the particular class of actions performed in a former birth which have occasioned the events that befall men in this present life, and prescribes the special expiation of each sin, one by one. It is of four kinds.

The first kind discloses the particular action which has brought a man into existence in one of the five classes into which mankind is divided, and the action which occasions the assumption of a male or female form. A *Kshatriya* who lives continently, will, in his next birth, be born a *Brahmin.* A *Vaisya* who hazards his transient life to protect a Brahmin, will become a *Kshatriya.* A *Sudra* who lends money without interest and does not defile his tongue by demanding repayment, will be born a *Vaisya.* A *Mlechchha* who serves a *Brahmin* and eats food from his house till his death, will become a *Sudra.* A *Brahmin* who undertakes the profession of a *Kshatriya* will become a *Kshatriya,* and thus a *Kshatriya* will become a *Vaisya,* and a *Vaisya* a *Sudra,* and a *Sudra* a *Mlechchha.* Whosoever accepts in alms . . . the bed on which a man has died[8] . . . will, in the next birth, from a man become a woman. Any woman or *Mlechchha,* who in the temple . . . sees the form of *Narayana,*[9] and worships him with certain incantations, will in the next birth, if a woman, become a man, and if a *Mlechchha,* a *Brahmin.* . . .

The second kind shows the strange effects of actions on health of body and in the production of manifold diseases.

---

[7]Abul Fazl is drawing an analogy for his Muslim readers. Just as Muslims consider all nonbelievers as outside the community of God, so Hindus regard the Mlechchha as outside their community.

[8]An "unclean" object.
[9]The personification of solar and cosmic energy underlying creation.

Madness is the punishment of disobedience to father and mother. . . .

Pain in the eyes arises from having looked upon another's wife. . . .

Dumbness is the consequence of killing a sister. . . .

Colic results from having eaten with an impious person or a liar. . . .

Consumption is the punishment of killing a *Brahmin*. . . .

The third kind indicates the class for actions which have caused sterility and names suitable remedies. . . .

A woman who does not menstruate, in a former existence . . . roughly drove away the children of her neighbors who had come as usual to play at her house. . . .

A woman who gives birth to only daughters is thus punished for having contemptuously regarded her husband from pride. . . .

A woman who has given birth to a son that dies and to a daughter that lives, has, in her former existence, taken animal life. Some say that she had killed goats. . . .

The fourth kind treats of riches and poverty, and the like. Whoever distributes alms at auspicious times, as during eclipses of the moon and sun, will become rich and bountiful (in his next existence). Whoso at these times, visits any place of pilgrimage . . . and there dies, will possess great wealth, but will be avaricious and of a surly disposition. Whosoever when hungry and with food before him, hears the supplication of a poor man and bestows it all upon him, will be rich and [generous].

Women and Islamic Law in the Ottoman Empire
▼▼▼

14 ▼ Khayr al-Din Ramli, *LEGAL OPINIONS*

Many of Muhammad's teachings were favorable to women. He taught the spiritual equality between men and women, and in his treatment of his own wives and daughters he exemplified his teachings about the moral and ethical dimensions of marriage. Women were among his earliest and most important followers. As Islam expanded and evolved, however, women's status declined. Women, especially from the upper classes, were secluded in their homes and expected to wear veils in public. Their role in religious affairs virtually disappeared, and vocational and educational opportunities declined. Some Islamic scholars came to believe that Heaven itself was closed to females.

As the following legal opinions show, however, women in the Ottoman Empire were not without legal rights and protections during the seventeenth century. The empire had a complex and sophisticated court system staffed by *qadi* (judges), whose job it was to interpret Islamic law, or Sharia, and apply it to specific cases. In making their decisions they drew on their knowledge of the Quran (the record of God's revelations to Muhammad) and Hadith (traditions connected with the life and teachings of Muhammad), collections of previous legal decisions, and various textbooks and commentaries on Islamic law. They also took into account *fatwas,* legal opinions provided by learned men known as *muftis*. Such legal opinions could be solicited by the judges themselves or by an individual involved in a court case. The resulting fatwa was not a binding legal judgment but rather one scholar's opinion that would be included in the record of the trial and might affect the judge's decision. In some provincial courts, however, the standing of a mufti might be so high that his fatwa would actually override a decision of the court.

The following fatwas were written by Kayhr al-Din Ramli (1585–1671), who, after studying in Cairo at al-Azhar, the outstanding school of Islamic studies in the region, returned to his native city of Ramla in Palestine, where he supported himself through farming, income from property, and the teaching of Islamic law. His fame, however, was based on his avocation as a jurisconsult, or mufti. Having written his first fatwa as a student in Cairo, he continued to do so after his return to Ramla. By the 1650s his reputation had spread throughout Syria and Palestine and was so great that no judge would go against one of his opinions. The following are examples of the many opinions he offered on questions having to do with women's position in society. They reveal judgments that took male dominance in society for granted, but also accorded legal rights and protections to women.

Many of the decisions involve marriage, a state into which every adult Muslim was expected to enter. Most marriages were arranged by legal guardians (usually fathers or grandfathers) while the future wife and in rare cases the future husband were still minors who had not reached puberty. On reaching puberty the young girl or boy had no choice but to acquiesce to his or her guardian's wishes and enter into the planned marriage. For marriages arranged for legal adults, however, individuals had the right to reject or consent to the proposed match. Similarly if a marriage was arranged by someone other than a father or grandfather for a minor, then on reaching legal majority the person could refuse.

Islamic law accepted the fact that no social good was served by continuing defective or unhappy marriages. Hence divorce was permissible and fairly common. A husband could divorce his wife by saying before her and a witness "I divorce you, I divorce you, I divorce you." This meant that the woman was irrevocably and finally divorced ("thrice-divorced") and could remarry if she wished. For a specified time or until the divorced wife remarried, the former husband was obligated to pay for her support. A woman could also demand a divorce by demonstrating in court that her husband had failed to fulfill his financial or sexual obligations. Or alternatively, she could convince her husband to annul the marriage by offering him financial concessions. For example, she might return some or all of the dowry payment she had received or release the husband from any support obligations after the annulment.

Other legal cases centered on relations between unmarried men and women (which were closely regulated), child custody (which accorded mothers and their families some rights), crimes against women, and sexuality. Together they provide many insights into male-female relations in seventeenth-century Syria-Palestine.

QUESTIONS FOR ANALYSIS

1. In making arrangements for marriage how much legal authority is exercised by the following: the future husband and wife; fathers and grandfathers; male relatives of the future husband and wife?

2. What do the divorce cases reveal about the obligations of husbands to their wives?
3. What rights does a married woman have against an abusive husband?
4. How did Khayr al-Din Ramli view rapists and abductors of women? What penalties are prescribed for such men?
5. What does the case about the widow who is appointed by her dying husband to be guardian of their children reveal about inheritance practices?
6. Taking all the cases together, what do they tell about women's legal standing in seventeenth-century Syria-Palestine? What situations and legal opinions underscore women's legal inferiority to men? What situations and decisions accord women legal rights in their dealings with men?

ARRANGING MARRIAGES

QUESTION: There is a minor girl whose brother married her off, and she came of age and chose annulment in her "coming-of-age" choice. Her husband claimed that her brother had acted as the agent of her father and she does not have a choice. She then claimed that [her brother] married her off during [her father's] brief absence on a journey. If the husband provides evidence for his claim, is her choice canceled or not? If he does not have evidence, and wants her oath on that, must she swear an oath?

ANSWER: Yes, if the husband proves his claim, then her choice is canceled. . . . Only the father's and grandfather's marriage arrangements cannot be canceled . . . [and] if the marriage was arranged by way of a proxy for her father, then she has no choice. If the marriage was arranged as a result of [the brother's] guardianship, then she has a choice.

▾▾▾

QUESTION: A virgin in her legal majority and of sound mind was abducted by her brother and married off to an unsuitable man. Does her father have the right to annul the marriage contract on the basis of the [husband's] unsuitability?

ANSWER: Yes, if the father asks for that, then the judge should separate the spouses whether or not the marriage was consummated, so long as she has not borne children, and is not pregnant, and did not receive the dower[1] before the marriage. . . . This is the case if her brother has married her off with her consent. But if she was given in marriage without her consent, she can reject [the marriage], and there is no need for the father [to ask for] separation [and raise] opposition, for he is not [in this case] a commissioned agent. [But] if she authorizes him to represent her, then he has the right to request from the judge an annulment of the marriage and a separation, and the judge should separate them. . . .

DIVORCE AND ANNULMENT

QUESTION: There is a poor woman whose husband is absent in a remote region and he left her without support or a legal provider, and she has suffered proven harm from that. She has made a claim against him for that [support], but the absent one is very poor. The resources [intended] for her support were left in his house and in his shop, but they are not sufficient for her to withstand her poverty. She therefore asked the Shafi[2] judge to annul the marriage, and he ordered her to bring proof. Two just men testified in conformity with what she had claimed, and so the judge annulled the marriage. . . . Then, following her waiting period, she married another man.

---

[1]In contrast to practice in Europe, according to Islamic law, dowry payments were paid by the husband to the wife.

[2]One of the four schools of Sunni Muslim jurisprudence; it tended to be more favorable to women seeking divorce.

Then the first husband returned and wanted to nullify the judgment. Can that be done for him, when it was all necessary and had ample justification?

ANSWER: When the harm is demonstrated and the evidence for that is witnessed, the annulment of the absent [one's marriage] is sound. . . . It is not for the Hanafi[3] or others to nullify this. . . .

▼▼▼

QUESTION: There is a poor man who married a virgin in her legal majority, but he did not pay her stipulated dower expeditiously, nor did he provide support, nor did he clothe her. This caused her great harm. Must he follow one of God's two commands: "Either you maintain her well or you release her with kindness?" And if the judge annuls the marriage, is it on account of the severe harm being done to her?

ANSWER: Yes, the husband should do one of the two things, according to God's command: "maintain her well or release her with kindness." . . . You cannot sustain [indefinitely] such needs through borrowing, and it appears that she does not have anyone to lend her money, and the husband has no actual wealth. . . .

▼▼▼

QUESTION: A man consummated his marriage with his virgin legally major wife, and then claimed that he found her deflowered. He was asked, "How was that?" And he said, "I had intercourse with her several times and I found her deflowered." What is the legal judgment on that?

ANSWER: The judgment is that all of the dower is required, and it is fully and entirely incumbent on him. Her testimony on her own virgin-

ity [is sufficient] to remove the shame. And if he accuses her without [evidence], he is punished and his testimony is not accepted, as is her right. If he defamed her with a charge of adultery, he must now make a sworn allegation of adultery if she so requests, [and take the consequences].[4] Such is the case, and God knows best.

VIOLENCE AGAINST WOMEN

QUESTION: A man approached a woman, a virgin in her legal majority who was married to someone else,[5] abducted her in the month of Ramadan, and took her to a village near her own village. He brought her to the shaykh[6] of the village, who welcomed him and gave him hospitality and protection. There the man consummated the "marriage," saying "between us there are relations." Such is the way of the peasants. . . . What is the punishment for him and the man who helped him? . . . Should Muslim rulers halt these practices of the peasants . . . even by combat and killing?[7]

ANSWER: The punishment of the abductor and his accomplice for this grave crime is severe beating and long imprisonment, and even worse punishment until they show remorse. It is conceivable that the punishment could be execution because of the severity of this act of disobedience to God. This practice — and one fears for the people of the region if it spreads and they do not halt it — will be punished by God. The one who commits this act, and those who remain silent about it, are like one who punches a hole in a ship, [an act] that will drown all the passengers. . . .

▼▼▼

QUESTION: There is a *muhsan*[8] criminal who kidnapped a virgin and took her virginity. She fled

---

[3]Another school of Sunni Muslim jurisprudence, less favorable to women seeking divorce.
[4]In order to prove adultery an accuser had to present four witnesses to testify that it occurred. A failure to prove such an accusation carried severe legal penalties.
[5]The marriage had been legally contracted but not consummated.

[6]In this context, the village leader, often a man with some religious training and standing.
[7]In other words, by sending in troops to enforce the law.
[8]A legally married person.

from him to her family and now her seducer wants to take her away by force. Should he be prevented, and what is required of him?

ANSWER: Yes, he should be prevented [from taking] her. If he claimed *shubha*[9] [judicial doubt], there is no *hadd* punishment but he must [pay] a fair dower. If he did not claim *shubha,* and admission and testimony prove [his actions], the specified *hadd* punishment[10] is required: if he is *muhsan,* then he is stoned; if not, he is flogged. In the event the *hadd* penalty is canceled, a dower is required.

▼ ▼ ▼

QUESTION: There is an evil man who harms his wife, hits her without right and rebukes her without cause. He swore many times to divorce her until she proved that a thrice divorce [a final and irrevocable divorce] had taken effect.

ANSWER: He is forbidden to do that, and he is rebuked and enjoined from her. If she has proved that a thrice divorce has taken place, it is permissible for her to kill him, according to many of the *'ulama'* [jurists] if he is not prevented [from approaching her] except by killing.

---

[10]A *hadd* punishment is one prescribed by Islamic law.

[9]An issue about which legal authorities disagree.

Chapter 3

▼▼▼

Europe in an Age of Conflict and Expansion

From the 1400s through the mid 1600s, European society changed in many ways. Centuries of religious uniformity under the Roman Catholic Church gave way to religious diversity as new Protestant churches cast off papal authority and rejected traditional Catholic doctrines. A political order characterized by local aristocratic power, decentralized authority, and weak monarchies yielded to a new political reality dominated by increasingly centralized and fiercely competitive nation-states. Armies grew in size, and battles were won and lost by soldiers armed with artillery and firearms, not longbows and lances. Intellectuals lost interest in the abstract theological and philosophical issues that had preoccupied their thirteenth-century predecessors, and inspired by new interests in Greek and Roman antiquity, broke new ground in science, moral philosophy, and political thought. Writers, artists, and architects developed new styles and themes, and explorers discovered new ocean routes that took them to Africa, Asia, and the Americas.

Taken together, these changes mark the end of the Middle Ages, that long, formative period of European civilization that began with the fall of the Western Roman Empire in the fifth century C.E. These changes are also generally viewed as indicators of progress, growth, and advancement in an age of renaissance, or rebirth, after centuries of medieval stagnation. Such a view is problematic in many respects. Aside from belittling the impressive achievements of the Middle Ages, it ignores the many tensions, doubts, and conflicts that accompanied the political, economic, and cultural changes of the immediate postmedieval era.

In many ways these years are better characterized as an "era of contradiction" or "an era of conflict" than as an age of rebirth. The emergence of Protestantism, for example, ultimately led to an acceptance of religious diversity and religious toleration in most of Europe, but in the sixteenth and early seventeenth centuries it was a source of war, rebellion, and bigotry. Tens of thousands of Europeans were exiled, imprisoned, or executed because of their religious convictions, and millions were killed in the religious wars that stretched from the 1520s to the mid 1600s. The discoveries of Copernicus, Kepler, Galileo, and others in the long run provided the foundation for one of Europe's most enduring achievements — experimental, mathematics-based science. In the short run, however, their rejection of revered ancient authorities and their many disagreements led many to the pessimistic view that humans could know little if anything with certainty. Nor did these scientists' discoveries dispel the irrational fears and superstitions of the age. The era saw a deepening fear of witchcraft, a fear so intense that it gave rise to witch hunts and witch trials that resulted in the execution of thousands of individuals, most of whom were women who confessed after protracted torture. Spectacular economic growth took place in the sixteenth century as a result of population growth, the influx of precious metals from the Americas, and Europe's growing share of world trade. This economic expansion generated new forms of business organization such as the joint stock company and created huge fortunes for many merchants and investors. But mounting inflation caused hardship for many sixteenth-century Europeans, and around 1600, plague, famine, war, and depression caused a decline in Europe's overall standard of living. Political changes also caused tensions. Advocates of strong centralized monarchy contended with defenders of local autonomy, divine right absolutists faced believers in regicide, and kings battled parliaments. Wars were fought to gain or protect territory, to advance the cause of Catholicism or Protestantism, to settle dynastic claims, or to fulfill personal ambitions. The Thirty Years' War from 1618 to 1648 involved every major European state and caused human suffering on a scale unmatched until the wars of the twentieth century.

Expansionist Europe was not, as one might have expected, a stable, cohesive and self-confident society. By sheer luck the Europeans in their efforts to reach Asia by sailing west discovered the Americas, whose peoples were easily subdued after millions of them died from imported Old World diseases. Elsewhere the Europeans' success in developing the military potential of gunpowder, in particular the ability to mount artillery on oceangoing ships, enabled them to expand their economic activities and establish their political power on the fringes of Africa and Asia. But these accomplishments, rightly deemed significant by historians, gave scant comfort to the majority of Europeans, who faced a troubled present and anticipated the future with more foreboding than hope.

Protestant Revolt and Catholic Response

During the High Middle Ages, "the age of faith," the esteem and devotion accorded the Catholic Church resulted in part from the clergy's moral example and leadership and in part from the Church's promise that its doctrines and practices, if followed, assured eternal salvation. During the fourteenth and fifteenth centuries, however, the Church was rocked by schism, scandal, deficits, political challenges, and uninspired and corrupt leadership. Anger over abuses intensified, especially in northern Europe, and many Europeans began to question the Church's ability to deliver the salvation they fervently sought. This doubt and alienation goes far in explaining the success of the sixteenth-century Protestant revolt, sparked in 1517 when a German friar, Martin Luther, openly challenged certain Catholic teachings, especially the doctrine that people could atone for their sins by purchasing indulgences. By 1650, Protestants dominated northern Germany, Scandinavia, England, Scotland, the Netherlands, and major Swiss cities, and were a significant minority in France and parts of central Europe.

No area of European life was unaffected by the Protestant Reformation. In the religious sphere, not only did new forms of Christianity take root, but efforts at Catholic reform revitalized an institution that had lost much of its spiritual focus and vitality. Education expanded throughout Europe because of the need of competing churches for educated leadership, and especially among Protestants because of their emphasis on Bible reading by the laity. The distinction between clergy and laity was narrowed because of the Protestant doctrine that devout laypersons were just as pleasing to God as priests and members of religious orders. Literacy among women increased as a result of Protestant educational efforts, and according to some historians, the Protestant affirmation of clerical marriage fostered a more positive view of women. Conversely, Protestant women saw no appreciable gains in their legal or economic status, and were just as likely as their Catholic sisters to be victimized by witch hunts and witch trials. The religious struggles of the Reformation era also profoundly affected politics. With religious passions exacerbating dynastic rivalries and internal conflicts, Europe endured a century of religious wars, many of which were both civil wars and wars between states.

Most significantly, the Reformation era contributed to the ongoing secularization of European politics, culture, and thought. In the short run, the Protestant and Catholic reformations intensified religious feeling and thrust religion into the forefront of European life. In the long run, however, the proliferation of competing faiths divided and weakened Europe's churches, and the long years of religious intolerance and war discredited religion in the eyes of many. The gradual acceptance of religious diversity within individual states and Europe as a whole was a sign of growing secularism. Paradoxically, the very intensity of the era's religious passions helped undermine the role of religion in European life and thought.

A Protestant View of Christianity
▼▼▼

15 ▼ Martin Luther, TABLE TALK

The Protestant Reformation had many voices, but its first prophet was Martin Luther (1483–1546), whose Ninety-Five Theses of 1517 initiated the momentous anti-Catholic rebellion. Born into the family of a German miner and educated at the University of Erfurt, the young Luther was preparing for a career as a lawyer when suddenly in 1505 he changed course and became an Augustinian friar. Luther's decision resulted from his dissatisfaction over his relationship with God and doubts about his personal salvation. He hoped that life as an Augustinian would protect him from the world's temptations and allow him to win God's favor by devoting himself to prayer, study, and the sacraments. His spiritual anxieties soon returned, however. Intensely conscious of his own inadequacies and failings, he became convinced that he could never earn his salvation or live up to the high standards of selflessness, charity, and purity prescribed by Jesus' teachings and the Catholic Church. He despaired of ever satisfying an angry, judging God and was terrorized by the prospect of eternal damnation in Hell.

During the 1510s, however, while teaching theology at the University of Wittenberg, Luther found spiritual peace through his reflections on the scriptures. He concluded that human beings, burdened as they were by weakness and sin, could never earn salvation by leading a blameless life and performing in the proper spirit the pious acts enjoined by the Catholic Church. Rather, salvation was an unmerited divine gift, resulting from God-implanted faith in Jesus, especially in the redemptive power of his death and resurrection. This fundamental Protestant doctrine of "justification by faith alone" inspired the Ninety-Five Theses, in which Luther attacked contemporary Catholic teaching. In particular he sought to discredit the doctrine of indulgences, which taught that people could atone for their sins and ensure their own and loved ones' salvation by contributing money to the Church. Within five years Luther was the recognized leader of a religious movement — Protestantism — that broke with the Catholic Church not just over salvation but also a host of other fundamental issues concerning Christianity and the Christian life.

QUESTIONS FOR ANALYSIS

1. According to Luther, what role should the Bible play in a Christian's life? How in his view does the Roman Catholic Church obscure the meaning and message of the Bible?
2. What does Luther mean by "good works"? Why does he believe that the Roman Church distorts the role of good works in a Christian's life?
3. What role does faith play in a Christian's life, according to Luther? Why is faith superior to external acts of devotion?
4. What criticisms does Luther offer of the papacy and other high officials of the Catholic Church?
5. How does Luther view marriage, in particular a woman's role in marriage?
6. Why does Luther single out monks and members of religious orders for special criticism? What are their shortcomings?

SALVATION AND DAMNATION

Because as the everlasting, merciful God, through his Word[1] and Sacraments,[2] talks and deals with us, all other creatures excluded, not of temporal things which pertain to this vanishing life . . . but as to where we shall go when we depart from here, and gives unto us his Son for a Savior, delivering us from sin and death, and purchasing for us everlasting righteousness, life, and salvation, therefore it is most certain, that we do not die away like the beasts that have no understanding; but so many of us . . . shall through him be raised again to life everlasting at the last day, and the ungodly to everlasting destruction.

▼ ▼ ▼

FAITH VERSUS GOOD WORKS

He that goes from the gospel to the law,[3] thinking to be saved by good works,[4] falls as uneasily as he who falls from the true service of God to idolatry; for, without Christ, all is idolatry and fictitious imaginings of God, whether of the Turkish Quran, of the pope's decrees, or Moses' laws; if a man think thereby to be justified and saved before God, he is undone.

▼ ▼ ▼

The gospel preaches nothing of the merit of works; he that says the gospel requires works for salvation, I say, flat and plain, is a liar.

Nothing that is properly good proceeds out of the works of the law, unless grace be present; for

---

[1]The *Word* is God's message, especially as revealed through Jesus' life.

[2]Sacraments are sacred rites or ceremonies that are signs or symbols of a spiritual reality. Of the seven Catholic sacraments, Luther retained two, baptism and the eucharist. Affirming Catholic tradition, he believed that these sacraments were a means of grace through which God bestows spiritual gifts.

[3]By *law* Luther meant religious rules and regulations; he believed that futile human efforts to live strictly according to the dictates of the law undermined true faith.

[4]All the ceremonies and pious activities such as pilgrimages, relic veneration, and attendance at Mass that the Catholic Church promoted as vehicles of God's grace and eternal salvation.

what we are forced to do, goes not from the heart, nor is acceptable.

▼▼▼

A Capuchin[5] says: wear a grey coat and a hood, a rope round thy body, and sandals on thy feet. A Cordelier says: put on a black hood; an ordinary papist says: do this or that work, hear mass, pray, fast, give alms, etc. But a true Christian says: I am justified and saved only by faith in Christ, without any works or merits of my own; compare these together, and judge which is the true righteousness.

▼▼▼

I have often been resolved to live uprightly, and to lead a true godly life, and to set everything aside that would hinder this, but it was far from being put in execution; even as it was with Peter,[6] when he swore he would lay down his life for Christ.

▼▼▼

I will not lie or dissemble before my God, but will freely confess, I am not able to effect that good which I intend, but await the happy hour when God shall be pleased to meet me with his grace.

▼▼▼

A Christian's worshiping is not the external, hypocritical mask that our friars wear, when they chastise their bodies, torment and make themselves faint, with ostentatious fasting, watching, singing, wearing hair shirts, scourging themselves, etc. Such worshiping God does not desire.

THE BIBLE

Great is the strength of the divine Word. In the epistle to the Hebrews,[7] it is called "a two-edged sword." But we have neglected and scorned the pure and clear Word, and have drunk not of the fresh and cool spring; we are gone from the clear fountain to the foul puddle, and drunk its filthy water; that is, we have sedulously read old writers and teachers, who went about with speculative reasonings, like the monks and friars.

▼▼▼

The ungodly papists prefer the authority of the church far above God's Word; a blasphemy abominable and not to be endured; void of all shame and piety, they spit in God's face. Truly, God's patience is exceeding great, in that they are not destroyed; but so it always has been.

THE PAPACY AND THE MONASTIC ORDERS

How does it happen that the popes pretend that they form the Church, when, all the while, they are bitter enemies of the Church, and have no knowledge, certainly no comprehension, of the holy gospel? Pope, cardinals, bishops, not a soul of them has read the Bible; it is a book unknown to them. They are a pack of guzzling, gluttonous wretches, rich, wallowing in wealth and laziness, resting secure in their power, and never, for a moment, thinking of accomplishing God's will.

▼▼▼

Kings and princes coin money only out of metals, but the pope coins money out of everything — indulgences, ceremonies, dispensations, pardons; all fish come to his net. . . .

▼▼▼

A gentleman being at the point of death, a monk from the next convent came to see what he could pick up, and said to the gentleman: Sir, will you give so and so to our monastery? The dying man,

---

[5]The Capuchins and Cordeliers were both branches of the Franciscan order noted for their austerity and strict poverty. A distinctive feature of the Capuchins' dress was their peaked hood, or *capuche*.
[6]One of Jesus' twelve apostles; following Jesus' arrest by Roman soldiers before his crucifixion, Peter three times

denied any relationship with Jesus, despite having vowed shortly before to lay down his life for his teacher. Eventually, Peter died a martyr in Rome.
[7]Paul's Letter to the Hebrews, a part of the Christian bible, or New Testament.

unable to speak, replied by a nod of the head, whereupon the monk, turning to the gentleman's son, said: You see, your father makes us this bequest. The son said to the father: Sir, is it your pleasure that I kick this monk down the stairs? The dying man nodded as before, and the son immediately drove the monk out of doors.

▼ ▼ ▼

The papists took the invocation of saints from the pagans, who divided God into numberless images and idols, and ordained to each its particular office and work. . . .

The invocation of saints is a most abominable blindness and heresy; yet the papists will not give it up. The pope's greatest profit arises from the dead; for the calling on dead saints brings him infinite sums of money and riches, far more than he gets from the living. . . .

▼ ▼ ▼

In Italy, the monasteries are very wealthy. There are but three or four monks to each; the surplus of their revenues goes to the pope and his cardinals.

▼ ▼ ▼

The fasting of the friars is more easy to them than our eating to us. For one day of fasting there are three of feasting. Every friar for his supper has two quarts of beer, a quart of wine, and spice-cakes, or bread prepared with spice and salt, the better to relish their drink. Thus go on these poor fasting brethren; getting so pale and wan, they are like the fiery angels.

▼ ▼ ▼

In Popedom they make priests, not to preach and teach God's Word, but only to celebrate mass, and to roam about with the sacrament. For, when a bishop ordains a man, he says: Take the power to celebrate mass, and to offer it for the living and the dead. But we ordain priests according to the command of Christ and St. Paul, namely, to preach the pure gospel and God's Word. The papists in their ordinations make no mention of preaching and teaching God's Word, therefore their consecrating and ordaining is false and wrong, for all worshiping which is not ordained of God, or erected by God's Word and command, is worthless, yea, mere idolatry.

THE REFORM OF THE CHURCH

The pope and his crew can in no way endure the idea of reformation; the mere word creates more alarm at Rome than thunderbolts from heaven or the day of judgment. A cardinal said the other day: Let them eat, and drink, and do what they will; but as to reforming us, we think that is a vain idea; we will not endure it. Neither will we Protestants be satisfied, though they administer the sacrament in both kinds, and permit priests to marry;[8] we will also have the doctrine of the faith pure and unfalsified, and the righteousness that justifies and saves before God, and which expels and drives away all idolatry and false-worshiping; with these gone and banished, the foundation on which Popedom is built also falls.

▼ ▼ ▼

The chief cause that I fell out with the pope was this: the pope boasted that he was the head of the church, and condemned all that would not be under his power and authority; . . . Further, he took upon him power, rule, and authority over the Christian church, and over the Holy Scriptures, the Word of God; no man must presume to expound the Scriptures, but only he, and according to his ridiculous conceits; this was not to be endured. They who, against God's word, boast of the church's authority, are mere idiots.

---

[8]Two of the many changes that Protestants demanded were allowing all Christians to receive the sacrament of the eucharist in the forms of bread and wine (in medieval Roman Catholic practice, only the priest drank the eucharistic wine) and allowing priests to marry. The principle behind both changes was Luther's teaching that all Christians are priests — that is, responsible for their own religious faith.

MARRIAGE AND CELIBACY

Who can sufficiently admire the state of conjugal union, which God has instituted and founded, and from which all human creatures, indeed, all states proceed. Where would we be if it did not exist? But neither God's ordinance, nor the gracious presence of children, the fruit of matrimony, moves the ungodly world, which sees only the temporal difficulties and troubles of matrimony, but sees not the great treasure that is hidden in it. We were all born of women — emperors, kings, princes, yea, Christ himself, the Son of God, did not disdain to be born of a virgin. Let the scoffers and rejecters of matrimony go hang, . . . and the papists, who reject married life, and yet have mistresses; if they need to scoff at matrimony, let them be consistent, and keep no concubines.

▼ ▼ ▼

Marrying cannot be without women, nor can the world subsist without them. To marry is medicine against unchastity. A woman is, or at least should be, a friendly, courteous, and merry companion in life; this is why they are named household-honors, the honor and ornament of the house, and inclined to tenderness; for this reason are they chiefly created, to bear children, and be the pleasure, joy, and solace of their husbands.

A Blueprint for Catholic Revival
▼▼▼

16 ▼ DECREES OF THE COUNCIL OF TRENT

The reform and revival of the Roman Catholic Church in the sixteenth century had many dimensions — the foundation of new religious orders such as the Society of Jesus; reforms initiated by dedicated popes, bishops, and leaders of religious orders; the political and military victories of arch-Catholic Spain; the emotional appeal of Baroque art and architecture; and the renewed dedication of countless individual Catholic men and women. Nothing, however, was more important than the Council of Trent, an assembly of Catholic churchmen that met on and off for almost twenty years between 1545 and 1563. Out of its debates and decisions there emerged a new Catholic Church more confident of its doctrines, clearer in its mission, and better prepared to meet the challenge of Protestantism.

Many times in the past, popes had convened Church councils to give bishops, archbishops, leaders of religious orders, and theologians an opportunity to debate and resolve fundamental theological and policy issues. In the 1520s, the strongest advocate of convening such a council was not the Pope but the Holy Roman Emperor, Charles V. He hoped that such a gathering, attended by both Protestants and Catholics, would encourage Protestants to return to the Catholic fold by ending abuses and achieving compromises on divisive theological issues. Such a strategy was at first opposed by many Catholics, including Pope Clement VII (1523–1534), who feared that a council would undermine the papacy's finances and threaten its authority.

Clement's successor, Paul III (1534–1549), who fully understood the gravity of the Church's situation and faced continuing pressure from Charles V, concluded that convening a Church council was necessary. Agreeing on a time, place, and agenda was difficult, however, and as a result, the long-awaited council did not begin until 1545 in the small northern Italian city of Trent. With its deliberations and votes increasingly controlled by the papacy and the numerically ascendant

Italian bishops, the council continued to meet until 1563, during which time it clarified numerous theological issues and approved a broad program of reform and renewal for the Church.

For Emperor Charles V and others hoping for reconciliation between Protestants and Catholics, the Council of Trent was a disappointment. Few Protestants attended, and in any case by the time the council met, theological disagreements had hardened to the point that meaningful compromises were unlikely. Instead of a vehicle for reconciliation, the Council of Trent affirmed traditional Catholic teachings and girded the Church for its struggle with Protestantism during the era of religious wars.

QUESTIONS FOR ANALYSIS

1. The council's declarations on justification affirm the importance of God's freely given grace as the beginning of the process of salvation. What else is required of the believer to gain salvation? How do such views differ from those of Luther?
2. What do the rules concerning prohibited books reveal about the Church's attitudes toward the printed book?
3. How openly do the council's statements admit that abuses existed among the clergy? What steps are proposed to deal with such abuses?
4. If Luther or one of his followers had been given the opportunity to comment on the decisions of the Council of Trent represented in this assignment, what might they have said about the following issues: individual salvation; the Bible; the nature of the priesthood; saints; indulgences?

CONCERNING JUSTIFICATION[1]

If anyone says that man can be justified before God by his own works, whether done by his own natural powers or through the teaching of the law, without divine grace through Jesus Christ, let him be anathema.[2] . . .

If anyone says that the sinner is justified by faith alone, meaning that nothing else is required . . . in order to obtain the grace of justification, and that it is not in any way necessary that he be prepared and disposed by the action of his own will, let him be anathema. . . .

If anyone says that the commandments of God are, even for one that is justified and constituted in grace, impossible to observe, let him be anathema. . . .

If anyone says that the justice received [from God] is . . . not increased before God through good works, but that those works are merely the fruits and signs of justification obtained, but not the cause of its increase, let him be anathema. . . .

CONCERNING PROHIBITED BOOKS

Since it is clear from experience that if the Sacred Books[3] are permitted everywhere and without discrimination in the vernacular, there will . . .

---

[1]The process by which a person is freed from the penalty of his or her sin and is accepted by God as worthy of being saved.

[2]Refers to a person made subject to excommunication and extreme condemnation by an official ecclesiastical authority.
[3]The Bible.

arise . . . more harm than good, the matter is . . . left to the judgement of the bishop or inquisitor;[4] who may . . . permit the reading of the Sacred Books translated into the vernacular by Catholic authors to those who they know will derive from such reading no harm but rather an increase of faith and piety, which permission they must have in writing. . . . Bookdealers who sell or in any other way supply Bibles written in the vernacular to anyone who has not this permission, shall lose the price of the books, which is applied by the bishop to pious purposes, and . . . they shall be subject to other penalties which are left to the judgement of the same bishop. . . .

Moreover, in all cities . . . the houses or places where the art of printing is carried on and the libraries offering books for sale, shall be visited often by persons appointed for this purpose by the bishop . . . or the inquisitor, so that nothing prohibited be printed, sold, or possessed.

All book-dealers and venders of books shall have in their libraries a list of books which they have for sale subscribed by said persons, and without the permission of the same appointed persons they may not under penalties of confiscation of the books and other penalties, . . . possess or sell or . . . supply other books. . . .

Finally, all the faithful are commanded not to presume to read or possess any books contrary to the prescriptions of these rules or the prohibition of this list. And if anyone should read or possess books by heretics . . . , he incurs immediately the sentence of excommunication.[5]

ON THE FOUNDING OF SEMINARIES

Since the age of youth, . . . unless educated from its tender years in piety and religion before the

habits of vice take possession of the whole man, will never perfectly and without the greatest and well-nigh extraordinary help of Almighty God persevere in ecclesiastical discipline, the holy council decrees that all cathedral and metropolitan churches[6] and churches greater than these shall be bound, . . . to provide for, to educate in religion, and to train in ecclesiastical discipline, a certain number of boys of their city and diocese, . . . in a college located near the said churches or in some other suitable place. . . . Into this college shall be received such as are at least twelve years of age, are born of lawful wedlock, who know how to read and write competently, and whose character and inclination justify the hope that they will dedicate themselves forever to the ecclesiastical ministry. . . . And that they may be better trained in . . . ecclesiastical discipline, they shall . . . always wear the tonsure[7] and the clerical garb; they shall study grammar, singing, ecclesiastical computation,[8] and other useful arts; shall be instructed in Sacred Scripture, ecclesiastical books, the homilies of the saints, the manner of administering the sacraments, especially those things that seem adapted to the hearing of confessions, and the rites and ceremonies. The bishop shall see to it that they are present every day at the sacrifice of the mass, confess their sins at least once a month, receive the body of our Lord Jesus Christ[9] in accordance with the directions of their confessor, and on festival days serve in the cathedral and other churches of the locality. . . .

ON CLERICAL CONDUCT

Since therefore the more these things contribute usefulness and honor in the Church of God, so the more zealously must they be observed, the

---

[4]An official approved by the Church to discover and suppress heresy, an opinion at variance with the authorized teaching of the Church.

[5]An ecclesiastical censure that excludes a person from communion with the faithful and prevents him or her from partaking in the sacraments of the Church.

[6]A cathedral church is the home church of a bishop; a metropolitan church is the church of an archbishop.

[7]The rite by which a layman becomes a member of the clergy; during the rite a small circular area is shaved on the top of the candidate's head.

[8]The process of determining the dates of Holy Days, especially Easter.

[9]In other words, to receive the consecrated communion wafer, believed by Catholics to have been transformed into the body of Christ.

holy council ordains that those things which have in the past been frequently and wholesomely enacted by the supreme pontiffs and holy councils concerning adherence to the life, conduct, dress, and learning of clerics, as also the avoidance of luxury, feastings, dances, gambling, sports, and all sorts of crime and secular pursuits shall in the future be observed under the same or greater penalties. . . .

It is to be desired that those who assume the episcopal office[10] know what are their duties, and understand that they have been called not for their own convenience, not for riches or luxury, but to labors and cares for the glory of God. . . . Wherefore, it commands not only that bishops be content with modest furniture and a frugal table, but also that they take heed that in the rest of their manner of living and in their whole house, nothing appears that is at variance with this holy ordinance, or that does not manifest simplicity, zeal for God and a contempt for vanities. But above all does it forbid them to attempt to enrich their relations or domestics from the revenues of the Church. . . . And what has been said of bishops . . . it decrees that it applies also to the cardinals[11] of the holy Roman Church.

How shameful and how unworthy it is of the name of clerics . . . to live in the filth of impurity and unclean cohabitation,[12] the thing itself sufficiently testifies by the common scandal of all the faithful and the supreme disgraces on the clerical order. Wherefore, that the ministers of the Church may be brought back to the continency and purity of life which is proper to them, . . . the holy council forbids all clerics whatsoever to presume to keep concubines or other women concerning whom suspicion can be had

in their house or elsewhere, or to presume to have any association with them; . . .

ON INDULGENCES

Since the power of granting indulgences[13] was conferred by Christ on the Church, . . . the holy council teaches and commands that the use of indulgences, . . . is to be retained in the Church, and it condemns . . . those who assert that they are useless or deny that there is in the Church the power of granting them. In granting them, however, it desires that . . . moderation be observed, lest by too great facility ecclesiastical discipline be weakened. But desiring that the abuses which have become connected with them . . . be amended and corrected, it ordains . . . that all evil traffic in them, which has been a most prolific source of abuses among the Christian people, be absolutely abolished. . . .

ON THE VENERATION OF SAINTS AND SACRED IMAGES

The holy council commands all bishops and others who hold the office of teaching and have charges of the [care of souls], that they instruct the faithful diligently, teaching them that the saints who reign together with Christ offer up their prayers to God for men, that it is good and beneficial . . . to invoke them and to have recourse to their prayers, assistance and support in order to obtain favors from God through His Son, Jesus Christ our Lord. . . . [Also,] those who maintain that veneration and honor are not due to the relics of the saints, or that these and other

---

[10]The office of bishop.

[11]High Church officials who serve as counselors and assistants of the pope and, as members of the College of Cardinals, elected new popes.

[12]Living with a woman.

[13]Connected with the sacrament of penance, an indulgence was originally a grant by the Church that exempted a person from the temporal penalties (the "acts of penance") imposed by a priest after confession. Crusaders were given a

plenary (full) indulgence for their participation in the Holy War against the Muslims. By the early sixteenth century indulgences could be purchased for one's own benefit and for the benefit of souls believed to be in Purgatory. The sale of indulgences became a major source of revenue for the Church, and many Christians came to believe the claims of indulgence preachers that salvation could be purchased through indulgences.

memorials are honored by the faithful without profit, and that the places dedicated to the memory of the saints for the purpose of obtaining their aid are visited in vain, are to be utterly condemned. . . . Moreover, that the images of Christ, of the Virgin Mother of God, and of the other saints are to be placed and retained especially in the churches, and that due honor and veneration is to be given them.

Art as Protestant Propaganda
▼▼▼

17 ▼ Hans Beham, AN ALLEGORY OF THE MONASTIC ORDERS; Anonymous, A MIRROR FOR THE BLIND; Lucas Cranach the Younger, TWO KINDS OF PREACHING: EVANGELICAL AND PAPAL

Some seventy years before Luther posted his Ninety-Five Theses in Wittenberg, in Mainz another German, Johannes Gutenberg (ca. 1395–1468), perfected a new method of printing books through movable metal type. Printing shops soon were established in hundreds of European towns and cities, and by the mid sixteenth century hundreds of thousands of books and pamphlets had been published.

Many of these publications played a key role in the Reformation era's religious struggles. The Ninety-Five Theses, intended by Luther to spark academic debate at the University of Wittenberg, brought him instant prominence when they were translated into German and made available in cheap printed editions. As the Reformation developed, Protestants, much more than Catholics, used the printed page to advance their ideas in Latin treatises for learned audiences and, more tellingly, in thousands of German books and pamphlets for the general population. Woodcuts and engravings were included in many of these works to illustrate Protestant teachings and make them accessible even to the illiterate. Many woodcuts and engravings were also printed separately and sold by booksellers for a few small coins. Several such illustrations are included in this section.

The first woodcut in this section was produced at the beginning of the Protestant movement by Hans Sebald Beham (1500–1550), a native of Nuremberg who studied under Albrecht Dürer, the most famous German artist of the era. An early supporter of Luther, Beham produced a number of pro-Lutheran woodcuts before he left Nuremberg for Frankfurt in the mid 1520s. *An Allegory of the Monastic Orders* focuses on a Roman Catholic monk who is being pulled back by three female figures representing pride, luxury, and avarice, three qualities directly opposed to the monastic ideal of chastity, obedience, and poverty. The monk is being pulled in the opposite direction by a poor peasant, who is being urged on by the figure of poverty. The peasant is yanking on the monk's forelock while forcing him to look at and ingest a book, probably the Bible. At the monk's feet is a discarded book, which may represent the rules of the monks' religious order.

The second woodcut, by an unknown artist, appeared in 1524 as the title page of a pro-Lutheran pamphlet "A Mirror for the Blind" by Heinrich Marschalk. It depicts a monk preaching to two figures representing the pope and a cathedral canon, an official charged with aiding a bishop in administering a diocese. The preaching monk, who is identified as Duns Scotus, a well-known medieval Catholic theologian, holds up a covered mirror that the two figures representing the pope and cathedral canon cannot see in any case since they are blindfolded. Behind the two clergymen are two laypersons, which can be identified from their clothing as a peasant and a well-off city dweller. They have turned away from the futile scene before them and are raising their arms toward the figure of Christ, depicted as lord of the world, seated in glory in the clouds.

The third woodcut, *Two Kinds of Preaching: Evangelical and Papal,* by far the most complex of the three examples in this section, was produced in 1547, and is the work of a life-long resident of Wittenberg and a close friend of Luther's, Lucas Cranach the Younger (1515–1586). It was distributed not as a book illustration but as a broadsheet — a single large printed sheet sold for a few small coins.

We have reproduced the woodcut on two pages, but in its original form it is undivided. The preacher facing left is Luther. Before him rests an open Bible, and on his side of the pulpit are words from the New Testament Book of Acts: "All prophets attest to this, that there is no other name in heaven than that of Christ." Above Luther is a dove, representing the Holy Spirit, the third person of the Holy Trinity whose major functions are illumination, solace, and sanctification. Luther is pointing to three heavenly figures: the Paschal Lamb (a symbol of the risen Christ), the crucified Christ, and God the Father, who holds an orb symbolizing his dominion over creation. The most important text consists of the words the crucified Christ directs toward God the Father: "Holy Father, save them. I have sacrificed myself for them with my wounds." Directly below is written, "If we sin, we have an advocate before God, so let us turn in consolation to this means of grace." In the center and lower left corner are depicted the two Lutheran sacraments, baptism and the eucharist. It is noteworthy that in celebrating the eucharist, the Lutheran pastor offers both the communion wafer and wine to the laity, as opposed to the Catholic practice of restricting the drinking of the wine to the priest. This Lutheran practice is supported by citation of Christ's words at the Last Supper according to Matthew 26: "Drink of it, all of you."

The right side of the woodcut is a Lutheran perspective on how Roman Catholicism has perverted Christianity. The preaching friar receives inspiration from the empty air blown into his ear by an imp-like demon. The words above his head summarize his message: The practices going on about him are free of heresy and offer an easy path to salvation. His audience consists largely of clergy, with only a handful of laypeople crowded in. In the upper right corner an angry God rains down thunderbolts while Francis of Assisi, the founder of the Franciscan order and a revered medieval saint, attempts in vain to intercede on behalf of wayward humanity. The rest of the scene illustrates in an exaggerated way Catholic practices rejected by Lutherans. They include, in the lower right corner, the sale of indulgences by the pope, who holds a sign reading: "Because the coin rings, the soul to heaven springs." The sign on the money bag reads: "This is shame and vice, squeezed from your donations." Directly behind the pope is a priest celebrating a private mass and an altar being consecrated by a bird-like demon. Still deeper in the background is a dying man having his hair clipped in the style of a monk and having a monk's cowl, or hood, placed on his head, steps that supposedly would ensure his salvation. The attending nun sprinkles the man with holy water and holds a banner reading: "The cowl, the tonsure, and the water aid you." To the right of this scene a bishop consecrates a bell. In the far background two pilgrims approach a small chapel, around which marches a procession honoring the saint depicted on the banner. To Lutherans, all these practices represent misguided rituals that replace faith with meaningless "works."

QUESTIONS FOR ANALYSIS

1. What is the main message of Beham's woodcut, *An Allegory of the Monastic Orders?*
2. What is the main message of the anonymous artist's *A Mirror for the Blind?*
3. In Beham's woodcut the monk is confronted by a peasant, and in the anonymous artist's woodcut, a peasant and a city-dweller are shown rejecting Catholic doctrine and looking to heaven. What message about Protestantism are the artists trying to put across by including these laypersons in their compositions?
4. In Cranach's woodcut, what differences do you see in the makeup of the crowds surrounding the pulpits on the two sides of the picture? What point is he trying to make?
5. What views of the Bible are presented in the woodcuts?
6. All three woodcuts depict the Catholic Church as full of abuses. What are these abuses, and how are they illustrated in each of the woodcuts?
7. How do the depictions of monks (identifiable by the tonsure, or shaven crown) in Cranach's woodcut compare with the message of Beham's woodcut and Luther's *Table Talk* (source 15)?

Hans Beham, An Allegory of the Monastic Orders

Anonymous, A Mirror for the Blind

Lucas Cranach the Younger, Two Kinds of Preaching: Evangelical

Lucas Cranach the Younger, Two Kinds of Preaching: Papal

European Exploration and Expansion: Goals and Motives

When students and scholars refer to the fifteenth and sixteenth centuries as an age of exploration and expansion, in almost every case they are referring to the state-sponsored transoceanic voyages of da Gama, Columbus, Magellan, and other European mariners. In many ways this is understandable and justifiable. Europe's overseas expansion was a turning point in history, with ramifications for the people of Eurasia, much of Africa, and especially for the Americas, whose 10,000-year isolation came to an end. Because of its importance, Europe's expansion has been studied and analyzed from the time it began to the present day. Nonetheless its meaning, significance, and context are frequently misunderstood.

One myth about expansion and exploration in the fifteenth and sixteenth centuries is that they were unique accomplishments of a handful of Western European states — primarily Portugal, Spain, England, France, and the Netherlands. In truth, many other societies were expanding during these years, and some were expanding into "unknown territory." The Ottoman Empire grew to incorporate northern Africa, the Arabian Peninsula, and southeastern Europe. Between 1405 and 1433 the Ming emperors of China sponsored a series of maritime expeditions under the direction of Admiral Zheng He designed to extend Chinese influence in the India Ocean basin. Beginning in the 1500s the Russians began to explore and expand to the east, not halting until they had conquered Siberia, reached the Pacific Ocean, and staked a claim to Alaska and parts of the North American west coast. The expansion of the Mughals in India, the Aztecs in central Mexico, and the Incas in South America could be added to the list.

Another myth is that Europe's expansion resulted from the superiority of Europeans over other peoples in the world. The Europeans, so it is argued, took the lead in overseas exploration and expansion because they had better ships, a more sophisticated economy, better organized states, and more effective weapons than anyone else in the world. Some go further to suggest it was the unique "adventurous spirit" of the Europeans that made the difference. Although it is true that European firearms, especially shipborne cannons, gave them an advantage in their early encounters with Africans, Native Americans, and merchants in the Indian Ocean, this is the only area in which one can convincingly argue that Europe's superiority made its expansion inevitable.

Instead, the causes of Europe's expansion are to be found in the confluence of several factors, including pressing economic needs (for gold and silver and a direct route to the spice markets of Asia); recent advances in shipbuilding and navigation (better maps; navigational instruments such as the compass and cross staff; ships outfitted with rear rudders and square and triangular sails); long-standing religious goals (to make converts in unknown lands and damage Muslim-dominated trade in the Indian Ocean and eastern Mediterranean); and rivalries among the European states (once Portuguese and Spaniards began to reap profits from overseas expansion it was only a matter of time before the French, English, and Dutch followed suit). It must also be remembered that the most notable discovery of the Europeans, namely the Americas, resulted largely from geographical circumstance. Living in the westernmost part of Eurasia, Europeans were in the best position to sail across the Atlantic. Luck also played a role. Columbus's goal had been Asia, but because most of his geographical theories were wrong, he discovered the Americas instead.

As the documents in this section show, motives for Europe's overseas expansion varied over time and differed from nation to nation and from individual to individual. Only by taking these variations into account can one gain an understanding of the background and causes of this major turning point in world history.

Why Portugal Began Exploring the African Coast

▼▼▼

18 ▼ Gomes Eannes de Azurara, *THE CHRONICLE OF GUINEA*

At the same time that Chinese fleets under Zhang He were sailing to India, the Arabian Peninsula, and east Africa, and Muslim sailors dominated the coastal trade of virtually every inhabited land washed by the Indian Ocean, Portuguese explorers began to inch their way down Africa's west coast. From 1419 onward, Prince Henry (1394–1460), the third son of King John I (r. 1385–1433), almost annually sent out a ship or two in an attempt to push farther toward the sub-Saharan land the Portuguese called *Guinea.* After they rounded Cape Bojador, on the western Sahara coast in 1434, the pace of exploration quickened, especially now that the Portuguese were coming to believe that it might be possible to reach Asia by sailing around Africa. By 1460 the Portuguese reached the coast of modern Sierra Leone, and in 1488 Bartolomeu Dias sailed around Africa's southern tip. Finally, on May 20, 1498, Vasco da Gama, seeking "Christians and spices," dropped anchor off Calicut on India's west coast after rounding Africa. Although da Gama lost two of his four ships and many of his crew in this enterprise, Portugal was now in the Indian Ocean to stay.

Da Gama's success was still almost a half century in the future when in 1452 Gomes Eannes de Azurara, a Portuguese royal official, began to compose a history of the life and work of Prince Henry, whose support for early Portuguese exploration has earned him the name "Prince Henry and Navigator." Azurara's history details Portuguese explorations down the African coast until 1448. Having completed *The Chronicle of Guinea* in 1453, Azurara turned to other duties in his service to the king, and he never completed an intended second volume. Nonetheless, his chronicle gives us a revealing picture of the spirit behind Portugal's first exploring ventures.

QUESTIONS FOR ANALYSIS

1. What event seems to have sparked Portuguese interest in exploring the oceans off Africa's west coast?
2. What were the anticipated economic benefits from the Portuguese voyages?
3. What religious goals did Henry hope to achieve? Does Azurara give the impression that Henry was motivated more by religion than economic gain?
4. What does the document reveal about the extent of Portuguese knowledge of Africa in the mid fifteenth century?

We imagine that we know a matter when we are acquainted with the doer of it and the end for which he did it. And since in former chapters we have set forth the Lord Infant[1] as the chief actor in these things, giving as clear an understanding of him as we could, it is meet that in this present chapter we should know his purpose in doing them. And you should note well that the noble spirit of this Prince, by a sort of natural constraint, was ever urging him both to begin and to carry out very great deeds. For which reason, after the taking of Ceuta[2] he always kept ships well armed against the Infidel, both for war, and because he had also a wish to know the land that lay beyond the isles of Canary and that Cape called Bojador, for that up to his time, neither by writings, nor by the memory of man, was known with any certainty the nature of the land beyond that Cape. Some said indeed that Saint Brendan[3] had passed that way; and there was another tale of two galleys rounding the Cape, which never returned. But this does not appear at all likely to be true, for it is not to be presumed that if the said galleys went there, some other ships would not have endeavored to learn what voyage they had made. And because the said Lord Infant wished to know the truth of this — since it seemed to him that if he or some other lord did not endeavor to gain that knowledge, no mariners or merchants would ever dare to attempt it — (for it is clear that none of them ever trouble themselves to sail to a place where there is not a sure and certain hope of profit) — and seeing also that no other prince took any pains in this matter, he sent out his own ships against those parts, to have manifest certainty of them all. And to this he was stirred up by his zeal for the service of God and of the King Edward his Lord and brother,[4] who then reigned. And this was the first reason of his action.

The second reason was that if there chanced to be in those lands some population of Christians, or some havens, into which it would be possible to sail without peril, many kinds of merchandise might be brought to this realm, which would find a ready market, and reasonably so, because no other people of these parts traded with them, nor yet people of any other that were known; and also the products of this realm might be taken there, which traffic would bring great profit to our countrymen.

The third reason was that, as it was said that the power of the Moors [Arab Muslims] in that land of Africa was very much greater than was commonly supposed, and that there were no Christians among them, nor any other race of men; and because every wise man is obliged by natural prudence to wish for a knowledge of the power of his enemy; therefore the said Lord Infant exerted himself to cause this to be fully discovered, and to make it known determinately how far the power of those infidels extended.

---

[1]A reference to Prince Henry. An *infante* was a younger son of a Portuguese king, and thus not a direct heir to the throne.

[2]A Muslim naval base in modern Morocco that Portugal captured in 1415.

[3]A wandering Irish monk of the sixth century.

[4]Reigned from 1433 to 1438.

The fourth reason was because during the one and thirty years that he had warred against the Moors, he had never found a Christian king, nor a lord outside this land, who for the love of our Lord Jesus Christ would aid him in the said war. Therefore he sought to know if there were in those parts any Christian princes, in whom the charity and the love of Christ was so ingrained that they would aid him against those enemies of the faith.

The fifth reason was his great desire to make increase in the faith of our Lord Jesus Christ and to bring to him all the souls that should be saved, — understanding that all the mystery of the Incarnation, Death, and Passion of our Lord Jesus Christ was for this sole end — namely the salvation of lost souls — whom the said Lord Infant by his travail and spending would fain bring into the true path. For he perceived that no better offering could be made unto the Lord than this; for if God promised to return one hundred goods for one, we may justly believe that for such great benefits, that is to say for so many souls as were saved by the efforts of this Lord, he will have so many hundreds of guerdons[5] in the kingdom of God, by which his spirit may be glorified after this life in the celestial realm. For I who wrote this history saw so many men and women of those parts turned to the holy faith, that even if the Infant had been a heathen, their prayers would have been enough to have obtained his salvation. And not only did I see the first captives,[6] but their children and grandchildren as true Christians as if the Divine grace breathed in them and imparted to them a clear knowledge of itself.

---

[5]Rewards.
[6]African slaves who had been captured and transported to Europe.

1492: What Columbus and His Patrons Hoped to Gain
▼▼▼

19 ▾ *KING FERDINAND AND QUEEN ISABELLA, AGREEMENTS WITH COLUMBUS OF APRIL 17 AND APRIL 30, 1492*

Among the many factors that contributed to Europe's expansion in the early modern period, perhaps none was more important than simple human ambition. There is no better example of this truth than Christopher Columbus, the Genoese mariner credited with the discovery of the New World. The best available evidence suggests that Columbus (Cristoforo Colombo in Italian; Cristóbal Colón in Spanish) was born in 1451 to a weaver and went to sea as a teenager. As a young man he gained wide experience as a sailor, with voyages as far north as Ireland, as far south as Mina on the Gulf of Guinea, and as far west as the Canary Islands, Madeira, and the Azores, all islands off Africa's coast. Having taught himself to read, he began to study geographical texts, maps, and even biblical passages that provided him with a set of assumptions concerning the circumference of the Earth, the size of Europe, and the distance of Japan from the Asian mainland. Although false, these assumptions convinced him it would be possible to reach Asia by sailing west into the Atlantic. In 1484 Columbus sought support for an exploratory voyage from King John II of Portugal (r. 1481–1495), but the king, who was convinced that sailing around Africa was the most promising route to Asia, refused.

Undeterred, in 1486 Columbus gained an audience with the Spanish monarchs Ferdinand and Isabella, who on hearing Columbus's proposal gave him a small stipend and appointed a commission of "learned men and mariners" to examine his plan. For five years Columbus followed the Spanish court from city to city, waiting for a final decision. Negotiations broke down in early 1492 when the king and queen balked at what they considered Columbus's excessive demands. With Columbus preparing to take his ideas to the king of France, however, a last-minute appeal to Isabella resulted in an agreement among the parties. In two "capitulations," excerpts from which follow, Ferdinand and Isabella in April 1492 promised Columbus a large share of any economic benefits that might accrue from his voyage and extensive authority over any lands he might discover. Preparations could now begin for Columbus's historic voyage that departed the Spanish port of Palos on August 3, 1492.

Columbus never realized his dreams of wealth and power. After his discoveries failed to produce either the gold or rich commercial opportunities he had promised, he lost favor at court, and from 1495 onward the monarchs ignored the agreements they had approved in 1492. Columbus made his fourth and last voyage across the Atlantic in 1502, four years before he died in Valladolid, Spain, still pressing his claims with the Crown and still convinced he had reached Asia.

QUESTIONS FOR ANALYSIS

1. What assumptions underlie Columbus's and the monarchs' statements about the authority they expect to exercise in the land Columbus discovers?
2. What kinds of authority will Columbus exercise over the lands he discovers? What role will be played by the monarchs?
3. What kind of material benefits do Columbus and the monarchs expect to gain from Columbus's promised discoveries? How will these gains be divided?
4. How do the stated and implied goals of Columbus's enterprise compare with the motives attributed by Gomes Eannes de Azurara to Prince Henry the Navigator (source 18)?

AGREEMENT OF APRIL 17, 1492

The things supplicated and which your Highnesses give and declare to Christopher Columbus in some satisfaction . . . for the voyage which now, with the aid of God, he is about to make therein, in the service of your Highnesses, are as follows:

Firstly, that your Highnesses as Lords that are of the said oceans, make from this time the said Don Christopher Columbus your Admiral in all those islands and mainlands which by his hand and industry shall be discovered or acquired in the said oceans, during his life, and after his death, his heirs and successors, from one to another perpetually, with all the pre-eminences and prerogatives belonging to the said office. . . .

Likewise, that your Highnesses make the said Don Christopher your Viceroy and Governor

General in all the said islands and mainlands and islands which as has been said, he may discover or acquire in the said seas; and that for the government of each one and of any one of them, he may make selection of three persons for each office, and that your Highnesses may choose and select the one who shall be most serviceable to you, and thus the lands which our Lord shall permit him to discover and acquire will be better governed, in the service of your Highnesses. . . .

Item, that all and whatever merchandise, whether it be pearls, precious stones, gold, silver, spices, and other things whatsoever, and merchandise of whatever kind, name, and manner it may be, which may be bought, bartered, discovered, acquired, or obtained within the limits of the said Admiralty, your Highnesses grant henceforth to the said Don Christopher, and will that he may have and take for himself, the tenth part of all of them, deducting all the expenses which may be incurred therein; so that of what shall remain free and clear, he may have and take the tenth part for himself, and do with it as he wills, the other nine parts remaining for your Highnesses. . . .

Item, that in all the vessels which may be equipped for the said traffic and negotiation each time and whenever and as often as they may be equipped, the said Admiral Don Christopher Columbus may, if be wishes, contribute and pay the eighth part of all that may be expended in the equipment. And also that he may have and take of the profit, the eighth part of all which may result from such equipment. . . .

These are executed and despatched with the responses of your Highnesses at the end of each article in the town of Santa Fe de la Vega de Granada, on the seventeenth day of April in the year of the nativity of our Savior Jesus Christ one thousand four hundred and ninety-two.

AGREEMENT OF APRIL 30, 1492

Forasmuch as you, Christopher Columbus, are going by our command, with some of our ships and with our subjects, to discover and acquire certain islands and mainland in the ocean, and it is hoped that, by the help of God, some of the said islands and mainland in the said ocean will be discovered and acquired by your pains and industry; and therefore it is a just and reasonable thing that since you incur the said danger for our service you should be rewarded for it . . . it is our will and pleasure that you, the said Christopher Columbus, after you have discovered and acquired the said islands and mainland in the said ocean, or any of them whatsoever, shall be our Admiral of the said islands and mainland and Viceroy and Governor therein, and shall be empowered from that time forward to call and entitle yourself Don Christopher Columbus, and that your sons and successors in the said office and charge may likewise entitle and call themselves Don, and Admiral and Viceroy and Governor thereof; and that you may have power to use and exercise the said office of Admiral, together with the said office of Viceroy and Governor of the said islands and mainland . . . and to hear and determine all the suits and causes civil and criminal appertaining to the said office of Admiralty, Viceroy, and Governor according as you shall find by law, . . . and may have power to punish and chastise delinquents, and exercise the said offices . . . in all that concerns and appertains to the said offices . . . and that you shall have and levy the fees and salaries annexed, belonging and appertaining to the said offices and to each of them, according as our High Admiral in the Admiralty of our kingdoms levies and is accustomed to levy them.

Why England Should Sponsor Colonies
▼▼▼

20 ▼ *Richard Hakluyt,*
A DISCOURSE ON WESTERN PLANTING

Although King Henry VII and a group of Bristol merchants had dispatched the Italian mariner John Cabot to North America in 1497 to search for a route to Asia, no further English exploration or colonization took place until the reign of Elizabeth I (1558–1603), when the political and religious conflicts connected with the English reformation abated. England's renewed efforts were not auspicious. Backed by a group of investors who formed the Company of Cathay (China), Martin Frobisher made three voyages to North America between 1576 and 1578 in search of gold and the Northwest Passage to Asia, but found neither. Five years later an effort promoted by Sir Humphrey Gilbert to colonize North America ended in tragedy when the expedition was lost at sea while sailing south from Newfoundland. These setbacks did not discourage a small group of merchants, mariners, and courtiers who continued to formulate plans for colonization and promote them at Elizabeth's court.

Included in this group was Richard Hakluyt (1552–1616), the son of a minor London merchant, who was orphaned at age five and raised by an older cousin, a lawyer. Through contacts with his cousin's friends and business associates, the young Hakluyt developed an interest in trade and exploration. Although he studied Greek and Latin at Oxford, his intellectual passion was geography, which he learned from books, maps, and reports from mariners, merchants, and explorers. Ordained a priest in the Church of England, Hakluyt still had time to write books on exploration and lobby royal officials and Queen Elizabeth herself on behalf of various proposals to colonize North America.

In 1584 Hakluyt wrote a lengthy memorandum to Queen Elizabeth in support of a proposal by Sir Humphrey Gilbert's half brother, Sir Walter Raleigh, to colonize the east coast of North America, known at the time as Norumbega. Elizabeth declined, pleading a lack of money, and thin funding was one of several reasons why the Roanoke Colony failed. Hakluyt and other supporters of English colonization continued to lobby on behalf of their ideas, however, and during the reign of James I (1603–1625) the chartering of the Virginia Company and the Plymouth Company marked the true beginnings of the successful English colonization of North America.

The following excerpt is the concluding summary to Hakluyt's memorandum to Elizabeth.

QUESTIONS FOR ANALYSIS

1. According to Hakluyt, what are the economic advantages England might expect from colonizing Norumbega?
2. According to Hakluyt, how will colonization strengthen England and weaken its rivals?

3. According to Hakluyt, how will colonization help solve England's domestic problems?
4. How important is religion in Hakluyt's thinking about colonization?
5. How much concrete knowledge of the Americas does Hakluyt seem to have?

A brief collection of certain reasons to induce her Majesty and the state to take in hand the western voyage and the planting there.

1. The soil yields and may be made to yield all the several commodities of Europe. . . .
2. The passage thither and home is neither too long nor too short, but easy, and to be made twice in the year.
3. The passage cuts not near the trade of any prince, nor near any of their countries or territories, and is a safe passage, and not easy to be annoyed [interfered with] by prince or potentate whatsoever.
4. The passage is to be performed at all times of the year, and in that respect passes our trades in the Levant Seas within the Straits of Gibraltar, and the trades in the seas within the King of Denmark's Strait,[1] and the trades to the ports of Norway and of Russia, etc. . . .
5. And where England now for certain hundred years last passed, by the peculiar [distinctive] commodity of wool, and of later years, by clothing of the same, has raised itself from meaner state to greater wealth and much higher honor, might, and power than before, to the equaling of the princes of the same to the greatest potentates of this part of the world; it comes now so to pass that by the great endeavor of the increase of the trade of wool in Spain and in the West Indies, now daily more and more multiplying, that the wool of England, and the cloth made of the same, will become base [inferior], and every day more base than [the]

other; which, prudently weighed, it behooves this realm, if it mean not to return to former old means and baseness, but to stand in present and late former honor, glory, and force, and not negligently and sleepingly to slide into beggary, to foresee and to plant at Norumbega or some like place, were it not for anything else but for the hope of the sale of our wool. . . .

6. This enterprise may stay the Spanish king from flowing over all the face of that waste [wild and uninhabited] firmament of America, if we seed and plant there in time. . . . And England possessing the purposed [proposed] place of planting, her Majesty may, by the benefit of the seat, having won good and royal havens, have plenty of excellent trees for masts, of goodly timber to build ships and to make great navies, of pitch, tar, hemp, and all things incident for a navy royal, and that for no price, and without money or request. How easy a matter may it be to this realm, swarming at this day with valiant youths, rusting [degenerating] and hurtful by lack of employment, and having good makers of cable and of all sorts of cordage,[2] and the best and most cunning shipwrights of the world, to be lords of all those seas, and to spoil Philip's Indian navy,[3] and to deprive him of yearly passage of his treasure to Europe, and consequently to abate the pride of Spain and of the supporter of the great Anti-christ of Rome,[4] and to pull him down in equality to his neighbor princes, and consequently to cut off the common mischiefs that come to all Europe

---

[1]The Levant Seas refers to the area of the eastern Mediterranean; the "seas within the King of Denmark's Strait" refers to the Baltic Sea.
[2]Ropes used in the rigging of sailing ships.

[3]Philip II, king of Spain from 1556 to 1598; his "Indian navy" refers to Spanish ships carrying gold, silver, and other commodities between Europe and the Americas.
[4]The pope.

by the peculiar abundance of his Indian treasure, and this without difficulty.

7. This voyage, albeit it may be accomplished by bark or smallest pinnace[5] . . . yet for the distance, for burden[6] and gain in trade, the merchant will not for profit's sake use it but by ships of great burden; so as this realm shall have by that means ships of great burden and of great strength for the defense of this realm. . . .

9. The great mass of wealth of the realm embarked in the merchants' ships, carried out in this new course, shall not lightly, in so far distant a course from the coast of Europe, be driven by winds and tempests into ports of any foreign princes, as the Spanish ships of late years have been into our ports of the West countries, etc. . . .

10. No foreign commodity that comes into England comes without payment of custom once, twice, or thrice, before it comes into the realm, and so all foreign commodities become dearer to the subjects of this realm; and by this course to Norumbega foreign princes' customs are avoided; and the foreign commodities cheaply purchased, they become cheap to the subjects of England, to the common benefit of the people, and to the saving of great treasure in the realm; whereas now the realm becomes poor by the purchasing of foreign commodities in so great a mass at so excessive prices.

11. At the first traffic [trade] with the people of those parts, the subjects of this realm for many years shall change many cheap commodities of these parts for things of high value there not esteemed; and this to the great enriching of the realm, if common use fail not.

12. By the great plenty of those regions the merchants and their factors [agents] shall lie there cheap, buy and repair their ships

cheap, and shall return at pleasure without stay or restraint of foreign prince; whereas upon stays and restraints the merchant raiseth his charge in sale over of his ware. . . .

13. By making of ships and by preparing of things for the same, by making of cables and cordage, by planting of vines and olive trees, and by making of wine and oil, by husbandry, and by thousands of things there to be done, infinite numbers of the English nation may be set on work, to the unburdening of the realm with many that now live chargeable to the state at home.

14. If the sea coast serve for making of salt, and the inland for wine, oils, oranges, lemons, figs, &c., and for making of iron, all which with much more is hoped, without sword drawn, we shall cut the comb[7] of the French, of the Spanish, of the Portuguese, and of enemies, and of doubtful friends, to the abating of their wealth and force, and to the greater saving of the wealth of the realm.

15. The substances serving, we may out of those parts receive the mass of wrought wares that now we receive out of France, Flanders, Germany, &c.; and so we may daunt [subdue] the pride of some enemies of this realm, or at the least in part purchase those wares, that now we buy dearly of the French and Flemish, better cheap; and in the end, for the part that this realm was wont to receive, drive them out of trade to idleness for the setting of our people on work.

16. We shall by planting there enlarge the glory of the gospel, and from England plant sincere religion, and provide a safe and a sure place to receive people from all parts of the world that are forced to flee for the truth of God's word.

17. If frontier wars there chance to arise, and if thereupon we shall fortify, it will occasion the training up of our youth in the disci-

---

[5]Barks and pinnaces are small sailing ships.
[6]Capacity of a ship for carrying cargo.

[7]Comb refers to the red crest of a rooster. To "cut one's comb" is to humble or humiliate someone.

pline of war, and make a number fit for the service of the wars and for the defence of our people there and at home.

18. The Spaniards govern in the Indies with all pride and tyranny; and like as when people of contrary nature at sea enter into galleys, where men are tied as slaves, all yell and cry with one voice, *Liberta, liberta,* as desirous of liberty and freedom, so no doubt whensoever the Queen of England, a prince of such clemency, shall seat upon that firmament of America, and shall be reported throughout all that tract to use the natural people there with all humanity, courtesy, and freedom, they will yield themselves to her government, and revolt clean from the Spaniard. . . .

19. The present short [insufficient] trades cause the mariner to be cast off, and often to be idle, and so by poverty to fall to piracy. But this course to Norumbega being longer, and a continuance of the employment of the mariner, doth keep the mariner from idleness and from necessity; and so it cuts off the principal actions of piracy, and the rather

because no rich prey for them to take comes directly in their course or anything near their course.

20. Many men of excellent wits and of diverse singular gifts, overthrown by suretyship [indebtedness] or by some folly of youth, that are not able to live in England, may there be raised again, and do their country good service; and many needful uses there may (to great purpose) require the saving of great numbers, that for trifles may otherwise be devoured by the gallows.

21. Many soldiers, in the end of the wars, that might be hurtful to this realm, may there be unladen, to the common profit and quiet of this realm, and to our foreign benefit there, as they may be employed.

22. The fry[8] of the wandering beggars of England, that grow up idly, and hurtful and burdenous to this realm, may there be unladen, better bred up, and may people waste countries to the home and foreign benefit, and to their own more happy state. . . .

---

[8]In this context, a "swarm" or crowd of insignificant persons.

▼▼▼

Marriage and Families in Early Modern Europe

The popular assumption that general progress marked Europe's transition from the Middle Ages to the Renaissance and early modern era is contradicted by the experiences of most European women. Although medieval women were far from having equality with men, they enjoyed more freedom and higher status than in antiquity and the postmedieval period. Aristocratic women in the Middle Ages often managed their family's estates while their husbands were on military campaigns, and some owned land themselves. Urban women joined guilds, were apprenticed to learn craft skills, and in some cities monopolized whole professions, such as leatherworking, brewing, and especially weaving and cloth finishing. Religious women were admired for their charity and piety, and many achieved distinction as models of spirituality.

During the fourteenth and fifteenth centuries, however, in the era that saw the decline of medieval civilization and the flowering of the Renaissance in Italy, women's economic and social prospects began to decline, and continued to do so in the early modern period. In cities guilds excluded women from membership, and municipal councils barred women from work as physicians and apothecaries. For more and more urban women work meant domestic service, spinning, shop-keeping, or prostitution, all poorly paid jobs with low status. In the countryside women's work was crucial to the peasant household's economic survival, as it had been throughout the Middle Ages. Women tended gardens, raised poultry, helped with planting and harvesting, cooked, preserved food, and cared for children and the elderly. Many also worked for wages as servants or laborers.

Irrespective of a woman's social status, there was universal agreement that her main purpose was to marry and have children. Large families, especially ones with more sons than daughters, were viewed as economic necessities by rich and poor alike. Peasants relied on children as workers, and wealthy aristocrats and busi-nessmen considered children as guarantees of the continuation of the family line and the preservation of its wealth and property. Moralists and religious leaders agreed that matrimony offered men and women the best opportunity for fulfill-ment and happiness and provided the foundation for a sound, God-fearing soci-ety. This was especially true among sixteenth-century Protestant writers, whose enthusiasm for marriage was linked to their rejection of the Catholic doctrine of clerical celibacy.

Many writers praised the institution of marriage so fervently because they were convinced that it was growing weaker. In Renaissance Italy upper-class parents deplored the reluctance of their sons to to marry. In northern Europe during the sixteenth century the age of first marriage steadily rose, and the proportion of unmarried individuals grew. Estimates of the number of single European women during the 1500s and early 1600s range from 20 to 40 percent, equally divided between widows and spinsters. For those who did marry, contemporary writers and preachers give the impression that more and more husbands and wives were unhappy. Many writers emphasized that a strong marriage depended on mutual affection and clearly defined spousal responsibilities and rights, but custom deprived young women of a meaningful say in the choice of a spouse, and laws clearly made wives subservient to husbands. The endless commentaries on unhappy marriages, abusive husbands, and disobedient wives suggest that har-monious marriages were far from universal.

The sources in this section, representing different parts of Europe and different socioeconomic groups, all focus on the institution of marriage in Renaissance and early modern Europe. Taken together they provide insight into the institution of marriage and in more general terms women's place in society.

Upper-Class Marriage in Renaissance Florence
▼▼▼

21 ▼ Leon Battista Alberti, BOOK OF THE FAMILY

More so than any other city, Florence was the heart and soul of the Italian Renaissance. During the fourteenth and fifteenth centuries its gifted painters, sculptors, and architects produced works of unsurpassed beauty, and its humanist scholars inspired a new appreciation and understanding of Greek and Roman antiquity. None of this would have been possible without the financial support and cultural interests of a relatively small number of elite Florentine families who had made fortunes in business and who under the guidance and control of the Medici family made up the city's political oligarchy. These families, along with the Catholic Church, provided the money to support the scholarship of humanists, the work of hundreds of painters and sculptors, and the construction and remodeling of countless buildings.

Some members of the Florentine elite were more than patrons; they were artists and scholars in their own right. Such was the case with Leon Battista Alberti (1404–1472), viewed by many as a personification of the ideal "Renaissance man." The illegitimate son of one of Florence's wealthiest merchants, Alberti studied at the universities of Padua and Bologna before assuming a position as papal secretary in Rome. He wrote books on mathematics, ancient literature, painting, and architecture, and designed churches and private residences in Florence and other Italian cities. He also wrote the *Book of the Family* (1443), a dialogue among Alberti men that supposedly took place in 1421 at the funeral of Alberti's father. Written in Italian rather than Latin and translated into the major European languages, Alberti's work expresses views of marriage and children common among wealthy and privileged Europeans of his era, especially those who had made their fortunes in business.

In the first section of the following excerpt from *Book of the Family,* Lionardo, a man in his late twenties or thirties, discusses marriage and the choice of wives; in the second section, an older gentleman, Gionnozzo, recalls the steps he took as a new husband to train his wife.

QUESTIONS FOR ANALYSIS

1. According to the speaker Lionardo, what discourages young men from marrying?
2. What is the main purpose of marriage, according to the characters in the dialogue?
3. In arranging marriages, how much input did the future wife and husband have? Who else influenced the final choice of a mate?
4. According to Lionardo, what considerations should affect the choice of a future wife? What qualities of a future wife are most important?

5. What did Gionnozzo hope to accomplish when he showed his new bride around the house, especially his private apartment?
6. What views of women underlie Alberti's description of marriage?

ARRANGING A MARRIAGE

Most times, the young do not appreciate the welfare of the family. Perhaps it seems to them that by bowing to matrimony they will lose much of their freedom in life. Perhaps they are overcome at times and caught in the clutches of a woman they love, as the comic poets are pleased to portray them. Perhaps the young find it most annoying having to maintain themselves, and therefore think that providing for a wife and children in addition to themselves is an overwhelming and hateful burden and are afraid they cannot properly take care of the needs which keep pace with the family's growth. Because of this, they consider the marriage bed too bothersome and avoid their duty honestly to enlarge the family. For these reasons, we must convince the young to marry by using reason, persuasion, rewards, and all other arguments so that the family may not be reduced to few members, which, as we said, is a most unfortunate condition, but grow in glory and the number of its young. . . .

▼ ▼ ▼

Once the young men have been persuaded through the efforts and advice of all the elders of the family, the mothers and other old relatives and friends, who know the customs and behavior of almost all the girls of the city from the time they were born, must select all the well-born and properly-raised girls and propose their names to the youth who is to be married. The latter will choose the one he prefers, and the elders must not reject her as a daughter-in-law, unless she brings with her the breath of scandal or blame. As for the rest, let the young man please himself, just as he will then have to please his bride. He should, however, follow the example of a good family-head who, when buying something, insists on examining the property many times before signing any contract. For every purchase and contract it is useful to seek information and advice, make inquiries of many persons, and use all possible diligence in order not to have to repent at a later time. One who wishes to marry must be even more diligent. My advice to him is to show forethought and, over a period of time and in various ways, learn what kind of woman his intended bride is, for he will be her husband and companion for the rest of his life. In his mind he must have two reasons for marrying: the first is to beget children, the other, to have a faithful and steadfast companion throughout his life. We must, therefore, seek a woman suited to childbearing and pleasant enough to be our constant companion.

For this reason, then, they say that in a wife we must seek beauty, family, and wealth. . . . The first prerequisite of beauty in a woman is good habits. It is possible for a foolish, ignorant, slovenly, and drunken woman to have a beautiful body, but no one will deem her to be a beautiful wife. . . . As for physical beauty, we should not only take pleasure in comeliness, charm, and elegance, but should try to have in our house a wife well built for bearing children and strong of body to insure that they will be born strong and robust. An ancient proverb states: "As you want your children, so choose their mother." . . . Physicians say that a wife should not be thin, but neither should she be burdened with fat, for the fat are very weak, have many obstructions, and are slow in conceiving. . . . They believe that a woman who is tall but full in all her limbs is very useful for begetting many children. They always prefer one of girlish age for many reasons, such as ease in conforming with her husband's wishes and others which we do not have to discuss here. Girls are pure because of their age, simple through inexperience, modest by nature and without malice. They are eager to learn their husbands' habits and desires and acquiesce without any reluctance. Thus we must follow all the precepts mentioned, for they are most useful for recognizing and choosing a prolific wife. To this we may add that it is a good sign for the girl to have many brothers, for you may then hope that she will be like her mother.

Thus we have finished speaking of beauty. Next comes the bride's family, and we shall consider what is suitable and to be preferred. I believe first of all we must examine with care the life and ways of all those who will become our relatives. Many marriages have been the cause of great misfortunes to families because they became related with quarrelsome, contentious, proud, and hateful men, as we hear and read every day. . . .

Therefore, to conclude this part of my argument in a few words, for I want to be very brief, let one try to find new relatives who are not of vulgar blood, little wealth, or humble profession. In other things let them be modest and not too far above you so that their greatness will not cast a shadow on your honor and dignity and will not disturb your family's peace and tranquility. Also, in case one of them should be ruined, you would be able to help and sustain him without too much discomfort and without suffering under a burden too heavy for your strength. Nor do I want these relatives to be inferior to you, for if it is an expense to aid the fallen relatives I mentioned above, these others will keep you in slavery. Let them, therefore, be your equals, modest, noble, and of honorable profession, as we have said.

Next comes the dowry,[1] which I believe should be modest, sure, and given at once rather than large, doubtful, and to be given in the future. . . . Let them not be too large, for the larger they are, the greater is the delay in receiving payment, the chance of litigation, and the reluctance to pay. In addition, in the case of a large dowry you will be much more inclined to

undergo great expense in order to collect it. Finally, one cannot say how unpleasant it is to have to pay a large dowry, which at times causes a family's ruin. Having discussed how a wife is to be chosen and how she is to be received, we must now learn how she is to be treated at home.

INSTRUCTIONS FOR A NEW WIFE

GIANNOZZO: You know, it has always seemed proper to me for the head of the family not only to do these things worthy of a man, but to avoid anything which should be done by women. We must leave unimportant household matters to the women, as I have done.

LIONARDO: You can be glad you had a most virtuous wife, perhaps more virtuous than others. I do not know where you could find another woman as industrious and prudent in managing the family as your wife was.

GIANNOZZO: She certainly was an excellent mother by nature and upbringing, but even more through my instruction.

LIONARDO: You taught her, then?

GIANNOZZO: In part.

LIONARDO: How did you go about it?

GIANNOZZO: I shall tell you. When after a few days my wife began to feel at ease in my house and did not miss her mother and family so much, I took her by the hand and showed her the whole house. I showed her that upstairs was the place for storing grain and down in the cellar that for wine and firewood. I showed her where the tableware was and everything else in the house, so that she saw where everything was kept and knew its use. Then we returned to my room, and there, after closing the door, I showed her our valuables, silver, tapestries, clothes, and jewels, and pointed out their proper storage places.

---

[1]Dowry payments in Europe were paid by the bride's family to the groom. During the marriage the money paid in the dowry was controlled by the husband, but if the husband predeceased the wife, the dowry returned to the wife under most circumstances. The size of dowries depended on the wealth of the families involved. Dowry payments increased steadily in Italy during the fifteenth century, and became a real hardship for families with several daughters. Daughters whose family could not raise a suitable dowry typically joined a religious order and entered a convent.

I kept only the ledgers and business papers, my ancestors' as well as mine, locked so that my wife could not read them or even see them then or at any time since. I never kept them in my pockets, but always under lock and key in their proper place in my study, almost as if they were sacred or religious objects. I never allowed my wife to enter my study either alone or in my company, and I ordered her to turn over to me at once any papers of mine she should ever find. . . .

No matter how trifling a secret I had, I never shared it with my wife or with any other woman. I disapprove of those husbands who consult their wives and do not know how to keep any secret to themselves. They are mad to seek good advice and wisdom in women, and even more so if they think a wife can guard a secret with greater jealousy and silence than her husband. O foolish husbands, is there ever a time when you chat with a woman without being reminded that women can do anything but keep silent? For this reason, then, I always took care that none of my secrets should ever become known to women. . . .

LIONARDO: What an excellent warning! And you are no less prudent than fortunate if your wife was never able to draw out any of your secrets.

GIANNOZZO: She never did, my dear Lionardo, and I shall tell you why. First of all, she was very modest, and so never cared to know more than she should. Then, I never spoke to her about anything but household matters, habits, and our children. Of these subjects I spoke to her often and at length so that she might learn what to do. . . . As for the household goods, I deemed it proper, then and later, to entrust them to my wife's care, but not entirely, for I often wanted to know and see where the least thing was kept and how safe it was. After my wife had seen and understood where everything was to be kept, I said to her: "My dear wife, you must take no less care than myself of those things which will be useful and convenient to you and to me both while we preserve them in good condition and whose neglect would bring harm and inconvenience. You have seen our possessions, which, thank God, are such that we can well be satisfied. If we know how to take care of them, they will be useful to you, to me, and to our children. Therefore, my dear wife, it is your duty as well as mine to be diligent and take care of them."

LIONARDO: What did your wife answer?

GIANNOZZO: She answered that she had learned to obey her father and mother, and that they had instructed her to obey me always. She was ready, therefore, to do whatever I commanded. And I said to her: "Well then, my dear wife, one who knows how to obey her father and mother will soon learn to satisfy her husband." . . .

Two Sixteenth-Century Commentaries on Marriage

▼▼▼

22 ▼ *Erhard Schön,*
NO MORE PRECIOUS TREASURE IS ON THE EARTH THAN A GENTLE WIFE WHO LONGS FOR HONOR;
Hans Sebald Beham,
A NUREMBERG COUPLE WOOING

Many Europeans were introduced to the new technology of printing not through books but through broadsheets. Printed on a single sheet and usually consisting of a woodcut illustration and a brief text, these inexpensive publications were meant for a mass audience. As seen earlier in this chapter, such broadsheets were used as instruments of propaganda during the Reformation, especially by Protestants. They also offered up satire, social commentary, moral instruction, and news about murders, witchcraft trials, astronomical portents, monsters, strange births, and countless other events and phenomena.

The following two broadsheets, both produced in Germany, address the issues of courtship and marriage. The first is the work of Erhard Schön (ca. 1491–1550), a Protestant from Nuremberg who produced hundreds of woodcuts for books and broadsheets. His woodcut *No More Precious Treasure Is on the Earth Than a Gentle Wife Who Longs for Honor* appeared in 1531. It shows, from left to right, a husband (pulling a cart that carries a laundry tub, probably filled with diapers), the wife, a young man, his sweetheart, an old woman wearing a fool's cap, and finally an old man. In a text from an unknown author the six figures state their opinions about marriage.

The second woodcut, *A Nuremberg Couple Wooing,* is by Hans Sebald Beham, the same Nuremberg artist who produced the woodcut *An Allegory of the Monastic Orders,* which is included earlier in this chapter in source 17. It shows a well-off young man and woman whose thinking about marriage is revealed in the rhymed verse written by the popular poet Hans Sachs (1494–1576).

QUESTIONS FOR ANALYSIS

1. On the basis of the Beham woodcut and the text by Hans Sachs, what conclusions can you draw about the courtship practices of upper-class German city-dwellers in the early sixteenth century? How do the roles of the young man and woman differ?
2. What qualities of his wife does the husband in Schön's woodcut most bitterly complain about?
3. What is the significance of the britches, purse, and sword that the wife holds in Schön's print?
4. According to Schön, how does the wife justify her actions and behavior? How do her justifications compare to the expectations about marriage set forth by the young girl?
5. Compare and contrast the arguments for and against marriage presented by the old man and the female fool in Schön's print. To what extent do the comments of the old man confirm the fears about marriage expressed by the young man?

Erhard Schön, No More Precious Treasure Is on the Earth Than a Gentle Wife Who Longs for Honor

NO MORE PRECIOUS TREASURE

The Wretched Idol {the Husband}
Oh woe, oh woe to me, wretched fool,
With what difficulty I pull this cart
To which point marriage has brought me.
I wish I had never thought of it!
A shrewish scold has come into my house
and has taken my sword, pants and purse.
Night and day I have no peace
And no good word from her.
My fidelity does not please her;
My words provoke hostility from her.
Thus is the fate of many a man
Who has, knows and can do nothing,
And yet in time must have a wife.

The Wife Speaks
Hey, beloved mate, but is this really true?
Be quiet! Or I will pull you by the hair.
If you want a nice and gentle wife
Who will always be subservient to you
Then stay at home in your own house
And stop your carousing.

Naked I go running around to peddle things,
Suffering from hunger and quaffing water.
It's difficult for a nice young wife
To maintain her wifely honor.
If you won't work to support me,
Then you have to wash, spin and pull the cart
And must let your back be bared.

The Journeyman
What do you say about this, young lady?
Would you like to be like her
And yourself hold sword, pants, purse and
    authority?
With words bite, rasp and cut?
That I should and would never suffer.
Should I fight and brawl with you,
Then perhaps I would end up
Pulling a cart like this poor man,
Who has lost all joy and pleasure.
Should I waste my life of freedom
With spinning, washing, cooking and carting?
I would rather swear off from taking up
    marriage.

The Girl

Boy, believe me on my honor.
I don't wish for such power.
If you want to fight over rank,
Then you will be the man in all things.
What a wife deserves,
To love, to experience hardship together and
   honor,
I will demand nothing besides this.
You should have no doubt about it.
I will devote my life to serving you
And love you in constant friendship.
And you won't be scolded by a single word.

The Woman Fool

Watch yourself, young man.
I, a poor fool speak the truth.
Much good is said about marriage
But it means more correctly "Woe."
You must suffer 'til you die
Much anxiety, uncertainty, worry and want.
From this no married person is spared.
Now when you see a pretty girl,

She will gladly do what you want
For a bottle of wine.
Afterwards you can let her go
And take on another.
A wife you have forever.

The Wise Man

Young man I will teach you better.
Do not listen to this woman fool.
Beware of the tricks of whores,
Who are always there to deceive you.
Take a young lady into marriage.
God will guide your lives.
Stay with her in love and pain
And always be patient.
If you experience aggravation,
Consider it to be God's will.
Provide for your wife by the sweat of your
   brow,
As God commands in the Book of Genesis.
Patience and suffering make a door
Through which we arrive at that place
Where the angels have their home.

Hans Sebald Beham, A Nuremberg Couple Wooing

A NUREMBERG COUPLE WOOING

The Young Lord

Tender Miss, to whom every honor is due,
Beauty so great and bearing so chaste
Was never before born of woman's body.
For this reason I have chosen
To court you faithfully and honorably.
And eternally to increase my joy by being with
   you.
I pray that you also hold me,
Young man that I am, equally dear.

The Young Girl

Young lord, although I can promise you
   nothing,
I also do not want to deny you anything.
Because I am not my own master,
I will not follow my own mind.
But rather, as is right to do,
Take counsel with my family,
For careless thought and action
Has often brought great regret and misfortune.

Stay Single, Be Happy
▼▼▼

23 ▼ *Anna Bijns,*
"UNYOKED IS BEST! HAPPY THE WOMAN WITHOUT A MAN"

Despite the obstacles society threw in their path, an increasing number of European women in the sixteenth and seventeenth centuries made names for themselves as poets, dramatists, and authors of works on religion, the classics, and education. In the Netherlands the best-known woman writer of the age was Anna Bijns (1493–1575), the daughter of an Antwerp tailor, who published three substantial volumes of poetry in her native Dutch dialect that were popular enough to go through several editions during and after her life. Biographical details about Anna Bijns are sparse. We know that after her father died in 1516, she and her brother Maarten opened a small school in Antwerp, which Anna ran independently after Maarten left in 1536. We also know that her younger sister married early and unhappily. Having never married herself, Anna died in 1575 in Antwerp and was given a pauper's service at the local Catholic church. Her poetry ranged over a wide variety of topics. She is best known for her robust poetic condemnations of Lutheranism and her blistering attacks on Luther himself. But she also wrote romantic lyrics, satirical verse, and poems on numerous social themes, including marriage. The following poem appeared in an anthology published at the end of her life.

QUESTIONS FOR ANALYSIS

1. What would appear to be the intended audience for the poem?
2. What are the major disadvantages of marriage to women, according to Bijns?
3. Are there disadvantages to remaining single?
4. How would you characterize the poet's attitudes toward men?

How good to be a woman, how much better to
  be a man!
Maidens and wenches, remember the lesson
  you're about to hear.
Don't hurtle[1] yourself into marriage far too
  soon.
The saying goes: "Where's your spouse? Where's
  your honor?"
But one who earns her board and clothes
Shouldn't scurry to suffer a man's rod.
So much for my advice, because I suspect —
Nay, see it sadly proven day by day —
'T happens all the time!
However rich in goods a girl might be,
Her marriage ring will shackle her for life.
If however she stays single
With purity and spotlessness foremost,
Then she is lord as well as lady. Fantastic,
Though wedlock I do not decry:
Unyoked is best! Happy the woman without a
  man.

Fine girls turning into loathly hags —
'Tis true! Poor sluts! Poor tramps! Cruel
  marriage!
Which makes me deaf to wedding bells.
Huh! First they marry the guy, luckless dears,
Thinking their love just too hot to cool.
Well, they're sorry and sad within a single year.
Wedlock's burden is far too heavy.
They know best whom it harnessed.
So often is a wife distressed, afraid.
When after troubles hither and thither he goes
In search of dice and liquor, night and day,
She'll curse herself for that initial "yes."
So, beware ere you begin.
Just listen, don't get yourself into it.
Unyoked is best! Happy the woman without a
  man.

A man oft comes home all drunk and pissed[2]
Just when his wife had worked her fingers to
  the bone

(So many chores to keep a decent house!),
But if she wants to get in a word or two,
She gets to taste his fist — no more.
And that besotted keg she is supposed to obey?
Why, yelling and scolding is all she gets,
Such are his ways — and hapless his victim.
And if the nymphs of Venus[3] he chooses to
  frequent,
What hearty welcome will await him home.
Maidens, young ladies: learn from another's
  doom,
Ere you, too, end up in fetters and chains.
Please don't argue with me on this,
No matter who contradicts, I stick to it:
Unyoked is best! Happy the woman without a
  man.

A single lady has a single income,
But likewise, isn't bothered by another's whims.
And I think: that freedom is worth a lot.
Who'll scoff at her, regardless what she does,
And though every penny she makes herself,
Just think of how much less she spends!
An independent lady is an extraordinary
  prize —
All right, of a man's boon she is deprived,
But she's lord and lady of her very own hearth.
To do one's business and no explaining sure is
  lots of fun!
Go to bed when she list,[4] rise when she list, all
  as she will,
And no one to comment! Grab tight your
  independence then.
Freedom is such a blessed thing.
To all girls: though the right Guy might come
  along:
Unyoked is best! Happy the woman without a
  man.

Regardless of the fortune a woman might bring,
Many men consider her a slave, that's all.
Don't let a honeyed tongue catch you off guard,

---

[1]Rush.
[2]Angry.

[3]Prostitutes.
[4]To choose.

Refrain from gulping it all down. Let them
  rave,
For I guess, decent men resemble white ravens.
Abandon the airy castles they will build for you.
Once their tongue has limed[5] a bird:
Bye bye love — and love just flies away.
To women marriage comes to mean betrayal
And the condemnation to a very awful fate.

All her own is spent, her lord impossible to
  bear.
It's *peine forte et dure*[6] instead of fun and games.
Oft it was the money, and not the man
Which goaded so many into their fate.
Unyoked is best! Happy the woman without a
  man.

---

[5]To smear a sticky substance on a twig to catch small birds.

[6]French for "severe and merciless pain" (i.e., torture).

▼▼▼

The Beginnings of the Scientific Revolution

Although European intellectuals during the Middle Ages and Renaissance had many disagreements and controversies, all but a few shared a number of common beliefs and assumptions. They believed that Christianity as interpreted by the Roman Catholic Church provided a complete revelation of God's purposes and true and perfect guidelines for human conduct. All of them revered antiquity. They looked to the Greeks for guidance in logic, philosophy, and science and to the Romans for inspiration in literature, government, and law. All believed that the Earth was the center of the universe and that on Earth Catholic Christians came closest to realizing God's design for humanity.

In the sixteenth and seventeenth centuries European thinkers were forced to reevaluate all these viewpoints. The secularism of the Renaissance, the religious divisions growing out of the Reformation, and surprising encounters with Africans, Native Americans, and Asians all challenged Europe's intellectual assumptions. As important as these developments were, however, none approached the significance of a series of remarkable scientific discoveries during the age that collectively have come to be known as the Scientific Revolution.

Science, or as it was known at the time, natural philosophy, was nothing new for Europeans in the 1500s and 1600s. Many medieval and Renaissance scholars had sought to understand the natural world, but their need to make science conform to Catholic doctrine and their conviction that everything worth knowing in science had already been revealed by the ancients discouraged speculation and hampered new discoveries.

The first major break from ancient Greek science was made by the Polish astronomer Nicholaus Copernicus, who, in his *On the Revolutions of the Heavenly Spheres,* theorized that the sun, not the Earth, was the center of the universe. By the time of Galileo Galilei (1564–1642), most scientists accepted Copernican heliocentrism, even though it raised perplexing theoretical questions. Most of these questions were answered by Isaac Newton (1642–1727), whose *Mathematical Principles of Natural Philosophy* (1687) explained planetary and earthly motion through the law of universal gravitation. Newton's work was the crowning achievement of a 150-year period in which European thinkers transformed their understanding of astronomy and mechanics, made spectacular advances in mathematics, invented the telescope, microscope, and many other scientific instruments, and achieved new insights in anatomy and chemistry.

As the two documents in this section show, the Scientific Revolution, like all revolutions, had wide-ranging effects. Galileo's letter to Grand Duchess Christina of Tuscany shows how the new theories clashed with orthodox Christian beliefs and according to some, challenged the literal truth of the Bible. The excerpts from Francis Bacon's *New Organon* reveal how the scientific enquiries of the age inspired new standards and methods for gaining knowledge and promoted a belief that progress was possible if nature could be understood and manipulated for the benefit of humanity.

Science and the Claims of Religion
▼▼▼

24 ▼ Galileo Galilei, LETTER TO THE GRAND DUCHESS CHRISTINA

The greatest European scientist in the early 1600s was the Italian physicist and astronomer Galileo Galilei (1564–1642). His most important work was in mechanics, in which he developed the theory of inertia and described the laws that dictate the movement of falling bodies. In astronomy he pioneered the use of the telescope and defended the theory of a sun-centered universe advanced by the Polish astronomer Nicholaus Copernicus in 1543. His public support of Copernicus disturbed Catholic clergymen and theologians, who were convinced it undermined correct belief and the authority of the Church. The Church officially condemned Copernican theory in 1616 and forced Galileo to renounce many of his ideas in 1632. His works continued to be read, however, and in the long run his writings contributed to the acceptance of Copernican theory and the new methodology of science.

In the following selection, Galileo, a devout Catholic, defends his approach to science in a published letter addressed to Christina, the grand duchess of Tuscany, in 1615.

QUESTIONS FOR ANALYSIS

1. According to Galileo, what are his enemies' motives? Why in his view do they use religious arguments against him?
2. According to Galileo, why is it dangerous to apply passages of scripture to science?
3. To Galileo, how does nature differ from the Bible as a source of truth?
4. In Galileo's view, what is the proper relationship between science and religion?

telescope

Some years ago, as Your Serene Highness well knows, I discovered in the heavens many things that had not been seen before our own age. The novelty of these things, as well as some consequences which followed from them in contradiction to the physical notions commonly held among academic philosophers, stirred up against me no small number of professors — as if I had placed these things in the sky with my own hands in order to upset nature and overturn the sciences. They seemed to forget that the increase of known truths stimulates the investigation, establishment, and growth of the arts; not their diminution or destruction.

Showing a greater fondness for their own opinions than for truth, they sought to deny and disprove the new things which, if they had cared to look for themselves, their own senses would have demonstrated to them. To this end they hurled various charges and published numerous writings filled with vain arguments, and they made the grave mistake of sprinkling these with passages taken from places in the Bible which they had failed to understand properly, and which were ill suited to their purposes.

Persisting in their original resolve to destroy me and everything mine by any means they can think of, these men are aware of my views in astronomy and philosophy. They know that as to the arrangement of the parts of the universe, I hold the sun to be situated motionless in the center of the revolution of the celestial orbs while the earth rotates on its axis and revolves about the sun. They know also that I support this position not only by refuting the arguments of Ptolemy[1] and Aristotle, but by producing many counter-arguments; in particular, some which relate to physical effects whose causes can perhaps be assigned in no other way. In addition there are astronomical arguments derived from many things in my new celestial discoveries that

plainly confute the Ptolemaic system while admirably agreeing with and confirming the contrary hypothesis. Possibly because they are disturbed by the known truth of other propositions of mine which differ from those commonly held, and therefore mistrusting their defense so long as they confine themselves to the field of philosophy, these men have resolved to fabricate a shield for their fallacies out of the mantle of pretended religion and the authority of the Bible. These they apply, with little judgment, to the refutation of arguments that they do not understand and have not even listened to.

First they have endeavored to spread the opinion that such propositions in general are contrary to the Bible and are consequently damnable and heretical. . . . Next, becoming bolder, . . . they began scattering rumors among the people that before long this doctrine would be condemned by the supreme authority.[2] They know, too, that official condemnation would not only suppress the two propositions which I have mentioned, but would render damnable all other astronomical and physical statements and observations that have any necessary relation or connection with these. . . .

To this end they make a shield of their hypocritical zeal for religion. They go about invoking the Bible, which they would have minister to their deceitful purposes. Contrary to the sense of the Bible and the intention of the holy Fathers, if I am not mistaken, they would extend such authorities until even in purely physical matters — where faith is not involved — they would have us altogether abandon reason and the evidence of our senses in favor of some biblical passage, though under the surface meaning of its words this passage may contain a different sense. . . .

The reason produced for condemning the opinion that the earth moves and the sun stands

---

[1]Ptolemy (ca. 100 to 170 C.E.), who spent most of his life in Alexandria, Egypt, was the Greek astronomer who propounded key aspects of the geocentric planetary system that prevailed in Europe until the time of Copernicus.

[2]The pope.

still is that in many places in the Bible one may read that the sun moves and the earth stands still. Since the Bible cannot err, it follows as a necessary consequence that anyone takes an erroneous and heretical position who maintains that the sun is inherently motionless and the earth movable.

With regard to this argument, I think in the first place that it is very pious to say and prudent to affirm that the holy Bible can never speak untruth — whenever its true meaning is understood. But I believe nobody will deny that it is often very abstruse, and may say things which are quite different from what its bare words signify. Hence in expounding the Bible if one were always to confine oneself to the unadorned grammatical meaning, one might fall into error. Not only contradictions and propositions far from true might thus be made to appear in the Bible, but even grave heresies and follies. Thus it would be necessary to assign to God feet, hands, and eyes, as well as corporeal and human affections, such as anger, repentance, hatred, and sometimes even the forgetting of things past and ignorance of those to come. These propositions uttered by the Holy Ghost were set down in that manner by the sacred scribes[3] in order to accommodate them to the capacities of the common people, who are rude and unlearned. . . .

This being granted, I think that in discussions of physical problems we ought to begin not from the authority of scriptural passages but from sense-experiences and necessary demonstrations; for the holy Bible and the phenomena of nature proceed alike from the divine Word, the former as the dictate of the Holy Ghost and the latter as the observant executrix of God's commands. It is necessary for the Bible, in order to be accommodated to the understanding of every man, to speak many things which appear to differ from the absolute truth so far as the bare meaning of the words is concerned. But Nature, on the other hand, is inexorable and immutable; she never transgresses the laws imposed upon her, or cares a whit whether her abstruse reasons and methods of operation are understandable to men. For that reason it appears that nothing physical which sense-experience sets before our eyes, or which necessary demonstrations prove to us, ought to be called in question (much less condemned) upon the testimony of biblical passages which may have some different meaning beneath their words. For the Bible is not chained in every expression to conditions as strict as those which govern all physical effects; nor is God any less excellently revealed in Nature's actions than in the sacred statements of the Bible.

---

[3]The Holy Ghost is the third divine person of the Trinity (God the Father, God the Son, God the Holy Ghost), who sanctifies and inspires humankind. Christians believe the authors of the Bible wrote under the sacred and infallible inspiration of the Holy Ghost.

The Promise of Science
▼▼▼

25 ▼ *Francis Bacon, NEW ORGANON*

Along with the Frenchman René Descartes (1596–1650), the English thinker Francis Bacon (1561–1626) was instrumental in formulating the strategies and methods of the new science. Both men rejected the medieval and Renaissance doctrine that scientific truth was attained by the careful study and analysis of authoritative texts from antiquity. Descartes, a superb mathematician and an advocate of the deductive method, stated in his *Discourse on Method* (1637) that humans could find scientific truth by carefully drawing conclusions from a few general, self-evident propositions. Bacon, a proponent of the inductive method, believed that experiment, observation, and the collection of data would reveal nature's laws. In his view, only after scientists had studied many individual phenomena could they generalize about the laws of nature. He also believed that an understanding of nature's laws would enable humans to use and control nature for the betterment of their condition.

Bacon's *New Organon* (1620), or "New Method of Inquiry," was meant to replace the "old organon," which refers to the "old method of inquiry" based on the system of logic devised by Aristotle. Written in Latin and hence directed to a learned audience, *New Organon* consists of 130 aphorisms — concise statements of principles — that summarize Bacon's views on scientific knowledge and its potential.

QUESTIONS FOR ANALYSIS

1. What does Bacon see as the major impediments to scientific progress?
2. According to Bacon, what are the roles of experiment, mathematics, and technology in scientific generalization?
3. What does Bacon mean when he says that a scientist must be like a bee rather than an ant or a spider?
4. What role in the future of humanity does Bacon see for science?
5. How do Bacon's concerns about potential roadblocks to scientific progress differ from those of Galileo?

1. Man, being the servant and interpreter of Nature, can do and understand so much and so much only as he has observed in fact or in thought of the course of nature: beyond this he neither knows anything nor can do anything.

2. Neither the naked hand nor the understanding left to itself can effect much. It is by instruments and helps that the work is done, which are as much wanted for the understanding as for the hand. And as the instruments of the hand either give motion or guide it, so the instruments of the mind supply either suggestions for the understanding or cautions.

3. Human knowledge and human power meet in one; for where the cause is not known the effect cannot be produced. Nature to be commanded must be obeyed; and that which in contemplation is as the cause is in operation as the rule. . . .

8. Even the works already known are due to chance and experiment rather than to sciences; for the sciences we now possess are merely systems for the peculiar arrangements and setting forth of things already invented; not methods of invention or directions for new works.

9. The cause and root of nearly all evils in the sciences is this — that while we falsely admire and extol the powers of the human mind we neglect to seek for its true helps. . . .

19. There are and can be only two ways of searching into and discovering truth. The one flies from the senses and particulars to the most general axioms, and from these principles, the truth of which it takes for settled and immovable, proceeds to judgment and to the discovery of middle axioms. And this way is now in fashion. The other derives axioms from the senses and particulars, rising by a gradual and unbro-

ken ascent, so that it arrives at the most general axioms last of all. This is the true way, but as yet untried. . . .

22. Both ways set out from the senses and particulars, and rest in the highest generalities; but the difference between them is infinite. For the one just glances at experiment and particulars in passing, the other dwells duly and orderly among them. The one, again, begins at once by establishing certain abstract and useless generalities, the other rises by gradual steps to that which is prior and better known in the order of nature. . . .

31. It is idle to expect any great advancement in science from the superinducing[1] and engrafting of new things upon old. We must begin anew from the very foundations, unless we would revolve for ever in a circle with mean and contemptible progress. . . .

36. One method of delivery alone remains to us; which is simply this: we must lead men to the particulars themselves, and their series and order; while men on their side must force themselves for a while to lay their notions by and begin to familiarize themselves with facts. . . .

95. Those who have handled sciences have been either men of experiment or men of dogmas. The men of experiment are like the ant; they only collect and use: the reasoners resemble spiders, who make cobwebs out of their own substance. But the bee takes a middle course; it gathers its material from the flowers of the garden and of the field, but transforms and digests it by a power of its own. Not unlike this is the true business of philosophy; for it neither relies solely or chiefly on the powers of the mind, nor does it take the matter which it gathers from natural history and mechanical experiments and lay it up in the memory whole, as it finds it; but lays it up in the understanding altered and digested. Therefore from a closer and purer league between these two faculties, the experimental and the rational, (such as has never yet been made) much may be hoped. . . .

108. So much then for the removing of despair and the raising of hope through the dismissal or rectification of the errors of past time. We must now see what else there is to ground hope upon. And this consideration occurs at once — that if many useful discoveries have been made by accident or upon occasion, when men were not seeking for them but were busy about other things; no one can doubt but that when they apply themselves to seek and make this their business, and that too by method and in order and not by desultory impulses, they will discover far more.

109. Another argument of hope may be drawn from this, — that some of the inventions already known are such as before they were discovered it could hardly have entered any man's head to think of; they would have been simply set aside as impossible. . . .

If, for instance, before the invention of ordnance,[2] a man had described the thing by its effects, and said that there was a new invention, by means of which the strongest towers and walls could be shaken and thrown down at a great distance; men would doubtless have begun to think over all the ways of multiplying the force of catapults and mechanical engines by weights and wheels and such machinery for ramming and projecting; but the notion of a fiery blast suddenly and violently expanding and exploding would hardly have entered into any man's imagination or fancy. . . .

In the same way, if before the discovery of silk, any one had said that there was a kind of thread discovered for the purposes of dress and furniture, which far surpassed the thread of linen or of wool in fineness and at the same time in strength, and also in beauty and softness; men would have begun immediately to think of some silky kind of vegetable, or of the finer hair of some animal, or of the feathers and down of birds; but of a web woven by a tiny worm, and that in such abundance, and renewing itself yearly, they would assuredly never have thought. Nay, if any one had

---

[1]To introduce a concept over and above some already existing concept.

[2]Cannon and artillery.

said anything about a worm, he would no doubt have been laughed at as dreaming of a new kind of cobwebs.

So again, if before the discovery of the magnet, any one had said that a certain instrument had been invented by means of which the quarters and points of the heavens could be taken and distinguished with exactness; men would have been carried by their imagination to a variety of conjectures concerning the more exquisite construction of astronomical instruments; but that anything could be discovered agreeing so well in its movements with the heavenly bodies, and yet not a heavenly body itself, but simply a substance of metal or stone, would have been judged altogether incredible. . . .

There is therefore much ground for hoping that there are still laid up in the womb of nature many secrets of excellent use, having no affinity or parallelism with any thing that is now known, but lying entirely out of the common track of our imagination, which have not yet been found out. They too no doubt will some time or other, in the course and revolution of many ages, come to light of themselves, just as the others did; only by the method of which we are now treating they can be speedily and suddenly and simultaneously presented and anticipated.

Chapter 4

▼▼▼

Africa and the Americas

Between the fifteenth and seventeenth centuries Africa and America became the first two major regions of the world to experience significant changes as a result of Europe's overseas expansion. On both sides of the Atlantic the arrival of Europeans changed agriculture and trade, recast governments, altered warfare, spread Christianity, and modified the size and composition of the population. But the magnitude of Europe's impact on the two regions was far different. Europeans affected Africa, but they transformed the Americas.

The European presence in Africa primarily meant trade — trade in which Europeans exchanged iron, hardware, textiles and other goods for pepper, gold, ivory and above all human beings. European involvement in the slave trade began in 1441, when a Portuguese raiding party captured twelve Africans on a small coastal island and sold them into slavery in Portugal. As the plantation system of agriculture spread from São Tomé, Cape Verde, and other South Atlantic islands to the West Indies and the Americas, the demand for slaves steadily grew from under 1,000 a year in the fifteenth century, to 7,500 per year in the mid seventeenth century, and over 50,000 per year in the eighteenth and early nineteenth centuries. The slave trade, however, did not translate into European political dominance or permanent European settlements. Except for small numbers of Dutch farmers who began to migrate to south Africa in 1652, Europeans who came to Africa stayed on the coast, completed their business, then departed. Missionary efforts were meager, and Portuguese dominance in Angola, in southwest Africa, is the only example of anything that approximated a European colony. As a result, despite the slave trade, Africans maintained control of their political lives and experienced few changes in their distinctive cultures and religions until the late nineteenth century, when a new wave of European expansion occurred.

In the Americas, however, the Europeans' arrival had immediate and catastrophic consequences for the indigenous peoples. By 1650 Spaniards and Portuguese directly ruled Mexico and Central and South America, and the English, French, Dutch, and other northern Europeans had begun to settle North America's Atlantic coast and the St. Lawrence River basin. In the 200 years after Columbus's discoveries, throughout the Western Hemisphere wealth was plundered, political structures were destroyed, millions of Native Americans were killed by Old World diseases, and traditional patterns of life and belief disappeared or managed only a tenuous survival.

Of the many factors that have been cited to explain the different experiences of Africa and the Americas during the age of European expansion, two stand out. First, unlike the Americas, where more than a half dozen European states from Portugal to Sweden competed for trade and territory, in Africa European involvement boiled down to Portuguese involvement only. Portugal led the way in African exploration and trade and by the end of the fifteenth century had already established commercial contacts and trading posts that discouraged potential European competitors. Only in the seventeenth century did other states, notably the Netherlands and England, show an interest in African trade. Second, Europeans, including the Portuguese, were convinced that in comparison to other parts of the world Africa offered few economic rewards other than trade in gold and slaves. Portugal's merchants and politicians concluded in the sixteenth century that their limited resources would be spent better on Indian Ocean trade and Brazilian development rather than on Africa. Neither they nor any other Europeans were willing to make the economic and military commitments necessary to overcome African resistance to European settlement and the establishment of European political authority.

Europeans faced a far different situation in the Americas. They soon discovered that the region contained easily exploitable sources of wealth such as gold, silver, and furs, and was capable of growing profitable crops such as tobacco and sugar. All these things were more or less theirs for the taking, not only in the thinly populated regions of North America and eastern and southern South America, but also in the more populous regions of Mexico, Peru, and the Caribbean.

Although the Europeans' guns, steel swords, and horses gave them an initial military advantage over the American Indians, superior technology was not the main reason for the relative ease of their conquests. In Mexico, for example, under normal circumstances several hundred Spaniards, even with their firearms and Native American allies, would have been no match for thousands of Aztec warriors with arrows, clubs, lances, and spears. But in the midst of fighting the Spaniards the Aztecs were struck by a debilitating smallpox epidemic, a disease introduced by the Spaniards. It was a sorely weakened and demoralized Aztec Empire that succumbed to the Spaniards and their allies in 1521.

Like the Aztecs, all American Indians had to contend with the bacteria, viruses, and parasites the Europeans carried in their bodies from across the Atlantic. Because of their long isolation they lacked immunity to Old World diseases such as diphtheria, measles, chicken pox, whooping cough, yellow fever, influenza, dysentery, and smallpox. Thus the arrival of a few Europeans and Africans had devastating consequences. On the island of Hispaniola, where Columbus established the first Spanish settlement in the New World, a population of 1 million fell to between 50,000 and 100,000 by the 1540s. Within fifty years after the arrival of the Spaniards in Mexico, the region's population fell by 90 percent, and in this case, millions, not tens of thousands, were victimized. No part of the Americas was untouched.

Such human devastation not only made it relatively easy for the Europeans to conquer or displace the Native Americans but also led to the enslavement of Africans in the New World. The epidemics created labor shortages that plantation and mine owners sought to overcome by importing enslaved Africans. Before the transatlantic slave trade ended, as many as 11 million Africans were sold into slavery in the Americas and millions more died in slave raids and the holds of slave ships. These Africans too were indirect victims of the bacilli, viruses, and parasites introduced to the New World in the early years of European expansion.

Africans and the Portuguese

When the Portuguese began sending ships into the Atlantic to explore Africa's offshore islands and west coast in the early fifteenth century, their goals were shaped by their limited and often inaccurate perceptions of Africa. They knew that North Africa was a Muslim stronghold, and that beyond it a vast desert existed. They also knew that south of the desert Africa was rich in gold and pepper, commodities that reached North Africa and Europe after crossing the desert in caravans. They also were convinced that somewhere beyond Islamic North Africa there was a large Christian country under the rule of Prester John, whose existence had intrigued Europeans ever since the twelfth century. Based on this small amount of information and legend, the Portuguese gambled that their voyages down the African coast would give them direct access to African gold and pepper and enable them to bypass Muslim traders in North Africa. They also dreamed of making contact with the rich and mighty ruler, Prester John, and joining him in a new crusade against their common Muslim enemy. Thus the Portuguese became involved in overseas exploration to make money and serve God.

In time Portuguese knowledge of Africa expanded, and as it did, some of their original goals were abandoned while new ones emerged. The Christian kingdom of Prester John was confirmed to be the east African kingdom of Ethiopia, but it proved to be a weak state with many political problems, including invasion by the neighboring Muslim state of Adal. No Portuguese-Ethiopian alliance would tip the balance of power in North Africa and the Middle East in favor of Christians. On Africa's west coast, the Portuguese discovered that Africa offered economic opportunities beyond trading for gold, pepper, and ivory. The sale of human beings also could generate profits. The ample rainfall and rich volcanic soil of the islands of Cape Verde, Madeira, and São Tomé made them ideal for growing and processing sugar, a commodity with a ready and expanding market in Europe. The sugar plantations of the South Atlantic islands created a market for African slaves, and by the 1500s the purchase, transport, and resale of slaves in the South Atlantic and later in Brazil had become a major Portuguese enterprise.

By the 1500s the Portuguese had made an even more important discovery, namely that by sailing around the Cape of Good Hope they could reach the rich markets of India, Southeast Asia, China, and Japan by an all-ocean route. This discovery immediately changed Portuguese thinking about Africa. Having direct access to the luxury goods and spices of Asia diminished the importance of trade in African pepper and generated opportunities for profit that trade in African products could not match. From the sixteenth century onward Africa came to be viewed as a source of slaves for the New World and a geographic obstacle to sail around in order to reach Asia.

Africa in the age of European discovery assumed a more prominent role in the world economy, but it resulted in the exploitation and denigration of millions of Africans rather then economic development. Out of the slave trade and New World slavery was born the myth of African moral and intellectual inferiority, used by defenders of slavery to justify a cruel and vicious institution. Thus the Europeans' involvement in Africa resulted in no massive epidemics, no toppling of empires, and no wholesale religious changes as in the Americas. It was, however, no less a tragedy.

Afro-Portuguese Trade and the Building of São Jorge da Mina

▼▼▼

26 ▼ Duarte Pacheo, *ESMERALDO DE SITU ORBIS*

Duarte Pacheo was a distinguished Portuguese navigator who made his first trip around Africa to India in 1500 under Admiral Pedro Cabral. Between 1505 and 1515 he composed his oddly named *Esmeraldo de Situ Orbis* (*Esmeraldo* is Portuguese for "emerald"; *de situ orbis* is Latin for "on the configuration of the world"), which was intended to be a practical guide for any Portuguese mariner making the trip from Europe to India by way of the Cape of Good Hope. It included a wealth of information on wind currents, distances, rivers, coastal settlements, and landmarks. Since it contained information meant for Portuguese mariners only, it never was published at the time it was written. When the manuscript was rediscovered and published in the nineteenth century, only the sections on the African coasts were still extant.

In this section Pacheo describes the building of the first Portuguese fortified trading post in Africa, São Jorge da Mina (St. George of the Mine), from which they were able to dominate trade on a 150-mile stretch of African coast on the Gulf of Guinea that today is a part of Ghana and the eastern fringe of Ivory Coast. The Portuguese called this stretch Mina, or mine, because it was a gold-producing region. The construction of the fort took place in 1481–1482 on land leased from two local peoples, the Fetu and the Comani. The fort, which was garrisoned by approximately sixty Portuguese troops, remained under royal control until it was taken by the Dutch in 1637.

The following excerpt from *De Situ Orbis* provides insights into the workings of Afro-Portuguese trade in the late fifteenth and sixteenth centuries.

QUESTIONS FOR ANALYSIS

1. What seems to have been the role of the Portuguese government in the building of São Jorge da Mina?
2. How profitable for the Portuguese is African trade according to Pacheo? What information does he provide that might explain this profitability?
3. What can one infer about African attitudes toward the Portuguese from the information Pacheo presents?
4. What evidence does the document provide about the obstacles faced by European merchants in Africa?

In the paragraph before last we related how the excellent prince, King Afonso V ordered the discovery of Mina and what captains and pilots he sent for the purpose. We must now tell how his son the most serene prince, King John of Portugal after the death of his father ordered the foundation of the Castle of S. [Jorge] da Mina. At the bidding of this magnanimous prince it was built by Dieguo d'Azambuja, a knight of his household. . . . On the 1st of January in the year of Our Lord 1482 he took with him nine caravels, each with its captain, very honorable men, under his command, together with two urcas[1] of 400 tons laden with lime and building stone and other material for this work. There was much trouble with the negroes, who wished to prevent the work, but it was finally finished, despite them, with all diligence and zeal, and it was necessary for the refuge and defence of all of us. At a later date the same King John, seeing that this was necessary, ordered the work to be added to. This, as we know, was the first stone building in the region of the Ethiopias of Guinea[2] since the creation of the world. Through this fortress trade so greatly increased by the favor of Our Lord that 170,000 doubloons[3] of good fine gold, and sometimes much more, are yearly brought thence to these realms of Portugal; it is bartered from the negro merchants who bring it thither from distant lands. These merchants belong to various tribes; the Bremus, Atis, Hacanys, Boroes, Mandinguas, Cacres, Andeses or Souzos, and many others which I omit for the sake of brevity. In exchange they take away much merchandise, such as "lanbens,"[4] which is the principal article of commerce . . . red and blue cloth, brass bracelets, handkerchiefs, corals, and certain red shells which they prize as we prize precious stones; white wine is also greatly prized, and blue beads, . . . and many other articles of various kinds. These people have hitherto been heathen, but some of them have now become Christians; I speak of those who dwell near the castle, for the merchants come from far and have not the same intercourse with us as these neighbors and accordingly continue in their false idolatry. The profit of this trade is five for one, or more, but the country is much subject to fever, and white men often die here. . . . Here there is an abundance of fish, upon which the negroes live, but they keep few cattle; however, there are many wild beasts such as ounces [leopards], elephants, buffaloes, gazelles and many other kinds, and also birds of various kinds, some of them being very beautiful. The negroes in this country go about naked, save for a loin-cloth or a piece of striped cloth, which they consider a very noble garment. They live on millet and palm-wine (though they prefer our wine) with fish and a little game. Our lord the King sends out yearly twelve small vessels laden with merchandise; these bring back to this realm the gold which the factor [agent] of his Highness obtains there by barter. Besides these vessels, three or four ships go out laden with provisions, wine and other articles which are needed there. The merchants who bring the gold to this fortress bring no asses or beasts of burden to carry away the merchandise, which they buy for three times and more its value in Portugal. Our people who are sent out by the most serene King in his ships buy slaves 200 leagues[5] beyond the castle, by rivers where there is a very large city called Beny, whence they are brought thither [to Mina]. What we have said of this is sufficient for our purpose, [which] solely concerns the commerce of our lord the King.

---

[1]A three-masted lightly armed transport ship mainly used to carry naval supplies and heavy bulky loads.

[2]*Guinea* was a general term for the regions of West Africa on the Atlantic from Gambia to Angola. *Ethiopia* was a general term for the regions of Africa inhabited by blacks.

[3]A Spanish gold coin.

[4]*Lanbens* is one of several Portuguese spellings of a word to describe brightly striped shawls produced in Tunis and other North African cities.

[5]A measurement of length; in the fifteenth century a league could vary from 2.4 to 4.6 miles.

Images of Europeans in the Art of Benin

▼▼▼

27 ▼ *A BENIN-PORTUGUESE SALTCELLAR and A BENIN WALL PLAQUE*

Over many centuries sub-Saharan Africans have produced some of the world's most impressive artworks, especially sculpture. Since at least 500 B.C.E., sculptors used clay, wood, ivory, and bronze to create masks, animal figures, ceremonial weapons, images of rulers, and religious objects that were of central importance to African society, politics, and religion. In some regions bronze casting and ivory carving were royal monopolies carried on by highly trained professionals.

Such was the case in Benin, a kingdom located on the west coast of tropical Africa in an area that today is part of Nigeria. Benin took shape in the 1200s and 1300s when a number of agricultural villages accepted the authority of an *oba,* or divine king, who ruled with a hierarchy of chiefs from the capital, Benin City. By the time the Portuguese arrived in 1485, Benin was a formidable military and commercial power and a center of state-sponsored artistic activity. Ivory carvers and bronze casters were organized into hereditary guilds and resided in their own neighborhoods in Benin City. They produced bronze heads, animal and human figures, pendants, plaques, musical instruments, drinking vessels, and armlets that were sold for profit or utilized for ceremonial purposes.

The arrival of the Portuguese in Benin affected the kingdom's artistic output in two ways. First, Portuguese merchants, prevented by the oba from establishing Benin as a source of slaves, turned to other commodities, including artworks, as objects of trade. They gave Benin ivory carvers numerous commissions to produce condiment sets, utensils, and hunting horns for sale in Europe. Second, the Portuguese stimulated the production of artworks for use in Benin itself by purchasing African goods with copper, a major component of the alloys used by Benin artists to create plaques and sculptures.

The two works pictured in this section provide opportunities to appreciate the skills of Benin artists and to gain insights into Benin attitudes toward Europeans. The first work, an ivory carving crafted in the sixteenth or early seventeenth century, is usually identified as a *salario,* or saltcellar. It depicts two Portuguese officials, flanked by two assistants. Above them is a Portuguese ship, with a man peering out of a crow's nest.

The second work is a sixteenth-century bronze plaque, approximately eighteen inches high, designed to be hung on a wall in the oba's palace in Benin City. The central figure is the oba, shown holding a spear and shield. On each of his sides are represented three subordinate chiefs. The one on the left is holding a bent iron bar, used as currency in trade; the figure next to him is holding a ceremonial sword; the figure on the far right is playing a flute-like musical instrument. The two figures in the background, on each side of the oba's head, represent the Portuguese. In one hand each figure holds a rectangular object, perhaps a glass

{text continues on page 121}

A Benin-Portuguese Saltcellar

A Benin Wall Plaque

mirror, and in the other hand what appears to be a goblet. These objects probably represent items the Portuguese offered in trade for Benin goods.

QUESTIONS FOR ANALYSIS

1. In the saltcellar, notice what hangs around the standing figure's neck, what he holds in his hands, and his facial expression. What is the sculptor trying to communicate about this figure?
2. Why might this image of the Portuguese official have appealed to the European purchasers for whom the carving was intended?
3. On the bronze plaque, what distinguishes the oba from the other figures? What details illustrate the oba's power and perhaps his divinity?
4. How does the representation of the Portuguese in the plaque differ from that of the saltcellar?
5. What might you infer from these works about Portuguese-Benin relations and attitudes of the Benin people toward the Portuguese?

Political Breakdown in the Kingdom of Kongo
▼▼▼

28 ▼ Nzinga Mbemba (Afonso I), LETTERS TO THE KING OF PORTUGAL

The largest state in central West Africa around 1500 was the Kingdom of Kongo, stretching along the estuary of the Congo River in territory that today lies within Angola and the Democratic Republic of Congo. In 1483 the Portuguese navigator Diogo Cão made contact with Kongo and several years later visited its inland capital. When he sailed home he was accompanied by Kongo emissaries, whom King Nzinga a Kuwu dispatched to Lisbon to learn European ways. They returned in 1491, along with Portuguese priests, artisans, and soldiers who brought numerous European goods, including a printing press. In the same year, the king and his son, Nzinga Mbemba, were baptized as Catholics.

Around 1506 Nzinga Mbemba, who took the name Afonso after his baptism, succeeded his father and ruled until about 1543. Afonso promoted the introduction of European culture in his kingdom by proclaiming Christianity the state religion (a step that affected few of his subjects), imitating the etiquette of Portuguese royalty, and using the Portuguese language in state business. His son Henrique was educated in Portugal and returned to serve as the region's Roman Catholic bishop. European firearms, horses, and cattle were introduced, and Afonso dreamed of achieving a powerful and prosperous state through cooperation with the Europeans. By the time of his death, however, his kingdom verged on disintegration, in no small measure because of the Portuguese. As many later African rulers were to discover, the introduction of European products and customs caused dissension and social instability. Worse, Portuguese involvement in the slave trade undermined Afonso's authority and made his subjects restive. In 1526 the king wrote the following letters to King John III of Portugal, urging him to control his rapacious subjects. The documents are part of a collection of twenty-four letters that Afonso and his Portuguese-educated, native secretaries dispatched to the kings of Portugal on a variety of issues.

QUESTIONS FOR ANALYSIS

1. According to Afonso, what have been the detrimental effects of the Portuguese presence in his kingdom?
2. What do the letters reveal about the workings of the slave trade in the kingdom? Who participated in it?
3. What do the letters reveal about Afonso's attitude toward slavery? Does he oppose the practice as such or only certain aspects of it?
4. What steps had the king taken to deal with the problems caused by the Portuguese? What do the letters suggest about the effectiveness of these steps?
5. How would you characterize Afonso's attitude toward the power and authority of the king of Portugal? Does he consider himself inferior to the Portuguese king or his equal?
6. How would you characterize King Afonso's conception of the ideal relationship between the Portuguese and his kingdom?

[handwritten: like Indians in Americas]

Sir, Your Highness should know how our Kingdom is being lost in so many ways that it is convenient to provide for the necessary remedy, since this is caused by the excessive freedom given by your agents and officials to the men and merchants who are allowed to come to this Kingdom to set up shops with goods and many things which have been prohibited by us, and which they spread throughout our Kingdoms and Domains in such an abundance that many of our vassals, whom we had in obedience, do not comply because they have the things in greater abundance than we ourselves; and it was with these things that we had them content and subjected under our vassalage and jurisdiction, so it is doing a great harm not only to the service of God, but the security and peace of our Kingdoms and State as well.

And we cannot reckon how great the damage is, since the mentioned merchants are taking every day our natives, sons of the land and the sons of our noblemen and vassals and our relatives, because the thieves and men of bad conscience grab them wishing to have the things and wares of this Kingdom which they are ambitious of; they grab them and get them to be sold; and so great, Sir, is the corruption and licentiousness that our country is being completely depopulated, and Your Highness should not agree with this nor accept it as in your service. And to avoid it we need from those (your) Kingdoms no more than some priests and a few people to teach in schools, and no other goods except wine and flour for the holy sacrament. That is why we beg of Your Highness to help and assist us in this matter, commanding your factors that they should not send here either merchants or wares, because it is *our will that in these Kingdoms there should not be any trade of slaves nor outlet for them {emphasis in original letter}*. Concerning what is referred [to] above, again we beg of Your Highness to agree with it, since otherwise we cannot remedy such an obvious damage. Pray Our Lord in His mercy to have Your Highness under His guard and let you do forever the things of His service. I kiss your hands many times.

[handwritten: Dom Afonso]

At our town of Kongo, written on the sixth day of July, João Teixeira[1] did it in 1526.
The King. Dom[2] Afonso.

{On the back of this letter the following can be read: To the most powerful and excellent prince Dom João, King our Brother.}

▼ ▼ ▼

Moreover, Sir, in our Kingdoms there is another great inconvenience which is of little service to God, and this is that many of our people, keenly desirous as they are of the wares and things of your Kingdoms, which are brought here by your people, and in order to satisfy their voracious appetite, seize many of our people, freed and exempt men, and very often it happens that they kidnap even noblemen and the sons of noblemen, and our relatives, and take them to be sold to the white men who are in our Kingdoms; and for this purpose they have concealed them; and others are brought during the night so that they might not be recognized.

And as soon as they are taken by the white men they are immediately ironed and branded with fire, and when they are carried to be embarked [on ships], if they are caught by our guards' men the whites allege that they have bought them but they cannot say from whom, so that it is our duty to do justice and to restore to the freemen their freedom, but it cannot be done if your subjects feel offended, as they claim to be.

And to avoid such a great evil we passed a law so that any white man living in our Kingdoms and wanting to purchase goods in any way should first inform three of our noblemen and officials of our court whom we rely upon in this matter, . . . who should investigate if the mentioned goods are captives or free men, and if cleared by them there will be no further doubt nor embargo [an act prohibiting the departure of a trading vessel] for them to be taken and embarked. But if the white men do not comply with it they will lose the aforementioned goods.

And if we do them this favor and concession it is for the part Your Highness has in it, since we know that it is in your service too that these goods are taken from our Kingdom, otherwise we should not consent to this. . . .

▼ ▼ ▼

Sir, Your Highness has been kind enough to write to us saying that we should ask in our letters for anything we need, and that we shall be provided with everything, and as the peace and the health of our Kingdom depend on us, and as there are among us old folks and people who have lived for many days, it happens that we have continuously many and different diseases which put us very often in such a weakness that we reach almost the last extreme; and the same happens to our children, relatives and natives owing to the lack in this country of physicians and surgeons who might know how to cure properly such diseases. And as we have got neither dispensaries nor drugs which might help us in this forlornness, many of those who had been already confirmed and instructed in the holy faith of Our Lord Jesus Christ perish and die; and the rest of the people in their majority cure themselves with herbs and breads and other ancient methods, so that they put all their faith in the mentioned herbs and ceremonies if they live, and believe that they are saved if they die; and this is not much in the service of God.

And to avoid such a great error and inconvenience, since it is from God in the first place and then from your Kingdoms and from Your Highness that all the good and drugs and medicines have come to save us, we beg of you to be agreeable and kind enough to send us two physicians and two apothecaries and one surgeon, so that they may come with their drugstores and all the necessary things to stay in our kingdoms, because we are in extreme need of them all and each of them. We shall do them all good and shall benefit them by all means, since they are sent by Your Highness, whom we thank for your

---

[1]One of Afonso's secretaries.

[2]Portuguese for "lord."

work in their coming. We beg of Your Highness as a great favor to do this for us, because besides being good in itself it is in the service of God as we have said above.

{Extracts from letter of King Afonso to the King of Portugal dated Oct. 18, 1526. By hand of Dom João Teixeira.}

Military Conflict in Southeast Africa

▼▼▼

29 ▼ *João dos Santos, EASTERN ETHIOPIA*

An example of African response to the Portuguese disruption of traditional trade patterns is provided by the military campaigns launched by the people known as the Zimba in the late sixteenth century. The *Zimba,* a term used by the Portuguese to describe any and all marauders from north of the Zambezi River, were in fact warriors of the Mang'aja tribe, whose attacks on the Portuguese and other African peoples to their east were ordered by their Lundu, or chief, in the late 1580s in response to disruption of their traditional trade. During the sixteenth century the market for Mang'aja ivory was ruined when the gold-obsessed Portuguese took over the coastal cities with which the Mang'aja had traded. The Zimba's military campaigns were intended to force the reopening of these markets. The Portuguese efforts to suppress the Zimba's attacks failed spectacularly. The Mang'aja continued their attacks until the early 1600s, but they never succeeded in re-establishing the traditional market for their ivory.

The following excerpt is from *Eastern Ethiopia* by João dos Santos, about whom little is known except that he was a Catholic clergyman who traveled along the east African coast and resided for a time in Sofala during the late sixteenth century. He uses the term *eastern Ethiopia* to include all of Africa's east coast from the Cape of Good Hope to the Red Sea.

QUESTIONS FOR ANALYSIS

1. According to dos Santos's account, why do the Portuguese decide to resist the Zimba?
2. What seems to have been the attitude of the Zimba toward the Portuguese?
3. How would you characterize the attitude of the African allies of the Portuguese toward the Zimba? How dedicated were the allies to the Portuguese themselves?
4. How great an advantage did Portuguese firearms give them over their enemy?
5. What tactics of the Zimba were most effective in the conflict with the Portuguese and their allies? What purposes did cannibalism play in their overall strategy?
6. What hints does dos Santos's account provide about the motives of the Zimba's military campaign?

Opposite the fort of Sena, on the other side of the river, live some Kaffirs,[1] lords of those lands, good neighbors and friends of the Portuguese, and always most loyal to them. It so happened at the time I was there that the Zimba Kaffirs, . . . who eat human flesh, invaded this territory and made war upon one of these friendly Kaffirs, and by force of arms took from him the kraal[2] in which he resided and a great part of his land, besides which they killed and ate a number of his people. The Kaffir, seeing himself thus routed and his power destroyed, proceeded to Sena[3] to lay his trouble before the captain, who was then André de Santiago, and to beg for assistance in driving out of his house the enemy who had taken possession of it. The captain, upon hearing his pitiful request, determined to assist him, both because he was very friendly to us and because he did not wish to have so near to Sena a neighbor as wicked as the Zimba.

Therefore, having made all necessary preparations for this war, he set out, taking with him a great number of the Portuguese of Sena with their guns and two pieces of heavy cannon from the fort. On arriving at the place where the Zimba were, they found them within a strong double palisade of wood, with its ramparts and loopholes for arrows, surrounded by a very deep and wide trench, within which the enemy were most defiant. André de Santiago, seeing that the enterprise was much more formidable than he had anticipated and that he had brought with him but few men to attack so strong an enemy and his fortress, fixed his camp on the bank of a rivulet which ran by the place, and sent a message to the captain of Tete, Pedro Fernandes de Chaves, to come to his assistance with the Por-

tuguese of Tete and as many Kaffir vassals of his fort as he could bring.

Pedro Fernandes de Chaves immediately prepared to go to the assistance of André de Santiago, and assembled more than a hundred men with their guns, Portuguese and half-castes,[4] and the eleven vassal chiefs. They all crossed to the other side of the river and proceeded by land until they were near the place where the Zimba had fortified themselves. These had information of their approach, and greatly feared their arrival. For this reason they sent out spies secretly upon the road, that when they approached they might see them, and report concerning the men who were coming. And learning from these spies that the Portuguese were in front of the Kaffirs in palanquins[5] and hammocks and not disposed in order of battle, they sallied out of their fortress by night secretly, without being heard by André de Santiago, and proceeded to conceal themselves in a dense thicket at about half a league's distance, through which the men of Tete would have to pass. When they were thus stationed the Portuguese came up nearly half a league in advance of the Kaffirs of their company, quite unsuspicious of what might befall them in the thicket. Just as they were entering it the Zimba fell upon them suddenly with such violence that in a short time they were all killed, not one surviving, and when they were dead the Zimba cut off their legs and arms, which they carried away on their backs with all the baggage and arms they had brought with them, after which they returned secretly to their fortress. When the chiefs reached the thicket and found all the Portuguese and their captain dead, they immediately turned back from the place and

---

[1]Based on the Arab word *kafir,* meaning "black," Kaffir was used to refer to the Bantu-speaking peoples of southeastern Africa and more generally to non-Muslim black Africans. Today in South Africa it is a derogatory term used by some whites for all blacks.

[2]Based on the Portuguese word *curral,* an enclosed pen for cattle, kraal refers to the enclosed area surrounding a royal residence.

[3]Sena and Tete were towns on the Zambesi River where the Portuguese had established trading posts.

[4]People of mixed Portuguese/African ancestry.

[5]Covered litters or couches that were mounted on long horizontal poles so they could be carried about.

retreated to Tete, where they related the lamentable event that had occurred.

At the time that preparations for this war were being made there was a friar of St. Dominic preaching at Tete, named Nicolau do Rosario, . . . a man who had reached perfection in many virtues. . . . In the ambush he was severely wounded, and seizing him yet alive the Zimba carried him away with them to put him to death more cruelly afterwards, which they did upon arriving at their fortress, where they bound him hand and foot to a tree and killed him with their arrows in the most cruel manner. This they did to him rather than to others because he was a priest and head of the Christians, as they called him, laying all the blame for the war upon him and saying that Christians did nothing without the leave and counsel of their cacis.[6] . . .

After the Zimba had put Father Nicolau to death they rested during the remainder of that sad day, and on the night that followed they celebrated their victory and success, playing upon many cornets and drums, and the next day at dawn they all sallied out of their fortress, the chief clothed in the chasuble[7] that the father had brought with him to say mass, carrying the golden chalice in his left hand and an assagai[8] in his right, all the other Zimba carrying on their backs the limbs of the Portuguese, with the head of the captain of Tete on the point of a long lance, and beating a drum they had taken from him. In this manner, with loud shouts and cries they came within sight of André de Santiago and all the Portuguese who were with him, and showed them all these things. After this they retired within their fortress, saying that what they had done to the men of Tete who had come to help their enemies, they would do to them, and that it was the flesh of those men that they were about to eat.

André de Santiago . . . was greatly shocked, as also were all the other Portuguese, at this most horrible and pitiful spectacle, for which reason they decided to retreat as soon as night came on.

In carrying this decision into execution they were in so great a hurry to reach the other side of the river that they were heard by the Zimba, who sallied out of their fortress and falling upon them with great violence killed many of them on the bank of the river. Among the slain was André de Santiago, who died as the valiant man he was. . . .

Thus these robbers and fierce Zimba killed one hundred and thirty Portuguese and half-castes of Tete and Sena and the two captains of these forts. This they accomplished with very little loss on their side, with their usual cunning, as they always took the Portuguese unawares, when they were unable to fight. This took place in the year 1592.

Great sorrow was felt at the death of Father Nicolau, whom all looked upon as a saint, and for all the Portuguese who lost their lives in this most disastrous war, both because some of them were married and left wives and children at these rivers, and because the Zimba were victorious, more insolent than before, and were within fortifications close to Sena, where with greater audacity they might in the future do much damage to the Portuguese who passed up and down these rivers with their merchandise. For these reasons Dom Pedro de Sousa, captain of Mozambique, determined to chastise these Zimba, conquer them, and drive them from the vicinity of Sena. . . .

After obtaining information of the condition of the Zimba, he commanded all the necessary preparations to be made for this war, and assembled nearly two hundred Portuguese and fifteen hundred Kaffirs, with whom he crossed to the other side of the Zambesi and proceeded by land to the fortress of the Zimba, where he formed a camp at the same place that André de Santiago had formed his. Then he commanded that the various pieces of artillery which he had taken with him for the purpose should be fired against the wall of the fortress, but this had no effect upon it, as it was made of large wood, strengthened within by a strong and wide rampart which

---

[6]Religious leaders.
[7]A chasuble is one of the vestments worn by a Catholic priest while celebrating mass.

[8]A spear.

the Zimba had constructed with the earth from the trench.

Dom Pedro, seeing that his artillery had no effect upon the enemy's wall, determined to enter the fortress and take it by assault, and for this purpose he commanded part of the trench to be filled up, which was done with great difficulty and danger to our men, as the Zimba from the top of the wall wounded and killed some of them with arrows. When this part of the trench was filled up, a number of men crossed over with axes in their hands to the foot of the palisade, which they began to cut down, but the Zimba from the top of the wall poured so great a quantity of boiling fat and water upon them that nearly all were scalded and badly wounded, especially the naked Kaffirs, so that no one dared go near the palisade, because they were afraid of the boiling fat and through fear of certain iron hooks similar to long harpoons, which the Zimba thrust through the loopholes in the wall and with which they wounded and caught hold of all who came near and pulled from within with such force that they drew them to the apertures, where they wounded them mortally. For this reason the captain commanded all the men to be recalled to the camp to rest, and the remainder of that day was spent in tending the wounded and the scalded.

The following day the captain commanded a quantity of wood and branches of trees to be collected, with which huge wicker-work frames were made, as high as and higher than the enemy's palisade, and he commanded them to be placed in front of the wall and filled with earth that the soldiers might fight on them with their guns, and the Zimba would not dare to appear on the wall or be able to pour boiling fat upon the men cutting down the palisade. When this stratagem of war was almost in readiness, another peaceful or cowardly device was planned in the following manner. The war had lasted two months, for which reason the residents of these rivers, who were there rather by force than of their own free will, being away from their homes and trade, which is their profession, and not war, pretended to have received letters from their wives in Sena relating the danger they were in from a rebel Kaffir who they said was coming with a number of men to rob Sena, knowing that the Portuguese were absent, for which reason they ought immediately to return home. This false information was spread through the camp, and the residents of Sena went to the captain and begged him to abandon the siege of the Zimba and attend to what was of greater importance, as otherwise they would be compelled to return to their homes and leave him.

Dom Pedro, seeing their determination and believing the information said to be given in the letters to be true, abandoned the siege and commanded the men to pass by night to the other side of the river and return to Sena, but this retreat could not be effected with such secrecy as to be unknown to the Zimba, who sallied out of their fortress with great cries, fell upon the camp, killed some men who were still there, and seized the greater part of the baggage and artillery, that had not been taken away.

With this defeat and disappointment the captain returned to Sena, and thence to Mozambique, without accomplishing what he desired; and the Zimba's position was improved and he became more insolent than before. . . .

Encounters in the Americas

For many millennia, perhaps beginning as early as 40,000 B.C.E., peoples from Asia crossed the land bridge linking northeast Siberia with the area of modern Alaska. Then after 10,000 B.C.E., as the Ice Age ended and the world's oceans rose, this single link between Eurasia and the Americas was submerged under the Bering Sea, and the peoples of the Americas were cut off from the rest of the world. This isolation ended after 1492, when Europeans and Africans, along with their animals, plants, and pathogens, began to arrive in the wake of Columbus's first voyage to the New World.

First in the West Indies, then in Mexico and Peru, and ultimately throughout the Americas, American Indians after 1492 faced the decision to resist or cooperate with the Europeans. Cooperation most commonly took the form of trade in which Native Americans exchanged dyes, foodstuffs, and furs for hardware, firearms, trinkets, and alcoholic beverages. Cooperation also took the form of military alliances. In Mexico, thousands of Mexican warriors fought on Cortés's side against their hated enemy, the Aztecs, while in North America, the Hurons allied with the French and the Iroquois allied with the Dutch and later the English in a long series of wars.

Many Native Americans chose to resist the Europeans until well into the late nineteenth century. In Mexico and Peru, however, military defeat came early with the conquest of the Aztec Empire by Cortés between 1519 and 1521 and the overthrow of the Inca Empire by Pizarro between 1531 and 1533. In North America, Indian raids inflicted considerable casualties and damage on the early European settlements in New England, the middle colonies, and the Chesapeake region. But the colonists' reprisals were equally bloody and destructive, and in conflicts such as the Pequot War (1637) in Connecticut and the Algonquin-Dutch wars (1643–1645) in modern New York and New Jersey, the Indians were routed and massacred. The long-term outcome of their resistance was never in doubt. The Europeans' single-mindedness, weaponry, and devastating biological effect made their victory inevitable.

The Battle for Tenochtitlán

▼▼▼

30 ▼ *Bernardino de Sahagún,* *GENERAL HISTORY OF THE* *THINGS OF NEW SPAIN*

Bernardino de Sahagún (ca. 1499–1590), a member of the Franciscan religious order, was one of the earliest Spanish missionaries in Mexico, arriving in 1529. He soon developed a keen interest in the culture of the peoples of Mexico, for whom he had deep affection and respect. Having mastered the Nahuatl language, spoken by the Aztecs and other central Mexican peoples, around 1545 he began to collect oral and pictorial information about Native Mexican culture. The result was his *General History of the Things of New Spain,* a major source of information about Mexican culture at the time of the Spanish conquest. Many Spaniards considered Sahagún's work dangerous because they feared his efforts to preserve the memory of native culture threatened their plans to exploit and Christianize the Indians. As a result, in 1578 his writings and notes were confiscated by royal decree and sent back to Spain, where they gathered dust in an archive until rediscovered and published in the nineteenth century.

The following selection comes from the twelfth and last book of the *General History*. Based on interviews with Aztecs who had lived through the conquest some twenty-five years earlier, Book Twelve, which exists in both Nahuatl and Spanish versions, recounts the conquest of Mexico from the time Cortés arrived on the Mexican coast in April 1519 until the days following the Aztecs' capitulation in August 1521. Although the exact role of Sahagún and his Indian assistants in composing and organizing Book Twelve has been hotly debated by scholars, most agree that it accurately portrays Aztec views and perceptions of the events that unfolded between 1519 and 1521.

The following excerpt picks up the story in November 1519. By then the Spaniards had gained as allies the Tlaxcalans, the Aztecs' bitter enemies, and were leaving Cholula, an ancient city that the Spaniards and their allies had sacked and looted because of its leaders' lack of cooperation. They were on their way to Tenochtitlán, the splendid Aztec capital on Lake Texcoco, for an anticipated meeting with Emperor Moctezuma.

QUESTIONS FOR ANALYSIS

1. What does the source reveal about the motives of the Spaniards and their Indian allies for their attack on the Aztecs?
2. What was Moctezuma's strategy to deal with the Spaniards? Why did it fail?
3. Aside from their firearms, what other military advantages did the Spaniards have over their opponents?
4. On several occasions the Aztecs routed the Spaniards. What explains these Aztec victories?
5. How did the Aztec view of war differ from that of the Spaniards?
6. What does the source reveal about Aztec religious beliefs and values?
7. What similarities and differences do you see between the Aztec-Spanish conflict and the armed clashes between the Zimba and the Portuguese (see source 29)?

And after the dying in Cholula, the Spaniards set off on their way to Mexico,[1] coming gathered and bunched, raising dust. . . .

Thereupon Moteucçoma[2] named and sent noblemen and a great many other agents of his . . . to go meet [Cortés] . . . at Quauhtechcac. They gave [the Spaniards] golden banners of precious feathers, and golden necklaces.

And when they had given the things to them, they seemed to smile, to rejoice and to be very happy. Like monkeys they grabbed the gold. It was as though their hearts were put to rest, brightened, freshened. For gold was what they greatly thirsted for; they were gluttonous for it, starved for it, piggishly wanting it. They came lifting up the golden banners, waving them

---

[1]*Mexico* refers to Tenochtitlán, the capital of the Aztec empire. *Mexica* (pronounced Mezh ee´ ka) refers to the people of Tenochtitlán and Tlatelolco, a suburb of Tenochtitlán.

[2]One of several spellings of the Aztec emperor's name, including Montezuma and Moctezuma.

from side to side, showing them to each other. They seemed to babble; what they said to each other was in a babbling tongue. . . .

Another group of messengers — rainmakers, witches, and priests — had also gone out for an encounter, but nowhere were they able to do anything or to get sight of [the Spaniards]; they did not hit their target, they did not find the people they were looking for, they were not sufficient. . . .

▷   Cortés and his entourage continue their march.

Then they set out in this direction, about to enter Mexico here. Then they all dressed and equipped themselves for war. They girded themselves, tying their battle gear tightly on themselves and then on their horses. Then they arranged themselves in rows, files, ranks.

Four horsemen came ahead going first, staying ahead, leading. . . .

Also the dogs, their dogs, came ahead, sniffing at things and constantly panting.

By himself came marching ahead, all alone, the one who bore the standard on his shoulder. He came waving it about, making it spin, tossing it here and there. . . .

Following him came those with iron swords. Their iron swords came bare and gleaming. On their shoulders they bore their shields, of wood or leather.

The second contingent and file were horses carrying people, each with his cotton cuirass,[3] his leather shield, his iron lance, and his iron sword hanging down from the horse's neck. They came with bells on, jingling or rattling. The horses, the deer,[4] neighed, there was much neighing, and they would sweat a great deal; water seemed to fall from them. And their flecks of foam splatted on the ground, like soapsuds splatting. . . .

The third file were those with iron crossbows, the crossbowmen. Their quivers went hanging at their sides, passed under their armpits, well filled, packed with arrows, with iron bolts. . . .

The fourth file were likewise horsemen; their outfits were the same as has been said.

The fifth group were those with harquebuses,[5] the harquebusiers, shouldering their harquebuses; some held them [level]. And when they went into the great palace, the residence of the ruler, they repeatedly shot off their harquebuses. They exploded, sputtered, discharged, thundered, disgorged. Smoke spread, it grew dark with smoke, everyplace filled with smoke. The fetid smell made people dizzy and faint.

Then all those from the various altepetl[6] on the other side of the mountains, the Tlaxcalans, the people of Tliliuhquitepec, of Huexotzinco, came following behind. They came outfitted for war with their cotton upper armor, shields, and bows, their quivers full and packed with feathered arrows, some barbed, some blunted, some with obsidian[7] points. They went crouching, hitting their mouths with their hands yelling, singing, . . . whistling, shaking their heads.

Some bore burdens and provisions on their backs; some used tump[8] lines for their forehead, some bands around their chests, some carrying frames, some board cages, some deep baskets. Some made bundles, perhaps putting the bundles on their backs. Some dragged the large cannons, which went resting on wooden wheels, making a clamor as they came.

▷   Cortés and his army entered Tenochtitlán in November 1519 and were amicably received by Moctezuma, who was nonetheless taken captive by the Spaniards. Cortés's army was allowed to

---

[3]A piece of armor covering the body from neck to waist.
[4]Having never seen horses, some Aztecs considered them to be large deer.
[5]A heavy matchlock gun that was portable but capable of being fired only with a support.

[6]The Nahuatl term for any sovereign state, especially for the local ethnic states of central Mexico.
[7]A volcanic glass, generally black.
[8]A strap or sling passed around the chest or forehead to help support a pack being carried on a person's back.

remain in a palace compound, but tensions grew the following spring. Pedro de Alvarado, in command while Cortés left to deal with a threat to his authority from the governor of Cuba, became concerned for the Spaniards' safety as the Aztecs prepared to celebrate the annual festival in honor of the god Huitzilopochtli.

And when it had dawned and was already the day of his[9] festivity, very early in the morning those who had made vows to him unveiled his face. Forming a single row before him they offered him incense; each in his place laid down before him offerings of food for fasting and rolled amaranth dough. And it was as though all the youthful warriors had gathered together and had hit on the idea of holding and observing the festivity in order to show the Spaniards something, to make them marvel and instruct them. . . .

When things were already going on, when the festivity was being observed and there was dancing and singing, with voices raised in song, the singing was like the noise of waves breaking against the rocks.

When it was time, when the moment had come for the Spaniards to do the killing, they came out equipped for battle. They came and closed off each of the places where people went in and out. . . . Then they surrounded those who were dancing, going among the cylindrical drums. They struck a drummer's arms; both of his hands were severed. Then they struck his neck; his head landed far away. Then they stabbed everyone with iron lances and struck them with iron swords. They struck some in the belly, and then their entrails came spilling out. They split open the heads of some, they really cut their skulls to pieces, their skulls were cut up into little bits. And if someone still tried to run it was useless; he just dragged his intestines along. There was a stench as if of sulfur. Those who tried to escape could go nowhere. When

anyone tried to go out, at the entryways they struck and stabbed him.

And when it became known what was happening, everyone cried out, "Mexica warriors, come running, get outfitted with devices, shields, and arrows, hurry, come running, the warriors are dying; they have died, perished, been annihilated, O Mexica warriors!" Thereupon there were war cries, shouting, and beating of hands against lips. The warriors quickly came outfitted, bunched together, carrying arrows and shields. Then the fighting began; they shot at them with barbed darts, spears, and tridents, and they hurled darts with broad obsidian points at them.

▷ The fighting that ensued drove the Spaniards and their allies back to the palace enclave. Without a reliable supply of food and water, in July 1520, Cortés, who had returned with his power intact, led his followers on a desperate nocturnal escape from the city, but they were discovered and suffered heavy losses as they fled. They retreated to the other side of the lake, and the Aztecs believed the Spanish threat had passed.

Before the Spanish appeared to us, first an epidemic broke out, a sickness of pustules.[10] . . . Large bumps spread on people; some were entirely covered. They spread everywhere, on the face, the head, the chest, etc. The disease brought great desolation; a great many died of it. They could no longer walk about, but lay in their dwellings and sleeping places, no longer able to move or stir. They were unable to change position, to stretch out on their sides or face down, or raise their heads. And when they made a motion, they called out loudly. The pustules that covered people caused great desolation; very many people died of them, and many just starved to death; starvation reigned, and no one took care of others any longer.

[9]A reference to the god Huitzilopochtli. An image of the god, made from amaranth seed flour and the blood of recently sacrificed victims, played a central role in the festival.

[10]The disease was smallpox.

On some people, the pustules appeared only far apart, and they did not suffer greatly, nor did many of them die of it. But many people's faces were spoiled by it, their faces and noses were made rough. Some lost an eye or were blinded.

This disease of pustules lasted a full sixty days; after sixty days it abated and ended. When people were convalescing and reviving, the pustules disease began to move in the direction of the Chalco.[11] And many were disabled or paralyzed by it, but they were not disabled forever. . . . The Mexica warriors were greatly weakened by it.

And when things were in this state, the Spaniards came, moving toward us from Tetzcoco. . . .

▷ Having resupplied his Spanish/Tlaxcalan army and having constructed a dozen cannon-carrying brigantines for use on the lake, Cortés resumed his offensive late in 1520. In April 1521 he reached Tenochtitlán and placed the city under a blockade.

When their twelve boats had come from Tetzcoco, at first they were all assembled at Acachinanco, and then the Marqués[12] moved to Acachinanco. He went about searching where the boats could enter, where the canals were straight, whether they were deep or not, so that they would not be grounded somewhere. But the canals were winding and bent back and forth, and they could not get them in. They did get two boats in; they forced them down the road coming straight from Xoloco. . . .

The Tlatelolca fought in Çoquipan, in war boats. And in Xoloco the Spaniards came to a place where there was a wall in the middle of the road, blocking it. They fired the big guns at it. At the first shot it did not give way, but the second time it began to crumble. The third time, at last parts of it fell to the ground, and the fourth time finally the wall went to the ground once and for all. . . .

Once they got two of their boats into the canal at Xocotitlan. When they had beached them, then they went looking into the house sites of the people of Xocotitlan. But Tzilacatzin and some other warriors who saw the Spaniards immediately came out to face them; they came running after them, throwing stones at them, and they scattered the Spaniards into the water. . . .

When they got to Tlilhuacan, the warriors crouched far down and hid themselves, hugging the ground, waiting for the war cry, when there would be shouting and cries of encouragement. When the cry went up, "O Mexica, up and at them!" the Tlappanecatl Ecatzin, a warrior of Otomi[13] rank, faced the Spaniards and threw himself at them, saying, "O Tlatelolca warriors, up and at them, who are these barbarians? Come running!" Then he went and threw a Spaniard down, knocking him to the ground; the one he threw down was the one who came first, who came leading them. And when he had thrown him down, he dragged the Spaniard off.

And at this point they let loose with all the warriors who had been crouching there; they came out and chased the Spaniards in the passageways, and when the Spaniards saw it the Mexica seemed to be intoxicated. The captives were taken. Many Tlaxcalans, and people of Acolhuacan, Chalco, Xochimilco, etc., were captured. A great abundance were captured and killed. . . .

Then they took the captives to Yacacolco, hurrying them along, going along herding their captives together. Some went weeping, some singing, some went shouting while hitting their hands against their mouths. When they got them to Yacacolco, they lined them all up. Each one went to the altar platform where the sacrifice was performed.[14] The Spaniards went first, going in the lead; the people of the different altepetl just followed, coming last. And when the sacrifice was over, they strung the Spaniards' heads on poles on skull racks; they also strung up the

---

[11]A city on the southeast corner of Lake Texcoco.
[12]Cortés.
[13]Elite warriors bound by oath never to retreat.

[14]Traditionally the sacrifice consisted of cutting the heart out of the victim.

horses' heads. They placed them below, and the Spaniards' heads were above them, strung up facing east. . . .

> ▷ Despite this victory, the Aztecs could not overcome the problems of shortages of food, water, and warriors. In mid July 1521 the Spaniards and their allies resumed their assault, and in early August the Aztecs decided to send into battle a quetzal-owl warrior, whose success or failure, it was believed, would reveal if the gods wished the Aztecs to continue fighting.

And all the common people suffered greatly. There was famine; many died of hunger. They no longer drank good, pure water, but the water they drank was salty. Many people died of it, and because of it many got dysentery and died. Everything was eaten: lizards, swallows, maize, straw, grass that grows on salt flats. And they chewed at wood, glue flowers, plaster, leather, and deerskin, which they roasted, baked, and toasted so that they could eat them, and they ground up medicinal herbs and adobe bricks. There had never been the like of such suffering. The siege was frightening, and great numbers died of hunger. . . .

And . . . the ruler Quauhtemoctzin[15] and the warriors Coyohuehuetzin, Temilotzin, Topantemoctzin, the Mixcoatlailotlac Ahuelitoctzin, Tlacotzin, and Petlauhtzin took a great warrior named Tlapaltecatl Opochtzin . . . and outfitted

him, dressing him in a quetzal-owl costume. . . . When they put it on him he looked very frightening and splendid. . . . They gave him the darts of the devil,[16] darts of wooden rods with flint tips. And the reason they did this was that it was as though the fate of the rulers of the Mexica were being determined.

When our enemies saw him, it was as though a mountain had fallen. Every one of the Spaniards was frightened; he intimidated them, they seemed to respect him a great deal. Then the quetzal-owl climbed up on the roof. But when some of our enemies had taken a good look at him they rose and turned him back, pursuing him. Then the quetzal-owl turned them again and pursued them. Then he snatched up the precious feathers and gold and dropped down off the roof. He did not die, and our enemies did not carry him off. Also three of our enemies were captured. At that the war stopped for good. There was silence, nothing more happened. Then our enemies went away. It was silent and nothing more happened until it got dark.

And the next day nothing more happened at all, no one made a sound. The common people just lay collapsed. The Spaniards did nothing more either, but lay still, looking at the people. Nothing was going on, they just lay still. . . .

> ▷ Two weeks passed before the Aztecs capitulated on August 13, 1521.

[15]Quauhtemoctzin was now the Aztec emperor.

[16]Darts sacred to Huitzilopochtli.

Conflict in New Netherlands
▼▼▼

31 ▼ *David Pieterzen DeVries,*
VOYAGES FROM HOLLAND TO AMERICA

As a result of the efforts of Henry Hudson, who explored what is now New York Harbor and the Hudson River in 1609, the Dutch claimed New Netherlands, an area that included Long Island, eastern New York, and parts of New Jersey and

Connecticut. To encourage colonization, the Dutch government granted wealthy Dutch colonists huge tracts of land, known as patroonships, with the understanding that each patroon would settle at least fifty tenants on the land within four years. At first, relations with the Algonquins and Raritans in the area around New Amsterdam (modern New York City) were generally cordial, but they deteriorated after the arrival of Willem Kieft as governor in 1642. He sought to tax the Algonquins to pay for the construction of a fort and attempted to force them off their land to create new patroonships, even though few existing patroonships had attracted the minimum number of tenants. When the Algonquins resisted, Kieft ordered the massacre described by David DeVries in the following excerpt from his work, *Voyages from Holland to America*. Born in Rochelle, France, in 1592 or 1593, DeVries spent most of his life as a merchant in the Netherlands before becoming a patroon in the Dutch colony in the early 1640s.

QUESTIONS FOR ANALYSIS

1. Why does DeVries oppose the governor's plan to attack the Algonquins?
2. What does this suggest about DeVries's attitude toward the Native Americans?
3. How did the Algonquins react immediately after the massacre?
4. What does the Algonquins' behavior suggest about their early relations with the Dutch?
5. What were the long-term results of the massacre?

The 24th of February, sitting at a table with the Governor, he [Governor Kieft] began to state his intentions, that he had a mind to *wipe the mouths* of the savages; that he had been dining at the house of Jan Claesen Damen, where Maryn Adriaensen and Jan Claesen Damen, together with Jacob Planck, had presented a petition to him to begin this work. I answered him that they were not wise to request this; that such work could not be done without the approbation of the Twelve Men;[1] that it could not take place without my assent, who was one of the Twelve Men; that moreover I was the first patroon, and no one else hitherto had risked there so many thousands, and also his person, as I was the first to come from Holland or Zeeland to plant a colony; and that he should consider what profit he could derive from this business, as he well

knew that on account of trifling with the Indians we had lost our colony in the South River at Swanendael, in the Hoere-kil, with thirty-two men, who were murdered in the year 1630; and that in the year 1640, the cause of my people being murdered on Staten Island was a difficulty which he had brought on with the Raritan Indians, where his soldiers had for some trifling thing killed some savages. . . . But it appeared that my speaking was of no avail. He had, with his co-murderers, determined to commit the murder, deeming it a Roman deed,[2] and to do it without warning the inhabitants in the open lands that each one might take care of himself against the retaliation of the savages, for he could not kill all the Indians. When I had expressed all these things in full, sitting at the table, and the meal was over, he told me he wished me to go to

---

[1] The board of directors responsible for governing New Netherlands.

[2] A glorious deed in the manner of the ancient Romans.

the large hall, which he had been lately adding to his house. Coming to it, there stood all his soldiers ready to cross the river to Pavonia to commit the murder. Then spoke I again to Governor Willem Kieft: "Let this work alone; you wish to break the mouths of the Indians, but you will also murder our own nation, for there are none of the settlers in the open country who are aware of it. My own dwelling, my people, cattle, corn, and tobacco will be lost." He answered me, assuring me that there would be no danger; that some soldiers should go to my house to protect it. But that was not done. So was this business begun between the 25th and 26th of February in the year 1643. I remained that night at the Governor's, sitting up. I went and sat by the kitchen fire, when about midnight I heard a great shrieking, and I ran to the ramparts of the fort, and looked over to Pavonia. Saw nothing but firing, and heard the shrieks of the savages murdered in their sleep. I returned again to the house by the fire. Having sat there awhile, there came an Indian with his squaw, whom I knew well, and who lived about an hour's walk from my house, and told me that they two had fled in a small skiff, which they had taken from the shore at Pavonia; that the Indians from Fort Orange had surprised them; and that they had come to conceal themselves in the fort. I told them that they must go away immediately; that this was no time for them to come to the fort to conceal themselves; that they who had killed their people at Pavonia were not Indians, but the Swannekens, as they call the Dutch, had done it. They then asked me how they should get out of the fort. I took them to the door, and there was no sentry there, and so they betook themselves to the woods. When it was day the soldiers returned to the fort, having massacred or murdered eighty Indians, and considering they had done a deed of Roman valor, in murdering so many in their sleep; where infants were torn from their mothers' breasts, and hacked to pieces

in the presence of the parents, and the pieces thrown into the fire and in the water, and other sucklings, being bound to small boards, were cut, stuck, and pierced, and miserably massacred in a manner to move a heart of stone. Some were thrown into the river, and when the fathers and mothers endeavored to save them, the soldiers would not let them come on land but made both parents and children drown — children from five to six years of age, and also some old and decrepit persons. Those who fled from this onslaught, and concealed themselves in the neighboring sedge, and when it was morning, came out to beg a piece of bread, and to be permitted to warm themselves, were murdered in cold blood and tossed into the fire or the water. Some came to our people in the country with their hands, some with their legs cut off, and some holding their entrails in their arms, and others had such horrible cuts and gashes, that worse than they were could never happen. And these poor simple creatures, as also many of our own people, did not know any better than that they had been attacked by a party of other Indians — the Maquas. After this exploit, the soldiers were rewarded for their services, and Director Kieft thanked them by taking them by the hand and congratulating them. At another place, on the same night, on Corler's Hook near Corler's plantation, forty Indians were in the same manner attacked in their sleep, and massacred there in the same manner. Did the Duke of Alva[3] in the Netherlands ever do anything more cruel? This is indeed a disgrace to our nation, who have so generous a governor in our Fatherland as the Prince of Orange,[4] who has always endeavored in his wars to spill as little blood as possible. As soon as the savages understood that the Swannekens had so treated them, all the men whom they could surprise on the farmlands, they killed; but we have never heard that they have ever permitted women or children to be killed. They burned all the houses, farms, barns, grain,

---

[3]Spanish general in the service of Philip II of Spain responsible for carrying out harsh anti-Protestant measures in the Netherlands in the 1560s.

[4]Frederick Henry, *stadholder,* or elected executive and military commander of the Netherlands.

haystacks, and destroyed everything they could get hold of. So there was an open destructive war begun. They also burnt my farm, cattle, corn, barn, tobacco-house, and all the tobacco. My people saved themselves in the house where I alone lived, which was made with embrasures, through which they defended themselves. Whilst my people were in alarm the savage whom I had aided to escape from the fort in the night came there, and told the other Indians that I was a good chief, that I had helped him out of the fort, and that the killing of the Indians took place contrary to my wish. Then they all cried out together to my people that they would not shoot them; that if they had not destroyed my cattle they would not do it, nor burn my house; that they would let my little brewery stand, though they wished to get the copper kettle, in order to make darts for their arrows; but hearing now that it had been done contrary to my wish, they all went away, and left my house unbesieged. When now the Indians had destroyed so many farms and men in revenge for their people, I went to Governor Willem Kieft, and asked him if it was not as I had said it would be, that he would only effect the spilling of Christian blood. Who would now compensate us for our losses? But he gave me no answer. He said he wondered that no Indians came to the fort. I told him that I did not wonder at it; "why should the Indians come here where you have so treated them?"

▼▼▼

Land and Labor in Spanish America

Throughout its more than 300 years of existence the Spanish empire in the Americas was based on the economic exploitation of Native Americans. Such exploitation began in the 1490s when Columbus sought to establish a permanent settlement on Hispaniola, an island he had discovered in 1492. The first Spanish settlers were determined to enrich themselves, and this spelled disaster for the island's Arawaks, who were robbed of their food, forced to work in the Spaniards' homes, fields, and mines, sold, enslaved, and, in the case of women, sexually abused. In 1497 Columbus attempted to curb the rapaciousness of his countrymen by allocating specific groups of Arawaks to individual Spaniards, who could demand tribute and labor from these Indians and these Indians alone. Abuse of the Arawaks continued, however, and in 1512 King Ferdinand of Spain issued the Laws of Burgos, which sought to regulate the Spaniards' treatment of Indians. Reasonable labor expectations, adequate food and housing, and restrictions on punishments and abuse were among its many provisions. The Laws of Burgos were difficult to enforce, and by the mid 1500s were irrelevant. By then imported African slaves, not Arawaks, were doing the Spaniards' work on Hispaniola. Victims of agricultural disruption, harsh labor, and epidemics, the Arawaks, who had numbered 1 million in 1492, had virtually disappeared.

Elsewhere in Spanish America the effects of forced labor on the native populations were less catastrophic, but economic realities were no different. Clearly, the New World would yield no income to the monarchy, nor would colonists be willing to settle in the Americas unless Amerindians were forced to work for the Spaniards, pay them tribute, or both. This rarely meant enslavement, which was illegal except in peripheral areas such as Chile, where persistent native resistance to Spanish authority seemed to justify it. Although not slaves, Indians could be assigned to an individual Spaniard, or *ecomendero;* required to pay tribute to individuals or the state; subjected to state-controlled labor drafts; or forced in the open market to accept pittance wages for their work.

This reliance on native labor raised perplexing and hotly debated questions among Spanish settlers, clergy, and royal officials. Through what mechanisms should the Indians be compelled to work for the Spaniards? What kind of work could they reasonably be asked to do? When did Indian labor cross the line from reasonable work to the kind of exploitation that led to the demise of the Arawaks? What responsibilities did royal officials have to protect Indians from mistreatment and abuse? Most fundamentally, how was it possible to reconcile the need to compel Indians to work with the Spaniards' responsibility to convert them to Christianity, civilize them, and treat them as human beings? The Spaniards never found satisfactory answers to these questions, even after 300 years of colonial rule.

Labor and Tribute in the Encomienda System
▼▼▼
32 ▾ *ENCOMIENDA RECORDS FROM NESTALPA, 1547–1565*

The mounds of encomienda records in archives throughout Spanish America testify to the importance of the system in early colonial society and the efforts of government officials to control it. The following selection provides a number of insights into how the encomienda system worked. It is a series of records compiled by various officials pertaining to an encomienda near Mexico City. The original encomenderos were Juan Galindo and Pedro Moreno, two soldiers who had come to Mexico with Cortés in 1519.

QUESTIONS FOR ANALYSIS

1. Summarize the changes in the obligations of the Indians from 1547 to 1575.
2. What evidence suggests that the Indians may have had a voice in the discussions concerning their labor and tribute?
3. Is there anything in the wording and tone of these documents that casts light on the sympathies of the government officials?
4. What aspects of the system may have discouraged productivity on the part of the Indians?
5. From your reading of these documents, what do you suspect were some of the major abuses in the encomienda system?

They [the Indians] are assessed each day two chickens and four loads of wood and two loads of maize, and fodder for the horses; and every eighty days twenty petticoats, and twenty shirts, and four loads of blankets of henequen,[1] and the labor on their plantings of peppers, beans, maize, and wheat, and the carrying of all this to the city,[2] and the completion of the house,[3] and they are not to be charged beyond this.

It appears that Sr. Lic.[4] Tejada, by commission of his highness, on February 11, 1547, with the consent of the parties, agreed that the Indians would give to Pedro Moreno and Juan Galindo, for the clothing and maize: thirty-two Indians in service, twelve of them in this city and twenty in the town to guard the animals . . . and two pesos of fodder of the Sr. viceroy's measure each day, and for the pepper planting ten loads of petates,[5] and the remainder of the assessment continued in force.

Signed by the said SR. LIC.; TAPIA, interpreter

▼▼▼

On April 21, 1553, by agreement, the services of the thirty-two Indians that they gave to their encomenderos were commuted, so that instead of them they are to give from now on 192 common gold pesos per year in payments made every eighty days, which, prorated, amount to 42 pesos, six tomines[6] per payment, and they are not to give anything else to Pedro Moreno and whoever has them in encomienda.

▼▼▼

In the city of Mexico on December 11, 1553, by agreement, the assessment of the town of Nestalpa was clarified. Pedro Moreno and Juan Galindo, now dead, have it in encomienda, and

the Indians give every day two chickens and four loads of wood; and because it appeared that for the petticoats and shirts and the two loads of maize included in the assessment they gave to their encomenderos thirty-two Indians of service, of whom twelve were given in this city and twenty in the pueblo,[7] . . . it was ordered that instead of the thirty-two Indians they are to give each year 100 pesos, five tomines. Also they are to make the plantings of peppers, beans, maize, and wheat as stated in the assessment, and they are to put all the proceeds of these plantings in the central part of the said town, and they are not to be compelled or forced to bring the goods to this city or to take them anywhere else under the penalties contained in the provisions and ordinances that are made, and the above is to be kept as the assessment, and neither the encomenderos nor any other person is to ask them for any other thing, under the penalties stated. . . .

▼▼▼

In the city of Mexico, on March 8, 1558, the visitation that was made of the town of Nestalpa was examined by the Srs. president and oidores[8] of the royal audiencia[9] of New Spain, for the Indians say that they cannot give to their encomenderos the tributes that they are taxed; in view of what appears in it and in view of the nature of the said town and the number of people that there are in it, the oidores said that from now on for a period of eight years the natives of the said town are to give in tribute to the said encomenderos each year 286 common gold pesos paid three times a year, and also they are to give in the cabecera[10] of the said town each day three loads of wood and three of fodder and one chicken, and also they are to give each year at harvest

---

[1]Fiber made from the leaves of a plant native to the Yucatan region of Mexico.
[2]Mexico City, where the goods would be sold.
[3]Presumably a house being built by the encomendero.
[4]Stands for Señor Licendiado ("honorable counselor"); a *licendiado* was a person with a university degree in law.
[5]Mats made from rough grass used in the unique system of irrigation agriculture practiced by the Mexicans known as *chinampa*. Crops were planted on the mats after they had

been piled with soil and rotten vegetation and floated on drained swamps or marshes.
[6]*Pesos* and *tomines* were silver coins.
[7]The village (of Nestalpa).
[8]Judges who were members of the *audiencia*.
[9]The *audiencia* was one of the first instruments of Spanish royal government in the New World. It was a court of law that also had executive functions.
[10]Municipal hall.

time one hundred fanegas[11] of wheat and four hundred fanegas of maize, and for this they are to make some common plantings where they may gather the said quantity, rather more than less, and what is left over will remain for the community of the said town, and nothing further is to be required or asked of them under penalty of the ordinances, and a copy of this modified assessment is to be given to the natives of the said town so that they may know how much they have to pay, and it is entered in the book of tributes, together with the fact that the chicken and fodder and wood are to be given when the encomenderos are in the town. The decree of the Srs. president and oidores was marked, and signed by Antonio de Turcios.

▼▼▼

In the city of Mexico on April 2, 1565, the Srs. president and oidores of the royal audiencia of New Spain, having seen the account and visitation that was made of the town of Nestalpa, which Pedro Moreno and Pedro Valdovinos are said to have in encomienda, in view of what appears there and in view of the number of people that there are in the said town, ordered that the natives give in tribute each year 964 pesos and seven tomines . . . of common gold, the payments to be made three times a year, and also 410¹/₂ fanegas of maize at harvest time, placed in the cabecera of the said town; of this the said encomenderos are to receive 821 common gold

pesos and all the maize, and the 153 pesos and seven tomines remaining are for the community of the said town, and this amount is to be placed in a box of three keys, of which the governor is to have one, one alcalde[12] another, and a mayordomo[13] the third, and all three are to be present when funds are taken out for necessary and convenient expenditures for the republic. They are to keep accounts so that these can be shown on demand. And in order to pay the said tribute each married tributary is to pay each year nine and one-half silver reales and one-half fanega of maize, and each widower, widow, bachelor, and spinster possessing and living on lands outside the parental jurisdiction is to pay [half that]; and they are not to be taxed or assessed or required to pay more tribute, service, or anything else under penalty of the ordinances, cedulas, and provisions of his majesty. Under the said penalties no tribute is to be collected from the unmarried young men who are with their parents so long as they do not marry or go out to live by themselves, nor from the old people, the blind, the crippled, and the sick, who are exempt for the said count; and they are to keep this assessment and it is to be entered in the book of tributes; and it is charged to the said encomenderos that they provide what is necessary for the maintenance of the divine cult and support of the clergy who are in charge of the religion of the natives of the said town. And thus it was pronounced and ordered, marked as by the royal audiencia.

---

[11]A measure equaling slightly more than 1.5 bushels.
[12]A government magistrate.

[13]A government steward.

Indian Abuse and the Courts
▼▼▼

33 ▼ *COMPLAINT OF THE INDIANS OF TECAMA AGAINST THEIR ECOMENDERO, JUAN PONCE DE LEÓN*

The development of Spain's Indian policy reflected a complex clash of interests and opinions, pitting a small group of uncompromising pro-Indian reformers against the encomenderos. The former, many of whom were members of Catholic religious orders, sought the suppression of the encomiendas, the end of all forms of Indian servitude, and the administration of Indian affairs by the clergy; the latter argued that without forced labor and tribute from the Indians, Spain's American empire would collapse. Royal officials conceded the encomenderos' point, but worried that if carried too far, exploitation would further reduce the Indian population, and if given too much authority, the encomenderos could develop into an entrenched aristocracy strong enough to challenge royal authority. As a result, the government pursued a middle course, allowing the encomienda system to continue but regulating it to protect Indian welfare. In the New Laws of 1542, it also provided for the gradual transfer of encomiendas from private to government control.

To enforce these and other laws pertaining to life in its American empire, the Spanish crown established a system of courts which ranged from small regional courts to *audiencias,* which served as supreme courts in their administrative districts. Staffed by royal appointees who served both as judges and as advisors to regional administrators, audiencias were probably the most important single civil institution in the Spanish American colonies.

The following excerpt, a summary of judicial proceedings that took place in Mexico City in 1550, confirms that legislation designed to protect Indians from abuse was often ignored. It also reveals, however, that Indians and their supporters could avail themselves of the court system to protect themselves from maltreatment. It is noteworthy that no less a person than Viceroy Don Luis de Velasco, the highest-ranking official in the large province of New Spain, presided over the proceedings. Unfortunately, the notary does not tell us how the case was decided, and one can only speculate about the final verdict.

QUESTIONS FOR ANALYSIS

1. The Indians begin their testimony by complaining about events that had occurred only a few days earlier. As they go on, they bring up grievances going back eight years. In what ways may this be significant?
2. What specific complaints do the Indians make about the treatment they have received?
3. On the basis of the Indians' testimony what conclusions can be drawn about the attitudes toward Indians on the part of the encomendero, Juan Ponce?

In the city of Mexico in New Spain on the 13th day of the month of December in the year of the birth of our Savior Jesus Christ 1550, in the presence of the illustrious Don Luis de Velasco, Viceroy and Governor of New Spain for His Majesty and President of the *Audiencia* and Royal Chancellery, which is resident in this city, and in the presence of me, Alonso Sanchez, notary of this Royal *Audiencia,* there appeared Martin Tlacuxtecal, Martin Mexicaltecatl, Tomas Teyagualcal, and Toribio [Tlayult], *principales*[1] of the *pueblo* [village] of Tecama, along with Pedro

---

[1] Members of the Indian aristocracy who ranked below chieftains; according to Indian custom they were entitled to collect tribute from commoners.

[and] Constantino, *macehuales*[2] of the said *pueblo*. And through Juan Frayle, the interpreter for this Royal *Audiencia,* they said that they were bringing a criminal complaint against Juan Ponce, their *encomendero,* and his brother Diego de Ordaz, and they related the case as follows: that the day before yesterday when their master, the said Juan Ponce, had asked them for fifty *tamemes* [carriers] to carry things to the mines of Zacatecas, because they said they did not want to give them since the *macehuales* would not serve as carriers, he took them by their hair and gave them many kicks, calling them dogs and sons of whores, and saying, "Are you not my slaves? You have to do it"; and when they, the *principales,* told the said Juan Ponce that the *pueblo* would be depopulated, he, responded that he did not care if it was. And also they made the complaint that the said Juan Ponce took and had taken from them much more than the hay that they are obliged to give in the assessment, adding a half *braza*[3] to each measure. And they also made the complaint against the interpreter of the said Juan Ponce, saying that he has been cutting their fruit trees and other things that they have in the *pueblo,* and when they tell him not to do this, he abuses them in words and kicks them. And the said Constantino and Pedro, *macehuales* of the *pueblo,* especially make the complaint that a dog belonging to the said Juan Ponce bit them on the arms, and one of them, Pedro, showed a bite that he had on his arm, and Constantino showed another bite on his hand that did not seem very serious. And they requested that the said Juan Ponce and Diego de Ordaz be punished and asked for justice.

▼▼▼

In the city of Mexico on the 19th day of the month of December in the year 1550 in the presence of the illustrious Don Luis de Velasco, Viceroy and Governor of New Spain, there appeared certain Indians who said through Hernando de Tapia, the interpreter of this Royal *Audiencia,* that they were named Martin Mexicaltecal, Martin Tlacaltecal, Toribio Tlaylutl, Tomas Teyaguacal, and Martin Tacotetle, *principales* and natives of the *pueblo* of Tecama, which is granted in *encomienda* to Juan Ponce; and they filed complaint for themselves and in the name of the other *principales* and natives, against the said Juan Ponce, for the following reasons:

First, for eight years, though they are obliged daily to give their master four of the measures of hay that were customarily given for the horses of the Viceroy Don Antonio de Mendoza in accord with the assessment, their master increased the amount they were obliged to give by half, and they have given him this for eight years without being paid for it.

Also, about a year ago, Bartolomé the constable [a colonial official] went to the *pueblo* to have them paid for the damage that the cattle of the said Juan Ponce had caused them, ordering them to be paid 17 pesos and 2 *tomines*[4] and giving them a silver pitcher as a pledge until they should be paid; and afterward he [Ponce] took the pitcher and said he would pay them in wheat, and he has not paid them anything for this.

Also, two or three months ago, some horses belonging to the said Juan Ponce did great damage in four fields of the *macehuales,* and they asked him to pay them for the damage they had done, and he said he would pay for it but never has done so.

Also, about a year ago, the said Juan Ponce, without any cause, began to abuse the *macehuales* while they were shaking out the ears of maize, and when three constables, who are called Martin Tlacatetle, Gaspar Tecpanecal, and Tomas Quamiscal,[5] interceded for them, he kicked and beat them, striking the said Gaspar with a rock and mistreating them badly in other ways, though they had the staff of office in their hands.

Also, the last Sunday, the said Juan Ponce ordered the *macehuales* to bring the wheat they are obliged to give, and because they did this they did not hear Mass.

---

[2]An Indian commoner; a peasant.
[3]A measure of length; approximately five and a half feet.
[4]Pesos and tomines were silver coins.

[5]Indian villagers given responsibility for dealing with minor crimes within their village.

Also, he has sometimes taken food from them without paying for it.

Also, that a black who is called Francisco, a slave of Juan Ponce, frequently takes their maize leaves from them [for] his master in the *pueblo,* going from house to house and taking from the *macehuales* the dried maize leaves that have been gathered for the tribute, and not paying anything for this.

In all of this, the abovesaid has committed a crime worthy of punishment, and they requested that the judges proceed against him in accord with the law and that their master be compelled to return and restore to them what he had taken in excess, and they swore to the complaint in proper form.

And concerning this they gave testimony in both complaints, and the said Juan Ponce was arrested and his confession [testimony] taken, and it seems that he was released on bail; and the licentiate Morones, the prosecutor (*fiscal*) of the Royal *Audiencia,* filed accusation against the said Juan Ponce in proper form in this matter, and the suit was argued by both parties in the Royal *Audiencia* until it was definitively concluded, and this is the present state of the said suit, which is in my possession and to which I refer. And I give the present in testimony of this at the request of the President and judges, dating it in the said city on the said 15th day of January of the said year 1552, as can be seen more fully in the original trial records, which are in my possession and to which I refer, and in conclusion I made my sign here in testimony of the truth.

ALONSO SANCHEZ.

The "Mountain of Silver" and the Mita System
▼▼▼

34 ▼ *Antonio Vazquez de Espinosa,*
COMPENDIUM AND DESCRIPTION
OF THE WEST INDIES

In 1545 an Indian herder lost his footing on a mountain in the eastern range of the Andes while chasing a llama. To keep from falling he grabbed a bush, which he uprooted to reveal a rich vein of silver. This is one story of how the world learned of the world's richest silver mine, at Potosí, in modern Bolivia. Located two miles above sea level in a cold, desolate region, Potosí became the site of the Western Hemisphere's first mining boom town. By the late 1500s Potosí had a racially mixed population of 160,000, making it the largest, wildest, gaudiest city in the New World. With one-fifth of its extracted silver going to the Spanish crown, Potosí was a major reason why Spanish kings were able to carry on massive military campaigns against Protestants in Europe and Muslims in the Mediterranean.

The backbone of the Potosí operation was a system of government-controlled draft labor known as the *repartimiento* ("distribution") system and widely practiced throughout Spanish America. In Peru it was known as the *mita* (Quechua for "time" or "distribution") system, a term used by the Incas for their own pre-conquest system of required state labor. In the repartimiento and mita systems native communities were ordered to supply a portion of their population at fixed intervals for assignment to particular tasks. In their original form these labor drafts may well have been less burdensome than what was required in the enco-mienda system. Required work was distributed more evenly throughout the community, and an individual might go months or even years without being called for labor service. But as revealed in the following document, the mita system still caused hardship and disruption for Indian communities and the individuals assigned to service.

The following description of the mita system is provided by Antonio Vazquez de Espinosa (d. 1630), a Spanish Carmelite friar who abandoned an academic career to perform priestly work in the Americas. During his retirement in the 1620s, he wrote several books on Spanish America and his experiences as a priest. His best-known work is his *Compendium and Description of the West Indies,* which recorded his observations of conditions in Mexico and Spanish South America. In this excerpt he describes mercury mining at Huancavelica and then the great silver mines of Potosí itself.

QUESTIONS FOR ANALYSIS

1. What was the range of annual wages for each laborer at Huancavelica? How do their wages compare with the annual salary of the royal hospital chaplain? How does the sum of the workers' annual wages compare with the cost of tallow candles at Potosí? Compare the wages of the mita workers at Potosí with the wages paid those Amerindians who freely hired themselves out. What do you conclude from all these figures?
2. What were the major hazards connected with the extraction and production of mercury and silver?
3. What evidence does this source provide of Spanish concern for the welfare of the Indian workers? What evidence of indifference does it provide? Where does the weight of the evidence seem to lie?
4. What does the document tell us about the impact of the mita system on native Peruvian society?

HUANCAVELICA

. . . It contains 400 Spanish residents, as well as many temporary shops of dealers in merchandise and groceries, heads of trading houses, and transients, for the town has a lively commerce. It has a parish church with vicar and curate,[1] a Dominican convent, and a Royal Hospital under the Brethren of San Juan de Diós for the care of the sick, especially Indians on the range; it has a chaplain with a salary of 800 pesos[2] contributed

by His Majesty; he is curate of the parish of San Sebastian de Indios, for the Indians who have come to work in the mines and who have settled down there. . . .

Every two months His Majesty sends by the regular courier from Lima[3] 60,000 pesos to pay for the mita of the Indians, for the crews are changed every two months, so that merely for the Indian mita payment (in my understanding of it) 360,000 pesos are sent from Lima every year, not to speak of much besides, which all

---

[1] A parish priest and his assistant priest.
[2] A standard Spanish coin worth eight *reals* (note 9).
[3] Lima was the capital city of the viceroyalty of Peru, one of the two major administrative units of Spanish America,

covering all of South America except part of the Caribbean coast. Appointed by the crown, the viceroy was the chief military and civil administrator.

crosses at his risk that cold and desolate mountain country which is the puna[4] and has nothing on it but llama ranches.

Up on the range there are 3,000 or 4,000 Indians working in the mine; it is colder up there than in the town, since it is higher. The mine where the mercury is located is a large layer which they keep following downward. When I was in that town [in 1616] I went up on the range and down into the mine, which at that time was considerably more than 130 stades[5] deep. The ore was very rich black flint, and the excavation so extensive that it held more than 3,000 Indians working away hard with picks and hammers, breaking up that flint ore; and when they have filled their little sacks, the poor fellows, loaded down with ore, climb up those ladders or rigging, some like masts and others like cables, and so trying and distressing that a man empty-handed can hardly get up them. That is the way they work in this mine, with many lights and the loud noise of the pounding and great confusion. Nor is that the greatest evil and difficulty; that is due to thievish and undisciplined superintendents. As that great vein of ore keeps going down deeper and they follow its rich trail, in order to make sure that no section of that ore shall drop on top of them, they keep leaving supports or pillars of the ore itself, even if of the richest quality, and they necessarily help to sustain and insure each section with less risk. This being so, there are men so heartless that for the sake of stealing a little rich ore, they go down out of hours and deprive the innocent Indians of this protection by hollowing into these pillars to steal the rich ore in them, and then a great section is apt to fall in and kill all the Indians, and sometimes the unscrupulous and grasping superintendents themselves, as happened when I was in that locality; and much of this is kept quiet so that it shall not come to

the notice of the manager and cause the punishment of the accomplices. . . .

POTOSÍ

According to His Majesty's warrant, the mine owners on this massive range have a right to the mita of 13,300 Indians in the working and exploitation of the mines, both those which have been discovered, those now discovered, and those which shall be discovered. It is the duty of the Corregidor[6] of Potosí to have them rounded up and to see that they come in from all the provinces between Cuzco over the whole of El Collao and as far as the frontiers of Tarija and Tomina;[7] this Potosí Corregidor has power and authority over all the Corregidors in those provinces mentioned; for if they do not fill the Indian mita allotment assigned each of them in accordance with the capacity of their provinces as indicated to them, he can send them, and does, salaried inspectors to report upon it, and when the remissness is great or remarkable, he can suspend them, notifying the Viceroy of the fact.

These Indians are sent out every year under a captain whom they choose in each village or tribe, for him to take them and oversee them for the year each has to serve; every year they have a new election, for as some go out, others come in. This works out very badly, with great losses and gaps in the quotas of Indians, the villages being depopulated; and this gives rise to great extortions and abuses on the part of the inspectors toward the poor Indians, ruining them and thus depriving the . . . chief Indians of their property and carrying them off in chains because they do not fill out the mita assignment, which they cannot do, for the reason given and for others which I do not bring forward.

---

[4]A high, cold plateau.
[5]A stade was a measure of length, approximately an eighth of a mile.

[6]A district military officer.
[7]This region consisted of approximately 139 villages.

These 13,300 are divided up every 4 months into 3 mitas, each consisting of 4,433 Indians, to work in the mines on the range and in the 120 smelters in the Potosí and Tarapaya areas; it is a good league[8] between the two. These mita Indians earn each day, or there is paid each one for his labor, 4 reals.[9] Besides these there are others not under obligation, who are mingados or hire themselves out voluntarily: these each get from 12 to 16 reals, and some up to 24, according to their reputation of wielding the pick and knowing how to get the ore out. These mingados will be over 4,000 in number. They and the mita Indians go up every Monday morning to the locality of Guayna Potosí which is at the foot of the range; the Corregidor arrives with all the provincial captains or chiefs who have charge of the Indians assigned them, and he there checks off and reports to each mine and smelter owner the number of Indians assigned him for his mine or smelter; that keeps him busy till 1 p.m., by which time the Indians are already turned over to these mine and smelter owners.

After each has eaten his ration, they climb up the hill, each to his mine, and go in, staying there from that hour until Saturday evening without coming out of the mine; their wives bring them food, but they stay constantly underground, excavating and carrying out the ore from which they get the silver. They all have tallow candles, lighted day and night; that is the light they work with, for as they are underground, they have need of it all the time. The mere cost of these candles used in the mines on this range will amount every year to more than 300,000 pesos, even though tallow is cheap in that country, being abundant; but this is a very great expense, and it is almost incredible, how much is spent for candles in the operation of breaking down and getting out the ore.

These Indians have different functions in the handling of the silver ore; some break it up with bar or pick, and dig down in, following the vein in the mine; others bring it up; others up above keep separating the good and the poor in piles; others are occupied in taking it down from the range to the mills on herds of llamas; every day they bring up more than 8,000 of these native beasts of burden for this task. These teamsters who carry the metal do not belong to the mita, but are mingados — hired.

So huge is the wealth which has been taken out of this range since the year 1545, when it was discovered, up to the present year of 1628, which makes 83 years that they have been working and reducing its ores, that merely from the registered mines, as appears from an examination of most of the accounts in the royal records, 326,000,000 assay[10] pesos have been taken out. At the beginning when the ore was richer and easier to get out, for then there were no mita Indians and no mercury process, in the 40 years between 1545 and 1585, they took out 111,000,000 of assay silver. From the year 1585 up to 1628, 43 years, although the mines are harder to work, for they are deeper down, with the assistance of 13,300 Indians whom His Majesty has granted to the mine owners on that range, and of other hired Indians, who come there freely and voluntarily to work at day's wages, and with the great advantage of the mercury process, in which none of the ore or the silver is wasted, and with the better knowledge of the technique which the miners now have, they have taken out 215,000,000 assay pesos. That, plus the 111 extracted in the 40 years previous to 1585, makes 326,000,000 assay pesos, not counting the great amount of silver secretly taken from these mines . . . to Spain, paying no 20 percent or registry fee, and to other countries outside Spain; and to the Philippines and China, which is beyond all reckoning; but I should venture to imagine and even assert that what has been taken from the Potosí range must be as

---

[8]Approximately three miles.
[9]A Spanish silver coin (see note 2).

[10]Measured so that silver content met official standards.

much again as what paid the 20 percent royal impost.[11]

Over and above that, such great treasure and riches have come from the Indies in gold and silver from all the other mines in New Spain and Peru, Honduras, the New Kingdom of Granada, Chile, New Galicia, New Vizcaya,[12] and other quarters since the discovery of the Indies, that they exceed 1,800 millions.

---

[11]The "20 percent royal impost" was the one-fifth of all New World silver owed to the Spanish crown.

[12]New Galicia and New Vizcaya were regions and administrative jurisdictions in New Spain located in north-central and northwestern Mexico.

Part Two

⋎⋎⋎

A World in Transition, from the Mid Seventeenth Century to the Early Nineteenth Century

Between 1633 and 1639, the Japanese shogun, Tokugawa Hitetada, in an effort to solidify his authority and further stabilize Japan, outlawed Christianity, expelled Spanish and Portuguese missionaries, and severely restricted trade with the English, Portuguese, Spanish, and Dutch. In 1640 the Portuguese decided to test the shogun's resolve by sending a trading ship to Japan. In response, the shogun ordered the execution of the captain and sixty members of the crew, leaving alive thirteen sailors to return to Macao, the Portuguese enclave in China, to tell what had happened. The Europeans all withdrew from Japan, except for the Dutch, who were permitted to send one ship a year to Japan as long as they accepted the strict conditions dictated by the shogun's government.

Two hundred years later another Asian state, China, sought to regulate trade with Europeans when in 1838 the emperor banned British opium sales to China, and in 1839 his official, Lin Zexu, coerced British merchants in Guangzhou to hand over without compensation about 3 million pounds of raw opium so it could be destroyed. This time the European response was quite different. Great Britain declared war and dispatched a force consisting of sixteen warships, four armed steamers, twenty-eight transports, and 4,000 troops to China. The British easily defeated the Chinese and in 1842 forced them to accept the humiliating Treaty of Nanjing, which ceded Hong Kong to the British, opened five ports to foreign trade, and required the Qing government to pay the British $21 million.

The vastly different outcomes of these two episodes show how much the world had changed between the seventeenth and early nineteenth centuries. In the first part of the seventeenth century, despite the Europeans' dominance of the New World, the states of Western Europe were in no position to challenge the great imperial states of Asia. Militarily, European armies were smaller than those of the Asian empires and in any case were fully engaged in the last of Europe's wars of religion, the Thirty Years' War (1618–1648). European governments, weakened by deepening conflict between kings and their powerful subjects, were struggling with declining revenues and rural violence. Economically, by the early 1600s Europeans had expanded their role in world trade, but when they built warehouses and wharves on the coasts of India, China, Southeast Asia, and Africa, they did so at the pleasure of local rulers and with the understanding they would follow the regulations set down by those same rulers. When they purchased Asian goods, they paid exclusively with silver, because they produced no manufactured or agricultural products that interested sophisticated Asian buyers.

By the early 1800s Europe and Europe's role in the world had both changed significantly. In the realm of ideas, intellectuals had largely abandoned the religious issues that had preoccupied their predecessors in the Medieval, Renaissance, and Reformation eras, and formulated views of society, politics, and human nature that were increasingly secular and scientific. In politics, revolutions had challenged royal authority, aristocratic privilege, and state-controlled churches, and introduced concepts of popular sovereignty, constitutionalism, legal equality, and freedom into the Europeans' political vocabulary. Nationalism emerged as a potent political force in the 1790s and early 1800s during the French Revolution and the Napoleonic era. In economics, population growth, urbanization, worldwide commercial expansion, and greater productivity in agriculture and manufacturing all contributed to impressive growth. Most importantly, beginning in the 1760s, the mechanization of the English textile and iron industries and the development of the steam engine heralded the beginning of the Industrial Revolution, which would give Europeans productive capacities unimagined in human history.

While Europe drew strength from the political, intellectual, and economic changes of the late seventeenth and eighteenth centuries, Asian empires had without exception grown weaker by 1800. By then the Safavid Empire no longer existed, and the Mughal Empire consisted of a small scrap of territory around the imperial capital of Delhi. Both empires had fallen victim to declining revenues, religious tensions, rebellions by provincial notables, and attacks by tribal warriors of Afghan or central Asian origin. The Ottoman Empire still existed despite a lengthening list of problems: chronic budgetary shortfalls, the de facto breakaway of provinces such as Egypt, stagnating trade, declining leadership, bureaucratic corruption, inflation, higher taxes, peasant violence, religiously inspired rebellion in Arabia, and a declining military. It was no longer the formidable power that had awed and worried Europeans in the 1500s.

In East Asia, decline came later. After more than a century of commercial growth, manageable population increases, and impressive military conquests, China faced a series of crises at the end of the eighteenth century. Military campaigns failed in Burma in the 1760s and Vietnam in 1788 and 1789; rural misery bred discontent as China's expanding population began to drive up rents and create land shortages; the bureaucracy, which had failed to expand to keep pace with China's growing population and territory, was hard pressed to carry out its functions effectively, and in any case, it increasingly was made up of officials more intent on profiting from graft and bribery than serving the emperor's subjects. The problems of Japan, still largely isolated from the outside world, seemed less severe, but even there, population growth, urbanization, and commercialization were putting strains on the social order.

By the early 1800s world relationships had undergone a historic shift in favor of a small group of states on the far western tip of the Eurasian landmass, a region that for millennia had played a minor role in history. By the early 1800s, however, these states had exported their languages, cultures, and ideas to two continents in the Western Hemisphere, gained political control of much of island Southeast Asia and parts of India, and established commercial ascendancy on the world's oceans. They had become the source of groundbreaking innovations in government and economics and were on the verge of establishing unprecedented dominance over the world.

Chapter 5

▼▼▼

Europe and the Americas in an Age of Science, Economic Growth, and Revolution

On October 24, 1648, the work of hundreds of diplomats and dozens of heads of state ended when signatures were affixed to the last agreements that collectively make up the Treaty of Westphalia, named after the northwest German territory where negotiations had taken place for the previous six years. With this, one of Europe's most devastating and demoralizing wars, the Thirty Years' War, came to an end. In no small measure because of this war's horrors and destructiveness, this was the last of the religious wars that had plagued Europe following the Protestants' break from the Roman Catholic Church in the sixteenth century. After a century of attempting to exterminate each other with armies, the executioner's axe, and instruments of the torture chamber, Protestants and Catholics accepted the permanence of Europe's religious divisions.

Religion was not the only area in which tensions eased in the second half of the seventeenth century. Conflicts between centralizing monarchs and independent-minded nobles and provinces ended in most European states with the triumph of absolute monarchs, who suppressed parliaments and claimed to rule by divine right. In only a handful of states, notably the Netherlands and England, were wealthy landowners and merchants successful in strengthening representative assemblies and limiting royal authority. In these states too, however, conflicts over fundamental, constitutional issues were resolved in the late 1600s.

A resolution of uncertainties also took place in the realm of ideas. The work of Isaac Newton (1642–1727) settled perplexing scientific issues that had emerged in the sixteenth century when Nicholaus Copernicus and others revealed the flaws of ancient Greek science but sought in vain for a coherent, all-encompassing model to replace it. Newton's theory of universal gravitation provided such a model. It enabled scientists to understand a host of natural phenomena, including the Earth's tides, the acceleration of falling bodies, and lunar and planetary movement. In the 1700s, the broad acceptance of Newton's theories along with advances in mathematics and other branches of science inspired confidence in human reason and the secularism of Europe's Age of Enlightenment.

Building on late-seventeenth-century foundations, in the eighteenth century Europe was more civil, more orderly, and more tranquil than it had been in hundreds of years. Wars were fought, but with military discipline tightened, religious tensions eased, and pitched battles rare, none matched the devastation of the Reformation era's religious wars. Steady economic growth, much of it fueled by trade with the Americas, modest inflation, and greater agricultural productivity, increased per capita wealth in Europe's expanding population. Peasant revolts and urban violence declined, and old class antagonisms seemed to have abated.

The Atlantic community's outward tranquility was deceptive, however. One does not have to look far below the surface to see tensions that led to anticolonial revolts in the Americas and revolutions in France and other European states at century's end. A host of issues — commercial, political, and ideological — increasingly divided the governments of Spain and Great Britain from colonists across the Atlantic who now considered themselves more American than European. In Europe discontent was also growing. Peasants, who as always were taxed to their limit and beyond, now faced land shortages and higher rents as a result of rural population growth. Artisans felt pinched by decades of gradual inflation. Many merchants, manufacturers, lawyers, and other members of the middle class prospered, but they resented the nobles' privileges and their rulers' ineptitude.

Their resentment, especially in France, was justified. While promoting themselves as defenders of liberty against royal tyranny, French nobles selfishly protected their privileges and tax exemptions even at the cost of bankrupting the state. Faced with spiraling deficits, Louis XV (r. 1715–1774) pursued his pleasures, and Louis XVI (r. 1774–1792) embraced then abandoned one solution after another. The intellectual atmosphere of the Age of Enlightenment, which fostered a belief in reason and progress, heightened political expectations, as did events in North America, where between 1776 and 1783 the thirteen colonies threw off British rule and established a new type of state based on constitutionalism and popular sovereignty. The meeting of the French representative assembly, the Estates General, in May 1789 was the first step toward a revolution in France that reverberated throughout Europe and ultimately affected every corner of the globe.

In England another revolution, an economic revolution, was also underway by century's end. The adoption of new spinning and weaving devices driven by water power and steam was transforming the textile industry, while new methods of smelting and casting brought fundamental changes to the production of iron. As guilds and domestic industry gave way to factory production, output soared, urban populations swelled, and work was redefined. These economic changes, collectively known as the Industrial Revolution, even more than the political revolution in France, reshaped the human condition.

▼▼▼

An Age of Science and Enlightenment

Although secularism had been a growing force in European intellectual life since the Italian Renaissance of the fourteenth and fifteenth centuries, only in the eighteenth century — the Age of Enlightenment — did it eclipse religion as the dominant influence on thought and culture. Organized churches, both Catholic and Protestant, still had millions of followers, and new religious movements such as Methodism in England were signs of continuing religious vitality. Nonetheless, the leading intellectuals of the eighteenth century were indifferent or openly hostile to religion, artists painted few religious scenes, and rulers gave little thought to religion in making political or diplomatic decisions.

The main inspiration for the secularism of the eighteenth century was the Scientific Revolution, especially the work of Isaac Newton (1642–1727). When Newton revealed the underlying physical laws that determined the movement of bodies throughout the universe, and did so without relying on religious inspiration or ancient authorities, he demonstrated to eighteenth-century intellectuals the full power of human reason. These intellectuals, known as *philosophes* (French for philosophers), were convinced that reason could be applied to social, political, and economic problems with results as spectacular as those achieved by seventeenth-century scientists. Specifically, reason could expose the weaknesses, flaws, and injustices inherited from Europe's "unenlightened" past. The philosophes were, therefore, social and political critics, known for their condemnation of their era's legal codes, schools, churches, government policies, wars, sexual mores, class privilege, and much else.

The Enlightenment was not, however, purely negative. The philosophes rejected passive acceptance of the status quo, and proclaimed that human beings through reason could plan and achieve a better future. They disagreed about what that future would be like, but none doubted that improvement of the human condition was not just possible, but inevitable, if only reason were given freedom to inquire, question, plan, and inspire.

Two Images of Seventeenth-Century Science
▼▼▼

35 ▼ *Sébastien Le Clerc,*
THE ROYAL ACADEMY AND ITS
PROTECTORS and A DISSECTION
AT THE JARDIN DES PLANTES

Many early participants in Europe's scientific revolution were solitary scholars who had relatively few contacts with others who shared their interests. By the late 1600s, however, the leading scientists were all members of one of several scientific societies, or academies, that supported and publicized their work and afforded opportunities for exchanging ideas. The four most prestigious academies were the Academy of Experiments (f. 1657), located in Florence and supported by Prince Leopold de Medici; the Royal Society of London (f. 1660), licensed but not financially supported by Charles II; the French Royal Academy of Sciences (f. 1661), supported by Louis XIV; and the Berlin Academy of Sciences (f. 1700), created under the auspices of King Frederick I of Brandenburg-Prussia. Although these academies varied in size and differed in their organization and activities, they all encouraged scientific investigation and contributed significantly to Europe's ongoing scientific development.

Many Europeans were introduced to the ideals and goals of the French Royal Academy of Sciences through the engravings of Sébastien Le Clerc (1637–1714), a gifted artist with a lifelong interest in mathematics and science. He made the engravings for many of the Academy's books and set a new standard for accurate scientific illustration. He also completed a series of engravings depicting the activities of the academicians themselves. These engravings appeared in several of the Academy's publications, with individual copies made for the king, interested courtiers, and collectors. Two of them are reproduced here.

The first, *The Royal Academy and Its Protectors* (1671), centers on Louis XIV, with two high nobles, the Prince of Condé and the Duke of Orléans, to his right and Colbert, the French controller general of finance, to his left. They are surrounded by members of the Academy and their scientific instruments. Through the window is seen a formal garden and the Royal Observatory, which is under construction. The second engraving is titled *A Dissection at the Jardin des Plantes* (1671). At the center two academicians are dissecting a fox, with their observations being recorded by the individual seated at their right. In the foreground Charles Perrault, a member of the Academy, points to a printed book where the results of the dissection will be published, and behind the table stands Le Clerc himself, who points to a page of his scientific engravings. On the far left two figures are making observations with a magnifying glass and a microscope, and on the right stand Colbert and another courtier.

Neither engraving is realistic. Louis XIV paid his first visit to the Academy in 1681, ten years after *The Royal Academy and Its Protectors* was engraved. And none of the Academy's rooms would have afforded a window view of the Royal Observatory. Furthermore, the room where dissections were carried out was notoriously rank, probably closer in appearance and smell to a butcher shop than the genteel scene portrayed by Le Clerc. The artist's goal, however, was not to depict the day-to-day reality of the Academy's activities but to communicate an idealized vision of the methods and purposes of contemporary science.

QUESTIONS FOR ANALYSIS

1. How many different pieces of scientific equipment can you identify in the engravings? What does the equipment and other paraphernalia reveal about the scientific interests and methodology of the academicians?
2. What is the significance of the picture toward which Colbert is pointing? What might be the significance of the map on the floor?
3. What point is Le Clerc trying to make about the Academy in the following details from the engraving of the dissection room: the two figures at the window, the figure pointing to the book, and the artist pointing to the page of engravings?
4. Note the formal gardens that can be seen through the windows in both engravings. What attitude toward nature is expressed in gardens such as these?

Sébastien Le Clerc, The Royal Academy and Its Protectors

Sébastien Le Clerc, A Dissection at the Jardin des Plantes

A Plea for Religious Understanding and Tolerance
▼▼▼

36 ▼ *Voltaire, TREATISE ON TOLERATION*

François-Marie Arouet (1694–1778), better known by his pen name, Voltaire, combined wit, literary elegance, and a passionate social conscience in a long literary career that best represents the values and spirit of the Age of Enlightenment. Born into a well-to-do Parisian bourgeois family, Voltaire published his first work, the tragic drama *Oedipus,* in 1717. In the next sixty-one years he wrote thousands of poems, histories, satires, novels, short stories, essays, and reviews. The European reading public avidly bought his works, making him one of the first authors to make a large fortune through the sale of his writings.

Although Voltaire's enormous output and popularity ensured his influence on the Enlightenment at many different levels, one particular contribution stands out: his devotion to the principles of toleration and freedom of thought. Voltaire was convinced that throughout history, the intolerance of organized religions, not just Christianity, had caused much of the world's suffering. He was angered that even in the "enlightened" eighteenth century, Protestant-Catholic enmity still resulted in episodes such as the torture and execution of Jean Calas, a French Protestant convicted unjustly of murdering his son, supposedly after learning of the son's intent to become a Catholic. Voltaire's devotion to toleration is revealed in the following selection, taken from his *Treatise on Toleration,* written in 1763 in response to the execution of Calas.

QUESTIONS FOR ANALYSIS

1. Does Voltaire believe that intolerance is a special trait of Christianity or that it characterizes other organized religions as well?
2. What point is Voltaire trying to make in his reference to the various dialects of the Italian language?
3. What does Voltaire suggest as the essence of a truly religious person?
4. What attitude toward humankind does Voltaire express in the "Prayer to God"?
5. What does the excerpt tell us about Voltaire's views of the nature of God?

OF UNIVERSAL TOLERANCE

No great art or studied eloquence is needed to prove that Christians should tolerate one another. I go even further and declare that we must look upon all men as our brothers. But the Turk, my brother? the Chinese, the Jew, the Siamese? Yes, of course; are we not all the children of one father and creatures of the same God?

But these people despise us; they call us idolators! Then I'll tell them they are quite wrong. I think I could at least shock the proud obstinacy of an imam[1] if I said to them something like this:

This little globe, nothing more than a point, rolls in space like so many other globes; we are lost in this immensity. Man, some five feet tall, is surely a very small part of the universe. One of these imperceptible beings says to some of his neighbors in Arabia or Africa: "Listen to me, for the God of all these worlds has enlightened me: there are nine hundred million little ants like us on the earth, but only my anthill is beloved of God; He will hold all others in horror through all eternity; only mine will be blessed, the others will be eternally wretched."

At that, they would cut me short and ask what fool made that stupid remark. I would be obliged to reply, "You yourselves." Then I would try to mollify them; but that would not be easy.

I would speak now to the Christians and dare say, for example, to a Dominican Inquisitor,[2] "My brother, you know that every province in Italy has its dialect, and people in Venice and Bergamo speak differently from those in Florence. The Academy della Crusca[3] has standardized the language; its dictionary is an inescapable authority, and Buonmattei's[4] grammar is an absolute and infallible guide; but do you believe that the head of the Academy and in his absence, Buonmattei, would have been able in all good conscience to cut out the tongues of all those from Venice and Bergamo who persisted in using their own dialect?"

The Inquisitor replies: "There is a great difference; here it's a question of your salvation. It's for your own good the Director of the Inquisition orders that you be seized on the testimony of a single person, no matter how infamous or criminal he may be; that you have no lawyer to defend you; that the very name of your accuser be unknown to you; that the Inquisitor promise you grace and then condemn you; that you undergo five different degrees of torture and then be whipped or sent to the galleys, or ceremoniously burned at the stake. . . .

I would take the liberty of replying: "My brother, perhaps you are right: I am convinced that you wish me well, but couldn't I be saved without all that?"

To be sure, these horrible absurdities do not soil the face of the earth everyday, but they are frequent enough, and a whole volume could easily be written about them much longer than the Gospels which condemn them. Not only is it very cruel to persecute in this brief existence of ours those who differ from us in opinion, but I am afraid it is being bold indeed to pronounce their eternal damnation. It hardly seems fitting for us atoms of the moment, for that is all we are, to presume to know in advance the decrees of our own Creator. . . .

Oh, sectarians of a merciful God, if you had a cruel heart, if, while adoring Him whose only law consists in the words: "Love God and thy neighbor as thyself (Luke X, 27)," you had overloaded this pure and holy law with sophisms and incomprehensible disputations; if you had lighted the torch of discord either over a new word or a single letter of the alphabet; if you had made eternal punishment the penalty for the omission of a few words or ceremonies which other nations could not know about, I would say to you, as I wept in compassion for mankind: "Transport yourselves with me to the day when all men will be judged and when God will do unto each man according to his works."

"I see all the dead of all centuries, past and present, appear before His presence. Are you quite sure that our Creator and Father will say to the wise and virtuous Confucius, to Solon the law-giver, to Pythagoras, Zaleucus, Socrates, and Plato, to the divine Antoninus, good Trajan, and

---

[1]In this context, a Muslim prayer leader at a mosque.
[2]A Catholic official responsible for uncovering and punishing erroneous belief, or heresy.

[3]The Florentine Academy of Letters, founded in 1582.
[4]A seventeenth-century Italian grammarian.

Titus, the flowering of mankind, to Epictetus and so many other model men:[5] "Go, you monsters; go and suffer punishment, limitless in time and intensity, eternal as I am eternal. And you, my beloved, Jean Chatel, Ravaillac, Damiens, Cartouche, etc.,[6] who died according to the prescribed formulas, share forever at my right hand my empire and my felicity."

You draw back in horror from these words, and since they escaped me, I have no more to say.

PRAYER TO GOD

I no longer address myself to men, but to thee, God of all beings, all worlds, and all ages. If indeed it is allowable for feeble creatures, lost in immensity and imperceptible to the rest of the universe, to dare ask anything of Thee who hast given all things, whose decrees are as immutable as they are eternal, deign to look with compassion upon the failings inherent in our nature, and grant that these failings lead us not into calamity.

Thou didst not give us hearts that we should hate each other or hands that we should cut each other's throats. Grant that we may help each other bear the burden of our painful and brief lives; that the slight difference in the clothing with which we cover our puny bodies, in our inadequate tongues, in all our ridiculous customs, in all our imperfect laws, in all our insensate opinions, in all our stations in life so disproportionate in our eyes but so equal in Thy sight, that all these little variations that differentiate the atoms called *man,* may not be the signals for hatred and persecution. . . .

May all men remember that they are brothers; may they hold in horror tyranny that is exercised over souls, just as they hold in execration the brigandage that snatches away by force the fruits of labor and peaceful industry. If the scourge of war is inevitable, let us not hate each other, let us not tear each other apart in the lap of peace; but let us use the brief moment of our existence in blessing in a thousand different tongues, from Siam to California, Thy goodness which has bestowed this moment upon us.

---

[5]These were moralists, enlightened political leaders, and philosophers who had lived before the coming of Christianity.

[6]Five notorious criminals from Voltaire's day.

An Affirmation of Human Progress

▼▼▼

37 ▼ *Marquis de Condorcet,* *SKETCH OF THE PROGRESS OF THE HUMAN MIND*

Throughout history most human beings have valued tradition and resisted change. Reform of governments and religious institutions was deemed possible, but it typically did not mean going forward to institute something new but going back to recapture features of a lost golden age. Thinkers who studied the past and contemplated the future concluded that the human condition had always been more or less the same, or that history ran in cycles, or that it was the story of gradual decline from a mythological state of perfection. Only in the West in the eighteenth and nineteenth centuries did intellectuals and much of the general populace come to believe that the past was a burden and that human beings could bring about changes in their condition that were beneficial, not destructive. In a word, people began to believe in progress.

The West's belief in progress can be traced back to the eighteenth-century Enlightenment, when many thinkers became convinced that well-intentioned human beings could employ reason to erase at least some of the cruelties, superstitions, and prejudices that had diminished the human condition in the past. By the end of the eighteenth century some went further and developed a theory of progress that saw humanity ascending from ignorance and darkness to a utopian future. The most famous prophet of progress was the Marquis de Condorcet (1743–1794), a mathematician, philosopher, and educational reformer. He supported the French Revolution but, like many moderates, fell afoul of the radical Jacobins and was forced to go into hiding in July 1793. It was then he wrote his *Sketch of the Progress of the Human Mind,* which traces human progress in ten stages from the dawn of history to the French Revolution and beyond. Having completed his work in March 1794, he emerged from hiding, was arrested immediately, and was found dead the next morning of unknown causes.

The following excerpts come from "The Ninth Epoch," in which he discusses developments from the mid seventeenth century to the beginning of the French Revolution, and "The Tenth Epoch," in which he describes the future.

QUESTIONS FOR ANALYSIS

1. What factors, according to Condorcet, have impeded progress in the past?
2. According to Condorcet, scientific achievement was the outstanding feature of humanity's "ninth stage." In what ways did science in this era change human thinking and affect human society?
3. Condorcet is not proud of the Europeans' record in dealing with the peoples of Asia, Africa, and the Americas. What groups does he blame for the Europeans' unenlightened behavior in these regions?
4. Why is Condorcet confident that Europeans will modify their behavior in Asia and Africa? What will be the result? Does Condorcet show any interest in preserving the customs and beliefs of the Asians and Africans?
5. What in Condorcet's view caused the oppression of women in the past? Why does he reject such oppression, and what positive results in his view will result from ending it?
6. What role will technology play in humanity's tenth stage? How are Condorcet's views on this issue similar to those expressed by Francis Bacon (source 25)?

NINTH EPOCH

From Descartes to the Formation
of the French Republic

Until now we have demonstrated the progress of philosophy only in those men who have culti-

vated, deepened, and perfected it: it now remains to reveal what have been its effects on general opinion, and how reason . . . learned how to preserve itself from the errors into which respect for authority and the imagination have often dragged it: at the same time it destroyed within the general mass of people the prejudices that have afflicted and corrupted the human race for so long a time.

Humanity was finally permitted to boldly proclaim the long ignored right to submit every opinion to reason, that is, to utilize the only instrument given to us for grasping and recognizing the truth. Each human learned with a sort of pride that nature had never destined him to believe the word of others. The superstitions of antiquity and the abasement of reason before the madness of supernatural religion disappeared from society just as they had disappeared from philosophy. . . .

If we were to limit ourselves to showing the benefits derived from the immediate applications of the sciences, or in their applications to man-made devices for the well-being of individuals and the prosperity of nations, we would be making known only a slim part of their benefits. The most important, perhaps, is having destroyed prejudices and re-established human intelligence, which until then had been forced to bend down to false instructions instilled in it by absurd beliefs passed on to the children of each generation by the terrors of superstition and the fear of tyranny. . . .

The advances of scientific knowledge are all the more deadly to these errors because they destroy them without appearing to attack them, while lavishing on those who stubbornly defend them the degrading taunt of ignorance. . . .

Finally this progress of scientific knowledge . . . results in a belief that not birth, professional status, or social standing gives anyone the right to judge something he does not understand. This unstoppable progress cannot be observed without having enlightened men search unceasingly for ways to make the other branches of learning follow the same path. It offers them at every step a model to follow, according to which they will be able to judge their own efforts and recognize false paths on which they have embarked. It protects them from skepticism, credulity, blind caution, and even exaggerated submission to the knowledgeable and famous. . . .

TENTH EPOCH

The Future Progress of the Human Mind

Our hopes for the future of the human species may be reduced to three important points: the destruction of inequality among nations; the progress of equality within nations themselves; and finally, the real improvement of humanity. Should not all the nations of the world approach one day the state of civilization reached by the most enlightened peoples such as the French and the Anglo-Americans? Will not the slavery of nations subjected to kings, the barbarity of African tribes, and the ignorance of savages gradually disappear? Are there on the globe countries whose very nature has condemned them never to enjoy liberty and never exercise their reason? . . .

If we cast an eye at the existing state of the globe, we will see right away that in Europe the principles of the French constitution are already those of all enlightened men. We will see that they are too widely disseminated and too openly professed for the efforts of tyrants and priests to prevent them from penetrating into the hovels of their slaves, where they will soon rekindle those embers of good sense and that muffled indignation that the habit of suffering and terror have failed to totally extinguish in the minds of the oppressed. . . .

Can it be doubted that either wisdom or the senseless feuds of the European nations themselves, working with the slow but certain effects of progress in their colonies, will not soon produce the independence of the new world; and that then the European population, spreading rapidly across that immense land, must either civilize or make disappear the savage peoples that now inhabit these vast continents?

If one runs through the history of our undertakings and establishments in Africa and Asia, you will see our commercial monopolies, our treacheries, our bloodthirsty contempt for people of a different color and belief; the insolence of our usurpations; the extravagant missionary activities and intrigues of our priests which destroy their feelings of respect and benevolence that the superiority of our enlightenment and the advantages of our commerce had first obtained. But the moment is approaching, without any doubt, when ceasing to present ourselves to these peoples as tyrants or corrupters, we will become instruments of their improvement and their noble liberators. . . .

> ▷ Slavery will be abolished, free trade established on the world's oceans, and European political authority in Asia and Africa ended.

Then the Europeans, limiting themselves to free trade, too knowledgeable of their own rights to show contempt for the rights of others, will respect this independence that until now they have violated with such audacity. Then their settlements, instead of being filled with government favorites by virtue of their rank or privileges who hasten by pillaging and dishonesty to amass fortunes so they can return to Europe to buy honors and titles, will be populated by hard-working men, seeking in these happy climates the affluence that eluded them in their homeland. . . . These settlements of robbers will become colonies of citizens who will plant in Africa and Asia the principles and the example of European liberty, enlightenment, and reason. In place of clergy who carry to these people nothing but the most shameful superstitions and who disgust them and menace them with a new form of domination, one will see men taking their place who are devoted to spreading among the nations useful truths about their happiness, and explaining to them both the concept of their own interest and of their rights. . . .

Thus the day will come when the sun will shine only on free men born knowing no other master but their reason; where tyrants and their slaves, priests and their ignorant, hypocritical writings will exist only in the history books and theaters; where we will only be occupied with mourning their victims and their dupes; when we will maintain an active vigilance by remembering their horrors; when we will learn to recognize and stifle by the force of reason the first seeds of superstition and tyranny, if ever they dare to appear! . . .

> ▷ Condorcet explains how education and scientific knowledge will be made available to all.

If we consider the human creations based on scientific theories, we shall see that their progress can have no limits; that the procedures in constructing them can be improved and simplified just like those of scientific procedures; that new tools, machines, and looms will add every day to the capabilities and skill of humans; they will improve and perfect the precision of their products while decreasing the amount of time and labor needed to produce them. Then the obstacles in the path of this progress will disappear, accidents will be foreseen and prevented, the unhealthful conditions that are due either to the work itself or the climate will be eliminated.

A smaller piece of land will be able to produce commodities of greater usefulness and value than before; greater benefits will be obtained with less waste; the production of the same industrial product will result in less destruction of raw materials and greater durability. We will be able to choose for each type of soil the production of goods that will satisfy the greatest number of wants and with the least amount of labor and expenditure. Thus without any sacrifice, the means of achieving conservation and limiting waste will follow the progress of the art of producing various goods, preparing them, and making them into finished products. Thus . . . each individual will work less but more productively and will be able to better satisfy his needs. . . .

Among the advances of the human mind we should reckon as most important for the general welfare is the complete destruction of those prejudices that have established an inequality of rights between the sexes, an inequality damaging even to the party it favors. One will look in vain for reasons to justify it on the basis of differences in physical make up, the strength of intellect, and moral sensibility. This inequality has no other root cause than the abuse of force, and it is to no purpose to try to excuse it through sophistical arguments. We will show how the abolition of practices condoned by this prejudice will increase the well-being of families and encourage domestic virtues, the prime foundation of all others; how it will favor the progress of education, and especially make it truly universal, partly because it will be extended to both sexes more equitably, and partly because it cannot be truly universal even for males without the cooperation of mothers in families. . . .

The most enlightened people, having seized for themselves the right to control their life and treasure, will slowly come to perceive war as the deadliest plague and the most monstrous of crimes. . . . They will understand that they cannot become conquerors without losing their liberty; that perpetual alliances are the only way to preserve independence; and that they should seek their security, not power. . . .

We may conclude then that the perfectibility of humanity is indefinite. However, until now, we have imagined humanity with the same natural abilities and physical make-up as at the present. How great will our certitude be, and how limitless our hopes, if one were to believe that these natural abilities themselves, this physical make-up, are also capable of improvement? This is the last question we shall consider.

The organic perfectibility or degeneration of species of plants and animals may be regarded as one of the general laws of nature. This law is also applicable to the human species. No one can doubt that progress in preventive medicine, the use of healthier food and housing, a way of living that increases strength through exercise without destroying it through excess, and finally, the destruction of the two most persistent causes of deterioration, poverty and excessive wealth, will lengthen for human beings the average life span and assure more good health and a stronger constitution. Clearly, improvements in medical practices resulting from the progress of reason and the order of society, will cause transmittable and contagious diseases to disappear as well as diseases caused by climate, nourishment, and certain vocations. . . . Would it be absurd then to imagine . . . that we will arrive at a time when death will be nothing more than the result of extraordinary accidents or of the gradual destruction of vital forces, and that as a result, the interval between birth and the time of that destruction will no longer have a fixed term? . . .

Finally, can we not also extend the same hopes to the intellectual and moral faculties? . . . Is it not also probable that education, while perfecting these qualities, will also influence, modify, and improve that bodily nature itself? Analogy, analysis of the development of human faculties, and even certain facts seem to prove the reality of such conjectures, which extend even further the limits of our hopes. . . .

How much does this picture of the human species, freed of all chains, released from the empire of blind fate and the enemies of progress, and marching with a firm and sure pace on the path of truth, virtue, and honor, present the philosopher with a scene that consoles him for the errors, crimes, and injustices that still defile the earth and often victimize him? In contemplation of this scene he receives the reward for his efforts on behalf of the advance of reason and the defense of liberty. . . . Such contemplation is a place of refuge where the memories of his persecutors cannot follow him, where living with the thought of humans established in their natural rights and dignity, he forgets the way greed, fear, and envy have tormented and corrupted them. It is there he truly exists with his fellow humans in an Elysium[1] which his reason has created and which his love of humanity adorns with the purest pleasures.

---

[1]In Greek mythology, Elysium, also known as the Elysian Fields or the Isles of the Blessed, was the dwelling place after death of virtuous mortals or those given immortality by divine favor.

▼▼▼

From Mercantilism to Laissez Faire

During the seventeenth and eighteenth centuries, European governments pursued a policy known as *mercantilism,* a system of economic regulation designed to strengthen the state and increase its gold and silver supply by encouraging industry, the growth of commerce, and self-sufficiency in agriculture and the production of raw materials. Although Europe's national and local governments had regulated economic activities since the Middle Ages, mercantilism was a new approach to regulation that reflected the growing competitiveness of the European state system and the authority of the absolutist state. Mercantilists viewed economic activity as a form of warfare in which each nation competed for economic advantages that would augment tax revenue, increase the amount of gold and silver in circulation, maintain high employment, and sustain a favorable balance of trade, all at the expense of its rivals. On balance, its early impact was positive, with government encouragement of commerce and protection of industries contributing to Europe's economic expansion.

By the eighteenth century, however, mercantilism had many critics who argued that it inflated prices, stifled innovation, and smothered the entrepreneurial spirit. In addition, mercantilism was opposed by many intellectuals connected with the Enlightenment who prized individual liberty, deplored government intrusiveness, and were convinced that a nation's economy, like nature itself, worked best when its own "natural laws" operated without interference. The critics of mercantilism in France were known as *Physiocrats,* a term rooted in the Greek words meaning the "rule of nature."

The most famous critic of mercantilism was a Scot, Adam Smith, whose *Wealth of Nations* (1776) called for free trade, the end of government regulation, and economic competition at every level. His disciples, the economic liberals of the nineteenth century, sought to convince governments to abandon mercantilism, and by doing so, freeing thousands of investors and entrepreneurs to take advantage of the unparalleled opportunities provided by industrialization.

The Advantages of Mercantilism

▼▼▼

38 ▼ *Jean-Baptiste Colbert,* "MEMORANDUM ON ENGLISH ALLIANCES" and "MEMORANDUM TO THE KING ON FINANCES"

Born to a family of merchants in Reims in 1619, Jean-Baptiste Colbert was the best known and most powerful minister of Louis XIV (r. 1643–1715). During the 1660s Colbert held several positions in the royal administration, the most important of which was controller-general of finance. Colbert's goal was to strengthen the French economy to provide Louis the resources necessary to fight his wars. No statesman better represents the policies of seventeenth-century mercantilism; for the French, the words *mercantilisme* and *Colbertisme* are virtually synonymous.

The following selection consists of excerpts from two memoranda Colbert prepared for King Louis XIV. The first, which dates from 1669, was written while French and English diplomats were secretly negotiating a possible Anglo-French alliance against their common commercial rival, the Dutch. The second, written in 1670, describes the goals and achievements of Colbert's economic policies during his tenure as controller-general.

QUESTIONS FOR ANALYSIS

1. Why is Colbert convinced that French commercial expansion can come only at the expense of France's economic competitors?
2. To what degree are Colbert's policies motivated by a wish to improve economic conditions among the French people?
3. What social and economic groups in France would stand to benefit most from Colbert's policies? Who would be hurt?
4. What is the basis of Colbert's conviction that international commerce is a form of war?
5. What industries is Colbert especially interested in encouraging? What do his choices reveal about the general purposes of French mercantilism?

MEMORANDUM ON ENGLISH ALLIANCES (1669)

The commerce of all Europe is carried on by ships of every size to the number of 20,000, and it is perfectly obvious that this number cannot be increased, because the number of people in all states remains the same and the consumption of goods also remains the same. . . .

It must be added that commerce causes a perpetual combat both in peacetime and during war among the nations of Europe as to who will win the most of it. . . . Each nation works incessantly to have its legitimate share of it and to gain an advantage over other nations. The Dutch currently are fighting this war with 15,000 to 16,000 ships, a government of merchants, all of whose principles and power are directed solely toward preservation and increase of their commerce, and more dedication, hard work, and thrift than any other nation.

The English fight with 3,000 to 4,000 vessels, less industriousness and attention, and more expenses. The French fight with 500 to 600 ships. The last two cannot improve their commerce except by increasing their number of vessels, and cannot increase this number except from the 20,000 that carry all the commerce, and consequently by cutting into the 15,000 or 16,000 of the Dutch.

MEMORANDUM TO THE KING ON FINANCES (1670)

. . . The well-being and economic recovery of the people depend on apportioning what they pay into the public treasury with the amount of money that circulates in commerce. This ratio has always been 150 million livres[1] to 45 million livres. At present it is at 120 million to 70 million. As a result, it is in excess by a wide margin, and as would be expected, the people are falling into great misery.

It will be necessary to do one of two things to stop this evil: either lower tax impositions and expenditures, or increase the amount of money in public commerce. For the first, impositions have been lowered already. . . . For the second, it consists of three parts: increase money in public commerce by attracting it from other lands; by keeping it inside the kingdom and keeping it from leaving; by giving the people the means to make a profit.

In these points consist the greatness and the power of the state and the magnificence of the king, . . . and this magnificence is all the greater in that it weakens at the same time all the neighboring states, because, there being only a given quantity of money circulating in all of Europe, and this quantity is increased from time to time by what comes in from the West Indies, it is certain and clear if there is only 150,000,000 livres that circulate publicly in France, that one cannot succeed in increasing it . . . without at the same time taking the same quantity from neighboring states; which is the cause of the double success of the past few years, the one increasing the power and greatness of your majesty, the other abasing that of his enemies and those who are jealous of him.

Thus in these three areas was concentrated all the work and attention to finances since the beginning of your majesty's administration; and since it is commerce alone and what depends on it that can produce such a great result, it was a task to introduce it into the realm because neither the general population nor individuals have applied themselves to it, and in a way it is even contrary to the genius of the nation. . . . For this,

it was necessary to see what was done to attract money into the kingdom and to keep it there; . . .

The Dutch, English, and other nations take from the kingdom wine, brandy, vinegars, linen, paper, articles of clothing, and wheat when needed. . . . But they brought us woolen cloth and other goods made of wool and animal hair; sugar, tobacco, and indigo from the Americas; all the spices, drugs, [illegible word] in oils, silks, cotton cloths, leather goods, and an infinity of other goods from the East Indies; the same merchandise from the Levant.[2] . . . All the merchandise necessary for ship construction, such as wood, masts, iron from Sweden and Galicia,[3] copper, tar, cannons, hemp, rope, tin coated sheet iron, brass, navigation instruments, musket balls, iron anchors, and generally everything necessary for the construction of vessels for the fleet for the king and for his subjects.

Gunpowder, fuses, muskets, cannon shot, lead, pewter, clothes, serge[4] from London, silk and wool stockings from London, barracans, damask, camlet, and other fabrics from Flanders, lacework from Venice and Holland, trimming from Flanders, camlet from Brussels, carpets of Flanders; beef and mutton from Germany, hides and horses from every land, silk fabrics from Milan, Genoa, and Holland. . . .

By these means . . . the Dutch, English, merchants of Hamburg, and others bring into the kingdom a quantity of merchandise much greater than they take away, withdraw the surplus in cash, which produced both their prosperity and the poverty of the kingdom, and as a result, unquestionably, added to their power and our weakness.

It is necessary next to examine the steps taken to change this fate. First, in 1662, your majesty sustained the right to 50 *sols*[5] for ton of freight carried on foreign vessels, which has had the

---

[1]The livre was the basic unit of French money.
[2]Lands along the eastern shore of the Mediterranean.
[3]A region of northwestern Spain.
[4]Serge is a fabric, as are barracan, damask, camlet, dimities,

and twills, all mentioned later in Colbert's memorandum.
[5]A *sol* was a French coin equal to one-twentieth of a livre. Colbert is referring to the royal tariff of 1662.

impressive result that the number of French ships has increased every year, and in seven or eight years the Dutch have been almost excluded from port-to-port commerce. . . . Finally, after carefully considering the matter, your majesty ordered the tariff of 1664, in which the duties are regulated by a completely different principle, that is, all the merchandise and manufactured goods of the realm were notably favored, and the prices of foreign goods increased; . . . this change began to offer the opportunity to manufacture these same items in the kingdom; and to this end:

The fabric manufacture of Sedan was re-established, and the number of looms increased from 12 to 62. New establishments have been built at Abbeville, Dieppe, Fecamp, and Rouen, at which there are presently more than 200 looms; the factory for barracan was established at Ferte-sous-Jouarre with 120 looms; a factory for small Brussels damask at Meaux, composed of 80 looms; a carpet factory in the same city with 20 looms; for camlets at Amiens and Abbeville with 120 looms; dimities and twills of Bruges and Brussels at Montmorin, St. Quentin, and Avranches, with 30 looms; for fine Dutch linens, at Bresle, Louviers, Laval, and other places, with 200 looms; serge of London at Gournay, Auxerre, Autun, and other places with 300 looms; English woolen stockings . . . in 32 towns and cities; that for tin in Nivernois; that for French lace in 52 towns and cities, in which more than 20,000 workers toil; the making of brass established in Champagne; brass wire in Burgundy; gold thread of Milan in Lyons; the manufacture of silks in the same city.

The search for saltpeter,[6] and at the same time the manufacture of gunpowder; that of match; the establishment of the manufacture of muskets and weapons of all sorts . . . ; the distribution of stud horses, which has produced and certainly will continue to produce the re-establishment of stud farms and will considerably decrease the import of foreign horses. . . .

And since your majesty wished to work hard for the restoration of his navy . . . it was absolutely necessary to try hard to find within the kingdom, or to establish everything needed for the great design.

To this end, the manufacture of tar was established at Médoc, Auvergne, Dauphiné and Provence; iron cannons in Burgundy, Nivernois, Saintonge, and Périgord; anchors in Dauphiné, Nivernois, Brittany, and Rochefort; sailcloth in Dauphiné; cloth for banners at Auvergne; pilots' instruments at Dieppe and la Rochelle; wood cutting for ships . . . ; wood for masts, which was unknown in the kingdom, has been found in Provence, Languedoc, Auvergne, Dauphiné, and in the Pyrenees. Iron, which was obtained from Sweden and Biscay, is now made within the kingdom. High quality hemp for rope, which came from Prussia and Piedmont, is now obtained from Burgundy, Maconnais, Bresse, and Dauphiné.

In a word, everything needed for the construction of vessels is at present established in the kingdom, so that your majesty can do without foreigners for the navy, and even in a short time can supply them with what they need and extract their money. . . .

In addition, to prevent the Dutch from profiting from American commerce, which they have gotten hold of and excluded the French, with annual profits of a million livres in gold, your majesty has established the West India Company and invested in it almost 4 million livres; he has also had the satisfaction of taking away from the Dutch that million livres per year that maintained more than 4,000 of their subjects who continually sailed among these islands on their 200 ships. . . . In addition, to prevent the same Dutch from taking more than 10 million livres out of the kingdom through all the goods they bring from the East Indies and the Levant, your majesty formed companies for the same areas, in which he has invested more than 5 million livres. . . .

---

[6]Potassium nitrate, used in making gunpowder.

All these great undertakings, however, and an infinity of others that are in a sense innovations . . . are still in their infancy and can be carried to perfection only with work and stubborn application and can exist only with the resources of the state, since considerable expenditures are always necessary to support all of this great system. . . .

Capitalism's Prophet
▼▼▼
39 ▼ Adam Smith, THE WEALTH OF NATIONS

Surprisingly few biographical details are known about Adam Smith, the economist famed for his devastating critique of mercantilism in *The Wealth of Nations.* Born in 1723 in a small Scottish fishing village and receiving his university education at Glasgow and Oxford, between 1751 and 1763 he held chairs in logic and moral philosophy at the University of Glasgow. The publication of his *Theory of Moral Sentiments* in 1759 ensured his literary and philosophical reputation. In 1763 he became the tutor of an English aristocrat's son and lived for three years in France, where he met many prominent French intellectuals. From 1767 to 1776 he lived in semiretirement in Scotland and finished *The Wealth of Nations,* published in 1776. In 1778 he became commissioner of customs in Scotland and died in Edinburgh in 1790.

The Wealth of Nations went through five English editions and was published in several European translations in the eighteenth century. Its importance lies in its general approach to economics, which brought systematic analysis to wages, labor, trade, population, rents, and money supply, and in its unrelenting assault on mercantilism. Unlike mercantilists like Colbert, who believed that wealth and overall economic activity were essentially fixed, Smith believed in economic growth, which could best be achieved not through regulation but through free competition among individuals and nations.

— free market

QUESTIONS FOR ANALYSIS

1. Smith denies that a nation's wealth consists of the amount of gold and silver it controls. What arguments does he present to defend his position, and what are their implications for trade policy?
2. Smith proposes that each individual by pursuing his or her own self-interest promotes the general welfare of society. What examples of this paradox does he provide? What implications does this paradox have for government policy?
3. What groups in society would you expect to be most enthusiastic about Smith's ideas? Why? What groups might be expected to oppose them?
4. The novelty of Smith's ideas can best be understood by comparing them with those of Colbert (source 38). How do the two men disagree about the following issues: (a) the benefits of government economic regulation, (b) economic competition among nations, and (c) the meaning of the balance of trade?

SELF-INTEREST AND THE FREE MARKET

1. This division of labor,[1] from which so many advantages are derived, is not originally the effect of any human wisdom, which foresees and intends that general opulence to which it gives occasion. It is the necessary, though very slow and gradual consequence of a certain propensity in human nature which has in view no such extensive utility; the propensity to truck,[2] barter, and exchange one thing for another.

2. . . . It is common to all men, and to be found in no other race of animals, which seem to know neither this nor any other species of contracts. . . . Nobody ever saw a dog make a fair and deliberate exchange of one bone for another with another dog. Nobody ever saw one animal by its gestures and natural cries signify to another, this is mine, that yours; I am willing to give this for that. . . . In almost every other race of animals each individual, which it is grown up to maturity, is entirely independent, and in its natural state has occasion for the assistance of no other living creature. But man has almost constant occasion for the help of his brethren, and it is in vain for him to expect it from their benevolence only. He will be more likely to prevail if he can interest their self-love in his favor, and show them that it is for their own advantage to do for him what he requires of them. Whoever offers to another a bargain of any kind, proposes to do this. Give me that which I want, and you shall have this which you want, is the meaning of every such offer; and it is in this manner that we obtain from one another the far greater part of those good offices which we stand in need of. It is not from the benevolence of the butcher, the brewer, or the baker, that we expect our dinner, but from their regard to their own interest. We address ourselves, not to their humanity but to their self-love, and never talk to them of our own necessities but of their advantages. . . .

PRICES AND THE FREE MARKET

. . . It is the interest of all those who employ their land, labor, or stock,[3] in bringing any commodity to market, that the quantity never should exceed the effectual demand; and it is the interest of all other people that it never should fall short of that demand.

If at any time it exceeds the effectual demand, some of the component parts of its price must be paid below their natural rate. If it is rent,[4] the interest of the landlords will immediately prompt them to withdraw a part of their land; and if it is wages or profit, the interest of the laborers in the one case, and of their employers in the other, will prompt them to withdraw a part of their labor or stock from this employment. The quantity brought to market will soon be no more than sufficient to supply the effectual demand. All the different parts of its price will rise to their natural rate, and the whole price to its natural price.

If, on the contrary, the quantity brought to market should at any time fall short of the effectual demand, some of the component parts of its price must rise above their natural rate. If it is rent, the interest of all other landlords will naturally prompt them to prepare more land for the raising of this commodity; if it is wages or profit, the interest of all other laborers and dealers will soon prompt them to employ more labor and stock in preparing and bringing it to market. The quantity brought thither will soon be sufficient to supply the effectual demand. All the different parts of its price will soon sink to their natural rate, and the whole price to its natural price. . . .

---

[1]This section follows Smith's discussion of the *division of labor.* He uses this term in reference to economic specialization, both in terms of different professions and in terms of the separate tasks carried out by different individuals in the process of manufacturing or preparing commodities for the market.

[2]A synonym for barter.

[3]Money or capital invested or available for investment or trading.

[4]In this sense, the cost of land; payments made by tenants to their landlord.

The monopolists, by keeping the market constantly under-stocked, by never fully supplying the effectual demand, sell their commodities much above the natural price, and raise their emoluments,[5] whether they consist in wages or profit, greatly above their natural rate.

The price of monopoly is upon every occasion the highest which can be got. The natural price, or the price of free competition, on the contrary, is the lowest which can be taken, not upon every occasion, indeed, but for any considerable time together. The one is upon every occasion the highest which can be squeezed out of the buyers, or which, it is supposed, they will consent to give: The other is the lowest which the sellers can commonly afford to take, and at the same time continue their business.

The exclusive privileges of corporations, statutes of apprenticeship,[6] and all those laws which restrain . . . the competition to a smaller number than might otherwise go into them, have the same tendency, though in a less degree. They are a sort of enlarged monopolies, and may frequently, for ages together and in whole classes of employments, keep up the market price of particular commodities above the natural price, and maintain both the wages of the labor and the profits of the stock employed about them somewhat above their natural rate.

MERCANTALIST FALLACIES

. . . A rich country, in the same manner as a rich man, is supposed to be a country abounding in money; and to heap up gold and silver in any country is supposed to be the readiest way to enrich it. . . .

In consequence of these popular notions, all the different nations of Europe have studied, though to little purpose, every possible means of accumulating gold and silver in their respective countries. Spain and Portugal, the proprietors of the principal mines which supply Europe with

those metals, have either prohibited their exportation under the severest penalties, or subjected it to a considerable duty. The like prohibition seems anciently to have [been] made a part of the policy of most other European nations. When those countries became commercial, the merchants found this prohibition, upon many occasions, extremely inconvenient. . . .

They represented [stated forcefully], first, that the exportation of gold and silver in order to purchase foreign goods, did not always diminish the quantity of those metals in the kingdom. . . .

They represented, secondly, that this prohibition could not hinder the exportation of gold and silver, which, on account of the smallness of their bulk in proportion to their value, could easily be smuggled abroad. . . .

Those arguments . . . were solid. . . . But they were sophistical in supposing, that either to preserve or to augment the quantity of those metals required more the attention of government, than to preserve or to augment the quantity of any other useful commodities, which the freedom of trade, without any such attention, never fails to supply in the proper quantity. . . .

A country that has no mines of its own must undoubtedly draw its gold and silver from foreign countries, in the same manner as one that has no vineyards of its own must draw its wines. It does not seem necessary, however, that the attention of government should be more turned towards the one than towards the other object. A country that has wherewithal to buy wine, will always get the wine which it has occasion for; and a country that has wherewithal to buy gold and silver, will never be in want of those metals. They are to be bought for a certain price like all other commodities, and as they are the price of all other commodities, so all other commodities are the price of those metals. We trust with perfect security that the freedom of trade, without any attention of government, will always supply us with the wine which we have occasion for:

---

[5]The returns from employment, usually in the form of compensation.

[6]Laws that restricted the number of individuals who could receive training in trades through apprenticeship.

and we may trust with equal security that it will always supply us with all the gold and silver which we can afford to purchase or to employ, either in circulating our commodities, or in other uses.

▾▾▾

By restraining, either by high duties, or by absolute prohibitions, the importation of such goods from foreign countries as can be produced at home, the monopoly of the home market is more or less secured to the domestic industry employed in producing them. . . . But whether it tends either to increase the general industry of the society, or to give it the most advantageous direction, is not, perhaps, altogether so evident. . . .

Every individual is continually exerting himself to find out the most advantageous employment for whatever capital he can command. It is his own advantage, indeed, and not that of the society, which he has in view. But the study of his own advantage, naturally, or rather necessarily, leads him to prefer that employment which is most advantageous to the society.

First, every individual endeavors to employ his capital as near home as he can, and consequently as much as he can in the support of domestic industry, provided always that he can thereby obtain the ordinary, or not a great deal less than the ordinary, profits of stock.

Secondly, every individual who employs his capital in the support of domestic industry, necessarily endeavors so to direct that industry, that its produce may be of the greatest possible value. . . .

As every individual, therefore, endeavors as much as he can both to employ his capital in the support of domestic industry, and so to direct that industry that its produce may be of the greatest value, every individual necessarily labors to render the annual revenue of the society as great as he can. He generally, indeed, neither intends to promote the public interest, nor knows how much he is promoting it. By preferring the support of domestic to that of foreign industry, he intends only his own security; and

by directing that industry in such a manner as its produce may be of the greatest value, he intends only his own gain, and he is in this, as in many other cases, led by an invisible hand to promote an end which was no part of his intention. . . . By pursuing his own interest he frequently promotes that of the society more effectually than when he really intends to promote it. . . .

What is the species of domestic industry which his capital can employ, and of which the produce is likely to be of the greatest value, every individual, it is evident, can, in his local situation, judge much better than any statesman or lawgiver can do for him. The statesman who should attempt to direct private people in what manner they ought to employ their capital, would not only load himself with a most unnecessary attention, but assume an authority which could safely be trusted, not only to no single person, but to no council or senate whatever, and which would nowhere be so dangerous as in the hands of a man who had folly and presumption enough to fancy himself fit to exercise it.

To give the monopoly of the home market to the produce of domestic industry, in any particular art or manufacture, is in some measure to direct private people in what manner they ought to employ their capital, and must, in almost all cases, be either a useless or a hurtful regulation. If the produce of domestic [industry] can be brought there as cheap as that of foreign industry, the regulation is evidently useless. If it cannot, it must generally be hurtful. It is the maxim of every prudent master of a family, never to attempt to make at home what it will cost him more to make than to buy. . . .

What is prudence in the conduct of every private family, can scarce be folly in that of a great kingdom. If a foreign country can supply us with a commodity cheaper than we ourselves can make it, better buy it of them with some part of the produce of our own industry, employed in a way in which we have some advantage. . . .

To expect, indeed, that the freedom of trade should ever be entirely restored in Great Britain, is as absurd as to expect that an Oceania or Utopia should ever be established in it. Not only the prejudices of the public, but what is much more unconquerable, the private interests of many individuals, irresistibly oppose it. . . .

The undertaker of a great manufacture, who, by the home markets being suddenly laid open to the competition of foreigners, should be obliged to abandon his trade, would no doubt suffer very considerably. That part of his capital which had usually been employed in purchasing materials and in paying his workmen might, without much difficulty perhaps, find another employment. But that part of it which was fixed in workhouses, and in the instruments of trade, could scarce be disposed of without considerable loss. The equitable regard, therefore, to his interest requires that changes of this kind should never be introduced suddenly, but slowly, gradually, and after a very long warning.

▼▼▼

Russia and the West in the Eighteenth Century

After two centuries of Mongol rule ended in the late 1400s, Russia embarked on a period of remarkable expansion in which the tsars consolidated their control of European Russia, then extended their authority eastward across the Urals into Siberia. By the 1630s Russia stretched all the way to the Pacific and was the largest nation in the world.

Russia's western border, however, remained insecure. The Livonian War (1558–1582), involving Poland and Sweden, resulted in territorial losses, and during the period of political breakdown known as the Time of Troubles (1604–1613), Poland and Sweden sent armies deep into Russian territory. In 1612 the Russians drove out the invaders, and for the next several decades the Thirty Years' War (1618–1648) diverted European rulers from Russian adventures. The Turks remained a threat, however, and in the late 1600s the Poles and the Swedes resumed their pressure.

Russia's inability to translate its enormous size into military victories against the Ottomans, Poles, and Swedes underscored the extent to which Russia lagged behind the states to its south and west in almost every activity that affects state power. Manufacturing was negligible, commerce was limited to small amounts of trade in amber, furs, and timber, and agricultural productivity was constrained by long Russian winters and inefficiencies inherent in a rural order based on the labor of serfs. With little economic development and an ineffective system of tax collection, Russia lacked the resources to match the weaponry and training of its rivals' armies. In the 1600s Russia seemed destined to exist in a state of permanent military and technological inferiority to the nations of Europe to the west and Persia and the Ottoman Empire to the south.

How to respond to their nation's perceived vulnerability and weakness deeply divided the Russian people in the eighteenth century. Some Russians, most notably Tsar Peter I, also known as Peter the Great (r. 1682–1725), advocated a range of strategies and actions that came be known as *Westernization.* Peter and his supporters were convinced that Russia could pull itself out of its backwardness only by adopting the institutions, customs, and attitudes of the technologically superior, wealthier, and ostensibly more successful nations of Western Europe. Inevitably, this would mean discarding much of Russia's distinctive past, but in Peter's view Russia had no choice. Many Russians disagreed. They treasured Russia's uniqueness and believed that in certain respects their country was superior to the nations of Western Europe. These lovers of Russia's Slavic traditions (later known as *Slavophiles*) argued that abandonment of Russia's past was too high a price to pay for Europeanization.

Variations of Russia's Westernizer-Slavophile debate later appeared among many peoples of Asia and Africa in the nineteenth and twentieth centuries. As Europeans forced themselves into their lives, these people too had to ask themselves how willing they were, if at all, to abandon cultural and religious traditions for the lure of Western science, military power, and material gain. They, like the Russians, would find no easy answer to this question.

Peter the Great's Blueprint for Russia
▼▼▼

40 ▼ Peter the Great, EDICTS AND DECREES

Peter the Great stands out as one of history's most significant figures during the past 300 years. This remarkable ruler developed an interest in Western Europe when as a boy he spent hours smoking and drinking in the German quarter, the Moscow district where visiting Europeans resided. His fascination grew in 1697 and 1698 during his visit to Western Europe, where Dutch and British commerce and naval technology especially impressed him.

But the urgency of Peter's efforts to Europeanize Russia indicates that he was motivated more by his sense of Russia's military vulnerability than a personal admiration of things European. The onset of the Great Northern War (1700–1721) with Sweden, especially Russia's early defeat at the Battle of Narva, spurred him into action. With characteristic energy and single-mindedness he embarked on a campaign to transform Russia, issuing in the next twenty-five years no fewer than 3,000 decrees on everything from the structure of government to male shaving habits. Several examples are included here.

QUESTIONS FOR ANALYSIS

1. What do these decrees reveal about Peter the Great's motives for his reforms?
2. What can be learned from these decrees about Russian social relationships and the state of the Russian economy?
3. Why do you think Peter believed it was necessary for Russians to change their dress, shaving habits, and calendar?

4. What evidence do these edicts provide about opposition or indifference to Peter's reforms on the part of his subjects?
5. What do these edicts reveal about Peter's views of the state and its relationship to his subjects?
6. What groups within Russia might have been most likely to oppose Peter's reforms? Why?

LEARNING FROM EUROPE

(Decree on the New Calendar {1699})

It is known to His Majesty that not only many European Christian lands, but also Slavic nations which are in total accord with our Eastern Orthodox Church . . . agree to count their years from the eighth day after the birth of Christ, that is from the first day of January, and not from the creation of the world,[1] because of the many difficulties and discrepancies of this reckoning. It is now the year 1699 from the birth of Christ, and from the first of January will begin both the new year 1700 and a new century; and so His Majesty has ordered, as a good and useful measure, that from now on time will be reckoned in government offices and dates be noted on documents and property deeds, starting from the first of January 1700. And to celebrate this good undertaking and the new century . . . in the sovereign city of Moscow . . . let the reputable citizens arrange decorations of pine, fir, and juniper trees and boughs along the busiest main streets and by the houses of eminent church and lay persons of rank. . . . Poorer persons should place at least one shrub or bough on their gates or on their house. . . . Also, . . . as a sign of rejoicing, wishes for the new year and century will be exchanged, and the following will be organized: when fireworks are lit and guns fired on the great Red Square, let the boyars,[2] the Lords of the Palace, of the Chamber, and the Council, and the eminent personages of Court, Army, and Merchant ranks, each in his own grounds, fire three times from small guns, if they have any, or from muskets and other small arms, and shoot some rockets into the air.

(Decree on the Invitation of Foreigners {1702})

Since our accession to the throne all our efforts and intentions have tended to govern this realm in such a way that all of our subjects should, through our care for the general good, become more and more prosperous. For this end we have always tried to maintain internal order, to defend the state against invasion, and in every possible way to improve and to extend trade. With this purpose we have been compelled to make some necessary and salutary changes in the administration, in order that our subjects might more easily gain a knowledge of matters of which they were before ignorant, and become more skillful in their commercial relations. We have therefore given orders, made dispositions, and founded institutions indispensable for increasing our trade with foreigners, and shall do the same in the future. Nevertheless we fear that matters are not in such a good condition as we desire, and that our subjects cannot in perfect quietness enjoy the fruits of our labors, and we have therefore considered still other means to protect our frontier from the invasion of the enemy, and to preserve the rights and privileges of our State, and the general peace of all Christians. . . .

To attain these worthy aims, we have endeavored to improve our military forces, which are the protection of our State, so that our troops

---

[1]Before January 1, 1700, the Russian calendar started from the date of the creation of the world, which was reckoned at 5508 B.C.E. The year began on September 1.

[2]Members of the hereditary nobility.

may consist of well-drilled men, maintained in perfect order and discipline. In order to obtain greater improvement in this respect, and to encourage foreigners, who are able to assist us in this way, as well as artisans profitable to the State, to come in numbers to our country, we have issued this manifesto, and have ordered printed copies of it to be sent throughout Europe. . . . And as in our residence of Moscow, the free exercise of religion of all other sects, although not agreeing with our church, is already allowed, so shall this be hereby confirmed anew in such manner that we, by the power granted to us by the Almighty, shall exercise no compulsion over the consciences of men, and shall gladly allow every Christian to care for his own salvation at his own risk.

(An Instruction to Russian Students Abroad Studying Navigation {1714})

1. Learn how to draw plans and charts and how to use the compass and other naval indicators.

2. Learn how to navigate a vessel in battle as well as in a simple maneuver, and learn how to use all appropriate tools and instruments; namely, sails, ropes, and oars, and the like matters, on row boats and other vessels.

3. Discover . . . how to put ships to sea during a naval battle. . . . Obtain from foreign naval officers written statements, bearing their signatures and seals, of how adequately you are prepared for naval duties.

4. If, upon his return, anyone wishes to receive from the Tsar greater favors, he should learn, in addition to the above enumerated instructions, how to construct those vessels [aboard] which he would like to demonstrate his skills.

5. Upon his return to Moscow, every foreign-trained Russian should bring with him at his own expense, for which he will later be reimbursed, at least two experienced masters of naval

science. They the returnees will be assigned soldiers, one soldier per returnee, to teach them what they have learned abroad. . . .

CREATING A NEW RUSSIAN

(Decree on Western Dress {1701})

Western dress shall be worn by all the boyars, members of our councils and of our court . . . gentry of Moscow, secretaries . . . provincial gentry, gosti,[3] government officials, streltsy,[4] members of the guilds purveying for our household, citizens of Moscow of all ranks, and residents of provincial cities . . . excepting the clergy and peasant tillers of the soil. The upper dress shall be of French or Saxon cut, and the lower dress . . . — waistcoat, trousers, boots, shoes, and hats — shall be of the German type. They shall also ride German saddles. Likewise the womenfolk of all ranks, including the priests', deacons', and church attendants' wives, the wives of the dragoons, the soldiers, and the streltsy, and their children, shall wear Western dresses, hats, jackets, and underwear — undervests and petticoats — and shoes. From now on no one of the above-mentioned is to wear Russian dress or Circassian[5] coats, sheepskin coats, or Russian peasant coats, trousers, boots, and shoes. It is also forbidden to ride Russian saddles, and the craftsmen shall not manufacture them or sell them at the marketplaces.

(Decree on Shaving {1705})

Henceforth, in accordance with this, His Majesty's decree, all court attendants . . . provincial service men, government officials of all ranks, military men, all the gosti, members of the wholesale merchants' guild, and members of the guilds purveying for our household must shave their beards and moustaches. But, if it happens that some of them do not wish to shave their beards and moustaches, let a yearly tax be collected from such persons; from court atten-

---

[3]Merchants who often served the tsar in some capacity.
[4]Members of the imperial guard stationed in Moscow.

[5]Circassia was a Russian territory between the Caspian and Black seas.

dants. . . . Special badges shall be issued to them from the Administrator of Land Affairs of Public Order . . . which they must wear. . . . As for the peasants, let a toll of two half-copecks[6] per beard be collected at the town gates each time they enter or leave a town; and do not let the peasants pass the town gates, into or out of town, without paying this toll.

MILITARY AND ECONOMIC REFORMS

(Decree on Promotion to Officer's Rank {1714})

Since there are many who promote to officer rank their relatives and friends — young men who do not know the fundamentals of soldiering, not having served in the lower ranks — and since even those who serve [in the ranks] do so for a few weeks or months only, as a formality; therefore . . . let a decree be promulgated that henceforth there shall be no promotion [to officer rank] of men of noble extraction or of any others who have not first served as privates in the Guards. This decree does not apply to soldiers of lowly origin who, after long service in the ranks, have received their commissions through honest service or to those who are promoted on the basis of merit, now or in the future. . . .

(Statute for the College of Manufactures[7] {1723})

His Imperial Majesty is diligently striving to establish and develop in the Russian Empire such manufacturing plants and factories as are found in other states, for the general welfare and prosperity of his subjects. He [therefore] most graciously charges the College of Manufactures

to exert itself in devising the means to introduce, with the least expense, and to spread in the Russian Empire these and other ingenious arts, and especially those for which materials can be found within the empire. . . .

His Imperial Majesty gives permission to everyone, without distinction of rank or condition, to open factories wherever he may find suitable. . . .

Factory owners must be closely supervised, in order that they have at their plants good and experienced [foreign] master craftsmen, who are able to train Russians in such a way that these, in turn, may themselves become masters, so that their produce may bring glory to the Russian manufactures. . . .

By the former decrees of His Majesty commercial people were forbidden to buy villages [i.e. to own serfs], the reason being that they were not engaged in any other activity beneficial for the state save commerce; but since it is now clear to all that many of them have started to found manufacturing establishments and build plants, . . . which tend to increase the welfare of the state . . . therefore permission is granted both to the gentry and to men of commerce to acquire villages for these factories without hindrance. . . .

In order to stimulate voluntary immigration of various craftsmen from other countries into the Russian Empire, and to encourage them to establish factories and manufacturing plants freely and at their own expense, the College of Manufactures must send appropriate announcements to the Russian envoys accredited at foreign courts. The envoys should then, in an appropriate way, bring these announcements to the attention of men of various professions, urge them to come to settle in Russia, and help them to move.

---

[6]One-twentieth a ruble, the basic unit of Russian money.

[7]One of several administrative boards created by Peter in 1717. Modeled on Swedish practice.

a lot for good of Russia although beard thing silly

A Russian Critic of Westernization

▼▼▼

41 ▼ *Mikhail Shcherbatov,*
ON THE CORRUPTION
OF MORALS IN RUSSIA

During the reign of Catherine the Great (1762–1796) Russian society continued to evolve along the lines laid down by Peter the Great. With the imperial court now in St. Petersburg, Peter's "window on the West," the German-born Catherine courted French intellectuals, encouraged the publication of Western European books, and proposed educational and political reforms inspired by Western models. Russian aristocrats spoke French, wore the latest European fashions, and congratulated themselves on Russia's growing prestige and their newly acquired sophistication and refinement. As the following selection reveals, however, some Russians had profound misgivings about Russia's transformation.

Prince Mikhail Shcherbatov (1733–1790) was born into a distinguished aristocratic family with a tradition of service to the state. Having developed a keen interest in Western European thought and literature through his knowledge of French, he moved as a young man from Moscow to St. Petersburg, where he contributed to literary journals and joined the political discussions sparked by Catherine's policies and proposals. His major work was a seven-volume *History of Russia from Earliest Times,* still unfinished at the time of his death. During the 1780s he experienced growing disillusionment with the changes in Russia since the reign of Peter the Great. He stated his reservations in his *On the Corruption of Morals in Russia,* written in 1787 but not published until 1897.

QUESTIONS FOR ANALYSIS

1. According to Shcherbatov, what were the salient characteristics of Russia before the reforms of Peter the Great?
2. What changes instituted by Peter does Shcherbatov approve of? Why?
3. Why does Shcherbatov have reservations about Peter's religious policies?
4. What is Shcherbatov's vision of the ideal Russian society and government?
5. According to Shcherbatov, what should Peter have done differently to prevent the moral decline of the Russian people?

I cannot but wonder at the short time in which morals in Russia have everywhere become corrupt. I can truly say that if, after entering later than other nations upon the path of enlightenment, nothing more remained for us than to follow prudently in the steps of nations previously enlightened, then indeed, in sociability and in various other things, it may be said that we have made wonderful progress and have taken gigantic steps to correct our outward appearance. But at the same time, with much greater speed, we have hastened to corrupt our morals, and have even come to this: that faith and God's Law have been extinguished in our hearts, Divine mysteries have fallen into disrepute and civil laws have become objects of scorn.

Children have no respect for parents, and are not ashamed to flout their will openly and to mock their old-fashioned behavior. Parents have no love for their offspring; . . . often they sacrifice them for profit, and many have become vendors of their daughters' honor for the sakes of ambition and luxury.[1] There is no genuine love between husbands and wives, who are often coolly indifferent to each other's adulteries; others, on some slight pretext, destroy the marriage concluded between them by the Church and are not merely unashamed but rather seem to take pride in this conduct. There is no family feeling, for the family name counts for nothing, and each lives for himself. There is no friendship, for everyone will sacrifice a friend for his own advantage. There is no loyalty to the monarch, for the chief aim of almost everyone is to deceive his sovereign, in order to receive from him ranks and lucrative rewards. There is no patriotism, for almost all men serve for their own advantage rather than for that of the nation. . . .

RUSSIA BEFORE PETER THE GREAT

Not only the subjects, but even our very monarchs led a very simple life. Their palaces were not large, as is attested by the old buildings that remain. Seven, eight, or at most, ten rooms, were sufficient for the monarch's accommodation.

These very palaces had no great embellishments, for the walls were bare, and the benches were covered with crimson cloth. . . .

For such a small number of rooms, not much lighting would be needed; but even here, they not only did not use, but considered it a sin to use wax candles,[2] and the rooms were lit by tallow candles, and even these were not set out in tens or hundreds; it was a large room indeed

where four candles were set out on candlesticks.

Now let us consider the Czars' clothing. . . . Their ceremonial robes glittered all over with gold, jewels and diamonds. But their normal apparel, in which they looked for comfort rather than magnificence, was simple, and hence could not give rise to voluptuousness; . . . Generally speaking, there were no exquisite or perishable articles of finery, nor a large number of outfits, but when the Czar or Czarina had five, six, or, at most, ten outfits, then this was considered sufficient, and even these clothes were worn until they wore out, unless they were given to someone by the monarch out of special favor. The chief luxury in the Czar's ordinary clothing consisted of the precious furs, which they used for lining and on the edges of their garments; but these furs were not purchased or imported from foreign states, but were a tribute, collected from the Siberian peoples. . . . The boyars and other dignitaries, according to their means, led a similar life, striving, however, out of respect for the Czar's rank, never to approach even this simple magnificence. But what kept them from voluptuousness most of all was the fact that they had no conception of changing fashions, but, what grandfathers wore, grandsons also wore and used, without considering themselves old-fashioned.

REIGN OF PETER THE GREAT

Peter the Great, in imitating foreign nations, not only strove to introduce to his realm a knowledge of sciences, arts and crafts, a proper military system, trade, and the most suitable forms of legislation; he also tried to introduce the kind of sociability, social intercourse and magnificence, which he first learnt from Lefort,[3] and which he later saw for himself.[4] Amid essen-

---

[1] A reference to the marriage of girls of noble birth into merchant families.

[2] Wax candles were to be used only in churches.

[3] Franz Lefort, a Genevan Swiss, was a mercenary in the Rus-

sian army who became Peter's close friend and advisor. He encouraged Peter's efforts to westernize Russia.

[4] A reference to Peter's protracted visit to Western Europe between March 1697 and September 1698.

tial legislative measures, the organization of troops and artillery, he paid no less attention to modifying the old customs which seemed crude to him. He ordered beards to be shaved off, he abolished the old Russian garments, and instead of long robes he compelled the men to wear German coats,[5] and the women to wear bodices, skirts, gowns and long dresses, and instead of skull-caps, to adorn their heads with fontanges and cornettes.[6] He established various assemblies where the women, hitherto segregated from the company of men, were present with them at entertainments.

It was pleasant for the female sex, who had hitherto been almost slaves in their own homes, to enjoy all the pleasures of society, to adorn themselves with clothes and fineries, which enhanced the beauty of their faces and set off their fine figures. It also gave them no small pleasure to be able to see in advance with whom they were to be joined for life, and that the faces of their husbands and betrothed were no longer covered with prickly beards.

And on the other hand, it was pleasant for men who were young and not set in the old ways to mix freely with the female sex and to be able to see in advance and make the acquaintance of their brides-to-be; for previously they married, relying on their parents' choice. . . . And this in itself meant that women, previously unaware of their beauty, began to realize its power; they began to try to enhance it with suitable clothes, and used far more luxury in their adornments than their ancestors.

If the passion to be pleasing produced such an effect on women, it could not fail to have an effect on men too, who wished to be attractive to them; thus, the same striving after adornment gave rise to the same luxury. And now they ceased to be content with one or two long coats,

but began to have many made, with galoon, embroidery and point-d'espagne.[7] . . .

With this change in the way of life, first of the leading officials of state, and then, by imitation, of the other nobles, and as expenditure reached such a point that it began to exceed income, people began to attach themselves more and more to the monarch and the grandees, as sources of riches and rewards.

PETER'S RELIGIOUS POLICIES

In Russia, the beard was regarded as being in the image of God, and it was considered a sin to shave it off, and through this, men fell into the heresy of the Anthropomorphites.[8] Miracles, needlessly performed, manifestations of icons,[9] rarely proven, were everywhere acclaimed, attracted superstitious idolatry, and provided incomes for dissolute priests.

Peter the Great strove to do away with all this. He issued decrees, ordering beards to be shaved off, and he placed a check on false miracles and manifestations and also on unseemly gatherings at shrines set up at crossways. . . .

But when did he do this? At a time when the nation was still unenlightened, and so, by taking superstition away from an unenlightened people, he removed its very faith in God's Law. This action of Peter the Great may be compared to that of an unskilled gardener, who, from a weak tree, cuts off the water-shoots which absorb its sap. If it had strong roots, then this pruning would cause it to bring forth fine, fruitful branches; but since it is weak and ailing, the cutting-off of these shoots . . . means that it fails. . . . Thus, the cutting-off of all superstitions did harm to the most basic articles of the faith; superstition decreased, but so did faith. The servile fear of Hell disappeared, but so did love of God and his

---

[5]Any coat tailored in the Western European style.
[6]Forms of a tall headdress for fashionable women in France in the late seventeenth and early eighteenth centuries.
[7]Galoon is a tightly woven braid of gold, silver, or silk thread; *point d'espagne* is French for a type of lace embroidery.
[8]Ascribing human characteristics to God.

[9]A religious image — usually of Christ, the Virgin Mary, or one of the saints — painted on a small wooden panel and used in the devotions of Orthodox Christians. Many icons were thought to have miracle-working qualities or even to have been produced in heaven.

Holy Law; and morals, which for lack of other enlightenment used to be improved by faith, having lost this support began to fall into dissolution.

And so, through the labors and solicitude of this monarch, Russia acquired fame in Europe and influence in affairs. Her troops were organized in a proper fashion, and her fleets covered the White Sea and the Baltic; with these forces she overcame her old enemies and former conquerors, the Poles and the Swedes, and acquired important provinces and sea-ports. Sciences, arts and crafts began to flourish there, trade began to

enrich her, and the Russians were transformed — from bearded men to clean-shaven men, from long-robed men to short-coated men; they became more sociable, and polite spectacles[10] became known to them.

But at the same time, true attachment to the faith began to disappear, sacraments began to fall into disrepute, resoluteness diminished, yielding place to brazen, aspiring flattery; luxury and voluptuousness laid the foundation of their power, and hence avarice was also aroused, and, to the ruin of the laws and the detriment of the citizens, began to penetrate the law-courts.

---

[10]Plays performed in a theater.

Revolutions in England and France

Revolutions involve more than changing leaders or replacing one ruling faction with another. Revolutions bring about fundamental changes in the political order itself, often resulting in the transfer of power from one social group to another. Moreover, they affect more than politics. Revolutions reshape legal systems, education, religious life, and economic practices and redefine relationships between rich and poor, males and females, old and young.

Because revolutions occur in societies already undergoing intellectual, economic, and social transformations, it is not surprising that history's first revolutions took place in Western Europe and the Americas in the seventeenth through the nineteenth centuries, when the growth of commerce and industry undermined old social hierarchies, and the emergence of new secular values weakened the foundations of divine right monarchies and privileged churches. Nor is it surprising that in recent history revolutions have spread to other parts of the world, as new ideologies and economic and social changes have affected one society after another.

In the 1600s England experienced two revolutions: the Puritan Revolution (also known as the English Revolution or English Civil War) in the 1640s and 1650s and the Glorious Revolution of 1688 and 1689. They limited royal authority, confirmed the fiscal and legislative powers of Parliament, and guaranteed many basic rights for the English people, especially those with property. They also affirmed the constitutional principle that governments must operate by established laws that apply to subjects and rulers alike, not according to the whims of individual rulers.

The French Revolution, which began in 1789, had a greater impact than the English revolutions. More social groups — peasants, urban workers, and women — participated, and it inspired more people around the globe. More important, the French Revolution went beyond liberalism and constitutionalism. It championed the democratic principles that every person, irrespective of social standing, should have a voice in government and that all people should be treated equally before the law. It also aroused the first nationalist movements in Europe and inspired disaffected groups throughout the world to seek political and social change through revolution.

The Foundations of Parliamentary Supremacy in England
▼▼▼

42 ▼ *ENGLISH BILL OF RIGHTS*

The acceptance of the English Bill of Rights in 1689 ended a clash between the Crown and Parliament that had convulsed English politics for almost a century. During the reigns of the first two Stuart kings, James I (r. 1603–1625) and his son Charles I (r. 1625–1649), the landowners, merchants, and lawyers who dominated the House of Commons fought the monarchy over religious, economic, diplomatic, and political issues that all centered on the fundamental question of Parliament's place in England's government.

A political impasse over new taxes led to civil war between Parliamentarians and Royalists in 1642. After a triumphant Parliament ordered the execution of Charles I in 1649, a faction of Puritans led by Oliver Cromwell seized power and for the next eleven years sought to impose its strict Protestant beliefs on the English people. The Puritans' grip on England loosened after the death of Cromwell in 1658 and was lost altogether when a newly elected Parliament restored the Stuarts in 1660.

Charles II (r. 1660–1685) and his brother James II (r. 1685–1688), however, alienated their subjects through pro-French and pro-Catholic policies and disregard for Parliament. James II was a professed Catholic, and when a male heir was born in 1688, it raised the possibility of a long line of English Catholic kings. Most of his predominantly Protestant subjects found this unacceptable, and the result was the Glorious Revolution of 1688–1689. In a change that resembled a coup d'état more than a revolution, Parliament offered the Crown to James's Protestant daughter Mary and her husband William of Orange of Holland. After James mounted only token resistance and then fled the country, his son-in-law and daughter became King William III and Queen Mary II after signing the English Bill of Rights, presented to them by Parliament in 1689. By doing so they accepted parliamentary limitations on royal authority that became a permanent part of England's constitution.

QUESTIONS FOR ANALYSIS

1. What abuses of royal power seem to have most disturbed the authors of the English Bill of Rights?
2. Were the authors most concerned with political, economic, or religious issues?
3. What role does the Bill of Rights envision for the English Crown?
4. When the Bill of Rights speaks of "rights," to whose rights does it refer?
5. In what ways might the common people of England benefit from the Bill of Rights?

Whereas the late King James the Second, by the assistance of diverse evil counselors, judges and ministers employed by him, did endeavor to subvert and extirpate the Protestant religion and the laws and liberties of this kingdom;

By assuming and exercising a power of dispensing with and suspending of laws and the execution of laws without consent of Parliament;

By committing and prosecuting diverse worthy prelates for humbly petitioning to be excused from concurring to the said assumed power;

By issuing and causing to be executed a commission under the great seal for erecting a court called the Court of Commissioners for Ecclesiastical Causes;[1]

By levying money for and to the use of the Crown by pretense of prerogative for other time and in other manner than the same was granted by Parliament;

By raising and keeping a standing army within this kingdom in time of peace without consent of Parliament, and quartering soldiers contrary to law;

By causing several good subjects being Protestants to be disarmed at the same time when papists were both armed and employed contrary to law;

By violating the freedom of election of members to serve in Parliament; . . .

And whereas of late years partial corrupt and unqualified persons have been returned and served on juries in trials, and particularly diverse jurors in trials for high treason which were not freeholders;

And excessive bail hath been required of persons committed in criminal cases to elude the benefit of the laws made for the liberty of the subjects;

And excessive fines have been imposed;

And illegal and cruel punishments inflicted;

And several grants and promises made of fines and forfeitures before any conviction or judgment against the persons upon whom the same were to be levied;

All which are utterly and directly contrary to the known laws and statutes and freedom of this realm;

And whereas the said late King James the Second having abdicated the government and the throne being thereby vacant, his Highness the prince of Orange (whom it hath pleased Almighty God to make the glorious instrument of delivering this kingdom from popery and arbitrary power) did . . . cause letters to be written to the Lords Spiritual and Temporal being Protestants, and other letters to the several counties, cities, universities, boroughs and cinque ports,[2] for the choosing of such persons to represent them as were of right to be sent to Parliament, to meet and sit at Westminster upon the two

---

[1] A special royal court established to try religious cases.
[2] Five maritime towns in southeast England that during the Middle Ages gained the right to send representatives to Parliament in return for aiding the naval defense of the realm.

and twentieth day of January in this year one thousand six hundred eighty and eight,[3] in order to make such an establishment as that their religion, laws and liberties might not again be in danger of being subverted, upon which letters elections having been accordingly made;

And thereupon the said Lords Spiritual and Temporal and Commons,[4] pursuant to their respective letters and elections, being now assembled . . . , taking into their most serious consideration the best means for attaining the ends aforesaid, do in the first place (as their ancestors in like case have usually done) for the vindicating and asserting their ancient rights and liberties declare;

That the pretended power of suspending of laws or the execution of laws by regal authority without consent of Parliament is illegal;

That the pretended power of dispensing with laws or the execution of laws by regal authority, as it hath been assumed and exercised of late, is illegal;

That the commission for erecting the late Court of Commissioners for Ecclesiastical Causes, and all other commissions and courts of like nature, are illegal and pernicious;

That levying money for or to the use of the Crown by pretense of prerogative, without grant of Parliament, for longer time, or in other manner than the same is or shall be granted, is illegal;

That it is the right of the Subjects to petition the king, and all commitments and prosecutions for such petitioning are illegal;

That the raising or keeping a standing army within the kingdom in time of peace, unless it be with consent of Parliament, is against law;

That the subjects which are Protestants may have arms for their defense suitable to their conditions and as allowed by law;

That election of members of Parliament ought to be free;

That the freedom of speech and debates or proceedings in Parliament ought not to be impeached or questioned in any court or place out of Parliament;

That excessive bail ought not to be required, nor excessive fines imposed nor cruel and unusual punishments inflicted;

That jurors ought to be duly impaneled and returned, and jurors which pass upon men in trials for high treason ought to be freeholders;[5]

That all grants and promises of fines and forfeitures of particular persons before conviction are illegal and void;

And that for redress of all grievances, and for the amending, strengthening and preserving of the laws, Parliaments ought to be held frequently. . . .

---

[3]Until the eighteenth century the English new year began on March 25, not January 1; by modern reckoning the year should be 1689.

[4]The Lords Spiritual were the prelates of the Anglican Church who sat in the House of Lords; the Lords Temporal were titled peers who sat in the House of Lords; Commons refers to the House of Commons, to which nontitled Englishmen were elected.

[5]Property holders.

A Program for Revolutionary Change in France
▼▼▼

43 ▼ *CAHIER OF THE THIRD ESTATE OF THE CITY OF PARIS*

The French Revolution began because of a problem that has plagued rulers since the beginning of organized government — King Louis XVI (r. 1774–1792) and his ministers could not balance their budget. Having exhausted every other solution,

in 1788 the king agreed to convene a meeting of the Estates General, France's representative assembly, which had last met in 1614. He hoped it would solve the government's fiscal plight by approving new taxes. The nobility, having fended off every effort to curtail its tax exemptions and privileges, saw the convening of the Estates General as an opportunity to increase its power at the expense of the monarchy. For both king and nobility the calling of the Estates General had unexpected results: The nobility lost its privileges, and the king lost most of his power and, in 1793, having been judged a traitor to the Revolution, his head.

Neither Louis nor the nobles had comprehended the French people's disgust with royal absolutism and aristocratic privilege. Nor had they sensed the degree to which the Enlightenment and the English and American revolutions had committed the people to fundamental change. Having convened in May 1789, within months the Estates General transformed itself into a National Assembly, dismantled the laws and institutions of the Old Regime, and set about creating a new political order based on constitutionalism, equality, and natural rights.

Even before the Estates General met, the French populace was in a high pitch of political excitement as a result of the procedures adopted for choosing delegates. The delegates representing the three orders of French society — the First Estate, or clergy; the Second Estate, or nobility; and the Third Estate, everyone else from peasants to wealthy city-dwellers — were chosen in a complicated process that began with village and neighborhood assemblies and ended at the level of *baillages,* larger districts based on divisions in the French judicial system. At each electoral meeting those attending were encouraged to draw up a *cahier de doléances,* a memorandum of grievances, in which all kinds of ideas on local and national affairs could be expressed. These were then passed on to editorial committees at the baillage level, whose members sifted through them and integrated them into final cahiers that were sent on to Versailles, where the Estates General would meet.

We have chosen to include excerpts from the cahier of the Third Estate of the city of Paris. A document largely created by lawyers and businessmen, it presents a fair sampling of the grievances and expectations of urban, upper-middle-class Frenchmen on the eve of the French Revolution.

QUESTIONS FOR ANALYSIS

1. What view of monarchy is expressed in the cahier? How does it compare with the views of monarchy expressed in the English Bill of Rights (source 42)?
2. What views are expressed in the cahier about the position of the nobility and clergy in the French society?
3. It has been said that the French Revolution was about legal privilege, not monarchy. Do the thoughts expressed in this cahier bear this out?
4. What solutions does the cahier offer for the government's fiscal crisis?
5. In what ways does this document represent the interests of the urban middle class? To what extent does it show concern for other groups in society?
6. What kind of government does the cahier envision for France?

CONSTITUTION

In the French monarchy, legislative power belongs to the nation conjointly with the king; executive power belongs to the king alone.

No tax can be established except by the nation.

The Estates General shall meet at three-year intervals.

Any person convicted of having done anything tending to prevent the meeting of the Estates General shall be declared a traitor to the nation, guilty of high treason, and punished as such. . . .

The order and form of the convening of the Estates General and of the national representation shall be fixed by law. . . .

The monarch's person is sacred and inviolable. The succession to the throne is hereditary in the reigning family, in the male line, by order of primogeniture, to the exclusion of women and their descendants, male or female, and can only fall on a prince born French, within lawful marriage. . . .

At the beginning of each new reign the king shall swear an oath to the nation, and the nation to the king; the form of which shall be determined by the Estates General.

No citizen may be arrested, nor his home violated, by virtue of *lettres de cachet*,[1] or any other order emanating from the executive power, . . . all persons who have solicited, countersigned, and executed them being subject to special prosecution and corporal punishment. . . .

The whole kingdom will be divided into provincial assemblies, made up of people who live in the province, elected freely by all the orders. . . .

Public administration, in all matters having to do with the allocation and collection of taxes, agriculture, commerce, manufacturing, communications, public works projects, construction, and public morals shall be entrusted to the provincial assemblies.

Cities, towns, and villages shall likewise have elected municipal authorities which, like the assemblies, shall administer local affairs.

Judicial authority shall be exercised in France in the name of the king by tribunals composed of members completely independent of any act by the executive power.

Nobles will be able to participate in commerce and other useful professions without losing their status.[2] The Estates General shall establish a civic and honorary award, personal and not hereditary, which will be conferred by the king without discrimination on citizens of any order who merit it by the loftiness of their patriotic virtue and by the importance of their public service.

The charter of the constitution shall be engraved on a public monument raised for this purpose. A reading of it shall be made to the king at the ascension to his throne, and then shall be followed by his oath. . . . All agents of the executive power, civil and military, all judicial magistrates, all municipal officers shall swear an oath to uphold the charter. Every year on the anniversary of its approval, the charter shall be read and posted in the churches, courts, schools, and at the headquarters of each regiment and on naval vessels. The day will be a day of solemn celebration in every country under French dominion.

FINANCES

The Estates General shall void every special tax, on persons or on property, such as the *taille*, the

---

[1]Literally "sealed letters"; a form of warrant issued under the king's signature for arbitrary arrest and imprisonment in prerevolutionary France.

[2]According to French law, members of the nobility lost their noble status if they participated in business activities involving commerce, manufacturing, and banking, all considered "middle class" professions. Nobles were expected to derive their income from landholding, investments, or government service.

franc-fief, head tax, military service, the *corvée,*[3] the billeting of troops, and others, and replace them as needed by general taxes, payable by all citizens of every order.

The Estates General in the outright replacement of taxes, shall consider principally direct taxes, which will bear equally on all citizens and all provinces and which will be simplest and less expensive to collect.

AGRICULTURE

The deputies will be especially charged to demand the total abolition of *capitaineries;*[4] they are in such contradiction to every principle of morality that they cannot be tolerated, even under the pretext of getting rid of some of their worst abuses.

It is the natural right of any proprietor of land to be able to destroy on his land destructive game and other animals.[5] In regard to hunting rights and the means of employing them, whether for their suppression or preservation, we look to the Estates General to suppress their abuses in a timely manner.

LEGISLATION

The object of the laws is to protect liberty and property. Their perfection is to be humane and just, clear and general, to be in keeping with the national character and morality, to protect people of every order and every class equally, and to punish without distinction of persons whoever violates the law.

TREATMENT OF CRIMINALS

No citizen can be arrested or obliged to appear before any judge without an order coming from a competent judge. Every accused person, even before his first interrogation, shall have the right to call a lawyer.

A law will be passed to suppress the use of all torture before a criminal is executed and all practices that add prolonged and cruel suffering to the execution.

The death penalty should be limited to the smallest number of cases as possible, and reserved for truly atrocious crimes.

Those guilty of the same crime, no matter what order of society they are from, should undergo the same punishment.

Prisons should have the purpose not of punishing prisoners but of securing their persons. Underground dungeons should be suppressed. Efforts should be made to make the interior of other prisons healthier, and to establish rules for the moral conduct of the prisoners.

The Estates General should consider the plight of black slaves and men of color, in the colonies as well as in France.

RELIGION

[Religion's] ministers, as citizens of the state, are subject to the law; as property owners, they must bear a share of all public expenditure.

The Christian religion ordains civil toleration; every citizen must enjoy private liberty of conscience, but the requirements of law and order require only one dominant religion. . . .

---

[3]*Taille:* a tax on land paid mainly by peasants; *franc-fief:* a fee paid by a nonnoble on the acquisition of land; *corvée:* unpaid labor demanded mainly from peasants by their landlords.
[4]Hunting monopolies granted mainly to members of the high nobility.

[5]Laws prevented peasants from destroying crop-damaging birds and rabbits; their purpose was to protect the supply of animals hunted by the nobility.

The Principles of the French Revolution
▼▼▼

44 ▼ DECLARATION OF THE RIGHTS OF MAN AND OF THE CITIZEN

The Estates General had its first meeting on May 5, 1789. By June 23, with the king's grudging approval, it had been transformed into the National Assembly, with the self-proclaimed goal of writing a constitution for France. This represented a crucial victory for the assembly's middle-class delegates, who now had an opportunity to end absolutism and the privileges of the nobility and the clergy. The approval of the Declaration of the Rights of Man and of the Citizen on August 27 was a step of exceptional importance. Drawing on the political principles of English constitutionalism, the American Revolution, and the Enlightenment, this document (which served as preamble to the Constitution of 1791) summarizes the political and social goals of the French revolutionaries of 1789 and countless others in the decades to follow.

QUESTIONS FOR ANALYSIS

1. In what specific ways does the declaration limit the power of the crown and the authority of government?
2. What rights and responsibilities does citizenship entail?
3. What does the declaration state about the origin and purpose of law?
4. How does the concept of rights in the declaration differ from the concept of rights in the English Bill of Rights (source 42)?
5. To what extent does the declaration reflect the political concerns of the authors of the cahier of the Parisian Third Estate (source 43)?

The representatives of the people of France, empowered to act as a national assembly, taking into consideration that ignorance, oblivion, or scorn of the rights of man are the only cause of public misery and the corruption of government, have resolved to state in a solemn declaration the natural, inalienable, and sacred rights of man, so that this declaration, continually offered to all the members of society, may forever recall them to their rights and duties; so that the actions of the legislative and executive power, able to be compared at every instant to the goal of any political institution, may be more respected; so that the demands of the citizens, from now on based on straightforward and incontestable prin-ciples, will revolve around the maintenance of the constitution and the happiness of everyone.

Consequently, the National Assembly recognizes and declares, in the presence and under the auspices of the Supreme Being, the following rights of man and citizen:

Article 1. Men are born and remain free and equal in rights; social distinctions can be established only for the common benefit.

2. The goal of every political association is the conservation of the natural and indefeasible rights of man; these rights are liberty, property, security, and resistance to oppression.

3. The source of all sovereignty is located

essentially in the nation; no body, no individual can exercise authority which does not emanate from it expressly.

4. Liberty consists in being able to do anything that does not harm another. Thus the exercise of the natural rights of each man has no limits except those which assure to other members of society the enjoyment of these same rights; these limits can be determined only by law.

5. The law has the right to prohibit only those actions harmful to society. All that is not prohibited by the law cannot be hindered, and no one can be forced to do what it does not order.

6. The law is the expression of the general will; all citizens have the right to concur personally or through their representatives in its formation; it must be the same for everyone, whether it protects or punishes. All citizens, being equal in its eyes, are equally admissible to all honors, offices, and public employments, according to their abilities and without any distinction other than those of their virtues and talents.

7. No man can be accused, arrested, or detained except in instances determined by the law, and according to the practices which it has prescribed. Those who solicit, draw up, carry out, or have carried out arbitrary orders must be punished; but any citizen summoned or seized by virtue of the law must obey instantly; he renders himself guilty by resisting.

8. The law must establish only penalties that are strictly and plainly necessary, and no one can be punished except in virtue of a law established and published prior to the offense and legally applied.

9. Every man being presumed innocent until he has been declared guilty, if it is judged indispensable to arrest him, all harshness that is not necessary for making secure his person must be severely limited by the law.

10. No one may be disturbed because of his opinions, even religious, provided that their public manifestation does not disturb the public order established by law.

11. The free communication of thoughts and opinions is one of the most precious rights of man: every citizen can therefore freely speak, write, and print, except he is answerable for abuses of this liberty in instances determined by the law.

12. The guaranteeing of the rights of man and citizen requires a public force; this force is therefore instituted for the advantage of everyone, and not for the private use of those to whom it is entrusted.

13. For the maintenance of the public force, and for the expenses of administration, a tax supported in common is indispensable; it must be apportioned among all citizens on grounds of their capacities to pay.

14. All citizens have the right to determine for themselves or through their representatives the need for taxation of the public, to consent to it freely, to investigate its use, and to determine its rate, basis, collection, and duration.

15. Society has the right to demand an accountability from every public agent of his management.

16. Any society in which guarantees of rights are not assured nor the separation of powers determined has no constitution.

17. Property being an inviolable and sacred right, no one may be deprived of it except when public necessity, legally determined, requires it, and on condition of a just and predetermined compensation.

Politics and Privilege in France before and after the French Revolution
▼▼▼

45 ▼ POLITICAL CARTOONS AND CARICATURES FROM THE FRENCH REVOLUTION

Political cartoons and caricatures first became popular in eighteenth-century England, where parliamentary government and lax censorship laws created an environment in which artists had free rein to express their political views. Their biting commentary on political issues and frequently scurrilous portrayals of politicians ranged from elaborately allegorical engravings to crude woodcuts, some of which were black-and-white and some colored with water-based paints. Such cartoons and caricatures were sold in bookstores and print shops (the technology did not exist to print them in newspapers) and provoked laughter and arguments in countless aristocratic clubs, taverns, and private homes. Cartoonists such as James Gilray (1756–1815), who produced many hundreds of political cartoons, became nationally known figures whose new works were eagerly anticipated.

Political cartoons and caricatures did not exist in France until 1787 and 1788, when censorship laws were eased during the nationwide political debate in the months leading up to the meeting of the Estates General in the spring of 1789. Once the revolution began, political excitement grew, and so did the market for inexpensive engravings that provided portraits of revolutionary leaders, depictions of events such as the swearing of the Tennis Court Oath and the fall of the Bastille, and above all, satire. Between 1789 and 1792 hundreds of political cartoons, mostly sympathetic to the revolution and many with biting messages, appeared. After 1793 their numbers declined, as censorship laws were reinstated by the radical Jacobins, the moderate Directory (1795–1799), and the regime of Napoleon (1799–1815), all of which appreciated the power of satire to shape public opinion.

The six cartoons that appear here — a mere sampling of the numerous political cartoons produced between 1787 and early 1793 — are all anonymous works that focus on the three estates of prerevolutionary France and their fate during the revolution. Legal categories rather than social classes, the three estates were the First Estate, the clergy; the Second Estate, the nobility; and the Third Estate, everyone else from poor peasants to wealthy businessmen. Membership in the first two estates brought with it privileges, including exemption from many taxes, preferential judicial treatment, and for members of the nobility, a monopoly on high offices in church and state. One of the first acts of France's revolutionary leaders was to abolish the first two estates' privileges and establish equality before the law.

The first pair of engravings, "The Past" and "The Present," appeared in many versions in 1790 and 1791. "The Past" shows a peasant carrying a clergyman and a nobleman on his back. The clergyman holds a moneybag entitled "the tithe," which was a tax paid by members of the Third Estate to the Church. In the nobleman's pockets are slips of paper on which are written the names of other taxes paid by peasants — the taille, a tax on land; the corvée, required labor on the lord's land; and various sales taxes. At the peasant's feet his crops are being devoured by rabbits and pigeons, two of many animals that were protected so they could be hunted by nobles. The nobleman's sword is inscribed with the words "reddened with blood." In contrast the peasant is keeping his balance by leaning on a tool, a pickaxe, labeled as representing "goodness." "The Present" engraving is of course quite different. The peasant is literally in the driver's seat, riding a nobleman who is being pulled along by a clergyman. The clergyman is carrying a small scale, representing justice. The paper on the left side of the scale has the words "the benefit of the people," while the paper on the right has "liberty and equality." The peasant is carrying a slip of paper with the inscription "peace and concord" while singing "Ca ira, Ca ira," the refrain from a popular revolutionary song usually translated as "it will go" or "it's speeding along."

The next pair of engravings presents a female version of the same theme. The first engraving, simply entitled "A Tenant Farmer in Drudgery," shows a noble-woman and a nun riding on the back of a peasant woman, who is holding a distaff used when spinning wool or flax. The second engraving of the pair is entitled "I Really Knew We Would Have Our Turn" with the inscription below, "Long Live the King, Long Live the Nation."

The final two cartoons continue the same themes. The fifth print, entitled "The Press," or in other versions, "The Fat Press," appeared after the revolutionary regime had confiscated church property in the summer of 1789 and used it as the basis for issuing a new paper currency, the assignats. In it a citizen and a soldier lead clergymen to a press that squeezes money from them into a treasure chest. The sixth print, "The Present," is based on Jesus' teaching that in the Kingdom of God "the first shall be last." The cartoon depicts a world literally turned upside down, with the figure representing the Third Estate bearing a sword and giving orders to a nobleman and a clergyman. The nobleman is dressed as an infantry soldier warily standing at attention, while the poor priest has literally been worked to the bone by his labors.

QUESTIONS FOR ANALYSIS

1. In their portrayal of social relationships of prerevolutionary France, how do the artists depict the clergy and the nobility?
2. How do they depict the members of the Third Estate?
3. What similarities and differences do you see in the way men and women are treated in the first two pairs of prints? What conclusions can be drawn about the status of French women on the basis of your comparisons?
4. What specific grievances of the Third Estate are represented in the various cartoons?
5. According to the cartoonists, what changed in French society as a result of the early events of the revolution?
6. How many themes in the Cahier of the Third Estate of the City of Paris (source 43) and the Declaration of the Rights of Man and of the Citizen (source 44) can you see represented in these political cartoons?

The Past

The Present

Costume & Caricature

La fermiere en Corpé.

A Tenant Farmer in Drudgery

Vive le Roi, Vive la Nation

J'savois ben Qu'jaurions not tour

I Really Knew We Would Have Our Turn

Le Pressoir

The Press

Le Tems present

Le Tiers Etat.   *La Noblesse*   *le Clergé*
C'est ici que les premiers sont les derniers.

The Present

▼▼▼

Anticolonialism and Revolution in the Americas

Despite the many contrasts between the British colonies of eastern North America and the Portuguese-Spanish colonies of Mexico and Central and South America, all of them won their independence between the 1770s and the 1830s. Although the independence movements in North and Latin America unfolded differently, throughout the Americas the rebels had similar grievances and ideals. Grievances included mercantilist restrictions on trade, high taxes, and a lack of self-government; the ideals were inspired by English constitutionalism, the Enlightenment, and, in the case of Latin America, the revolutions in North America and France.

The governments that emerged after the revolutions differed markedly. In the northern thirteen colonies, opponents of British rule coalesced in a unified movement under the Continental Congress and George Washington, and after independence this unity was ultimately preserved in the U.S. Constitution. In South America, where struggles for independence were waged on a regional basis under generals such as Simón Bolívar, Bernardo O'Higgins, and José de San Martín, the end of Spanish and Portuguese authority resulted in more than a dozen independent states. In North America, federal and state governments drew on the principles of English constitutionalism to guarantee basic freedoms and extend political rights to a majority of adult white males. In Latin America, with its traditions of Spanish/Portuguese absolutism and aristocracy, wealthy landowners controlled the new states and excluded the peasant masses from politics.

Social and economic relationships also differed markedly in the postcolonial era. Although the new U.S. government preserved slavery and continued to restrict women's legal and political rights, property holding was widespread. A fluid class structure and economic expansion ensured that not just the political elite but the common people too would benefit from independence. In Latin America, however, continuation of the colonial class structure meant that the economic and social chasm between the mass of propertyless Indian peasants and the narrow elite of white property owners remained. More so than in North America, the independence movement in Latin America ended colonialism but was not a true revolution.

"Simple Facts, Plain Arguments, and Common Sense"

▼▼▼

46 ▼ Thomas Paine, *COMMON SENSE*

After more than a decade of growing tensions over taxes, British imperial policy, the power of colonial legislatures, and a host of other emotionally charged issues, in April 1775 the American Revolution began with the clash between British regulars and American militiamen at the Battle of Lexington and Concord. In May the Green Mountain Boys under Ethan Allen took Fort Ticonderoga on Lake Champlain, and in June the British defeated colonial troops in the Battle of Bunker Hill outside of Boston at the cost of more than a thousand casualties.

Despite these events, in the summer and fall of 1775 most Americans still supported compromise and reconciliation with Great Britain. They were convinced that evil ministers, not the king, were responsible for British policy and that views of conciliatory British politicians such as Edmund Burke would prevail. Then in January 1776 there appeared in Philadelphia a thirty-five page pamphlet entitled *Common Sense,* written by Thomas Paine (1737–1809), a bankrupt one-time corset-maker, sailor, tobacconist, and minor customs official, who had immigrated to Pennsylvania from England only fourteen months earlier to escape debtor's prison. Despite his background, Paine produced what was far and away the most brilliant political pamphlet written during the American Revolution, and perhaps ever in the English language.

In three months *Common Sense* sold more than 100,000 copies, one for every eight or ten adults in the colonies. It "burst from the press," wrote Benjamin Rush, the Pennsylvania physician and signer of the Declaration of Independence, "with an effect which has rarely been produced in any age or country." Written with passion and vivid imagery, Paine's pamphlet brought into focus American reservations about England and expressed American aspirations for creating a newer, freer, more open society as an independent nation. It accelerated the move toward the events of July 2, 1776, when the delegates to the Second Continental Congress created the United States of America, and of July 4, when they signed the Declaration of Independence.

During the Revolutionary War Paine fought in Washington's army and composed pamphlets to bolster American spirits. In the late 1780s he returned to England but in 1792 was forced to flee to France after his public support of the French Revolution led to his indictment for sedition. Chosen as a delegate to the French National Convention (although he knew no French), Paine was later imprisoned for ten months during the Reign of Terror, and on his release resided with James Monroe, the American ambassador to France. While in France he attacked Christianity in his pamphlet *The Age of Reason,* the notoriety of which was such that on his return to the United States in 1802 he was vilified as an atheist. Impoverished and disgraced, he died unheralded in New York City in 1809.

QUESTIONS FOR ANALYSIS

1. What are Paine's views of the origins and defects of monarchy as a form of government and hereditary succession as a principle of government?
2. What are his views of King George III?
3. What characteristics does Paine ascribe to Great Britain in general and the British government in particular? How might his background explain his negative views?
4. How does Paine counter the arguments of Americans who still sought reconciliation with Great Britain?

5. Despite Paine's rejection of the British government, do his ideas in *Common Sense* owe a debt to the principles of the English Bill of Rights?
6. What is there about the pamphlet's language, tone, and arguments that might explain its enormous popularity?

REMARKS ON THE ENGLISH CONSTITUTION

Absolute governments (though the disgrace of human nature) have this advantage with them, they are simple; if the people suffer, they know the head from which their suffering springs; know likewise the remedy; and are not bewildered by a variety of causes and cures. But the constitution of England is so exceedingly complex that the nation may suffer for years together without being able to discover in which part the fault lies; some will say in one and some in another, and every political physician will advise a different medicine.

An inquiry into the *constitutional errors* in the English form of government is at this time highly necessary; for as we are never in a proper condition of doing justice to others while we continue under the influence of some leading partiality, so neither are we capable of doing it to ourselves while we remain fettered by any obstinate prejudice. And as a man who is attached to a prostitute is unfitted to choose or judge of a wife, so any prepossession in favor of a rotten constitution of government will disable us from discerning a good one.

OF MONARCHY AND HEREDITARY SUCCESSION

Government by kings was first introduced into the world by the heathens, from whom the children of Israel copied the custom. It was the most prosperous invention the Devil ever set on foot for the promotion of idolatry. The heathens paid divine honors to their deceased kings, and the Christian world has improved on the plan by doing the same to their living ones.[1] How impious is the title of sacred Majesty applied to a worm, who in the midst of his splendor is crumbling into dust! . . .

To the evil of monarchy we have added that of hereditary succession; and as the first is a degradation and lessening of ourselves, so the second, claimed as a matter of rights, is an insult and imposition on posterity. For all men being originally equals, no *one* by *birth* could have a right to set up his own family in perpetual preference to all others forever, and though himself might deserve *some* decent degree of honors of his contemporaries, yet his descendants might be far too unworthy to inherit them. . . .

Secondly, as no man at first could possess any other public honors than were bestowed upon him, so the givers of those honors could have no power to give away the right of posterity, and though they might say "we choose you for our head," they could not without manifest injustice to their children say "that your children and your children's children shall reign over our's forever." Because such an unwise, unjust, unnatural compact might perhaps, in the next succession put them under the government of a rogue or a fool. . . .

This is supposing the present race of kings in the world to have had an honorable origin; whereas it is more than probable that, could we take off the dark covering of antiquity and trace them to their first rise, we should find the first of them nothing better than the principal ruffian of some restless gang. . . .

The most plausible plea which hath ever been offered in favor of hereditary succession is that it preserves a nation from civil wars; and were this true, it would be weighty; whereas, it is the most barefaced falsity ever imposed upon man-

---

[1]The reference is to the theory of divine right monarchy, which asserted that kings were God's specially chosen lieutenants to rule his subjects, and were even in some limited sense divine figures themselves.

kind. The whole history of England disowns the fact. Thirty kings and two minors have reigned in that distracted kingdom since the conquest,[2] in which time there have been (including the Revolution) no less than eight civil wars and nineteen rebellions. Wherefore instead of making for peace, it makes against it, and destroys the very foundation it seems to stand upon. . . .

In short, monarchy and succession have laid (not this or that kingdom only) but the world in blood and ashes. 'Tis a form of government which the word of god bears testimony against, and blood will attend it.

THOUGHTS ON THE PRESENT STATE OF AMERICAN AFFAIRS

In the following pages I offer nothing more than simple facts, plain arguments, and common sense; and have no other preliminaries to settle with the reader, than that he will divest himself of prejudice and prepossession, and suffer his reason and his feelings to determine for themselves; that he will put on, or rather that he will not put off, the true character of a man, and generously enlarge his views beyond the present day.

Volumes have been written on the subject of the struggle between England and America. Men of all ranks have embarked in the controversy, from different motives, and with various designs; but all have been ineffectual, and the period of debate is closed. Arms as the last resource decide the contest; the appeal was the choice of the king, and the continent has accepted the challenge. . . .

The sun never shined on a cause of greater worth. 'Tis not the affair of a city, a county, a province, or a kingdom; but of a continent — of at least one-eighth part of the habitable globe. 'Tis not the concern of a day, a year, or an age; posterity are virtually involved in the contest, and will be more or less affected even to the end

of time by the proceedings now. Now is the seedtime of continental union, faith, and honor. The least fracture now will be like a name engraved with the point of a pin on the tender rind of a young oak; the wound would enlarge with the tree, and posterity read it in full grown characters. . . .

I have heard it asserted by some, that as America has flourished under her former connection with Great Britain, the same connection is necessary towards her future happiness. . . . Nothing can be more fallacious than this kind of argument. We may as well assert that because a child has thrived upon milk, that it is never to have meat, or that the first twenty years of our lives is to become a precedent for the next twenty. But even this is admitting more than is true; for I answer roundly that America would have flourished as much, and probably much more, had no European power taken any notice of her. The commerce by which she hath enriched herself are the necessaries of life, and will always have a market while eating is the custom of Europe.

But she has protected us, say some. That she hath engrossed[3] us is true, and defended the continent at our expense as well as her own is admitted; and she would have defended Turkey from the same motive, viz., for the sake of trade and dominion. . . .

We have boasted the protection of Great Britain without considering that her motive was *interest,* not *attachment;* and that she did not protect us from *our enemies* on *our account,* but from her enemies on her own account, from those who had no quarrel with us on any *other account,* and who will always be our enemies on the *same account.* . . .

As I have always considered the independency of this continent an event which sooner or later must arrive, so from the late rapid progress of the continent to maturity, the event cannot be far off. Wherefore, on the breaking out of hostil-

---

[2]A reference to the conquest of England in 1066 by the Duke of Normandy, who reigned as King William I until his death in 1087.

[3]To occupy with troops.

ities, it was not worth the while to have disputed a matter which time would have finally redressed, unless we meant to be in earnest; otherwise it is like wasting an estate on a suit at law, to regulate the trespasses of a tenant whose lease is just expiring. No man was a warmer wisher for a reconciliation than myself, before the fatal nineteenth of April, 1775, but the moment the event of that day was made known, I rejected the hardened, sullen-tempered Pharaoh of England[4] forever; and disdain the wretch, that with the pretended title of FATHER OF HIS PEOPLE can unfeelingly hear of their slaughter, and composedly sleep with their blood upon his soul.

But admitting that matters were now made up, what would be the event? I answer, the ruin of the continent. And that for several reasons.

First. The powers of governing still remaining in the hands of the king, he will have a negative[5] over the whole legislation of this continent. And as he hath shown himself such an inveterate enemy to liberty, and discovered such a thirst for arbitrary power, is he, or is he not, a proper person to say to these colonies, *You shall make no laws but what I please!* . . .

Secondly. That as even the best terms which we can expect to obtain can amount to no more than a temporary expedient, or a kind of government by guardianship, which can last no longer than till the colonies come of age, so the general face and state of things in the interim will be unsettled and unpromising. Emigrants of property will not choose to come to a country whose form of government hangs but by a thread, and who is every day tottering on the brink of commotion and disturbance; and numbers of the present inhabitants would lay hold of the interval to dispose of their effects, and quit the continent. . . .

If there is any true cause of fear respecting independence, it is because no plan is yet laid down. Men do not see their way out. Wherefore, as an opening into that business I offer the following hints; at the same time modestly affirming that I have no other opinion of them myself

than that they may be the means of giving rise to something better. . . .

Let the assemblies be annual, with a president only. The representation more equal, their business wholly domestic, and subject to the authority of a continental congress.

Let each colony be divided into six, eight, or ten, convenient districts, each district to send a proper number of delegates to congress, so that each colony send at least thirty. The whole number in congress will be at least 390. Each congress to sit and to choose a president by the following method. When the delegates are met, let a colony be taken from the whole thirteen colonies by lot, after which let the congress choose (by ballot) a president from out of the delegates of that province. In the next congress, let a colony be taken by lot from twelve only, omitting that colony from which the president was taken in the former congress, and so proceeding on till the whole thirteen shall have had their proper rotation. And in order that nothing may pass into a law but what is satisfactorily just, not less than three fifths of the congress to be called a majority. He that will promote discord, under a government so equally formed as this, would have joined Lucifer in his revolt. . . .

But where, say some, is the king of America? I'll tell you, friend, he reigns above, and doth not make havoc of mankind like the Royal Brute of Great Britain. Yet that we may not appear to be defective even in earthly honors, let a day be solemnly set apart for proclaiming the charter; let it be brought forth placed on the divine law, the Word of God; let a crown be placed thereon, by which the world may know, that so far as we approve of monarchy, that in America THE LAW IS KING. For as in absolute governments the king is law, so in free countries the law *ought* to BE king, and there ought to be no other. But lest any ill use should afterwards arise, let the crown at the conclusion of the ceremony be demolished, and scattered among the people whose right it is. . . .

---

[4]A reference to King George III of England.

[5]A veto.

Ye that tell us of harmony and reconciliation, can ye restore to us the time that is past? Can ye give to prostitution its former innocence? Neither can ye reconcile Britain and America. The last cord now is broken, the people of England are presenting addresses against us. There are injuries which nature cannot forgive; she would cease to be nature if she did. As well can the lover forgive the ravisher of his mistress, as the continent forgive the murders of Britain. . . .

O ye that love mankind! Ye that dare oppose not only the tyranny but the tyrant, stand forth! Every spot of the old world is overrun with oppression. Freedom hath been hunted round the globe. Asia and Africa have long expelled her. Europe regards her like a stranger, and England hath given her warning to depart. O receive the fugitive, and prepare in time an asylum[6] for mankind.

---

[6]A place of refuge and protection.

Bolívar's Dreams for Latin America
▼▼▼

47 ▼ *Simón Bolívar, THE JAMAICA LETTER*

Simón Bolívar, the most renowned leader of the Latin American independence movement, was born to a wealthy Venezuelan landowning family in 1783. Orphaned at an early age, he was educated by a private tutor who inspired in his pupil an enthusiasm for the principles of the Enlightenment and republicanism. After spending three years in Europe, Bolívar returned to New Spain in 1803, where the death of his new bride plunged him into grief and caused his return to France and Italy. In 1805 in Rome he took a vow to dedicate his life to the liberation of his native land. On his return he became a leading member of the republican-minded group in Caracas that in 1808 began to agitate for independence and in 1810 deposed the colonial governor. Until his death in 1830, Bolívar dedicated himself to the Latin American independence movement as a publicist, diplomat, theoretician, and statesman. His greatest contribution was as the general who led the armies that defeated the Spaniards and liberated the northern regions of South America.

The so-called Jamaica Letter was written in 1815 during a self-imposed exile in Jamaica. It was addressed to "an English gentleman," probably the island's governor, the Duke of Manchester. The Venezuelan Republic had collapsed in May as a result of a viciously fought Spanish counteroffensive, divisions among the revolutionaries, and opposition from many Indians, blacks, and mulattos, who viewed the Creole landowners, not the Spaniards, as their oppressors. The letter was written in response to a request from the Englishman for Bolívar's thoughts about the background and prospects of the liberation movement.

QUESTIONS FOR ANALYSIS

1. Why does Bolívar believe that Spain's efforts to hold on to its American territories are doomed?

2. What Spanish policies, according to Bolívar, made Spanish rule odious to him and other revolutionaries?
3. In Bolívar's view, what complicates the task of predicting Spanish America's political future?
4. Does Bolívar's letter reveal concern for the economic and social condition of South America's nonwhite population? What are some of the implications of Bolívar's attitudes?
5. Based on your reading of Bolívar, what guesses can you make about the reasons why the new nations of South America found it difficult to achieve stable republican governments?

With what a feeling of gratitude I read that passage in your letter in which you say to me: "I hope that the success which then followed Spanish arms may now turn in favor of their adversaries, the badly oppressed people of South America." I take this hope as a prediction, if it is justice that determines man's contests. Success will crown our efforts, because the destiny of America has been irrevocably decided; the tie that bound her to Spain has been severed. Only a concept maintained that tie and kept the parts of that immense monarchy together. That which formerly bound them now divides them. The hatred that the Peninsula[1] inspired in us is greater than the ocean between us. It would be easier to have the two continents meet than to reconcile the spirits of the two countries. The habit of obedience; a community of interest, of understanding, of religion; mutual goodwill; a tender regard for the birthplace and good name of our forefathers; in short, all that gave rise to our hopes, came to us from Spain. As a result there was born a principle of affinity that seemed eternal, notwithstanding the misbehavior of our rulers which weakened that sympathy, or, rather, that bond enforced by the domination of their rule. At present the contrary attitude persists: we are threatened with the fear of death, dishonor, and every harm; there is nothing we have not suffered at the hands of that unnatural stepmother — Spain. The veil has been torn asunder.

We have already seen the light, and it is not our desire to be thrust back into darkness. . . .

It is . . . difficult to foresee the future fate of the New World, to set down its political principles, or to prophesy what manner of government it will adopt. . . . We inhabit a world apart, separated by broad seas. We are young in the ways of almost all the arts and sciences, although, in a certain manner, we are old in the ways of civilized society. . . . But we scarcely retain a vestige of what once was; we are, moreover, neither Indian nor European, but a species midway between the legitimate proprietors of this country and the Spanish usurpers. In short, though Americans by birth we derive our rights from Europe, and we have to assert these rights against the rights of the natives, and at the same time we must defend ourselves against the invaders. This places us in a most extraordinary and involved situation. . . .

The role of the inhabitants of the American hemisphere has for centuries been purely passive. Politically they were non-existent. We are still in a position lower than slavery, and therefore it is more difficult for us to rise to the enjoyment of freedom. . . . States are slaves because of either the nature or the misuse of their constitutions; a people is therefore enslaved when the government, by its nature or its vices, infringes on and usurps the rights of the citizen or subject. Applying these principles, we find that America

---

[1]Refers to the Iberian Peninsula, consisting of Spain and Portugal.

was denied not only its freedom but even an active and effective tyranny. Under absolutism there are no recognized limits to the exercise of governmental powers. The will of the great sultan, khan, bey, and other despotic rulers is the supreme law, carried out more or less arbitrarily by the lesser pashas, khans, and satraps of Turkey and Persia, who have an organized system of oppression in which inferiors participate according to the authority vested in them. To them is entrusted the administration of civil, military, political, religious, and tax matters. But, after all is said and done, the rulers of Isfahan are Persians; the viziers of the Grand Turk are Turks; and the sultans of Tartary are Tartars. . . .

How different is our situation! We have been harassed by a conduct which has not only deprived us of our rights but has kept us in a sort of permanent infancy with regard to public affairs. If we could at least have managed our domestic affairs and our internal administration, we could have acquainted ourselves with the processes and mechanics of public affairs. . . .

Americans today, and perhaps to a greater extent than ever before, who live within the Spanish system occupy a position in society no better than that of serfs destined for labor, or at best they have no more status than that of mere consumers. Yet even this status is surrounded with galling restrictions, such as being forbidden to grow European crops, or to store products which are royal monopolies, or to establish factories of a type the Peninsula itself does not possess. To this add the exclusive trading privileges, even in articles of prime necessity, and the barriers between American provinces, designed to prevent all exchange of trade, traffic, and understanding. In short, do you wish to know what our future held? — simply the cultivation of the fields of indigo, grain, coffee, sugar cane, cacao, and cotton; cattle raising on the broad plains; hunting wild game in the jungles; digging in

the earth to mine its gold — but even these limitations could never satisfy the greed of Spain.

So negative was our existence that I can find nothing comparable in any other civilized society, examine as I may the entire history of time and the politics of all nations. Is it not an outrage and a violation of human rights to expect a land so splendidly endowed, so vast, rich, and populous, to remain merely passive?

As I have just explained, we were cut off and, as it were, removed from the world in relation to the science of government and administration of the state. We were never viceroys or governors, save in the rarest of instances; seldom archbishops and bishops; diplomats never; as military men, only subordinates; as nobles, without royal privileges. In brief, we were neither magistrates nor financiers and seldom merchants — all in flagrant contradiction to our institutions. . . .

It is harder, Montesquieu[2] has written, to release a nation from servitude than to enslave a free nation. This truth is proven by the annals of all times, which reveal that most free nations have been put under the yoke, but very few enslaved nations have recovered their liberty. Despite the convictions of history, South Americans have made efforts to obtain liberal, even perfect, institutions, doubtless out of that instinct to aspire to the greatest possible happiness, which, common to all men, is bound to follow in civil societies founded on the principles of justice, liberty, and equality. But are we capable of maintaining in proper balance the difficult charge of a republic? Is it conceivable that a newly emancipated people can soar to the heights of liberty, and, unlike Icarus, neither have its wings melt nor fall into an abyss? Such a marvel is inconceivable and without precedent. There is no reasonable probability to bolster our hopes.

More than anyone, I desire to see America fashioned into the greatest nation in the world, greatest not so much by virtue of her area and

---

[2]Montesquieu (1689–1755) was a French philosopher, historian, and jurist best known for his *Spirit of the Laws* (1755) and his theory that the powers of government — executive,

legislative, and judicial — must be separated to ensure individual freedom.

wealth as by her freedom and glory. Although I seek perfection for the government of my country, I cannot persuade myself that the New World can, at the moment, be organized as a great republic. Since it is impossible, I dare not desire it; yet much less do I desire to have all America a monarchy because this plan is not only impracticable but also impossible. Wrongs now existing could not be righted, and our emancipation would be fruitless. The American states need the care of paternal governments to heal the sores and wounds of despotism and war. . . .

From the foregoing, we can draw these conclusions: The American provinces are fighting for their freedom, and they will ultimately succeed. Some provinces as a matter of course will form federal and some central republics; the larger areas will inevitably establish monarchies, some of which will fare so badly that they will disintegrate in either present or future revolutions. To consolidate a great monarchy will be no easy task, but it will be utterly impossible to consolidate a great republic. . . .

When success is not assured, when the state is weak, and when results are distantly seen, all men hesitate; opinion is divided, passions rage, and the enemy fans these passions in order to win an easy victory because of them. As soon as we are strong and under the guidance of a liberal nation which will lend us her protection, we will achieve accord in cultivating the virtues and talents that lead to glory. Then will we march majestically toward that great prosperity for which South America is destined. . . .

Chapter 6

▼▼▼

Africa, Southwest Asia, and India in the Seventeenth and Eighteenth Centuries

Around 1600, Southwest Asia and India, regions dominated by the large and powerful Ottoman, Safavid, and Mughal empires, would seem to have had little in common with Africa, a continent that was divided into hundreds of kingdoms, confederations, chiefdoms, independent cities, and large regions with no formal states. Southwest Asia and India, moreover, had but two major religions, Islam and Hinduism, while Africa had many — Islam in the Mediterranean north, the Sudan, and the east coast, Christianity in Ethiopia, and numerous varieties of animism throughout the continent. In comparison to Africa, India and Southwest Asia were more densely populated and more urbanized, and had more commercial and cultural contacts with Europe and East Asia.

Despite these many differences, during the seventeenth and eighteenth centuries, Africa, Southwest Asia, and India shared a number of common historical experiences. All three areas, for example, experienced increasing political instability leading in some cases to the collapse of once formidable states. The Persian Safavid Empire was overrun and disappeared in the 1730s, and in India the Mughal Empire was reduced to impotence and irrelevance by the mid 1700s. The Ottoman Empire survived, but with shrunken borders, a demoralized populace, and an army that was a shadow of the force that had marched from victory to victory in the fifteenth and sixteenth centuries. In Africa the Songhai Empire in West Africa fell apart after a major defeat by invading Moroccans in 1591, and in the southeast the Kingdom of Monomotapa disintegrated after it was overrun by a former client state, the Changamire Kingdom, in

1685. Other African states survived but experienced civil war, invasion, or the erosion of central authority. These included Ethiopia, the Christian state in east Africa; Benin, a kingdom on the Gulf of Guinea; and Kanem-Bornu, in the central Sudan. Political decline in Africa was not universal. Dahomey, the Asante Confederation, and Oyo all emerged as formidable powers, and throughout the continent hundreds of chieftainships preserved their traditional authority. Overall, however, African political life became less stable and more subject to conflict in the 1600s and 1700s.

Increased European pressure and involvement is another common thread in the histories of the three regions. In some cases this involvement was subtle and indirect. In the Ottoman Empire, for example, European traders used ever-greater amounts of American silver to purchase agricultural products and manufactured goods, and by creating shortages and causing inflation, added to the woes of Ottoman society. In other cases European involvement meant actual political control. In India in the eighteenth century, officials of the British East India Company took advantage of the Mughal Empire's disintegration by established their authority over Bengal in the northeast and other regions on the subcontinent's east coast. In Africa the 1600s and 1700s saw the beginnings of permanent white settlement on the continent and a dramatic increase in the transatlantic slave trade. European settlement began in 1652 when Dutch farmers arrived at the southern tip of Africa and soon began to push into the interior in search of land and slaves. Meanwhile on Africa's west coast Europeans presided over a substantial increase in the transatlantic slave trade in response to demands for slaves from West Indian and Brazilian sugar producers. As many as 6 million Africans were transported to the Americas as slaves in the 1700s. On Africa's east coast slave exports also increased. By the end of the eighteenth century Dutch, Portuguese, Arab, and French merchants were selling many thousands of African slaves per year to buyers in the Middle East, India, and French-controlled islands in the Indian Ocean. This spectacular growth in the slave trade underlined Africa's vulnerability in an age of growing global interaction.

Africa's Curse: The Slave Trade

Slavery has been practiced throughout history, in every corner of the globe. Slavery has existed in small farming villages in China and great imperial cities such as ancient Rome; it has been practiced by pastoral nomads, plantation owners, small farmers, emperors, and modern totalitarian dictators. Slavery is mentioned in ancient Sumerian law codes from the fourth millennium B.C.E., and is still the lot of millions of human beings today despite its official condemnation by the world's governments.

In recent history slavery has uniquely affected the people of Africa, who became a source of unpaid labor in many parts of the world, especially the Americas. The transatlantic slave trade began in the fifteenth century under the Portuguese, who at first made small shipments of Africans to Portugal to serve as domestics and then larger shipments to the Canary Islands, the Madeiras, and São Tomé to work on sugar plantations. By 1500, approximately 500 slaves were exported each year. That number grew appreciably in the mid 1500s, when the plantation system was established in Brazil and subsequently spread to Spanish America, the West Indies, and British North America. By the eighteenth century, when Great Britain became the leading purveyor of slaves, the transatlantic slave trade peaked, with more than 6 million slaves transported to the Americas.

Almost every aspect of modern African slavery is the subject of debate among historians. Did the enslavement of Africans result from racism, or were Africans enslaved because they were available and convenient to the market across the Atlantic? Did the loss of millions of individuals to slavery over 500 years have serious or minimal demographic consequences for Africa? Was the political instability of African states linked to the slave trade or other factors? Did reliance on selling slaves to Europeans impede Africa's economic development? Did European governments abolish the slave trade because of humanitarianism or hard-headed economic calculation?

One thing is certain. For the millions of Africans who were captured, shackled, wrenched from their families, branded, sold, packed into the holds of ships, sold once more, and put to work in American mines and fields, enslavement meant pain, debasement, and fear. For them, slavery was an unmitigated and terrible curse.

The Path to Enslavement in America
▼▼▼

48 ▼ *Olaudah Equiano,*
THE INTERESTING NARRATIVE
OF OLAUDAH EQUIANO
WRITTEN BY HIMSELF

In 1789 no fewer than 100 abolitionist books and pamphlets were published in England, but none was more widely read than the autobiography of the former slave Olaudah Equiano. In his memoir Equiano relates that he was born in 1745 in Iboland, an area east of the Niger River delta that today is part of Nigeria. He also describes how he was captured and sold into slavery when he was about eleven years old, and having survived the harrowing Atlantic crossing, served three masters, including Michael Henry Pascal, an officer in the British navy; an English sea captain who took him to the West Indian island of Montserrat; and finally Robert King, a Quaker merchant from Philadelphia.

In many ways Equiano's experiences as a slave were exceptional. He never served as a plantation slave, and while owned by Pascal he learned to read and write. Under his three masters he made numerous trips back and forth across the Atlantic and in the process learned skills relating to navigation, bookkeeping, and commerce. Having purchased his freedom from King in 1766, he took up residence in England, where he supported himself as a barber, servant, and crew member on sea voyages to the Mediterranean and around the Atlantic. In the 1770s he joined the English abolitionist movement, and as a result of the contacts he made with the movement's leaders, in the late 1780s he was given a government post with the responsibility of arranging the transfer of food and other provisions to Sierra Leone, a newly founded colony that abolitionists hoped would serve as an African homeland for freed slaves. Dismissed after a year, Equiano turned to writing his autobiography, which with the financial support of leading abolitionists, was published in 1789. Heavily promoted by Equiano on a lecture tour that took him to dozens of British towns and cities, his book went through eight editions in the 1790s. It is generally acknowledged that it strengthened the abolitionist cause, and must be given at least some of the credit for the act of Parliament in 1807 that abolished the British slave trade.

How factual is Equiano's narrative? Historians must ask this question of any historical source, especially autobiographies, whose authors cannot be expected to be totally objective when writing about themselves or to be totally accurate in recalling childhood events. Equiano's memoirs, furthermore, were written with a specific purpose, namely to discredit slavery and garner support for the abolitionist cause. One scholar, Vincent Carretta from the University of Maryland, has recently suggested that Equiano fabricated the account of his kidnapping in Africa and his voyage across the Atlantic on the slave ship. A baptismal certificate and a Royal Navy document, he argues, show that Equiano was actually born in South Carolina, not Africa.

Other scholars reject Carretta's evidence as inconclusive and continue to believe that Equiano's memoir is generally accurate. Certainly a comparison of Equiano's description of his slave experience with what we know from other sources suggests that his work is free of exaggeration and distortion. This includes the following excerpt in which he describes his harsh introduction to slavery.

QUESTIONS FOR ANALYSIS

1. On the basis of Equiano's account, describe the role of Africans in the slave trade.
2. What does Equiano's account reveal about the effect of slavery and the slave trade on African society?
3. What were the characteristics of slavery that Equiano encountered?
4. Once aboard the slave ship, what in the slaves' experiences contributed to their despair and demoralization, according to Equiano?
5. What factors might have contributed to the brutal treatment of the slaves by the ship's crew?

TAKEN CAPTIVE

Generally when the grown people in the neighborhood were gone far in the fields to labor, the children assembled together in some of the neighbors' premises to play, and commonly some of us used to get up a tree to look out for any assailant or kidnapper that might come upon us, for they sometimes took those opportunities of our parents' absence to attack and carry off as many as they could seize. . . . One day, when all our people were gone out to their work as usual and only I and my dear sister were left to mind the house, two men and a woman got over our walls, and in a moment seized us both, and without giving us time to cry out or make resistance they stopped our mouths and ran off with us into the nearest wood. . . .

For a long time we had kept to the woods, but at last we came into a road which I believed I knew. I had now some hopes of being delivered, for we had advanced but a little way before I discovered some people at a distance, on which I began to cry out for their assistance: but my cries had no other effect than to make them tie me faster and stop my mouth, and then they put me into a large sack. They also stopped my sister's mouth and tied her hands, and in this manner we proceeded till we were out of the sight of these people. When we went to rest the following night they offered us some victuals, but we refused it, and the only comfort we had was in being in one another's arms all that night and bathing each other with our tears. But alas! we were soon deprived of even the small comfort of weeping together. The next day proved a day of greater sorrow than I had yet experienced, for my sister and I were then separated while we lay clasped in each other's arms. It was in vain that we besought them not to part us; she was torn from me and immediately carried away, while I was left in a state of distraction not to be described. I cried and grieved continually, and for several days I did not eat anything but what they forced into my mouth. At length, after many days' traveling, during which I had often changed masters, I got into the hands of a chieftain in a very pleasant country. This man had two wives and some children, and they all used me extremely well and did all they could to comfort me, particularly the first wife, who was something like my mother. . . . This first master of mine, as I may call him, was a smith, and my principal employment was working his bellows, which were the same kind as I had seen in my vicinity. . . . I believe it was gold he worked, for it was of a lovely bright yellow color and was worn by the women on their wrists and ankles. I was there I suppose about a month, and they at last used to trust me some little distance from the house. This liberty I used in embracing every opportunity to inquire the way to my own home: and I also sometimes, for the same purpose, went with the maidens in the cool of the evenings to bring pitchers of water from the springs for the use of the house.

▷ Equiano escapes but terrified of being alone in the forest at night returns to his household.

Soon after this my master's only daughter and child by his first wife sickened and died, which affected him so much that for some time he was almost frantic, and really would have killed himself had he not been watched and prevented. However, in a small time afterwards he recovered and I was again sold. I was now carried to the left of the sun's rising, through many different countries and a number of large woods. The people I was sold to used to carry me very often when I was tired either on their shoulders or on their backs. I saw many convenient well-built sheds along the roads at proper distances, to accommodate the merchants and travelers who lay in those buildings along with their wives, who often accompany them; and they always go well armed.

▷ Equiano encounters his sister, but again they are quickly separated.

I was now more miserable, if possible, than before. The small relief which her presence gave me from pain was gone, and the wretchedness of my situation was redoubled by my anxiety after her fate and my apprehensions lest her sufferings should be greater than mine, when I could not be with her to alleviate them. Yes, thou dear partner of all my childish sports! thou sharer of my joys and sorrow! happy should I have ever esteemed

myself to encounter every misery for you, and to procure your freedom by the sacrifice of my own. . . .

I did not long remain after my sister [departed]. I was again sold and carried through a number of places till, after traveling a considerable time, I came to a town called Tinmah in the most beautiful country I had yet seen in Africa. . . . I was sold here . . . by a merchant who lived and brought me there. I had been about two or three days at his house when a wealthy widow, a neighbor of his, came there one evening, and brought with her an only son, a young gentleman about my own age and size. Here they saw me; and, having taken a fancy to me, I was bought of the merchant, and went home with them. . . . The next day I was washed and perfumed, and when meal-time came I was led into the presence of my mistress, and ate and drank before her with her son. This filled me with astonishment; and I could scarce help expressing my surprise that the young gentleman should suffer me, who was bound, to eat with him who was free; and not only so, but that he would not at any time either eat or drink till I had taken first, because I was the eldest, which was agreeable to our custom. Indeed everything here, and all their treatment of me, made me forget that I was a slave. . . . There were likewise slaves daily to attend us, while my young master and I with other boys sported with our darts and bows and arrows, as I had been used to do at home. In this resemblance to my former happy state I passed about two months; and I now began to think I was to be adopted into the family, and was beginning to be reconciled to my situation, and to forget by degrees my misfortunes, when all at once the delusion vanished; for without the least previous knowledge, one morning early, while my dear master and companion was still asleep, I was wakened out of my reverie to fresh sorrow, and hurried away. . . .

At last I came to the banks of a large river, which was covered with canoes in which the people appeared to live with their household utensils and provisions of all kinds. I was beyond measure astonished at this, as I had never before seen any water larger than a pond or a rivulet: and my surprise was mingled with no small fear when I was put into one of these canoes and we began to paddle and move along the river. We continued going on thus till night, and when we came to land and made fires on the banks, each family by themselves, some dragged their canoes on shore, others stayed and cooked in theirs and laid in them all night. . . . Thus I continued to travel, sometimes by land, sometimes by water, through different countries and various nations, till at the end of six or seven months after I had been kidnapped I arrived at the sea coast.

THE SLAVE SHIP

The first object which saluted my eyes when I arrived on the coast was the sea, and a slave ship which was then riding at anchor and waiting for its cargo. These filled me with astonishment, which was soon converted into terror when I was carried on board. I was immediately handled and tossed up to see if I were sound by some of the crew, and I was now persuaded that I had gotten into a world of bad spirits and that they were going to kill me. Their complexions too differing so much from ours, their long hair and the language they spoke (which was very different from any I had ever heard) united to confirm me in this belief. Indeed such were the horrors of my views and fears at the moment that, if ten thousand worlds had been my own, I would have freely parted with them all to have exchanged my condition with that of the meanest slave in my own country. When I looked round the ship too and saw a large furnace or copper boiling and a multitude of black people of every description chained together, every one of their countenances expressing dejection and sorrow, I no longer doubted of my fate; and quite overpowered with horror and anguish, I fell motionless on the deck and fainted. When I recovered a little I found some black people about me, who I believed were some of those who had brought me on board and had been receiving their pay; they talked to me in order to cheer me, but all in vain. . . .

I was soon put down under the decks, and there I received such a salutation in my nostrils as I had never experienced in my life: so that with the loathsomeness of the stench and crying together, I became so sick and low that I was not able to eat, nor had I the least desire to taste anything. I now wished for the last friend, death, to relieve me; but soon, to my grief, two of the white men offered me eatables, and on my refusing to eat, one of them held me fast by the hands and laid me across I think the windlass, and tied my feet while the other flogged me severely. I had never experienced anything of this kind before, and although, not being used to the water, I naturally feared that element the first time I saw it, yet nevertheless could I have got over the nettings I would have jumped over the side, but I could not; and besides, the crew used to watch us very closely who were not chained down to the decks, lest we should leap into the water: and I have seen some of these poor African prisoners most severely cut for attempting to do so, and hourly whipped for not eating. This indeed was often the case with myself. In a little time after, amongst the poor chained men I found some of my own nation, which in a small degree gave ease to my mind. I inquired of these what was to be done with us; they gave me to understand we were to be carried to these white people's country to work for them. I then was a little revived, and thought if it were no worse than working, my situation was not so desperate: but still I feared I should be put to death, the white people looked and acted, as I thought, in so savage a manner; for I had never seen among my people such instances of brutal cruelty, and this not only shown towards us blacks but also to some of the whites themselves. One white man in particular I saw, when we were permitted to be on deck, flogged so unmercifully with a large rope near the foremast that he died in consequence of it; and they tossed him over the side as they would have done a brute. This made me fear these people the more, and I expected nothing less than to be treated in the same manner. . . .

At last, when the ship we were in had got in all her cargo, they made ready with many fearful noises, and we were all put under deck so that we could not see how they managed the vessel. But this disappointment was the last of my sorrow. The stench of the hold while we were on the coast was so intolerably loathsome that it was dangerous to remain there for any time, and some of us had been permitted to stay on the deck for the fresh air; but now that the whole ship's cargo were confined together it became absolutely pestilential. The closeness of the place and the heat of the climate, added to the number in the ship, which was so crowded that each had scarcely room to turn himself, almost suffocated us. This produced copious perspirations, so that the air soon became unfit for respiration from a variety of loathsome smells, and brought on a sickness among the slaves, of which many died, thus falling victims to the improvident avarice, as I may call it, of their purchasers. This wretched situation was again aggravated by the galling of the chains, now become insupportable, and the filth of the necessary tubs, into which the children often fell and were almost suffocated. The shrieks of the women and the groans of the dying rendered the whole a scene of horror almost inconceivable. Happily perhaps for myself I was soon reduced so low here that it was thought necessary to keep me almost always on deck, and from my extreme youth I was not put in fetters. . . .

One day, when we had a smooth sea and moderate wind, two of my wearied countrymen who were chained together (I was near them at the time), preferring death to such a life of misery, somehow made through the nettings and jumped into the sea: immediately another quite dejected fellow, who on account of his illness was suffered to be out of irons, also followed their example; and I believe many more would very soon have done the same if they had not been prevented by the ship's crew, who were instantly alarmed. Those of us that were the most active were in a moment put down under the deck, and there was such a noise and confusion amongst the people of the ship as I never heard before, to stop her and get the boat out to go after the slaves.

However two of the wretches were drowned, but they got the other and afterwards flogged him unmercifully for thus attempting to prefer death to slavery. In this manner we continued to undergo more hardships than I can now relate, hardships which are inseparable from this accursed trade. Many a time we were near suffocation from the want of fresh air, which we were often without for whole days together. This and the stench of the necessary tubs carried off many. . . .

At last we came in sight of the island of Barbados, at which the whites on board gave a great shout and made many signs of joy to us. We did not know what to think of this, but as the vessel drew nearer we plainly saw the harbor and other ships of different kinds and sizes, and we soon anchored amongst them off Bridgetown. Many merchants and planters now came on board, though it was in the evening. They put us in separate parcels and examined us attentively. They also made us jump, and pointed to the land, signifying we were to go there. . . .

We were not many days in the merchant's custody before we were sold after their usual manner, which is this: On a signal given, (as the beat of a drum) the buyers rush at once into the yard where the slaves are confined, and make choice of that parcel they like best. The noise and clamor with which this is attended and the eagerness visible in the countenances of the buyers serve not a little to increase the apprehensions of the terrified Africans, who may well be supposed to consider them as the ministers of that destruction to which they think themselves devoted. In this manner, without scruple, are relations and friends separated, most of them never to see each other again. I remember in the vessel in which I was brought over, in the men's apartment there were several brothers who, in the sale, were sold in different lots; and it was very moving on this occasion to see and hear their cries at parting. O, ye nominal Christians! might not an African ask you, learned you this from your God who says unto you, Do unto all men as you would men should do unto you?

The Economics of the Slave Trade on Africa's Coast

▼▼▼

49 ▼ Thomas Phillips, *A JOURNAL OF A VOYAGE MADE IN THE HANNIBAL OF LONDON IN 1694*

As Olaudah Equiano's memoirs reveal, the road to slavery in the Americas for millions of Africans began in thousands of inland villages where as a result of military defeat, slave raids, or the decision of a chieftain or king, they were wrenched from their homes and marched to a slave market on the coast. There, while they were herded together in closely guarded holding pens or prison-like structures, complex and sometimes lengthy business negotiations took place between European merchants whose ships lay anchored off the coast and African slave merchants, many of whom were kings or major chieftains. Many European merchants recorded their experiences in such negotiations in memoirs or journals, and their recollections provide a wealth of information about the economics of the slave trade. They also offer many insights into how African and European slave traders viewed each other and their profession. They reveal that for millions of Africans the transatlantic slave trade was a nightmare, but for many others — Europeans, Americans, Africans, and indirectly even Asians — it was one more way to make a profit in an increasingly commercialized world.

Thomas Phillips, the author of the following account of a slave voyage from England to Africa to the Barbados Islands in the Caribbean in 1693 and 1694, was an English merchant. In 1693 he purchased the slave ship *Hannibal* in partnership with a number of London merchants who were members of the Royal African Company, a trading company chartered by King Charles II in 1672. The *Hannibal,* along with five other ships, departed England late in 1693 for Whydah, a kingdom on the Guinea Coast, which is located in the modern nation of Benin some 200 miles east of the city of Lagos, Nigeria. Whydah, the coastal village where the king resided, was rapidly developing into a major slave market and had been the site of an English trading station, or "factory," since 1682. The events Phillips describes took place in May 1694.

QUESTIONS FOR ANALYSIS

1. What evidence does the source provide about the attitudes of the Whydah king and nobility toward Europeans? Did they consider themselves equal, inferior, or superior to Europeans?
2. What do Phillips' words and actions reveal about his views of Africans?
3. What does the source reveal about Africans as businessmen? What did they hope to gain from trading with Europeans? How would you describe their business methods?

4. What can you infer from Phillips' account about the impact of the Whydah slave trade on Africa's interior?
5. Compile a list of individuals or groups of individuals who benefited economically from the slave trade. Do not limit yourself to Europeans or simply to merchants and investors. You should end up with at least some Asians on your list.
6. Compare the attitudes toward slavery of the king of Whydah and his nobility with those of King Afonso of Kongo (source 28) some 200 years earlier. How might one account for these differences?

Our factory [at Whydah] lies about three miles from the sea-side, where we were carry'd in hamocks, which the factor [agent] Mr. Joseph Peirson, sent to attend our landing, with several arm'd blacks that belong'd to him for our guard; . . .

Our factory . . . stands low near the marshes, which renders it a very unhealthy place to live in; the white men the African company send there, seldom returning to tell their tale: 'tis compass'd round with a mudwall, about six foot high, and on the southside is the gate; within is a large yard, a mud thatch'd house, where the factor lives, with the white men; also a store-house, a trunk [a prison-like holding area] for slaves, and a place where they bury their dead white men, call'd, very improperly, the hog-yard; there is also a good forge, and some other small houses. . . .

As soon as the king understood of our landing, he sent two of his cappasheirs, or noblemen, to compliment us at our factory, where we design'd to continue, that night, and pay our devoirs [respects] to his majesty next day . . . ; whereupon he sent two more of his grandees to invite us there that night, saying he waited for us, and that all former captains used to attend him the first night: whereupon being unwilling to infringe the custom, or give his majesty any offence, we took our hamocks, and Mr. Peirson, myself, Capt. Clay, our surgeons, pursers,[1] and about 12 men, arm'd for our guard, were carry'd to the king's town, which contains about 50 houses. . . .

We returned him thanks by his interpreter, and assur'd him how great affection our masters, the royal African company of England, bore to him, for his civility and fair and just dealings with their captains; and that notwithstanding there were many other Places, more plenty of negro slaves that begg'd their custom [business patronage], yet they had rejected all the advantageous offers made them out of their good will to him, and therefore had sent us to trade with him, to supply his country with necessaries, and that we hop'd he would endeavour to continue their favour by his kind usage and fair dealing with us in our trade, that we may have our slaves with all expedition. . . . He answer'd that the African company was a very good brave man; that he lov'd him; that we should be fairly dealt with, and not impos'd upon; But he did not prove as good as his word; . . . so after having examin'd us about our cargoe, what sort of goods we had, and what quantity of slaves we wanted, etc., we took our leaves and return'd to the factory. . . .

According to [our] promise we attended his majesty [the next morning] with samples of our goods, and made our agreement about the prices, tho' not without much difficulty . . . ; then we had warehouses, a kitchen, and lodgings assign'd us . . . next day we paid our customs to the king and cappasheirs, as will appear hereafter; then the bell was order'd to go about to give notice to all people to bring their slaves to the trunk to sell us. . . .

---

[1]A ship's officer responsible for keeping accounts and business papers.

Capt. Clay [the captain of another English ship] and I had agreed to go to the trunk to buy the slaves by turns, each his day, that we might have no distraction or disagreement in our trade, as often happens when there are here more ships than one, and . . . their disagreements create animosities, underminings, and out-bidding each other, whereby they enhance the prices to their general loss and detriment, the blacks well knowing how to make the best use of such opportunities, and as we found make it their business, and endeavour to create and foment misunderstandings and jealousies between commanders, it turning to their great account in the disposal of their slaves.

When we were at the trunk, the king's slaves, if he had any, were the first offer'd to sale, . . . and we must not refuse them, tho' as I observ'd they were generally the worst slaves in the trunk, and we paid more for them than any others, which we could not remedy, it being one of his majesty's prerogatives: then the cappasheirs each brought out his slaves according to his degree and quality, the greatest first, etc. and our surgeon examin'd them well in all kinds, to see that they were sound wind and limb, making them jump, stretch out their arms swiftly, looking in their mouths to judge of their age; for the cappasheirs are so cunning, that they shave them all close before we see them, so that let them be never so old we can see no grey hairs in their heads or beards; and then having liquor'd[2] them well and sleek with palm oil, 'tis no easy matter to know an old one from a middle-age one. . . .

When we had selected from the rest such as we liked, we agreed in what goods to pay for them, the prices being already stated before the king, how much of each sort of merchandize we were to give for a man, woman, and child, which gave us much ease, and saved abundance of disputes and wranglings . . . ; then we mark'd the slaves we had bought in the breast, or shoulder, with a hot iron, having, the letter of the ship's name on it, the place being before anointed with a little palm oil, which caus'd but little pain, the mark being usually well in four or five days, appearing very plain and white after. . . .

When our slaves were come to the sea-side, our canoes were ready to carry them off to the longboat, if the sea permitted, and she convey'd them aboard ship, where the men were all put in irons, two and two shackled together, to prevent their mutiny, or swimming ashore.

The negroes are so wilful and loath to leave their own country, that they have often leap'd out of the canoes, boat and ship, into the sea, and kept under water till they were drowned, to avoid being taken up and saved by our boats, which pursued them; they having a more dreadful apprehension of Barbadoes than we can have of hell, tho' in reality they live much better there than in their own country; but home is home, etc. . . .

I have been inform'd that some commanders have cut off the legs and arms of the most wilful, to terrify the rest, for they believe if they lose a member, they cannot return home again: I was advis'd by some of my officers to do the same, but I could not be persuaded to entertain the least thought of it, much less put in practice such barbarity and cruelty to poor creatures, who, excepting their want of Christianity and true religion (their misfortune more than fault) are as much the works of God's hands, and no doubt as dear to him as ourselves; nor can I imagine why they should be despis'd for their colour, being what they cannot help, and the effect of the climate it has pleas'd God to appoint them. I can't think there is any intrinsick value in one colour more than another, nor that white is better than black, only we think so because we are so, and are prone to judge favourably in our own case, as well as the blacks, who in odium [hatred and loathing] of the colour, say, the devil is white, and so paint him. . . .

After we are come to an agreement for the prices of our slaves, ere the bell goes round to order all people to bring their slaves to the trunk

---

[2]To dress (as leather) with oil or grease.

to be sold, we are oblig'd to pay our customs to the king and cappasheirs for leave to trade, protection and justice; which for every ship are as follow, *viz.*

To the king six slaves value in cowries,[3] or what other goods we can persuade him to take, but cowries are most esteem'd and desir'd; all which are measur'd in his presence, and he would wrangle with us stoutly about heaping up the measure.

To the cappasheirs in all two slaves value, as above. . . .

The best goods to purchase slaves here are cowries, the smaller the more esteem'd; . . .

The next in demand are brass neptunes or basons [plates], very large, thin, and flat; for after they have bought them they cut them in pieces to make anilias or bracelets, and collars for their arms legs and necks.

The other preferable goods are blue paper sletias, cambricks or lawns, caddy chints, broad ditto [all types of cloth], coral, large, smooth, and of a deep red, rangoes [beads] large and red, iron bars, powder [gunpowder], and brandy . . . but without the cowries and brass they will take none of the last goods, and but small quantities at best, especially if they can discover that you have good store of cowries and brass aboard, then no other goods will serve their turn, till they have got as much as you have; and after, for the rest of the goods they will be indifferent, and make you come to their own terms, or else lie [offshore] a long time for your slaves, so that those you have on board are dying while you are buying others ashore; therefore every man that comes here, ought to be very cautious in making his report to the king at first, of what sorts and quantities of goods he has, and be sure to say his cargo consists mostly in iron, coral, rangoes, chints, etc. so that he may dispose of those goods as soon as he can, and at last his cowries and brass will bring him

slaves as fast as he can buy them; but this is to be understood of a single ship: or more, if the captains agree, which seldom happens; for where there are divers [various] ships, and of separate interests, about buying the same commodity they commonly undermine, betray, and out-bid one the other; and the Guiney [Guinea] commanders words and promises are the least to be depended upon of any I know use the sea; for they would deceive their fathers in their trade if they could. . . .

When our slaves are aboard we shackle the men two and two, while we lie in port, and in sight of their own country, for 'tis then they attempt to make their escape, and mutiny; to prevent which we always keep sentinels upon the hatchways, and have a chest full of small arms, ready loaden [loaded] and prim'd, constantly lying at hand upon the quarterdeck. . . . Their chief diet is call'd dabbadabb, being Indian corn ground as small as oat-meal, in iron mills, which we carry for that purpose; and after mix'd with water, and boil'd well in a large copper furnace, till 'tis as thick as a pudding, about a peckful of which in vessels, call'd crews, is allow'd to 10 men, with a little salt, malagetta [pepper], and palm oil, to relish; they are divided into messes of ten each, for the easier and better order in serving them: Three days a week they have horse-beans boil'd for their dinner and supper, great quantities of which the African company do send aboard us for that purpose; these beans the negroes extremely love and desire, beating their breast, eating them, and crying Pram! Pram! which is Very good! they are indeed the best diet for them, having a binding quality, and consequently good to prevent the flux [diarrhea], which is the inveterate distemper that most affects them, and ruins our voyages by their mortality. . . . We often at sea in the evenings would let the slaves come up into the sun to air them-

---

[3]*Cowrie* is a term for any number of marine snails that live in the coastal waters of the Indian and Pacific oceans. The snails produce thick polished shells many of which are brightly colored and speckled. Particularly prized in Africa was a one-inch long yellow shell produced off the Maldive Islands in the Indian Ocean. Many tons of these shells were harvested and processed for sale to Europeans who transported them to Europe as ballast in the holds of their ships. In Europe they were repurchased by slave traders before leaving for Africa.

selves, and make them jump and dance for an hour or two to our bagpipes, harp, and fiddle, by which exercise to preserve them in health; but notwithstanding all our endeavour, 'twas my hard fortune to have great sickness and mortality among them.

Having bought my compliment of 700 slaves, *viz.* 480 men and 220 women, and finish'd all my business at Whidaw, I took my leave of the old king, and his cappasheirs, and parted, with many affectionate expressions on both sides, being forced to promise him that I would return again the next year, with several things he desired me to bring him from England; and having sign'd bills of lading [loading] to Mr. Peirson, for the negroes aboard, I set sail the 27th of July in the morning. . . .

I deliver'd alive at Barbadoes to the company's factors 372, which being sold, came out at about nineteen pounds per head. . . .

Political Change in the Islamic World

Empires are forged through military conquest, and most disintegrate in the wake of military defeat. So it was for the Muslim empires of Southwest Asia, Africa, and India from the late sixteenth century onward. The Songhai Empire of Africa, which had dominated the western Sudan since the late fifteenth century, fell apart and was replaced by a number of small regional states after a musket-bearing Moroccan army defeated its forces at the Battle of Tondibi outside of Gao in 1591. The Safavid Empire came to an abrupt end in 1722 when Afghan warriors took the capital city of Isfahan, and the Safavids fled to the hills, leaving the empire open to Ottoman invasion, decades of anarchy, and the establishment of the weak Qajar Dynasty in the 1790s. The Mughal Empire in India broke apart when the warlord Nadir Shah, who had seized power in Persia, invaded India in 1739, and sacked Delhi, the Mughal capital. The Ottoman Empire outlasted the other Islamic empires, but in the end it too disappeared in the wake of military defeat, in this case in World War I.

In each of these empires decay had set in long before military defeat led to their demise. Like countless previous empires, all of them faced deteriorating financial situations once their expansion ended. Large armies were still needed to defend borders and maintain authority over newly conquered ethnic and religious groups, many of whom resented their new rulers and resisted integration into the new state. Rulers themselves added to the financial strain by spending large sums on court life, the arts, and ambitious building projects. When these empires were expanding, such costs could be met by confiscating the wealth of newly conquered peoples and adding them to the tax rolls. After expansion ended, expenses could be met only by raising taxes, running deficits, and selling offices and titles. Such expedients impeded economic growth, encouraged government corruption and inefficiency, and simply put off the day of fiscal reckoning.

All of these empires were plagued by succession struggles and deteriorating leadership. In the Ottoman and Safavid empires the practice of raising the rulers' sons as indulged prisoners in the palace to prevent rebellions contributed to a long series of uninformed, inexperienced, and often debauched sultans and shahs. In Songhai, of the eight sixteenth-century rulers who followed the empire's founders, Sunni Ali (r. 1469–1492) and Askia Muhammad (r. 1493–1528), all but three were murdered in office or deposed. Leadership also was a problem in Mughal India. Aurangzeb's (r. 1658–1707) persecution of his Hindu subjects and his costly military campaigns in the south set the stage for the mutinies and rebellions that undermined Mughal authority in the eighteenth century.

Although the causes of political decline in these empires were broadly similar, the consequences differed. After the breakup of the Songhai Empire, the western Sudan was ruled by a number of small regional states, some of which were conquered and merged around 1800 into a larger state, the Sokoto Caliphate. Persia survived the civil wars of the immediate post-Safavid Era, but then languished for another century and a half under the Zand and Qajar dynasties. The Ottoman Empire continued, but efforts of reforming sultans and ministers failed to halt territorial losses or prevent growing Western interference in its political and economic affairs. The fall of the Mughal Empire had the most significant consequences. It paved the way for the gradual British takeover of the Indian subcontinent — the first time a European state was able to extend its authority over an ancient center of civilization in Asia. It also marked the beginning of a new wave of European imperialism that by the late nineteenth century would bring Africa and much of Asia under Western control.

An Insider's View of Ottoman Decline
▼▼▼

50 ▼ Mehmed Pasha, THE BOOK OF COUNSEL FOR VIZIERS AND GOVERNORS

Along with battlefield defeats, fiscal crises, internal turmoil, and palace intrigues, another sign of Ottoman decline in the seventeenth and eighteenth centuries was the appearance of numerous treatises that offered plans for reviving the empire's fortunes. Among the most candid and insightful works of this type was *The Book of Counsel for Viziers and Governors*, written in the early eighteenth century by an Ottoman treasury official, Mehmed Pasha. Although few facts are known about Mehmed Pasha's early life, it is likely that he was born into the family of a petty merchant in Istanbul in the 1650s. While in his teens, he became an apprentice for an official in the Ottoman treasury department, a branch of government in which he worked for the rest of his career. His long service was rewarded in 1702, when he was named chief *defterdar,* or treasurer of the empire. Over the next fifteen years Mehmed Pasha lost and regained this office no fewer than seven times as different factions became ascendant in the sultan's administration. In 1717 he was executed on order of the sultan when his enemies blamed him for the loss of a fortress in the Balkans.

It is unknown when exactly Mehmed Pasha wrote *The Book of Counsel for Viziers and Governors,* but internal evidence suggests it was around 1703 or 1704. It is a book written by a man who had firsthand knowledge of the failings of the Ottoman state and was deeply disturbed by what he knew.

QUESTIONS FOR ANALYSIS

1. Mehmed Pasha cites several examples of how the sultan's subjects suffer as a result of government policies and practices. What examples does he cite and what are their causes?
2. What, according to the author, are the reasons for the government's financial problems? What solutions does he propose?
3. How does Mehmed Pasha's description of the Ottoman military and government differ from the observations made by Ogier Ghiselin de Busbecq in the sixteenth century (source 9)?
4. What do Mehmed Pasha's comments reveal about the economic situation in the Ottoman Empire around 1700?
5. Little was done to implement the changes suggested by Mehmed Pasha and other Ottoman reformers. What do you think made it so difficult to achieve meaningful reforms?

THE RESULTS OF BRIBERY

It is essential to guard against giving office through bribery to the unfit and to tyrannical oppressors. For giving office to such as these because of bribes means giving permission to plunder the property of the subjects. An equivalent for the bribe which is given must be had. In addition to what is given as a bribe, he must make a profit for himself and his followers. Bribery is the beginning and root of all illegality and tyranny, the source and fountain of every sort of disturbance and sedition, the greatest of calamities. . . . There is no more powerful engine of injustice and cruelty, for bribery destroys both faith and state. . . .

If it becomes necessary to give a position because of bribes, in this way its holder has permission from the government for every sort of oppression. Stretching out the hand of violence and tyranny against the poor subjects along his route of travel[1] and spreading fear among the

poor, he destroys the wretched peasants and ruins the cultivated lands. As the fields and villages become empty of husbandmen, day by day weakness comes to land and property, which remain destitute of profits, revenues, harvest, and benefit. In addition to the fact that it causes a decline in the productivity of the subjects and in the revenues of the Treasury, through neglect of the employment of tilling and lack of the work of agriculture, there is the greatest probability . . . that will cause scarcity, dearth, mishaps and calamities.

FINANCIAL ISSUES

The business of the Treasury is among the most important and essential affairs of the Exalted Government. The man who is chief treasurer needs to know and understand . . . the Treasury employees who for their own advantage are the cause of ruin and destruction to the government

---

[1]Officials traveling on government business were entitled to horses, food, and lodging from the people of the districts they visited.

service in obtaining tax farms.[2] He must know how they behave in getting money from the Treasury through "invalid receipts"[3] and in other cases, and he must understand what are their tricks and wiles. . . . Every one of them is waiting and watching in the corner of opportunity, taking care . . . to cause certain matters outside the regular procedure to appear correct. . . . In case the chief treasurer is not informed about such persons, they cause the wasting of the public wealth through various frauds, and of disordering affairs. . . .

Those who are chief treasurers should be extremely circumspect in behavior, upright and devout, devoid of avarice and spite. . . . They . . . should strive to increase the income of the Treasury and to diminish expenditures.

But the reduction of expenditures cannot come about through the care and industry of the chief treasurer alone. These must be supplemented by the Sovereign and personal help of his imperial majesty the sultan, who is the refuge of the universe, and by the good management of his excellency the grand vizier.[4] . . .

Certain tax concessions, instead of being farmed out, should be committed to the charge of trustworthy and upright persons on government account.[5]

Let the janissary corps[6] not be increased. Let them be well disciplined, few but elite, and all present in time of need. In this connection also it is fitting to be extremely careful and to be attentive in keeping their rolls in proper order and in having the soldiers actually present. The late Lutfi Pasha, who was formerly grand vizier, has

written: "Fifteen thousand soldiers are a great many soldiers. It is a heroic deed to pay the wages year by year of fifteen thousand men with no decrease." But under the present conditions the soldiers and pensioned veterans . . . who get pay and rations have exceeded all limits.

In order that the income and expenditure of the Treasury may be known and the totals inspected, the rolls of the bureaus must be investigated and the numbers known. There are on a war footing 53,200 janissary footmen, consisting of janissaries of the imperial court and pensioned veterans, including those who are in the fortresses protecting the ever-victorious frontier. There are 17,133 cavalrymen of the sipahis, silihdars,[7] and four other regiments of cavalry. The armorers of the imperial court and artillerymen and artillery drivers and bostanjis[8] of the bodyguard . . . and the aghas[9] of the imperial stirrup and müteferriqas[10] and sergeants and gatemen and those who belong to the imperial stables and the flourishing kitchens and to the dockyard and to the peikan[11] and to other units, making up 17,716 persons, the total of all these amounts to 96,727 persons.

The expense for meat and value of the winter allowance[12] together with the yearly pay of the janissaries of the lofty court and armorers and artillerymen and artillery drivers in the fortresses on the ever-victorious frontier exceeds a total of ten thousand purses of aspers.[13] And in addition to these, the local troops in the fortresses on the ever-victorious frontier number seventy thousand persons and certain veterans pensioned from the income of the custom house and tax farms, to-

---

[2]Tax farms were purchased by private individuals who in return for paying the government a lump sum received the right to collect taxes owed the government.

[3]Forged documents showing that a person had paid taxes he owed.

[4]A *vizier* was a government minister. The *grand vizier* was chief minister.

[5]In other words, tax farming should be abandoned and taxes collected directly by government officials. The author does not develop this point further.

[6]Infantry fighters in the Ottoman army, originally recruited from the sultan's Christian subjects who were converted to Islam and given over to military training. Their effectiveness had severely declined by the eighteenth century.

[7]*Sipahis* and *silihdars* were cavalry troops supported by land grants from the sultan.

[8]Infantry troops who maintained the palace grounds in Istanbul.

[9]Generals.

[10]Mounted bodyguards who accompanied diplomats on missions.

[11]An elite bodyguard numbering thirty to forty men who wore distinctive gilded helmets.

[12]Payments over and above the troops' regular salary.

[13]A *purse* was a unit of money made up of approximately 420 *piasters*; one piaster equaled 120 *aspers*.

gether with those who have the duty of saying prayers amount to twenty-three thousand five hundred. Their yearly pay amounts to five thousand nine hundred and ten purses. Those who are on the government galleys total six thousand persons and their yearly pay eight hundred purses. Accordingly, the total of those who receive pay and have duties is 196,227 and their yearly pay amounts to 16,710 purses.[14]

In addition to these salaries there are incomes of the illustrious princes and princesses and the grand vizier and the yearly allowance of the Tatar princes[15] and of the commanders of the sea and the expenditures of the imperial kitchens and stables, of the flourishing dockyards, of the prefect of the capital, of the chief butcher, of the agha of Istanbul, of the chief biscuit maker, of the cannon factory, some expenditures of müteferriqas, and in addition to these, chance expenditures which do not come to mind. . . . For this reason the income does not cover the expenditure, and of necessity the farmed taxes, and other taxes such as the capitation tax,[16] have each fallen a year or two in arrears.

THE STATE OF THE MILITARY

The troops on the frontiers are actually too numerous on their rolls and in the summaries given, although it is certain that in their appointed places each battalion is deficient, some being perhaps half lacking and others even more, nevertheless they let the salaries be sent from here for all. As for the extra money which they get, they have agreed to divide it among themselves. Care and thought and trustworthiness and uprightness in the officers is needed for the separation and distinguishing of those who are present and those who are absent. . . .

Everyone knows that there are very many people outside the corps who pretend they are janissaries. Especially in recent times, because of the long continuance of campaigns which have taken place against the Magyars[17] and in various other regions according to the necessity of the moment, outsiders have joined and mixed themselves among this janissary corps more than among all the others. Becoming mingled with all sorts of people, the janissaries have broken down their fixed regulations. In the towns and villages situated on the coasts of Anatolia and in many regions of Rumelia[18] likewise, many of the subject population, in order to free their necks from the obligations which are incumbent upon them, have changed their dress.[19] Because of their pretensions of being janissaries and because of aid from the commanders of the latter,[20] the civilians cannot be separated from the janissaries. There is no distinction between this sort of men and the faithful guardians of the frontier, veterans who have undergone fatigue and hard usage on campaigns, who have perhaps been several times wounded and injured, who have suffered cuts and bruises for the welfare of faith and state, who have pillowed their heads on stones and lain down to sleep upon the ground. . . .

At the present time special care is necessary in the repairing of castles. If they be built solidly they will not become dilapidated, and frequent repairs will not be needed. But the execution of repairs must not be committed to any chance person, for the appropriation from the Treasury may be embezzled and wasted. It must be committed to a man who abstains from profiteering and avarice.

When either the glorious commander-in-chief or the generals go on campaign their true purpose should be the animating of religion and the

---

[14]A sum that exceeded the estimated annual income of the government.
[15]Chieftains on the borders of the empire who were allies of the Ottomans.
[16]A tax on individuals; a head tax.
[17]The term *Magyar,* meaning Hungarian, was used to refer to any of the Ottomans' Christian enemies in southeastern Europe.

[18]An area north of Greece, including the regions of Albania, Macedonia, and Thrace.
[19]The people have purchased and wear the uniforms of the janissaries and claim to be members of the corps to avoid taxes.
[20]The commanders have accepted bribes to enter their names on the corps' roles.

execution of the words of the Prophet. . . . Let them not be unjust or oppressive to any one, but just and equitable, and let them seek to win affection and praises. While not oppressing or tyrannizing over the military corps, let them safeguard proper discipline.

For when soldiers are charged with a campaign, they join in bands and agree together to consider one of themselves as chief. Practicing brigandage, they are not satisfied with free fodder for their horses and food for their own bellies from the villages they meet. They covet the horse-cloth and rags of the peasants, and if they can get their hands on the granaries they become joyful, filling their sacks with barley and oats for provisions and fodder. While they behave in this way, . . . the sighs and groans of mankind attain the heavens and it is certain that they will be accursed. . . .

ECONOMIC REGULATIONS

It is essential at all times for every ruler to keep track of the small things relating to the general condition of the people. He must set the proper market prices. Everything must be sold at the price it is worth. For in case the sultan and the viziers say: "The fixing of market prices, though part of the public business, is insignificant," and are not diligent about it, the city judge alone cannot carry it out. . . . Under such circumstances everyone buys and sells as he pleases. Through senseless avarice the venom of vipers is added to lawful goods. The most contemptible of the people, useless both for the services of the sultan and for warfare, become possessors of all the wealth . . . while the great men of the people who deserve respect, becoming poor and powerless, pursue the road of bankruptcy. Then, when it comes about that both horsemen and footmen who go on campaign must sell all their property,[21] it is troublesome and difficult to determine all at once how to restrain those men who have them by the throat and how to change their demeanor and diminish their arrogance (may God forbid it!). . . . The fruiterers and merchants put a double price on provisions and supplies and reap a harvest of profits. They rob the people. It is apparent that neglect in this matter redounds to the harm of believers in time of trouble and to the benefit of fruiterers and merchants.[22]

---

[21]Many soldiers paid for their own military equipment and provisions before a campaign. They hoped to recoup their expenses through plunder.

[22]Many merchants were Christian Armenians or Jews.

The Beginnings of Britain's Indian Empire

▼▼▼

51 ▼ Robert Clive,
LETTER TO WILLIAM PITT, 1759

As the Mughal Empire disintegrated in the eighteenth century, the relationship between India and Europe underwent a dramatic change. Until then Portuguese, Dutch, French, and English merchants had stayed out of Indian politics, content to trade from coastal cities, where with the approval of the emperor and local rulers they built wharves, warehouses, and offices. As Mughal authority deteriorated, agents of the British East India Company, founded in 1600, and the French East India Company, founded in 1664, sought to expand their commercial activities by entering into agreements with local princes. By mid century they were laying plans for actual territorial conquest.

Competition for commercial dominance in India was just one source of the ongoing Anglo-French rivalry that pitted the two dominant European powers against one another in the War of the Austrian Succession (1740–1748) and the Seven Years' War (1756–1763). The issue in India was decided in 1757 at the Battle of Plassey, when an army commanded by Robert Clive, an agent of the British East India Company, defeated the army of his French rival, Joseph François Dupleix, and his ally, Siraj-ud-Daula, the Indian governor, or nawab, of the large northeastern state of Bengal. After placing Mir Ja'far, their own puppet nawab, in power in Bengal, British officials of the East India Company became the de facto rulers of Bengal and immediately set about plundering their new dependency in the interest of company profit and their own personal fortunes. Such was the beginning of the British Empire in India, the achievement of merchants working more for their directors, shareholders, and themselves than for their government.

The architect of British empire-building in India, Robert Clive (1725–1774), was the son of an English landowner and politician; at age eighteen he entered the service of the East India Company and sailed to India after an unspectacular career as a student. Commissioned in the company army four years later, he distinguished himself by helping defeat the French and their Indian supporters at the Battle of Arcot in 1751. Six years later he led British forces in their decisive victory at Plassey. After becoming governor of Bengal, he instituted the practice by which the British gained the right of collecting taxes in return for making annual payments to the Mughal emperor.

The following letter, written on January 7, 1759, is directed to William Pitt the Elder, later Earl of Chatham (1708–1778), who since 1757 had been the government minister responsible for directing the fighting against France in the Seven Years' War. In it Clive describes the situation in India two years after the Battle of Plassey.

QUESTIONS FOR ANALYSIS

1. What is Clive's vision of the role of Great Britain in India?
2. Why is Clive convinced that the British will encounter little difficulty in establishing their political authority in India?
3. According to Clive, what benefits will accrue to Great Britain once it establishes its authority in India?
4. What does Clive's letter reveal about the state of the Mughal Empire in the mid 1700s?
5. What does the letter reveal about Clive's attitudes toward the Indians and their rulers?

The close attention you bestow on the affairs of the British nation in general has induced me to trouble you with a few particulars relative to India, and to lay before you an exact account of the revenues of this country, the genuineness whereof you may depend upon, as it has been faithfully extracted from the Minister's books.

The great revolution that has been effected here by the success of the English arms, and the vast advantages gained to the Company[1] by a

---

[1]The East India Company.

treaty concluded in consequence thereof, have, I observe, in some measure, engaged the public attention; but much more may yet in time be done, if the Company will exert themselves in the manner the importance of their present possessions and future prospects deserves. I have represented to them in the strongest terms the expediency of sending out and keeping up constantly such a force as will enable them to embrace the first opportunity of further aggrandizing themselves; and I dare pronounce, from a thorough knowledge of this country's government, and of the genius of the people, acquired by two years' application and experience, that such an opportunity will soon offer. The reigning Subah,[2] whom the victory at Plassey invested with the sovereignty of these provinces, still, it is true, retains his attachment to us, and probably, while he has no other support, will continue to do so; but Muslims are so little influenced by gratitude, that should he ever think it his interest to break with us, the obligations he owes us would prove no restraint: and this is very evident from his having lately removed his Prime Minister, and cut off two or three principal officers, all attached to our interest, and who had a share in his elevation. Moreover, he is advanced in years; and his son is so cruel, worthless a young fellow, and so apparently an enemy to the English, that it will be almost unsafe trusting him with the succession. So small a body as two thousand Europeans will secure us against any apprehensions from either the one or the other; and, in case of their daring to be troublesome, enable the Company to take the sovereignty upon themselves.

There will be the less difficulty in bringing about such an event, as the natives themselves have no attachment whatever to particular princes; and as, under the present Government, they have no security for their lives or properties, they would rejoice in so happy an exchange as that of a mild for a despotic Government: and

there is little room to doubt our easily obtaining the Mughal's grant in confirmation thereof, provided we agreed to pay him the stipulated allotment out of the revenues, viz. fifty lacs[3] annually. This has, of late years, been very ill-paid, owing to the distractions in the heart of the Mughal Empire, which have disabled that court from attending to their concerns in the distant provinces: and the Vizier[4] has actually wrote to me, desiring I would engage the Nawab to make the payments agreeable to the former usage. . . . That this would be agreeable to the Mughal can hardly be questioned, as it would be so much to his interest to have these countries under the dominion of a nation famed for their good faith, rather than in the hands of people who, a long experience has convinced him, never will pay him his proportion of the revenues, unless awed into it by the fear of the Imperial army marching to force them thereto.

But so large a sovereignty may possibly be an object too extensive for a mercantile Company; and it is to be feared they are not of themselves able, without the nation's assistance, to maintain so wide a dominion. I have therefore presumed, Sir, to represent this matter to you, and submit it to your consideration, whether the execution of a design, that may hereafter be still carried to greater lengths, be worthy of the Government's taking it into hand. I flatter myself I have made it pretty clear to you, that there will be little or no difficulty in obtaining the absolute possession of these rich kingdoms; and that with the Mughal's own consent, on condition of paying him less than a fifth of the revenues thereof. Now I leave you to judge, whether an income yearly of upwards of two millions sterling, with the possession of three provinces abounding in the most valuable productions of nature and of art, be an object deserving the public attention; and whether it be worth the nation's while to take the proper measures to secure such an acquisition —

---

[2]A synonym for nawab, or provincial governor of an Indian province. The individual to whom Clive refers is Mir Ja'far, the British puppet named nawab of Bengal after the Battle of Plassey.

[3]Synonymous with lakh, meaning 100,000. Clive states that the British will pay 5 million rupees, in British currency approximately 260,000 pounds, per year to the emperor.
[4]A high official in the emperor's administration.

an acquisition which, under the management of so able and disinterested a minister, would prove a source of immense wealth to the kingdom, and might in time be appropriated in part as a fund towards diminishing the heavy load of debt under which we at present labor. Add to these advantages the influence we shall thereby acquire over the several European nations engaged in the commerce here, which these could no longer carry on but through our indulgence, and under such limitations as we should think fit to prescribe. It is well worthy of consideration, that this project may be brought about without draining the mother country, as has been too much the case with our possessions in America. A small force from home will be sufficient, as we always make sure of any number we please of black [Indian] troops, who, being both much better paid and treated by us than by the country powers, will very readily enter into our service. . . .

The greatest part of the troops belonging to this establishment are now employed in an expedition against the French in Deccan; and, by the accounts lately received from thence, I have great hopes we shall succeed in extirpating them from the province of Golconda,[5] where they have reigned lords paramount so long, and from whence they have drawn their principal resources during the troubles upon the coast. . . .

May the zeal and the vigorous measures, projected from the service of the nation, which have so eminently distinguished your ministry, be crowned with all the success they deserve, is the most fervent wish of him who is, with the greatest respect,

Sir,

Your most devoted humble servant,

(Signed) Robert Clive

Calcutta,
7th January, 1759

---

[5] A region of central India.

▼▼▼

The Continuing Vitality of Islam

The resurgence of Islam in the late twentieth century, characterized by political militancy, intensification of personal devotion, and a drive to create societies based on Islamic law and teaching, has precedents that go far back in Islamic history. Time and again the religion has been revitalized and renewed by movements inspired by visionaries and reformers who have exhorted believers to purify doctrine and ritual and to rededicate their lives to God. Many of these reformers spoke of the need for *jihad,* Arabic for exertion or struggle. In formal religious terms this means the struggle of Muslims to overcome unbelief and sin. It can also mean holy war against unbelievers.

The eighteenth century was such a period of Islamic revitalization despite the demoralizing political and military failures of the major Muslim empires. While the Ottomans were losing battles to European armies and the Safavid and Mughal empires were falling apart, Islam continued to make converts in Southeast Asia and Africa and spread into areas such as eastern Bengal through migration. In addition, movements of reform and renewal took root in many parts of the Islamic world, including the religion's historic center in Arabia and its outermost fringes in Southeast Asia and West Africa.

Given the widely different backgrounds of these movements, it is not surprising that their doctrines and impact varied greatly. Most were led by legal or Quranic scholars or by Muslims with ties to Sufism, the mystical movement within Islam that emphasizes personal experience and closeness to God through devotion. Many reformers traveled widely and drew inspiration from ideas they encountered in religious centers such as Baghdad, Cairo, Mecca, and Medina. Some called for a purification of Muslim practices and a return to Islam's fundamentals as revealed in the Quran and the teachings and deeds of Muhammad. Many were convinced that Islam had been tainted by accommodating itself to local religious customs and beliefs. Some urged Muslims to seek social justice, while others preached a message of puritanical rigor and personal regeneration. A few called on their followers to take up the sword against unbelievers and heretics.

Eighteenth-century Islamic reform movements were not anti-Western in any meaningful sense. They did, however, affect interactions between the West and the Islamic world in the nineteenth and twentieth centuries. In the early history of Islam, many Muslim intellectuals and religious leaders considered certain Western and Islamic views compatible, and they had integrated aspects of Western thought, especially ancient Greek science, into Islamic learning. The message of many eighteenth-century reformers, however, was that Islam was sufficient unto itself. It should be more exclusivist, more centered on its own writings and traditions, and more suspicious of outside ideas and practices. Such views were one of many factors that shaped the tone of interactions between the Muslim and Western worlds in the modern era.

A Call to Recapture Islam's Purity

▼▼▼

52 ▼ *'Abdullah Wahhab,*
THE HISTORY AND DOCTRINES
OF THE WAHHABIS

Muhammad ibn-Abd al-Wahhab (1703–1792) was a native of Nejd, a region in the east central part of the Arabian Peninsula, who as a student and teacher visited Mecca, Medina, Basra, Damascus, and Baghdad. In the course of his studies he embraced the ideas of Ahmad ibn Hanbal, the ninth-century jurist and founder of the *Hanbali* school of Sunni Muslim law, which asserted that the sole source of Islamic law was the Quran and *hadith,* Muhammad's sayings and practices as recorded by those who knew him. After returning to Arabia, Wahhab began to denounce the Arabs' religious failings. These included magical rituals, faith in holy men, worship of saints and their tombs, and veneration of supposedly sacred wells and trees. Rejecting Sufi mysticism and rationalist attempts to understand God's nature and purposes, he sought to recapture the pure faith revealed to Muhammad and set forth in Hanbali doctrines. Wahhab urged his listeners to focus on Islam's central doctrine that only God was worthy of worship. Calling themselves *Muwahhidin,* or "unitarians," to emphasize their exclusive devotion to Allah, Wahhab's followers gained military backing when an Arabian chieftain, Muhammad ibn-Saud, accepted their message and dedicated himself to spreading it by force.

In 1803, eleven years after Abd al-Wahhab's death, his followers captured the holy city of Mecca, the immediate aftermath of which is described in the following selection. It is the work of the founder's grandson, 'Abdullah Wahhab, who participated in the conquest of Mecca and was executed when an army sent by the Ottoman sultan took the city in 1818. He wrote it to answer critics and to clarify the beliefs of the Muwahhidin.

QUESTIONS FOR ANALYSIS

1. In the Wahhabi view what are the most serious threats to the purity of Islam?
2. How did the Wahhabis attempt to change Mecca after they captured it? What do their acts reveal about their beliefs and purposes?
3. The Wahhabis have been characterized as puritanical and intolerant. Is such a view justified on the basis of this document?
4. The Wahabbis strongly opposed Shiism and the use of logic as a means of discovering religious truth. Why? (See the introduction to source 12 for a discussion of Shiism.)
5. How do the Wahabbis perceive their role in the history of Islam?

In the name of God, the compassionate and merciful! Praise be to God, the Lord of the Universe, and blessing and peace be upon our prophet Muhammad, the faithful, and on his people and his companions, and those who lived after them, and their successors of the next generation! Now I was engaged in the holy war, carried on by those who truly believe in the Unity of God, when God, praised be He, graciously permitted us to enter Mecca, the holy, the exalted, at midday, on the 6th day of the week on the 8th of the month Muharram, 1218, Hijrí.[1] Before this, Saud, our leader in the holy war, whom the Lord protect, had summoned the nobles, the divines, and the common people of Mecca; for indeed the leaders of the pilgrims and the rulers of Mecca had resolved on battle, and had risen up against us in the holy place, to exclude us from the house of God. But when the army of the true believers

advanced, the Lord filled their hearts with terror, and they fled hither and thither. Then our commander gave protection to everyone within the holy place, while we, with shaven heads and hair cut short,[2] entered with safety, crying "Labbayka,"[3] without fear of any created being, and only of the Lord God. Now, though we were more numerous, better armed and disciplined than the people of Mecca, yet we did not cut down their trees, neither did we hunt,[4] nor shed any blood except the blood of victims, and of those four-footed beasts which the Lord has made lawful by his commands.

When our pilgrimage was over, we gathered the people together on the forenoon of the first day of the week, and our leader, whom the Lord saves, explained to the divines what we required of the people, . . . namely, a pure belief in the Unity of God Almighty. He pointed out to them

---

[1] April 1803.
[2] A custom during the pilgrimage to Mecca.
[3] The loud cry uttered by Muslims as they begin their pilgrimage activities in Mecca.

[4] Not cutting down a defeated enemy's trees or hunting the enemy's animals was considered an act of mercy by the victor.

that there was no dispute between us and them except on two points, and that one of these was a sincere belief in the unity of God, and a knowledge of the different kinds of prayer of which *dua*[5] was one. He added that to show the significance of *shirk,*[6] the prophet (may he be blessed!) had put people to death on account of it; that he had continued to call upon them to believe in the Unity of God for some time after he became inspired, and that he had abandoned shirk before the Lord had declared to him the remaining four pillars[7] of Islam. . . .

. . . They then acknowledged our belief, and there was not one among them who doubted or hesitated to believe that that for which we condemned men to death, was the truth pure and unsullied. And they swore a binding oath, although we had not asked them, that their hearts had been opened and their doubts removed, and that they were convinced whoever said, "Oh prophet of God!" or "Oh Ibn 'Abbes!" or "Oh 'Abdul Qadir!"[8] or called on any other created being, thus entreating him to turn away evil or grant what is good, (where the power belongs to God alone) such as recovery from sickness, or victory over enemies, or protection from temptation, etc.; he is a *Mushrik,*[9] guilty of the most heinous form of shirk, his blood shall be shed and property confiscated. Nor is it any excuse that he believes the effective first cause in the movements of the universe is God, and only supplicates those mortals . . . to intercede for him or bring him nearer the presence of God, so that he may obtain what he requires from Him through them or through their intercession. Again, the

tombs which had been erected over the remains of the pious, had become in these times as it were idols where the people went to pray for what they required; they humbled themselves before them, and called upon those lying in them, in their distress, just as did those who were in darkness before the coming of Muhammad.

When this was over, we razed all the large tombs in the city which the people generally worshipped and believed in, and by which they hoped to obtain benefits or ward off evil, so that there did not remain an idol to be adored in that pure city, for which God be praised. Then the taxes and customs we abolished, all the different kinds of instruments for using tobacco we destroyed, and tobacco itself we proclaimed forbidden.[10] Next we burned the dwellings of those selling *hashish,* and living in open wickedness, and issued a proclamation, directing the people to constantly exercise themselves in prayer. They were not to pray in separate groups according to the different Imams;[11] but all were directed to arrange themselves at each time of prayer behind any Imam who is a follower of any of the four Imams (may the Lord be pleased with them!). For in this way the Lord would be worshiped by as it were one voice, the faithful of all sects would become friendly disposed towards each other, and all dissensions would cease. . . .

We believe that good and evil proceed from God, the exalted; that nothing happens in His kingdom, but what He commands; . . . We believe that the faithful will see Him in the end, but we do not know under what form, as it was beyond our comprehension. And in the same way

---

[5]A personal prayer uttered by a Muslim.

[6]*Shirk* is the opposite of surrender to God and the acceptance and recognition of His reality. It may mean atheism, paganism, or polytheism. It is the fundamental error at the root of all sin and transgression.

[7]The first pillar of Islam is the creed, which affirms "There is no god but God, and Muhammad is the messenger of God." The four other pillars are daily prayer; almsgiving; fasting during the month of Ramadan; and pilgrimage, at least once in every Muslim's life if possible, to Mecca, the city of Muhammad's birth and revelation.

[8]Calling out in prayer the name of Muhammad or these early caliphs in the Abbasid line detracted from the majesty of God.

[9]A person guilty of shirk.

[10]The Wahhabis saw no Quranic basis for the use of tobacco; its use is still rare in modern Saudi Arabia, where Wahhabism is predominant.

[11]The author uses the term *imam* to refer to the founders of the four major schools of Sunni Muslim jurisprudence: Abu Hanifah (d. 767), founder of the Hanafite school; Malik ibn Anas (d. 795), founder of the Malikite school; al-Shafi (d. 820), founder of the Shafiite school; and Ahmad ibn Hanbal (d. 855), founder of the Hanbali school. The Wahhabis were Hanbalis, but did not reject the authority of the other schools.

we follow Imam Ahmad Ibn Hanbal in matters of detail; but we do not reject anyone who follows any of the four Imams, as do the Shias, the Zaidiyyahs, and the Imamiyyahs,[12] &c. Nor do we admit them in any way to act openly according to their vicious creeds; on the contrary, we compelled them to follow one of the four Imams. We do not claim to exercise our reason in all matters of religion, and of our faith, save that we follow our judgment where a point is clearly demonstrated to us in either the Quran or the Sunnah. . . . We do not command the destruction of any writings except such as tend to cast people into infidelity to injure their faith, such as those on Logic, which have been prohibited by all Divines. But we are not very exacting with regard to books or documents of this nature, if they appear to assist our opponents, we destroy them. . . . We do not consider it proper to make Arabs prisoners of war, nor have we done so, neither do we fight with other nations. Finally, we do not consider it lawful to kill women or children. . . .

We consider pilgrimage is supported by legal custom, but it should not be undertaken except to a mosque, and for the purpose of praying in it. Therefore, whoever performs pilgrimage for this purpose, is not wrong, and doubtless those who spend the precious moments of their existence in invoking the Prophet, shall, according to Hadith,[13] obtain happiness in this world and the next, and he will dispel their sorrows. We do not deny miraculous powers to the saints, but on the contrary allow them. They are under the guidance of the Lord, so long as they continue to follow the way pointed out in the laws and obey the prescribed rules. But whether alive or dead, they must not be made the object of any form of worship. . . .

We prohibit those forms of Bidah[14] that affect religion or pious works. Thus drinking coffee, reciting poetry, praising kings, do not affect religion or pious works and are not prohibited. . . .

All games are lawful. Our prophet allowed play in his mosque. So it is lawful to chide and punish persons in various ways; to train them in the use of different weapons; or to use anything which tends to encourage warriors in battle, such as a war-drum. But it must not be accompanied with musical instruments. These are forbidden, and indeed the difference between them and a war drum is clear. . . .

Whoever is desirous of knowing our belief, let him come to us at al Diriyya,[15] and he will see what will gladden his heart, and his eyes will be pleased in reading the compilations on the different kinds of knowledge. . . . He will see God praised in a pleasing manner; the assistance He gives in establishing the true faith; the kindness, which He exerts among the weak and feeble, between inhabitants and travelers. . . . He is our Agent, our Master, our Deliverer. May peace and the blessing of God be upon our prince Muhammad and on his family and his companions!

'Abdullah, son of Muhammad, son of 'Abdul-Wahhab, wrote this in Muharram, 1218.

[April 1803]

---

[12]Zaidiyyahs and Imamiyyahs were Shia sects.

[13]The tradition, or written record, of the thought and deeds of Muhammad as recorded by his companions.

[14]Erroneous or improper customs that grew after the third generation of Muslims died out.

[15]The Wahhabi capital, some fifteen miles northeast of Riyadh.

Jihad in the Western Sudan
▼▼▼

53 ▼ Usman dan Fodio,
SELECTIONS FROM HIS WRITINGS

Although merchants and teachers from North Africa and Arabia had introduced Islam to Africa's western and central Sudan as early as the tenth century, by 1800 Islam was not truly dominant in these regions. It was still a religion of the cities, where resident Muslim merchants had established Islamic communities, built mosques, introduced Arabic, and made converts. Many converts, however, continued non-Muslim religious rites and festivals, and in rural areas peasants and herders remained animists. Rulers became Muslims in name, but often less for religious reasons than to ingratiate themselves with the merchant community and to attract Islamic scholars to their service as advisors, interpreters, and scribes. Most rulers tolerated their subjects' pagan practices, and many participated in such practices themselves.

This all changed as a result of a series of *jihads,* or holy wars, that swept across the Sudan in the eighteenth and especially the nineteenth centuries. Dedicated Muslims took up arms against non-Muslim and nominal Muslim rulers and, after seizing power, imposed a strict form of Islam on their new subjects. In a matter of decades, these movements redrew the political and religious map of the Sudan.

The first major jihad of the era, known as the Sokoto Jihad, took place in Hausaland in the early nineteenth century under the leadership of Usman dan Fodio (1754–1817). Hausaland, an area that straddles the Niger River and today makes up the northern part of Nigeria, had been settled by Hausa speakers in the tenth century but also had a substantial population of Fulani, pastoralists who had begun to migrate into the area in the 1500s. It was divided into approximately a dozen principalities that had emerged after the Songhai Empire's collapse around 1600.

Usman dan Fodio, a member of a Fulani clan with a tradition of Islamic scholarship and teaching, was a member of the *Qadiriyya,* a Sufi brotherhood dating from the twelfth century. Beginning in the 1770s, he began to travel and preach in Hausaland, denouncing corrupt Islamic practices and the tyrannical and venal rulers who tolerated them. His calls for religious and political renewal gained him many followers among the Fulani, who considered themselves oppressed by their rulers, and some Hausa farmers, who were feeling the effects of drought and land shortages. In 1804 when the Sultan of Gobir denounced Usman and prepared to attack his followers, Usman called on his supporters to take up arms and begin a jihad against Hausaland's rulers. By the late 1810s, Usman controlled Hausaland and established the Kingdom of Sokoto. After his retirement from public life Usman's son and brother extended the campaign to the south and east of the kingdom. The era of Sudanese jihads had begun in earnest.

Usman wrote close to 100 treatises on politics, religion, marriage customs, and education. Brief excerpts from four of them are included here. Together they provide a sampling of his thoughts on religion, government, and society.

QUESTIONS FOR ANALYSIS

1. What policies and values of the Hausa sultans does Usman criticize? Why?
2. How do the religious failings of the Hausa princes prevent them from being just and equitable rulers?
3. What groups in Hausa society would have been most likely to respond positively to Usman's criticisms of the sultans?
4. What is Usman's message concerning the treatment of Muslim women? Is it a message of equality with men?

THE FAULTS OF THE HAUSA RULERS[1]

And one of the ways of their government is the building of their sovereignty upon three things: the people's persons, their honor, and their possessions; and whomsoever they wish to kill or exile or violate his honor or devour his wealth they do so in pursuit of their lusts, without any right in the *Sharia*.[2] . . . One of the ways of their government is their intentionally eating whatever food they wish, whether it is religiously permitted or forbidden, and wearing whatever clothes they wish, whether religiously permitted or forbidden, and drinking what beverages they wish, whether religiously permitted or forbidden, and riding whatever riding beasts they wish, whether religiously permitted or forbidden, and taking what women they wish without marriage contract, and living in decorated palaces, whether religiously permitted or forbidden, and spreading soft carpets as they wish, whether religiously permitted or forbidden.

. . . One of the ways of their government is to place many women in their houses, until the number of women of some of them amounts to one thousand or more. . . . One of the ways of their government is to delay in the paying of a debt, and this is injustice. One of the ways of their government is what the superintendent of the market takes from all the parties to a sale, and the meat which he takes on each market day from the butchers, . . . and one of the ways of their government is the cotton and other things which they take in the course of the markets. . . . One of the ways of their government is the taking of people's beasts of burden without their permission to carry the sultan's food to him.

. . . One of the ways of their government which is also well known is that whoever dies in their country, they take his property, and they call it "inheritance," and they know that it is without doubt injustice.[3] One of the ways of their government is to impose tax on merchants, and other travellers. One of the ways of their government, which is also well known, is that one may not pass by their farms, nor cross them without suffering bad treatment from their slaves. One of the ways of their government, which is also well known, is that if the people's animals go among their animals, they do not come out again unless they give a proportion of them, and if the sultan's animals stray, and are found spoiling the cultivated land and other things, they are not driven off. . . .

One of the ways of their government, which is also well known, is that if you have an adversary in law and he precedes you to them, and gives them some money, then your word will not be accepted by them, even though they know for a certainty of your truthfulness, unless you give them more than your adversary gave. One of the ways of their government is to shut the door in the face of the needy. . . . Therefore do not follow

---

[1]An excerpt from *Kitab al-farq,* "The Book of Difference between the Government of Muslims and Unbelievers," probably written around 1806.

[2]*Sharia,* literally "path" in Arabic, is the word for Islamic law.

[3]A grievance of foreign Muslim merchants who might die while residing in a Hausa city.

their way in their government, and do not imitate them. . . .

ROYAL RELIGION[4]

It is well known that in our time Islam in these countries mentioned above is widespread among people other than the sultans. As for the sultans, they are undoubtedly unbelievers, even though they may profess the religion of Islam, because they practice polytheistic rituals and turn people away from the path of God and raise the flag of worldly kingdom above the banner of Islam. . . .

The government of a country is the government of its king without question. If the king is a Muslim, his land is Muslim; if he is an Unbeliever, his land is a land of Unbelievers. In these circumstances it is obligatory for anyone to leave it for another country.[5] There is no dispute that the sultans of these countries venerate certain places, certain trees, and certain rocks and offer sacrifice to them. This constitutes unbelief according to the consensus of opinion.[6]

I say this on the basis of the common practice known about them, but I do not deny the existence of some Muslims here and there among them. Those however are rare and there is no place for what is rare in legal decisions.

THE TREATMENT OF WOMEN AND SLAVES[7]

Most of our educated men leave their wives, their daughters, and the slaves morally abandoned, like beasts, without teaching them what God prescribes should be taught them, and without instructing them in the articles of the Law which concern them. Thus, they leave them ignorant of the rules regarding ablutions,[8] prayer, fasting, business dealings, and other duties which they have to fulfil, and which God commands that they should be taught.

Men treat these beings like household implements which become broken after long use and which are then thrown out on the dung-heap. This is an abominable crime! Alas! How can they thus shut up their wives, their daughters, and their slaves in the darkness of ignorance? . . .

Muslim women — Do not listen to the speech of those who are misguided and who sow the seed of error in the heart of another; they deceive you when they stress obedience to your husbands without telling you of obedience to God and to his Messenger,[9] (May God show him bounty and grant him salvation), and when they say that the woman finds her happiness in obedience to her husband.

They seek only their own satisfaction, and that is why they impose upon you tasks which the Law of God and that of his Prophet have never especially assigned to you. Such are — the preparation of food-stuffs, the washing of clothes, and other duties which they like to impose upon you, while they neglect to teach you what God and the Prophet have prescribed for you.

Yes, the woman owes submission to her husband, publicly as well as in intimacy, even if he is one of the humble people of the world, and to disobey him is a crime, at least so long as he does not command what God condemns; in that case she must refuse, since it is wrong of a human creature to disobey the Creator.

THE CALL TO HOLY WAR[10]

That to make war upon the heathen king who does not say "There is no God but Allah" on account of the custom of his town, and who makes no profession of Islam, is obligatory by assent,[11]

---

[4]From *Tanbih al-ikhwan 'ala ahwal ard al-Sudan*, "Concerning the Government of Our Country and Neighboring Countries in the Sudan," written around 1811.
[5]Usman did just this when he led his followers out of the sultanate of Gobir after its ruler had turned against him.
[6]Consensus of the Muslim community, usually interpreted to mean the opinions of leading legal scholars.
[7]From *Nur al-albab*, "Light of the Intellects."

[8]Washing one's body as part of a religious rite.
[9]Muhammad.
[10]From *Wathiqat ahl al-Sudan wa man sha' Allah min al-ikhwan*, "Dispatch to the Folk of the Sudan and to Whom so Allah Wills among the Brethren," probably written in 1804 or 1805.
[11]"By assent" refers to the consensus of the Muslim community.

and that to take the government from him is obligatory by assent.

And that to make war upon the king who is an apostate, and who has abandoned the religion of Islam for the religion of heathendom is obligatory by assent, and that to take the government from him is obligatory by assent; And that to make war against the king who is an apostate — who has not abandoned the religion of Islam as far as the profession of it is concerned, but who mingles the observances of Islam with the observances of heathendom, like the kings of Hausa-land for the most part — is also obligatory by assent, and that to take the government from him is obligatory by assent.

And to make war upon backsliding Muslims who do not own allegiance to any of the Emirs of the Faithful,[12] is obligatory by assent, if they be summoned to give allegiance and they refuse, until they enter into allegiance; . . .

And to enslave the freeborn among the Muslims is unlawful by assent, whether they reside in the territory of Islam, or in enemy territory. . . .

---

[12]"Emirs of the faithful" were Usman's lieutenants.

Chapter 7

Change and Continuity in East Asia and Oceania

For the Ottoman, Safavid, and Mughal empires, the seventeenth and eighteenth centuries were times of decline and defeat after an era of strength and expansion. In East Asia, this pattern was reversed. For Japan the sixteenth century was an era of civil war and social discord, made worse by the arrival of Europeans, who introduced firearms and converted tens of thousands of Japanese to Christianity. China entered into a period of dynastic decline at the end of the sixteenth century when the quality and effectiveness of Ming emperors declined just when the empire was faced with pressing new financial and diplomatic problems. Factionalism paralyzed the central administration, and peasant violence escalated in the face of rising taxes, higher rents, natural catastrophes, and government corruption. The collapse of central authority and the suicide of the last emperor paved the way for the invasion of China by the Manchus, who poured into China from their homeland to the northeast and established a new dynasty, the Qing, in 1644.

During the seventeenth century, however, conflicts and tensions abated in both China and Japan. In Japan, recovery began in 1603, when the Tokugawa clan took power and ended the decades-long civil war, while in China it began soon after the Manchu conquest. Although China and Japan did not lack problems in the seventeenth and eighteenth centuries, in comparison to what had occurred earlier and what would follow, these were years of orderly government and social harmony.

These were also years in which European pressures on the region eased. China's rulers continued to limit European merchants' activities to Macao and Guangzhou, and beginning in the early 1700s they curtailed European missionary activity. The Manchus also checked Russian expansion in the Amur Valley. In 1689 they negotiated the Treaty of Nerchinsk, by which the Russians abandoned their trading posts in Manchuria in return for modest commercial privileges in Beijing. In Japan during the first half of the seventeenth century the Tokugawa shoguns expelled all foreigners, outlawed Christianity, and limited trade with Europeans to one Dutch ship a year. In the East Indies the Dutch, after forcing out the Portuguese and establishing a political base in Java, were content after the mid 1600s to protect rather than expand their gains. Spain's involvement in the region never extended beyond the Philippines.

By the end of the 1700s, however, signs of change were evident. In Japan economic expansion, urbanization, and political tranquility created new tensions by enriching merchants while undermining the function and financial base of the military aristocracy. In China continuing population growth caused hardship among the peasant masses by driving up the cost of land; moreover, around 1800 budgetary shortfalls, higher taxes, abuses of the civil service examination system, and neglect of roads, bridges, and dikes were signs of impending dynastic decline.

In addition, European pressures in the region once more were growing. In the 1780s, the English began to settle Australia and New Zealand. French missionaries increased their activities in Vietnam. In 1800 the Dutch government stripped the Dutch East India Company of its administrative responsibilities in the East Indies and tightened its grip on the region's agriculture and trade. From their base in India British merchants opened a new chapter in the history of trade with China after finding a product that millions of Chinese deeply craved. The product, grown and processed in India, packed into 133-pound chests, shipped to Guangzhou, and sold for silver to Chinese traders who sold it to millions of addicts, was opium. For East and Southeast Asians and for the peoples of the South Pacific islands, a new era of upheaval was about to begin.

China's Revival under the Qing

After the last Ming emperor hanged himself in April 1644 and the bandit-emperor Li Zicheng fled Beijing in June, Manchu invaders placed the child emperor Shunzhi on the throne, and China's last dynasty, the Qing, began its rule. During the next thirty-five years, Manchu armies fought from Burma to Taiwan, hunting down and executing Ming supporters, crushing their armies, and suppressing rebellion. By 1680 the Manchus controlled China and could fully attend to the challenge of ruling their new subjects.

The Manchus made it clear from the start that they were the rulers and the Chinese their subjects. They ordered courtiers and officials to abandon the loose-fitting robes of the Ming for the high-collared tight jackets favored by the Manchus. They also required all males to shave their foreheads and braid their hair in the back in a style despised by the Chinese.

In most other ways, however, the Manchus adapted to Chinese culture. They embraced the Chinese principle of centralized monarchy, learned Chinese, and supported Confucian scholarship. They reinstated the civil service examinations, which had been abandoned during the last decades of Ming rule. Although Manchus were disproportionately represented in the bureaucracy, Chinese were allocated half of all important offices, and gradually Chinese scholar-officials began to support and serve the new foreign dynasty.

From 1661 through 1799, China had but three emperors: Kangxi (r. 1661–1722), Yongzhen (r. 1722–1736), and Qianlong (r. 1736–1796), who resigned as emperor in 1796 to avoid exceeding the long reign of his grandfather Kangxi but who actually ruled until 1799. By any standard, the years of their rule were among the most impressive in all of Chinese history. China reached its greatest size as a result of military campaigns in central Asia. Agriculture flourished, trade expanded, and China's population grew (how much and how fast it grew is a matter of ongoing scholarly debate). China's cultural vitality was no less remarkable. The era's literary output included China's greatest novel, *The Dream of the Red Chamber* by Cao Xueqin, and painting and scholarship flourished under Qing patronage. Kangxi sponsored a dictionary of the Chinese language and an encyclopedia that reached 5,000 volumes. Qianlong supported scholars and copyists who compiled an anthology of 3,450 historical, literary, and philosophical texts that totaled 36,000 volumes.

Toward the end of Qianlong's reign, however, problems began to appear. Rural poverty worsened, military effectiveness declined, and factionalism and favoritism at the imperial court resurfaced. Nonetheless, it was neither farfetched nor fanciful when France's leading eighteenth-century writer, Voltaire, described Qing China as a model of moral and ethical government and praised Qianlong as the ideal philosopher-king.

Emperor Kangxi Views His World
▼▼▼

54 ▼ Kangxi, SELF-PORTRAIT

In 1661 a seven-year-old boy became the second emperor of the Qing Dynasty after the unexpected death of his father, Shunzhi. He took as his reign name Kangxi, and during his long reign, which lasted until 1722, he brought order to China after decades of Ming misrule, revolt, and invasion. He crushed the last vestiges of Ming resistance, fortified China's borders, revitalized the civil service examination system, won the support of China's scholar-officials, managed to ease tensions between ethnic Chinese and their Manchu conquerors, and brought new vigor and direction to government. A generous supporter of writers, artists, poets, scholars, and craftsmen, Kangxi himself was a scholar and writer of distinction. He studied Confucianism, Latin, music, mathematics, and science and left behind a rich store of writings, including poems, essays, aphorisms, and letters.

In 1974, the historian Jonathan Spence drew on these writings and statements to compile a self-portrait of the emperor. In the following excerpts the emperor expresses his views on justice, government administration, and Europeans, with whom China's relations worsened during his reign.

Since the late sixteenth century, members of the Society of Jesus, a Catholic religious order, had provided an intellectual and cultural link between China and the West. Prized for their knowledge of astronomy and mathematics and their skills as cartographers, artists, and architects, the Jesuit fathers had been welcomed at the imperial court in Beijing, where they wore Chinese garb, learned Chinese, and paid homage to the emperor. They also managed to convert some 200 court officials, who in keeping with a policy initiated by the founder of the Jesuit mission in China, Matteo Ricci (see source 7), were permitted to continue traditional ceremonies in honor of deceased ancestors and offer public homage to Confucius. Kangxi had an avid interest in Western learning, and in 1692 he granted toleration to Christianity and permission to the Jesuits to preach outside Beijing. By the early eighteenth century as many as 300,000 Chinese may have been Roman Catholics.

In the early 1700s, however, the Catholic missionary effort experienced a fatal schism. Members of the Franciscan and Dominican religious orders, fresh from their successful missionary efforts in the Philippines and relative newcomers to the field of Chinese missions, attacked the Jesuit position on Confucian rites and won over Pope Clement XI to their point of view. In 1706 a papal envoy to China, Charles de Tournon, announced the pope's decision that traditional Confucian ceremonies were religious, not civil, rites and henceforth would be prohibited for Chinese Catholics. An angry Kangxi responded with a ban on Christian preaching, and the Qing assault on Christianity was under way. Under Kangxi's successor, the Jesuits lost their position at Beijing, and the main source of contact between the imperial court and the intellectual world of the West disappeared.

QUESTIONS FOR ANALYSIS

1. What does Kangxi's treatment of delinquent and dishonest government officials reveal about his philosophy of government?
2. How do Confucian values affect Kangxi's decisions about whether to be lenient to men accused of killing their wives?
3. What are Kangxi's views of the civil service examination system? What ideas did he have about improving the system?
4. What role do eunuchs play in Kangxi's administration? How does this compare with the situation during the late Ming Era (source 4)?
5. According to Kangxi, what are the strengths and limitations of Western science and mathematics?
6. According to Kangxi, what specific issues were involved in the dispute over Chinese rites?
7. What other characteristics and actions of the missionaries led to Kangxi's decision to ban further Christian preaching?

AN EMPEROR'S RESPONSIBILITIES

Giving life to people and killing people — those are the powers that the emperor has. He knows that administrative errors in government bureaus can be rectified, but that a criminal who has been executed cannot be brought back to life any more than a chopped string can be joined together again. He knows, too, that sometimes people have to be persuaded into morality by the example of an execution. . . .

Hu Jianzheng was a subdirector of the Court of Sacrificial Worship whose family terrorized their native area in Jiangsu, seizing people's lands and wives and daughters, and murdering people after falsely accusing them of being thieves. . . . I ordered . . . that he be executed with his family and in his native place, so that all the local gentry might learn how I regarded such behavior. Corporal Yambu was sentenced to death for gross corruption in the shipyards. I not only agreed to the penalty but sent guards officer Uge to supervise the beheading, and ordered that all shipyard personnel from generals down to private soldiers

kneel down in full armor and listen to my warning that execution would be their fate as well unless they ended their evil ways. . . .

The final penalty of lingering death[1] must be given in cases of treason, as the Legal Code requires. . . . When Ilaguksan Khutuktu, who had had his spies in the lamas' residences so that they would welcome Galdan's[2] army into China, and had plotted with Galdan and encouraged him in his rebellion, was finally caught, I had him brought to Beijing and cut to death in the Yellow Temple, in the presence of all the Manchu and Mongol princes, and the senior officials, both civil and military. . . .

Of all the things that I find distasteful, none is more so than giving a final verdict on the death sentences that are sent to me for ratification. . . .

Each year we went through the lists, sparing sixteen out of sixty-three at one session, eighteen out of fifty-seven at another, thirty-three out of eighty-three at another. For example, it was clear to me that the three cases of husbands killing wives that came up . . . were all quite different. The husband who hit his wife with an ax because

---

[1] A slow, painful, and humiliating punishment in which a person dies from the administration of numerous cuts on the body.

[2] A lama was a Buddhist priest or monk in Tibet, Mongolia, and western China. Galdan was a leader of a Western Mon-

gol tribe who in the late seventeenth century conquered much of Chinese Turkestan and Outer Mongolia; when he threatened Beijing, Kangxi raised an army and defeated him in 1696.

she nagged at him for drinking, and then murdered her after another domestic quarrel . . . how could any extenuating circumstances be found? But Baoer, who killed his wife for swearing at his parents; and Meng, whose wife failed to serve him properly and used foul language so that he killed her — they could have their sentences reduced. . . .

EUNUCHS AND BUREAUCRATS

You have to define and reward people in accordance with their status in life. If too much grace is shown to inferiors they become lazy and uppity and will be sure to stir up trouble — and if you neglect them they will abuse you behind your back. That was why I insisted on such strictness when the eunuch Jian Wenzai beat a commoner to death, saying strangulation was not enough. For eunuchs are basically Yin[3] in nature. They are quite different from ordinary people; when weak with age they babble like babies. In my court I never let them get involved with government — even the few eunuchs-of-the-presence with whom I might chatter or exchange family jokes were never allowed to discuss politics. I only have about four hundred, as opposed to the immense numbers there were in the Ming, and I keep them working at menial jobs; I ignore their frowns and smiles and make sure that they stay poor. Whereas in the later Ming Dynasty, besides being so extravagant and reckless, they obtained the power to write endorsements on the emperors' memorials, for the emperors were unable to read the one- or two-thousand-character memorials that flowed in; and the eunuchs in turn passed the memorials on to *their* subordinates to handle.

▾ ▾ ▾

There are too many men who claim to be pure scholars and yet are stupid and arrogant; we'd be better off with less talk of moral principle and more practice of it. Even in those who have been the best officials in my reign there are obvious failings. . . .

This is one of the worst habits of the great officials, that if they are not recommending their teachers or their friends for high office then they recommend their relations. This evil practice used to be restricted to the Chinese: they've always formed cliques and then used their recommendations to advance the other members of the clique. Now the practice has spread to the Chinese Bannermen[4] like Yu Chenglong, and even the Manchus, who used to be so loyal, recommend men from their own Banners, knowing them to have a foul reputation, and will refuse to help the Chinese. . . .

In 1694 I noted that we were losing talent because of the ways the exams were being conducted: even in the military exams most of the successful candidates were from Zhejiang and Jiangnan, while there was only one from Henan and one from Shanxi.[5] The successful ones had often done no more than memorize old examination answer books, whereas the best *should* be selected on the basis of riding and archery. Yet it is always the strong men from the western provinces who are eager to serve in the army, while not only are troops from Zhejiang and Jiangnan among the weakest, they also pass on their posts to their relatives who are also weak.

Even among the examiners there are those who are corrupt, those who do not understand basic works, those who ask detailed questions about practical matters of which they know nothing, those who insist entirely on memorization of the *Classics*[6] and refuse to prescribe essays, those who put candidates from their own geographical area

---

[3] In East Asian thought, Yin and Yang were the two complementary principles or forces that make up all aspects and phenomena of life. Yin is conceived of as Earth, female, dark, passive, and absorbing.

[4] The banner system was a method of military organization under the Qing in which fighting men were grouped in divisions identified by different colored banners. Bannermen were given grants of land and small stipends for their ser-

vice. Chinese (as opposed to Manchu) bannermen were originally drawn from the ranks of Chinese soldiers and officers who had surrendered to the Manchus and joined their cause early in their struggle against Ming supporters.

[5] Zhejiang and Jiangnan were southeast coastal regions of China; Henan and Shanxi were north-central provinces.

[6] A set of writings from Chinese antiquity, thought to embody Confucian wisdom.

at the top of the list, or those who make false claims about their abilities to select the impoverished and deserving. . . . Other candidates hire people to sit [take] the exams for them, or else pretend to be from a province that has a more liberal quota than their own. It's usually easy enough to check the latter, since I've learnt to recognize the accents from thirteen provinces, and if you watch the person and study his voice you can tell where he is really from. As to the other problems, one can overcome some of them by holding the exams under rigorous armed supervision and then reading the exam papers oneself.

DEALING WITH EUROPEANS

The rare can become common, as with the lions and other animals that foreign ambassadors like to give us and my children are now accustomed to; . . .

Western skills are a case in point: in the late Ming Dynasty, when the Westerners first brought the gnomon,[7] the Chinese thought it a rare treasure until they understood its use. And when the Emperor Shunzhi got a small chiming clock in 1653, he kept it always near him; but now we have learned to balance the springs and to adjust the chimes and finally to make the whole clock, so that my children can have ten chiming clocks each to play with, if they want them. Similarly, we learned in a short time to make glassware that is superior to that made in the West, and our lacquer would be better than theirs, too, were it not that their wet sea climate gives a better sheen than the dry and dusty Chinese climate ever could. . . .

I realized, too, that Western mathematics has its uses. . . . I ordered the Jesuits Thomas, Gerbillon, and Bouvet to study Manchu also, and to compose treatises in that language on Western arithmetic and the geometry of Euclid.[8] In the early 1690's I often worked several hours a day with them. With Verbiest I had examined each stage of the forging of cannons, and made him build a water fountain that operated in conjunction with an organ, and erect a windmill in the court; with the new group — who were later joined by Brocard and Jartoux, and worked in the Yangxin Palace under the general direction of my Eldest Son Yinti — I worked on clocks and mechanics. Pereira taught me to play the tune, *"P'u-yen-chou"* on the harpsichord and the structure of the eight-note scale, Pedrini taught my sons musical theory, and Gherardini painted portraits at the Court. I also learned to calculate the weight and volume of spheres, cubes, and cones, and to measure distances and the angle of river banks. On inspection tours later I used these Western methods to show my officials how to make more accurate calculations when planning their river works. . . . I showed them how to calculate circumferences and assess the area of a plot of land, even if its borders were as jagged as dogs' teeth, drawing diagrams for them on the ground with an arrow; and calculated the flow of river water through a lock gate by multiplying the volume that flowed in a few seconds to get a figure for the whole day. . . .

But I was careful not to refer to these Westerners as "Great Officials." . . . For even though some of the Western methods are different from our own, and may even be an improvement, there is little about them that is new. The principles of mathematics all derive from the *Book of Changes,*[9] and the Western methods are Chinese in origin: this algebra — "A-erh-chu-pa-erh" — springs from an Eastern word.[10] And though it was indeed the Westerners who showed us something our ancient calendar experts did not know —

---

[7] A sundial.

[8] The ancient Greek mathematician who lived around 300 B.C.E. and laid the foundation for the study of geometry.

[9] One of the Classics, the *Book of Changes* was a work of divination that relied on the analysis of trigrams and hexagrams.

[10] *Algebra* is derived from the Arabic word *Al-jabr.* Kangxi is correct when he asserts that China had a long tradition of achievement in algebra, geometry, and trigonometry dating back at least as far as the Han Dynasty (206 B.C.E.–220 C.E.).

namely how to calculate the angle of the northern pole — this but shows the truth what Zhu Xi[11] arrived at through his investigation of things: the earth is like the yolk within an egg.

▼ ▼ ▼

On the question of the Chinese Rites that might be practiced by the Western missionaries, de Tournon[12] would not speak, though I sent messages to him repeatedly. I had agreed with the formulation the Beijing fathers had drawn up in 1700: that Confucius was honored by the Chinese as a master, but his name was not invoked in prayer for the purpose of gaining happiness, rank, or wealth; that worship of ancestors was an expression of love and filial remembrance, not intended to bring protection to the worshiper; and that there was no idea when an ancestral tablet was erected, that the soul of the ancestor dwelt in that tablet. And when sacrifices were offered to Heaven it was not the blue existent sky that was addressed, but the lord and creator of all things. If the ruler Shang-ti was sometimes called Heaven, *T'ien,* that had no more significance than giving honorific names to the emperor.

If de Tournon didn't reply, the Catholic Bishop Maigrot[13] did, . . . telling me that Heaven is a material thing and should not be worshiped, and that one should invoke only the name "Lord of Heaven" to show the proper reverence. Maigrot wasn't merely ignorant of Chinese literature, he couldn't even recognize the simplest Chinese characters; yet he chose to discuss the falsity of the Chinese moral system. . . .

Even little animals mourn their dead mothers for many days; these Westerners who want to treat their dead with indifference are not even equal to animals. How could they be compared with Chinese? We venerate Confucius because of his doctrines of respect for virtue, his system of education, his inculcation of love for superiors and ancestors. Westerners venerate their own saints because of their actions. They paint pictures of men with wings and say, "These represent heavenly spirits, swift as if they had wings, though in reality there are no men with wings." I do not find it appropriate to dispute this doctrine, yet with superficial knowledge Maigrot discussed Chinese sanctity. . . .

Every country must have some spirits that it reveres. This is true for our dynasty, as for Mongols or Mohammedans, Miao or Lolo,[14] or other foreigners. Just as everyone fears something, some snakes but not toads, some toads but not snakes; and as all countries have different pronunciations and different alphabets. But in this Catholic religion, the Society of Peter[15] quarrels with the Jesuits, . . . and among the Jesuits the Portuguese want only their own nationals in their church while the French want only French in theirs. This violates the principles of religion. Such dissension cannot be inspired by the Lord of Heaven but by the Devil, who, I have heard the Westerners say, leads men to do evil since he can't do otherwise.

▼ ▼ ▼

Since I discovered on the Southern Tour of 1703 that there were missionaries wandering at will over China, I had grown cautious and determined to control them more tightly: to bunch them in the larger cities and in groups that included men from several different countries, to catalogue their names and residences, and to permit no new establishments without my express permission. . . . I made all missionaries who wanted to stay on in China sign a certificate, stating that they would remain here for life and fol-

---

[11]Zhu Xi (1130–1200 C.E.), a famous commentator on Confucius, was China's leading philosopher after the classical age.

[12]Charles de Tournon (1668–1710) was a papal envoy sent to India and China to oversee Catholic missions. His demand that Chinese Christians abandon traditional rites was deeply offensive to Kangxi. The emperor ordered him to prison, where he died in 1710.

[13]Charles Maigrot (1652–1730) was the apostolic vicar to China. His opposition to the Jesuit position on rites led to his expulsion from China in 1707.

[14]The Miao (also known as the Hmong) and Lolo were peoples of southwest China and upland Southeast Asia.

[15]There is no such religious order as the "Society of Peter." Kangxi is probably referring to supporters of the papal position on rites; according to Roman Catholics the authority of the pope can be traced back to the apostle Peter.

low Ricci on the Rites. Forty or fifty who refused were exiled to Guangzhou; de Tournon was sent to Macao,[16] his secretary, Appiani, we kept in prison in Beijing.

Despite these sterner restrictions, the Westerners continued to cause me anxiety. Our ships were being sold overseas; reports came of ironwood for keel blocks being shipped out of Guangdong; Luzon and Batavia[17] became havens for Chinese outlaws; and the Dutch were strong in the Southern Seas. I ordered a general inquiry among residents of Beijing who had once lived on the coast, and called a conference of the coastal governors-general. "I fear that some time in the future China is going to get into difficulties with these various Western countries," I said. "That is my prediction."

---

[16]Macao was the trading settlement near Guangzhou whereby imperial order Western merchants were permitted to do business.

[17]Luzon was the major island of the Spanish-ruled Philippines; Batavia was the Dutch name for the island of Java in the East Indies.

Negotiating with the Qianlong Emperor
▼▼▼

55 ▼ *Sir Henry Dundas,*
LETTER TO LORD GEORGE MACARTNEY,
SEPTEMBER 8, 1792

Chinese restrictions on Western commerce in the eighteenth century increasingly frustrated and angered the British, who were strenuously seeking to expand their trade in East Asia. According to the government's Guangzhou System, agents of the British East India Company and other European merchants could do business in the environs of only one city, Guangzhou and only during the trading season, which ran from October to March. Subject to Chinese laws, they were barred from entering Guangzhou's city limits, learning Chinese, being accompanied by their wives, and much else. Furthermore, they were required to deal exclusively with a small number of merchant companies that formed a merchants' guild, the Cohong, which had a government monopoly on trading with Westerners. Any grievance or dispute had to be referred to these Chinese merchants, who would pass it on to the Hoppo, a government-appointed trade official who oversaw Guangzhou trade. The Hoppo might make a decision himself, forward the grievance to Beijing, or simply ignore it.

Efforts by the East India Company to have the system modified got nowhere. When the company sent James Flint to China in 1759 to negotiate trade issues with the emperor, the unfortunate envoy was imprisoned for three years on charges of learning Chinese, sailing to unapproved ports, and improperly addressing the emperor.

With demand for Chinese tea soaring, at the urging of Sir Henry Dundas, president of the board of the East India Company and home minister in the government of William Pitt the Younger, the company and the government decided to dispatch another embassy to Beijing in 1792. Chosen to head the mission was Lord George Macartney, a friend of Dundas and an experienced diplomat. Unlike previous emissaries to Beijing, Macartney would be the official representative of the king, not the East India Company. The government's meticulous planning for the trip included the following set of instructions prepared for Macartney by Dundas. Written in the form of a letter, it provides useful information on the British goals for the mission and insights into British thinking on how Macartney should approach the emperor and his officials.

QUESTIONS FOR ANALYSIS

1. What specific complaints about China's trade policies are expressed in the letter of instruction?
2. What are the specific goals of Macartney's mission?
3. If these goals had been attained, how would they have improved the situation of the English merchants trading with China?
4. According to the letter, what must Macartney do to have the best chance of having successful negotiations with the Chinese government? What should he avoid?
5. What British views of the Chinese underlie the instructions given to Macartney?
6. Which British proposals do you think the Chinese found most objectionable? Why?

WHITEHALL 8TH SEPTEMBER 1792

My Lord.

Having to signify to your Excellency His Majesty's Commands and Instructions on the subject of the Embassy to which he has been pleased to appoint you, I shall introduce them by recalling to your attention the occasion and object of this measure. . . .

The measures lately taken by Government [of Great Britain] respecting the Tea trade, having more than trebled the former legal importation of this article into Great Britain, it is become particularly desirable to cultivate a friendship, and increase the communication with China, which may lead to such a vent [market] throughout that extensive Empire, of the manufactures of the mother Country, and of our Indian Territories, as beside contributing to their prosperity will out of the sales of such produce, furnish resources for the investment to Europe, now re-

quiring no less an annual sum than one million, four hundred thousand pounds.

Hitherto, however, Great Britain has been obliged to pursue the Trade with that Country under circumstances the most discouraging, hazardous to its agents employed in conducting it, and precarious to the various interests involved in it. The only place where His Majesty's subjects have the privilege of a factory [trading station] is Canton [Guangzhou]. The fair competition of the Market is there destroyed by associations of the Chinese; our Supercargoes[1] are denied open access to the tribunals of the Country, and to the equal execution of its laws, and are kept altogether in a most arbitrary state of depression, ill suited to the importance of the concerns which are entrusted to their care, and scarcely compatible with the regulations of civilized society. . . .

His Majesty from his earnest desire to promote the present undertaking and in order to give the greater dignity to the Embassy, has been gra-

---

[1]An officer on a merchant ship in charge of the commercial concerns of the voyage.

ciously pleased to order one of His Ships of War to convey you and your Suite [entourage] to the Coast of China. With the same view he has ordered a Military Guard to attend your Person, to be composed of chosen Men from the light Dragoons, Infantry and Artillery, with proper Officers. . . . This guard will add splendour and procure respect to the Embassy; the order, appearance and evolutions of the Men may convey no useless idea of our military Character and discipline, and if it should excite in the Emperor a desire of adopting any of the exercise or maneuvers, among the Troops, an opportunity thus offers to him, for which a return of good offices on his part is natural to be expected. . . .

Should your answer be satisfactory, and I will not suppose the contrary, you will then assume the Character and public appearance of His Majesty's Ambassador Extraordinary, and proceed with as much ceremony as can be admitted without causing a material delay, or incurring an unreasonable expense. . . .

I am satisfied you will be too prudent and considerate, to let any trifling punctilio [point of honor] stand in the way of the important benefits which may be obtained by engaging the favourable disposition of the Emperor and his Ministers. You will take the earliest opportunity of representing to His Imperial Majesty, that your Royal Master, already so justly celebrated in Foreign Countries on account of the voyages projected under his immediate auspices, for the acquisition and diffusion of knowledge, was from the same disposition desirous of sending an embassy to the most civilized as well as most ancient and populous Nation in the World in order to observe its celebrated institutions, and to communicate and receive the benefits which must result from an unreserved and friendly intercourse between that Country and his own. You will take care to express the high esteem which His Majesty has conceived for the Emperor, from the wisdom and virtue with which his character has been distinguished. . . .

I do not mean to prescribe to you the particular mode of your negotiation; much must be left to

your circumspection, and the judgement to be formed upon occurrences as they arise; but upon the present view of the matter, I am inclined to believe that instead of attempting to gain upon the Chinese Administration by representations founded upon the intricacies of either European or Indian Politicks, you should fairly state, after repeating the general assurances of His Majesty's friendly and pacific inclinations towards the Emperor, and his respect for the reputed mildness of his Administration, first the mutual benefit to be derived from a trade between the two Nations, in the course of which we receive beside other articles to the amount of twenty millions of Pounds weight of a Chinese herb [tea], which would find very little vent, as not being in general use in other Countries, European or Asiatic, and for which we return woolens, cottons, and other articles useful to the Chinese, but a considerable part is actually paid to China in bullion.

Secondly, that the great extent of our commercial concerns in China, requires a place of security as a depot for such of our Goods as cannot be sold off or shipped during the short season that is allowed for our shipping to arrive and depart, and that for this purpose we wish to obtain a grant of a small tract of ground or detached Island, but in a more convenient situation than Canton, where our present warehouses are at a great distance from our Ships, and where we are not able to restrain the irregularities which are occasionally committed by the seamen of the Company's Ships, and those of private traders.

Thirdly, that our views are purely commercial, having not even a wish for territory; that we desire neither fortification nor defense but only the protection of the Chinese Government for our Merchants or their agents in trading or travelling thro the Country and a security to us against the encroachments of other powers, who might ever aim to disturb our trade; and you must here be prepared to obviate any prejudice which may arise from the argument of our present dominions in India by stating our situation in this respect to have arisen without our intending it, from the necessity of our defending ourselves against the oppressions of the revolted Nabobs,[2] who entered into Cabals [small, secret conspiratorial groups] to our prejudice with other Nations of Europe, and disregarded the privileges granted to us by different Emperors, or by such other arguments as your own reflections upon the subject will suggest. . . .

If any favorable opportunity should be afforded to your Excellency it will be advisable that the difficulties with which our trade has long laboured at Canton should be represented; but in making such a representation you will endeavour to convince the Emperor that it is [far] from His Majesty's [the king of Britain] design only to appease [apprise?] his Imperial Majesty that such difficulties do exist, in full confidence that from his wisdom and justice they will not hereafter be experienced.

Should a new establishment be conceded you will take it in the name of the King of Great Britain. You will endeavour to obtain it on the most beneficial terms, with a power of regulating the police, and exercising jurisdiction over our own dependents, for which competent powers would be given so as effectually to prevent or punish the disorders of our people, which the Company's Supercargos in their limited sphere of action must see committed with impunity. . . .

It is necessary you should be on your Guard against one stipulation which, perhaps, will be demanded from you: which is that of the exclusion of the trade of opium from the Chinese dominions as being prohibited by the Laws of the Empire; if this subject should come into discussion, it must be handled with the greatest circumspection. It is beyond a doubt that no inconsiderable portion of the opium raised within our Indian territories actually finds its way to China: but if it should be made a positive requisition or any article of any proposed commercial treaty, that none of that drug should be sent by us to China, you must accede to it, rather than risk any essential benefit by contending for a liberty in this respect in which case the sale of our opium in Bengal must be left to take its chance in an open market, or to find a consumption in the dispersed and circuitous traffic of the eastern Seas. . . .

In case the embassy should have an amicable and prosperous termination, it may be proposed to his Imperial Majesty to receive an occasional or perpetual Minister from the King of Great Britain, and to send one on his own part to the Court of London, in the assurance that all proper honours will be paid to any person who may be deputed in that sacred character. . . .

Sincerely wishing your Excellency a prosperous voyage and complete success in the very important objects of it, I have the honour to be with great regard, My Lord,

Your Excellency's most obedient
and most humble Servant
Henry Dundas.

---

[2]Another spelling of *nawab,* a term for an Indian provincial prince.

Qianlong's Rejection of British Demands
▼▼▼

56 ▾ *Emperor Qianlong,* *EDICT ON TRADE WITH GREAT BRITAIN*

Lord Macartney departed for China in September 1792 with an entourage of scientists, servants, artists, guards, and translators on a heavily armed man-of-war accompanied by two support ships. The support ships were loaded with 600 boxes of gifts for the eighty-two-year-old emperor and high Chinese officials designed to show the sophistication and quality of British manufacturing and instrument making. The British delegation reached Beijing in June 1793, and after reaching a compromise on the issue of whether Macartney could kneel and bow before the emperor rather than prostrate himself in the ritual known as the kowtow, Macartney presented his case to the emperor and his chief officials. Shortly thereafter, Qianlong issued the following edict to King George III in which he rejected each and every British proposal. Macartney's mission had failed, and Sino-British relations continued to deteriorate until the Opium War (1839– 1842) settled the two nations' many disputes through force rather than diplomacy.

QUESTIONS FOR ANALYSIS

1. What views of China's place in the world is revealed in Qianlong's letter?
2. What does the letter reveal about Qianlong's views of foreigners in general and the British in particular?
3. What are the emperor's stated reasons for rejecting any expansion of trade with Great Britain?
4. What unstated reasons might also have influenced his decision?

You, O King, from afar have yearned after the blessings of our civilization, and in your eagerness to come into touch with our converting influence have sent an Embassy across the sea bearing a memorial.[1] I have already taken note of your respectful spirit of submission, have treated your mission with extreme favor and loaded it with gifts, besides issuing a mandate to you, O King, and honoring you with the bestowal of valuable presents. Thus has my indulgence been manifested.

Yesterday your Ambassador petitioned my Ministers to memorialize me regarding your trade with China, but his proposal is not consistent with our dynastic usage and cannot be entertained. Hitherto, all European nations, including your own country's barbarian merchants, have carried on their trade with our Celestial Empire at Guangzhou. Such has been the procedure for many years, although our Celestial Empire possesses all things in prolific abundance and lacks no product within its own borders. There was therefore no need to import the manufactures of outside barbarians in exchange for our own produce. But as the tea, silk, and porcelain which the Celestial Empire produces are absolute necessities to European nations and to yourselves, we have permitted, as a signal mark of favor, that *hongs*[2] should be established at Guangzhou, so that your wants might be supplied and your country thus participate in our beneficence. But your Ambassador has now put forward new requests which completely fail to recognize the Throne's principle to "treat strangers from afar with indulgence," and to exercise a pacifying control over barbarian tribes the world over. Moreover, our dynasty, ruling over the myriad races of the globe, extends the same benevolence towards all. Your England is not the only nation trading at Guangzhou. If other nations, following your bad example, wrongfully importune my ear with further impossible requests, how will it

[1]Memorandum.
[2]Approximately ten Chinese merchant guilds that alone were licensed to trade with Westerners.

be possible for me to treat them with easy indulgence? Nevertheless, I do not forget the lonely remoteness of your island, cut off from the world by intervening wastes of sea, nor do I overlook your excusable ignorance of the usages of our Celestial Empire. I have consequently commanded my Ministers to enlighten your Ambassador on the subject, and have ordered the departure of the mission. But I have doubts that after your Envoy's return he may fail to acquaint you with my view in detail or that he may be lacking in lucidity, so that I shall now proceed . . . to issue my mandate on each question separately. In this way you will, I trust, comprehend my meaning. . . .

Your request for a small island near Zhoushan,[3] where your merchants may reside and goods be warehoused, arises from your desire to develop trade. As there are neither *hongs* nor interpreters in or near Zhoushan, where none of your ships has ever called, such an island would be utterly useless for your purposes. Every inch of the territory of our Empire is marked on the map and the strictest vigilance is exercised over it all: even tiny islets and far-lying sand-banks are clearly defined as part of the provinces to which they belong. Consider, moreover, that England is not the only barbarian land which wishes to establish . . . trade with our Empire: supposing that other nations were all to imitate your evil example and beseech me to present them each and all with a site for trading purposes, how could I possibly comply? This also is a flagrant infringement of the usage of my Empire and cannot possibly be entertained.

The next request, for a small site in the vicinity of Guangzhou city, where your barbarian merchants may lodge or, alternatively, that there be no longer any restrictions over their movements at Macao,[4] has arisen from the following causes. Hitherto, the barbarian merchants of

Europe have had a definite locality assigned to them at Macao for residence and trade, and have been forbidden to encroach an inch beyond the limits assigned to that locality. . . . If these restrictions were withdrawn, friction would inevitably occur between the Chinese and your barbarian subjects, and the results would militate against the benevolent regard that I feel towards you. From every point of view, therefore, it is best that the regulations now in force should continue unchanged. . . .

Regarding your nation's worship of the Lord of Heaven, it is the same religion as that of other European nations. Ever since the beginning of history, sage Emperors and wise rulers have bestowed on China a moral system and inculcated a code, which from time immemorial has been religiously observed by the myriads of my subjects.[5] There has been no hankering after heterodox doctrines. Even the European officials[6] in my capital are forbidden to hold intercourse with Chinese subjects; they are restricted within the limits of their appointed residences, and may not go about propagating their religion. The distinction between Chinese and barbarian is most strict, and your Ambassador's request that barbarians shall be given full liberty to disseminate their religion is utterly unreasonable.

It may be, O King, that the above proposals have been wantonly made by your Ambassador on his own responsibility, or peradventure you yourself are ignorant of our dynastic regulations and had no intention of transgressing them when you expressed these wild ideas and hopes. . . . If, after the receipt of this explicit decree, you lightly give ear to the representations of your subordinates and allow your barbarian merchants to proceed to Zhejiang and Tianjin,[7] with the object of landing and trading there, the ordinances of my Celestial Empire are strict in the extreme, and the local officials, both civil and military, are

---

[3]A group of islands in the East China Sea at the entrance to Hangzhou Bay.
[4]Island colony west of Hong Kong where Europeans were allowed to carry on their trade.

[5]A reference to Confucianism.
[6]Missionaries.
[7]Two Chinese port cities.

bound reverently to obey the law of the land. Should your vessels touch the shore, your merchants will assuredly never be permitted to land or to reside there, but will be subject to instant expulsion. In that event your barbarian merchants will have had a long journey for nothing. Do not say that you were not warned in due time! Tremblingly obey and show no negligence! A special mandate!

▼▼▼

Social and Economic Change in Tokugawa Japan

Tokugawa Ieyasu and his immediate successors as shogun implemented a four-part plan to strengthen their authority and stabilize Japan. They tightened control of powerful *daimyo* families, who maintained authority in their domains but whose ability to launch rebellions was crippled; they severed almost all contacts between Japan and the outside world; they officially sanctioned and supported Confucianism, with its conservativism and respect for authority; and they sought to freeze class divisions with military aristocrats at the top and farmers, artisans, and merchants below them. These policies were remarkably successful. Their subjects, who yearned for order as much as their rulers, experienced internal peace and stable government under the Tokugawa until 1867, when the regime was overthrown.

Paradoxically, the demise of the Tokugawa regime resulted in part from its success. Decades of peace fostered economic expansion accompanied by population growth, urbanization, and social mobility. Japan's population grew from approximately 18 million in 1600 to 30 million by the 1750s, and Edo (modern Tokyo) grew from a small village into a city with over a million inhabitants. These changes increased demand for all types of goods, especially rice, and as a result certain groups such as richer peasants and merchants prospered. Most peasants, however, could not take advantage of the commercialization of agriculture, and in the eighteenth century, many experienced hardships from land shortages and rising rents. In addition, Japan's military aristrocrats, the daimyo and samurai, failed to benefit from the economic boom. Lavish personal spending and the daimyo's need to maintain residences in both Edo and their own domain led to massive indebtedness.

While economic change was undermining the social basis of the Tokugawa regime, intellectual ferment was eroding its ideological underpinnings. As the memory of earlier civil wars faded, the conservativism of Confucianism lost some of its appeal, and foreign ideas seemed less dangerous. In the eighteenth century two intellectual developments challenged state-sponsored Confucianism. Proponents of National Learning, or *Kokugaku*, rejected Chinese influence, especially Confucianism, and dedicated themselves to the study and glorification of Japan's ancient literature and religious beliefs. Other Japanese developed an interest in European ideas, especially in medicine but also in botany, cartography, and gunnery. These endeavors were known as *Dutch Studies* because the main source of information about Europe came from the Dutch, who continued to trade on a limited basis with Japan even after the seclusion policy was adopted. By the late eighteenth century those who were dissatisfied with the Tokugawa regime did not lack models for a different future, something that solidly Confucian China did not have.

A Japanese Merchant Views His World
▼▼▼

57 ▼ *Mitsui Takafusa,* *SOME OBSERVATIONS ON MERCHANTS*

Among the hundreds of family businesses begun in the early Tokugawa period, none can match the long-term economic success and political clout of the multi-faceted business enterprise founded by the Mitsui family. With interests at first in *sake* brewing, pawnbrokering, and money changing, the family opened a dry goods store in Edo in 1673 and continued to diversify into banking, shipping, rice marketing, and mining. By 1800 it employed 1,000 workers in its Edo shops alone, and a century later it was Japan's largest business conglomerate and a powerful force in creating the new industrialized Japan.

None of this could have been foreseen by Mitsui Takahira (1653–1737), the second head of the family business. He had seen too many new businesses flourish at the start only to fail because of high living and poor business decisions on the part of second- and third-generation owners. In the hope that the Mitsui firm would avoid such a fate, in 1722 he drew up the Mitsui Family Code, a set of precepts of personal and business behavior for members of the family. He also compiled a set of sketches of approximately fifty business families, from Osaka, Edo, and Kyoto, whose businesses had failed. The purpose of these sketches was to illustrate the points he had made in the code. Sometime in the late 1720s Mitsui Takahira's son, Takafusa, collated and edited his father's sketches and added an introduction and conclusion. Posterity has credited the son with the authorship of *Some Observations on Merchants,* even though it mainly contains his father's recollections and ideas. It is an invaluable source of information about the business world of early Tokugawa Japan and the values and experiences of the merchants who were part of it.

QUESTIONS FOR ANALYSIS

1. What is the message of the source concerning the ideal qualities of a successful merchant?
2. What is likely to lead to business failure?
3. What does the source reveal about the level of commercialization in the Japanese economy?
4. What perspectives does the source offer concerning the merchant's place in Japanese society, in particular the relationship of merchants to the daimyo and samurai?

5. **What differences and similarities do you see in the views of merchants of Mitsui and those of the Chinese writer Zhang Han (source 3)?**

QUALITIES OF A SUCCESSFUL MERCHANT

There was a man of Edo rather ill-favored by nature. He had, nevertheless, a considerable fortune. Once when he met with other persons of the same status, they all asked: "What should we do to make money like yourself? Please pass on the formula." Thereupon he replied, "If only you are fond of money, you can do it any time." The people answered that there was no one who was not fond of money. "In that case," the man inquired, "if each of you now had as much money as he wanted, what would you do? I would like to have your reflections on the subject." They each gave their views, that if they had so much money they would put so much aside and with the rest restore their unsightly houses or pay off their debts and so on. "Since this is how you all feel," the man said, "you cannot have money. You actually are planning to spend it before you even have it. I do not worry about the state of my house. Nor do I have clothes made. The only thing I am keen on is money." How truly right these golden words are. This little story should be weighed thoroughly.

▼▼▼

When a deficiency appears in their financial positions, they should own up immediately to their poverty and declare their inability to pay. This should be the time to make plans to stay in business, but what they do is to think first of their reputations and borrow as much as they can to cover up their financial position. When at their wit's end, they are exposed and thus wind up like this [bankrupt]. . . . This is the meaning of the maxim that a bud may be nipped with the hand but if left will later have to be chopped with an axe.

▼▼▼

Whatever business you get your start in, you must always continue to recognize the value of that business and put your heart and soul into it. Most people, however, when they have made a fortune, with large holdings of gold and silver, forget where it came from and think that the way to make a living is to engage in financing, which does not require many assistants. They leave their former business clerks and think they can live at ease through financing, but it is scarcely possible to make a living as easily as that. There are many examples in this world of people eventually going bankrupt by risking not only their own capital but even borrowed money. After all, though it may be a slower process, if you pay for all your personal expenses out of the profits of the trade in which you originally prospered, regard the money which you have as your stock in trade and work single-mindedly at your own business, it is only natural that as a divine reward your house will continue. . . .

MERCHANTS' MISSTEPS

This business of lending to daimyo is like gambling. Instead of being cut in the first place while they are small, losses become a kind of bait. Using the argument that if further loans are made the original ones will be reactivated, the officials and financial agents of daimyo who raise loans decoy the lenders with specious talk. This is like setting fried bean curd for mice, as the saying has it, and finally they are caught in the trap. They thus incur heavier losses than before. Such being the case, one should give up making loans of this sort. However, no gambler places a bet expecting from the beginning that he will lose. . . . If in lending to daimyo the dealings go according to contract, certainly there is no better business. It does not require a large staff. With one account book and one pair of scales, the thing is settled. This is really genuinely making money while you sleep. As the classical saying goes, however, "for every profit there is a loss." Such a fine business as this is liable to turn out very badly in the end. Consider well that you should never rely on lending to daimyo.

▾ ▾ ▾

Samurai employ stratagems with victory as their sole aim. To do so is their military duty. Merchants may think that they can make profits to a reasonable extent and write off their losses. Samurai, however, are the highest of the four social classes, and their officials, who combine cleverness with cunning, see through your tricks and turn the tables on you. As soon as they have what they want out of the other party, they seize control and default. The bamboo spears of merchants, you might say, are pitted against the true swords of samurai, and you are no match for your adversary. . . . In books on military strategy, it is said that only he who knows the enemy as well as his own side can be called a great general. Any merchant who tries to trick samurai does not know his enemy.

▾ ▾ ▾

Many in times both past and present have ruined their families through becoming involved in speculative ventures. In Edo, by so-called gold extraction,[1] or the smelting of gold from copper, people obtained some gold from bar copper and showed it to amateurs, whom they tricked into putting a lot of money into the idea. Eventually those "gold extractors" absconded with the money they had raised. They say that a little gold generally can be extracted by processing copper. If the cost of charcoal and laborers is taken into account, however, it hardly provides a living. I am told that in Holland they do smelt gold from copper. In Japan, though how to do this is known, it does not pay for the above reason, and so the copper is handed over as it is.

As regards gold mines, they say that small amounts of gold and silver exist everywhere but that the mining of them is not a commercial proposition because, as with the extraction of gold from copper, the yield is too small. Despite this, just because someone shows them something supposed to be ore from a mine and talks glibly, there are many people about who, being somewhat rash by nature, are ready to risk everything and, finally being talked into it, and by losing what little they had.

THE MERCHANT'S PLACE IN SOCIETY

The Jūemon I and Jūemon II[2] possessed many fine household articles which they had bought. One of these was the "Misoya Katatsuki" tea container, which was bought from Kameya someone or other for a thousand gold pieces. They say the purchase money was loaded on a cart and dragged around in broad daylight to make the payment and take delivery.

Jūemon II built a Zen temple at Narutaki, on the western side of Kyoto. He deposited with the temple an image of Hitomaro[3] and built for it a hall called Hitomaro Hall. The interior of this he lined with gold brocade. It is commonly known as the Gold Brocade Hall of Narutaki. Through his interest in Japanese poetry, he, though a merchant, mixed with distinguished Court nobles, forgot the real nature of his status and finally lost his large fortune. He was one who did not know his proper station.

▾ ▾ ▾

Again, a merchant called Ishikawa Rokubei, of Edo, who started off in the brokerage business, had a wife who was extraordinarily extravagant and went to the limit in finery. Retribution finally caught up with them. Along the route of the valiant [the shogun's heir apparent], when this

---

[1]The process of extracting gold or silver from copper ore by smelting it with the addition of lead was introduced to Japan by Europeans in the late sixteenth century.

[2]"Jūemon I" is Itoya Jūemon, a Kyoto-based rice trader. "Jūemon II" and "Jūemon III" were his son and grandson, respectively.

[3]Kakinomoto Hitomaro was a famous poet of the late seventh and the early eighth centuries venerated as the God of Poetry.

Rokubei's wife and her servants were all decked out, the valiant prince, thinking that she was the wife of a daimyo or of some family of high rank, graciously had his aides make inquiries and was told that she was the wife of that fellow [the merchant]. After he had returned to the palace, Rokubei and his wife were summoned to the office of the town magistrate. It was considered that their extravagance beyond their station and particularly their lack of respect for their superiors were outrageous. Their family property was forfeited, and, by the Shogun's mercy, they got off with banishment from Edo.

As they say, a curse always falls on the house where the hen does the crowing. If a wife is extravagant in defiance of her husband and runs the household just as she likes, it is the same as for a hen to crow the time. This must be the meaning of the golden words which say that such a house invariably perishes. . . .

THE MERCHANT'S CALLING

. . . When great men are extravagant, they lose their territories, but lesser folk lose their livelihood. Even if one cannot add further profits to the money which one's forebear, acquiring merit through difficulties, accumulated by sweating away at money-making day and night, one at least should reflect on the debt of gratitude owing to one's forebear and take good care to keep his fortune intact. What can we say of one who does neither of these things and finally ruins his family through extravagance! Losses through miscalculation in trading, as well as losses in financial operations, may be due to insufficient concentration of one's proper calling. This is your livelihood, however, and as such cannot be shirked. Understand thoroughly that these things are only matters of prudence. . . . It is the law of nature that birds and beasts and in fact all things which dwell between heaven and earth — and above all, human beings — should seek their sustenance by working at their callings. This being so, such behavior on the part of people far from being in their dotage displays ignorance of the will of heaven.

The Social Ills of Tokugawa Japan
▼▼▼

58 ▼ *Honda Toshiaki,*
A SECRET PLAN OF GOVERNMENT

Honda Toshiaki, born in northern Japan in 1721, was a perceptive critic of late Tokugawa society and a prophet of Japan's future. After studying and teaching mathematics, astronomy, and fencing in Edo, he devoted most of his life to observing and analyzing the state of contemporary Japan. In his travels he was particularly interested in observing conditions among the poor and learning the reasons for their misery. He concluded that as a small island nation, Japan needed to expand its commerce and colonize, rather than concentrate on agriculture, as a large continental country like China could do. In his view Japan's seclusion policy should be abandoned and efforts made to teach the Japanese modern navigation and weaponry. Honda publicized his ideas to students and correspondents, but his influence on Japan's political leaders came only after his death. His only government service was as advisor to the lord of Kaga, a minor daimyo. In 1821 he died in Edo.

Honda's *A Secret Plan for Government*, written in 1798, is his most important work. In it he elaborates an economic and political plan for Japan based on what he called the "four imperative needs": to learn the effective use of gunpowder, to develop metallurgy, to increase trade, and to colonize both nearby islands and distant lands. The following excerpt comes at the end of a long discourse on Japanese history in which Honda analyzes the roots of Japan's problems.

QUESTIONS FOR ANALYSIS

1. What is Honda's view of the daimyo? How does it compare to Mitsui's views of the daimyo (source 57)?
2. How do merchants contribute to Japan's problems, according to Honda?
3. How does Honda justify his assertion that fifteen-sixteenths of all Japanese rice production goes to the merchants? Are his arguments plausible?
4. Why is Europe rather than China the better model for Japan's revival, according to Honda?
5. What Confucian influence is evident in Honda's *Plan?* In what ways does Honda reject Confucianism?

Not until Tokugawa Ieyasu used his power to control the strong and give succor to the weak did the warfare that had lasted for three hundred years without a halt suddenly abate. Arrows were left in their quivers and spears in their racks. If now, in a time of peace, the country were ruled in accordance with the four imperative needs, the prices of all commodities would be stabilized, and the discontent of the people would thus be cut off at the root. This is the true method of establishing a permanent foundation for the nation, so that the people will become honest in their hearts and cultivate orderly ways even if they are not governed. It must have been because he realized how difficult it would be to preserve the empire for all ages to come if the people were not honest in their hearts that Ieyasu, in his testament, exhorted shoguns who would succeed him to abstain from any irregularities in government, and to rule on a basis of benevolence and honesty. It was his counsel that the shoguns should serve as models to the people, and by their honesty train the people in the ways of humanity and justice. He taught that

the shogun should not compel obedience merely by the use of force, but by his acts of benevolence should keep the nation at peace. . . .

He taught the daimyo that the duties of a governor consisted in the careful attempt to guide the people of their domains in such a way as both to bring about the prosperity of the land and to encourage the literary and military arts.

However, in recent days there has been the spectacle of lords confiscating the allocated property of their retainers on the pretext of paying back debts to the merchants. The debts do not then decrease, but usually seem rather to grow larger. One daimyo with an income of 60,000 *koku*[1] so increased his borrowings that he could not make good his debts, and there was a public suit. The court judgment in the case was said to have been over 1,180,000 *ryo.*[2] Even if repayment had been attempted on the basis of his income of 60,000 koku, the debt would not have been completely settled for fifty or sixty years, so long a time that it is difficult to imagine the day would actually come.

[1] A *koku* is approximately five bushels of rice and was used to measure daimyo income.

[2] A measurement of the weight of gold.

All the daimyo are not in this position, but there is not one who has not borrowed from the merchants. Is this not a sad state of affairs? The merchant, watching this spectacle, must feel like a fisherman who sees a fish swim into his net. Officials of the daimyo harass the farmers for money, which they claim they need to repay the daimyo's debts, but the debts do not diminish. Instead, the daimyo go on contracting new ones year after year. The [daimyo's] officials are blamed for this situation, and are dismissed as incompetent. New officials then harass and afflict the farmers in much the same way as the old ones, and so it goes on. . . .

No matter how hard the daimyo and their officials rack their brains, they do not seem to be able to reduce the debts. The lords are "sunk in a pool of debts," as it is popularly said, a pool from which their children and grandchildren will be unable to escape. Everything will be as the merchants wish it. The daimyo turn over their domains to the merchants, receiving in return an allowance with which to pay their public and private expenses. Such daimyo give no thought at all to Heaven, to fulfilling their duties as samurai, or to the proper way of looking after the farmers.

Many fields have turned into wasteland since the famine of 1783, when thousands of farmers starved to death. Wherever one goes . . . , one hears people say, "There used to be a village here. . . . The land over there was once part of such-and-such a county, but now there is no village and no revenue comes from the land." . . . When so many farmers starved, reducing still further their already insufficient numbers, the amount of uncultivated land greatly increased. If the wicked practice of infanticide, now so prevalent, is not stopped, the farming population will dwindle until it tends to die out altogether. Generous protective and relief measures must be put into effect immediately if this evil practice is to be stamped out.

A wise ruler could end this practice in short order and create an atmosphere favorable to the prosperity of the nation by establishing a system based on generosity and compassion. When a woman of one of the lower classes becomes pregnant, a government agent should be sent to investigate the situation. The mother of the child should then be given two sacks of rice each year from the month the child is born until he is ten years old. The practice of infanticide would soon stop. Thus by spending a mere twenty sacks of rice over a period of ten years, the country would at the same time gain a good farmer and atone for the misery caused in the past. . . .

The Confucian scholars of ancient and modern times have talked a great deal about benevolence and compassion, but they possess neither in their hearts. Officials and authorities talk about benevolent government, but they have no understanding of what that means. Whose fault is it that the farmers are dying of starvation and that good fields are turning into wasteland? The fault lies entirely with the ruler. . . .

▷ There follows an enthusiastic but often inaccurate account of Europe's accomplishments.

Because astronomy, calendar making, and mathematics are considered the ruler's business, the European kings are well versed in celestial and terrestrial principles, and instruct the common people in them. Thus even among the lower classes one finds men who show great ability in their particular fields. The Europeans as a result have been able to establish industries with which the rest of the world is unfamiliar. It is for this reason that all the treasures of the world are said to be attracted to Europe. There is nowhere the Europeans' ships do not go in order to obtain the different products and treasures of the world. They trade their own rare products, superior implements, and unusual inventions for the precious metals and valuable goods of others, which they bring back to enrich their own countries. Their prosperity makes them strong, and it is because of their strength that they are never invaded or pillaged, whereas for their part they have invaded countless non-European countries. . . .

There is no place in the world to compare with Europe. It may be wondered in what way this supremacy was achieved. In the first place, the European nations have behind them a history of five to six thousand years. In this period they have delved deep into the beauties of the arts, have divined the foundations of government, and have established a system based on a thorough examination of the factors that naturally make a nation prosperous. Because of their proficiency in mathematics, they have excelled also in astronomy, calendar making, and surveying. They have elaborated laws of navigation such that there is nothing simpler for them than to sail the oceans of the world. . . .

In spite of this example, however, the Japanese do not look elsewhere than to China for good or beautiful things, so tainted are the customs and temperament of Japan by Chinese teachings. . . .

China is a mountainous country that extends as far as Europe and Africa. It is bounded by the ocean to the south, but water communication within the country is not feasible. Since it is impossible to feed the huge population of cities when transport can be effected only by human or animal strength, there are no big cities in China away from the coast. China is therefore a much less favored country than Japan, which is surrounded by water, and this factor shows in the deficiencies and faults of Chinese state policies. China does not merit being used as a model. Since Japan is a maritime nation, shipping and trade should be the chief concerns of the ruler. Ships should be sent to all countries to obtain products needed for national consumption and to bring precious metals to Japan. A maritime nation is equipped with the means to increase her national strength.

By contrast, a nation that attempts to get along on its own resources will grow steadily weaker. . . . To put the matter more bluntly, the policies followed by the various ruling families until now have determined that the lower classes must lead a hand-to-mouth existence. The best part of the harvests of the farmers who live on the domains of the empire is wrenched away from them. The lords spend all they take within the same year, and if they then do not have enough, they oppress the farmers all the more cruelly in an effort to obtain additional funds. This goes on year after year. . . .

It is a great shame that such conditions prevail, but it is said that "even the thoughts of an ant may reach up to Heaven." Though their conditions differ, the highest and the lowest alike are human beings, and the rulers ought to think about those who are less fortunate than themselves. Soon all the gold and silver currency will pass into the hands of the merchants, and only merchants will be deserving of the epithets "rich" and "mighty." Their power will thus grow until they stand first among the four classes. When I investigated the incomes of present-day merchants, I discovered that fifteen-sixteenths of the total income of Japan goes to the merchants, with only one-sixteenth left for the samurai. As proof of this statement, I cite the following case. When there are good rice harvests at Yonezawa in Dewa or in Semboku-gun in Akita[3] the price is five or six *mon* for one *sho*.[4] The rice is sold to merchants who ship it to Edo, where the price is about 100 mon, regardless of the original cost. At this rate, if one bought 10,000 ryos worth of rice in Dewa, sent it to Edo, and sold it there, one's capital would be increased to 160,000 ryo. If the 160,000 ryo in turn were used as capital, the return in Edo would be 2,560,000 ryo. With only two exchanges of trade it is possible to make enormous profits.

It may be claimed that of this sum part must go for shipping expenses and pack-horse charges, but the fact remains that one gets back sixteen times what one has paid for the rice. It is thus apparent that fifteen-sixteenths of the nation's income goes to the merchants. In terms of the production of an individual farmer, out of thirty days a month he works twenty-eight for the merchants and two for the samurai; or, out of 360

---

[3]Dewa and Akita are provinces in northern Honshu.

[4]A *mon* was a copper coin; a *sho* was about 3.2 pints.

days in a year, he works 337½ for the merchants and 22½ for the samurai. Clearly, then, unless the samurai store grain it is impossible for them to offer any relief to the farmers in years of famine. This may be why they can do no more than look on when the farmers are dying of starvation. And all this because the right system has not been established. It is a most lamentable state of affairs that the farmers have to shoulder the weight of this error and die of starvation as inevitably as "water collecting in a hollow."

By means of the plans outlined in the account of the four imperative needs . . . the present corrupt and jejune society could be restored to its former prosperity and strength. The ancient glories of the warrior-nation of Japan would be revived. Colonization projects would gradually be commenced and would meet with great success. . . . Then, under enlightened government, Japan could certainly be made the richest and strongest country in the world.

▼▼▼

The Opening of Oceania

Slowly, in a process that began as long as 40,000 or even 60,000 years ago when people from Asia reached Australia and ended only in 900 C.E. when the Maori settled New Zealand, human beings populated the thousands of islands stretching across the South Pacific from Asia to the Americas. The details of this process are dimly understood, but one thing is certain: Once established, these island societies existed in isolation from the rest of the world until the 1700s. The single exception is the Chamorro people of Guam and the Marianas, islands that were conquered and occupied by the Spaniards in the late 1600s to serve as refreshment stations for their galleons crossing the Pacific. Even in Australia, which is not far from the East Indies and the Southeast Asian mainland, native Australians had no documented contact with outsiders from approximately 8000 B.C.E. until the arrival of the Dutch explorer Abel Janszoon Tasman in 1642. Tasman and his backers, the merchants of the Dutch East India Company, concluded that the island had few economic prospects, and the next outsiders to visit Australia were Englishmen commanded by Captain James Cook, who claimed the subcontinent for Great Britain in 1770.

Cook's Pacific voyages, which took him to Tahiti, New Zealand, Hawaii, and dozens of other Pacific islands between 1768 and 1779, initiated a new era of European and U.S. involvement in Oceania. Although ignored in many histories, it is nonetheless an interesting and significant story. Because the Western move into the Pacific was rapid and on a comparatively small scale, it provides sharp insights into the phenomenon of Western expansion. One extreme is represented by the seal hunters who were among the first Westerners attracted to New Zealand, Australia, and Tasmania. Their slaughter of seals was so intense that the seal population was all but exterminated within a generation. Their treatment of the Maori and Aborigines was not much different. They kidnapped and sexually abused the women, enslaved the men, and subjected both to punishment or death for minor acts of theft or disobedience. When the seals were gone, most of the hunters moved on.

On the other extreme were the missionaries, most of whom were Protestants from Great Britain and the United States. These missionaries were for the most part sincere idealists who endured great hardship to carry Christianity and the supposed benefits of civilization to the Pacific Islanders. Yet the germs they carried in their bodies and the ideas they carried in their minds were lethal to the peoples they encountered, no matter how noble their intentions. The missionaries from the West did a measure of good but, like the sealers, also a measure of harm.

Early Reports from New Zealand

▼▼▼

59 ▼ Committee of the Church of England Missionary Society, *MEMORANDUM TO THE EARL OF BATHURST, SECRETARY OF STATE OF THE COLONIES*

The islands that make up modern New Zealand were uninhabited by humans until the Maori, a Polynesian people, arrived during the ninth century C.E. They numbered approximately 250,000 when the Dutch explorer Abel Janszoon Tasman visited in 1642. More than a century later, after the Englishman James Cook charted the islands in 1769, whalers and sealers from Australia, Europe, and the United States were drawn to New Zealand's shores, and permanent settlers on the islands soon followed.

Missionary efforts in New Zealand sponsored by the Church of England began in 1814 under the direction of Reverend Samuel Marsden (1764–1838), the son of a blacksmith. As a young man Marsden abandoned his studies at Cambridge University to minister to convicts who had been shipped to Australia. When he shifted his activities to New Zealand, he and his assistants concentrated on ministering to the Maori. They had three goals: to protect the Maori from abuse, to teach them agricultural and craft skills, and to convert them to Christianity.

As the following letter written in 1817 shows, Marsden and the other missionaries faced formidable obstacles. Massacres of the Maori and other abuses prompted hardened Maori resistance despite British government efforts to curb excesses. Conversions came slowly, and a series of bloody wars was fought before the Maori acquiesced to English rule. The Maori survived their encounter with the Europeans. Today they number approximately 300,000 and comprise 10 percent of New Zealand's population. Some of them are Christians.

QUESTIONS FOR ANALYSIS

1. How do the authors view the intellectual and moral capacities of the Maori?
2. What solutions do the authors suggest to end the abuses they describe?

3. How does the document depict Maori attitudes toward the Europeans?
4. On the basis of the examples cited, what were the causes of the conflicts between the Maori and the Europeans?

The memorial[1] of the Committee of the Church of England Missionary Society for Africa and the East humbly sheweth, —

That the Church Missionary Society has been engaged for eight years in endeavoring to propagate the knowledge of the Christian religion among the idolatrous nations of Africa and the East, and thereby to promote their civilization, as well as their spiritual and eternal welfare.

That in the prosecution of these designs the Society has directed its attention to the inhabitants of the islands of the South Seas, and especially to those of New Zealand, whose active and intelligent character appeared to offer a favorable field for their exertions. In the course of the year 1814, having obtained a grant of land from one of the chiefs of the country, the Society established a settlement in the Bay of Islands in New Zealand, at which three missionary settlers, with their families, have been since resident.

That the efforts of these settlers, as far as it has been possible hitherto to extend them, have been attended with most encouraging success. They have found the natives in the vicinity of a frank and affectionate character, desirous to cultivate their friendship, and to receive instruction, and the Society entertain a confident hope that by the establishment of schools and by other means of instruction they shall in due time be enabled, under the Divine blessing, to diffuse the knowledge of Christianity throughout this populous and benighted [unenlightened] land, and to rescue a noble race of men from the horrible superstitions and savage customs by which they are now degraded. The Society feels warranted also to hope that its exertions will tend in other ways to meliorate the condition of the islanders. Their settlers have already introduced among them the cultivation of wheat and other grain, and a foundation may perhaps be thus laid for the agricultural improvement of this fertile and productive country, which may hereafter render it not an unimportant object of commercial attention.

That the hopes which your memorialists thus entertain have been greatly checked by the intelligence [information] continually received by them of the atrocities committed by the European traders in the South Seas, by which not only the most grievous injuries are inflicted on the natives, but their minds are exasperated to acts of barbarous revenge, all tendency to a milder and more civilized character is repressed, confidence in the character and designs of the European settlers is weakened, and the lives of themselves and their families are seriously endangered. . . .

In the year 1810 the ship *Boyd* sailed from Port Jackson to Whangarooa in New Zealand with some natives on board, one of them the son of the head chief of the place. These persons were very ill used during the voyage. The young chief, who had fallen sick and was unable to work as a sailor, was severely flogged, treated with great indignity, and sent on shore, lacerated with stripes. When the treatment which he had received became known to his friends and people it roused them to fury; they seized the ship, and put the captain and all the crew to death. Soon after this Tippahee, a chief belonging to the Bay of Islands, and who was well known and respected at Port Jackson, was accused of having been concerned in the massacre. In consequence of this report, the whalers, who were on the coast, manned and armed seven boats, landed on the island of Tippahee, and shot every man, woman, and child that came in their

---

[1]A statement of facts addressed to a government, often accompanied by a petition or request.

way. Tippahee was severely wounded. It has since been ascertained that this chief so far from being guilty of the crime imputed to him, he exerted himself to save the lives of the crew. His people must have been known to be guiltless, for their territory was forty miles distant from Whanga-rooa; yet thus have the unoffending inhabitants of a whole island been exterminated by a lawless act of private vengeance.

A year or two before this the captain of an English ship which was sailing by one of the islands fired, without any provocation, five or six large guns, loaded with grape shot, among a multitude of natives, men, women, and children, who were assembled on the beach to look at the vessel, and killed and wounded several of them. When remonstrated with for this act of wanton barbarity he only said it was necessary to strike terror into the minds of these natives, and convince them of what power we possessed.

In 1812 the schooner *Parramatta* put into the Bay of Islands, in distress, for provisions and water. She was supplied by the natives with potatoes, pork, and fish to the extent of their wants, and when they required payment they were thrown overboard, fired at, and wounded. The schooner immediately weighed anchor, but was soon after driven on shore in a storm, and the islanders revenged themselves by putting the crew to death. . . .

That your memorialists will not dwell on the various instances in which potato grounds (the chief culture of these islands) have been destroyed, and the produce stolen; in which the property of the natives has been forcibly taken or fraudulently obtained, under pretence of purchase, and no equivalent given; in which their chiefs have been imprisoned and ill treated in order to extort a ransom; and all these misdeeds too often accompanied by circumstances of wanton cruelty.

That in a recent case proceedings have been instituted at Port Jackson[2] against the captain of a trading vessel for acts of oppression and cruelty against the chiefs and other natives of one of the Marquesas Islands,[3] in which after a full investigation a conviction took place on the whole of the charges; but the party convicted has escaped with impunity, on account of the inadequacy of the powers vested in the Magistrates to punish the offence.

That your memorialists are informed that there is no competent jurisdiction in New South Wales for the cognizance and punishment of such offences as have been enumerated, nor any adequate means for their prevention; and that no remedy at present exists but sending persons charged with the perpetration of such enormities to be tried at the Admiralty Sessions in England.[4] . . .

That even the establishment of a tribunal with adequate power of punishment in New South Wales would not in all cases be effectual to remedy the evil . . . and that some further measure seems therefore requisite for the protection of the islanders, and the prevention of the crimes by which the moral character of Great Britain is degraded by the conduct of her subjects trading in those seas.

That, in consequence of the want at present of any sufficient provision by colonial tribunals or otherwise for the prevention or the punishment of crimes committed in the islands of the South Seas, your memorialists submit that not only the lives of the missionaries and settlers in those islands are exposed to the most imminent hazard, but that all endeavors to extend the blessings of Christianity and civilization among the natives must thereby be in a great measure frustrated, and the reasonable hope of advantage which might be derived therefrom even to our own country is destroyed.

---

[2]Sydney's original name.
[3]An island group just south of the equator and to the east of Hawaii.

[4]A court that handled cases involving ships on the seas.

The Plight of the Tasmanians

▼▼▼

60 ▼ *George A. Robinson,* *REPORT TO THE LIEUTENANT GOVERNOR-GENERAL OF TASMANIA*

The island of Tasmania, off the southeastern coast of Australia and about the size of West Virginia, was first inhabited by humans 20,000 years ago when a land-bridge connected it to the Australian mainland. When the seas rose 10,000 years later, the bridge disappeared, and the Tasmanian Aborigines were isolated until the arrival of Europeans in the seventeenth century. Hunters and gatherers who were organized into approximately ten tribes, the Tasmanian Aborigines numbered 4,000 to 6,000 around 1800.

In the early nineteenth century Australian, British, and American seal hunters established bases on the island's northern shore, and the British began sending convicts to three new penal colonies. Conflicts with the Aborigines erupted immediately over such issues as kangaroo hunting and soon intensified when farmers and sheepherders took over much of the island in the 1820s. By 1830 Tasmania supported nearly 25,000 settlers, more than 500,000 sheep, but only 2,000 Aborigines, whose numbers had shrunk as a result of disruption and disease.

In the 1830s English administrators attempted to solve the "Aborigine problem" by forcing native Tasmanians to live in one area where they could be protected and taught Christianity, and kept out of the way. Many Aborigines were killed resisting captivity, so that only several hundred were shipped to the aboriginal settlement on Flinders Island, off Tasmania's north shore. The settlement's director was George A. Robinson, a carpenter who had come to Tasmania in 1824 and had directed the roundup of Aborigines in the early 1830s. A religious man who viewed the Aborigines as "brothers in Christ," he believed they would benefit from living on Flinders Island. He wrote the following letter to the lieutenant governor-general of Tasmania in 1837, three years after the founding of the colony.

None of the letter's optimistic predictions came true. Infection, alcoholism, and poor diet further diminished the Aborigine population, and the colony on Flinders Island was disbanded in the early 1840s. Many whites now concluded the Aborigines were beyond redemption. The survivors of Flinders Island were sent to the village of Oyster Cove, where the last full-blooded male Aborigine died in 1868, and the last female, Truganini, died in 1871. Her skeleton was displayed as a scientific curiosity in a Hobart museum until 1947, when public opposition forced the Royal Society of Tasmania to put it in storage. In 1976, after appeals from Tasmanians of mixed Aborigine-European descent, her remains were cremated and scattered on the beach where she had played as a girl.

QUESTIONS FOR ANALYSIS

1. What encouraging signs does Robinson claim to have seen in the first years of the Flinders Island colony's existence?
2. What are Robinson's views of the skills and mental capacities of the Aborigines?
3. In Robinson's view, what are the concrete signs that the Aborigines are becoming "civilized"?
4. According to Robinson, what general lessons pertaining to colonial policy can be learned from the experience at Flinders Island?
5. Despite Robinson's rosy picture of Flinders Island, the colony soon failed. From reading Robinson's letter, what can you surmise about the reasons?

Sir,

. . . I have much satisfaction in stating that the wants of the aborigines are amply and abundantly supplied, and that the provisions furnished by the Government are of the best description; and though, notwithstanding, the fatality to which I have heretofore alluded is of painful character, still it must be conceded that the same is quite providential [caused by an act of Providence, or God], and might have occurred in their own native districts; . . . and hence, amid the calamity that has happened, it is a pleasing reflection to know that everything has been done which ingenuity could devise or humanity suggest to alleviate their condition, and of which the aborigines themselves have marked their appreciation, and oft repeated their acknowledgements for . . . the kind intention of the Government towards them.

The advantages to the aborigines by their removal have been manifold, and many of them of the highest order. In their native forests they were without the knowledge of a God, hence but little removed from the brute themselves. Their mode of life was extremely precarious, and to the juveniles distressing in the extreme; and though in their insidious and deadly attacks on the white inhabitants they invariably eluded pursuit, yet they themselves were not without dangers and alarms, and might reasonably be said to exist by excitement alone. . . . Anterior to their arrival . . . they were in a deplorable state of mental degradation. Such is not now the case: they not only possess the knowledge of a Deity, but are acquainted with the principles of Christianity.

From the time I first took charge of the settlement, now near two years since, religious knowledge has been daily imparted to them, and religious principles inculcated. In this laudable object the whole of the officers and my family have untiredly assisted, a duty in which they have evinced the greatest aptitude and delight; and I myself can testify with what avidity and eagerness they have attended to and sought after religious knowledge. . . .

DOMESTIC ECONOMY

Their time is wholly employed in useful labor, harmless amusements, in their attendance at school, and religious exercises, and not, as heretofore, wandering about the settlement with listless and careless indifference to what was going on; but on the contrary, evinced by their general conduct, their prompt attention to instruction, and their persevering industry, that they have an interest in the affairs of the settlement, [in] which it has ever been my aim on all occasions to bring them to participate. They are no longer idle spectators, but actors and ready agents to assist, as far as strength and ability will permit, in every useful undertaking.

I have already alluded to their proficiency in useful arts, viz. knitting and fancy network, and though from the paucity of their numbers the manufacture cannot be done to any great extent, still in whatever light we view it, whether as a branch of useful industry, or as an amusement, one thing is certain, that it displays a precocity of intellect of no ordinary kind, and proves that those whom civilized men despised as beings without mind, are, like all God's creatures, perfect in every form, and which only requires the adoption of proper means, when the latent intellect of the degraded savage will be made manifest, and be developed.

There are many and numerous incidents that might be cited to mark their improvement in domestic economy: suffice to say, they are not now, as formerly, content to sit upon the ground, but require seats, both as an article of convenience and a preservation from soiling their clothes. Those among them who have knives and forks habitually use them, and which the residue are anxious to possess; they now also confine themselves more closely to their domiciles, and not interchanging or crouching under bushes or lolling about in idleness.

The aborigines are becoming cleanly in their persons; they now perform the necessary ablutions daily, and the greater part of them have shorn beards; they are not now satisfied as heretofore with one garment, *i.e.,* a frock coat, but require trousers also, and their raiment [garments] is in general kept in clean and proper order.

The females are equally as anxious to possess clothes of a European fashion. Several pieces of print [printed cotton fabric] bought on their account, and sold at the market, were purchased with avidity [enthusiasm] and manufactured into gowns; they likewise wear under garments, which they keep in clean and good order. They now evince great desire for domestic comforts, and which, though amply supplied, can only be attained by industry and good conduct. Their primitive habits are now all but forgotten: the use of ochre[1] and grease, with which they used formerly to bedaub themselves, is now entirely abolished. Their nocturnal orgies . . . , which hurt the repose of the settlement and impaired the health of the natives . . . never occur.

ABORIGINAL POLICE

The police of this establishment consists of four special constables, and their two chiefs, to whom the conservation of the aborigines is confided. The constables are chosen from each of the two remnant tribes in full assembly, convened for the occasion.

The constables act under the orders of their chiefs; the latter determine all points of disputes, and on several occasions have displayed tact and judgment highly creditable, and in every instance have administered impartial justice. When this police was first established, it was done as an experiment, and solely with a view to assimilate the natives as much as it was possible to the customs and usages of Europeans. . . .

CHRISTIAN INSTRUCTION

The work of Christian instruction and civilization, which has taken place under the auspices of the local government at this settlement, has succeeded beyond the most sanguine expectation, and has determined a question hitherto deemed impracticable.

If, as is made evident, so much has been effected for a people said to possess so little intellectual capacity, a people reputed to be but one remove from the brute creation, and of whom it was said they were but a link between the human and brute species; if so much has been done for such a people, how much more might be performed with those of a different character; and I do trust that the time is not far distant when the experiment will be tried among the numerous tribes inhabiting New Holland; for from the appalling accounts received, and from what I myself have witnessed, as well as from information

---

[1]An earthy clay containing iron ore, usually reddish in color.

heretofore communicated, there appears a prompt necessity that some efficient protection be extended to those ill-used and persecuted people. Humanity, religion, and justice require that every effort should be made on their behalf.

The primeval occupants of Van Diemen's Land[2] are not deserving of the obloquy which has been heaped upon them. The hostile feeling evinced by them towards the whites, and their attacks upon the lonely settlement of the colony, are only considered as just retaliation for the wrongs due to them and to their progenitors. They are now well disposed and bear no ill-will or animosity to the white inhabitants. . . .

The effects that have been produced on the minds of these people will forever put to silence the cavils of the most sceptical and prejudicially minded; and if (as I understand) in the sister colony the attempts hitherto brought into operation for the amelioration of the aborigines have failed, it can only be attributed to a defect in the system, and not to the people themselves.

---

[2]After finding Tasmania in 1642, the Dutch explorer Tasman named it Van Diemen's Land in honor of the governor-general of the Dutch East India Company in Jakarta.

Part Three

▾▾▾

The World in the Age of Western Dominance: 1800–1914

The direction of world history during the nineteenth century is perhaps best symbolized by the experience of Africa. In 1800, except for the far southern regions settled by the Dutch and the areas on each coast where slaves were traded, Africa was largely untouched by Europeans. A century later, except for Ethiopia and Liberia, the whole continent was under the political control of European powers, who accomplished their takeover with scant regard for the interests and wishes of the Africans. In 1884 and 1885 rules for dividing up Africa were established at the Berlin West Africa Conference, with the rule makers diplomats representing fourteen European nations and the United States. They agreed that each power had to give the others proper notice if it intended to annex African lands and, on doing so, could not simply ink in its name on a map. It had to have real troops or administrators on the scene. Only three decades later, during World War I, Africa's colonial masters dispatched thousands of Africans to battlefronts in Africa, Europe, and the Middle East, where many gave their lives for their European overlords.

The Europeans' land grab in Africa was striking in terms of its suddenness, rapidity, and magnitude, but it was not unique. Burma, India, Vietnam, Cambodia, Laos, Malaya, the East Indies, and many South Pacific islands also came under direct European or U.S. control in the nineteenth century. Other states such as Cuba, Nicaragua, Haiti, the Dominican Republic, the Ottoman Empire, Egypt, and China, although independent, were forced to accept varying degrees of Western control of their finances and foreign policy. Australia and New Zealand became European settler colonies. Canada, South Africa, the Philippines, and most of the West Indies remained parts of pre-nineteenth-century empires, although Canada in 1867 and South Africa in 1910 were granted extensive powers of self-government and the Philippines in 1898 changed masters from Spain to the United States. Mexico and most Central and South American nations retained full political sovereignty but saw many of their economic assets — banks, railroads, mines, and grazing lands — taken over by Western investors. Only Japan, by adopting the technology, military organization, and industrial economy of the West, avoided subservience to the West and became an imperialist power itself.

Never had world economic and political relationships been as one-sided as they were when World War I began in 1914. A handful of nations led by Great Britain, France, and the newly emerging powers, Germany and the United

States, were masters of Africa and large parts of Asia and exerted political influence throughout the world. These same nations controlled much of the world's economy and channeled a disproportionate amount of the world's wealth and resources to their own societies.

The West's expansion resulted in part from the inner dynamics of capitalism, with its drive for new markets, resources, and investment opportunities. It also resulted from nationalist rivalries among the Western powers themselves, most of whose leaders and citizens were convinced that prestige and prosperity depended on empire building and overseas investment. It also resulted from the huge disparity between the military and economic strength of Europe and the United States and that of the rest of the world. During the nineteenth century once powerful states, such as the Ottoman Empire and China, faced formidable internal problems and others, like Mughal India, had collapsed even earlier. Europe and the United States, however, continued to industrialize, develop new technologies, and build the most powerful armies and navies in history. Thus the Western nations faced no effective resistance when they sought to extend their economic grasp and political authority throughout the world.

The people of Asia and Africa now faced questions and, to the degree it was within their power to do so, made choices similar to those confronting the Russians during and after the reign of Peter the Great. Do we want to Westernize? If so, how thoroughly? At what human cost? How? How quickly? People found no easy answers to these questions, but ignoring the West was no longer an option.

Chapter 8

▼▼▼

The West in the Age of Industrialization and Imperialism

As far-reaching as the transformation of Western civilization since the Renaissance had been, no one around 1800 could have predicted the even greater changes about to occur in the nineteenth century. When Napoleon met defeat at Waterloo in 1815, Europe's population was 200 million, with as many as 25 million people of European descent living in the rest of the world. By 1914, when World War I began, these numbers had increased to 450 million and 150 million, respectively. In 1815 a large majority of Europeans and Americans lived in rural villages and worked the land; by 1914, in highly industrialized nations such as Great Britain, a majority of the population lived in cities and worked in factories or offices. In 1815, despite two decades of democratic revolution, most governments were still aristocratic and monarchical; in 1914 representative government and universal manhood suffrage were the norms in most of Europe, the United States, and the British dominions of Canada, Australia, and New Zealand. In 1815 most governments limited their activities to defense, the preservation of law and order, and some economic regulation; in 1914 governments in industrialized states subsidized education, sponsored scientific research, oversaw public health, monitored industry, provided social welfare care, maintained huge military establishments, and, as a result, had grown enormously.

Europe's global role also changed dramatically. In 1815 European political authority around the world appeared to be declining. Great Britain no longer ruled its thirteen American colonies, Portugal and Spain were losing their colonies in Mexico and Central and South America, and France recently had lost Haiti and sold 800,000 square miles of North American territory to the United States through the Louisiana Purchase. Decisions of several European states to outlaw the slave trade seemed to be a step toward a diminished European role in Africa, and there was little to suggest that Western nations had the ability or inclination to extend their power in the Middle East or East Asia. Only the continuing expansion of Great Britain in India hinted at what the nineteenth century would bring — the Western nations' takeover of Africa and Southeast Asia, their intrusion into the politics of China and the Middle East, and their dominance of the world's economy.

Many factors contributed to the West's transformation and expansion in the nineteenth century. But the single most important cause was the Industrial Revolution — that series of wide-ranging economic changes involving the application of new technologies and energy sources to manufacturing, communication, and transportation. The Industrial Revolution began in England in the late eighteenth century when a series of inventions transformed the textile industry. By 1914 industrialization had taken root in Europe, Japan, and the United States and was spreading to Canada, Russia, and parts of Latin America. As much as the discovery of agriculture many centuries earlier, industrialization profoundly altered the human condition.

▼▼▼

Middle Class and Working Class in Early Industrial Europe

The English were the first and, for many decades, the only people in the world to experience the material benefits and social costs of industrialization. Favored by an abundant labor supply, strong domestic and foreign markets, rich coal deposits, plentiful capital, a sound banking system, good transportation, a favorable business climate, and government stability, England began to industrialize in the eighteenth century. By the 1760s mechanical devices for spinning and weaving were beginning to transform the textile industry, and by the early 1800s coal-burning steam engines were being applied not only to textile manufacture but also to iron smelting, brewing, milling, and a host of other industrial processes. In 1830, the first public railroad line opened between Liverpool and Manchester, and within two decades railroads were moving people and goods throughout England.

During the nineteenth century industrialization spread from England to continental Europe, the United States, and Japan, and in the process changed considerably. In the late nineteenth century small family-owned businesses gave way to large corporations, monopolies, and cartels; new energy sources such as petroleum and electricity were introduced; and, most important, new scientific discoveries, especially in chemistry, transformed thousands of industrial processes.

The Industrial Revolution was a revolution in every sense of the term. It affected politics, work, people's standards of living, marriage patterns, child-rearing, leisure, and the structure of society itself. In preindustrial Europe landowning aristocrats dominated society and politics, and peasants were the largest socioeconomic group. Preindustrial cities consisted of a middle class, or bourgeoisie, made up of merchants and professionals at the top and artisans and small shopkeepers below them. They also contained numerous servants and unskilled workers who earned wages as porters and laborers.

Society after the Industrial Revolution looked quite different. Cities had grown enormously, especially industrial centers like Birmingham, England, which grew from 73,000 to 250,000 between 1801 and 1850, and Liverpool, which grew from 77,000 to 400,000 in the same half-century. Europe in 1800 had twenty-one cities with populations over 100,000. By 1900 the number of such cities had reached 120. Within these cities there had emerged a new class of factory workers, the "proletariat," who took their place in the working class alongside skilled tradesmen, servants, and day laborers. Industrialization and urbanization also increased the size, diversity, and wealth of the middle class. To the ranks of merchants, lawyers, doctors, and shopkeepers, there now were added industrialists, managers, government officials, white-collar workers, and skilled professionals in such fields as engineering, architecture, accounting, the sciences, and higher education.

This new and expanding middle class dominated the nineteenth century. Its members controlled Europe's liberal, parliamentary governments, set the standards of taste in literature, music, and art, and drove forward and reaped the benefits from Europe's industrialization. They considered themselves responsible for the material and moral progress of the age. To others, however, the rise of the middle class had a different meaning. To Karl Marx, the German socialist, the bourgeoisie were selfish materialists, exploiters and oppressors of the workers, and responsible for the poverty and squalor of the industrial age. Marx and his followers looked forward to the coming revolution in which workers would rise up and destroy the bourgeoisie, end class exploitation, and initiate a new era of cooperation, harmony, and equality.

English Workers in the Early Industrial Revolution

▼▼▼

61 ▼ *TESTIMONY BEFORE PARLIAMENTARY COMMITTEES ON WORKING CONDITIONS IN ENGLAND*

A key to England's early industrial growth was the large pool of workers willing to accept low wages for long hours of labor in factories and mines. Many of these workers were displaced farmers or farm workers, forced from rural areas because of land shortages caused by population growth and the consolidation of small farms into large estates by wealthy landowners. Rural families moved to cities or coal-mining towns, where they provided the workforce for the early Industrial Revolution. Few avoided poverty, crowded housing, and poor health.

Eventually, the British government responded by passing laws to protect factory workers and miners, especially children, from exploitation. When considering legislation, parliamentary committees held hearings to gather testimony from workers, employers, physicians, clergy, and local officials. Their statements, some of which are included in the following excerpts, present a vivid picture of working-class conditions in the first half of the nineteenth century.

Section 1 includes testimony from the records of the Sadler Committee, chaired by Michael Thomas Sadler in 1831 and charged with investigating child labor in cotton and linen factories; section 2 includes testimony taken by a parliamentary commission appointed in 1833 to investigate working conditions in other textile industries; section 3 presents evidence taken in 1842 by a committee investigating conditions in coal mines.

QUESTIONS FOR ANALYSIS

1. What differences were there between working conditions in the mines and in the cotton factories?
2. As revealed by the questions they asked, what did the committee members consider the worst abuses of working conditions in the factories and mines?
3. What does the testimony of Hannah Richardson and George Armitage reveal about (a) the economic circumstances of working-class families and (b) attitudes of working-class families toward their children?
4. Consider the testimony of the workers themselves. Do the workers express anger? Do they demand changes? What might explain their attitudes?
5. For what reasons do William Harter and Thomas Wilson oppose factory laws? In what ways do their views reflect the economic philosophy of Adam Smith in the *Wealth of Nations* (source 39)?

▷   1. Testimony before the Sadler Committee, 1831

ELIZABETH BENTLEY

What age are you? — Twenty-three. . . .

What time did you begin to work at a factory? — When I was six years old. . . .

What kind of mill is it? — Flax-mill. . . .

What was your business in that mill? — I was a little doffer.[1]

What were your hours of labor in that mill? — From 5 in the morning till 9 at night, when they were thronged [busy].

For how long a time together have you worked that excessive length of time? — For about half a year.

What were your usual hours of labor when you were not so thronged? — From 6 in the morning till 7 at night.

What time was allowed for your meals? — Forty minutes at noon.

_____
[1]A worker, usually a young child, whose job was to clean the machines used in textile manufacturing.

Had you any time to get your breakfast or drinking? — No, we got it as we could.

And when your work was bad, you had hardly any time to eat it at all? — No; we were obliged to leave it or take it home, and when we did not take it, the overlooker took it, and gave it to his pigs.

Do you consider doffing a laborious employment? — Yes.

Explain what it is you had to do. — When the frames are full, they have to stop the frames, and take the flyers off, and take the full bobbins off, and carry them to the roller; and then put empty ones on, and set the frames on again.

Does that keep you constantly on your feet? — Yes, there are so many frames and they run so quick.

Your labor is very excessive? — Yes; you have not time for any thing.

Suppose you flagged a little, or were too late, what would they do? — Strap us.

Are they in the habit of strapping those who are last in doffing? — Yes.

Constantly? — Yes.

Girls as well as boys? — Yes.

Have you ever been strapped? — Yes.

Severely? — Yes.

Could you eat your food well in that factory? — No, indeed, I had not much to eat, and the little I had I could not eat it, my appetite was so poor, and being covered with dust; and it was no use to take it home, I could not eat it, and the overlooker took it, and gave it to the pigs. . . .

Did you live far from the mill? — Yes, two miles.

Had you a clock? — No, we had not.

Supposing you had not been in time enough in the morning at the mills, what would have been the consequence? — We should have been quartered.

What do you mean by that? — If we were a quarter of an hour too late, they would take off half an hour; we only got a penny an hour, and they would take a halfpenny more. . . .

Were you generally there in time? — Yes, my mother has been up at 4 o'clock in the morning, and at 2 o'clock in the morning; the colliers used to go to their work about 3 or 4 o'clock, and when she heard them stirring she has got up out of her warm bed, and gone out and asked them the time, and I have sometimes been at Hunslet Car at 2 o'clock in the morning, when it was streaming down with rain, and we have had to stay till the mill was opened. . . .

▷ 2. *Commission for Inquiry into the Employment of Children in Factories,* Second Report, 1833

JOHN WRIGHT [A silk mill worker in his mid thirties]

Are silk-mills clean in general? — They are; they are swept every day, and whitewashed once a year.

What is the temperature of silk-mills? — I don't know exactly the temperature, but it is very agreeable.

Is any artificial heat required? — In the winter it is heated by steam.

To what degree? — I cannot speak positively; but it is not for the work, only to keep the hands warm and comfortable.

Why, then, are those employed in them said to be in such a wretched condition? — In the first place, the great number of hands congregated together, in some rooms forty, in some fifty, in some sixty, and I have known some as many as 100, which must be injurious to both health and growing. In the second place, the privy is in the factory, which frequently emits an unwholesome smell; and it would be worth while to notice in the future erection of mills, that there be betwixt the privy door and the factory wall a kind of a lobby of cage-work. 3dly, The tediousness and the everlasting sameness in the first process preys much on the spirits, and makes the hands spiritless. 4thly, the extravagant number of hours a child is compelled to labor and confinement, which for one week is seventy-six hours, which makes 3,952 hours for one year, we deduct 208 hours for meals within the factory which makes the net labor for one year 3,744; but the labor and confinement together of a child between ten years of age and twenty is 39,520 hours, enough to fritter away the best constitution. 5thly, About six months in the year we are obliged to use either gas, candles, or lamps, for the longest portion of that time, nearly six hours a day, being obliged to work amid the smoke and soot of the same; and also a large portion of oil and grease is used in the mills.

What are the effects of the present system of labor? — From my earliest recollections, I have found the effects to be awfully detrimental to the well-being of the operative; I have observed frequently children carried to factories, unable to walk, and that entirely owing to excessive labor and confinement. The degradation of the workpeople baffles all description: frequently have two of my sisters been obliged to be assisted to the factory and home again, until by-and-by they could go no longer, being totally crippled in their legs. . . .

WILLIAM HARTER [The owner of silk mill in Manchester]

What effect would it have on your manufacture to reduce the hours of labor to ten? — It would instantly much reduce the value of my mill and machinery, and consequently far prejudice my manufacture.

How so? — They are calculated to produce a certain quantity of work in a given time. Every machine is valuable in proportion to the quantity of work which it will turn off in a given time. It is impossible that the machinery could produce as much work in ten hours as in twelve. If the tending of the machines were a laborious occupation, the difference in the quantity of work might not always be in exact proportion to the difference of working time; but in my mill, and silk-mills in general, the work requires the least imaginable labor; therefore it is perfectly impossible that the machines could produce as much work in ten hours as in twelve. The produce would vary in about the same ratio as the working time.

What may be said about the sum invested in your mill and machinery? — It is not yet near complete, and the investment is a little short of 20,000 pounds.

Then to what extent do you consider your property would be prejudiced by a bill limiting the working hours to ten? — All other circumstances remaining the same, it is obvious that any property in the mill and machinery would be prejudiced to the extent of one-sixth its value, or upwards of 3,000 pounds.

How would the reduction in the hours of labor affect the cost of your manufactures? — The cost of our manufactures consists in the price of the raw material and of the expense of putting that said material into goods. Now the mere interest of the investment in buildings and machinery, and the expense of keeping the same in repair, forms a large item in the cost of manufacturing. Of course it follows, that the *gross* charge under this head would be the same upon a production of 10,000 pounds and 12,000 pounds, and this portion of the cost of manufacturing would consequently be increased by about 16%.

Do you mean to say, that to produce the same quantity of work which your present mill and machinery is capable of, it requires an additional outlay of upwards of 3,000 pounds? — I say distinctly, that to produce the same quantity of work under a ten-hours bill will require an additional outlay of 3,000 or 4,000 pounds; therefore a ten-hours bill would impose upon me the necessity of this additional outlay in such perishable property as buildings and machinery, or I must be content to relinquish one-sixth portion of my business.

▷   3. *Testimony before the Ashley Committee on the Conditions in Mines, 1842*

EDWARD POTTER

I am a coal viewer, and the manager of the South Hetton colliery. We have about 400 bound people (contract laborers), and in addition our bank people (foremen), men and boys about 700.

In the pits 427 men and boys; of these, 290 men. . . .

Of the children in the pits we have none under eight, and only three so young. We are constantly beset by parents coming making application to take children under the age, and they are very anxious and very dissatisfied if we do not take the children; and there have been cases in times of brisk trade, when the parents have threatened to leave the colliery, and go elsewhere if we did not comply. At every successive binding, which takes place yearly, constant attempts are made to get the boys engaged to work to which they are not competent from their years. In point of fact, we would rather not have boys until nine years of age complete. If younger than that, they are apt to fall asleep and get hurt: some get killed. It is no interest to the company to take any boys under nine. . . .

HANNAH RICHARDSON

I've one child that works in the pit; he's going on ten. He is down from 6 to 8. . . . He's not much tired with the work, it's only the confinement that tires him. He likes it pretty well, for he'd rather be in the pit than go to school. There is not much difference in his health since he went into the pit. He was at school before, and can read pretty well, but can't write. He is used pretty well; I never hear him complain. I've another son in the pit, 17 years old. . . . He went into the pit at eight years old. It's not hurt his health nor his appetite, for he's a good size. It would hurt us if children were prevented from working till 11 or 12 years old, because we've not jobs enough to live now as it is. . . .

MR. GEORGE ARMITAGE

I am now a teacher at Hoyland school; I was a collier at Silkstone until I was 22 years old and worked in the pit above 10 years. . . . I hardly know how to reprobate the practice sufficiently of girls working in pits; nothing can be worse. I have no doubt that debauchery is carried on, for

which there is every opportunity; for the girls go constantly, when hurrying, to the men, who work often alone in the bank-faces apart from every one. I think it scarcely possible for girls to remain modest who are in pits, regularly mixing with such company and hearing such language as they do — it is next to impossible. I dare venture to say that many of the wives who come from pits know nothing of sewing or any household duty, such as women ought to know — they lose all disposition to learn such things; they are rendered unfit for learning them also by being overworked and not being trained to the habit of it. I have worked in pits for above 10 years, where girls were constantly employed, and I can safely say it is an abominable system; indecent language is quite common. I think, if girls were trained properly, as girls ought to be, that there would be no more difficulty in finding suitable employment for them than in other places. Many a collier spends in drink what he has shut up a young child the whole week to earn in a dark cold corner as a trapper. The education of the children is universally bad. They are generally ignorant of common facts in Christian history and principles, and, indeed, in almost everything else. Little can be learned merely on Sundays, and they are too tired as well as indisposed to go to night schools. . . .

THE REV. ROBERT WILLAN, CURATE OF ST. MARY'S, BARNSLEY

I have been resident here as chief minister for 22 years. I think the morals of the working classes here are in an appalling state. . . . The ill manners and conduct of the weavers are daily presented to view in the streets, but the colliers work under ground and are less seen, and we have less means of knowing. . . . The master-sin among the youths is that of gambling; the boys may be seen playing at pitch-and-toss on the Sabbath and on week-days; they are seen doing this in all directions. The next besetting sin is promiscuous sexual intercourse; this may be much induced by the manner in which they sleep — men, women, and children often sleeping in one bed-room. I have known a family of father and mother and 12 children, some of them up-grown, sleeping on a kind of sacking and straw bed, reaching from one side of the room to the other, along the floor; they were an English family. Sexual intercourse begins very young. This and gambling pave the way; then drinking ensues, and this is the vortex which draws in every other sin.

THOMAS WILSON, ESQ., OWNER OF THREE COLLIERIES

I object on general principles to government interference in the conduct of any trade, and I am satisfied that in the mines it would be productive of the greatest injury and injustice. The art of mining is not so perfectly understood as to admit of the way in which a colliery shall be conducted

being dictated by any person, however experienced, with such certainty as would warrant an interference with the management of private business. I should also most decidedly object to placing collieries under the present provisions of the Factory Act[2] with respect to the education of children employed therein. First, because, if it is contended that coal-owners, as employers of children, are bound to attend to their education, this obligation extends equally to all other employers, and therefore it is unjust to single out one class only; secondly, because, if the legislature asserts a right to interfere to secure education, it is bound to make that interference general; and thirdly, because the mining population is in this neighborhood so intermixed with other classes, and is in such small bodies in any one place, that it would be impossible to provide separate schools for them.

---

[2]The Factory Act of 1833, which regulated employment of children and women, applied to textile factories.

Middle-Class Success and How to Achieve It
▼▼▼
62 ▼ Samuel Smiles, SELF-HELP and THRIFT

No writer expressed the hopes, fears, expectations, and values of nineteenth-century Europe's middle class more faithfully and successfully than the Scottish-born biographer, essayist, and businessman Samuel Smiles (1812–1904). Born into the family of a papermaker and shopkeeper, Smiles received a medical degree, worked as a journalist in Leeds, and held several managerial posts in the railroad industry. He wrote biographies, histories, and travel narratives, and achieved worldwide fame through his inspirational books on morality and personal behavior. Although it had been rejected by six publishers, his book *Self-Help* (1859) became a bestseller that went through dozens of editions and was translated into seventeen languages, including Arabic, Chinese, and Japanese. With an upbeat message that hard work, discipline, and high moral standards guaranteed success, *Self-Help* was followed by *Character* (1871), *Thrift* (1875), and *Duty* (1880). With his life spanning the century that saw the triumph of the middle-class values he championed, he died in 1904 at the age of ninety-three.

In the following excerpt, the first two sections, "Self-Help and Individualism" and "Habits of Successful Men," are from *Self-Help;* the third section, "Faults of the Poor," is from *Thrift.*

QUESTIONS FOR ANALYSIS

1. Why does Smiles consider government incapable of solving the social and economic problems confronting early industrial England? In his view what should be government's proper role and function?
2. How would Smiles define the word *individualism?*
3. What are the components of the "middle-class ethic" discussed by Smiles?
4. According to Smiles, who is responsible for the poverty in England? In his view, what can be done about it?
5. If given a chance to testify before one of the parliamentary committees about the effects of industrialization on the working class, what might Smiles have said?
6. How do Smiles's views resemble and differ from those of Adam Smith in *The Wealth of Nations?* (See source 39.)

SELF-HELP AND INDIVIDUALISM

"Heaven helps those who help themselves" is a well-tried maxim, embodying in a small compass the results of vast human experience. The spirit of self-help is the root of all genuine growth in the individual; and, exhibited in the lives of many, it constitutes the true source of national vigor and strength. . . . Whatever is done *for* men or classes, to a certain extent takes away the stimulus and necessity of doing for themselves; and where men are subjected to over-guidance and over-government, the inevitable tendency is to render them comparatively helpless.

Even the best institutions can give a man no active help. Perhaps the most they can do is, to leave him free to develop himself and improve his individual condition. But in all times men have been prone to believe that their happiness and well-being were to be secured by means of institutions rather than by their own conduct. Hence the value of legislation as an agent in human advancement has usually been much over-estimated. . . . Moreover, it is every day becoming more clearly understood, that the function of Government is negative and restrictive, rather than positive and active; being resolvable principally into protection — protection of life, liberty, and property. Laws, wisely administered, will secure men in the enjoyment of the fruits of their labor, whether of mind or body, at a com-

paratively small personal sacrifice; but no laws, however stringent, can make the idle industrious, the thriftless provident, or the drunken sober. Such reforms can only be effected by means of individual action, economy, and self-denial; by better habits, rather than by greater rights. . . .

National progress is the sum of individual industry, energy, and uprightness, as national decay is of individual idleness, selfishness, and vice. What we are accustomed to decry as great social evils, will for the most part be found to be but the outgrowth of man's own perverted life; and though we may endeavor to cut them down and extirpate them by means of Law, they will only spring up again with fresh luxuriance in some other form unless the conditions of personal life and character are radically improved. If this view be correct, then it follows that the highest patriotism and philanthropy consist, not so much in altering laws and modifying institutions as in helping and stimulating men to elevate and improve themselves by their own free and independent individual action.

HABITS OF SUCCESSFUL MEN

. . . On the whole, it is not good that human nature should have the road of life made too easy. Better to be under the necessity of working hard and faring meanly, than to have every thing done ready to our hand and a pillow of down to repose upon. Indeed, to start in life with comparatively small means seems so necessary as a stimulus to work, that it may almost be set down as one of the conditions essential to success in life. Hence, an eminent judge, when asked what contributed most to success at the bar, replied, "Some succeed by great talent, some by high connections, some by miracle, but the majority by commencing without a shilling."

The necessity of labor may, indeed, be regarded as the main root and spring of all that we call progress in individuals, and civilization in nations; and it is doubtful that any heavier curse could be imposed on a man than the gratification of all his wishes without effort on his part, leaving nothing for his hopes, desires, or struggles. . . .

Attention, application, accuracy, method, punctuality, and dispatch are the principal qualities required for the efficient conduct of business of any sort. . . . They are little things, it is true; but human life is made up of comparative trifles. It is the repetition of little acts which constitutes not only the sum of human character, but which determines the character of nations. And where men or nations have broken down, it will almost invariably be found that neglect of little things was the rock on which they split. Every human being has duties to be performed, and, therefore, has need of cultivating the capacity for doing them; whether the sphere of action be the management of a household, the conduct of a trade or profession, or the government of a nation. . . .

Men of business are accustomed to quote the maxim that Time is money; but it is more; the proper improvement of it is self-culture, self-improvement, and growth of character. An hour wasted daily on trifles or in indolence, would, if devoted to self-improvements, make an ignorant man wise in a few years, and, employed in good works, would make his life fruitful, and death a harvest of worthy deeds. Fifteen minutes a day devoted to self-improvement, will be felt at the end of the year.

---

[1] The Bank of England, England's central bank.

FAULTS OF THE POOR

England is one of the richest countries in the world. Our merchants are enterprizing, our manufacturers are industrious, our labourers are hardworking. There is an accumulation of wealth in the country to which past times can offer no parallel. The Bank[1] is gorged with gold. There never was more food in the empire; there never was more money. There is no end to our manufacturing productions, for the steam-engine never tires. And yet, notwithstanding all this wealth, there is an enormous mass of poverty. Close alongside the Wealth of Nations, there gloomily stalks the Misery of Nations, — luxurious ease resting upon a dark background of wretchedness.

Parliamentary reports have again and again revealed to us the miseries endured by certain portions of our working population. They have described the people employed in factories, workshops, mines, and brickfields, as well as in the pursuits of country life. We have tried to grapple with the evils of their condition by legislation, but it seems to mock us. Those who sink into poverty are fed, but they remain paupers. Those who feed them, feel no compassion; and those who are fed, return no gratitude. . . . Thus the Haves and the Have-nots, the opulent and the indigent, stand at the two extremes of the social scale, and a wide gulf is fixed between them. . . .

With respect to the poorer classes, — what has become of them in the midst of our so-called civilization? An immense proportion of them remain entirely uncivilized. . . .

They work, eat, drink, and sleep: that constitutes their life. They think nothing of providing for tomorrow, or for next week, or for next year. They abandon themselves to their sensual appetites; and make no provision whatever for the future. The thought of adversity, or of coming sorrow, or of the helplessness that comes with years and sickness, never crosses their minds. In these respects, they resemble the savage tribes, who know no better, and do no worse. Like the North American Indians, they debase themselves by the vices which accompany civilization, but make no use whatever of its benefits and advantages. . . .

Hence, the skilled workman, unless trained in good habits, may exhibit no higher a life than that of the mere animal; and the earning of increased wages will only furnish him with increased means for indulging in the gratification of his grosser appetites. . . .

This habitual improvidence — though of course there are many admirable exceptions — is the real cause of the social degradation of the artisan. This too is the prolific source of social misery. But the misery is entirely the result of human ignorance and self-indulgence. For though the Creator has ordained poverty, the poor are not necessarily, nor as a matter of fact, the miserable. Misery is the result of moral causes, — most commonly of individual vice and improvidence. . . .

Complaining that the laws are bad, and that the taxes are heavy, will not mend matters. Aristocratic government, and the tyranny of masters, are nothing like so injurious as the tyranny of vicious appetites. Men are easily led away by the parade of their miseries, which are for the most part voluntary and self-imposed, — the results of idleness, thriftlessness, intemperance, and misconduct. To blame others for what we suffer, is always more agreeable to our self-pride, than to blame ourselves. But it is perfectly clear that people who live from day to day without plan, without rule, without forethought — who spend all their earnings, without saving anything for the future — are preparing beforehand for inevitable distress. . . . What hope can there be for a people whose only maxim seems to be, "Let us eat and drink, for tomorrow we die"?

All this may seem very hopeless; yet it is not entirely so. The large earnings of the working classes is an important point to start with. The gradual diffusion of education will help them to use, and not abuse, their means of comfortable living. The more extended knowledge of the uses of economy, frugality, and thrift, will help them to spend their lives more soberly, virtuously, and religiously. . . . Social improvement is always very slow. . . . It requires the lapse of generations before its effect can be so much as discerned; for a generation is but as a day in the history of civilization. . . . From the days in which our British progenitors rushed to battle in their war-paint, — or those more recent times when the whole of the labouring people were villeins and serfs, bought and sold with the soil which they tilled, — to the times in which we now live, — how wide the difference, how gratifying the contrast. Surely it ought not to be so difficult to put an end to the Satanic influences of thriftlessness, drunkenness, and improvidence!

▼▼▼

New Perspectives on Humanity and Society

In October 1873, the English naturalist Charles Darwin wrote a letter to the German philosopher and revolutionary Karl Marx in which he stated, "I believe we both earnestly desire the extension of human knowledge; and this in the long run is sure to add to the happiness of mankind." Whether Marx and Darwin added to human happiness is difficult to judge, but there is no doubting their enormous influence. Although nineteenth-century Europe produced more scientists, philosophers, artists, composers, novelists, poets, historians, critics, and social theorists than ever before, and although these intellectuals produced an abundance of provocative new ideas, none matched the wide-ranging influence of these two men.

Darwin (1809–1882) did not invent the theory of evolution. Several Europeans before him had hypothesized that species were mutable and that all plants and animals, including humans, evolved from more primitive forms. Darwin's contribution was the wealth of scientific data he marshaled to support the idea of evolution and his theory that evolution resulted not from a divine plan but through natural selection. Thus Darwin cast doubt on the creation story set forth in the book of Genesis, in which God creates the whole universe, including the first humans, Adam and Eve, in seven days. Darwin's theories outraged biblical literalists and, ever since, Darwinism has been an emotion-charged issue involving the competing claims of religion and science. Darwinism also forced philosophers and other intellectuals to re-examine long-accepted notions about nature, morality, permanence versus change, and of course, humanity itself. Finally, Darwinism had important political ramifications. Imperialists, free traders, nationalists, and fascists were just a few of the groups who used (or misused) Darwinism to bolster their beliefs.

Just as Darwin was not the first proponent of evolution, Marx was not the first socialist. The first socialists were early-nineteenth-century idealists and visionaries, subsequently dubbed "utopians," whose dreams of equality and justice lacked philosophical rigor and practical political sense. Marx shared the utopians' moral outrage over the poverty and cutthroat competition engendered by the Industrial Revolution. He was also, however, an academically trained philosopher knowledgeable in history, economics, and science. His goal was to establish the intellectual foundation of *scientific socialism* and describe the mechanism by which socialism would ultimately replace capitalism.

For both Darwin and Marx, conflict and competition were key concepts. For Darwin it was competition among members of a species; for Marx it was conflict among social and economic classes. Through class conflict, in a process Marx referred to as the *dialectic,* society develops through stages until it reaches the age of industrial capitalism when the oppressor class, the bourgeoisie, clashes with the factory workers, the proletariat. The conflict ends, argues Marx, with the proletariat's triumph, because capitalism itself, an intrinsically flawed system, will create the conditions for the proletarian revolution, the end of the dialectic, and a classless society.

Even the most dedicated disciples of Marx and Darwin concede that much of what they wrote was incomplete, incorrect, and hypothetical. Well before the collapse of most of the world's Marxist governments in the late twentieth century, critics could point out many ways in which Marx misjudged capitalism, workers' attitudes, and the causes of revolution. Opponents of Darwinism contend that its theories cannot be proved and that natural selection is not the most credible explanation for evolution. Nonetheless, Darwin and Marx remain a part of that small group of nineteenth-century European thinkers whose work has left an indelible mark on history and contemporary thought.

The Marxist Critique of Industrial Capitalism
▼▼▼

63 ▼ *Karl Marx and Friedrich Engels,* THE COMMUNIST MANIFESTO

Karl Marx (1818–1883) was born in Trier, a German city on the Rhine River that had been occupied by Napoleon in 1803 and assigned to the Kingdom of Prussia by the Congress of Vienna in 1815. Marx's parents both came from long lines of Jewish rabbis, but in 1817 his father, Herschel Levi, converted the family to Christianity and changed its name to Marx to protect his career as a lawyer. Young Marx studied law at the University of Bonn before enrolling at the University of Berlin, where he was influenced by the thought of the famous philosopher G. W. F. Hegel (1770–1831), especially his theory that history unfolded toward a specific goal in an ongoing process driven by the clash and resolution of antagonistic ideas. After losing his job as a journalist for a Cologne newspaper because of his political views, in 1844 Marx moved to Paris, where he argued doctrine with other radicals and would-be revolutionaries and continued his studies of economics and history. He also made the acquaintance of another German, Friedrich Engels (1820–1895), an ardent critic of capitalism despite the fortune he amassed from managing a textile mill in Manchester, England. In 1847, Marx and Engels joined the Communist League, a revolutionary society dominated by German political exiles in France and England. In 1848, a year of revolution in France, Germany, Austria, Hungary, and Italy, the two men wrote *The Communist Manifesto* to publicize the League's program. It soon became the most widely read socialist tract in history.

After 1848, Marx and Engels remained friends, with Engels giving the impoverished Marx enough money to continue his writing and political activities while living in London. Both men continued to write on behalf of socialism, but Marx's works, especially his masterpiece, *Das Kapital (Capitalism),* assumed the far greater role in shaping modern socialist thought. Furthermore, Marx's views of history, human behavior, and social conflict have influenced not only politics but also philosophy, religion, literature, and all the social sciences.

QUESTIONS FOR ANALYSIS

1. How do Marx and Engels define class, and what do they mean by the "class struggle"?
2. According to Marx and Engels, how does the class struggle in nineteenth-century Europe differ from class struggles in previous eras?
3. According to Marx and Engels, what are the characteristics of the bourgeoisie?
4. Marx and Engels believe that bourgeois society is doomed and that the bourgeoisie will be the cause of their own destruction. Why?
5. The authors dismiss the importance of ideas as a force in human affairs. On what grounds? Ultimately, what is the cause of historical change in their view?

6. What may explain the popularity and influence of *The Communist Manifesto* among workers and those who sympathized with their plight?
7. How does *The Communist Manifesto*'s vision of the past and future resemble that of Condorcet's *Sketch of the Progress of the Human Mind* (source 37)? How does it differ?
8. How would Marx and Engels have responded to the point of view represented by Samuel Smiles in *Self-Help* and *Thrift* (source 62)?

I. THE BOURGEOISIE AND PROLETARIAT

The history of all hitherto existing society is the history of class struggles.

Freeman and slave, patrician and plebeian, lord and serf, guild-master and journeyman, in a word, oppressor and oppressed, stood in constant opposition to one another, carried on an uninterrupted, now hidden, now open fight, a fight that each time ended, either in a revolutionary reconstitution of society at large, or in the common ruin of the contending classes. . . .

The modern bourgeois society that has sprouted from the ruins of feudal society has not done away with class antagonisms. It has but established new classes, new conditions of oppression, new forms of struggle in place of the old ones.

Our epoch, the epoch of the bourgeoisie, possesses, however, this distinctive feature: It has simplified the class antagonisms. Society as a whole is more and more splitting up into two great hostile camps, into two great classes directly facing each other — bourgeoisie and proletariat.

From the serfs of the Middle Ages sprang the chartered burghers of the earliest towns. From these burgesses the first elements of the bourgeoisie were developed.

The discovery of America, the rounding of the Cape, opened up fresh ground for the rising bourgeoisie. The East-Indian and Chinese markets, the colonization of America, trade with the colonies, the increase in the means of exchange and in commodities generally, gave to commerce, to navigation, to industry, an impulse never before known, and thereby, to the revolutionary element in the tottering feudal society, a rapid development.

The feudal system of industry, in which industrial production was monopolized by closed guilds, now no longer sufficed for the growing wants of the new markets. The manufacturing system took its place. The guild-masters were pushed aside by the manufacturing middle class; division of labor between the different corporate guilds vanished in the face of division of labor in each single workshop.

Meantime the markets kept ever growing, the demand ever rising. Even manufacture no longer sufficed. Thereupon, steam and machinery revolutionized industrial production. The place of manufacture was taken by the giant, modern industry, the place of the industrial middle class by industrial millionaires, the leaders of whole industrial armies, the modern bourgeois. . . .

We see, therefore, how the modern bourgeoisie is itself the product of a long course of development, of a series of revolutions in the modes of production and of exchange. . . .

The bourgeoisie, historically, has played a most revolutionary part.

The bourgeoisie, wherever it has got the upper hand, has put an end to all feudal, patriarchal, idyllic relations. It has pitilessly torn asunder the motley feudal ties that bound man to his "natural superiors," and has left no other nexus between man and man than naked self-interest, than callous "cash payment." . . . It has resolved personal worth into exchange value, and in place of the numberless indefeasible chartered freedoms, has set up that single, unconscionable freedom — Free Trade. In one word, for exploitation, veiled by religious and political illusions, it has substituted naked, shameless, direct, brutal exploitation. . . .

We see then: the means of production and of exchange, on whose foundation the bourgeoisie built itself up, were generated in feudal society. At a certain stage in the development of these means of production and of exchange, the conditions under which feudal society produced and exchanged, the feudal organization of agriculture and manufacturing industry, in one word, the feudal relations of property became no longer compatible with the already developed productive forces; they became so many fetters. They had to be burst asunder; they were burst asunder.

Into their place stepped free competition, accompanied by a social and political constitution adapted to it, and by the economic and political sway of the bourgeois class.

A similar movement is going on before our own eyes. Modern bourgeois society with its relations of production, of exchange and of property, a society that has conjured up such gigantic means of production and of exchange, is like the sorcerer who is no longer able to control the powers of the nether world whom he has called up by his spells. For many a decade past the history of industry and commerce is but the history of the revolt of modern productive forces against modern conditions of production, against the property relations that are the conditions for the existence of the bourgeoisie and of its rule. It is enough to mention the commercial crises that by their periodical return put the existence of the entire bourgeois society on its trial, each time more threateningly. In these crises a great part not only of the existing products, but also of the previously created productive forces, are periodically destroyed. In these crises there breaks out an epidemic that, in all earlier epochs, would have seemed an absurdity — the epidemic of overproduction.

And how does the bourgeoisie get over these crises? On the one hand, by enforced destruction of a mass of productive forces; on the other, by the conquest of new markets, and by the more thorough exploitation of the old ones. That is to say, by paving the way for more extensive and more destructive crises, and by diminishing the means whereby crises are prevented.

The weapons with which the bourgeoisie felled feudalism to the ground are now turned against the bourgeoisie itself.

But not only has the bourgeoisie forged the weapons that bring death to itself; it has also called into existence the men who are to wield those weapons — the modern working class — the proletarians. . . .

Modern industry has converted the little workshop of the patriarchal master into the great factory of the industrial capitalist. Masses of laborers, crowded into the factory, are organized like soldiers. As privates of the industrial army they are placed under the command of a perfect hierarchy of officers and sergeants. Not only are they slaves of the bourgeois class, and of the bourgeois state; they are daily and hourly enslaved by the machine, by the overseer, and, above all, by the individual bourgeois manufacturer himself. The more openly this despotism proclaims gain to be its end and aim, the more petty, the more hateful and the more embittering it is. . . .

The lower strata of the middle class — the small tradespeople, shopkeepers, and retired tradesmen generally, the handicraftsmen and peasants — all these sink gradually into the proletariat, partly because their diminutive capital does not suffice for the scale on which modern industry is carried on, and is swamped in the competition with the large capitalists, partly because their specialized skill is rendered worthless by new methods of production. Thus the proletariat is recruited from all classes of the population.

But with the development of industry the proletariat not only increases in number; it becomes concentrated in greater masses, its strength grows, and it feels that strength more. The various interests and conditions of life within the ranks of the proletariat are more and more equalized, in proportion as machinery obliterates all distinctions of labor, and nearly everywhere reduces wages to the same low level. The growing competition among the bourgeois, and the resulting commercial crises, make the wages of the workers ever more fluctuating. The unceasing improvement of machinery, ever more rapidly developing, makes their livelihood more and more precarious; the collisions between individual workmen and individual bourgeois take more and more the character of collisions between two classes. Thereupon the workers begin to form combinations (trade unions) against the bourgeois; they club together in order to keep up the rate of wages; they found permanent associations in order to make provision beforehand for these occasional revolts. Here and there the contest breaks out into riots.

Now and then the workers are victorious, but only for a time. The real fruit of their battle lies, not in the immediate result, but in the ever expanding union of the workers. This union is helped on by the improved means of communication that are created by modern industry, and that place the workers of different localities in contact with one another. It was just this contact that was needed to centralize the numerous local struggles, all of the same character, into one national struggle between classes. . . .

This organization of the proletarians into a class, and consequently into a political party, is continually being upset again by the competition between the workers themselves. But it ever rises up again, stronger, firmer, mightier. . . .

Further, as we have already seen, entire sections of the ruling classes are, by the advance of industry, precipitated into the proletariat, or are at least threatened in their conditions of existence. These also supply the proletariat with fresh elements of enlightenment and progress.

Finally, in times when the class struggle nears the decisive hour, the process of dissolution going on within the ruling class, in fact within the whole range of old society, assumes such a violent, glaring character, that a small section of the ruling class cuts itself adrift, and joins the revolutionary class, the class that holds the future in its hands. Just as, therefore, at an earlier period, a section of the nobility went over to the bourgeoisie, so now a portion of the bourgeoisie goes over to the proletariat, and in particular, a portion of the bourgeois ideologists, who have raised themselves to the level of comprehending theoretically the historical movement as a whole.

II. PROLETARIANS AND COMMUNISTS

The distinguishing feature of communism is not the abolition of property generally, but the abolition of bourgeois property. But modern bourgeois private property is the final and most complete expression of the system of producing and appropriating products that is based on class antagonisms, on the exploitation of the many by the few.

In this sense, the theory of the Communists may be summed up in the single sentence: Abolition of private property. . . .

You are horrified at our intending to do away with private property. But in your existing society, private property is already done away with for nine-tenths of its population; its existence for the few is solely due to its nonexistence in the hands of those nine-tenths. You reproach us, therefore, with intending to do away with a form of property, the necessary condition for whose existence is the nonexistence of any property for the immense majority of society.

In one word, you reproach us with intending to do away with your property. Precisely so; that is just what we intend. . . .

The Communists are further reproached with desiring to abolish countries and nationality.

The working men have no country. We cannot take from them what they have not got. . . .

National differences and antagonism between peoples are daily more and more vanishing, owing to the development of the bourgeoisie, to freedom of commerce, to the world market, to uniformity in the mode of production and in the conditions of life corresponding thereto.

The supremacy of the proletariat will cause them to vanish still faster. United action of the leading civilized countries at least, is one of the first conditions for the emancipation of the proletariat.

In proportion as the exploitation of one individual by another is put an end to, the exploitation of one nation by another will also be put an end to. In proportion as the antagonism between classes within the nation vanishes, the hostility of one nation to another will come to an end.

The charges against communism made from a religious, a philosophical and, generally, from an ideological standpoint, are not deserving of serious examination.

Does it require deep intuition to comprehend that man's ideas, views, and conceptions, in one word, man's consciousness, change with every change in the conditions of his material existence, in his social relations and in his social life?

What else does the history of ideas prove, than that intellectual production changes its character in proportion as material production is changed? The ruling ideas of each age have ever been the ideas of its ruling class. . . .

IV. POSITION OF THE COMMUNISTS IN RELATION TO THE VARIOUS EXISTING OPPOSITION PARTIES

The Communists turn their attention chiefly to Germany, because that country is on the eve of a bourgeois revolution that is bound to be carried out under more advanced conditions of European civilization and with a much more developed proletariat than that of England was in the seventeenth, and of France in the eighteenth century, and because the bourgeois revolution in Germany will be but the prelude to an immediately following proletarian revolution.

In short, the Communists everywhere support every revolutionary movement against the existing social and political order of things.

In all these movements they bring to the front, as the leading question in each, the property question, no matter what its degree of development at the time. . . .

The Communists disdain to conceal their views and aims. They openly declare that their ends can be attained only by the forcible overthrow of all existing social conditions. Let the ruling classes tremble at a communist revolution. The proletarians have nothing to lose but their chains. They have a world to win.

Working men of all countries, unite!

The Principles of Darwinism
▼▼▼

64 ▼ *Charles Darwin,*
ON THE ORIGIN OF SPECIES and THE DESCENT OF MAN

After pursuing his university education at Edinburgh and Cambridge, Charles Darwin spent five years on the HMS *Beagle* as chief naturalist on a scientific expedition that explored the South Pacific and the western coast of South America. Darwin observed the bewildering variety of nature and began to speculate on how millions of species of plants and animals had come into existence. On his return to England he developed his theory of evolution, basing his hypothesis on his own formidable biological knowledge, recent discoveries in geology, work on the selective breeding of plants and animals, and the suggestion of several authors that competition was the norm for all living things. In 1859 he published his theories in *On the Origin of Species,* followed in 1871 by *The Descent of Man.*

QUESTIONS FOR ANALYSIS

1. What does Darwin mean by the terms *struggle for existence* and *natural selection?*
2. How does Darwin defend himself from religiously motivated attacks on his work?
3. What were some implications of Darwin's work for nineteenth-century views of progress? Of nature? Of human nature?
4. Defenders of laissez-faire capitalism sometimes drew upon Darwinian concepts in their arguments against socialism. Which concepts might they have used?
5. Similarly, Darwinian concepts were used to defend militarism and late-nineteenth-century Western imperialism. Which of Darwin's theories might have proved useful in such a defense?

ON THE ORIGIN OF SPECIES

Chapter III   Struggle for Existence

It has been seen in the last chapter that amongst organic beings in a state of nature there is some individual variability: indeed I am not aware that this has ever been disputed. . . . But the mere existence of individual variability and of some few well-marked varieties, . . . helps us but little in understanding how species arise in nature. How have all those exquisite adaptations of one part of the organization to another part, and to the conditions of life, and of one organic being to another being, been perfected? We see these beautiful co-adaptations most plainly in the woodpecker and the mistletoe;[1] and only a little less plainly in the humblest parasite which clings to the hairs of a quadruped or feathers of a bird; in the structure of the beetle which dives through the water: in the plumed seed which is wafted by the gentlest breeze; in short, we see beautiful adaptations everywhere and in every part of the organic world.

Again, it may be asked, how is it that varieties, which I have called incipient species, become ultimately converted into good and distinct species, which in most cases obviously differ from

each other far more than do the varieties of the same species? . . . All these results . . . follow from the struggle for life. Owing to this struggle, variations, however slight and from whatever cause proceeding, if they be in any degree profitable to the individuals of a species, in their infinitely complex relations to other organic beings and to their physical conditions of life, will tend to the preservation of such individuals, and will generally be inherited by the offspring. The offspring, also, will thus have a better chance of surviving, for, of the many individuals of any species which are periodically born, but a small number can survive. I have called this principle, by which each slight variation, if useful, is preserved, by the term Natural Selection, in order to mark its relation to man's power of selection. But the expression often used by Mr. Herbert Spencer[2] of the Survival of the Fittest is more accurate, and is sometimes equally convenient. . . .

{The term, struggle for existence, used in a large sense}
I should premise that I use this term in a large and metaphorical sense including dependence of one being on another, and including (which is more important) not only the life of the individual, but success in leaving progeny. Two canine

---

[1] In a previous chapter Darwin had discussed how perfectly the structures of mistletoe and the woodpecker suited them for survival as a parasitic plant and as a bird that pecked insects out of trees.

[2] An English philosopher (1820–1903) influenced by Darwin's work.

animals, in a time of dearth, may be truly said to struggle with each other which shall get food and live. But a plant on the edge of a desert is said to struggle for life against the drought, though more properly it should be said to be dependent on the moisture. A plant which annually produces a thousand seeds, of which only one of an average comes to maturity, may be more truly said to struggle with the plants of the same and other kinds which already clothe the ground. The mistletoe is dependent on the apple and a few other trees, but can only in a far-fetched sense be said to struggle with these trees, for, if too many of these parasites grow on the same tree, it languishes and dies. But several seedling mistletoes, growing close together on the same branch, may more truly be said to struggle with each other. . . . In these several senses, which pass into each other, I use for convenience's sake the general term of Struggle for Existence.

{Geometrical ratio of increase} A struggle for existence inevitably follows from the high rate at which all organic beings tend to increase. Every being, which during its natural lifetime produces several eggs or seeds, must suffer destruction during some period of its life, and during some season or occasional year, otherwise . . . its numbers would quickly become so inordinately great that no country could support the product. Hence, as more individuals are produced than can possibly survive, there must in every case be a struggle for existence, either one individual with another of the same species, or with the individuals of distinct species, or with the physical conditions of life. It is the doctrine of Malthus[3] applied with manifold force to the whole animal and vegetable kingdoms; for in this case there can be no artificial increase of food, and no prudential restraint from marriage. Although some species may be now increasing, more or less rapidly, in numbers, all cannot do so, for the world would not hold them.

THE DESCENT OF MAN

Chapter II On the Manner of Development of Man from Some Lower Form

In this chapter we have seen that as man at the present day is liable, like every other animal, to multiform individual differences or slight variations, so no doubt were the early progenitors of man; the variations being formerly induced by the same general causes, and governed by the same general and complex laws as at present. As all animals tend to multiply beyond their means of subsistence, so it must have been with the progenitors of man; and this would inevitably lead to a struggle for existence and to natural selection. . . .

Chapter VI On the Affinities and Genealogy of Man

Now as organisms have become slowly adapted to diversified lines of life by means of natural selection, their parts will have become more and more differentiated and specialized for various functions, from the advantage gained by the division of physiological labor. The same part appears often to have been modified first for one purpose, and then long afterwards for some other and quite distinct purpose; and thus all the parts are rendered more and more complex. But each organism still retains the general type of structure of the progenitor from which it was aboriginally derived. In accordance with this view it seems, if we turn to geological evidence, that organization on the whole has advanced throughout the world by slow and interrupted steps. In the great kingdom of the Vertebrata it has culminated in man. . . .

The most ancient progenitors in the kingdom of the Vertebrata, at which we are able to obtain an obscure glance, apparently consisted of a group of marine animals, resembling the larvae of existing Ascidians.[4] These animals probably gave rise to a group of fishes, as lowly organized as the lancelet;[5] and from these the Ganoids,[6] and

---

[3]An English philosopher (1766–1834), whose *Essay on the Principle of Population* (1798) warned that human population growth, if unchecked, would lead to catastrophic famine.
[4]Saclike marine animals.

[5]Marine animals with a rodlike primitive backbone.
[6]Boney fish such as the sturgeon and gar, covered with large armorlike scales.

other fishes must have developed. From such fish a very small advance would carry us on to the Amphibians. We have seen that birds and reptiles were once intimately connected together; and the Monotremata[7] now connect mammals with reptiles in a slight degree. But no one can at present say by what line of descent the three higher and related classes, namely, mammals, birds, and reptiles, were derived from the two lower vertebrate classes, namely, amphibians and fishes. In the class of mammals the steps are not difficult to conceive which led from the ancient Monotremata to the ancient Marsupials,[8] and from these to the early progenitors of the placental mammals. We may thus ascend to the Lemuridae,[9] and the interval is not very wide from these to the Simiadae.[10] The Simiadae then branched off into two great stems, the New World and Old World monkeys; and from the latter, at a remote period, Man, the wonder and glory of the Universe, proceeded.

Chapter XXI General Summary and Conclusion

I am aware that the conclusions arrived at in this work will be denounced by some as highly irreligious; but he who denounces them is bound to show why it is more irreligious to explain the origin of man as a distinct species by descent from some lower form, through the laws of variation and natural selection, than to explain the birth of the individual through the laws of ordinary reproduction. The birth both of the species and of the individual are equally parts of that grand sequence of events, which our minds refuse to accept as the result of blind chance. The understanding revolts at such a conclusion, whether or not we are able to believe that every slight variation of structure, — the union of each pair in marriage, — the dissemination of each seed, —

and other such events, have all been ordained for some special purpose. . . .

The main conclusion arrived at in this work, namely that man is descended from some lowly organized form, will, I regret to think, be highly distasteful to many. But there can hardly be a doubt that we are descended from barbarians. The astonishment which I felt on first seeing a party of Fuegians[11] on a wild and broken shore will never be forgotten by me, for the reflection at once rushed into my mind — such were our ancestors. These men were absolutely naked and bedaubed with paint, their long hair was tangled, their mouths frothed with excitement, and their expression was wild, startled, and distrustful. They possessed hardly any arts, and like wild animals lived on what they could catch; they had no government, and were merciless to every one not of their own small tribe. He who has seen a savage in his native land will not feel much shame, if forced to acknowledge that the blood of some more humble creature flows in his veins. For my own part I would as soon be descended from that heroic little monkey, who braved his dreaded enemy in order to save the life of his keeper, or from that old baboon, who descending from the mountains, carried away in triumph his young comrade from a crowd of astonished dogs — as from a savage who delights to torture his enemies, offers up bloody sacrifices, practices infanticide without remorse, treats his wives like slaves, knows no decency, and is haunted by the grossest superstitions.

Man may be excused for feeling some pride at having risen, though not through his own exertions, to the very summit of the organic scale; and the fact of his having thus risen, instead of having been aboriginally placed there, may give him hope for a still higher destiny in the distant future. But we are not here concerned with hopes or fears, only with the truth as far as our reason

---

[7]Order of egg-laying mammals such as the platypus.
[8]Mammals, such as the kangaroo, whose females lack placentas and carry their young in an abdominal pouch.
[9]Largely nocturnal tree-dwelling mammals distinct from monkeys.

[10]Apes and monkeys.
[11]Inhabitants of Tierra del Fuego, an island at the southernmost tip of South America.

permits us to discover it; and I have given the evidence to the best of my ability. We must, however, acknowledge, as it seems to me, that man with all his noble qualities, with sympathy which feels for the most debased, with benevolence which extends not only to other men but to the humblest living creature, with his god-like intellect which has penetrated into the movements and constitution of the solar system — with all these exalted powers — Man still bears in his bodily frame the indelible stamp of his lowly origin.

▾▾▾

The Fight for Women's Political Rights

Women's political and legal rights emerged as a subject of public debate and controversy for the first time during the French Revolution, an event in which women played a prominent role. In October 1789 thousands of women marched from Paris to the palace grounds at Versailles, where their demonstrations forced the king and the National Assembly to relocate to Paris, the center of revolutionary fervor and agitation. In 1790 women began to form their own political clubs and demanded an end to the laws and customs that were the foundation of France's patriarchal society. In response, legislators passed laws giving women the right to own property, marry without parental consent, initiate divorce, and take legal action against fathers of illegitimate children. In 1793, however, Jacobin revolutionaries outlawed women's political clubs and flatly rejected women's demands for political equality with men. Giving women the right to vote, hold public office, and serve in the army would, so it was argued, undermine the family and divert women from their calling as wives and mothers. Women experienced further setbacks in the late 1790s when more conservative revolutionary leaders rescinded most of the laws that had improved women's legal status. Under Napoleon, the Civil Code of 1804, later known as the Napoleonic Code, unequivocally reaffirmed women's legal inferiority to men.

In the conservative atmosphere of the 1820s and 1830s, women's political activism in Europe diminished, and prevailing opinion consigned middle-class women to a domestic role centered on child care, housekeeping, supervising servants, and providing husbands with a tranquil haven where they could escape the rigors of business and politics. By midcentury, however, women on both sides of the Atlantic, many of whom were veterans of the temperance and antislavery movements, once more began to speak out and organize on behalf of women's political and legal rights. A landmark in the history of nineteenth-century feminism (a word coined in France in the 1830s) was the women's rights convention held in the upstate New York town of Seneca Falls in 1848, which adopted resolutions proclaiming the equality of men and women and demanding for women the vote, divorce and property rights, and equal employment and educational opportunities. Such issues became the focus of feminists in England in the 1850s and in France and Germany later in the century.

By the end of the nineteenth century some gains had been made, especially in the areas of women's education and legal status. In addition, professions such as nursing and teaching provided new opportunities for many middle-class women, and a few women established careers as doctors and lawyers. Granting women full political rights, however, met stiff resistance, and only minor gains were made before World War I. By then only Australia, New Zealand, Finland, Norway, and several states in the western United States had granted women full voting privileges. Elsewhere women were permitted to vote only in municipal elections or, more commonly, not at all.

The efforts of nineteenth-century suffragists were not in vain, however. After World War I, women received the right to vote in most democratic states, and those who carried on the struggle for women's equality with men in the twentieth century continued to draw inspiration from their ideals and actions.

American Women Demand Equality
▼▼▼

65 ▼ *Ohio Women's Convention of 1850,* *RESOLUTIONS*

In 1850, two years after the first U.S. women's rights convention was held in Seneca Falls, New York, a group of Ohio women met in Salem, in eastern Ohio, to draw up resolutions on the status of women for submission to a forthcoming convention that was to consider amendments to the state constitution. The Salem meeting has a special place in the history of feminist movements because, although men attended, they were not allowed to speak, vote, or make proposals. At the close of the meeting the men in attendance organized their own association, and as their first act, voted to endorse the resolutions the women had just approved. The resolutions were received less favorably at the constitutional convention, where the delegates, all men, ignored them.

QUESTIONS FOR ANALYSIS

1. What specific demands do the resolutions make in the areas of education, the family, politics, and employment?
2. For the authors of the resolutions, *dependency* is a key concept in their views of women's place in society. What do they mean by this term, and what social and political practices contribute to it?
3. What specific demands do the resolutions make in the areas of political rights, employment, education, and the family?
4. The authors admit that not all women share their views. How do they view women who are content to accept their "idle lives" and "sterile submission"? How do they explain these women's indifference to women's plight?

Whereas, all men are created equal and endowed with certain God-given rights, and all just government is derived from the consent of the governed; and whereas, the doctrine that "man shall pursue his own substantial happiness" is acknowledged by the highest authority to be the great precept of Nature; and whereas, this doctrine is not local, but universal, being dictated by God himself; therefore,

Resolved, That the prohibition of Woman from participating in the enactment of the laws by which she is governed is a direct violation of this precept of Nature, as she is thereby prevented from occupying that position which duty points out, and from pursuing her own substantial happiness by acting up to her conscientious convictions; and that all statutes and constitutional provisions which sanction this prohibition are null and void.

Resolved, That all rights are *human* rights, and pertain to human beings, without distinction of sex; therefore justice demands that all laws shall be made, not for man, or for woman, but for mankind, and that the same legal protection be afforded to the one sex as to the other.

Resolved, That the servile submission and quiet indifference of the Women of this country in relation to the unequal and oppressive laws by which they are governed, are the fruit either of ignorance or degradation, both resulting legitimately from the action of those laws.

Resolved, That the evils arising from the present social, civil, and religious condition of women proclaim to them in language not to be misunderstood, that not only their *own* welfare, but the highest good of the race demands of them, as an imperative duty, that they should secure to themselves the elective franchise.

Resolved, That in those laws which confer on man the power to control the property and person of woman, and to remove from her at will the children of her affection, we recognize only the modified code of the slave plantation; and that thus we are brought more nearly in sympathy with the suffering slave, who is despoiled of all his rights.

Resolved, That we, as human beings, are entitled to claim and exercise all the rights that belong by nature to any members of the human family.

Resolved, That all distinctions between men and women in regard to social, literary, pecuniary, religious or political customs and institutions, based on a distinction of sex, are contrary to the laws of Nature, are unjust, and destructive to the purity, elevation and progress in knowledge and goodness of the great human family, and ought to be at once and forever abolished.

Resolved, That the practice of holding women amenable to a different standard of propriety and morality from that to which men are held amenable, is unjust and unnatural, and highly detrimental to domestic and social virtue and happiness.

Resolved, That the political history of Woman demonstrates that tyranny, the most degrading, cruel and arbitrary, can be exercised and produced the same in effect under a mild and republican form of government as by an hereditary despotism.

Resolved, That while we deprecate thus earnestly the political oppression of Woman, we see in her social condition, the regard in which she is held as a moral and intellectual being, the fundamental cause of that oppression.

Resolved, That amongst the principal causes of such social condition we regard the public sentiment which withholds from her all, or almost all, lucrative employment, and enlarged spheres of labor.

Resolved, That in the difficulties thus cast in the way of her self-support, and in her consequent *dependence* upon man, we see the greatest influence at work in imparting to her that tone of character which makes her to be regarded as the "weaker vessel." . . .

Resolved, That we regard those women who content themselves with an idle, aimless life, as involved in the guilt as well as the suffering of their own oppression; and that we hold those who go forth into the world, in the face of the frowns and the sneers of the public, to fill larger spheres of labor, as the truest preachers of the cause of Woman's Rights.

Whereas, one class of society dooms woman to a life of drudgery, another to one of dependence and frivolity; and whereas, the education she generally receives is calculated to cultivate vanity and dependence, therefore,

Resolved, That the education of woman should be in accordance with responsibility in life, that she may acquire the self-reliance and true dignity so essential to the proper fulfillment of the important duties devolving on her.

Resolved, That as woman is not permitted to hold office, nor have any voice in the government, she should not be compelled to pay taxes out of her scanty wages to support men who get eight dollars a-day for *taking* the right to *themselves* to enact laws *for* her.

Resolved, That we, the Women of Ohio, will hereafter meet annually in Convention to consult upon and adopt measures for the removal of various disabilities — political, social, religious, legal and pecuniary — to which women as a class are subjected, and from which results so much misery, degradation, and crime.

Women's Suffrage: A Woman's Protest
▼▼▼

66 ▼ *Mrs. Humphry Ward,*
AN APPEAL AGAINST WOMEN'S SUFFRAGE

Organized efforts by English women to gain the vote can be traced back to the mid nineteenth century. In 1847 a group of Sheffield women founded the Female Political Association and collected signatures on a prosuffrage petition that they submitted to the House of Lords. Four years later, in 1851, Harriet Hardy Mill (1807–1858), the wife of philosopher John Stuart Mill, wrote a widely read pamphlet entitled the "Enfranchisement of Women." Nine years after her death, in 1867 John Stuart Mill, then a member of the House of Commons, proposed an amendment to a voting reform bill that would have given women the vote. It was rejected 194 to 73, a setback that led directly to the founding of the National Society for Women's Suffrage in 1868. Although women received the right to vote in municipal and school board elections in the 1860s and 1870s, women's suffrage continued to be a subject of acrimonious and emotional debate until 1918, when English women finally received the right to vote in parliamentary elections.

In the long battle over women's political rights, opponents of women's suffrage included both men and women. One woman who opposed giving women the vote was Mrs. Humphry Ward, who in 1889 published the following "Appeal against Women's Suffrage" in the journal *The Nineteenth Century*. Born into a distinguished literary family, Mary Augusta Arnold attended boarding schools before marrying in 1872 Humphry Ward, who became a literary critic for the London *Times*. While pursuing a literary career (in which she produced twenty-five novels, three plays, an autobiography, and many articles and essays), she raised three children and devoted herself to charitable causes on behalf of poor children, working-class families, and the physically handicapped. Although she worked to secure women full access to universities and approved women's right to vote in local elections, she strongly opposed giving women the right to vote in parliamentary elections. Ward wrote the following resolution in response to a proposal in Parliament to give the vote in parliamentary elections to unmarried women of property. The proposal was killed, and soon women's struggle to win the vote became increasingly violent and militant under the leadership of Emmeline Pankhurst and the organization she founded, the Women's Social and Political Union. Ward countered by founding the Women's National Anti-Suffrage League in 1908. She died in 1920.

QUESTIONS FOR ANALYSIS

1. The author refers to the "special work" women have to do for the state. What does this special work involve and how does it differ from men's work?
2. What qualities of men and women dictate the type of work they do for the state? Are these qualities inherent or the result of custom and tradition?
3. The author argues that women can influence government policy without being able to vote. How do they exercise this influence, and in your view, how is it likely to be successful?
4. What effect, according to Ward, will the granting of full voting rights to women have on the family and on women themselves?
5. The author approves of women's right to vote in municipal and school board elections but not in parliamentary elections. What is her rationale for this assertion?
6. How would the authors of the resolutions of the Ohio Women's Convention (source 65) respond to Ward's arguments?

We, the undersigned, wish to appeal to the common sense and the educated thought of the men and women of England against the proposed extension of the Parliamentary suffrage to women.

1. While desiring the fullest possible development of the powers, energies, and education of women, we believe that their work for the State, and their responsibilities towards it, must always differ essentially from those of men, and that therefore their share in the working of the State machinery should be different from that assigned to men. Certain large departments of the national life are of necessity worked exclusively by men. To men belong the struggle of debate and legislation in Parliament; the hard and exhausting labour implied in the administration of the national resources and powers; the conduct of England's relations towards the external world; the working of the army and navy; all the heavy, laborious, fundamental industries of the State, such as those of mines, metals, and railways; the lead and supervision of English commerce, the management of our vast English finance, the service of that merchant fleet on which our food supply depends. In all these spheres women's direct participation is made impossible either by the disabilities of sex, or by strong formations of custom and habit resting ultimately upon physical difference, against which it is useless to contend. They are affected indeed, in some degree, by all these national activities; therefore they ought in some degree to have an influence on them all. This influence they already have, and will have more and more as the education of women advances. But their direct interest in these matters can never equal that of men, whose whole energy of mind and body is daily and hourly risked in them. . . .

At the same time we are heartily in sympathy with all the recent efforts which have been made to give women a more important part in those affairs of the community where their interests and those of men are equally concerned; where it is possible for them not only to decide but to help in carrying out, and where, therefore, judgment is weighted by a true responsibility, and can be guided by experience and the practical information which comes from it. As voters for or members of School Boards, Boards of Guardians, and other important public bodies, women have now opportunities for public usefulness which must promote the growth of character, and at the same time strengthen among them the social sense and habit. All these changes of recent years, together with the great improvements in women's education which have accompanied them, we cordially welcome. But we believe that the emancipating process has now reached the limits fixed by the physical constitution of women, and by the fundamental difference which must always exist between their main occupations and those of men. The care of the sick and the insane; the treatment of the poor; the education of children: in all these matters, and others besides, they have made good their claim to larger and more extended powers. We rejoice in it. But when it comes to questions of foreign or colonial policy, or of grave constitutional change, then we maintain that the necessary and normal experience of women — speaking generally and in the mass — does not and can never provide them with such materials for sound judgment as are open to men.

To sum up: we would give them their full share in the State of social effort and social mechanism; we look for their increasing activity in that higher State which rests on thought, conscience, and moral influence; but we protest against their admission to direct power in that State which *does* rest upon force — the State in its administrative, military and financial aspects — where the physical capacity, the accumulated experience and inherited training of men ought to prevail without the harassing interference of those who, though they may be partners with men in debate, can in these matters never be partners with them in action.

2. If we turn from the *right* of women to the suffrage — a right which on the grounds just given we deny — to the effect which the possession of the suffrage may be expected to have on their character and position and on family life, we find ourselves no less in doubt. It is urged that the influence of women in politics would tell upon the side of morality. We believe that it does so tell already, and will do so with greater force as women by improved education fit themselves to exert it more widely and efficiently. But it may be asked, On what does this moral influence depend? We believe that it depends largely on qualities which the natural position and functions of women as they are at present tend to develop, and which might be seriously impaired by their admission to the turmoil of active political life. These qualities are, above all, sympathy and disinterestedness. Any disposition of things which threatens to lessen the national reserve of such forces as these we hold to be a misfortune. It is notoriously difficult to maintain them in the presence of party necessities and in the heat of party struggle. Were women admitted to this struggle, their natural eagerness and quickness of temper would probably make them hotter partisans than men. As their political relations stand at present, they tend to check in them the disposition to partisanship, and to strengthen in them the qualities of sympathy and disinterestedness. We believe that the admission to the suffrage would precisely reverse this condition of things, and that the whole nation would suffer in consequence. For whatever may be the duty and privilege of the parliamentary vote for men, we hold that citizenship is not dependent upon or identical with the possession of the suffrage. Citizenship lies in the participation of each individual in effort for the good of the community. And we believe that woman will be more valuable citizens, will contribute more precious elements to the national life without the vote than with it. The quickness to feel, the willingness to lay aside

prudential considerations in a right cause, which are amongst the peculiar excellencies of women, are in their right place when they are used to influence the more highly trained and developed judgment of men. But if this quickness of feeling could be immediately and directly translated into public action, in matters of vast and complicated political import, the risks of politics would be enormously increased, and what is now a national blessing might easily become a national calamity. . . .

3. Proposals for the extension of the suffrage to women are beset with grave practical difficulties. If votes be given to unmarried women on the same terms as they are given to men, large numbers of women leading immoral lives will be enfranchised on the one hand, while married women, who, as a rule, have passed through more of the practical experiences of life than the unmarried, will be excluded. To remedy part of this difficulty it is proposed by a large section of those who advocate the extension of the suffrage to women, to admit married women with the requisite property qualification. This proposal — an obviously just one if the suffrage is to be extended to women at all — introduces changes in family life, and in the English conception of the household, of enormous importance, which have never been adequately considered. . . .

4. A survey of the manner in which this proposal has won its way into practical politics leads us to think that it is by no means ripe for legislative solution. A social change of momentous gravity has been proposed; the mass of those immediately concerned in it are notoriously indifferent; there has been no serious and general demand for it, as is always the case if a grievance is real and reform necessary; the amount of information collected is quite inadequate to the importance of the issue; and the public has gone through no sufficient discipline of discussion on the subject. Meanwhile pledges to support female suffrage have been hastily given in the hopes of strengthening existing political parties by the female vote. No doubt there are many

conscientious supporters of female suffrage amongst members of Parliament; but it is hard to deny that the present prominence of the question is due to party considerations of a temporary nature. . . .

5. It is often urged that certain injustices of the law towards women would be easily and quickly remedied were the political power of the vote conceded to them; and that there are many wants, especially among working women, which are now neglected, but which the suffrage would enable them to press on public attention. We reply that during the past half century all the principal injustices of the law towards women have been amended by means of the existing constitutional machinery; and with regard to those that remain, we see no signs of any unwillingness on the part of Parliament to deal with them. On the contrary, we remark a growing sensitiveness to the claims of women, and the rise of a new spirit of justice and sympathy among men, answering to those advances made by women in education, and the best kind of social influence, which we have already noticed and welcomed. . . .

In conclusion: nothing can be further from our minds than to seek to depreciate the position or the importance of women. It is because we are keenly alive to the enormous value of their special contribution to the community, that we oppose what seems to us likely to endanger that contribution. We are convinced that the pursuit of a mere outward equality with men is for women not only vain but demoralising. It leads to a total misconception of women's true dignity and special mission. It tends to personal struggle and rivalry, where the only effort of both the great divisions of the human family should be to contribute the characteristic labour and the best gifts of each to the common stock.

▷ One hundred four women, all with aristocratic or upper-middle-class backgrounds, had their names listed in support of the appeal. After their names this statement followed.

In furtherance of the foregoing Appeal . . . — the accompanying proposed protest is laid before the readers of the *Nineteenth Century,* with the request that such ladies among them as agree with it will be kind enough to sign the opposite page and return it, *when detached,* to the Editor of this Review. . . .

Female Suffrage: A Women's Protest

The undersigned protest strongly against the proposed Extension of the Parliamentary Franchise to Women, which they believe would be a measure distasteful to the great majority of the women of the country — unnecessary — and mischievous both to themselves and to the State.

▼▼▼

Nationalism and Imperialism in the Late Nineteenth Century

Nationalism, simply defined, is dedication to and identification with the interests, purposes, and well-being of one's nation-state, a political entity consisting ideally of individuals with a common language, history, and values. As such, nationalism takes precedence over competing loyalties to religion, locality, and even family. No other political force in modern history has matched its ability to inspire heroism and self-sacrifice, both for good and ill.

Nationalism emerged during the French Revolution when the French people transformed themselves from "subjects" to "citizens" by abolishing class privilege and establishing a regime based on equality and popular sovereignty. When war broke out in 1792 between republican France and antirevolutionary Austria and Prussia, previously apathetic Frenchmen eagerly volunteered to fight, and defense of the Revolution became a national crusade. In 1792 and 1793 their patriotism saved the revolution, and in the early 1800s it contributed to the stunning victories of Napoleon that gave France control of most of Europe by 1810. French conquests in turn aroused nationalism among Germans, Italians, Poles, and Russians, who fought to throw off French rule and establish self-government.

Although successful in defeating France on the battlefield, nationalists had their hopes dashed in 1815 at the Congress of Vienna. Diplomats gave Norway to Sweden, Belgium to the Netherlands, and much of Italy to Austria; divided Poland among Russia, Prussia, and Austria; and kept Germany fragmented. But nationalism could not be snuffed out by redrawing maps and making diplomatic compromises. Strengthened by romanticism, Darwinist notions of competition and struggle, economic rivalries, and popular journalism, nationalism intensified in the nineteenth century, not only in areas of foreign rule and political fragmentation, but also in long-established states such as Great Britain and France. It contributed to some of the nineteenth century's most important political developments: the revolutions of 1830 and 1848, the unification of Italy in 1870 and of Germany in 1871, runaway militarism among the Great Powers, the emergence of new states in the Balkans, and what concerns us in this section, late-nineteenth-century imperialism.

Unlike nationalism, a new historical phenomenon, European imperialism has a history that goes back to the medieval crusades and the sixteenth-century conquests of the Americas. Europe's overseas expansion continued in the late eighteenth and early nineteenth centuries despite the loss of American colonies by France, Great Britain, Portugal, and Spain. The British extended their authority in India, the French subdued Algeria between 1830 and 1847, and the European powers led by England forced China to open its ports to foreign trade after the Opium War (1839–1842). Then in the closing decades of the 1800s — the Era of Imperialism — the long history of Western expansion culminated in an unprecedented and astounding land grab. Between 1870 and 1914 Great Britain added 4.25 million square miles of territory and 66 million people to its empire; France, 3.5 million square miles of territory and 26 million people; Germany, 1 million square miles and 13 million people; and Belgium, 900,000 square miles and 13 million people. Italy, the United States, and the Netherlands also added colonial territories and subjects.

These acquisitions were made possible by a number of key technological developments. The replacement of sailing vessels by metal-hulled steamships reduced two-month ocean voyages to two weeks; undersea telegraph lines enabled governments and businessmen to communicate in seconds, not weeks or months; medical advances and new drugs protected Europeans from diseases that flourished in warm, humid climates; rapid-fire rifles and machine guns gave Western troops an insurmountable advantage over any Africans or Asians who resisted the invaders of their lands.

Technological capability alone, however, cannot explain the expansionist fever that swept through the West in the late 1800s. Anticipated economic gains, missionary fervor, racism, and a faith in the West's civilizing mission all contributed. But the most important cause was nationalism. Politicians, journalists, and millions of people from every walk of life were convinced that foreign conquests brought respect, prestige, and a sense of national accomplishment. To have colonies was a sure sign of Great Power status.

Racism, Militarism, and the New Nationalism

▼▼▼

67 ▼ Heinrich von Treitschke, Extracts from HISTORY OF GERMANY IN THE NINETEENTH CENTURY and HISTORICAL AND POLITICAL WRITINGS

As nationalism grew in nineteenth-century Europe, it also changed. In the first half of the century, when nationalists saw conservative monarchical governments as the main obstacle to national self-determination, nationalism was linked to republicanism and liberalism. During the middle of the century, especially in Germany and Italy, nationalism was championed by pragmatic and moderate leaders who believed that hard-headed politics, not romantic gestures and lofty republican ideals, would bring about national unification and independence from foreign rule. By century's end nationalism was increasingly associated with conservative if not reactionary groups that used it to justify large military outlays, imperialism, and aggressive foreign policies. It also would lure the masses away from socialism and democracy.

The German historian Heinrich von Treitschke (1834–1896) represents this later link between nationalism and militarism, racism, and authoritarianism. The son of a Prussian general, Treitschke taught history at several universities, including the prestigious University of Berlin. He also was a member of the German representative assembly, the Reichstag, from 1871 to 1884. His best-known work is his seven-volume *History of Germany in the Nineteenth Century.* In this and his numerous other writings, lectures, and speeches, Treitschke acclaimed militarism, authoritarianism, and war as the path to German greatness. His views struck a responsive chord among many Germans who feared socialism and democracy and yearned for the day when Germany would be recognized as the world's most powerful nation.

QUESTIONS FOR ANALYSIS

1. What, according to Treitschke, is the relationship between the state and the individual?
2. Why, according to Treitschke, is monarchy superior to democracy?
3. What qualities of Germans set them apart from other peoples, especially the English and the Jews, according to Treitschke?
4. Early nineteenth-century nationalists believed that all nations had a contribution to make to human progress. What is Treitschke's view?
5. What, according to Treitschke, is the value of war for a nation?

ON THE GERMAN CHARACTER

Depth of thought, idealism, cosmopolitan views; a transcendent philosophy which boldly oversteps (or freely looks over) the separating barriers of finite existence, familiarity with every human thought and feeling, the desire to traverse the world-wide realm of ideas in common with the foremost intellects of all nations and all times. All that has at all times been held to be characteristic of the Germans and has always been praised as the essence of German character and breeding.

The simple loyalty of the Germans contrasts remarkably with the lack of chivalry in the Eng-

lish character. This seems to be due to the fact that in England physical culture is sought, not in the exercise of noble arms, but in sports like boxing, swimming, and rowing, sports which undoubtedly have their value, but which obviously tend to encourage a brutal and purely athletic point of view, and the single and superficial ambition of getting a first prize.[1]

ON THE STATE

The state is a moral community, which is called upon to educate the human race by positive achievement. Its ultimate object is that a nation

---

[1]Treitschke is correct in drawing a distinction between English and German sports. The English prized competitive athletic contests, while the Germans favored group calisthenics and exercises.

should develop in it, a nation distinguished by a real national character. To achieve this state is the highest moral duty for nation and individual alike. All private quarrels must be forgotten when the state is in danger.

At the moment when the state cries out that its very life is at stake, social selfishness must cease and party hatred be hushed. The individual must forget his egoism, and feel that he is a member of the whole body.

The most important possession of a state, its be-all and end-all, is power. He who is not man enough to look this truth in the face should not meddle in politics. The state is not physical power as an end in itself, it is power to protect and promote the higher interests. Power must justify itself by being applied for the greatest good of mankind. It is the highest moral duty of the state to increase its power. . . .

Only the truly great and powerful states ought to exist. Small states are unable to protect their subjects against external enemies; moreover, they are incapable of producing genuine patriotism or national pride and are sometimes incapable of *Kultur*[2] in great dimensions. Weimar produced a Goethe and a Schiller;[3] still these poets would have been greater had they been citizens of a German national state.

ON MONARCHY

The will of the state is, in a monarchy, the expression of the will of one man who wears the crown by virtue of the historic right of a certain family; with him the final authority rests. Nothing in a monarchy can be done contrary to the will of the monarch. In a democracy, plurality, the will of the people, expresses the will of the state. A monarchy excels any other form of government, including the democratic, in achieving unity and power in a nation. It is for this reason that monarchy seems so natural, and that it makes such an appeal to the popular understanding. We Germans had an experience of this in the first years of our new empire.[4] How wonderfully the idea of a united Fatherland was embodied for us in the person of the venerable Emperor! How much it meant to us that we could feel once more: "That man is Germany; there is no doubting it!"

ON WAR

The idea of perpetual peace is an illusion supported only by those of weak character. It has always been the weary, spiritless, and exhausted ages which have played with the dream of perpetual peace. A thousand touching portraits testify to the sacred power of the love which a righteous war awakes in noble nations. It is altogether impossible that peace be maintained in a world bristling with arms, and even God will see to it that war always recurs as a drastic medicine for the human race. Among great states the greatest political sin and the most contemptible is feebleness. . . .

War is elevating because the individual disappears before the great conception of the state. The devotion of the members of a community to each other is nowhere so splendidly conspicuous as in war.

Modern wars are not waged for the sake of goods and resources. What is at stake is the sublime moral good of national honor, which has something in the nature of unconditional sanctity, and compels the individual to sacrifice himself for it. . . .

The grandeur of war lies in the utter annihilation of puny man in the great conception of the State, and it brings out the full magnificence of the sacrifice of fellow-countrymen for one another. In war the chaff is winnowed from the wheat. Those who have lived through 1870 cannot fail to understand Niebuhr's[5] description of his feelings in 1813, when he speaks of how no one who

---

[2]German for *culture* or *civilization.*
[3]Johann Wolfgang von Goethe (1749–1832) and Johann von Schiller (1759–1805) were poets and dramatists who lived before Germany became a unified state. They both

spent much of their adult lives in Weimar, the capital of the Duchy of Saxe-Weimar.
[4]When Germany became a unified state in 1871, the king of Prussia, William I, became emperor of Germany.

has entered into the joy of being bound by a common tie to all his compatriots, gentle and simple alike, can ever forget how he was uplifted by the love, the friendliness, and the strength of that mutual sentiment.

It is war which fosters the political idealism which the materialist rejects. What a disaster for civilization it would be if mankind blotted its heroes from memory. The heroes of a nation are the figures which rejoice and inspire the spirit of its youth, and the writers whose words ring like trumpet blasts become the idols of our boyhood and our early manhood. He who feels no answering thrill is unworthy to bear arms for his country. To appeal from this judgment to Christianity would be sheer perversity, for does not the Bible distinctly say that the ruler shall rule by the sword, and again that greater love hath no man than to lay down his life for his friend? To Aryan[6] races, who are before all things courageous, the foolish preaching of everlasting peace has always been in vain. They have always been man enough to maintain with the sword what they have attained through the spirit. . . .

ON THE ENGLISH

The hypocritical Englishman, with the Bible in one hand and a pipe of opium[7] in the other, possesses no redeeming qualities. The nation was an ancient robber-knight, in full armor, lance in hand, on every one of the world's trade routes.

The English possess a commercial spirit, a love of money which has killed every sentiment of honor and every distinction of right and wrong.

English cowardice and sensuality are hidden behind unctuous, theological fine talk which is to us free-thinking German heretics among all the sins of English nature the most repugnant. In England all notions of honor and class prejudices vanish before the power of money, whereas the German nobility has remained poor but chivalrous. That last indispensable bulwark against the brutalization of society — the duel — has gone out of fashion in England and soon disappeared, to be supplanted by the riding whip.[8] This was a triumph of vulgarity. The newspapers, in their accounts of aristocratic weddings, record in exact detail how much each wedding guest has contributed in the form of presents or in cash; even the youth of the nation have turned their sports into a business, and contend for valuable prizes, whereas the German students wrought havoc on their countenances for the sake of a real or imaginary honor.[9]

ON JEWS

The Jews at one time played a necessary role in German history, because of their ability in the management of money. But now that the Aryans have become accustomed to the idiosyncrasies of finance, the Jews are no longer necessary. The international Jew, hidden in the mask of different nationalities, is a disintegrating influence; he can be of no further use to the world. It is necessary to speak openly about the Jews, undisturbed by the fact that the Jewish press befouls what is purely historical truth.

---

[5]Barthold Georg Niebuhr (1776–1831) was a Prussian civil servant and historian. He lectured for a time at the University of Berlin and is best known for his three-volume history of Rome.

[6]Today, the term *Aryan,* or Indo-Iranian, refers to a branch of the Indo-European family of languages, which also includes Baltic, Slavic, Armenian, Greek, Celtic, Latin, and Germanic. Indo-Iranian includes Bengali, Persian, Punjabi, and Hindi. In Treitschke's day *Aryan* was used not only to refer to the prehistoric language from which all these languages derive but also to the racial group that spoke the language and migrated from its base in central Asia to Europe and India in the distant past. In the racial mythology that grew in connection with the term and later was embraced by

Hitler and the Nazis, the Aryans provided Europe's original racial stock.

[7]Treitschke is making a point about what he considers the hypocrisy of the British, professed Christians who nonetheless sell opium to the Chinese.

[8]Aristocratic males frequently settled disputes concerning their honor by dueling. To Treitschke, abandoning the duel for less manly pursuits such as hunting and horseback riding was a sign of decadence.

[9]Treitschke is again using examples from sports to underscore the differences between the Germans and English. English sports such as rugby and football (American soccer) were organized into professional leagues; the Germans were still willing to be scarred in duels to defend their honor.

Jewish Nationalism and the Birth of Zionism
▼▼▼

68 ▼ Theodor Herzl, THE JEWS' STATE

Zionism, which officially began at the World Zionist Congress held in Basel, Switzerland, in 1897, was the last nationalist movement to appear in nineteenth-century Europe. It was also the most ambitious. Jews had not had their own state since 586 B.C.E., when the Kingdom of Judah in Palestine had been conquered by the Babylonians, and from the time of their expulsion from their homeland by the Romans in the first century C.E., they had come to live in communities scattered across the Middle East, North Africa, Europe, and the Americas. During the many centuries of their dispersal Jews held fast to the dream of returning to their homeland in Palestine, the Land of Zion, which according to Hebrew scriptures, was theirs by virtue of their covenant with God. This pious hope, expressed in traditional Jewish prayers and religious writings, in the twentieth century became a highly organized political movement that in 1949 resulted in the foundation of the modern state of Israel.

Zionism originated in Europe, where in the late eighteenth and nineteenth centuries many discriminatory laws against Jews were lifted and Jews gained the freedom to participate fully in their nation's economic, political, and cultural life. Old anti-Jewish prejudices were difficult to eradicate, however, and in an atmosphere of rapid social change, growing nationalism, new racial theories, and simple jealousy of the many successful Jewish physicians, businessmen, journalists, and academics, anti-Semitism intensified in the late 1800s. In France, the trial, conviction, and ultimate exoneration of the Jewish army officer Alfred Dreyfus for treason dragged on from 1894 to 1906 and revealed the depths of anti-Jewish feeling in what was supposedly Europe's most tolerant and liberal state. German politicians routinely attacked the Jews, and in 1895 voters in Vienna elected Karl Lüger, an outspoken anti-Semite, as their mayor. Russia's tsarist government issued new anti-Jewish laws, and to divert attention away from its own failures, encouraged mob attacks (*pogroms*) on Jewish communities in Russia itself and in Poland, Ukraine, and Lithuania, three regions that were part of its empire and the home of the vast majority of Europe's Jews.

The founder of Zionism, Theodor Herzl, was born into the family of a wealthy businessman in Budapest in 1860. At age eighteen he and his family moved to Vienna, where he attended the University of Vienna and earned his doctorate in law. Spurning a legal career, he spent several years writing plays and fiction before accepting a job as a correspondent for the *Neue Freie Presse*, a Viennese newspaper. Although not deeply religious, during the 1880s Herzl became increasingly troubled by growing signs of anti-Semitism in Europe, and in the 1890s he became convinced by the Dreyfus affair and the election of Lüger that Jews had no future unless they had a state of their own outside of Europe. After publishing *Der Judenstaat* (*The Jews' State,* or as it is also translated, *The Jewish State*) in 1896, he organized the first World Zionist Congress in Basel. Until his death in 1904 he worked tirelessly to strengthen Zionism by lecturing, organizing, writing books and articles, and seeking the support of wealthy philanthropists and important political leaders. In 1949, forty-five years after his death, his remains were flown from Vienna to Jerusalem, where they were reburied in the new state of Israel.

QUESTIONS FOR ANALYSIS

1. Herzl states at the outset that the Jews "are a people, *one* people." In his view why have the Jews maintained this unity despite living in communities scattered across several continents?
2. According to Herzl, what are the concrete signs of continuing anti-Semitism in late-nineteenth-century Europe?
3. How does Herzl explain the persistence of anti-Semitism?
4. According to Herzl, why are "staying put" and "assimilation" not viable options for Europe's Jews?
5. According to Herzl, why is a Jews' state the only means for the Jews to escape their predicament in Europe?
6. What role does religion play in Herzl's arguments? What role, according to Herzl, should it play in the future Jews' state?

PREAMBLE AND INTRODUCTION

The concept with which I am dealing in this paper is very old. It is the establishment of the Jews' State.

The world resounds with clamor against Jews, and that arouses this concept out of its sleep. . . .

I consider the issue of the Jews neither in social nor religious terms, even though these things do come into it. It is a national issue, and if we are to find a solution, we must make it a political question for the whole world, to be tackled in counsel with all civilized peoples.

We are a people, *one* people.

We have tried everywhere in all honesty to assimilate into the communities around us, while preserving the faith of our fathers. We are not allowed to. We are faithful and often even over-enthusiastic patriots — in vain. We make the same sacrifices in life and limb as our countrymen — in vain. We do our utmost to further the reputation of our home countries in the fields of arts and science — in vain. We toil to increase the wealth of our lands with our commerce and trade — in vain. In our home countries, where we have been living for centuries, we are decried as foreign, often by those whose forebears were not even living there when our forebears were already being persecuted. . . . Therefore we are good patriots everywhere in vain, just like the Huguenots,[1] who were forced to go elsewhere. If they only left us in peace. . . .

But I believe they will not leave us in peace.

For deep down within the feelings of peoples there are old prejudices anchored against us. If you want evidence, you only need to listen where the people express themselves simply and truthfully: folktales and proverbs are antisemitic. . . .

The collective personality of the Jews as a people, however, cannot, will not, and must not perish. It cannot perish, because external enemies hold it together. It will not perish; it has demonstrated that during two millennia under enormous suffering. It must not perish; that is what I seek to demonstrate in this publication after many other Jews who never gave up hope. Whole

---

[1]Huguenots were Protestants in predominantly Catholic France who were granted religious toleration in 1598 only to have it revoked under Louis XIV in 1685. In response large numbers of Huguenots left France and settled in England, the Netherlands, and Prussia, where many became successful in business.

branches of Jewry may well die away and fall off; the tree lives. . . .

No one person has sufficient strength or wealth to transplant a whole people from one domicile to another. Only an idea is powerful enough to do that. The idea of the state has such power. For the whole night of their history Jews have not stopped dreaming the royal dream. "Next year in Jerusalem" is our ancient watchword. The question now is to demonstrate that the dream can be turned into an idea as bright as day. . . .

THE ISSUE OF THE JEWS

Day by day, attacks on Jews increase in the parliaments, at meetings, in the press, on the pulpit, in the street; when they travel, they are denied entry into hotels or places of amusement. The character of these persecutions varies, depending on country or social circle. In Russia they plunder Jewish villages, in Rumania they beat a few people to death, in Germany Jews are on the receiving end of a good thrashing now and again, in Austria public life is terrorized by antisemites, in Algeria there are preachers roaming the countryside extolling hatred, in Paris high society closes ranks and shuts itself off against Jews. The variety is endless. However, this is not an attempt to provide a melancholy list of all Jewish hardships. We will not worry about details, however painful.

It is not my intention to create an atmosphere sympathetic to us. All that would be useless, in vain, and unworthy of us. For me it is sufficient to ask the Jews: is it not a fact that in countries where we live in significant numbers, the position of Jewish lawyers, doctors, technicians, teachers and all types of public servants is becoming increasingly unbearable? Is it not a fact that our whole Jewish middle class is under serious threat? Is it not a fact that all the passions of the lower classes are being marshalled against our wealthy people? Is it not a fact that the poor among us suffer much more than the rest of the proletariat? . . .

The fact is that it amounts to the same thing everywhere, and it can be summarized in the classic slogan of the Berliners: Away with the Jews!

I will now express the issue of the Jews in its most concise form: if we must be away, then where to?

Or can we still stay put? And for how long?

Let us first tackle the question of staying put. Can we hope for better times, can we be patient, put our faith in God and wait until the rulers and peoples of the world get into a more benign mood towards us? I say we cannot expect a turnaround in the general trend. Why not? Kings and emperors cannot protect us, even if they wished to treat us equally. They would only inflame hatred against the Jews if they showed the Jews too much sympathy. And this "too much sympathy" would at any rate still amount to less than what is normally due to every normal citizen or social group.

The peoples with whom Jews live are all antisemites, without exception, discreetly or brazenly. . . .

EFFECTS OF ANTI-SEMITISM

The pressure exerted upon us does not make us any better. We are no different from other human beings. It is quite true that we do not love our enemies. . . . Pressure naturally evokes in us hostility against our oppressors; and then our hostility in turn increases the pressure. It is impossible to break the vicious circle.

"Nevertheless," so the gentle daydreamers will say, "nevertheless, it is possible by working patiently to draw out what is good in people."

Do I really still have to demonstrate that this is just sentimental twaddle? If you wanted to improve your situation by relying on the good will of people, you would certainly be writing a utopian romance.

I have already mentioned our "assimilation." I do not say for a moment that I want it. Our national character is historically too famous and, despite all humiliation, too proud to wish for its demise. But perhaps we could merge without a trace into the peoples around us if we were left in peace for a couple of generations. They will not leave us in peace. After short spells of tolerance the hostility against us awakens anew. There seems to be something in our prosperity that irritates people, because the world has been accustomed to seeing us as the most despised among the poor. At the same time they do not notice, whether from ignorance or narrowmindedness, that our prosperity weakens us as Jews and dissipates our character. Only pressure keeps us close to the old tribe, only the hatred that surrounds us turns us into strangers. . . .

We are a people — the enemy turns us into one against our wishes — that has been the same throughout history. In oppression we stand together, and then we suddenly discover our power. Yes, we have the power to create a state, even a state that would stand as a model for all. We possess all the necessary human and material means.

THE PLAN

In its basic form the whole plan is infinitely simple: it just has to be if it is to be understood by everyone.

We should be given sovereignty over a piece of the earth's surface sufficient for the legitimate needs of our people. We will look after everything else. . . .

As I have already said, the departure of the Jews should not be seen as a sudden phenomenon. It will occur gradually and will take decades. First the poorest Jews will go and make the land arable. In accordance with a previously developed concept they will build the streets, bridges and railways, they will construct the telegraph system, they will regulate the rivers and build homes for themselves. Their work will lead to business, business will bring markets, markets will entice new immigrants to come. Everyone will come of their own free will, and bear their own costs and risks. . . . Jews will not take long to realize that a new and lasting target has been opened up for their spirit of enterprise, for which hitherto they have been hated and despised. . . .

If the Great Powers are prepared to grant the Jews as a people sovereignty over a neutral land, then the Society will enter into negotiations about the land which is to be selected. Two regions will be considered: Palestine and Argentina. . . .

In terms of natural resources Argentina is one of the wealthiest countries in the world, enormous in size, sparsely populated, and with a moderate climate. It would be in the interest of the Argentinian republic to cede us a piece of territory. Unfortunately, the present infiltration of Jews has created ill feeling there; we would have to explain to Argentina the fundamental difference of the new Jewish migration.

Palestine is our unforgettable historical home. This very name would already be an enormously powerful rallying cry for our people. If His Majesty the Sultan were to give us Palestine, we could undertake the responsibility of putting the finances of Turkey completely in order. To Europe we would represent a part of the barrier against Asia; we would serve as the outpost of civilization against barbarism. As a neutral state we would remain allied to all of Europe, which in turn would have to guarantee our existence. An internationally acceptable arrangement would be found to guarantee the extra-territorial status of the holy places of Christendom. We would form the guard of honor around the holy places, and guarantee the execution of this duty with our very existence. This guard of honor would be the great symbol of the solution of the issue of the Jews after eighteen centuries of agony.

THE TRANSPLANT

Up to now we have simply indicated how the emigration is to be effected without economic upheaval. However, such an emigration is also associated with strong, deep, personal disorientation. There are old customs, and memories which tie us people to specific places. We have cradles, we have graves, and we know the place of graves in the hearts of Jews. The cradles we will take with us — in them slumbers our smiling and rosy future. Our dear graves will have to be left behind — I believe this separation will weigh heavily on our possessive people. But it must be.

Economic distress, political oppression, and social hatred already separate us from our home towns and from our graves. Jews already leave one country for the next at every moment; a strong movement even leads overseas to the United States, where we are not welcome either. Where will we ever be welcome, so long as we do not have a country to call our own?

We, however, want to give the Jews a home country. Not by tearing them forcibly out of their present land. No, by lifting them carefully with all their roots and transplanting them into a better soil. Just as we want to create new conditions in the economic and political sphere, we will respect the sanctity of old ways in the cultural sphere. . . .

THEOCRACY

Will we end up having a theocracy? No! Faith will hold us together, science makes us free. We will not even allow the theocratic inclinations of our spiritual leaders to raise their ugly heads. We will know how to keep them in their temples, just as we will know how to keep our professional army in the barracks. Army and clerics will be highly honored, as much as is right and proper in the light of their beautiful functions. They have no say in the state which treats them with deference, for they will only conjure up external and internal difficulties.

Everybody is as free and unfettered in practicing his belief or unbelief as he is in his nationality. And should it come to pass that persons of other faiths or nationalities live among us, then we will accord them honorable protection and equality before the law. Tolerance we have learnt in Europe, and I am not even being sarcastic when I say this. Only in a few isolated instances can you equate modern antisemitism with the old religious intolerance. It is in most cases a movement among the civilized peoples, with which they want to ward off a ghost from their own past.

A Defense of French Imperialism
▼▼▼

69 ▾ *Jules Ferry,*
SPEECH BEFORE THE
FRENCH NATIONAL ASSEMBLY

Jules Ferry (1832–1893), a French politician and ardent imperialist, twice served as premier of France. During his premierships (1880–1881, 1883–1885) France annexed Tunisia and parts of Indochina and began exploring parts of Africa. In debates in the French National Assembly he frequently defended his policies against socialist and conservative critics who opposed French imperialism. In the following selection from a speech on July 28, 1883, he summarizes his reasons for supporting French expansionism; it also sheds light on his opponents' views.

QUESTIONS FOR ANALYSIS

1. According to Ferry, what recent developments in world trade have made France's need for colonies more urgent?
2. What arguments against imperialism are proposed by Ferry's critics? How does Ferry counter them?

3. Aside from providing markets for French goods, what other economic advantages do colonies offer, according to Ferry?
4. How does Ferry's appeal for colonies reflect nineteenth-century nationalism?
5. Given the opportunity to have heard Ferry's speech, how might Condorcet have reacted to it (source 37)?

M. JULES FERRY Gentlemen, it embarrasses me to make such a prolonged demand upon the gracious attention of the Chamber, but I believe that the duty I am fulfilling upon this platform is not a useless one: It is as strenuous for me as for you, but I believe that there is some benefit in summarizing and condensing, in the form of arguments, the principles, the motives, and the various interests by which a policy of colonial expansion may be justified; it goes without saying that I will try to remain reasonable, moderate, and never lose sight of the major continental interests which are the primary concern of this country. What I wish to say, to support this proposition, is that in fact, just as in word, the policy of colonial expansion is a political and economic system; I wish to say that one can relate this system to three orders of ideas: economic ideas, ideas of civilization in its highest sense, and ideas of politics and patriotism.

In the area of economics, I will allow myself to place before you, with the support of some figures, the considerations which justify a policy of colonial expansion from the point of view of that need, felt more and more strongly by the industrial populations of Europe and particularly those of our own rich and hard working country: the need for export markets. Is this some kind of chimera? Is this a view of the future or is it not rather a pressing need, and, we could say, the cry of our industrial population? I will formulate only in a general way what each of you, in the different parts of France, is in a position to confirm. Yes, what is lacking for our great industry, drawn irrevocably on to the path of exportation by the (free trade) treaties of 1860,[1] what it lacks more and more is export markets. Why? Because next door to us Germany is surrounded by barriers, because beyond the ocean, the United States of America has become protectionist, protectionist in the most extreme sense, because not only have these great markets, I will not say closed but shrunk, and thus become more difficult of access for our industrial products, but also these great states are beginning to pour products not seen heretofore into our own markets. . . . It is not necessary to pursue this demonstration any further. . . .

. . . Gentlemen, there is a second point, a second order of ideas to which I have to give equal attention, but as quickly as possible, believe me; it is the humanitarian and civilizing side of the question. On this point the honorable M. Camille Pelletan[2] has jeered in his own refined and clever manner; he jeers, he condemns, and he says "What is this civilization which you impose with cannon-balls? What is it but another form of barbarism? Don't these populations, these inferior races, have the same rights as you? Aren't they masters of their own houses? Have they called upon you? You come to them against their will, you offer them violence, but not civilization." There, gentlemen, is the thesis; I do not hesitate to say that this is not politics, nor is it history: it is political metaphysics. ("Ah, Ah" *on far left*.)[3]

. . . Gentlemen, I must speak from a higher and more truthful plane. It must be stated openly that, in effect, superior races have rights over inferior races. (*Movement on many benches on the far left.*)

M. JULES MAIGNE Oh! You dare to say this in the country which has proclaimed the rights of man!

---

[1]Refers to a treaty between Great Britain and France that lowered tariffs between the two nations.
[2]Pelletan (1846–1915) was a radical republican politician noted for his strong patriotism.

[3]Going back to a tradition begun in the legislative assemblies of the French Revolution, democrats and republicans sat on the left, moderates in the center, and conservatives on the right. By the 1880s the "left" also included socialists.

M. DE GUILLOUTET This is a justification of slavery and the slave trade!

M. JULES FERRY If M. Maigne is right, if the declaration of the rights of man was written for the blacks of equatorial Africa, then by what right do you impose regular commerce upon them? They have not called upon you.

M. RAOUL DUVAL We do not want to impose anything upon them. It is you who wish to do so!

M. JULES MAIGNE To propose and to impose are two different things!

M. GEORGES PERIN[4] In any case, you cannot bring about commerce by force.

M. JULES FERRY I repeat that superior races have a right, because they have a duty. They have the duty to civilize inferior races. . . . *(Approbation from the left. New interruptions from the extreme left and from the right.)* . . .

That is what I have to answer M. Pelletan in regard to the second point upon which he touched.

He then touched upon a third, more delicate, more serious point, and upon which I ask your permission to express myself quite frankly. It is the political side of the question. The honorable M. Pelletan, who is a distinguished writer, always comes up with remarkably precise formulations. I will borrow from him the one which he applied the other day to this aspect of colonial policy.

"It is a system," he says, "which consists of seeking out compensations in the Orient with a circumspect and peaceful seclusion which is actually imposed upon us in Europe."

I would like to explain myself in regard to this. I do not like this word "compensation," and, in effect, not here but elsewhere it has often been used in a treacherous way. If what is being said or insinuated is that a republican minister could possibly believe that there are in any part of the world compensations for the disasters which we have experienced,[5] an injury is being inflicted . . . and an injury undeserved by that government.

(Applause at the center and left.) I will ward off this injury with all the force of my patriotism! *(New applause and bravos from the same benches.)*

Gentlemen, there are certain considerations which merit the attention of all patriots. The conditions of naval warfare have been profoundly altered. ("Very true! Very true!")

At this time, as you know, a warship cannot carry more than fourteen days' worth of coal, no matter how perfectly it is organized, and a ship which is out of coal is a derelict on the surface of the sea, abandoned to the first person who comes along. Thence the necessity of having on the oceans provision stations, shelters, ports for defense and revictualling. *(Applause at the center and left. Various interruptions.)* And it is for this that we needed Tunisia, for this that we needed Saigon and the Mekong Delta, for this that we need Madagascar, that we are at Diégo-Suarez and Vohemar[6] and will never leave them! *(Applause from a great number of benches.)* Gentlemen, in Europe as it is today, in this competition of so many rivals which we see growing around us, some by perfecting their military or maritime forces, others by the prodigious development of an ever growing population; in a Europe, or rather in a universe of this sort, a policy of peaceful seclusion or abstention is simply the highway to decadence! Nations are great in our times only by means of the activities which they develop; it is not simply "by the peaceful shining forth of institutions" *(Interruptions on the extreme left and right)* that they are great at this hour. . . .

As for me, I am astounded to find the monarchist parties becoming indignant over the fact that the Republic of France is following a policy which does not confine itself to that ideal of modesty, of reserve, and, if you will allow me the expression, of bread and butter *(Interruptions and laughter on the left)* which the representatives of fallen monarchies wish to impose upon France. *(Applause at the center.)* . . .

---

[4]Maigne, Guilloutet, Duval, and Perin were all members of the assembly.
[5]Refers to France's defeat by Prussia and the German states in the Franco-Prussian War of 1870–1871.

[6]Madagascar port cities.

(The Republican Party) has shown that it is quite aware that one cannot impose upon France a political ideal conforming to that of nations like independent Belgium and the Swiss Republic; that something else is needed for France: that she cannot be merely a free country, that she must also be a great country, exercising all of her rightful influence over the destiny of Europe, that she ought to propagate this influence throughout the world and carry everywhere that she can her language, her customs, her flag, her arms, and her genius. *(Applause at center and left.)*

Images of Imperialism in Great Britain
▼▼▼

70 ▼ *ADVERTISEMENTS AND ILLUSTRATIONS FROM BRITISH BOOKS AND PERIODICALS*

Although late-nineteenth-century imperialism had its critics, there is no doubt that in the major imperialist states it had broad support, not just from investors, missionary groups, and civil servants who had direct interests in Africa and Asia but also from the general populace. Imperialism had this appeal for several reasons. For many it confirmed their faith in progress and their belief in the superiority of white, Christian Europeans over the rest of the world's peoples. For ardent nationalists it was an endeavor that tested and demonstrated the nation's strength and vigor. For those who found their lives in industrial society drab and tedious, it provided vicarious adventure, excitement, and a sense of the exotic.

Late-nineteenth-century popular culture provides ample evidence of the public's enthusiasm for imperialism. Especially in Great Britain, the premier imperialist power, novels, poetry, plays, children's books, advertisements, music hall entertainment, and publications of missionary societies were filled with positive imperialist images, themes, and motifs. Youth organizations such as the Boy Scouts (f. 1908) and the Girl Guides (f. 1910) sought to inculcate the values of service to Britain's imperial cause. This constant exposure of the public to material connected with the British Empire reinforced imperialism's appeal and strengthened support for the government's expansionist policies.

The selections in this section provide several examples of how British popular culture propagated imperial values. The first group of illustrations (page 306) appeared in *An ABC for Baby Patriots* by Mrs. Earnest Ames. Designed to be read to young children, it was published in 1898 in London and went through several printings. The illustration that accompanies the letter *N* depicts a British naval officer showing off a flotilla of Royal Navy ships on maneuvers off Spithead in the English Channel. The foreigners are a German on the left and a Frenchman on the right.

The second illustration (page 307, top) is taken from *The Kipling Reader,* a collection of stories written for young adults by Rudyard Kipling (1865–1936); it was published in 1908 and illustrated by J. Macfarlane. Kipling, one of the most popular British writers of the era, is best remembered for his strong support of imperialism and his glorification of the heroism of the British soldier in India and

Burma. This particular illustration depicts Scott, a character in the story "William the Conqueror." Set in India during a famine, the story centers on the romance between Scott and a young woman nicknamed "William" while they toil to save Indians from starvation. Scott has saved hundreds of babies by feeding them milk from a herd of goats he has managed to maintain. In this illustration he approaches William, who sees "a young man, beautiful as Paris, a god in a halo of gold dust, walking slowly at the head of his flocks, while at his knee ran small naked Cupids."

The third illustration (page 307, bottom) is an advertisement for Lipton Teas, which appeared in 1897 in the popular weekly the *Illustrated London News.* The Lipton Company was founded in Glasgow, Scotland, by the son of a poor Irish shopkeeper, Thomas Lipton (1850–1931). He opened a small food shop in Glasgow in 1871 and by 1890 owned 300 food stores throughout Great Britain. In 1890 the multimillionaire decided to cash in on the British taste for tea. Growing tea on plantations he owned in India and Ceylon and marketing it in inexpensive small packets that guaranteed freshness, the Lipton Company soon became synonymous with tea drinking throughout Europe and the United States. Advertisements for its tea appeared regularly in the *Illustrated London News* during the 1890s and early 1900s.

The fourth and fifth illustrations (page 308) are cartoons published in the popular English humor magazine *Punch,* founded in 1841. Although noted for its political radicalism in its early years, by the late nineteenth century *Punch* had adopted a more moderate political stance, one that reflected the perspectives of its largely middle-class readers. The first cartoon, "On the Swoop," was published in 1894, a time when the European powers were consolidating their territorial claims in Africa. It shows an eagle representing Germany about to pounce on an African village. By then it was clear that the German acquisition of Tanganyika had ruined the British imperialists' dream of establishing a string of contiguous British colonies in east Africa that stretched from Cairo in Egypt to Cape Town in South Africa. The second cartoon, "Britannia and Her Suitors," was published in 1901, a time when Great Britain was still studiously avoiding entanglements in the diplomatic alliances then taking shape among the continental powers. It shows Britannia dancing with a figure representing its colonies, while in the background the German emperor Wilhelm II, then allied only with weak Austria-Hungary, looks on unhappily. Further in the background Tsar Nicholas II of Russia dances with a figure representing France, with whom Russia had been allied since 1894.

QUESTIONS FOR ANALYSIS

1. What views of Africans and Asians are being communicated in each of the illustrations?
2. What message is being communicated about the benefits colonial subjects are accruing from their status?
3. What images are being communicated about the British in their role as imperialists?

(text continued on p. 307)

From *An ABC for Baby Patriots*

N.

N is the Navy
We keep at Spithead,
It's a sight that makes foreigners
Wish they were dead.

I.

I is for India,
Our land in the East
Where everyone goes
To shoot tigers and feast.

W.

W is the Word
Of an Englishman true;
When given, it means
What he says, he will do.

4. What concrete examples of nationalism can you see in the various illustrations?
5. How many of the justifications for imperialism presented in Jules Ferry's speech (source 69) can you find represented in the illustrations?
6. Using evidence in the illustrations alone, what conclusions can you draw about the reasons for imperialism's popularity within the general British population?

From The Kipling Reader

Advertisement for Lipton Teas, which appeared in the Illustrated London News, *a weekly publication*

PARTNERS.

Britannia. "After all, my dear, we needn't trouble ourselves about the others."
Colonia. "No; we can always dance together, you and I!"

"Britannia and Her Suitors," from Punch, *1901*

ON THE SWOOP!

"On the Swoop," from Punch, *1894*

Chapter 9

Western Pressures, Nationalism, and Reform in Africa, Southwest Asia, and India in the 1800s

Africa, Southwest Asia, and India all shared a common experience in the nineteenth century: All three were engulfed in a tidal wave of change set off by the political, economic, and cultural onslaught of Europe. Until the 1800s, contact with Europeans for the peoples and rulers of these regions mainly had meant dealing with merchants, who did their business on the coast and traded with the indulgence of local rulers who often benefited from their activities. Only in the case of the Ottoman Empire were relations with Europeans marked by territorial conflict and war. And only in India were Europeans, in this instance the British in the eighteenth century, able to establish extensive political authority.

By the early twentieth century the politics of all three regions had been transformed as a result of European penetration. In the 1800s the British extended their Indian empire until it encompassed the whole Indian subcontinent. Africa also lost its independence. The main difference was that India had but one colonial master; Africa ended up with half a dozen. Persia experienced growing British and Russian interference in its affairs, culminating in the Anglo-Russian Agreement of 1907, which divided the country into a Russian-dominated north, a British-dominated south, and a nominally independent center.

The Ottoman Empire survived but lost thousands of square miles of territory. In North Africa, which was still part of the

Ottoman Empire despite the near independence of its rulers, Algeria and Tunisia became French colonies and Egypt became a British protectorate. In southeastern Europe, Greece, Serbia, Romania, Bulgaria, Montenegro, and Albania all gained their independence from Ottoman rule, often with the aid of European powers. In addition, Europeans seriously compromised the sovereignty of the Ottoman state itself. Foreign businessmen, who controlled the empire's banks, railroads, and mines, regulated Ottoman tariff policy and were exempt from many of the empire's laws and taxes. Beginning in 1881 Europeans supervised the collection and disbursement of state revenues through the Ottoman Public Debt Administration, an agency established mainly to guarantee payment of government debts to European creditors.

In all three regions European penetration threatened ruling elites and traditional political institutions, making some irrelevant, destroying others, and inspiring reform in a few. It also undermined these regions' traditional economies. Europeans built railroads and telegraph lines, undertook huge engineering projects such as the Suez Canal, created new demands for raw materials and agricultural goods, and aggressively marketed their own manufactured products. Europeans also introduced unsettling new ideas and values through intensified missionary activity, the introduction of the printing press, and the promotion of Western education and science. In a matter of decades, the peoples of Africa, Southwest Asia, and India were wrenched from their past and forced to face an uncertain future.

▼▼▼

The European Assault on Africa

Paradoxically, the century that saw the near total submission of Africa to European rule began with an effort by Europeans to outlaw their main business in Africa, the slave trade. Responding to both humanitarian and economic arguments, several states, including Denmark, France, the United States, and, most important, Great Britain, banned slave trading around 1800. Unexpectedly, this led to more, not less, European involvement in Africa. Palm oil, ivory, cocoa, coffee, rubber, and other goods replaced slaves as items of trade, and by the 1850s this "legitimate" trade was more profitable for the British than the old slave trade. Then in the closing decades of the nineteenth century, African-European relations underwent a radical transformation, and the whole continent except Liberia and Ethiopia succumbed to European rule.

The takeover took just two decades. It began in earnest in 1878, when King Leopold II of Belgium (r. 1865–1909) and his business associates gained control of lands in the Congo River basin through the efforts of their representative, Welsh explorer Henry M. Stanley (1841–1904). In 1880 Italian-born explorer Pierre Savorgnan de Brazza (1852–1905) signed the first of hundreds of treaties with African chieftains that laid the basis for what became the sprawling colony of French Equatorial Africa. In 1881 France established a protectorate over Tunisia, and in 1882 Great Britain occupied Egypt. In 1884 and 1885 thirteen European nations and the United States attended the Berlin West Africa Conference, which established guidelines for the European conquest of Africa. By 1914, when World War I began, Africa had become a vast European colony.

Africans did not passively acquiesce to the European onslaught. Many Africans fought back, but the Europeans' artillery, high-explosive shells, and machine guns doomed their efforts. In 1898 the Battle of Omdurman in modern Sudan resulted in some 11,000 casualties for the Sudanese and forty for the British and their Egyptian troops.

"With the View of Bettering . . . Our Country"
▼▼▼
71 ▼ *Royal Niger Company, STANDARD TREATY*

During the partition of Africa, African chieftains signed hundreds of treaties that effectively gave European states or trading companies control of African lands and resources. The following document is an example of such a treaty.

This "standard treaty" was utilized in the late 1880s by representatives of the Royal Niger Company, founded in 1879 as the United African Company by the merchant adventurer George Goldie Taubman. Competing with the French for trade on the Niger River, the company was commissioned by Queen Victoria in 1886 as the Royal Niger Company and given a trade monopoly and the right to exercise political authority in the region. After receiving the royal charter, the company's representatives had to move quickly to head off the French, so they drew up a set of standard treaties in which one needed only to fill in the blanks. Using templates such as the one that appears here, British representatives of the trading companies concluded no fewer than 373 treaties with chieftains of the region between 1884 and 1892. These treaties served as the basis for the Niger Districts Protectorate, which in turn became the British colony of Nigeria.

QUESTIONS FOR ANALYSIS

1. By accepting this treaty, what were the chieftains giving up?
2. What benefits were the Africans to receive by signing the treaty?
3. What does use of the standard treaty signify about English attitudes toward and knowledge of the Africans?
4. What does the treaty indicate about the motives of the British in Africa?

We, the undersigned Chiefs of ____, with the view to the bettering of the condition of our country and people, do this day cede to the Royal Niger Company, for ever, the whole of our territory extending from ____.

We also give to the said Royal Niger Company full power to settle all native disputes arising from any cause whatever, and we pledge ourselves not to enter into any war with other tribes without the sanction of the said Royal Niger Company.

We understand that the said Royal Niger Company have full power to mine, farm, and build in any portion of our country.

We bind ourselves not to have any intercourse with any strangers or foreigners except through the said Royal Niger Company.

In consideration of the foregoing, the said Royal Niger Company (Chartered and Limited) bind themselves not to interfere with any of the native laws or customs of the country, consistently with the maintenance of order and good government.

The said Royal Niger Company agree to pay native owners of land a reasonable amount for any portion they may require.

The said Royal Niger Company bind themselves to protect the said Chiefs from the attacks of any neighboring aggressive tribes.

The said Royal Niger Company also agree to pay the said Chiefs ____ measures native value.

We, the undersigned witnesses, do hereby solemnly declare that the ____ Chiefs whose names are placed opposite their respective crosses have in our presence affixed their crosses of their own free will and consent, and that the said ____ has in our presence affixed his signature.

Done in triplicate at ____, this ____ day of ____, 188____.

Declaration by interpreter I, ____, of ____, do hereby solemnly declare that I am well acquainted with the language of the country, and that on the ____ day of ____, 188____, I truly and faithfully explained the above Agreement to all the Chiefs present, and that they understood its meaning.

The Realities of Legitimate Trade on the Oil Rivers

▼▼▼

72 ▼ *PETITION OF KING OCKIYA AND THE CHIEFS OF BRASS TO LORD DERBY, FEBRUARY 1877 and MEMORANDUM OF THE BRASS CHIEFS, JUNE 1895*

Between 1792 and 1836 one by one the maritime states of Europe and the United States outlawed the slave trade, and although smuggling continued (no fewer than 3 million slaves were sent to the Americas in the 1800s), the centuries-old dependency of many African merchants and rulers on the transatlantic slave trade came to an end. Great Britain, the world's leading slave-trading nation in the 1700s, took the lead in enforcing the new antislaving laws in the early 1800s by dispatching ships of the Royal Navy to patrol the African coast. The British also sought to persuade African kings and chieftains to end their dependence on selling slaves and provisioning slave ships in favor of "legitimate trade." For merchants of the villages on the Niger River delta and the regions just to its east and west, legitimate trade primarily meant trade in palm oil, produced from the nut of the oil palm, a tree that flourished in a relatively small region just beyond the coastal swamplands. A traditional African food, palm oil had been one of the products Africans sold to European slavers, who added it along with pepper to the gruel they served slaves bound for the Americas. In the nineteenth century demand for palm oil soared in Europe, where it was used as a lubricant and as an ingredient in soap and candles. By the 1860s more than 40,000 tons of palm oil were being exported from Africa annually, and the many creeks and rivers in the Niger delta and its vicinity came to be known as the "oil rivers."

This shift to legitimate trade in palm oil was a mixed blessing for Africans. Producing palm oil was arduous, labor-intensive work, involving harvesting and sorting palm nuts, cooking them, boiling them, skimming off the oil, and pouring the finished product into thirty-six-pound tins that were transported to the coast in large canoes. As a result of the heavy demand for labor, domestic slavery in palm oil–producing regions actually increased in the 1800s. In addition, the palm oil trade heightened tensions and conflict among the numerous small city-states of the region, whose merchant-chieftains purchased the oil in the hinterland, transported it to the coast, and sold it to Europeans. Finally, as the following documents show, African merchants were at a disadvantage in their dealings with the Royal Niger Company, which with the backing of British officials imposed and enforced a host of new trade duties and regulations. Such regulations and duties became especially burdensome from the 1880s onward when the introduction of petroleum-based lubricants in Europe softened the market for palm oil.

The following two memoranda reveal some of the problems and frustrations faced by African palm-oil merchants in their dealings with the British. Both memoranda were produced by the king and chiefs of Brass (also known as Nembe), a city-state on the Niger delta with a long history of involvement in trade. More so than other African traders, the Brassmen resisted the British. They complained to British officials, evaded regulations, and occasionally attacked British steamboats and trading facilities. British authorities fined the merchants of Brass for their smuggling and attacks on British property, but they ignored their many petitions of grievance.

QUESTIONS FOR ANALYSIS

1. On the basis of information contained in the two memoranda, describe the economic changes experienced by the merchants of Brass as a result of their dealings with the British in the nineteenth century.
2. What specific grievances do the Brass chiefs have in their dealings with the British? What specific changes in British policy do they seek?
3. In what respects are the Brass traders at a disadvantage in their dealings with the British?
4. How do the Brass traders perceive themselves in their relationship with the British? Do they consider themselves the equals of the British? How do their attitudes compare with those of the African slave traders described in source 48?

KING OCKIYA AND THE CHIEFS OF BRASS TO LORD DERBY, FEBRUARY 1877

Many years ago we used to make our living by selling slaves to Europeans which was stopped by your Government and a Treaty made between you and our country that we discontinue doing so, and that we should enter into a legitimate trade and that if we did so an allowance . . . should be paid us by the traders on all produce bought. This we did and our trade gradually increased. . . . We shipped . . . about 4,500 to 5,000 tons of palm oil per annum.

To do all this we had to open up place[s] on the Niger, trading Stations or markets as we call them up as far [as] a place called Onitha [*sic*] on the Niger. Some years ago the White men began trading on the Niger with the intention of opening up this River, this did us no harm as they went up a long way farther than we could go in their Steamers and also bought a different kind of produce to what we were buying, but lately within the last six years they have begun putting trading Stations at our places and consequences [*sic*] they have stopped our trade completely as well as of those in the Lower part of the River Niger, our living made out of the brokerage and formerly when we sent nearly 5,000 tons of oil away we do not send 1,500 per annum. This means starvation to my people as well as Natives of the Niger under my rule I have about 8,000 people and there are another 8,000 in the lower part of the Niger suffering with me. . . .

We have no land where we can grow plantains or yams and if we cannot trade we must starve, and we earnestly beg and pray that you will take our case into consideration, we do not want anything that is not fair, we only want the markets that we and our money [?] have made to be secured to us and that the white men who have had nothing to do with opening up the Palm Oil trade shall not come and reap all our benefits.

One of the steamers has just been up the Niger and the people over whom I have no rule and who are starving have fought with her and the white men now accuse me and my people of having done it although I assure them I have nothing to do with it. . . . I can truly say that I have never myself nor have I ever allowed my people to break the treaty we have with England nor will I allow them to do so again. I beg that you will look into this affair for me and my people. What we want is that the markets we have made between the river and Onitha should be left to ourselves. . . .

The duties and Regulations of the Company mean to us ruin; of this there is no doubt.

We do not deny that we have smuggled, but under the circumstances can this be wondered at?

We have suffered many hardships from the Company's Regulations. Our people have been fired upon by the Company's launches, they have been fired upon from the Company's hulks, our canoes have been seized and goods taken, sometimes when engaged in what white men call smuggling, and sometimes when not. . . .

Within the last few weeks the Niger Company has sent messengers to the Ejohs and other tribes with whom we have always traded and said that any of them who traded with us at all, or who paid us their debts, would be severely punished, and their villages burnt.

We have evidence to prove all this, which we would like to lay before the big man who has been sent by the Queen.

All these unjust things that have been done to us, the many times we have been told to be patient and have been so, and the wrongs which we consider we have suffered are now worse than ever, all these drove us to take the law into our own hands and attack the Company's factories at Akassa.

We know now we have done wrong, and for this wrong we have been severely punished; but we submit that the many unjust oppressions we have borne have been very great, and it is only in self-defence, and with a view to have our wrongs inquired into, that we have done this thing. . . .

Traders we are, have been, and always will be.

The soil of our country is too poor to cultivate sufficient food for all our people, and so if we do not trade and get food from other tribes we shall suffer great want and misery.

We fervently hope and pray that some arrangements may be arrived at which will enable us to pursue our trade in peace and quietness.

> Warri, his x mark.
> Karemm, ditto.
> Thomas Okea, ditto.
> Nathaniel Hardstone, ditto.

MEMORANDUM OF THE BRASS CHIEFS, JUNE 1895

. . . The Company which is now known as the Niger Company, has done us many injuries . . . ; for some time after the Charter was granted they drove us away from our markets in which we and our forefathers had traded for generations, and did not allow us to get in our trust, or trade debts, some of which remain unpaid to this day. Neither will they permit the Ejoh or market people to come down and pay us.

In 1889, Major Macdonald, now our big Consul, came to us, and we told him of all these things, and he promised that he would lay our complaints before the Queen's Government. . . .

In 1891, he, Major MacDonald, came again and explained to us that it was the intention of the Queen's Government to send Consuls to these rivers and that we should then have a Consul of our own who would specially look after our interests. He pointed out to us that this could not be done without money, and explained how the money could be raised by means of duty, and asked whether we consented to pay these duties. At first we refused, because we could get no satis-factory answer about our markets; but eventually we signed, but begged the Major that he would do what he could to get some of our markets back for us. . . .

Since then we have seen the Major many times, and he has always told us to be patient, but latterly [recently] things have gone from bad to worse, and the markets that we have are quite insufficient to maintain us.

We thoroughly understand that all markets are free, and open to everybody, black and white man alike; and we are quite willing to trade side by side with the white man at those markets. We do not now ask for any exclusive privileges whatever; but only that we may be allowed to trade without molestation at the places we and our fathers have traded in days gone by. . . .

We submit that, if we have to go to Akassa, a distance of nearly 40 miles, to pay our duties, and are only allowed to trade at certain places selected by the Niger Company called 'ports of entry,' and have to take out trade and spirit licences, and pay a very heavy duty going into the territories and a heavy duty coming out, it is the same thing as if we were forbidden to trade at all.

The Niger Company say, 'We (the Company) have to do these things, why not you?'

We can only say that, with our resources, to carry out these Regulations, and pay these duties means ruin to us.

The Niger Company are cleverer than we are. We humbly submit that we have a right, confirmed by our Treaty, to go and trade freely in the places we have traded at for all these generations. We are ready to pay to do so, but let us pay a fair duty, and conform to fair Regulations.

The Fate of the Ndebele
▼▼▼

73 ▼ *Ndansi Kumalo, HIS STORY*

If one seeks proof of the remarkable changes in Africa during the nineteenth and twentieth centuries, consider the fate of the Ndebele (pronounced en-duh-bee'-lee) and the life of one of their sons, Ndansi Kumalo. In the early nineteenth century the Ndebele were pastoralists living in southeastern Africa, a region of political turmoil and economic hardship as a result of overpopulation and drought. In the 1820s they fled from the warriors of the Zulu chieftain Shaka, who in just a few years created a large and formidable Zulu state in southeastern Africa. The Ndebele moved to a region north of the Vaal River but ten years later were forced off their land by Boer *trekkers,* Dutch pioneers from the south who sought grazing land for their cattle. The Ndebele moved north of the Limpopo River to a region that is part of modern Zimbabwe. Despite their years of flight, they were able to subdue other groups in the region and establish a sizable kingdom with a population of 100,000.

But the Ndebele could not escape danger. This time it came from the British, who, under the famous imperialist Cecil Rhodes, were anxious to exploit the region's mineral wealth. In 1888 the Ndebele chieftain, Lobengula, signed an agreement with Rhodes that gave the South Africa Company mining rights in exchange for 1,000 rifles and a monthly stipend of 100 pounds. Friction grew when European settlers began establishing farmsteads around 1890, and war broke out in 1893. The Ndebele were defeated, and they were defeated again when they rose up against the British in 1897. The Ndebele then made one last journey to a vast but arid reservation their new masters provided.

One of the Ndebele who made this journey was Ndansi Kumalo. Born in the late 1870s, he was raised as a warrior to protect Ndebele land and raid neighbors for wives and cattle. He fought against the British in the 1890s and took up farming after the Ndebele's defeat. In 1932 he caught the attention of a British filmmaker who was in Southern Rhodesia to make *Rhodes of Africa,* on the life of Cecil Rhodes. He was recruited to play the part of Lobengula, the Ndebele chieftain. To complete the film he traveled to England, where he took in the sights of London and made his first plane flight. He also related his life story to the English Africanist Margery Perham, whose transcription of it serves as the basis for the following excerpt. *Rhodes of Africa* was a modest success, and after it opened, Ndansi Kumalo returned to Africa, where he rejoined his large family. In the following excerpt he describes events of the 1890s.

QUESTIONS FOR ANALYSIS

1. Who was to blame for the outbreak of hostilities between the Ndebele and the British in 1893?
2. How did conditions following the war lead to the 1897 rebellion?
3. The condition of the Ndebele rapidly deteriorated after the suppression of the rebellion. Why?
4. Aside from raising revenue, what might the British have hoped to achieve by imposing, then raising, taxes on the Ndebele?
5. What economic changes did the Ndebele experience as a result of their subjection to the Europeans?
6. Do you agree with Ndansi Kumalo that the arrival of Europeans was a mixed blessing? Why?

We were terribly upset and very angry at the coming of the white men, for Lobengula . . . was under her . . . [The Queen's] protection and it was quite unjustified that white men should come with force into our country.[1] . . . Lobengula had no war in his heart: he had always protected the white men and been good to them. If he had meant war, would he have sent our regiments far away to the north at this moment? As far as I know the trouble began in this way. Gandani, a chief who was sent out, reported that some of the Mashona[2] had taken the king's cattle; some regiments were detailed to follow and recover them. They followed the Mashona to Ziminto's people. Gandani had strict instructions not to molest the white people established in certain parts and to confine himself to the people who had taken the cattle. The commander was given a letter which he had to produce to the Europeans and tell them what the object of the party was. But the members of the party were restless and went without reporting to the white people and killed a lot of Mashonas. The pioneers were very angry and said, "You have trespassed into our part." They went with the letter, but only after they had killed some people, and the white men said, "You have done wrong, you should have brought the letter first and then we should have given you permission to follow the cattle." The commander received orders from the white people to get out, and up to a certain point which he could not possibly reach in the time allowed. A force followed them up and they defended themselves. When the pioneers turned out there was a fight at Shangani and at Bembezi. . . .

The next news was that the white people had entered Bulawayo; the King's kraal[3] had been burnt down and the King had fled. Of the cattle very few were recovered; most fell into the hands of the white people. Only a very small portion were found and brought to Shangani where the King was, and we went there to give him any assistance we could. . . . Three of our leaders mounted their horses and followed up the King and he wanted to know where his cattle were; they said they had fallen into the hands of the whites, only a few were left. He said, "Go back and bring them along." But they did not go back again; the white forces had occupied Bulawayo and they went into the Matoppos. Then the white people came to where we were living and sent word round that all chiefs and warriors should go into Bulawayo and discuss peace, for the King had gone and they wanted to make peace. . . . The white people said, "Now that your King has deserted you, we occupy your country. Do you submit to us?" What could we do? "If you are sincere, come back and bring in all your arms, guns, and spears." We did so. . . .

So we surrendered to the white people and were told to go back to our homes and live our usual lives and attend to our crops. But the white men sent native police who did abominable things; they were cruel and assaulted a lot of our people and helped themselves to our cattle and goats. These policemen were not our own people; anybody was made a policeman. We were treated like slaves. They came and were overbearing and we were ordered to carry their clothes and bundles. They interfered with our wives and our daughters and molested them. In fact, the treatment we received was intolerable. We thought it best to fight and die rather than bear it. How the rebellion started I do not know; there was no organization, it was like a fire that suddenly flames up. We had been flogged by native police and then they rubbed salt water in the wounds. There was much bitterness because so many of our cattle were branded and taken away from us; we had no property, nothing we could call our own. We said, "It is no good living under such conditions; death would be better — let us fight." Our King

---

[1] In the agreement Lobengula signed with Rhodes in 1888 the British government (Her Majesty's government) guaranteed there would be no English settlers on Ndebele land and no decrease of Lobengula's authority. Lobengula's conces-sions angered many of his warriors, who began to press for war against the Europeans.
[2] Pastoralists subject to the Ndebele.
[3] The stockade where the king lived.

gone, we had submitted to the white people and they ill-treated us until we became desperate and tried to make an end of it all. We knew that we had very little chance because their weapons were so much superior to ours. But we meant to fight to the last, feeling that even if we could not beat them we might at least kill a few of them and so have some sort of revenge.

I fought in the rebellion. We used to look out for valleys where the white men were likely to approach. We took cover behind rocks and trees and tried to ambush them. We were forced by the nature of our weapons not to expose ourselves. I had a gun, a breech-loader. They — the white men — fought us with big guns and Maxims[4] and rifles.

I remember a fight in the Matoppos when we charged the white men. There were some hundreds of us; the white men also were as many. We charged them at close quarters: we thought we had a good chance to kill them but the Maxims were too much for us. We drove them off at the first charge, but they returned and formed up again. We made a second charge, but they were too strong for us. I cannot say how many white people were killed, but we think it was quite a lot. . . . Many of our people were killed in this fight: I saw four of my cousins shot. One was shot in the jaw and the whole of his face was blown away — like this — and he died. One was hit between the eyes; another here, in the shoulder; another had part of his ear shot off. We made many charges but each time we were beaten off, until at last the white men packed up and retreated. But for the Maxims, it would have been different. . . .

So peace was made. Many of our people had been killed, and now we began to die of starvation; and then came the rinderpest[5] and the cattle that were still left to us perished. We could not help thinking that all these dreadful things were brought by the white people. We struggled, and the Government helped us with grain; and by degrees we managed to get crops and pulled

through. Our cattle were practically wiped out, but a few were left and from them we slowly bred up our herds again. We were offered work in the mines and farms to earn money and so were able to buy back some cattle. At first, of course, we were not used to going out to work, but advice was given that the chief should advise the young people to go out to work, and gradually they went. At first we received a good price for our cattle and sheep and goats. Then the tax came. It was 10s.[6] a year. Soon the Government said, "That is too little, you must contribute more; you must pay £1." We did so. Then those who took more than one wife were taxed; 10s. for each additional wife. The tax is heavy, but that is not all. We are also taxed for our dogs; 5s. for a dog. Then we were told we were living on private land; the owners wanted rent in addition to the Government tax; some 10s. some £1, some £2 a year. . . .

Would I like to have the old days back? Well, the white men have brought some good things. For a start, they brought us European implements — plows; we can buy European clothes, which are an advance. The Government has arranged for education and through that, when our children grow up, they may rise in status. We want them to be educated and civilized and make better citizens. Even in our own time there were troubles, there was much fighting and many innocent people were killed. It is infinitely better to have peace instead of war, and our treatment generally by the officials is better than it was at first. But, under the white people, we still have our troubles. Economic conditions are telling on us very severely. We are on land where the rainfall is scanty, and things will not grow well. In our own time we could pick our own country, but now all the best land has been taken by the white people. We get hardly any price for our cattle; we find it hard to meet our money obligations. If we have crops to spare we get very little for them; we find it difficult to make ends meet

---

[4]Invented by the American-born engineer Hiram S. Maxim, the Maxim gun was an early machine gun.

[5]An acute infectious disease of cattle.

[6]s. = shilling, one-twentieth of a pound.

and wages are very low. When I view the position, I see that our rainfall has diminished, we have suffered drought and have poor crops and we do not see any hope of improvement, but all the same our taxes do not diminish. We see no prosperous days ahead of us. There is one thing we think an injustice. When we have plenty of grain the prices are very low, but the moment we are short of grain and we have to buy from Europeans at once the price is high. If when we have hard times and find it difficult to meet our obligations some of these burdens were taken off us it would gladden our hearts. As it is, if we do raise anything, it is never our own: all, or most of it, goes back in taxation. We can never save any money. If we could, we could help ourselves: we could build ourselves better houses; we could buy modern means of traveling about, a cart, or donkeys or mules.

As to my own life, I have had twelve wives altogether, five died and seven are alive. I have twenty-six children alive, five have died. Of my sons five are married and are all at work farming; three young children go to school. I hope the younger children will all go to school. I think it is a good thing to go to school.

There are five schools in our district. Quite a number of people are Christians, but I am too old to change my ways. In our religion we believe that when anybody dies the spirit remains and we often make offerings to the spirits to keep them good-tempered. But now the making of offerings is dying out rapidly, for every member of the family should be present, but the children are Christians and refuse to come, so the spirit-worship is dying out. A good many of our children go to the mines in the Union, for the wages are better there. Unfortunately a large number do not come back at all. And some send money to their people — others do not. Some men have even deserted their families, their wives, and children. If they cannot go by train they walk long distances.

▼▼▼

Southwest Asia under Siege

Each decade of the nineteenth century confirmed what had been apparent for at least a century, namely that years of misgovernment, economic stagnation, and military neglect had enfeebled the once-powerful and culturally sophisticated Persian and Ottoman empires. The Ottoman Empire lost its territories in north Africa and southeastern Europe, and escaped embarrassing and potentially fatal military defeats by Russia and its one-time province, Egypt, only because Great Britain and France dreaded the consequences of its disintegration and intervened on its behalf. Under the Qajar Dynasty, Persia lost territory on each side of the Caspian Sea to Russia and lands around the Persian Gulf to Great Britain. At times Russian and British consular officials in Teheran, not the shah and his officials, appeared to be in charge of Persian affairs.

What economic development occurred in the region mainly benefited European businessmen. Ottoman, Persian, and Egyptian governments all welcomed European investors and borrowed heavily from European financiers, who then "rescued" them from their unpayable debts in return for monopolies, control of governmental expenditures, and a cut of tax revenues. When in 1876 the Egyptian government failed to make required payments on its loans, two officials, one British and one French, took over its finances and became the real rulers of Egypt. They hired well-paid Europeans to administer the country and made debt liquidation the fiscal priority of the state. In 1882, following anti-European demonstrations and an attempted military revolt led by Colonel Ahmad Urabi, the British bombarded Alexandria, occupied Cairo, and established a protectorate over Egypt, making it for all intents and purposes a British colony until 1936.

Intellectuals, military men, and religious leaders throughout the region debated the causes and significance of these developments, and government officials, especially within the Ottoman state, took action by implementing reforms. Such reformers loosely fit into one of two categories. Moderates, or as they are sometimes called, "conservative modernizers," sought to reorganize the army, end corruption, improve tax collection, and reform the judiciary while preserving the authority of traditional rulers. Reformers in this camp cautiously approved greater intellectual and cultural contacts with the West and accepted the need for European investment. By the 1870s, other more progressive reformers, such as the Young Ottomans, went beyond proposals for military and administrative reform; they sought greater acceptance of Western science and secularism and demanded parliaments, written constitutions, elections, and guarantees of individual freedoms.

Reformers in both camps faced formidable obstacles. Powerful families and well-placed officials who benefited from the status quo naturally opposed them. So did many religious leaders, who feared that all reforms at some level were European-inspired and thus inevitably would weaken Islam by encouraging secularization. True reform, they believed, would come not from modern weapons and new law codes, but from rededication to Islam. Many Islamic religious leaders thus supported the autocratic and reactionary rule of the Ottoman sultan Abbul Hamid II (1876–1909) and undercut the parliamentary regime established by the Persian Revolution of 1906 by demanding a legal system based on Islamic law rather than Western legal codes.

The reformers' biggest obstacle was lack of money. The costs of modern armies, schools, roads, telegraph lines, bridges, and steamships outstripped revenues, forcing governments to rely on European loans and investments and to accept European control of taxes and expenditures. In other words, the reformers' policies fostered greater economic dependency on the West, one of the things they most wished to avoid.

In the end, reformers and revolutionaries in the Middle East were unable to halt Western intervention or stave off political disaster. Egypt remained a British protectorate. In 1907 Persia was divided into a Russian north and British south, with only the central portion under the control of the Qajars, who were overthrown by a military coup in 1925. The Ottoman Empire lost all but a tiny sliver of its European territories as a result of the Balkan Wars of 1912 and 1913 and lost its Arab provinces during World War I. It disappeared altogether when the sultan's government was overthrown by Turkish nationalists in 1920 and replaced by the modern state of Turkey.

Ottoman Reforms in the Tanzimat Era

▼▼▼

74 ▼ *Sultan Abdul Mejid, IMPERIAL RESCRIPT*

Serious efforts to reverse the Ottoman Empire's political and military decline can be traced back to the reign of Selim III (r. 1789–1807), who sought to revitalize the Ottoman army by importing foreign officers, updating weapons, and tightening discipline. These modest reforms were bitterly opposed by many Islamic religious leaders and by the janissaries, once the elite of the Ottoman army, but now mainly concerned with protecting their privileges. As a result, Selim was deposed in 1807 and then murdered. Mahmud II (r. 1808–1839) achieved some permanent military and administrative reforms, largely because of his destruction of the reactionary janissary corps in 1826 and his success in weakening some of the authority of conservative Islamic judges. Despite his efforts, his armies were badly defeated when he sent them into battle against the forces of the Egyptian pasha Muhammad Ali in 1832 and 1839. Yet another era of reform began during the reign of Abdul Mejid (r. 1839–1861). Inspired by the sultan's foreign minister and later grand vizier, Mustafa Reshid, it came to be known as the era of *Tanzimat,* which literally means restructuring. This movement, which maintained its momentum until the reign of Abdul Hamid II (r. 1876–1909), sought to save the empire by administrative reform, expansion of education, and the adoption of Western legal concepts and practices.

Two of the most important documents in the Tanzimat Era were proclamations issued by Sultan Abdul Mejid. The first, known as the Noble Rescript, was issued shortly after he became sultan in 1839. In it he committed himself to ending government corruption, confirming the rights of non-Muslims, and protecting all subjects from arbitrary arrest. Seventeen years later, in 1856, he made a second, broader statement, known as the Imperial Rescript. This represented the high point of efforts to reform the Ottoman Empire while maintaining its authoritarian government and traditional mix of Muslim, Christian, and Jewish subjects.

QUESTIONS FOR ANALYSIS

1. What benefits were the sultan's non-Muslim subjects to receive as a result of this proclamation?
2. What efforts were to be made to improve the empire's system of justice?
3. What do the decrees dealing with the economy suggest about the state of the empire's economic situation?
4. To what extent does this document extend meaningful political rights to the sultan's subjects?
5. In what respects does this document reflect Western liberal ideals of individual freedom and religious toleration?

Let it be done as herein set forth. . . . It being now my desire to renew and enlarge still more the new Institutions ordained with the view of establishing a state of things conformable with the dignity of my Empire and — . . . by the kind and friendly assistance of the Great Powers, my noble Allies,[1] . . . The guarantees promised on our part by the Hatti-Humaïoun of Gülhané,[2] and in conformity with the Tanzimat, . . . are today confirmed and consolidated, and efficacious measures shall be taken in order that they may have their full and entire effect.

All the privileges and spiritual immunities granted by my ancestors from time immemorial, and at subsequent dates, to all Christian communities or other non-Muslim persuasions established in my empire, under my protection, shall be confirmed and maintained.

Every Christian or other non-Muslim community shall be bound within a fixed period, and with the concurrence of a commission composed . . . of members of its own body, to proceed with my high approbation and under the inspection of my Sublime Porte,[3] to examine into its actual immunities and privileges, and to discuss and submit to my Sublime Porte the reforms required by the progress of civilization and of the age. The powers conceded to the Christian Patriarchs and Bishops[4] by the Sultan Mehmed II[5] and his successors, shall be made to harmonize with the new position which my generous and beneficient intentions ensure to these communities. . . . The ecclesiastical dues, of whatever sort of nature they be, shall be abolished and replaced by fixed revenues of the Patriarchs and heads of communities. . . . In the towns, small boroughs, and villages, where the whole population is of the same religion, no obstacle shall be offered to the repair, according to their original plan, of buildings set apart for religious worship, for schools, for hospitals, and for cemeteries. . . .

Every distinction or designation tending to make any class whatever of the subjects of my Empire inferior to another class, on account of their religion, language, or race, shall be forever effaced from Administrative Protocol. The laws shall be put in force against the use of any injurious or offensive term, either among private individuals or on the part of the authorities. . . .

As all forms of religion are and shall be freely professed in my dominions, no subject of my Empire shall be hindered in the exercise of the religion that he professes. . . . No one shall be compelled to change their religion . . . and . . . all the subjects of my Empire, without distinction of nationality, shall be admissible to public employments. . . . All the subjects of my Empire, without distinction, shall be received into the civil and military schools of the government. . . . Moreover, every community is authorized to establish public schools of science, art, and industry. . . .

All commercial, correctional, and criminal suits between Muslims and Christian or other non-Muslim subjects, or between Christian or other non-Muslims of different sects, shall be referred to Mixed Tribunals. The proceedings of these Tribunals shall be public; the parties shall be confronted, and shall produce their witnesses, whose testimony shall be received, without distinction, upon an oath taken according to the religious law of each sect. . . .

Penal, correctional, and commercial laws, and rules of procedure for the Mixed Tribunals, shall be drawn up as soon as possible, and formed into a code. . . . Proceedings shall be taken, for the reform of the penitentiary system. . . .

The organization of the police . . . shall be revised in such a manner as to give to all the peace-

[1]During the Crimean War (1853–1856) the Ottoman Empire was allied with Great Britain and France against Russia. France and Great Britain at the time were encouraging Ottoman military reform to offset the power of Russia in the region.
[2]This refers to the Noble Rescript of 1839.
[3]"Sublime Porte" refers to the building that housed the grand vizier and other high officials of the Ottoman state. It is a translation of the Turkish words *Bab-i-Ali,* or "high gate." The term is used to refer to Ottoman leadership in much the same way that the "White House" refers to the American presidency.
[4]The reference is to ruling officials of the Greek and Armenian churches in the Ottoman Empire.
[5]Ottoman ruler from 1451 to 1481.

able subjects of my Empire the strongest guarantees for the safety both of their persons and property. . . . Christian subjects, and those of other non-Muslim sects, . . . shall, as well as Muslims, be subject to the obligations of the Law of Recruitment [for military service]. The principle of obtaining substitutes, or of purchasing exemption, shall be admitted.

Proceedings shall be taken for a reform in the constitution of the Provincial and Communal Councils, in order to ensure fairness in the choice of the deputies of the Muslim, Christian, and other communities, and freedom of voting in the Councils. . . .

As the laws regulating the purchase, sale, and disposal of real property are common to all the subjects of my Empire, it shall be lawful for foreigners to possess landed property in my dominions. . . .

The taxes are to be levied under the same denomination from all the subjects of my Empire, without distinction of class or of religion. The most prompt and energetic means for remedying the abuses in collecting the taxes, and especially the tithes, shall be considered. The system of direct collection shall gradually, and as soon as possible, be substituted for the plan of farming,[6] in all the branches of the revenues of the state.

A special law having been already passed, which declares that the budget of the revenue and the expenditure of the state shall be drawn up and made known every year, the said law shall be most scrupulously observed. . . .

The heads of each community and a delegate, designated by my Sublime Porte, shall be summoned to take part in the deliberations of the Supreme Council of Justice on all occasions which might interest the generality of the subjects of my Empire. . . .

Steps shall be taken for the formation of banks and other similar institutions, so as to effect a reform in the monetary and financial system, as well as to create funds to be employed in augmenting the sources of the material wealth of my empire.

Everything that can impede commerce or agriculture shall be abolished. To accomplish these objects means shall be sought to profit by science, the art, and the funds of Europe, and thus gradually to execute them.

---

[6]Tax farming, in which the government contracted with private financiers who collected taxes for a profit.

Persian Opposition to the Tobacco Concession
▼▼▼

75 ▼ Sayyid Jamal ad-Din, *LETTER TO HASAN SHIRAZI*

European imperialism did not always involve gunboats, invading armies, and control by colonial administrators. It frequently was more economic than political. Both the Ottoman Empire and Persia remained independent states in the 1800s, but their finances and economies were increasingly controlled and manipulated by European bondholders, bankers, businessmen, and speculators. Their experience is as much a part of the West's imperialist expansion as that of India, Africa, and Southeast Asia.

For Persia, economic imperialism was epitomized by the numerous concessions granted to foreign businessmen by the shah's government. These agreements gave Europeans control of a sector of the nation's economy, usually in return for a one-time payment and an annual percentage of profits. Viewed as a painless way to attract foreign capital, solve budget problems, and generate bribes, such arrangements were irresistible to Persia's shahs and their ministers. Hundreds of concessions were granted for activities ranging from railroad construction to the founding and administration of a national lottery. By far the most ambitious such agreement was the concession granted in 1872 to Baron Julius de Reuter, a British subject. De Reuter gained control of much of Persia's economy — factories, minerals, irrigation works, agricultural improvements, and virtually any other enterprise that had to do with Persia's economic modernization — for a period of seventy years. The Russians and many Persians were outraged, and largely because of their opposition, government officials found reasons to withdraw the concession, although keeping the payments (legal and illegal) de Reuter had made.

Despite the outcry over the de Reuter concession, the number of concessions granted by Shah Nasir al-Din and his ministers mounted in the 1870s and 1880s. Many Persians experienced deep frustration over their inability to dissuade their autocratic and concession-loving ruler from selling off the nation's economic future to foreigners. This changed, however, in 1891, when for the first and only time in history a government abandoned an unpopular policy after the adult population "kicked the habit" and gave up tobacco smoking.

In 1891 Persians learned of a new concession granted to the British Imperial Tobacco Corporation for the purchase, processing, and sale of tobacco, for which it paid the shah 15,000 pounds and promised him 25 percent of annual profits. The English expected to reap huge profits, but the Persians expected to pay inflated prices for a product they grew, used heavily, and previously had marketed themselves. Persia erupted with demonstrations, angry sermons, calls for boycotts, destruction of tobacco warehouses, and denunciations of the shah. Then in December Persia's most prominent Shia religious leader, Hasan Shirazi, ordered Persians to give up tobacco smoking until the concession was lifted. The nation obeyed, and within only a few days the concession was canceled.

A key figure in the campaign against the tobacco concession was the Islamic intellectual Sayyid Jamal ad-Din "al Afghani," who since 1889 had resided in Teheran. Born in 1838 or 1839 in Persia and raised as a Shia, he was educated in Persia, learned of the West while visiting British India and Europe, and traveled and taught throughout the Middle East. In his many writings and speeches Jamal ad-Din blended Islamic traditionalism and a selective acceptance of Western science, technology, and values. He taught that only a religious and intellectual revival that transcended state boundaries and sectarian differences could save Islam from subservience to the West.

From the time he moved to Teheran, Jamal ad-Din was a vocal critic of the shah. Fearing arrest, he sought sanctuary at a holy shrine, but the shah's soldiers forcefully removed him in January 1891 and deported him to Ottoman territory. From exile, in April 1891 he wrote the following letter to Hasan Shirazi. It is unclear how much influence Jamal ad-Din's letter had, but as Jamal ad-Din had hoped, Shirazi did abandon his apolitical stance by denouncing the shah and then issuing the antismoking decree.

The shah stayed in power and the foreigners remained, but for the first time in their modern history, all Persians, rural and urban, religious and secular, had united for a political end. Such unity of purpose reappeared in the Persian Revolution of 1906, which, for a time, established a parliamentary government for Persia.

QUESTIONS FOR ANALYSIS

1. What strategies does Jamal ad-Din use to convince Hasan Shirazi that he should speak out against the shah? What does he claim would be the consequences of inaction?
2. According to Jamal ad-Din, what are the personal faults of the shah? Are his criticisms based more on religious or nonreligious considerations?
3. What has been the result of the shah's fiscal and economic policies, according to the author?
4. What view of the West is expressed in the letter?
5. What seems to be Jamal ad-Din's vision of Persia's future?
6. What differences do you see between the ideas and spirit of Jamal ad-Din's letter and those of the rescript of Sultan Abdul Mejid (source 74)?
7. What does the letter reveal about the prospects and progress of reform in Persia, as compared to the Ottoman Empire?

. . . Hasan Shirazi — may God protect by your means the fold of Islam, and avert the plots of the vile unbelievers! —

God . . . has chosen you out of the true communion, and has committed to your hands the reins to guide the people obediently to the most luminous Law, and thus to protect their rights, and to guard their hearts from errors and doubts. He has entrusted to you out of all mankind (so that you have become the heir of the Prophet) the care of those weighty interests by which the people shall prosper in this world and attain happiness in the hereafter. He has assigned to you the throne of authority, and has bestowed on you such supremacy over his people as empowers you to save and defend their country and testify for them to the ways of those who have gone before. . . .

O most mighty Religious Guide! Verily the Shah's purpose wavers, his character is impure, his perceptions are failing and his heart is corrupt. He is incapable of governing the land, or managing the affairs of his people, and has en-trusted the reins of government in all things great and small to the hands of a wicked free-thinker,[1] a tyrant and usurper, who reviles the Prophets openly, and heeds not God's Law, who counts for nothing the religious authorities, curses the doctors of the Law, rejects the pious, condemns honorable Sayyids[2] and treats preachers as one would treat the vilest of mankind. Moreover since his return from Europe he . . . drinks wine openly,[3] associates with unbelievers and displays enmity toward the virtuous. Such is his private conduct; but in addition to this he has sold to the foes of our Faith the greater part of the Persian lands and the profits derived from them, for example, the mines, the roads leading to them, the roads connecting them with the frontiers of the country, the inns about to be built by the side of these extensive means of travel which will spread out through all parts of the kingdom, and the gardens and fields surrounding them. Also the river Karun[4] and the guesthouses which will arise on its banks up to its very source, and the gardens and meadows which ad-

---

[1]Amin al-Sultan, the shah's grand vizier.
[2]Descendants of Muhammad.
[3]A forbidden act according to the Quran.

[4]In 1888 an Englishman had been granted a concession to open steamship traffic on the river.

join it, and the highway from Ahwaz to Teheran, with the buildings, inns, gardens, and fields surrounding it. Also tobacco, with the chief centers of its cultivation, the lands on which it is grown, and the warehouses, carriers, and sellers, wherever these are found. He has similarly disposed of the grapes used for making wine, and the shops, factories, and winepresses pertaining to this trade throughout the whole of Persia; and so likewise soap, candles, and sugar, and the factories connected with their manufacture. Lastly there is the Bank:[5] what must you understand about the Bank? It means the complete handing over of the reins of government to the enemy of Islam, the enslaving of the people to that enemy, the surrendering of them and of all dominion and authority into the hands of the foreign foe.

After this the ignorant traitor, desiring to pacify the people by his futile arguments, pretended that these agreements were temporary, and these compacts were only for a limited period which would not exceed a hundred years! God! what an argument, the weakness of which amazed even the traitors! . . .

In short this criminal has offered the provinces of Persia to auction among the Powers,[6] and is selling the realms of Islam and the abodes of Muhammad and his household (on whom be greeting and salutation) to foreigners. But by reason of the vileness of his nature and meanness of his understanding he sells them for a paltry sum and at a wretched price. . . .

And you, O Proof, if you will not arise to help this people, and will not unite them in purpose, and pluck them forth, by the power of the Holy Law from the hands of this sinner, verily the realms of Islam will soon be under the control of foreigners, who will rule . . . as they please and do what they will. If this opportunity is lost . . . and this thing happens while you are alive, verily you will not leave behind . . . a fair record in the register of time and on the pages of history. And you know that the *ulama*[7] of Persia and the Persian people . . . with one accord (their spirits being troubled and their hearts distressed) await a word from you with which they shall behold their happiness and by which their deliverance shall be effected. How then can it seem that one on whom God has bestowed such power as this to be so reluctant to use it or to leave it suspended?

I further assure Your Eminence . . . that the Ottoman Government will rejoice in your undertaking of this effort and will aid you in it, for it is well aware that the intervention of Europeans in the Persian domains and their ascendancy there will assuredly prove injurious to its own dominions. Moreover all the ministers and lords of Persia will rejoice in a word in this sense uttered by you, seeing that all of them naturally detest these innovations and are constitutionally opposed to these agreements, which your actions will give them the opportunity to annul, that perhaps they may restrain this evil of covetousness which has been sanctioned and approved. . . . All is from you, by you and in you, and you are responsible for all before God and men. . . .

As for my own story and what that ungrateful tyrant did to me . . . the wretch [the shah] commanded me to be dragged, when I was in sanctuary in the shrine of Shah 'Abdu'l-'Azim and grievously ill, through the snow to the capital with such circumstances of disrespect, humiliation and disgrace as cannot be imagined for wickedness. . . .

Thereafter his miserable lackeys placed me, despite my illness, on a pack-saddle, loading me with chains, and this in the winter season, amid the snow-drifts and bitter, icy blasts, and a company of horsemen conveyed me to Khaniqin,[8] guarded by an escort. And he had previously written to the . . . Turkish governor, requesting him to remove me to Basra, knowing well that, if he left me alone, I should come to you. . . . For he knew for a certainty that, should I succeed in meeting you, it would not be possible for him to continue in his office, involving as it does the ruin of the country, the destruction of the people, and the encouragement of unbelief. . . . What is

---

[5]The Imperial Bank of Persia had been granted a sixty-year concession to issue bank notes and carry on other banking activities.

[6]The Great Powers of Europe.
[7]Those learned in religion; the Muslim clergy.
[8]A Turkish frontier post on the road from Persia to Baghdad.

this weakness? What this cowardice? How is it possible that a low-born vagabond and contemptible fool should be able to sell the Muslims and their lands for a vile price and a paltry sum, scorn the *ulama,* treat with disrespect the descendants of the Prophet, and slander in such fashion Sayyids of the House of 'Ali? Is there no hand able to pluck up this evil root and so to appease the wrathful indignation of the Muslims, and avenge the descendants of the Chief of God's Apostles (upon whom and whose household be blessings and salutation)? . . .

The Beginnings of Arab Nationalism

▼▼▼

76 ▼ *ANNOUNCEMENT TO THE ARABS, SONS OF QAHTAN*

Of all the non-Turkish ethnic groups in the Ottoman Empire, the Arabs were the sultan's least troublesome during the nineteenth century. Attached to the Ottoman state through deeply ingrained habits of loyalty and the perception of the sultan/caliph as protector of the Islamic community, or *umma,* the Arabs, unlike the Balkan Christians, Kurds, and Armenians, experienced no surge of nationalism and made no demands for independence or greater autonomy. This changed in the years directly preceding the outbreak of World War I, when Arab nationalism suddenly intensified. It gained strength during the Arab revolt against the Ottomans in World War I and has continued to be a significant part of the region's politics to the present day.

Although Arab nationalism became a political force only on the eve of World War I, its roots can be traced back to the nineteenth century, when publications of Arabic language printing houses and the establishment of schools and universities in major Arab cities under the auspices of French Jesuit and American Prostestant missionaries sparked renewed interest in Arab history and literature. These same missionary schools also introduced Arab students to Western science and Western ideas of constitutionalism and liberalism. Continued Ottoman misrule and military losses in the Balkans also encouraged the growth of Arab consciousness. The Ottoman Empire, some suggested, was no longer capable of defending the interests of Islam, and a few went further to suggest that the Islamic community would continue to decline until its founders and natural leaders, the Arabs, regained control.

Arab discontent intensified after the Young Turk Revolution of 1908. Although many Arabs had supported the Young Turks' political agenda before the revolution, they turned against the new regime after it replaced Arab officials with Turks, stripped many old Arab families of their local authority, mandated the use of Turkish throughout the empire, and encouraged the further secularization of education and the law. Arab political organizations formed in Cairo, Beirut, Damascus, Baghdad, and Aleppo, with some advocating greater Arab autonomy within the empire, and others demanding Arab independence.

Independence clearly was the goal of the author or authors of the following "announcement" to the Arabs, which appeared in Cairo in the summer of 1914. It may have been written by a supporter of Major Aziz Ali-al-Misri, a decorated Arab officer in the Ottoman Army and founder of the Covenant, an organization of Arab officers dedicated to Arab independence. Arrested and condemned to death by Ottoman officials in early 1914, he was released later in the year and allowed to go to Cairo as a result of foreign pressure and public outcry among the Arabs.

QUESTIONS FOR ANALYSIS

1. The author's nationalism is directed against both the Turks and the West. What, specifically, are his views of each?
2. Does he have a deeper aversion for the Turks or for the Western nations? Why?
3. In the view of the author, what lessons can the Arabs learn from the Armenians?
4. How does the author define "Arab"?
5. What role does religion play in connection with the author's nationalism? How committed is he to Islam?
6. What are the author's goals for the Arab people? How does he believe these goals can be attained?

O Sons of Qahtan! O Descendants of Adnan![1] Are you asleep? And how long will you remain asleep? . . . When will you realize the truth? When will you know that your country has been sold to the foreigner? See how your natural resources have been alienated from you and have come into the possession of England, France, and Germany. Have you no right to these resources? You have become humiliated slaves in the hands of the usurping tyrant; the foreigner unjustly dispossesses you of the fruit of your work and labor and leaves you to suffer the pangs of hunger. How long will it be before you understand that you have become a plaything in the hand of him who has no religion but to kill the Arabs and forcibly to seize their possessions? The Country is yours, and they say that rule belongs to the people, but those who exercise rule over you in the name of the Constitution[2] do not consider you part of the people, for they inflict on you all kinds of suffering, tyranny, and persecution. How, then, can they concede to you any political rights? In their eyes you are but a flock of sheep whose wool is to be clipped, whose milk is to be drunk, and whose meat is to be eaten. . . .

The Armenians, small as their numbers are when compared to yours, have won their administrative autonomy in spite of the opposition of the Turkish state, and they will presently become independent.[3] Their people will then become

---

[1]Qahtan, or Kahtan, was supposedly the ancient ancestor of all south Arabs; Adnan was the ancestor of north Arabs.

[2]The Constitution of 1876, restored for a time by the Young Turks.

[3]These claims are exaggerated. Slightly more than 1 million Armenians were Ottoman subjects, with most of them living in eastern Anatolia. An upsurge in Armenian nationalism at the end of the nineteenth century led to a proliferation of Armenian political groups, antigovernment terrorism, and public demonstrations against Turkish rule. Abdul Hamid's government responded by ordering, or at least condoning, massacres of perhaps as many as one hundred thousand Armenians by Ottoman troops and mobs between 1894 and 1897. Another massacre of approximately twenty thousand Armenians took place in the village of Adana in 1909. Such atrocities outraged world opinion, and European governments pressured the Ottomans to implement reforms on behalf of the Armenians. A plan worked out in 1914 that established two large provinces with heavy Armenian populations in eastern Anatolia and placed them under the administrative authority of Europeans was agreed upon by the Ottoman government and the European powers. With the outbreak of World War I, however, the plan was dropped. During the war government-ordered evacuations of Armenians from their homelands and attacks on Armenian communities resulted in more than a million Armenian deaths.

self-governing, free and advanced, free and active in the social organization of humanity, in contrast to you, who will remain ever enslaved to the descendants of Genghis and Hulagu[4] who brought to an end your advanced Arab government in Baghdad, the Abode of Peace; and to the descendants of Tamerlane[5] who built a tower composed of the heads of eighty thousand Arabs in Aleppo. Till when will you go on acquiescing in this utter humiliation, when your honor is made free of, your wives raped, your children orphaned, your habitations destroyed, so that the Byzantine capital should be defended, your money taken to be spent in the palaces of Constantinople, full as they are with intoxicating drink, musical instruments, and all kinds of wealth and luxury, and your young men driven to fight your Arab brethren. . . . Has your Arab blood become congealed in your veins, and has it changed into dirty water? You have become, by God, a byword among the nations, a laughingstock of the world, a subject of mockery and derision among the peoples. You have almost become proverbial in your humility, weakness, and acquiescence in great loss.

Compare how well the Turks treat the Armenians and how they seek to humor them, with the harsh treatment which they reserve for you Arabs. See how the Turkish government adopts the stance of obedience before them, how it humbly begs them to accept more than their due share of parliamentary representation. As for you, O how we grieve for you! The government directs against you those armies which had been defeated on the Russian front and in the Balkans,[6] in order to kill you, destroy your liberty, destroy your noble Arab race, and finally to finish you off, as though it can have no power but over you. . . .

O sons of Qahtan! Do you not know that man is meant to live here on earth a goodly life, in honor and prosperity, a life full of spiritual values, and that he founds states which safeguard these things, the most precious gift of God to the sons of Adam, to which they hold very fast? What, then, is the value of life, when honor is stained, possessions robbed, and souls destroyed? What is the meaning of a life spent in humiliation and subjection, without honor, without possessions, without enjoyment of liberty and independence? . . .

O ye Arabs! Warn the people of the Yemen, of Asir, of Nejd, and of Iraq[7] against the intrigues of your enemies. Be united, in the Syrian and Iraqi provinces, with the members of your race and fatherland. Let the Muslims, the Christians, and the Jews be as one in working for the interest of the nation and of the country. You all dwell in one land, you speak one language, so be also one nation and one land. Do not become divided against yourselves according to the designs and purposes of the troublemakers who feign Islam, while Islam is really innocent of their misdeeds. . . .

Unite then and help one another, and do not say, O ye Muslims: This is a Christian, and this is a Jew, for you are all God's dependents, and religion is for God alone. God has commanded us, in his precious Arabic Book and at the hand of his Arab Adnanian Prophet, to follow justice and equality, to deal faithfully with him who does not fight us, even though his religion is different, and to fight him who uses us tyrannously. Who, then, have tyrannized over the Arabs? Have the Christian Arabs or any others sent armed expeditions to the Yemen, to Nejd, or to Iraq? Is it not the band of Constantinople who fight you and

---

[4]Chinggis Khan (1167–1227) was the Mongol ruler who conquered northern China, central Asia and Persia; his grandson Hulagu, or Hülegü, led the armies that sacked Baghdad in 1258, killing an estimated two hundred thousand inhabitants and bringing an end to the Abbasid Dynasty.
[5]Tamerlane (ca. 1336–1405) was a conqueror of Turko-Mongol ancestry. His armies carved out a short-lived empire that stretched from Asia Minor to India. His most notorious custom was to pile his victims' skulls in huge pyramids after a city had been sacked.

[6]The Ottoman government had been fighting and losing wars in the Balkans since the 1820s; their most recent defeat had come in the Balkan War of 1912–1913. The last major war with Russia had been fought in 1877 and 1878 with disastrous results for the Ottomans.
[7]Yemen, Asir, and Nejd are all regions of the Arabian Peninsula; Iraq was a province centered on the Tigris/Euphrates rivers. The Ottoman government had sent troops to all these regions to quell disturbances or control local Arab rulers.

seek to exterminate some of the Arabs by means of sword and fire, and others by means of quarrels and dissensions, following the maxim "divide and rule"? . . .

Every tyrannical government is an enemy and a foe to Islam; how more so, then, if the government destroys Islam, considers it lawful to shed the blood of the people of the Prophet of Islam, and seeks to kill the language of Islam in the name of Islamic government and the Islamic caliphate? . . . Therefore, he who supports these unionists[8] because he considers them Muslims is in clear error, for none of them have done a good deed for Islam. . . . Fanatic in its cause, they fight the Quran and the tradition of the Arabic Prophet. Is this the Islam which it is incumbent on them to respect? It is not notorious that they seek to kill the Arabic language? Did they not write books to show that it must be abandoned, and that prayers and the call to prayers should be made in Turkish? And if Arabic dies, how can the Quran and the traditions live? And if the Book and the traditions cease to be known, what remains of Islam?

And O ye Christian and Jewish Arabs, combine with your brethren the Muslim Arabs, and do not follow in the footsteps of him who says to you, whether he be one of you or not: The Arab Muslims are sunk in religious fanaticism, therefore we prefer the irreligious Turks. This is nonsensical speech which proceeds from an ignorant man who knows neither his own nor his people's interest. . . . Our ancestors were not fanatical in

this sense, for Jews and Christians used to study in the mosques of Baghdad and the Andalus like brethren. Let them, both sides, aim at tolerance and at the removal of these ugly fanaticisms. For you must know that those who do not speak your tongue are more harmful to you than the ignorant fanatics among the Arabs, since you can reach understanding with the Arabs who are your brethren in patriotism and race, while it is difficult for you to reach agreement with these contemptible creatures who are at the same time your enemies and the enemies of the Muslim Arabs. See how, when you are friendly to them, they maltreat you, look down on you, and withhold your rights. Combine with your fellow countrymen and your kin, and know that ugly fanaticism will inevitably disappear. A day will come when fanaticism will disappear from our country, leaving no trace, and that day shall be when our affairs will be in our own hands, and when our affairs, our learning, and the verdicts of our courts will be conducted in our own language. If we are united, such a day is not far off. . . .

The reform of which we speak is not on the principle of decentralization coupled with allegiance to the minions of Constantinople, but on the principle of complete independence and the formation of a decentralized Arab state which will revive our ancient glories and rule the country on autonomous lines, according to the needs of each province.

---

[8]Refers to the Committee of Union and Progress, the political party of the Young Turks.

▼▼▼

India under British Domination

As Great Britain took control of India during the nineteenth century, British administrators, policymakers, and the general public all agreed that this new colony should serve the economic interests of the mother country. It would be a source of raw materials, an area for investment, and a market for British manufactured goods.

Other issues, however, sparked lively debate. Most of the British assumed that at some point they would leave India, and their colony would become a self-governing, independent state. They had no timetable for leaving, however, and they disagreed about how to prepare their subjects for that day of independence. They would bring some Indians into the colonial administration, but how many and at what levels? They would provide India with schools and colleges, but would they offer Western or traditional Indian learning? They would attempt to "civilize" the Indians, but in doing so, how much traditional Indian culture were they willing to suppress?

The debate among the British was complicated by sharp disagreements among Indians about their relationship with their colonial masters. Many Indians at first believed that British rule was a blessing that would enable them to benefit from Western science, constitutional government, and economic development. Such views persisted into the twentieth century, but by the late 1800s only a minority embraced them. Many Indians came to resent the British assumption that Western ways were superior to centuries-old Indian beliefs and practices. They also were offended by Britain's one-sided economic policies, which drained India's resources, stifled development, and damaged traditional industries. Finally, they were angered by Great Britain's reluctance to consider seriously Indian self-rule.

As the following documents reveal, an evaluation of the benefits and harm of British rule in India is no simple matter. Historians continue to debate the issue down to the present day.

A Plea for Western Schools
▼▼▼

77 ▼ *Rammohun Roy,*
LETTER TO LORD AMHERST

Rammohun Roy, the father of modern India, was born into a devout high-caste Hindu family in 1772. He showed an early genius for languages and a keen interest in religions. By the age of twenty he had learned Arabic, Persian, Greek, and Sanskrit (the ancient language of India) and had spent five years wandering through India seeking religious enlightenment. He then learned English and entered the service of the British East India Company, ultimately attaining the highest administrative rank possible for an Indian. In 1814, at the age of forty-two, he retired to Calcutta, where he founded several newspapers and a number of schools, and campaigned to abolish the practice of widow burning, or *sati*. He also established the Society of God, dedicated to combining Christian ethical teaching with certain Hindu beliefs. He spent his final years in England, where he died in 1833.

Roy wrote the following letter in 1823 to the British governor-general of India, Lord Amherst (1773–1857), to oppose a British plan to sponsor a school in Calcutta to teach Sanskrit and Hindu literature. Roy believed that Indians should study English and receive a Western education.

In 1835 the debate over Indian education was settled when a British government committee decided that Indian schools should offer an English-style education. In the words of the committee's chair, Thomas B. Macaulay (1800–1859), the goal was to produce young men who were "Indian in blood and color, but English in taste, in opinions, in morals, and in intellect."

QUESTIONS FOR ANALYSIS

1. How would you characterize Roy's attitude toward the British? Does he seem comfortable offering the British advice? Explain your answer.
2. What does he especially admire in Western civilization?
3. What does he consider to be the weaknesses of an education based on traditional Indian learning?
4. According to Roy, what implications would a Hindu-based educational system have for India's political future?

To His Excellency the Right Honorable Lord Amherst, Governor-General in Council

My Lord,

Humbly reluctant as the natives of India are to obtrude upon the notice of government the sentiments they entertain on any public measure, there are circumstances when silence would be carrying this respectful feeling to culpable excess. The present rulers of India, coming from a distance of many thousand miles to govern a people whose language, literature, manners, customs, and ideas, are almost entirely new and strange to them, cannot easily become so intimately acquainted with their real circumstances as the natives of the country are themselves. We should therefore be guilty of a gross dereliction of duty to ourselves and afford our rulers just grounds of complaint at our apathy did we omit, on occasions of importance like the present, to supply them with such accurate information as might enable them to devise and adopt measures calculated to be beneficial to the country, and thus second by our local knowledge and experience their declared benevolent intentions for its improvement.

The establishment of a new Sanskrit School in Calcutta evinces the laudable desire of govern-

ment to improve the natives of India by education — a blessing for which they must ever be grateful, and every well-wisher of the human race must be desirous that the efforts made to promote it should be guided by the most enlightened principles, so that the stream of intelligence may flow in the most useful channels.

When this seminary of learning was proposed, we understood that the government in England had ordered a considerable sum of money to be annually devoted to the instruction of its Indian subjects. We were filled with sanguine hopes that this sum would be laid out in employing European gentlemen of talent and education to instruct the natives of India in mathematics, natural philosophy, chemistry, anatomy, and other useful sciences, which the natives of Europe have carried to a degree of perfection that has raised them above the inhabitants of other parts of the world.

While we looked forward with pleasing hope to the dawn of knowledge thus promised to the rising generation, our hearts were filled with mingled feelings of delight and gratitude, we already offered up thanks to Providence for inspiring the most generous and enlightened nations of the West with the glorious ambition of planting in Asia the arts and sciences of modern Europe.

We find that the government are establishing a Sanskrit school under Hindu pandits[1] to impart such knowledge as is already current in India. This seminary (similar in character to those which existed in Europe before the time of Lord Bacon)[2] can only be expected to load the minds of youth with grammatical niceties and metaphysical distinctions of little or no practical use to the possessors or to society. The pupils will there acquire what was known two thousand years ago with the addition of vain and empty subtleties since then produced by speculative men such as is already commonly taught in all parts of India.

The Sanskrit language, so difficult that almost a lifetime is necessary for its acquisition, is well known to have been for ages a lamentable check to the diffusion of knowledge, and the learning concealed under this almost impervious veil is far from sufficient to reward the labor of acquiring it. But if it were thought necessary to perpetuate this language for the sake of the portion of valuable information it contains, this might be much more easily accomplished by other means than the establishment of a new Sanskrit College; for there have been always and are now numerous professors of Sanskrit in the different parts of the country engaged in teaching this language, as well as the other branches of literature which are to be the object of the new seminary. Therefore their more diligent cultivation, if desirable, would be effectually promoted, by holding out premiums and granting certain allowances to their most eminent professors, who have already undertaken on their own account to teach them, and would by such rewards be stimulated to still greater exertion. . . .

Neither can much improvement arise from such speculations as the following which are the themes suggested by the Vedanta.[3] In what manner is the soul absorbed in the Deity? What relation does it bear to the Divine Essence? Nor will youths be fitted to be better members of society by the Vedantic doctrines which teach them to believe that all visible things have no real existence, that as father, brother, etc., have no real entity, they consequently deserve no real affection, and therefore the sooner we escape from them and leave the world the better. . . .

If it had been intended to keep the British nation in ignorance of real knowledge, the Baconian philosophy would not have been allowed to displace the system of the schoolmen which was the best calculated to perpetuate ignorance. In the same manner the Sanskrit system of education would be the best calculated to keep this country in darkness, if such had been the policy of the British legislature. But as the improvement of the native population is the object of the government, it will consequently promote a more liberal and enlightened system of instruction, embracing mathematics, natural philosophy, chemistry, anatomy, with other useful sciences, which may be accomplished with the sums proposed by employing a few gentlemen of talent and learning educated in Europe and providing a college furnished with necessary books, instruments, and other apparatus.

In presenting this subject to your Lordship, I conceive myself discharging a solemn duty which I owe to my countrymen, and also to that enlightened sovereign and legislature which have extended their benevolent care to this distant land, actuated by a desire to improve the inhabitants, and therefore humbly trust you will excuse the liberty I have taken in thus expressing my sentiments to your Lordship.

I have the honor, etc.,

Rammohun Roy

---

[1] Wise and learned men of Hindu India.

[2] A reference to the English philosopher and prophet of science, Francis Bacon (1561–1626). Excerpts from his *New Organon* are included in source 25.

[3] A major school of Hindu philosophy based on the study and analysis of three ancient texts, the *Upanishads,* the *Vedanta-sutras,* and the *Bhagavad Gita.* The various schools of Vedanta have different views concerning the nature of Brahman, the relationship of the individual to Brahman, and the nature and means of liberation from the cycle of reincarnation.

A Call to Expel the British

▼▼▼

78 ▼ *THE AZAMGARH PROCLAMATION*

On May 10, 1857, in Meerut in northern India, soldiers from three Indian infantry regiments that were part of the army maintained by the British East India Company shot their British officers, released all prisoners from jail, and marched on the nearby city of Delhi, which fell on May 11. In June and July similar mutinies occurred across northern India, and with scattered support from peasants, landowners, and a few native princes, for a time the rebellion appeared to threaten the very basis of British authority in India. In the following months, however, British forces regrouped, and with the help of loyal Indian troops, crushed the rebels in 1858. Though brief, the Indian Mutiny, or as it is also known, the Sepoy Rebellion, was bitterly fought, with atrocities committed by both sides. Two months after it ended, Parliament passed the India Act, which stripped the East India Company of its political authority and placed India directly under the Crown.

The significance of the Indian Mutiny continues to be widely debated. To some historians it represents the first true expression of Indian nationalism; to others, it was simply a series of army mutinies that never garnered much support outside the north. There is more unanimity about its causes. It was triggered by growing discontent among the Indian troops (sepoys) in the East India Company's Bengal army, discontent that boiled over into rebellion when the British introduced new cartridges greased with cow fat, which made them obnoxious to Hindu soldiers, and pig fat, which made them obnoxious to Muslims. This was only the spark, however. The rebellion gained support from many different groups, some with specific grievances over British rule, and some with vague fears about British intentions. Some of these grievances and concerns are revealed in the following document.

The document, known as the Azamgarh Proclamation, was issued in the summer of 1857, supposedly by one of the grandsons of the eighty-two-year-old king of Delhi, Bahadur Shah. Although the king had little authority, even in Delhi itself, he was a descendant of the great Mughal rulers of previous centuries and still was considered "emperor of India," since the Mughal Empire had never been officially abolished. Some of the rebels, including the author of the Azamgarh Proclamation, harbored the unrealistic dream of restoring Mughal authority once the British had been expelled. Primarily for this reason, the Indian Act, which stripped the East India Company of its political authority, also abolished the Mughal Empire.

QUESTIONS FOR ANALYSIS

1. What incentives does the author of the proclamation offer to those who would join the rebellion?
2. For each of the groups discussed (zamindars, merchants, artisans) what, according to the proclamation, have been the detrimental effects of British rule?
3. What role does religion play in the proclamation?

4. How do the views of the author of the proclamation differ from those of Rammohun Roy (source 77)?
5. What solutions for India's problems does the proclamation suggest?

It is well known to all that in this age the people of Hindustan,[1] both Hindus and Muslims, are being ruined under the tyranny and oppression of the infidel and treacherous English. It is therefore the bounden duty of those who have any sort of connection with any of the Muslim royal families, and are considered the pastors and masters of the people, to stake their lives and property for the well-being of the public. With the view of effecting this general good, several princes belonging to the royal family of Delhi have dispersed themselves in the different parts of India, Iran, Turan [Turkestan], and Afghanistan, and have been long since taking measures to compass their favorite end; and it is to accomplish this charitable object that one of the aforesaid princes has, at the head of an army of Afghanistan, etc., made his appearance in India; and I, who am the grandson of Abul Muzuffer Sarajuddin Bahadur Shah Ghazee, emperor of India,[2] having . . . come here to extirpate the infidels residing in the eastern part of the country, and to liberate and protect the poor helpless people now groaning under their iron rule, have, by the aid of the Mujahidins [fighters for Islam against infidels] . . . raised the standard of Mohammad, and persuaded the orthodox Hindus who had been subject to my ancestors, and have been and are still accessories in the destruction of the English, to raise the standard of Mahavir.[3]

Several of the Hindu and Muslim chiefs, who have long since left their homes for the preservation of their religion, and have been trying their best to root out the English in India, have presented themselves to me, and taken part in the reigning Indian crusade, and it is more than probable that I shall very shortly receive more help from the west. Therefore, for the information of the public, the present proclamation, con-

sisting of several sections, is put in circulation, and it is the imperative duty of all to take it into their careful consideration, and abide by it. Parties anxious to participate in the common cause, but having no means to provide for themselves, shall receive their daily subsistence from me; and be it known to all, that the ancient works, both of the Hindus and Muslims, the writings of the miracle-workers, and the calculations of the astrologers, pundits, and fortune-tellers, all agree in asserting that the English will no longer have any footing in India or elsewhere. . . .

No person, at the misrepresentation of the well-wishers of the British government, ought to conclude from the present slight inconveniences usually attendant on revolutions, that similar inconveniences and troubles should continue when the royal government is established on a firm basis; and parties badly dealt with by any sepoy (soldier) or plunderer, should come up and represent their grievances to me, and receive redress at my hands; and for whatever property they may lose in the reigning disorder, they will be recompensed from the public treasury when the royal government is well fixed.

Section I. — Regarding Zamindars [landholders]. — It is evident that the British government, in making settlements with zamindars, have imposed exorbitant jummas (taxes), and have disgraced and ruined several zamindars by putting up their estates to public auction for arrears of rent, insomuch that on the institution of a suit by a common farmer, a maidservant, or a slave, the respectable zamindars are summoned into court, arrested, put in jail, and disgraced. In litigations regarding zamindars, the immense value of stamps, and other unnecessary expenses of the civil courts, which are pregnant with all sorts of crooked dealings, and the practice of allowing, a

---

[1]A term used at the time to refer to northern India.
[2]Also the King of Delhi, Bahadur Shah.

[3]Great Hero. In this context a name for the Hindu god Vishnu.

case to hang on for years, are all calculated to impoverish the litigants. Besides this, the coffers of the zamindars are annually taxed with subscriptions for schools, hospitals, roads, etc. Such extortions will have no manner of existence in the royal government; but, on the contrary, the taxes will be light, the dignity and honour of the zamindars safe, and every zamindar will have absolute rule in his own territory.

Section II. — Regarding Merchants. — It is plain that the infidel and treacherous British government have monopolised the trade of all the fine and valuable merchandise, such as indigo, cloth, and other articles of shipping, leaving only the trade of trifles to the people, and even in this they are not without their share of the profits, which they secure by means of customs and stamp fees, etc., in money suits, so that the people have merely a trade in name. . . . When the royal government is established, all these aforesaid fraudulent practices shall be dispensed with, and the trade of every article, without exception, both by land and water, shall be open to the native merchants of India, who will have the benefit of the government steam-vessels and steam carriages for the conveyance of the merchandise gratis; and merchants having no capital of their own shall be assisted from the public treasury. . . .

Section III. — Regarding Public Servants. — It is not a secret thing, that under the British government, natives employed in the civil and military services, have little respect, low pay, and no manner of influence; and all the posts of dignity and emolument [reward] in both the departments, are exclusively bestowed on Englishmen. . . . But under the royal government, . . . the posts . . . which the English enjoy at present . . . will be given to the natives . . . together with landed estates, ceremonial dress, tax-free lands, and influence. Natives, whether Hindus or Muslims, who fall fighting against the English, are sure to go to heaven; and those killed fighting for the English, will, doubtless, go to hell. Therefore, all the natives in the British service ought to be alive to their religion and interest, and, abjuring their loyalty to the English, side with the royal government and obtain salaries of 200 or 300 rupees per month for the present, and be entitled to high posts in future.

Section IV. — Regarding Artisans. — It is evident that the Europeans, by the introduction of English articles into India, have thrown the weavers, the cotton-dressers, the carpenters, the blacksmiths, and the shoemakers, &c., out of employ, and have engrossed [taken over] their occupations, so that every description of native artisan has been reduced to beggary. But under the royal government the native artisans will exclusively be employed in the services of the kings, the rajahs, and the rich; and this will no doubt insure their prosperity. Therefore the artisans ought to renounce the English services, and assist the Mujahidins . . . engaged in the war, and thus be entitled both to secular and eternal happiness.

Section V. — Regarding Pundits, Fakirs,[4] and other learned persons. — The pundits and fakirs being the guardians of the Hindu and Muslim religions respectively, and the Europeans being the enemies of both religions, and as at present a war is raging against the English on account of religion, the pundits and fakirs are bound to present themselves to me, and take their share in this holy war, otherwise they will stand condemned. . . .

Lastly, be it known to all, that whoever, out of the above-named classes, shall, after the circulation of this Ishtahar, still cling to the British government, all his estates shall be confiscated, and his property plundered, and he himself, with his whole family, shall be imprisoned, and ultimately put to death.

---

[4]*Pundit* and *fakir* are both vague terms. Pundits were learned men; fakirs were mystics.

Chapter 10

▼▼▼

East and Southeast Asia Confront the West

During the nineteenth century ancient patterns of life in East and Southeast Asia were irrevocably altered by upheavals that felled governments, intensified social conflict, introduced new ideas and technologies, and transformed long-standing relationships among states. These changes were caused in part by social and political forces generated from within these societies themselves, but new pressures from the West also played a major role. Until the nineteenth century, Western involvement in the region had been limited to commerce and a modicum of generally ineffectual missionary activity. The only major exceptions were the Philippines, which since the sixteenth century had been ruled by the Spaniards, and the island of Java, where in the eighteenth century the Dutch established indirect and informal control in cooperation with indigenous rulers. Only the Filipinos converted to Catholicism in large numbers. Elsewhere the region's rulers and their subjects remained politically independent and culturally indifferent to the West.

This changed in the nineteenth century. By the time World War I began in 1914, Burma, Laos, Cambodia, Vietnam, Singapore, the states of the Malay Peninsula, and many islands of the East Indies had all joined the Philippines and Java as parts of Western empires. Thailand remained independent but lost territory to France and Great Britain.

China faced severe internal problems and experienced relentless economic and military pressures from Britain, France, Russia, Germany, the United States, and Japan. Previous Chinese regimes had survived domestic turbulence and foreign threats before, but this time China's problems proved fatal, not just to the Qing Dynasty but also to China's 2,000-year tradition of imperial rule. When the last Qing emperor was overthrown in the Revolution of 1911, no new dynasty was established, and China faced an uncertain future without the authority of an emperor, the rule of scholar-officials, and the guidance of official Confucian ideology.

Japan also faced internal conflict and foreign threats in the nineteenth century, but otherwise its experience differed sharply from China's. Midcentury, after an intense debate over Japan's future, a group of patriotic aristocrats overthrew the Tokugawa shogunate in 1867, restored the emperor, and began laying plans for Japan's rapid modernization. By the 1890s Japan had escaped becoming a victim of imperialism and was well on its way to becoming an imperialist power itself.

▼▼▼

The Disintegration of Imperial China

In 1842, only a half century after the Qianlong emperor sent King George III of England his condescending rejection of the British appeal for trade concessions (see source 56), the Daoguang emperor (r. 1821–1850) was forced to sign the Treaty of Nanjing, which required the Chinese government to open five Chinese ports to British merchants, cede Hong Kong to the British, lower tariffs, pay an indemnity of $21 million to the London government, and free all British prisoners. Acceptance of this humiliating treaty followed defeat in the Opium War (1839–1842), the climax of early Chinese efforts to halt the British sale of opium to China.

The Treaty of Nanjing was only a foretaste of the galling indignities the Chinese experienced during the rest of the nineteenth century. As a result of foreign pressures and military defeats, the government was forced to open additional coastal cities to foreign trade, lost control of Korea, granted foreigners the right to collect customs duties, lost legal authority over resident foreigners, and promised to protect the lives and property of Christian missionaries. In 1899 and 1900 resentment of the hated "foreign devils" exploded in the Boxer rebellion, the uprising in which rebels murdered foreigners and Chinese Christians and besieged foreign embassies in Beijing. After a multinational force of British, French, German, Russian, U.S., and Japanese troops crushed the rebellion, the government was forced to sign yet another punitive treaty, which among other things demanded an indemnity payment of $333 million, to be paid over a forty-year period with terms of interest that more than doubled the amount.

Even without the foreign onslaught, nineteenth-century China faced enormous problems, many of them resulting from its spiraling population. By midcentury, its population reached 450 million, more than three times greater than in 1500. The inevitable results were land shortages, famine, and deepening poverty among the peasantry. Heavy taxes, inflation, and bureaucratic corruption compounded the peasants' woes. Meanwhile the government neglected public works and the military, and as bureaucratic efficiency declined, landowners, secret societies, and military strongmen took over local affairs by default. Reform programs such as the Self-Strengthening Movement, which flourished in the 1860s and 1870s, and the One Hundred Days' Reforms in 1898 were frustrated by conservative opposition and the difficulty of blending Confucian values with modern technology and Western political ideas. Rebellion, lawlessness, and foreign exploitation continued to plague the Qing regime until the Revolution of 1911 caused the regime, and China's ancient imperial tradition, to pass into history.

The Curse of Opium

▼▼▼

79 ▼ Lin Zexu,
LETTER TO QUEEN VICTORIA, 1839

Although the opium poppy was grown in China and opium derivatives had been used in Chinese medicine for centuries, smoking opium as a narcotic dates from the seventeenth century, shortly after the Spanish and Portuguese introduced tobacco smoking in China. Opium use increased dramatically in the late 1700s when British and Indian merchants with access to one of the world's greatest poppy-growing areas in north and northwest India began to import large amounts of opium into China. By the early 1800s millions of Chinese at every social and economic level were addicted to opium, and almost 2 million pounds of opium were being sold in China every year.

Chinese officials viewed the social and economic consequences of opium addiction with increasing alarm, but there was no agreement on what should be done. Some advocated the legalization of opium and the expansion of poppy growing in China to lessen the country's dependence on imports. Others recommended a total ban on opium imports and use, an approach that won the support of the Daoguang emperor, who issued an imperial ban on opium use in 1838. One year later he sent one of his officials, Lin Zexu (1785–1850), to Guangzhou to confiscate the foreign merchants' stock of opium and halt their trade in opium altogether. Lin had served in the Hanlin Academy, China's leading center for Confucian studies in Beijing, and had held various provincial posts, including terms in Hubei and Hunan, where he had tried to suppress opium smoking. On arrival in Guangzhou he launched a campaign of moral persuasion and force to discourage opium smoking among Chinese and end the sale of opium by Chinese and foreign merchants. Insight into his thinking is provided by a letter he wrote to Great Britain's Queen Victoria in 1839, imploring her to halt her subjects' sale of opium.

Nothing came of his letter, and the refusal of British merchants in Guangzhou to cooperate drove Lin to more drastic steps. He arrested the leading English opium trader and blockaded the foreign quarter until its merchants agreed to hand over 20,000 chests of opium. On receiving the opium, he had it mixed with water, salt, and lime and flushed into the sea. On learning of these events, the British government dispatched a fleet and mobilized Indian troops to protect British interests in

China. While the flotilla of almost fifty vessels was en route in late 1839, fighting between the Chinese and the English had already started around Guangzhou; the Opium War was under way.

QUESTIONS FOR ANALYSIS

1. What does Lin's letter reveal about Chinese views of foreign relations and the relationship between the Chinese emperor and other rulers?
2. What differences does Lin see in the motives of Chinese and Europeans in regard to trade?
3. What moral arguments does Lin use to persuade Victoria to order the end of opium trading? What other arguments does he use?
4. What seems to be Lin's understanding of the powers of Victoria as queen of England?
5. How does Lin view the world outside of China? How do his views differ from and resemble those of the Qianlong emperor (source 56)?

His Majesty the Emperor comforts and cherishes foreigners as well as Chinese: he loves all the people in the world without discrimination. Whenever profit is found, he wishes to share it with all men; whenever harm appears, he likewise will eliminate it on behalf of all of mankind. His heart is in fact the heart of the whole universe.

Generally speaking, the succeeding rulers of your honorable country have been respectful and obedient. Time and again they have sent petitions to China, saying: "We are grateful to His Majesty the Emperor for the impartial and favorable treatment he has granted to the citizens of my country who have come to China to trade," etc. I am pleased to learn that you, as the ruler of your honorable country, are thoroughly familiar with the principle of righteousness and are grateful for the favor that His Majesty the Emperor has bestowed upon your subjects. Because of this fact, the Celestial Empire, following its traditional policy of treating foreigners with kindness, has been doubly considerate towards the people from England. You have traded in China for almost 200 years, and as a result, your country has become wealthy and prosperous.

As this trade has lasted for a long time, there are bound to be unscrupulous as well as honest traders. Among the unscrupulous are those who bring opium to China to harm the Chinese; they succeed so well that this poison has spread far and wide in all the provinces. You, I hope, will certainly agree that people who pursue material gains to the great detriment of the welfare of others can be neither tolerated by Heaven nor endured by men. . . .

Your country is more than 60,000 li[1] from China. The purpose of your ships in coming to China is to realize a large profit. Since this profit is realized in China and is in fact taken away from the Chinese people, how can foreigners return injury for the benefit they have received by sending this poison to harm their benefactors? They may not intend to harm others on purpose, but the fact remains that they are so obsessed with material gain that they have no concern whatever for the harm they can cause to others. Have they no conscience? I have heard that you strictly prohibit opium in your own country, indicating unmistakably that you know how harmful opium is.[2] You do not wish opium to harm your own coun-

---

[1]A Chinese measurement of distance, approximately one-third of a mile.

[2]Actually, the use of opium was not prohibited in England when Lin wrote his letter.

try, but you choose to bring that harm to other countries such as China. Why?

The products that originate from China are all useful items. They are good for food and other purposes and are easy to sell. Has China produced one item that is harmful to foreign countries? For instance, tea and rhubarb[3] are so important to foreigners' livelihood that they have to consume them every day. Were China to concern herself only with her own advantage without showing any regard for other people's welfare, how could foreigners continue to live? Foreign products like woolen cloth and beiges[4] rely on Chinese raw materials such as silk for their manufacturing. Had China sought only her own advantage, where would the foreigners' profit come from? The products that foreign countries need and have to import from China are too numerous to enumerate: from food products such as molasses, ginger, and cassia[5] to useful necessities such as silk and porcelain. The imported goods from foreign countries, on the other hand, are merely playthings which can be easily dispensed with without causing any ill effect. Since we do not need these things really, what harm would come if we should decide to stop foreign trade altogether? The reason why we unhesitantly allow foreigners to ship out such Chinese products as tea and silk is that we feel that wherever there is an advantage, it should be shared by all the people in the world. . . .

I have heard that you are a kind, compassionate monarch. I am sure that you will not do to others what you yourself do not desire. I have also heard that you have instructed every British ship that sails for Guangzhou not to bring any prohibited goods to China. It seems that your policy is as enlightened as it is proper. The fact that British ships have continued to bring opium to China results perhaps from the impossibility of making a thorough inspection of all of them owing to their large numbers. I am sending you this letter to reiterate the seriousness with which we enforce the law of the Celestial Empire and to make sure that merchants from your honorable country will not attempt to violate it again.

I have heard that the areas under your direct jurisdiction such as London, Scotland, and Ireland do not produce opium; it is produced instead in your Indian possessions such as Bengal, Madras, Bombay, Patna, and Malwa. In these possessions the English people not only plant opium poppies that stretch from one mountain to another but also open factories to manufacture this terrible drug. As months accumulate and years pass by, the poison they have produced increases in its wicked intensity, and its repugnant odor reaches as high as the sky. Heaven is furious with anger, and all the gods are moaning with pain! It is hereby suggested that you destroy and plow under all of these opium plants and grow food crops instead, while issuing an order to punish severely anyone who dares to plant opium poppies again. If you adopt this policy of love so as to produce good and exterminate evil, Heaven will protect you, and gods will bring you good fortune. Moreover, you will enjoy a long life and be rewarded with a multitude of children and grandchildren! In short, by taking this one measure, you can bring great happiness to others as well as yourself. Why do you not do it? . . .

For every government, past or present, one of its primary functions is to educate all the people living within its jurisdiction, foreigners as well as its own citizens, about the law and to punish them if they choose to violate it. Since a foreigner who goes to England to trade has to obey the English law, how can an Englishman not obey the Chinese law when he is physically within China? The present law calls for the imposition of the death sentence on any Chinese who has peddled or smoked opium. Since a Chinese could not peddle or smoke opium if foreigners had not brought it to China, it is clear that the true culprits of a Chinese's death as a result of an opium conviction are the opium traders from foreign

---

[3]Rhubarb roots were used in medicines.
[4]A soft wool fabric unbleached and undyed, thus having a tan color.

[5]A spice similar to cinnamon.

countries. Being the cause of other people's death, why should they themselves be spared from capital punishment? A murderer of one person is subject to the death sentence; just imagine how many people opium has killed! This is the rationale behind the new law which says that any foreigner who brings opium to China will be sentenced to death by hanging or beheading. Our purpose is to eliminate this poison once and for all and to the benefit of all mankind.

Our Celestial Empire towers over all other countries in virtue and possesses a power great and awesome enough to carry out its wishes. But we will not prosecute a person without warning him in advance; that is why we have made our law explicit and clear. If the merchants of your honorable country wish to enjoy trade with us on a permanent basis, they must fearfully observe our law by cutting off, once and for all, the supply of opium. Under no circumstance should they test our intention to enforce the law by deliberately violating it. You, as the ruler of your honorable country, should do your part to uncover the hidden and unmask the wicked. It is hoped that you will continue to enjoy your country and become more and more respectful and obeisant. How wonderful it is that we can all enjoy the blessing of peace!

The Plight of the Emperor's Subjects
▼▼▼

80 ▼ Zeng Guofan,
MEMORANDUM TO EMPEROR XIANFENG

Zeng Guofan (1811–1872) was one of nineteenth-century China's truly impressive statesmen. Born into a farm family in the province of Hunan, Zeng received a Confucian education and passed the highest civil service examination at age twenty-eight. As a government official, his greatest achievement was the organization and leadership of a potent military force, the Xiang Army, which was instrumental in suppressing the Taiping Rebellion, a massive peasant revolt that raged through China between 1850 and 1864. Knowing well the problems of the regime, especially the cause of unrest among the peasantry, Zeng drew up the following memorandum on February 7, 1852, for Emperor Xianfeng (r. 1851–1861). It provides a clear and balanced assessment of China's problems at midcentury.

QUESTIONS FOR ANALYSIS

1. According to Zeng, what is the key to keeping China peaceful and secure?
2. Which aspects of the government's tax policies does Zeng deplore?
3. How, according to Zeng, does the behavior of local officials, soldiers, and magistrates affect the lives of the Chinese people?
4. Zeng states at the end of his memorandum that he will draft a plan to address the shortcomings of the tax system. What do you guess he will propose?
5. How does Zeng propose to remedy the problem of corruption? Does his solution have a reasonable chance of success? Why or why not?

For a period of fifteen years [1662–1677], from the first to the sixteenth year of Kangxi during the present dynasty, the Yellow River broke its dikes every year with the exception of one, and flood damage was extremely heavy over a large region. . . . As if this were not enough, the Three Viceroys' Rebellion erupted[1] and ravaged nine provinces; it took the government seven years to suppress it. By then the treasury was almost empty, emptier than it is today. Yet the dynasty remained secure and the country undisturbed. Why? Because the Saintly Progenitor [Kangxi] loved the people more than he did himself, and the people, in response, continued to pledge to him their unswerving allegiance and rallied for his support. Though Your Majesty undeniably loves your subjects to the same extent as the Saintly Progenitor loved his, local officials, being indifferent to the plight of their charges, have failed in conveying your compassionate sentiments to the people and bringing to your attention their grievances. Because of this lack of communication, your humble servant wishes to take this opportunity to describe in some detail the ills from which our people suffer most.

The first ill concerns the high price of silver which affects adversely the peasants' ability to fulfill their tax obligations. The tax load in Suzhou, Songjiang, Zhangzhou, and Jinjiang[2] is the heaviest in the nation, and the people in these districts also suffer most. The yield for each *mou* of land [one sixth an acre] is anywhere from 15 to 20 pecks[3] of polished rice, and the landowner, after dividing it with his tenant on a fifty-fifty basis, receives approximately 8 pecks as his rent. Though his regular tax is only 2 pecks per *mou,* he has to pay another 2 pecks as rice tribute and 2 pecks more for miscellaneous requisitions, totaling 6 pecks altogether. Thus, for each *mou* of land he owns, his net income is only 2 pecks of polished rice per year. If all these taxes could be paid in rice, the situation would not be so serious. But most of them have to be paid in silver. . . . Since a farmer reaps only rice, he has to sell his harvest for standard coins [copper] in order to obtain the necessary cash; since the price of standard coins is high in terms of rice, he has understandable grievances. Moreover, in order to pay his taxes, he has to convert his standard coins into silver. . . . Formerly, selling 3 pecks of rice would bring enough silver to pay taxes for one *mou* of land; now, selling 6 pecks will not be enough to achieve the same purpose. While the return to the government remains the same, the burden to the people has been doubled. Besides, there are additional taxes on houses and family cemeteries, all of which have been doubled in terms of rice because they, like most of other taxes, have also to be paid in silver.

Under the circumstances it is not surprising that a large number of taxpayers have become delinquent, despite local governments' effort to enforce payment. Often special officials are assigned to help tax collections, and day and night soldiers are sent out to harass taxpayers. Sometimes corporal punishments are imposed upon tax delinquents; some of them are so badly beaten to exact the last penny that blood and flesh fly in all directions. Cruel though it is, this practice does not necessarily reflect the evil nature of local officials who, more often than not, do not believe that they have a better choice. If they fail to collect 70 percent of the amount due, not only will they be impeached and punished as a matter of routine, they may also have to pay the balance with their own money, that sometimes amounts to thousands of taels,[4] and ruin their families in the process. In short, they are forced to do what they loathe. . . .

Under the circumstances it is not surprising that the people are complaining and angry, and often the resistance to tax payment bursts forth and mushrooms into full-fledged riot. . . .

The second ill of our nation is the great number of bandits which threaten the security of our law-abiding citizens. . . . Lately your humble

---

[1]Also known as the Revolt of the Three Feudatories, 1673–1681.
[2]All are located in the south-central region of China.

[3]One peck equals one-quarter of a bushel.
[4]Chinese silver coins, each weighing approximately 1¼ ounces.

servant has heard that the bandits have become bolder and more numerous, robbed and raped in broad daylight, and kidnapped people for ransom. Whenever an act of banditry is reported to the government, the local official announces in advance his intention to send troops against the bandits and advertises it in public proclamations, so as to make sure that the bandits know the soldiers are coming. Upon arriving at the village where the banditry took place, the official-in-charge expects to learn from the village chiefs, who are afraid of the bandits, that the offenders have already fled. Without anything worthwhile to do, he orders the burning of some of the houses in the village before his departure, so as to impress the villagers with the power of his office. Meanwhile his soldiers use a variety of excuses to exact payment from the bandits' victim, who by then is only too regretful that he reported the banditry to the government in the first place. While the soldiers are busy taking away from his house whatever they can carry, the bandits are still at large, hiding somewhere in the village. Sometimes the official announces that the responsible bandit has in fact been killed and that the case is therefore closed; then he proceeds to show off the bandit's body, after killing some prisoner in his jail who has nothing to do with this particular crime. Not only does the bandits' victim fail to get his grievances redressed and his stolen properties restored; he may also lose everything he has and go bankrupt. After all this, he will probably swallow his tears in silence and make no more complaint, since by then he is no longer financially able to make any appeals.

Suppose he does appeal and that the government responds by mobilizing a large force in its attempt to arrest the bandits. Since these soldiers have always been in collusion with the bandits, they will release the offenders soon after their capture, in return for a handsome bribe, and the offenders will quickly disappear without leaving a trace. Sometimes the soldiers use the reported presence of bandits as an excuse to blackmail the villagers; if the latter refuse to pay the bribes they demand, they will accuse them as the bandits' accomplices, burn their houses, and bring them to the city in chains. . . .

The third ill which your humble servant wishes to stress is the great number of cases in which innocent men are condemned and the inability on the part of the people to have a wrong redressed. Since his appointment at the Ministry of Justice, your humble servant has reviewed several hundred cases of appeal. . . . In most cases, . . . it was the plaintiffs who received punishment in the end, on the ground that they had made false accusations, while the defendants went through the whole litigation unscathed and free. Generally speaking, the officials-in-charge invoke the following rules in the law as legitimate ground to impose heavy penalties upon the plaintiffs. First, the plaintiff has failed to present the truth in his petition, and for such failure he is to receive one hundred blows by a striking rod. Second, the case he presents is not serious enough for him to bypass the local courts and to go straight to the nation's capital, and for such offense he is to be punished by banishment to the frontier as a soldier. Third, he intimidates the government under the pretense of offering constructive suggestions, and for such offense he is to be punished by banishment to a nearby area as a soldier. Fourth, he harbors personal grudges against the official under whose jurisdiction he lives and falsely accuses him of wrongdoing before the latter's superior. For this offense he is to be punished by banishment to the malarious regions as a soldier. . . .

Who can believe that when an ordinary citizen is a plaintiff and a government official a defendant, the defendant is always right and the plaintiff always wrong? The answer to both questions would have to be a clear "No one" if we had conscientious, enlightened officials sitting on the bench as judges. . . .

These three ills are the most serious the nation faces today, and the search for their cure is our most urgent task. Insofar as the second and the third ills — the widespread banditry and the condemnation of innocent men — are concerned, Your Majesty is hereby requested to issue a strict order to all the governors-general and governors to think carefully about them and to devise ways for their cure. As for the first ill or the increasingly higher price of silver, we should find remedies in terms of stabilizing the existing price.

Your humble servant is at present drafting a proposal aimed at the attainment of this goal, which, when completed, will be presented to Your Majesty for reference purposes.

A Revolutionary Formula for China's Revival
▼▼▼

81 ▼ Sun Yat-sen,
THE THREE PEOPLE'S PRINCIPLES AND THE FUTURE OF THE CHINESE PEOPLE

By 1900 the prognosis for the Qing Dynasty had deteriorated from poor to critical. It had survived massive peasant revolts, military defeats at the hands of the British, French, and Japanese, and a series of one-sided treaties that made a mockery of China's self-image as the world's greatest power. But the government was doing little more than surviving. In 1898 a desperate attempt to revamp government, encourage education, promote agriculture and commerce, and strengthen the armed forces resulted in a flurry of decrees from the Guangxu emperor during the period known as the One Hundred Days' Reforms. The emperor's efforts, however, were scuttled by court reactionaries led by the Empress Dowager Cixi. Cixi then lent her support to the antiforeign secret societies known as the Boxers, who in 1899 went on a rampage against foreigners and Chinese Christians and in 1900 besieged the foreign embassies in Beijing. The Boxer Rebellion was suppressed by a multinational force, and China was forced to accept another humiliating treaty — one that included an indemnity of $333 million. Support for the government virtually disappeared, and many intellectuals, students, generals, secret society members, and Chinese living abroad began plotting the downfall of the Qing.

The leading revolutionary was Sun Yat-sen (1866–1925), a man far different from previous Chinese reformers. Born to a poor rural family near Guangzhou, Sun was educated in Hawaiian and Chinese missionary schools and developed a worldview more Western than Confucian. Galled by China's military impotence and Qing ineptitude, in 1894 he founded the secret Revive China Society, which in 1895 laid plans to overthrow the government. The plot was uncovered, and Sun was forced into exile. After sixteen years of traveling, planning, writing, and organizing, his hopes for radical change were realized when the revolution that ended the Qing era broke out in 1911.

On his return to China from the United States, he was elected provisional president of the United Provinces of China on December 30, 1911. Sun's moment of glory was short-lived. Without an armed force or an organized political party to back him up, Sun resigned as president in 1912 in favor of the military strongman Yuan Shikai, who one year later sent Sun into exile as part of his plan to establish a dictatorship. Sun returned to Guangzhou in 1917 and attempted to establish a parliamentary government, but by then China had descended into the chaos of warlord rule. When Sun died in 1925 the prospects of national unity and orderly government for China still seemed dim.

In the following selection Sun presents an early formulation of his "three people's principles," which served as the ideology of the United League, an organization he founded in 1905 in Tokyo that combined members of Chinese secret societies, overseas Chinese groups, and Chinese students in Japan. When the United League joined several other groups to form the Guomindang, or Nationalist, party in 1912, Sun's three principles provided the platform for the new party. Sun presented the following analysis of his three principles in a speech to the United League in Tokyo in 1906 to help celebrate the first anniversary of the League's publication, *Min Pao (The People's Journal)*.

QUESTIONS FOR ANALYSIS

1. What is meant by Sun's principle of nationalism? Against whom are his nationalist sentiments directed? How is his principle of nationalism linked to the principle of democracy?
2. What does he mean by the principle of democracy, and why does he feel it is so important to the future of China?
3. What, according to Sun, have been the good and bad effects of "the advances of civilization"? Why have the benefits of these advances been so poorly distributed?
4. Briefly describe Sun's "land valuation procedure" and its relation to the principle of livelihood. What are its strengths and weaknesses?
5. What is Sun's attitude toward the West? How and in what ways will the future government and society of China be superior to those of the West?
6. To what extent are Sun's ideas inspired by Western ideologies and to what extent do they draw on traditional Chinese thought and practice?

A person always recognizes his parents and never confuses them with strangers. Nationalism is analogous to this. It has to do with human nature and applies to everyone. Today, more than 260 years have passed since the Manchus entered China proper, yet even as children we Han[1] would certainly not mistake them for fellow Han. This is the root of nationalism. On the other hand, we should recognize that nationalism does not mean discriminating against people of different nationality. It simply means not allow-ing such people to seize our political power, for only when we Han are in control politically do we have a nation. . . .

The population of the globe is only one billion, several hundred million; we Han, being 400 million, comprise one-fourth of that population. Our nation is the most populous, most ancient, and most civilized in the world, yet today we are a lost nation. Isn't that enormously bizarre? The African nation of the Transvaal has a population of only 200,000, yet when Britain tried to de-

---

[1] *Han* in the Chinese language means the Chinese people, defined as those who speak Chinese and share a common Chinese culture and history.

stroy it, the fighting lasted three years.[2] The Philippines have a population of only several million, but when America tried to subdue it, hostilities persisted for several years.[3] Is it possible that the Han will gladly be a lost nation?

We Han are now swiftly being caught up in a tidal wave of nationalist revolution, yet the Manchus continue to discriminate against the Han. They boast that their forefathers conquered the Han because of their superior unity and military strength and that they intend to retain these qualities so as to dominate the Han forever. . . . Certainly, once we Han unite, our power will be thousands of times greater than theirs, and the success of the nationalist revolution will be assured.

As for the Principle of Democracy, it is the foundation of the political revolution. In the future, to be sure, the vicious politics of today will be swept away after the nationalist revolution triumphs, but it will also be necessary to eradicate the roots of such politics. For several thousand years China has been a monarchical autocracy, a type of political system intolerable to those living in freedom and equality. A nationalist revolution is not itself sufficient to get rid of such a system. Think for a moment: When the founder of the Ming dynasty expelled the Mongols and restored Chinese rule, the nationalist revolution triumphed, but his political system was only too similar to those of the Han, Tang, and Song dynasties.[4] Consequently, after another three hundred years, foreigners again began to invade China. This is the result of the inadequacy of the political system, so that a political revolution is an absolute necessity. . . . The aim of the political revolution is to create a constitutional, democratic political system. In the context of the current political situation in China, a revolution would be necessary even if the monarch were a Han. . . .

▼ ▼ ▼

Now, let me begin by discussing the origins of the Principle of the People's Livelihood, a principle that began to flourish only in the latter part of the nineteenth century. Before that it did not flourish because civilization was not as highly developed. . . . As civilization advanced, people relied less on physical labor and more on natural forces, since electricity and steam could accomplish things a thousand times faster than human physical strength. For example, in antiquity a single man tilling the land could harvest at best enough grain to feed a few people, notwithstanding his toil and trouble. Now, however, as a result of the development of scientific agriculture, one man can grow more than enough to feed a thousand people because he can use machinery instead of his limbs, with a consequent increase in efficiency. . . .

▼ ▼ ▼

Everyone in Europe and America should be living in a state of plenty and happiness undreamed of in antiquity. If we look around, however, we see that conditions in those countries are precisely the opposite. Statistically, Britain's wealth has increased more than several thousandfold over the previous generation, yet poverty of the people has also increased several thousandfold over the previous generation. Moreover, the rich are extremely few, and the poor extremely numerous. This is because the power of human labor is no match for the power of capital. In antiquity, agriculture and industry depended completely on human labor; but now, with the development of

---

[2]A reference to the South African War, also known as the Boer War (1899–1902), fought between Great Britain and Transvaal and the Orange Free State, the two Afrikaner, or Boer, states in South Africa. It resulted from cultural friction and political conflict between the British settlers and administrators in the region and the Dutch settlers of the two states.

[3]Between 1899 and 1901 Filipinos under Emilio Aguinaldo fought against their new colonial master, the United States, after the United States took over the Philippines from Spain at the conclusion of the Spanish-American War.
[4]The Han (206 B.C.E.–220 C.E.), Tang (618–907 C.E.), and Song (960–1279 C.E.) were dynastic periods in Chinese history.

natural forces that human labor cannot match, agriculture and industry have fallen completely into the hands of capitalists. . . . Unable to compete, the poor have naturally been reduced to destitution. . . .

Indeed, this constitutes a lesson for China. . . . Civilization yields both good and bad fruits, and we should embrace the good and reject the bad. In the countries of Europe and America, the rich monopolize the good fruits of civilization, while the poor suffer from its evil fruits. . . .

Why have Europe and America failed to solve their social problems? Because they have not solved their land problem. Generally speaking, wherever civilization is advanced, the price of land increases with each passing day. . . . In China capitalists have not yet emerged, so that for several thousand years there has been no increase in land prices. . . . After the revolution, however, conditions in China will be different. For example, land prices in Hong Kong and Shanghai are currently as much as several hundred times higher than those in the interior. This increment is the result of the advance of civilization and the development of communications. It is inevitable that, as the entire nation advances, land prices everywhere will rise accordingly. . . . This is evidence of the clearest sort, from which we can see that in the future the rich will get richer every day, and the poor, poorer. In another ten years, social problems will become even more pressing. . . . Consequently, we must come up with a solution now. . . .

With respect to a solution, although the socialists have different opinions, the procedure I most favor is land valuation. For example, if a landlord has land worth 1,000 dollars, its price can be set at 1,000 or even 2,000 dollars. Perhaps in the future, after communications have been developed, the value of his land will rise to 10,000 dollars; the owner should receive 2,000, which entails a profit and no loss, and the 8,000 increment will go to the state. Such an arrangement will greatly benefit both the state and the people's livelihood. Naturally, it will also eliminate the shortcomings that have permitted a few rich people to monopolize wealth. This is the simplest, most convenient, and most feasible method. . . .

Once we adopt this method, the more civilization advances, the greater the wealth of the nation, and then we can be sure our financial problems will not become difficult to handle. After the excessive taxes of the present have been abolished, the price of consumer goods will gradually fall and the people will become increasingly prosperous. We will forever abolish the vicious taxation policies that have prevailed for several thousand years. Even Europe, America, and Japan, although rich and powerful, impose taxes and rents that are too heavy on their people. After China's social revolution is accomplished, private individuals will never again have to pay taxes. The collection of land revenues alone will make China the richest nation on earth. . . .

▼ ▼ ▼

Obviously, . . . it is necessary to give considerable attention to what the constitution of the Republic of China should be. . . . The British constitution embodies the so-called separation of powers into executive, legislative, and judicial, all mutually independent. . . . The Frenchman Montesquieu[5] later embraced the British system and melded it with his own ideals to create his own school of thought. The American constitution was based on Montesquieu's theories but went further in clearly demarcating the separation of powers. . . . As to the future constitution of the Republic of China, I propose that we introduce a new principle, that of the "five separate powers."

Under this system, there will be two other powers in addition to the three powers just discussed. One is the examination power. . . . American officials are either elected or appointed. Formerly there were no civil service examinations, which led to serious shortcomings with

---

[5]Montesquieu (1689–1755) was a French political philosopher whose *Spirit of the Laws* (1748) described the separation of powers as a means to protect individual liberty.

respect to both elected and appointed officials. With respect to elections, those endowed with eloquence ingratiated themselves with the public and won elections, while those who had learning and ideals but lacked eloquence were ignored. Consequently, members of America's House of Representatives have often been foolish and ignorant people who have made its history quite ridiculous. As for appointees, they all come and go with the president. The Democratic and Republican parties have consistently taken turns holding power, and whenever a president is replaced, cabinet members and other officials, comprising no fewer than 60,000–70,000 people, including the postmaster general, are also replaced. As a result, the corruption and laxity of American politics are unparalleled among the nations of the world. . . . Therefore, the future constitution of the Republic of China must provide for an independent branch expressly responsible for civil service examinations. Furthermore, all officials, however high their rank, must undergo examinations in order to determine their qualifi-

cations. . . . This procedure will eliminate such evils as blind obedience, electoral abuses, and favoritism. . . .

The other power is the supervisory power, responsible for monitoring matters involving impeachment. For reasons that should be evident to all, such a branch is indispensable to any nation. The future constitution of the Republic of China must provide for an independent branch. Since ancient times, China had a supervisory organization, the Censorate,[6] to monitor the traditional social order. Inasmuch as it was merely a servant of the monarchy, however, it was ineffectual. . . .

With this added to the four powers already discussed, there will be five separate powers. That constitution will form the basis of the sound government of a nation that belongs to its own race, to its own citizens, and to its own society. This will be the greatest good fortune for our 400 million Han people. I presume that you gentlemen are willing to undertake and complete this task. It is my greatest hope.

---

[6]The Censorate, or Board of Censors, was a unique feature of Ming and Qing government. Board members reviewed the conduct of officials and reported to the emperor any dereliction of duty. They were considered the "eyes and ears" of the emperors.

▼▼▼

The Emergence of Modern Japan

In the late nineteenth century the Japanese accomplished what no other people had or has been able to do. Within only three decades and without recourse to foreign loans or investments, Japan changed from a secluded, preindustrial society vulnerable to foreign exploitation into a powerful, industrialized nation that shocked the world by winning wars against China in 1895 and Russia in 1905. What made this transformation even more remarkable was that it was accompanied by little social upheaval and that, despite its magnitude, the Japanese retained many of their hallowed ideals and beliefs.

Japan's transformation began in 1867 when a faction of aristocrats led a rebellion that abolished the Tokugawa shogunate and then orchestrated the move of the previously secluded and ceremonial emperor from Kyoto to Edo to assume titular authority over a government that they controlled. This is known as the Meiji

Restoration, based on the Japanese word for "brilliant rule," *meiji,* chosen by Emperor Mutsuhito as his reign name.

The Meiji Restoration came after almost a century in which the foundations of Tokugawa society had been weakened by population growth, urbanization, intellectual ferment, social change, and the erosion of Confucian values. Peasant revolts, urban riots, and bolder and more frequent denunciations of the shogun by restive aristocrats all were signs of a troubled regime.

Then in July 1853 an event that many Japanese had feared for decades finally occurred. Into Edo Bay steamed four naval vessels, flying U.S. colors and under the command of the forceful and flamboyant Commodore Matthew Perry. Perry demanded that the Japanese agree to open their ports to U.S. merchants, and Japan acquiesced. Within a decade, Japan also granted trading privileges to the Netherlands, Russia, Great Britain, and France.

Patriotic Japanese now bitterly turned against a government lacking the will, strength, and broad-based support to protect them from such indignities. Opponents of the shogun raised the cry "Honor the Emperor, Expel the Barbarians!" They were convinced that only the semidivine emperor could inspire the national effort needed to overcome the foreigners. On January 3, 1868 (by the Japanese calendar, the ninth day of the twelfth month of 1867), forces led by the Satsuma and Chosu clans seized the shogun's palace and declared the restoration of the emperor. Mutsuhito accepted the invitation of the rebels to head the government, and after his supporters crushed the shogun's resistance, more than 250 years of Tokugawa rule ended. Japan now entered the Meiji Era, a period of transformation unparalleled in recent history.

Eastern Ethics and Western Science
▼▼▼

82 ▼ *Sakuma Shozan,*
REFLECTIONS ON MY ERRORS

After Commodore Perry left Tokyo in the summer of 1853, promising to return within a year to receive answers to his demands, government officials, daimyo, samurai, intellectuals, merchants, and courtiers entered into an intense debate about the crisis at hand and their nation's future. Although the immediate reaction was to reject all things Western and "Expel the Barbarians," many soon realized that threats were no match for superior ships and firepower. Thus, as the debate went on (ending only in 1868 with the collapse of the shogunate), increasing numbers of Japanese were willing to consider the ideas of Sakuma Shozan, whose philosophy is summarized by the motto he made famous: "Eastern ethics and Western science."

Born into a samurai family in 1811, Sakuma received a Confucian education before entering the service of one of Japan's leading aristocrats, Sanada Yukitsura. When the shogun put Sanada in charge of Japan's coastal fortifications in 1841, Sakuma was pushed into the world of artillery, naval strategy, and shipbuilding. He learned Dutch, read all he could of Western science, and became an advocate of adopting Western weaponry. In the 1840s such views were unpopular within the shogun's government, and as a result both Sakuma and his lord were dismissed from the shogun's service. Sakuma experienced more problems in 1854, when at his urging a student of his attempted to stow away on one of Perry's ships as it left Japan. According to the Seclusion Laws (see source 6), this was a capital offense, but through his aristocratic connections, Sakuma and his student received jail sentences of only several months.

Sakuma wrote his deceptively titled *Reflections on My Errors* on his release from prison. Far from being an apology for his "errors," it was a vigorous defense of his opinions made up of fifty-two brief commentaries on various issues. Although he claimed that the work was to be "locked up in a box" and shown only to his descendants, it was widely circulated among Japan's military and political leaders.

After completing *Reflections,* Sakuma continued to advocate the opening of Japan and cooperation between shogun and emperor. His views angered those who sought to abolish the shogunate completely and they arranged his assassination in 1864.

QUESTIONS FOR ANALYSIS

1. What is the meaning of the parable about the "man who is grieved by the illness of his lord or his father"? What is the meaning of the story concerning Zao Wei?
2. What does Sakuma mean by Eastern ethics? Does he see any difficulty reconciling them with Western science?
3. What does Sakuma see as the weaknesses of Japan's military leaders and Confucian scholars? How can their deficiencies be rectified?
4. Why does Sakuma consider the study of mathematics and science to be so important?
5. Aside from his admiration of Western science, how would you characterize Sakuma's attitude toward the West?
6. What similarities and differences do you see between Sakuma's ideas and those of Honda Toshiaki (source 58)?

During my seven months of imprisonment, I pondered over my errors, and, as a result, there were things that I should have liked to say concerning them. However, brush and ink-stone were forbidden in the prison, and I was therefore unable to keep a manuscript. Over that long period, then, I forgot much. Now that I have come out, I shall record what I remember. . . .

▼▼▼

Take, for example, a man who is grieved by the illness of his lord or his father, and who is seeking medicine to cure it. If he is fortunate enough to secure the medicine, and is certain that it will be efficacious, then, certainly, without questioning either its cost or the quality of its name, he will beg his lord or father to take it. Should the latter refuse on the grounds that he dislikes the name, does the younger man make various schemes to give the medicine secretly, or does he simply sit by and wait for his master to die? There is no question about it: the feeling of genuine sincerity and heartfelt grief on the part of the subject or son makes it absolutely impossible for him to sit idly and watch his master's anguish; consequently, even if he knows that he will later have to face his master's anger, he cannot but give the medicine secretly. . . .

▼▼▼

The gentleman has five pleasures, but wealth and rank are not among them. That his house understands decorum and righteousness and remains free from family rifts — this is one pleasure. That exercising care in giving to and taking from others, he provides for himself honestly, free, internally, from shame before his wife and children, and externally, from disgrace before the public — this is the second pleasure. That he expounds and glorifies the learning of the sages, knows in his heart the great Way, and in all situations contents himself with his duty, in adversity as well as in prosperity — this is the third pleasure. That he is born after the opening of the vistas of science by the Westerners, and can therefore understand principles not known to the sages and wise men of old — this is the fourth pleasure. That he employs the ethics of the East and the scientific technique of the West, neglecting neither the spiritual nor material aspects of life, combining subjective and objective, and thus bringing benefit to the people and serving the nation — this is the fifth pleasure. . . .

▼▼▼

The principal requisite of national defense is that it prevents the foreign barbarians from holding us in contempt. The existing coastal defense installations all lack method; the pieces of artillery that have been set up are improperly made; and the officials who negotiate with the foreigners are mediocrities who have no understanding of warfare. The situation being such, even though we wish to avoid incurring the scorn of the barbarians, how, in fact, can we do so? . . .

▼▼▼

Of the men who now hold posts as commanders of the army, those who are not dukes or princes or men of noble rank, are members of wealthy families. As such, they find their daily pleasure in drinking wine, singing, and dancing; and they are ignorant of military strategy and discipline. Should a national emergency arise, there is no one who could command the respect of the warriors and halt the enemy's attack. This is the great sorrow of our times. For this reason, I have wished to follow in substance the Western principles of armament, and, by banding together loyal, valorous, strong men of old, established families not in the military class — men of whom one would be equal to ten ordinary men — to form a voluntary group which would be made to have as its sole aim that of guarding the nation and protecting the people. Anyone wishing to join the society would be tested and his merits examined; and, if he did not shirk hardship, he would then be permitted to join. Men of talent in military strategy, planning, and administration would be advanced to positions of leadership, and then, if the day should come when the country must be defended, this group could be gathered together and organized into an army to await official commands. It is to be hoped that they would drive the enemy away and perform greater service than those who now form the military class. . . .

▼▼▼

Mathematics is the basis for all learning. In the Western world after this science was discovered military tactics advanced greatly, far outstripping that of former times. . . . In the *Art of War*[1] of Sunzi, the statement about "estimation, determination of quantity, calculation, judgment, and victory" has reference to mathematics. However, since Sunzi's time neither we nor the Chinese have ceased to read, study, and memorize his teachings, and our art of war remains exactly as it was then. It consequently cannot be compared

---

[1] A classic work on military strategy written during the early fourth century B.C.E.

with that of the West. There is no reason for this other than that we have not devoted ourselves to basic studies. At the present time, if we wish really to complete our military preparations, we must develop this branch of study. . . .

▼▼▼

What do the so-called scholars of today actually do? . . . Do they, after having learned the rites and music, punishment and administration, the classics and governmental system, go on to discuss and learn the elements of the art of war, of military discipline, of the principles of machinery? Do they make exhaustive studies of conditions in foreign countries? Of effective defense methods? Of strategy in setting up strongholds, defense barriers, and reinforcements? Of the knowledge of computation, gravitation, geometry, and mathematics? If they do, I have not heard of it! Therefore I ask what the so-called scholars of today actually do. . . .

▼▼▼

In order to master the barbarians there is nothing so effective as to ascertain in the beginning conditions among them. To do this, there is no better first step than to be familiar with barbarian tongues. Thus, learning a barbarian language is not only a step toward knowing the barbarians, but also the groundwork for mastering them. . . .

▼▼▼

Last summer the American barbarians arrived in the Bay of Uraga[2] with four warships, bearing their president's message. Their deportment and manner of expression were exceedingly arrogant, and the resulting insult to our national dignity was not small. Those who heard could but gnash their teeth. A certain person on guard in Uraga suffered this insult in silence, and, having been ultimately unable to do anything about it, after the barbarians had retired, he drew his knife and slashed to bits a portrait of their leader, which they had left as a gift. Thus he gave vent to his rage. In former times Zao Wei of Song,[3] having been demoted, was serving as an official in Shensi, and when he heard of the character of Chao Yuanhao, he had a person skillful in drawing paint Chao's image. Zao looked at this portrait and knew from its manly appearance that Chao would doubtless make trouble on the border in the future. Therefore Zao wished to take steps toward preparing the border in advance, and toward collecting together and examining men of ability. Afterwards, everything turned out as he had predicted. Thus, by looking at the portrait of his enemy, he could see his enemy's abilities and thereby aid himself with his own preparations. It can only be regretted that the Japanese guard did not think of this. Instead of using the portrait, he tore it up. In both cases there was a barbarian; in both cases there was a portrait. But one man, lacking the portrait, sought to obtain it, while the other, having it, destroyed it. Their depth of knowledge and farsightedness in planning were vastly different.

---

[2]A small bay at the mouth of Tokyo Bay.

[3]The Chinese Song Dynasty ruled from 960 to 1279 C.E.

Patriotic Duty and Business Success
▼▼▼

83 ▼ *Iwasaki Yataro,*
LETTER TO MITSUBISHI EMPLOYEES

From the moment they seized power, the Meiji reformers sought ways to modernize Japan's economy, especially in those industries on which modern military power depended. After a rocky start in the 1870s, Japanese industrialization proceeded rapidly, and by 1900 the nation had become a major economic power through a combination of government subsidies and individual entrepreneurship.

The greatest success story in Japan's economic transformation was Iwasaki Yataro (1835–1885), the founder of one of the nation's most powerful business conglomerates, Mitsubishi. Born into a poor farming family, Iwasaki gained a rudimentary education and held several low-level business jobs before he found employment as an official in the service of the aristocratic Tosa family in the mid 1860s. He was given the task of managing and reducing the Tosa domain's huge debt, which had resulted from massive purchases of firearms and artillery. His policies, which included paying some debtors with counterfeit money, quickly eliminated the domain's deficit. In 1871, when the domain abandoned its direct ownership of business enterprises, it gave Iwasaki eleven steamships and all the assets connected with its enterprises in the silk, coal, tea, and lumber industries. In return, Iwasaki was expected to pay off some new Tosa debts and provide employment for former samurai. With this to build on, he systematically wiped out foreign and domestic competition and, through a series of shrewd (and frequently cutthroat) business moves, turned Mitsubishi into Japan's second largest conglomerate, with interests in shipbuilding, mining, banking, insurance, and manufacturing.

Iwasaki wrote the following letter to his employees in 1876 during Mitsubishi's battle with the British Peninsula and Oriental Steam Navigation Company over control of Japanese coastal trade. He had just cut fares in half but had also reduced wages by a third.

QUESTIONS FOR ANALYSIS

1. Why does Iwasaki believe that the Japanese must prevent foreigners from becoming involved in the coastal trade?
2. According to Iwasaki, what is at stake in the competition for control of Japan's coastal trade?
3. What advantages and disadvantages does Iwasaki's company have in its rivalry with the Peninsula and Oriental Steam Navigation Company?
4. How does Iwasaki attempt to inspire greater dedication and effort from his workers?
5. To what extent is Iwasaki's letter similar in spirit to Sakuma Shozan's *Reflections on My Errors* (source 82)?

Many people have expressed differing opinions concerning the principles and advantages of engaging foreigners or Japanese in the task of coastal trade. Granted, we may permit a dissenting opinion which suggests that in principle both foreigners and Japanese must be permitted to engage in coastal trade, but once we look into the question of advantages, we know that coastal trade is too important a matter to be given over to the control of foreigners. If we allow the right of coastal navigation to fall into the hands of foreigners in peacetime it means loss of business opportunities and employment for our own people, and in wartime it means yielding the vital right of information to foreigners. In fact, this is not too different from abandoning the rights of our country as an independent nation.

Looking back into the past, in Japan at the time when we abandoned the policy of seclusion and entered into an era of friendly intercourse and commerce with foreign nations, we should have been prepared for this very task. However, due to the fact that our people lack knowledge and wealth, we have yet to assemble a fleet sufficient to engage in coastal navigation. Furthermore, we have neither the necessary skills for navigation nor a plan for developing maritime transportation industry. This condition is the cause of attracting foreign shipping companies to occupy our major maritime transport lines. Yet our people show not a sense of surprise at it. Some people say that our treaties with foreign powers contain an express provision allowing foreign ships to proceed from Harbor A to Harbor B, and others claim that such a provision must not be regarded as granting foreign ships the right to coastal navigation inasmuch as it is intended not to impose unduly heavy taxes on them. While I am not qualified to discuss it, the issue remains an important one.

I now propose to do my utmost, and along with my 35 million compatriots, perform my duty as a citizen of this country. That is to recover the right of coastal trade in our hands, and not to delegate that task to foreigners. Unless we propose to do so, it is useless for our government to revise the unequal treaties[1] or to change our entrenched customs. We need people who can respond, otherwise all the endeavors of the government will come to naught. This is the reason why the government protects our company, and I know that our responsibilities are even greater than the full weight of Mt. Fuji[2] thrust upon our shoulders. There have been many who wish to hinder our progress in fulfilling our obligations. However,

we have been able to eliminate one of our worst enemies, the Pacific Mail Company of the United States, from contention by application of appropriate means.[3] Now, another rival has emerged. It is the Peninsula & Oriental Steam Navigation Company of Great Britain which is setting up a new line between Yokohama and Shanghai, and is attempting to claim its right over the ports of Nagasaki, Kobe, and Yokohama. The P & O Company comes to compete for the right of coastal navigation with us. How can we decline the challenge? Heretofore, our company has received protection from the government, support from the nation, and hard work from its employees through which it has done its duty. However, our company is young and not every phase of its operation is well conducted. In contrast, the P & O Company is backed by its massive capital, its large fleet of ships, and by its experiences of operations in Oriental countries. In competing against this giant, what methods can we employ?

I have thought about this problem very carefully and have come to one conclusion. There is no other alternative but to eliminate unnecessary positions and unnecessary expenditures. This is a time-worn solution and no new wisdom is involved. Even though it is a familiar saying, it is much easier said than done, and this indeed has been the root cause of difficulties in the past and present times. Therefore, starting immediately I propose that we engage in this task. By eliminating unnecessary personnel from the payroll, eliminating unnecessary expenditures, and engaging in hard and arduous work, we shall be able to solidify the foundation of our company. If there is a will there is a way. Through our own effort, we shall be able to repay the government for its protection and answer our nation for its confidence shown in us. Let us work together in discharging our responsibilities and not be ashamed of ourselves. Whether we succeed or fail, whether we

---

[1]The various commercial treaties the shogunate signed after Admiral Perry's mission.
[2]The highest mountain in Japan, near Tokyo.
[3]The American firm abandoned its effort to crack the

Japanese market when it found it could not compete with Mitsubishi's low prices, made possible largely by government subsidies.

can gain profit or sustain loss, we cannot anticipate at this time. Hopefully, all of you will join me in a singleness of heart to attain this cherished goal, forebearing and undaunted by setbacks to restore to our own hands the right to our own coastal trade. If we succeed it will not only be an accomplishment for our company alone but also a glorious event for our Japanese Empire, which shall let its light shine to all four corners of earth. We can succeed or fail, and it depends on your effort or lack of effort. Do your utmost in this endeavor!

Images of the West in Late Tokugawa and Meiji Japan
▼▼▼

84 ▼ *PRINTS AND DRAWINGS, 1853–1887*

In the decades after the first Europeans arrived in Japan in 1542, their ideas, dress, weapons, and religion proved attractive to many Japanese. As many as 500,000 Japanese converted to Catholicism, military leaders put European firearms to use in their civil wars, and in the 1580s and 1590s some Japanese showed an interest in European fashion and cuisine. After the Tokugawa suppressed Christianity and implemented the seclusion policy in the seventeenth century, however, knowledge of the West soon came to be limited to the merchants who traded with the Dutch in Nagasaki and a handful of intellectuals who maintained interest in European thought. For most Japanese, memory of the South Sea Barbarians disappeared.

The arrival of Commodore Perry in 1853 and the opening of Japan to foreign trade in 1854 changed this dramatically. Inspired by a mixture of fear, awe, and curiosity, the Japanese developed a deep interest in the West, and a flood of printed material about Europe and the United States appeared in the 1850s and 1860s. Then after the Meiji Restoration of 1868, imitation of the West became a patriotic duty. Employing Western science, technology, military organization, and government practices would make Japan strong and prosperous; adopting Western fashion, etiquette, grooming habits, architecture, and culture would make the Japanese respected and admired. In the late 1880s, however, a reaction against overzealous Westernization set in. Since then, the Japanese have managed to strike a balance between borrowing from the West what was necessary for their modernization and preserving the essentials of their traditional culture.

The six following illustrations, covering the period from the 1850s to the late 1880s, provide insights into changing Japanese views of the West. They also serve as reminders that these changes in attitudes underlay the political, military, and economic transformation that made Japan a world power.

The first two illustrations (page 358) are tile prints that appeared shortly after the arrival of Commodore Perry in 1853. Forerunners of modern newspapers, tile prints were produced quickly and anonymously after newsworthy events and sold for a few cents. The first print depicts one of Perry's "black ships," so called because of the dark smoke that belched from their smokestacks. The Japanese text provides information on the ship's dimensions and the length of its voyage to Japan. The second print depicts Commander Henry Adams, Perry's second-in-command.

The next two illustrations both appeared when the drive to emulate Europeans was fully under way. The first illustration (page 359) is part of a series of wood-block prints published in the 1880s entitled *Self-Made Men Worthy of Emulation.* The individual depicted here is Fukuchi Gen'ichiro (1841–1909), a journalist who served as editor-in-chief of Tokyo's first daily newspaper. He is shown as a war correspondent covering the Satsuma Rebellion of 1877, a rebellion by disgruntled samurai against the new Meiji order that was suppressed by the imperial army. The accompanying text (with an erroneous birthdate) reads:

> Fukuchi Gen'ichiro was born in Nagasaki in 1844. An exceptionally bright child, he could recognize characters at the age of five and had begun to read and write at about the age of seven. He resolved to enter the service of the shogunate and, upon coming of age, entered the government, in the service of which he traveled three times to Europe. He then entered into a successful business career. In 1874 he became president of the Reporters' Association. He personally covered the Satsuma Rebellion in the south. Received by the emperor, he respectfully reported his observations to the throne. His style seemed almost supernatural in its logic, force, and lucidity. He is one of the truly great men of Meiji.

The next illustration (page 360) appeared in a popular book, written by Kanaga-ki Robun and published in serial form in the 1870s. Entitled *Hiking through the West,* it relates the adventures of two Japanese travelers during a trip to London and back. The illustration depicts, from right to left, an "unenlightened man," dressed in the garb of a samurai, a "half-enlightened man," and an "enlightened man."

Even in the years when the Japanese enthusiasm for things Western reached its height, some opposed Japan's headlong rush to Westernize. Government censorship caused most of these critics to remain silent, but a few managed to get their ideas into print. Cartoonists Honda Kinkichiro and Kobayashi Kyochika were two such individuals. Honda's cartoons, usually accompanied by English captions and a Japanese text, appeared in the 1870s and 1880s in the weekly humor magazine *Marumara Chimbun.* His cartoon "Monkey Show Dressing Room" (page 360) was published in 1879, shortly after Dr. Edward S. Morse introduced Darwin's theory of evolution in a series of lectures at the newly founded Department of Zoology at Tokyo University. The text reads, "Mr. Morse explains that all human beings were monkeys in the beginning. In the beginning — but even now aren't we still monkeys? When it comes to Western things we think the red beards [a Japanese nickname for Westerners] are the most skillful at everything."

Kobayashi, who contributed cartoons to *Marumara Chimbun* in the 1880s, published his cartoon (page 361) in the *Tokyo Daily News* in 1891. It depicts the New Year's Dance held in the Rokumeikan, a pavilion built by the government in 1883 to serve as a venue for fancy-dress balls and other entertainments involving Westerners and Japan's elite. Above the dance floor, dominated by ill-matched Western and Japanese couples, is a sign that reads, "Hands Dance, Feet Stomp, Call Out Hurrah!"

One of Commodore Perry's Black Ships

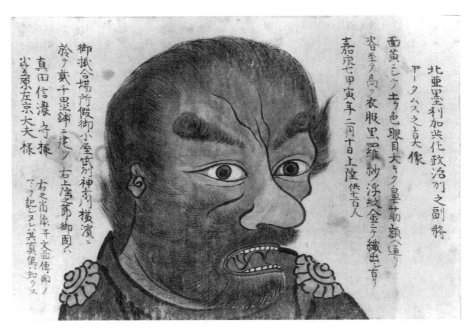

Commodore Perry's Second-in-Command, Commander Henry Adams

Kobayashi Kyochika, *Fukuchi Gen'ichiro*

Kanagaki Robun, *Hiking through the West*

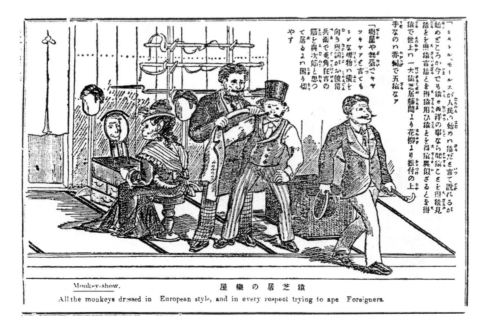

Monkey-show.

All the monkeys dressed in European style, and in every respect trying to ape Foreigners.

Honda Kinkichiro, *"Monkey Show Dressing Room"*

Kobayashi Kiyochika, *"Hands Dance, Feet Stomp, Call Out Hurrah!"*

QUESTIONS FOR ANALYSIS

1. What impression of the West is conveyed by the prints of Perry's ship and his second-in-command, Commander Adams? What specific details help convey this impression?
2. In the top illustration on page 360, what are the most significant differences between the three figures? How does the artist convey a sense of the "enlightened man's" superiority?
3. What is there in the drawing of Fukuchi Gen'ichiro and in the accompanying text that makes him "a man worthy of emulation"?
4. Why do you think the artist chose to depict Fukuchi while he was covering the Satsuma Rebellion?
5. What messages are Honda and Kobayashi attempting to convey about Japan's campaign to Westernize?
6. Compare and contrast the depiction of Westerners in "Hands Dance . . ." with the earlier depiction of Commander Adams.

▼▼▼

Southeast Asia in the Era of Imperialism

The Western takeover of Southeast Asia in the nineteenth century was more gradual than the European seizure of Africa but was motivated by the same mixture of nationalism, anticipated economic benefits, missionary zeal, and perceived strategic imperatives. The British move into Burma, which took place in three stages following wars fought in the 1820s, 1850s, and 1880s, was to prevent Burmese interference in India and head off French influence in the region. In contrast, economic motives inspired the British takeover of the Malay Peninsula. The British annexed Singapore in 1819 after they discovered that Malacca, taken from the Dutch in 1795, had lost much of its commercial prominence. They gradually extended their authority over the remainder of the peninsula to protect their interests in the region's tin mines and rubber plantations.

The French subjugation of Vietnam, which began in 1862 with the takeover of Saigon and the southern provinces, was ostensibly for religious reasons. The French intervened to protect Vietnamese Christians and European Catholic missionaries from persecution by the Vietnamese government. They subsequently took over northern Vietnam, Laos, and Cambodia, and lumped these territories into their colony of Indochina.

The Dutch extended their political authority in the East Indies in the late nineteenth century to head off European competitors and to exploit the islands' tin, oil, rubber, and agricultural products. Finally, the United States became an imperialist power in the region when it took over the Philippines from Spain after the Spanish American War of 1898.

Western colonialism in most of Southeast Asia was relatively brief, lasting on average only a century or less, but it was still significant. In politics it brought administrative cohesion to diverse island groupings such as the East Indies, and throughout the region it weakened or eliminated the authority of traditional leaders. It also altered the region's economy by stimulating enterprises such as tin mining and rubber production, introducing new crops such as the oil palm, improving communications, and promoting the building of new harbors and rail systems. In part because of economic development, the region's population soared from approximately 26 million in 1830 to 123 million in the 1940s. Western colonialism also expanded education and introduced the ideologies of nationalism, liberalism, and democracy. Inevitably, these developments inspired anticolonial movements and, after World War II, the emergence of independent states throughout the region.

Reform from Above in Thailand

▼▼▼

85 ▼ King Chulalongkorn, EDICTS AND PROCLAMATIONS

Unlike the rulers of Burma, who underestimated the British threat, and the rulers of Vietnam, who provoked the French by persecuting Christians, the kings of Thailand pursued a policy of compromise with the West and a program of European-inspired reform. As a result, Thailand lost territory in the imperialist era, but not its independence.

Thailand had been largely immune from Western interference since the 1600s, but in the 1820s the British began to petition for trading privileges, and missionaries, many of them American Protestants, increased their activities. Missionaries made few converts among Thailand's devout Buddhists, but they introduced Western medicine, science, and the country's first printing press. They also influenced King Mongkut (r. 1851–1868), the ruler who oversaw Thailand's early response to the West. Before becoming king, Mongkut spent twenty-seven years in a Buddhist monastery, where in addition to his religious studies he learned Western languages and developed an interest in Western science and mathematics. As king, he sought to modernize Thailand's army and economy and to accommodate Western powers by opening Thailand to trade.

Mongkut's policies were continued under his son Chulalongkorn (one of the eighty children Mongkut fathered after abandoning monastic celibacy at age forty-seven), who reigned from 1868 to 1910. Chulalongkorn's experiences included trips to India, Java, and Malaya and two visits to Europe. He delicately balanced his diplomatic relations with Great Britain, colonial master of Burma and Malaya, and France, which dominated Indochina. He also introduced railroad, postal, and telegraph systems, founded schools, and abolished slavery.

The following excerpts from Chulalongkorn's speeches and writings provide insights into his motives and style as a reformer. The first selection is from a speech to his advisors in 1864 on the subject of slavery, a centuries-old institution in Thailand. Large numbers of Thais sold themselves into slavery to cancel debts or escape poverty, and all their children became slaves. The state put a value on slaves at various ages, and slaves could gain their freedom if they paid their master their worth. Few could do this, so most slaves were slaves for life. Chulalongkorn gradually liberalized Thailand's slavery laws and in 1895 abolished slavery altogether.

The other two sections deal with education, the expansion of which was important to Chulalongkorn's plans to modernize his country. He advocated not only the teaching of Western languages, mathematics, and science, but also Thailand's cultural and literary heritage.

QUESTIONS FOR ANALYSIS

1. What motivated Chulalongkorn to improve the lot of slaves in Thailand?
2. Why does he believe that immediately ending slavery would be a mistake?
3. What were Chulalongkorn's convictions about education, and how were they linked to his strategy for ending slavery?
4. What kind of person should Thailand's educational system seek to produce, according to Chulalongkorn?
5. In Chulalongkorn's view, what are the major deficiencies of missionary schools?
6. How does Chulalongkorn's approach to reform resemble and differ from that of Russia's Peter the Great (source 40)?

I wish to see whatever is beneficial to the people accomplished gradually according to circumstances and unjust, though well-established, customs abolished. But, as it is impossible to change everything overnight, steady pruning is necessary to lighten the burden. If this practice is adopted, things will proceed smoothly and satisfactorily as time goes by. As far as slavery is concerned, children born to slaves in their creditors' houses are considered by present legislation to be slaves. For this purpose, male slaves born in such circumstances from the age of 26 to 40 are worth each, according to present legislation, 14 *tamlungs*,[1] while female ones are worth each 12 *tamlungs*. In the case of male slaves of more than 40 and female ones of more than 30, value declines gradually with advancing age until at 100 male slaves are worth 1 *tamlung* while female ones 3 *baht*.

I feel that children born to slaves in their creditor's houses, who are slaves as from the time of delivery and are worth something even beyond 100, have not been treated kindly. Children thus born have nothing to do with their parents' wrongdoing. The parents have not only sold themselves into slavery but also dragged their innocent children into lifetime slavery and suffering on their behalf. But to emancipate them straight away now would put them into the danger of being neglected and being left to die by themselves, since unkind creditors, seeing no use

in letting mothers look after their children, will put these mothers to work. It is therefore felt that, if these children are of no use to their parents' creditors, they will meet with no kindness. If the burden borne at present is so reduced as to allow them to become free, it seems advisable. Slaves' children aged from 8 upwards can be depended upon to work, and thus their full worth should be calculated as from this age. With advancing years their worth should be reduced until at 21 they are emancipated just in time for ordination as priests and for embarking on their careers. Similarly, female slaves are emancipated just in time to get married and have children. . . . Thus at 21 they are emancipated, and, in view of the fact that they have served their masters up to 20, enough advantage has been derived by their masters. . . .

▷ Chulalongkorn expresses his hope that all slavery might be abolished.

However, I do not think that my proposal can be carried to its logical conclusions, since pressure exists in the direction of making people want to become slaves despite our desire to see the contrary. Slaves do not have to pay high State dues and do not have to engage in any regular occupation, since they are maintained by their masters. They work when work comes to them;

---

[1] A unit of Thai currency; one tamlung equaled four baht.

otherwise they are unoccupied. When there is nothing to do and they happen to come by a bit of money, they gamble, since there is no risk of losing their means of subsistence. . . . If my proposal really succeeds, I can think of one other thing which can effectively liberate slaves' children from slavery. Slaves' children are compelled to serve their masters from an early age and know nothing other than what pleases their masters. Instead of getting vocational training, they spend their free time in gambling from early childhood so that this habit becomes ingrained, thereby preventing them from seeing any value in having a career. If they really have to quit slavery, they do not possess sufficient knowledge to improve their status and are compelled to return to slavery. It is because of this that there should be an institution for education similar to the old almshouse where, by royal command, education was given to children. There have been a good many men educated in this manner, and many available clerks at the time came from such institution. . . . At the present time, there are not enough clerks [literate people] to go round. Literate people are in great demand among the noblemen and will not readily remain slaves. This is why I feel that education can really free slaves. . . . Once they can read and write, various subjects including those derived from translated European texts can be taught. At 17 or 18 they should be able to apply their knowledge to various branches of the civil service as petty officials or clerks, or secure employment outside the civil service. . . . But school education is an increasingly expensive undertaking, and should begin in a small way with possibilities of gradual expansion. This will not only reduce the number of slaves but will also bring prosperity to the country, paving the way for a more drastic reform in the future. . . .

ROYAL PROCLAMATION ON EDUCATION

. . . Chulalongkorn, Lord of Siam, considers that, though the long-established practice in educa-tion in Siam has been to use the monastery as the seat of learning and the home as the center of vocational training in the family, in modern times the increasing tempo of international communications by means of steamers at sea and railways on land and the increasing international contacts caused by the necessity of nations to exchange commodities, have dictated a reorientation of academic and technical training in a correct and useful manner and also a proper adjustment of outmoded disciplines and arts. . . .

The Government has for some time maintained schools; but the original purpose of training people for the needs of the civil service has misled some into thinking that learning is meant exclusively for those destined for the civil service and that it is no part of the masses' duty to seek knowledge. . . .

In actual fact, education leads to intelligence and proper behavior and skill in earning one's living. No matter what a person's career is, whether it be in teaching, medicine, trade or mechanics, prior learning is essential for success in life. . . .

From now on it shall be the duty of parents and guardians to teach their children and afford them such opportunity for education as their status and financial means allow. The Government will, for its part, lay down the framework of national education as a guideline to be announced later by officials of the Ministry of Education. The purpose of such education and training shall be to inculcate the following qualities: inquisitiveness for knowledge to whet intelligence and capability, good and righteous behavior, concern for family welfare, generosity to relatives, unity and harmony with spouses, faithfulness to friends, economy, kindness to others, regard for the public good, compliance with laws, willingness to serve the country with courage, loyalty to the throne in times of need, and gratefulness and loyalty to the throne at all times.

When all these elements of responsibility have become so deeply rooted in one's nature as to be manifested in all outward behavior, then training and education may be said to have succeeded, and any one who has successfully undergone the process may be said to be an eminently worthy citizen of Siam.

LETTER TO THE THAI MINISTER OF EDUCATION, 1910

Dear Praya Paisal,

I have one more thing to tell you. At the celebration of my birthday the Kulstree School[2] for royal ladies sent me 6 copies of the Wadhana Widhaya magazine, which is a monthly and which you may have seen yourself. . . .

My reaction as I went through the magazine was initially that these missionaries had a working knowledge of Siamese and that our girl students had a working knowledge of English. On reflection, however, it was seen that the knowledge of contributors was confined to narrow limits, since there were many errors in respect, for instance, to geography and history about which nothing was known. What was known concerned only religion taught by teachers, and it is a pity that students should be thus confined. . . .

My conclusion from this was that, though the teaching of missionaries could bring about knowledge and intelligence in some matters, it could hardly foster patriotism, since the basic approach was already destructive of this. . . . In one

place mention was made of liberty, which the Siamese were unlikely to understand when it was also made of riots in India. This is something we are not accustomed to and must be a novelty. . . . I think it should be our principle to think out the approach to education that will promote the welfare of that part of the globe in which we live rather that which missionaries set up. What they preach will be different from the principles of learning in particular countries. Do they all preach this in all places and do they succeed elsewhere? I do not think they do. They can only deceive softhearted and ignorant women into following them. Even then these people are in the minority and in an embarrassing position. They feel abashed to pay respect to Buddhist monks in the presence of Europeans, and are equally shameful to let the Siamese know their European faith. There are many such Siamese, and it is not in the nature of our good citizens to be so. Remember this. Religion is not important, and any religion is out of date in the context of the present day, unless we establish up-to-date religions. But, as we cannot establish religions, we should plan to keep up with the times and forget about an up-to-date religion. It is a waste of time to argue about something which is 2,000 years old.

---

[2]A school sponsored by the Anglican Church, England's state church, for educating princesses and daughters of the high nobility.

The Fall of Vietnam
▼▼▼

86 ▼ *Phan Thanh Gian,*
LETTER TO EMPEROR TU DUC and
LAST MESSAGE TO HIS ADMINISTRATORS

In 1802 decades of civil war ended in Vietnam when Nguyen Anh unified the country after his conquest of Hanoi. Taking the name Emperor Gia Long, he and his successors attempted to govern the country according to the principles of Confucianism, which had played an important role in Vietnamese politics and thought for many centuries. The Nguyen emperors' efforts to stabilize Vietnam and turn it into a model Confucian society led directly to the persecution of Vietnamese Catholics, who, as a result mainly of efforts by French missionaries, numbered 300,000 by the nineteenth century. When Vietnamese Catholics were implicated in a rebellion in 1833, Emperor Minh Mang ordered the imprisonment and execution of converts and European missionaries. Three years later he closed Vietnamese ports to European shipping. These steps caused the French, who sixty years earlier had helped the Nguyen Dynasty gain power, to send naval vessels and troops to Vietnam, ostensibly to protect Christianity but also to advance French imperialism. Fighting broke out in earnest in 1858, and although the Vietnamese staunchly resisted, Emperor Tu Duc accepted a settlement in 1862 by which he ceded to the French three southern provinces around Saigon.

Four years later, an anti-French rebellion broke out in a district west of Saigon, then under the governorship of Phan Thanh Gian (1796–1867), one of Vietnam's leading statesmen and head of a delegation sent to Paris in 1863 to negotiate with the French government. When he failed to suppress the revolts, the French sent in troops and demanded control of the provinces. In 1867 Phan Thanh Gian acquiesced and then committed suicide, but not before he wrote the following two letters, one to Emperor Tu Duc and the other to administrators in his district.

QUESTIONS FOR ANALYSIS

1. What is the basis of Phan Thanh Gian's hope that the emperor can save Vietnam from further humiliation at the hands of the French?
2. What is Phan Thanh Gian's view of the French?
3. What evidence of Phan Thanh Gian's Confucian training do you see in the letter?
4. Why did Phan Thanh Gian decide to acquiesce to the French?

LETTER TO EMPEROR TU DUC

8, July 1867

I, Phan Thanh Gian, make the following report, in expressing frankly, with my head bowed, my humble sentiments, and in soliciting, with my head raised, your discerning scrutiny.

During the period of difficulties and misfortunes that we are presently undergoing, rebellion is rising around the capital, the pernicious influence[1] is expanding on our frontiers. The territorial question is rapidly leading to a situation that it is impossible to end.

My duty compels me to die. I would not dare to live thoughtlessly, leaving a heritage of shame

to my Sovereign and my Father. Happily, I have confidence in my Emperor, who has extensive knowledge of ancient times and the present and who has studied profoundly the causes of peace and of dissension: . . . In respectfully observing the warnings of Heaven and in having pity on the misery of man . . . in changing the string of the guitar, in modifying the track of the governmental chariot, it is still possible for you to act in accordance with your authority and means.

At the last moment of life, the throat constricted, I do not know what to say, but, in wiping my tears and in raising my eyes toward you affectionately, I can only ardently hope that this wish will be realized. With respect, I make this

---

[1]The French.

report, Tu Duc, twentieth year, sixth moon, seventh day, Phan Thanh Gian.

LAST MESSAGE TO HIS ADMINISTRATORS

Mandarins and people,

It is written: He who lives in accordance with the will of Heaven lives in virtue; he who does not live according to the will of Heaven lives in evil. To work according to the will of Heaven is to listen to natural reason. . . . Man is an intelligent animal created by Heaven. Every animal lives according to his nature, as water flows to low ground, as fire goes out on dry ground. . . . Men, to whom Heaven has given reason, must apply themselves to live in obedience to this reason which Heaven has given them.

The empire of our king is ancient. Our gratitude toward our kings is complete and always ardent; we cannot forget them. Now, the French are come, with their powerful weapons of war to cause dissension among us. We are weak against them; our commanders and our soldiers have been vanquished. Each battle adds to our misery. . . . The French have immense warships, filled with soldiers and armed with huge cannons. No one can resist them. They go where they want, the strongest ramparts fall before them.

I have raised my spirit toward Heaven and I have listened to the voice of reason. And I have said: "It would be as senseless for you to wish to defeat your enemies by force of arms as for a young fawn to attack a tiger. You attract uselessly great misfortunes upon the people whom Heaven has confided to you. I have thus written to all the mandarins and to all the war commanders to break their lances and surrender the forts without fighting.

But, if I have followed the Will of Heaven by averting great evils from the head of the people, I am a traitor to our king in delivering without resistance the provinces which belong to him. . . . I deserve death. Mandarins and people, you can live under the command of the French, who are only terrible during the battle, but their flag must never fly above a fortress where Phan Thanh Gian still lives."

Part Four

▼▼▼

The Global Community and Its Challenges in the Twentieth and Twenty-first Centuries

What will future historians have to say about the last 100 years of human history? How will they interpret the wars, revolutions, economic transformations, new ideologies, technological breakthroughs, demographic trends, cultural changes, and all the other events and developments that took place? What part will recent events such as the terrorist attacks of September 11, 2001, and the U.S.-led invasion of Iraq in 2003 play in their accounts? How will they explain the seeming contradiction between humankind's stupendous achievements and abysmal failures? From the perspective of the early twenty-first century no one can answer questions such as these. Future historians' views of our past will be shaped by events that have not yet occurred and by values and concerns unique to their own era. What seems of great consequence to us, therefore, may be insignificant to them, while developments we barely perceive may be important parts of their stories.

It would be surprising, however, if future historians did not note the importance of the dramatic shift in world relationships that took place in the middle of the twentieth century. The world of the early 1900s was a Eurocentric world. Europeans were the best-educated and wealthiest people on Earth, and a few European states — Great Britain, Germany, Russia, and France, along with the Netherlands, Portugal, Belgium, Italy, and a European offshoot, the United States — were the masters of Africa and much of Asia. When one spoke of Great Powers, they were all European states. Despite its new industrial might and a few colonies, the United States was still not a major player on the world scene. After the Second World War, Europe's primacy ended. The Europeans' colonial empires disintegrated, their paramount role in international relations shifted to the Soviet Union and the United States, and their economic importance declined in the face of global competition.

Future historians undoubtedly will also highlight the phenomenon of *globalization,* a word and concept that came into common usage at the end of the twentieth century to describe the unprecedented scale of integration and interaction that had come to dominate relationships among the world's peoples. Human interaction, of course, was nothing new. Long-distance trade, migration, travel, missionary activity, wars of conquest, and the diffusion of new ideas and technologies all had been part of history for thousands of years. But interaction on a global scale did not begin to increase rapidly until the fifteenth and sixteenth centuries, when Europeans first sailed to Africa, the Americas, and Asia and opened a new era in commerce, migration, and biological exchange.

During the twentieth century, however, breakthroughs in communications and transportation virtually obliterated the limitations of time and space, and the exchange of goods and ideas among the world's peoples reached undreamed-of levels. It became the age of *world* wars, *multinational* corporations, *global* communication networks, the *World Wide Web,* and thousands of *international* organizations.

Historians assuredly will also note other developments: the ongoing rush of scientific, medical, and technological discoveries; the spectacular expansion of the world's population (from approximately 1.7 billion in 1900 to 6.4 billion in 2003); the decline of the world's rural population and the growth of cities, best represented by megacities such as Tokyo, Mexico City, São Paulo, and Bombay; and the emergence at least superficially of a shared global culture, symbolized by the Internet and the ubiquity of McDonald's restaurants, blue jeans, American popular music, and twenty-four-hour cable news networks.

What else historians will say about the twentieth century is open to conjecture. They undoubtedly will take note of our recent history's inhumanities and cruelties: its appalling war casualties, its use of torture, and its genocides, not just against Jews in World War II but also against Armenians in World War I, Cambodians in the 1970s, and Bosnians, Kosovars, and Tutsi in the 1990s. Will such developments be described as aberrations or the beginning of a new trend toward brutality and callousness in human relationships? Historians surely will discuss the emergence of over 100 new independent states in Africa and Asia after the demise of colonialism. Will their stories be celebrations of economic and political achievement or tales of failure and disillusionment? They will note that the twentieth century was marked by signs of both growing religious fervor and indifference; environmental disasters and growing environmental consciousness; and the globalization of culture and the continued appeal of nationalism and ethnic identification.

In looking toward the future, optimists affirm their faith in progress, holding fast to the dream that reasonable human beings are capable of shaping a future of peace, harmony, and a just sharing of the world's wealth. Pessimists ponder population projections, inevitable energy shortages, worsening pollution, and perhaps a nuclear winter, and warn of the coming of a new "dark age." However things develop, recent history has launched humankind on new paths that will determine its future for years to come.

Chapter 11

▼▼▼

The Industrialized World in Crisis

In 1922 the French intellectual Paul Valéry spoke these words in a speech to a university audience in Switzerland:

> The storm has died away, and still we are restless, uneasy, as if the storm is about to break. Almost all the affairs of men remain in terrible uncertainty. We think of what has disappeared, we are almost destroyed by what has been destroyed; we do not know what will be born, and we fear the future, not without reason. We hope vaguely, we dread precisely; . . . we confess that the charm of life is behind us, abundance is behind us, but doubt and disorder are in us and with us. There is no thinking man, however shrewd or learned he may be, who can hope to overcome this anxiety, to escape this darkness, to measure the probable duration of this period when the vital relations of humanity are disturbed profoundly.[1]

How stark a contrast between Valéry's despondency and the previous generation's limitless optimism! Before World War I the wealth, power, and scientific achievements of the West reached unimagined heights, and most Americans and Europeans were self-satisfied and proud to the point of arrogance. They took for granted their moral and intellectual superiority and were confident their world dominance would last indefinitely. The people of Japan, a successful new entrant into the ranks of industrialized nations, had a different perspective on the future, but like the people of the West they looked forward to that future with high expectations. Only a few years later assurance gave way to doubt, hope to despair, and moderation to fanaticism.

The turning point, especially for Europe, was World War I — the four-year exercise in death that resulted in 30 million casualties, billions of squandered dollars, and a disturbing realization that human inventiveness had potentially dark and

---

[1] Paul Valéry, *Variety* (New York: Harcourt-Brace, 1927), p. 252.

devastating consequences. The war and the postwar treaties set the stage for three decades marked by worldwide economic depression, totalitarianism, diplomatic failure, contempt for human rights, and finally, a second world war with a legacy of 50 to 60 million dead, the attempted annihilation of Europe's Jews, and the dropping of the first atomic bombs.

Interwar intellectuals who shared Paul Valéry's anxiety and gloom prophesied the fall of Western civilization and drew analogies between the decline of the West in the twentieth century and the fatal problems of fifth-century Rome. Developments after World War II discredited much of their bleak pessimism. The industrialized nations, even devastated Germany and Japan, recovered from the decades of war and depression and have retained many of their distinctive characteristics. What changed was their role in the world. Empires disappeared, and formerly colonial peoples reestablished their political independence. The traumatic events that unfolded between 1914 and 1945 were largely responsible for these changes.

▼▼▼

The Trauma of World War I

Why did Europeans find World War I so demoralizing, so unsettling, so devoid of any quality or result that might have justified its appalling costs and casualties? War, after all, was nothing new for Europeans. Dynastic wars, religious wars, commercial wars, colonial wars, civil wars, wars to preserve or destroy the balance of power, wars of every conceivable variety fill the pages of European history books. Some of these wars involved dozens of states, and some can even be considered world wars. The Seven Years' War (1756–1763) was fought in Europe, the Americas, and India. The wars of the French Revolution and Napoleonic Era spilled over from Europe into Egypt and had reverberations in the Americas, South Africa, and Southeast Asia. Yet, as the sources in this section seek to show, none of these experiences prepared Europeans for the war they fought between 1914 and 1918.

The sheer number of battlefield casualties goes far to explain the war's devastating impact. The thirty-two nations that participated in the war mobilized approximately 65 million men, of whom just under 10 million were killed and slightly more than 20 million were wounded. To present these statistics in another way, this means that for approximately 1,500 consecutive days during the war, on average 6,000 men were killed. Losses were high on both the eastern and western fronts, but those in the west were more troubling. Here, after the Germans almost took Paris in the early weeks of fighting, the war became a stalemate until the armistice on November 11, 1918. Along a 400-mile front stretching from the

English Channel through Belgium and France to the Swiss border, defense — a combination of trenches, barbed wire, land mines, poison gas, and machine guns — proved superior to offense — massive artillery barrages followed by charges of troops sent over the top across no man's land to overrun enemy lines. Such attacks produced unbearably long casualty lists but minuscule gains of territory.

Such losses would have been easier to endure if the war had led to a secure and lasting peace. But the hardships and antagonisms of the postwar years rendered such sacrifice meaningless. After the war, winners and losers alike faced inflation, high unemployment, and, after a few years of prosperity in the 1920s, the affliction of the Great Depression. Embittered by their defeat and harsh treatment by the victorious allies in the Versailles Treaty, the Germans abandoned their democratic Weimar Republic for Hitler's Nazi dictatorship in 1933. Japan and Italy, though on the winning side, were disappointed with their territorial gains, and this resentment played into the hands of ultranationalist politicians. The Arabs, who had fought against Germany's ally, the Turks, in the hope of achieving nationhood, were embittered when Great Britain and France denied their independence. The United States, disillusioned with war and Great Power wrangling, withdrew into diplomatic isolation, leaving Great Britain and France to enforce the postwar treaties and face the fearsome problems caused by the reordering of Europe and Russia's Bolshevik Revolution. Britain and France expanded their colonial empires in Africa and the Middle East, but this was scant compensation for their casualties, expenditures, and postwar problems of inflation, indebtedness, and loss of economic leadership. There were no true victors in World War I.

The Romance of War
▼▼▼

87 ▼ *POPULAR ART AND POSTER ART FROM GERMANY, ENGLAND, AND AUSTRALIA*

When the soldiers marched off to war in the summer of 1914, crowds cheered, young men rushed to enlist, and politicians promised that "the boys would be home by Christmas." Without having experienced a general war since the defeat of Napoleon in 1815 and with little thought to the millions of casualties in the American Civil War, Europeans saw the war as a glorious adventure — an opportunity to fight for the flag or kaiser or queen, to wear splendid uniforms, and to win glory in battles that would be decided by élan, spirit, and bravery. The war they fought was nothing like the war they imagined, and the disparity between expectations and reality was one of many reasons why the four-year struggle was fraught with such disillusionment and bitterness.

The four illustrations shown here portray the positive attitudes toward the war that all belligerents shared at the outset and that governments sought to perpetuate as the war dragged on. The first (page 375, left), entitled *The Departure,* shows a German troop train departing for the battlefront in late summer 1914. The work of B. Hennerberg, an artist originally from Sweden, it originally appeared in the German periodical *Simplicissimus* in August 1914. That *Simplicissimus* would publish such an illustration indicates the depth of the nationalist emotions the war generated. Noted before the war for its irreverent satire and criticism of German militarism, *Simplicissimus,* once the fighting started, lent its full support to the war effort.

The second illustration (page 375, right) is one of a series of war-related cards that the Mitchell Tobacco Company included in its packs of Golden Dawn Cigarettes in 1914 and early 1915. It shows a sergeant offering smokes to the soldiers under his command before battle. Tobacco advertising with military themes reached a saturation point in England during the war years.

An Australian recruitment poster issued in 1915 serves as the third illustration (page 376, left). Although Australia, like Canada, had assumed authority over its own internal affairs by the time the war started, its foreign policy was still controlled by Great Britain. Hence when Great Britain went to war, so did Australia. The Australian parliament refused to approve conscription, however, so the government had to work hard to encourage volunteers. This particular poster appeared at a time when Australian troops were heavily involved in the Gallipoli campaign, the allied effort to knock the Ottoman Empire out of the war. Directing its message to the many young men who were members of sports clubs, it promised them an opportunity to enlist in a battalion made up entirely of fellow sportsmen. Such battalions had already been formed in England.

The fourth poster was produced and distributed by the newly formed British Ministry of Munitions in early 1917 to encourage women to accept jobs in the munitions industry. This was just one example of the broad government attempt from 1915 onward to enlist women in the war effort as medical workers, police, agricultural workers, porters, drivers, foresters, members of the Women's Auxiliary Army Corps, and, most important, factory laborers. This particular poster shows a young and attractive English woman offering a jaunty salute to a passing soldier as she arrives for work. It gives no hint of the dangers of munitions work. During the war approximately 300 "munitionettes" were killed in explosions or from chemical-related sicknesses. Women who worked with TNT came to be known as "canaries" because of the yellow color of their skin. Despite such hazards and relatively low pay, approximately 950,000 women were working in munitions factories by war's end.

QUESTIONS FOR ANALYSIS

1. What message about the war does each of the four illustrations seek to convey?
2. In what specific ways does each poster romanticize the life of a soldier or female munitions worker?
3. What impression of battle does the English tobacco card communicate?
4. What does a comparison of Hennerberg's painting and the English poster of the munitions worker suggest about changing views of women's role during the war and in society at large?

Advertisement card from Golden Dawn Cigarettes

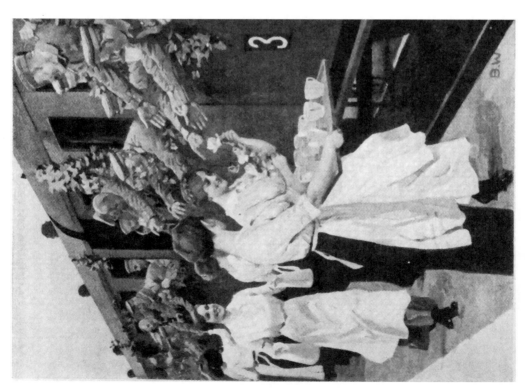

B. Hennerberg, *The Departure*

Septimus Scott, *These Women Are Doing Their Bit*

Australian recruitment poster

Twenty-four Hours on the Western Front
▼▼▼

88 ▼ *Henry S. Clapham,*
MUD AND KHAKI, MEMOIRS
OF AN INCOMPLETE SOLDIER

Until 1914 Henry S. Clapham had led a conventional life, notably lacking in adventure or excitement. Born in 1875 in the town of Hull, he graduated from Queen's College in Taunton, a boarding school for the sons of well-to-do families. After clerking in a law office, he married and began a career as a solicitor in London. His favorite entertainment was the card game bridge. In the fall of 1914, however, he answered the call to enlist and by January 1915 was a soldier in the British army fighting to hold back the Germans in northern Belgium. He fought there until October 1915, when a hand wound made him unfit for further service. On his return to England he resumed his career as a lawyer and, like many other returning soldiers, prepared his diary notes for publication as a book, which appeared in 1917 with the title *Mud and Khaki.* It went through several printings and was republished in 1930.

Clapham's book describes his experiences fighting in and around the northern Belgian city of Ypres, a commercial city of some 200,000 in the low, wet, largely unforested region that abuts the English Channel. It was the site of three major battles, one in the fall of 1914, another in 1915, and the last and bloodiest in 1917. Clapham fought in the so-called Second Battle of Ypres, which began in April 1915 when General Erich von Falkenhayn ordered a German attack on the entrenched English, Canadian, French, and French colonial troops to firm up German lines and divert allied troops from an anticipated offensive further to the south. After the Germans abandoned their major offensive in late May, fighting continued in the region, as Clapham's memoir clearly shows.

The Second Battle of Ypres saw the introduction of poison gas on the Western Front. Chlorine gas, a product of the German dyestuff industry and developed by the giant German chemical company IG Farben, could be released from cylinders or delivered by artillery shells. It stimulated the lungs to produce fluid, causing the victim to drown. Thousands of soldiers around Ypres died as a result of German gas attacks, but the effectiveness of the new weapon diminished when soldiers were supplied with respirators, or gas masks, and learned that holding a wet (often urine-soaked) handkerchief over one's nose and mouth provided some protection. Such countermeasures stimulated both sides to develop other types of poison gas, including phosgene, which causes asphyxiation, and mustard gas, which causes severe blistering.

QUESTIONS FOR ANALYSIS

1. As far as can be determined by Clapham's account, what were the actual results of the one day of fighting he describes?

2. What aspects of the fighting did Clapham and the other men find most unnerving?
3. Wars inevitably cause immense human suffering. But the suffering in World War I for soldiers and civilians alike was especially traumatic and unbearable. What is there in Clapham's account that may explain this phenomenon?

JUNE 19, 1915

We started again at dusk and passed down the railway cutting, but, instead of turning off into the fields, we went on as far as the Menin Road, at what is known as "Hell Fire Corner." A few hundred yards down the road we found a resting place for the night in some shallow "jumping off" trenches, a few yards back from the front line. It was very dark, and the trench was small, and sitting in a huddle I got a cramp and felt miserable.

The Huns[1] started by putting over big crumps[2] all around us. They seemed to aim for the relics of a building a hundred yards in the rear, and there the bricks were flying. . . . Then at 2:50 A.M. our own guns started and kept up a heavy bombardment of the trenches in front until 4:15, by which time it was quite light. . . .

At 4.15 a whistle blew. The men in the front line went over the top, and we scrambled out and took their places in the front trench. In front of us was a small field . . . split diagonally by an old footpath. On the other side of the field was a belt of trees in which lay the Hun trench.

In a few moments flags went up there, to show that it had been captured and that the troops were going on. Another whistle, and we ourselves scrambled over the parapet[3] and sprinted across the field. Personally I was so overweighted that I could only amble. . . . I took the diagonal path, as the line of least resistance, and most of my section did the same.

When I dropped into the Hun trench I found it a great place, only three feet wide, and at least eight deep, and beautifully made of white sandbags, back and front. At that spot there was no sign of any damage by our shells, but a number of dead Huns lay in the bottom. There was a sniper's post just where I fell in, a comfortable little square hole, fitted with seats and shelves, bottles of beer, tinned meats, and a fine helmet hanging on a hook.

Our first duty was to change the [barbed] wire, so . . . I slipped off my pack, and, clambering out again, started to move the wire from what was now the rear, to the new front of the trench. It was rotten stuff, most of it loose coils. . . . What there was movable of it, we got across without much difficulty, and we had just finished when we were ordered to move down the trench, as our diagonal advance had brought us too far to the right.

We moved down along the belt of woodland, which was only a few yards broad, to a spot where one of our companies was already hard at work digging a communication trench[4] back to our old front line. Here there was really no trench at all. One or more of our own big shells had burst in the middle, filling it up for a distance of ten yards and practically destroying both parapet and parados.[5] Some of us started building up the

---

[1] A derogatory term for German soldiers in World War I. The Huns were a nomadic people of Central Asia whose invasions of the fourth and fifth century C.E. contributed to the fall of the Western Roman Empire. The Huns were legendary for their cruelty and ferocity.

[2] A heavy German shell that burst with a cloud of black smoke on explosion.

[3] A mound built to protect the front of a trench.

[4] A shallow trench built from the front line to a relatively safe area in the rear. Used to supply front-line troops with food and ammunition and to transport killed and wounded soldiers away from the fighting.

[5] A mound built to protect the rear of a trench.

parapet with sandbags, and I saw the twins [two men in Clapham's unit] merrily at work hauling out dead Huns at least twice their own size.

There was a hedge along the back of the trench, so I scrambled through a hole in it, piled my pack, rifle, and other things, including the helmet, on the farther side, and started again on the wire. Hereabouts it was much better stuff, and it took us some time to get it across and pegged down. We had just got the last knife-rest across, when I saw a man who was placing sandbags on the parapet from the farther side swivel round, throw his legs into the trench, and collapse in a heap in the bottom. Several others were already lying there, and for the first time I realized that a regular hail of machine-gun bullets was sweeping over the trench.

. . . We all started work at a feverish pace, digging out the trench and building up some sort of shelter in front. One chap, a very nice kid, was bowled over almost at once with a bullet in the groin, and lay in the trench, kicking and screaming while we worked. . . .

The attacking battalions had carried several more trenches and we were told that two at least had been held, but our own orders were to consolidate and hold on to the trench we were in at all costs. . . .

I had just filled a sandbag and placed it on the top of the parapet when I happened to glance down, and saw a slight movement in the earth between my feet. I stooped and scraped away the soil with my fingers and found what seemed like palpitating flesh. It proved to be a man's cheek, and a few minutes' work uncovered his head. I poured a little water down his throat, and two or three of us dug out the rest of him. He was undamaged except for his feet and ankles, which were a mass of pulp, and he recovered consciousness as we worked. The first thing he said was in English: "What Corps are you?" He was a big

man, and told us he was forty-five and had only been a soldier for a fortnight.

We dragged him out and laid him under the hedge. There was nothing else we could do for him. He had another drink later, but he must have died in the course of the day. I am afraid we forgot all about him, but nothing could have lived there until evening.

The Captain was the next to go. He insisted on standing on the parados, directing operations, and got a bullet in the lungs. He could walk, and two men were detailed to take him down to the dressing-station. One came back, to be killed later in the day, but the other stopped a bullet *en route,* and followed the Captain.

When we had got our big Hun out, he left a big hole in the ground, and we found a dead arm and hand projecting from the bottom. We dug about, but did not seem to be able to find the body, and when I seized the sleeve and pulled, the arm came out of the ground by itself. We had to dig deeper for our own sake, but there was nothing else left, except messy earth, which seemed to have been driven into the side of the trench. The man helping me turned sick, for it wasn't pretty work. . . .

About 5.30 A.M. the Huns started shelling, and the new communication trench soon became a death-trap. A constant stream of wounded who had come down another trench from the north, passed along the rear. The Huns made a target of the two traverses (unluckily including our own), from which the communication trench opened, and numbers of the wounded were caught just behind us. The trench itself was soon choked with bodies. . . .

The shelling got worse as the day wore on and several more of our men went down. They plastered us with crumps, shrapnel, and whizz-bangs.[6] One of the latter took off a sandbag from the top of the parapet and landed it on my head.

---

[6]*Shrapnel* were hollow shells filled with bullets or pieces of metal that scattered on explosion. *Whizz-bangs* were shells fired by light German field guns.

It nearly broke my neck and I felt ill for some time after. . . .

The worst of it was the inaction. Every minute several shells fell within a few yards and covered us with dust, and the smell of the explosives poisoned my mouth. All I could do was to crouch against the parapet and pant for breath, expecting every moment to be my last. And this went on for hours. I began to long for the shell which would put an end to everything, but in time my nerves became almost numbed, and I lay like a log until roused.

I think it must have been midday when something happened. An alarm was given and we manned the parapet, to see some scores of men retreating at a run from the trench in front. They ran right over us, men of half a dozen battalions, and many dropped on the way. As they passed, something was said of gas, but it appeared that nearly all the officers in the two front trenches had been killed or wounded, someone had raised an alarm of gas, and the men had panicked and run.

A lot of the runaways insisted on gathering by the hedge just behind us, in spite of our warnings not to do so, and I saw at least twenty hit by shrapnel within a few yards of us.

The Brigade-Major arrived, cursing, and called upon some of our own men to advance and reoccupy the trench in front. He led them himself, and they made a very fine dash across. I do not think more than twenty fell, and they reoccupied the trench and, I believe, the third also, before the Huns realized that they were empty. . . .

Soon the runaways began to return. They had been turned back, in some cases, at the point of the revolver, but when their first panic had been overcome, they came back quite willingly, although they must have lost heavily in the process. They crowded into our trench, and there was hardly room to move a limb.

It was scorchingly hot and no one could eat, although I tried to do so. All day long we were constantly covered with debris from the shell-bursts. Great pieces fell all about us, and, packed like herrings, we crowded in the bottom of the trench. Hardly anything could be done for the wounded. If their wounds were slight, they gen-erally risked a dash to the rear. Every now and then we stood to in expectation of a counter-attack, but none developed.

About 6.0 P.M. the worst moment of the day came. The Huns started to bombard us with a shell which was quite new to us. It sounded like a gigantic fire-cracker, with two distinct explosions. These shells came over just above the parapet, in a flood, much more quickly than we could count them. After a quarter of an hour of this sort of thing, there was a sudden crash in the trench and ten feet of the parapet, just beyond me, was blown away and everyone around blinded by the dust. With my first glance I saw what looked like half a dozen bodies, mingled with sandbags, and then I smelt gas and realized that these were gas-shells. I had my respirator on in a hurry and most of our own men were as quick. The others were slower and suffered for it. One man was sick all over the sandbags and another was coughing his heart up. We pulled four men out of the debris unharmed. One man was unconscious, and died of gas later. Another was hopelessly smashed up and must have got it full in the chest.

We all thought that this was the end and almost hoped for it, but luckily the gas-shells stopped, and after a quarter of an hour we could take off our respirators. I started in at once to build up the parapet again, for we had been laid open to the world in front, but the gas lingered about the hole for hours, and I had to give up delving in the bottom for a time. As it was it made me feel very sick.

A counter-attack actually commenced as soon as the bombardment ceased, and we had to stand to again. . . . As we leaned over the parapet, I saw the body of a Hun lying twenty yards out in front. It commenced to writhe and finally half-sat up. I suppose the gas had caught him. The man standing next me — a corporal in a county battalion — raised his rifle, and before I could stop him, sent a bullet into the body. It was a rotten thing to see, but I suppose it was really a merciful end for the poor chap, better than his own gas, at any rate.

The men in the front trenches had got it as badly as we had, and if the counter-attack was pressed, it did not seem humanly possible, in the condition we were in, to offer a successful defence. . . . Fortunately, our own guns started and apparently caught the Huns massing. The counterattack accordingly crumpled up.

In the midst of it all, someone realized that the big gap in the parapet could not be manned, and four of us, including myself, were ordered to lie down behind what was left of the parados and cover the gap with our rifles. It was uncomfortable work, as . . . the place was a jumble of dead bodies. We could not stand up to clear them away,

and in order to get a place at all, I had to lie across the body of a gigantic Hun. . . .

We managed to get some sort of parapet erected in the end. It was more or less bullet-proof, at any rate. At dusk some scores of men came back from the front line, wounded or gassed. They had to cross the open at a run or a shamble, but I did not see any hit. Then the Brigade-Major appeared, and cheered us by promising a relief that night. It still rained shells, although not so hard as before dusk, and we did not feel capable of standing much more of it.

The Peace That Failed
▼▼▼

89 ▼ *COMMENTS OF THE GERMAN DELEGATION TO THE PARIS PEACE CONFERENCE ON THE CONDITIONS OF PEACE, OCTOBER 1919*

On January 19, 1919, thousands of diplomats, ministers, journalists, and observers gathered in Paris for the first session of the peace conference given the task of reordering the world after World War I. Participants included delegates from the thirty-two nations on the winning side, observers from the defeated Central Powers, and observers from numerous ethnic and religious groups — Arabs, Egyptians, Kurds, Irish, Zionists, Persians, Indians, Vietnamese, Africans, African-Americans, and Armenians. Women's organizations and even supporters of the tsarist cause in Russia were also represented.

Many in attendance hoped the postwar treaties would reflect the vision of the U.S. president, Woodrow Wilson, who in January 1918 had issued his famous Fourteen Points in regard to the peace. Wilson had called for open diplomacy, free trade, reduced armies, a "readjustment" of colonial claims, and national self-determination in Europe. Although Germany would be required to return Alsace-Lorraine to France and abandon conquered territories in Russia and Belgium, there was no talk of punishing Germany or blocking "in any way her legitimate influence and power." Wilson also called for the founding of a "general association of nations" whose purpose would be to preserve peace and guarantee the integrity of great and small nations alike.

British prime minister David Lloyd George and French premier Georges Clemenceau had different ideas. Clemenceau wanted to protect French security by weakening and punishing Germany. Lloyd George was more flexible, but whatever moderate inclinations he might have had were outweighed by his recent election promises to "hang the emperor" and "squeeze the German lemon until the pips squeak." Their views prevailed rather than Wilson's, and the result was the harsh Treaty of Versailles, grudgingly signed by Germany on June 28, 1919.

Germany lost all of its colonies, 13 percent of its land, and 10 percent of its population. Alsace and Lorraine, won from France in 1871, were returned to France. Northern Schleswig went to Denmark, parts of Posen and West Prussia went to Poland, while smaller bits of territory went to Belgium and Czechoslovakia. The coal mines of the Saar Basin were given to France for fifteen years, at which time the German government could buy them back; the Saar region itself was to be administered by the League of Nations. East Prussia was cut off from the rest of Germany by territory ceded to Poland, and the largely German port of Danzig on the Baltic Sea came under Polish economic control. The Germans were permitted to have no air force, a navy of approximately two dozen ships, and a volunteer army of no more than 100,000 officers and men. Article 231, the "war-guilt" clause, held Germany and its allies responsible for causing the war. On the basis of this claim, Germany was held accountable for all Allied losses and damages, and would be required to pay reparations. In 1921 the sum was set at $33 billion. The humiliated Germans deeply resented the Treaty of Versailles. In the 1920s nationalist and antidemocratic politicians learned to play on these resentments and in doing so undermined the democratic government that had signed the treaty. Of those politicians the most successful was Adolf Hitler, whose Nazis took power in 1933.

The reasons for German anger are spelled out in the following comments and observations. They were submitted in October 1919 by the German delegation to the Paris Peace Conference, which continued to meet after the signing of the Versailles Treaty until January 21, 1920.

QUESTIONS FOR ANALYSIS

1. In Germany's view, how would the country have been treated differently if the principles they attribute to President Wilson had been applied?
2. What does the document reveal about the difficulty of applying the principle of ethnic self-determination in Europe?
3. To what higher "fundamental" laws does the document appeal in order to strengthen German assertions?
4. What view of colonialism is expressed in the document? Why do the authors claim that Germany has a right to its colonies?
5. According to the authors of the German complaint, how will various provisions of the treaty hurt Germany's economy?
6. Do you agree with the authors of the document that Germany was being poorly treated? What response to their complaints might defenders of the treaty have made?

Although President Wilson, in his speech of October 20th, 1916, has acknowledged that "no single fact caused the war, but that in the last analysis the whole European system is in a deeper sense responsible for the war, with its combination of alliances and understandings, a complicated texture of intrigues and espionage that unfailingly caught the whole family of nations in its meshes," . . . Germany is to acknowledge that Germany and her allies are responsible for all damages which the enemy Governments or their subjects have incurred by her and her allies' aggression. . . . Apart from the consideration that there is no incontestable legal foundation for the obligation for reparation imposed upon Germany, the amount of such compensation is to be determined by a commission nominated solely by Germany's enemies, Germany taking no part. . . . The commission is plainly to have power to administer Germany like the estate of a bankrupt.[1]

As there are innate rights of man, so there are innate rights of nations. The inalienable fundamental right of every state is the right of self-preservation and self-determination. With this fundamental right the demand here made upon Germany is incompatible. Germany must promise to pay an indemnity, the amount of which at present is not even stated. The German rivers are to be placed under the control of an international body upon which Germany's delegates are always to be but the smallest minority. Canals and railroads are to be built on German territory at the discretion of foreign authorities.

These few instances show that that is not the just peace we were promised, not the peace "the very principle of which," according to a word of President Wilson, "is equality and the common participation in a common benefit. . . ."

In such a peace the solidarity of human interests, which was to find its expression in a League of Nations, would have been respected. How often Germany has been given the promise that this League of Nations would unite the belligerents, conquerors as well as conquered, in a permanent system of common rights! . . .

. . . But in contradiction to them, the Covenant of the League of Nations has been framed without the cooperation of Germany. Nay, still more. Germany does not even stand on the list of those States that have been invited to join the League

of Nations. . . . What the treaty of peace proposes to establish, is rather a continuance of the present hostile coalition which does not deserve the name of "League of Nations." . . . The old political system based on force and with its tricks and rivalries will thus continue to thrive!

Again and again the enemies of Germany have assured the whole world that they did not aim at the destruction of Germany. . . .

In contradiction to this, the peace document shows that Germany's position as a world power is to be utterly destroyed. The Germans abroad are deprived of the possibility of keeping up their old relations in foreign countries and of regaining for Germany a share in world commerce, while their property, which has up to the present been confiscated and liquidated, is being used for reparation instead of being restored to them. . . .

In this war, a new fundamental law has arisen which the statesmen of all belligerent peoples have again and again acknowledged to be their aim: the right of self-determination. To make it possible for all nations to put this privilege into practice was intended to be one achievement of the war. . . .

Neither the treatment described above of the inhabitants of the Saar[2] region as accessories to the [coal] pits nor the public form of consulting the population in the districts of Eupen, Malmédy and Prussian Moresnet[3] — which, moreover, shall not take place before they have been put under Belgian sovereignty — comply in the least with such a solemn recognition of the right of self-determination.

The same is also true with regard to Alsace-Lorraine. If Germany has pledged herself "to right the wrong of 1871," this does not mean any renunciation of the right of self-determination of the inhabitants of Alsace-Lorraine. A cession of

[1]A Reparations Commission appointed by the Peace Conference set the final sum at $33 billion in 1921.
[2]After fifteen years, the people of the Saar would have a plebiscite to decide if they would remain under the administration of a League of Nations commission or become part of France or Germany. In 1935 they voted to become part of Germany.

[3]Moresnet, an area of some 1,400 acres and the site of a valuable zinc mine, was annexed outright by Belgium. In Eupen and Malmédy, those who objected to the transfer of the areas to Belgium could sign their names in a public registry. On the basis of this "plebiscite," both areas became Belgian.

the country without consulting the population would be a new wrong, if for no other reason, because it would be inconsistent with a recognized principle of peace.

On the other hand, it is incompatible with the idea of national self-determination for two and one-half million Germans to be torn away from their native land against their own will. By the proposed demarcation of the boundary, unmistakably German territories are disposed of in favor of their Polish neighbors. Thus, from the Central Silesian districts of Guhrau and Militsch certain portions are to be wrenched away, in which, beside 44,900 Germans, reside at the utmost 3,700 Poles. . . .

This disrespect of the right of self-determination is shown most grossly in the fact that Danzig[4] is to be separated from the German Empire and made a free state. Neither historical rights nor the present ethnographical conditions of ownership of the Polish people can have any weight as compared with the German past and the German character of that city. . . . Likewise the cession of the commercial town of Memel, which is to be exacted from Germany, is in no way consistent with the right of self-determination. The same may be said with reference to the fact that millions of Germans in German-Austria are to be denied the union with Germany which they desire and that, further, millions of Germans dwelling along our frontiers are to be forced to remain part of the newly created Czecho-Slovakian State.

Even as regards that part of the national territory that is to be left to Germany, the promised right of self-determination is not observed. A Commission for the execution of the indemnity[5] shall be the highest instance for the whole State.

Our enemies claim to have fought for the great aim of the democratization of Germany. To be sure, the outcome of the war has delivered us from our former authorities, but instead of them we shall have in exchange a foreign, dictatorial power whose aim can and must be only to exploit the working power of the German people for the benefit of the creditor states. . . .

The fact that this is an age in which economic relations are on a world scale, requires the political organization of the civilized world. The German Government agrees with the Governments of the Allied and Associated Powers in the conviction that the horrible devastation caused by this war requires the establishment of a new world order, an order which shall insure the "effective authority of the principles of international law," and "just and honorable relations between the nations." . . .

There is no evidence of these principles in the peace document which has been laid before us. Expiring world theories, emanating from imperialistic and capitalistic tendencies, celebrate in it their last horrible triumph. As opposed to these views, which have brought unspeakable disaster upon the world, we appeal to the innate sense of right of men and nations, under whose token the English State developed, the Dutch People freed itself, the North American nation established its independence, France shook off absolutism. The bearers of such hallowed traditions cannot deny this right to the German people, that now for the first time has acquired in its internal polities the possibility of living in harmony with its free will based on law.

---

[4]Danzig was administered by the League of Nations, but its economy would be controlled by Poland.
[5]This concern was well-founded. After the Germans fell behind in their payments in 1923, the French-controlled Reparations Commission ordered French, Belgian, and Italian personnel into Germany's Ruhr region to collect coal and transport it to the border under military protection.

The Russian Revolution and the Foundation of the Soviet State

One of the most important results of World War I was the downfall of Russia's tsarist regime and its replacement by a Bolshevik dictatorship inspired by the doctrines of Karl Marx. Tsar Nicholas II, facing defeat on the battlefield, defections within the army, and rioting in Petrograd, abdicated in March 1917. Tsarist autocracy was replaced by a liberal provisional government that sought to govern Russia until a constituent assembly could meet and devise a new constitution. Seven months later, the Bolsheviks wrested power from the provisional government, and after four years of civil war, established the world's first communist state.

Nicholas II's Russia was full of discontent. Its millions of peasants were no longer serfs, but they still lived in abysmal poverty. Some moved to Moscow or St. Petersburg to work in Russia's new factories, but without political power or unions, most exchanged the squalor of the rural village for the squalor of the urban slum. Meanwhile many intellectuals, mostly from the ranks of Russia's small middle class, became deeply alienated from the tsar's regime and threw their support to political causes ranging from anarchism to constitutional monarchy. With the fervor of religious zealots, they argued, organized, hatched plots, planned revolution, assassinated government officials (including Tsar Alexander II in 1881), published pamphlets by the thousands, and tried, not always successfully, to stay a step ahead of the secret police.

Nicholas II raised his subjects' hopes in 1905, when after rioting broke out in St. Petersburg (renamed Petrograd after World War I began) he promised constitutional reforms and a parliament. Russians soon realized, however, that their tsar had no intention of abandoning control of such crucial areas as finance, defense, and ministerial appointments. Meanwhile workers and peasants cursed their government, and revolutionaries continued to plot. World War I provided the final push to a regime teetering on the brink of collapse.

After the Bolsheviks seized power in 1917 and survived the civil war that ended in 1921, their leaders faced the challenge of establishing the world's first Marxist state. After a decade of experiment and controversy, in the 1930s Soviet leaders created a framework of government that lasted until the breakup of the Soviet Union in the late 1980s. The Soviet Union became a major industrial power and a highly centralized, one-party dictatorship that tolerated no dissent. Freedom and individual initiative played no role in this new society, based, so their leaders claimed, on the principles of Karl Marx.

The Basic Tenets of Leninism
▼▼▼

90 ▼ Lenin, "WHAT IS TO BE DONE?"

The founder of the Soviet Union was Vladimir Ilyich Ulyanov (1870–1924), better known by his adopted revolutionary name, Lenin. The son of a government official, Lenin dedicated himself to revolution after the government executed his brother for plotting the assassination of Tsar Alexander III. After joining the Marxist-inspired Social-Democratic Party, founded in 1898, in 1903 he became the leader of the "majority men," or Bolsheviks, who, in opposition to the "minority men," or Mensheviks, demanded highly centralized party leadership, noncooperation with bourgeois liberals, and single-minded devotion to revolution.

Lenin described his ideas about revolutionary tactics in 1902 in a pamphlet entitled "What Is to Be Done?" It was directed against ideological enemies Lenin called "Economists," Marxists who believed that because Russia had just begun to industrialize, it was not ready for socialism. Social-Democrats, the Economists believed, should seek short-term economic gains for workers rather than revolution. Published in Germany, smuggled into Russia, and read by thousands of Social-Democrats, "What Is to Be Done?" established Lenin as a major party theoretician and a man to be reckoned within the Social-Democratic Party. It marked the beginning of that distinctive variant of Marxism known as Leninism.

QUESTIONS FOR ANALYSIS

1. According to Lenin, how does the "critical Marxism" of men such as Bernstein endanger the socialist movement?
2. In Lenin's view how are the goals and purposes of trade unionism similar to and different from those of the Social-Democratic Party?
3. Why, according to Lenin, have the workers been unable to develop true revolutionary consciousness? What does he believe must be done to change this?
4. What advantages does Lenin see in restricting the party to a small corps of dedicated revolutionaries?
5. What kinds of activities will these professional revolutionaries carry on to further the cause of revolution?
6. Compare and contrast the views of Lenin and Marx (see source 63) on the following topics: revolution, the working class, the role of the party.

[SOCIALIST DIVISIONS]

In fact, it is no secret for anyone that two trends have taken form in present-day international Social-Democracy. . . . The essence of the "new" trend, which adopts a "critical" attitude towards "obsolete dogmatic" Marxism, has been clearly enough *presented* by Bernstein and *demonstrated* by Millerand.[1]

Social-Democracy must change from a party of

---

[1]Eduard Bernstein (1850–1932) was a German socialist identified with revisionism, the idea that socialists should seek their goals not by revolution but through the demo-cratic process. Alexandre Millerand (1859–1943) was the first French socialist to take a cabinet seat in a nonsocialist government.

social revolution into a democratic party of social reforms. Bernstein has surrounded this political demand with a whole battery of well-attuned "new" arguments and reasonings. Denied was the possibility of putting socialism on a scientific basis and of demonstrating its necessity and inevitability from the point of view of the materialist conception of history. Denied was the fact of growing impoverishment, the process of proletarization, and the intensification of capitalist contradictions; the very concept, *"ultimate aim,"* was declared to be unsound, and the idea of the dictatorship of the proletariat was completely rejected. Denied was the antithesis in principle between liberalism and socialism. Denied was *the theory of the class struggle,* on the alleged grounds that it could not be applied to a strictly democratic society governed according to the will of the majority, etc. . . .

[THE WORKERS AND REVOLUTION]

We have said that *there could not have been* Social-Democratic consciousness among the workers. It would have to be brought to them from without. The history of all countries shows that the working class, exclusively by its own effort, is able to develop only trade-union consciousness, i.e., the conviction that it is necessary to combine in unions, fight the employers, and strive to compel the government to pass necessary labor legislation, etc. . . .

The overwhelming majority of Russian Social-Democrats have of late been almost entirely absorbed by this work of organising the exposure of factory conditions. . . . — so much so, indeed, that they have lost sight of the fact that this, *taken by itself,* is in essence still not Social-Democratic work, but merely trade union work. As a matter of fact, the exposures merely dealt with the relations between the workers *in a given trade* and their employers, and all they achieved was that the sellers of labor-power learned to sell their "commodity" on better terms and to fight the purchasers over a purely commercial deal. These exposures could have served . . . as a begin-

ning and a component part of Social-Democratic activity; but they could also have led . . . to a "purely trade union" struggle and to a non-Social-Democratic working-class movement. Social-Democracy leads the struggle of the working class, not only for better terms for the sale of labor-power, but for the abolition of the social system that compels the propertyless to sell themselves to the rich. Social-Democracy represents the working class, not in its relation to a given group of employers alone, but in its relation to all classes of modern society and to the state as an organised political force. . . . We must take up actively the political education of the working class and the development of its political consciousness. . . .

Why do the Russian workers still manifest little revolutionary activity in response to the brutal treatment of the people by the police, the persecution of religious sects, the flogging of peasants, the outrageous censorship, the torture of soldiers, the persecution of the most innocent cultural undertakings, etc.? Is it because the "economic struggle" does not "stimulate" them to this, because such activity does not "promise palpable results," because it produces little that is "positive"? . . . We must blame ourselves, our lagging behind the mass movement, for still being unable to organize sufficiently wide, striking, and rapid exposures of all the shameful outrages. When we do that (and we must and can do it), the most backward worker will understand, *or will feel,* that the students and religious sects, the peasants and the authors are being abused and outraged by those same dark forces that are oppressing and crushing him at every step of his life. Feeling that, he himself will be filled with an irresistible desire to react, and he will know how to heckle the censors one day, on another day to demonstrate outside the house of a governor who has brutally suppressed a peasant uprising . . . etc. As yet we have done very little, almost nothing, *to bring* before the working masses prompt exposures on all possible issues. Many of us as yet do not recognize this as our *bounden duty* but trail spontaneously in the wake of the "drab everyday struggle," in the narrow confines of factory life. . . .

[THE PARTY AND ITS PURPOSES]

If we begin with the solid foundation of a strong organisation of revolutionaries, we can ensure the stability of the movement as a whole and carry out the aims both of Social-Democracy and of trade unions proper. If, however, we begin with a broad workers' organisation, which is supposedly most "accessible" to the masses (but which is actually most accessible to the gendarmes and makes revolutionaries most accessible to the police), we shall achieve neither the one aim nor the other; . . . because we remain scattered and our forces are constantly broken up by the police, we shall only make trade unions of the Zubatov and Ozerov[2] type the more accessible to the masses. . . .

"A dozen wise men can be more easily wiped out than a hundred fools." This wonderful truth (for which the hundred fools will always applaud you) appears obvious only because in the very midst of the argument you have skipped from one question to another. You [the skeptical reader] began by talking and continued to talk of the unearthing of a "committee," of the unearthing of an "organization," and now you skip to the question of unearthing the movement's "roots" in their "depths." The fact is, of course, that our movement cannot be unearthed, for the very reason that it has countless thousands of roots deep down among the masses. . . . But since you raise the question of *organizations* being unearthed and persist in your opinion, I assert that it is far more difficult to unearth a dozen wise men than a hundred fools. This position I will defend, no matter how much you instigate the masses against me for my "anti-democratic" views, etc. As I have stated repeatedly, by "wise men," in connection with organization, I mean *professional revolutionaries.* . . . I assert: (1) that no revolutionary movement can endure without a stable organization of leaders maintaining continuity; (2) that the broader the popular mass drawn spontaneously into the struggle, which forms the basis of the movement and participates in it, the more urgent the need for such an organization, and the more solid this organization must be (for it is much easier for all sorts of demagogues to side-track the more backward sections of the masses); (3) that such an organization must consist chiefly of people professionally engaged in revolutionary activity; (4) that in an autocratic state, the more we *confine* the membership of such an organization to people who are professionally engaged in revolutionary activity and who have been professionally trained in the art of combating the political police, the more difficult will it be to unearth the organization; and (5) the *greater* will be the number of people from the working class and from the other social classes who will be able to join the movement and perform active work in it.

I shall deal only with the last two points. The question as to whether it is easier to wipe out "a dozen wise men" or "a hundred fools" reduces itself to the question, above considered, whether it is possible to have a mass *organization* when the maintenance of strict secrecy is essential. . . . To concentrate all secret functions in the hands of as small a number of professional revolutionaries as possible does not mean that the latter will "do the thinking for all" and that the rank and file will not take an active part in the *movement.* . . . Centralization of the secret functions of the *organization* by no means implies centralization of all the functions of the *movement.* . . . The active and widespread participation of the masses will not suffer; on the contrary, it will benefit by the fact that a "dozen" experienced revolutionaries, trained professionally no less than the police, will centralize all the secret aspects of the work — the drawing up of leaflets, the working out of approximate plans; and the appointing of bodies of leaders for each urban district, for each factory district, and for each educational institution. . . . Centralization of the most secret functions in an organization of revolutionaries will not diminish,

---

[2]S. V. Zubatov (1864–1917), a colonel in the Moscow state police, was an ardent foe of revolutionary movements best known for his efforts to establish "depoliticized" trade unions under the control of the police; he shot himself when the tsarist government fell during the Russian Revolution. I. K. Ozerov was a professor at the University of Moscow who supported Zubatov's "police socialism."

but rather increase the extent and enhance the quality of the activity of a large number of other organizations, that are intended for a broad public and are therefore as loose and as non-secret as possible, such as workers' trade unions; workers' self-education circles[3] and circles for reading illegal literature; and socialist, as well as democratic, circles among *all* other sections of the population; etc., etc. We must have such circles, trade unions, and organizations everywhere in *as large a number as possible* and with the widest variety of functions; but it would be absurd and harmful *to confound* them with the organization of *revolutionaries,* . . . to make still more hazy the all too faint recognition of the fact that in order to "serve" the mass movement we must have people who will devote themselves exclusively to Social-Democratic activities, and that such people must *train* themselves patiently and steadfastly to be professional revolutionaries.

Yes, this recognition is incredibly dim. Our worst sin with regard to organization consists in the fact that *by our primitiveness we have lowered the prestige of revolutionaries in Russia.* A person who is flabby and shaky on questions of theory, who has a narrow outlook, who pleads the spontaneity of the masses as an excuse for his own sluggishness,

who resembles a trade-union secretary more than a spokesman of the people, who is unable to conceive of a broad and bold plan that would command the respect even of opponents, and who is inexperienced and clumsy in his own professional art — the art of combating the political police — such a man is not a revolutionary, but a wretched amateur!

Let no active worker take offense at these frank remarks, for as far as insufficient training is concerned, I apply them first and foremost to myself. I used to work in a study circle that set itself very broad, all-embracing tasks; and all of us, members of that circle, suffered painfully and acutely from the realization that we were acting as amateurs at a moment in history when we might have been able to say, varying a well-known statement: "Give us an organization of revolutionaries, and we will overturn Russia!" The more I recall the burning sense of shame I then experienced, the bitterer become my feelings towards those pseudo-Social-Democrats whose preachings "bring disgrace on the calling of a revolutionary," who fail to understand that our task is not to champion the degrading of the revolutionary to the level of an amateur, but *to raise* the amateurs to the level of revolutionaries.

---

[3]Regular meetings of workers, intellectuals, or students to discuss and plan strategies to overcome Russia's social and political problems.

The Soviet Model of Economic Planning
▼▼▼

91 ▼ Joseph Stalin, THE RESULTS OF THE FIRST FIVE-YEAR PLAN

Joseph Stalin (1879–1953), the son of a shoemaker from the Russian province of Georgia, was a candidate for the priesthood before he abandoned Christianity for Marxism and became a follower of Lenin in 1903. In 1917 he was named Bolshevik party secretary, an office he retained after the revolution. Following Lenin's death in 1924, Stalin won the battle for party control with Leon Trotsky (1879–1940), the leader of the Red Army during the civil war and Lenin's heir apparent. Shortly after taking power in 1928 Stalin launched a bold restructuring of the Soviet economy.

In 1928 the New Economic Policy (NEP), which Lenin had instituted in 1921, still guided Soviet economic life. Through the NEP, Lenin had sought to restore agriculture and industry after seven years of war, revolution, and civil strife. Although the state maintained control of banks, foreign trade, and heavy industry, peasants could sell their goods on the open market, and small businessmen could hire labor, operate small factories, and keep their profits. The NEP saved the Soviet Union from economic collapse, but its acceptance of private profit and economic competition troubled Marxist purists, and it did little to foster industrialization. Thus in 1928 Stalin abandoned the NEP and replaced it with the first Five-Year Plan, which established a centralized planned economy in which Moscow bureaucrats regulated agriculture, manufacturing, finance, and transportation. In agriculture, the plan abolished individual peasant holdings and combined them into large collectives and state farms. This meant the obliteration of the class of prosperous and successful peasant farmers known as *kulaks*. In manufacturing, the plan emphasized heavy industry and the production of goods such as tractors, trucks, and machinery. Second and third Five-Year Plans were launched in 1933 and 1938.

Despite its enormous human costs, measured in terms of economic growth and industrial development, the Soviet experiment in central planning can be called a success. During the 1930s, when the Depression was devastating Western capitalist economies, the Soviet economy grew at an annual rate of 27 percent and achieved impressive increases in the production of iron and steel, oil and electricity, tractors, trucks, and chemicals. To many observers central planning seemed to be the solution to the challenge of rapid industrialization. In the second half of the twentieth century, it became the economic model throughout the communist world and for many newly independent states in Asia and Africa that were seeking rapid industrialization and economic development.

In the following report, delivered to the Central Committee of the Communist Party of the Soviet Union in January 1933, Stalin outlines the goals and achievements of the first Five-Year Plan.

QUESTIONS FOR ANALYSIS

1. What were the overriding reasons, according to Stalin, for adopting the Five-Year Plan? Does socialist theory or the defense of the Soviet Union seem more important to him?
2. Why, in the industrial area, was it necessary to concentrate on heavy industry?
3. According to Stalin, why was the collectivization of agriculture such a key component of the Five-Year Plan?
4. What were the main obstacles to the success of the Five-Year Plan, according to Stalin?
5. In Stalin's view, how have the Soviet people benefited from the Five-Year Plan? What sacrifices have they been asked to make?
6. According to Stalin, how does the success of the Five-Year Plan prove that communism is superior to capitalism?

The fundamental task of the Five-Year Plan was to convert the U.S.S.R. from an agrarian and weak country, dependent upon the caprices of the capitalist countries, into an industrial and powerful country, fully self-reliant and independent of the caprices of world capitalism.

The fundamental task of the Five-Year Plan was, in converting the U.S.S.R. into an industrial country, fully to eliminate the capitalist elements, to widen the front of socialist forms of economy, and to create the economic base for the abolition of classes in the U.S.S.R., for the construction of socialist society.

The fundamental task of the Five-Year Plan was to create such an industry in our country as would be able to re-equip and reorganize, not only the whole of industry, but also transport and agriculture — on the basis of socialism.

The fundamental task of the Five-Year Plan was to transfer small and scattered agriculture to the lines of large-scale collective farming, so as to ensure the economic base for socialism in the rural districts and thus to eliminate the possibility of the restoration of capitalism in the U.S.S.R.

Finally, the task of the Five-Year Plan was to create in the country all the necessary technical and economic prerequisites for increasing to the utmost the defensive capacity of the country, to enable it to organize determined resistance to any and every attempt at military intervention from outside. . . . In order to carry out such a plan it is necessary first of all to find its main link; for only after this main link has been found and grasped can all the other links of the plan be raised. . . .

The main link in the Five-Year Plan was heavy industry, with machine building at its core. For only heavy industry is capable of reconstructing industry as a whole, as well as the transport system and agriculture, and of putting them on their feet. . . .

But the restoration and development of heavy industry, particularly in such a backward and poor country as our country was at the beginning of the Five-Year Plan period, is an extremely difficult task; for, as is well known, heavy industry calls for enormous financial expenditures and the availability of a certain minimum of experienced technical forces, without which, speaking generally, the restoration of heavy industry is impossible. Did the party know this, and did it take this into consideration? Yes, it did. . . . The party declared frankly that this would call for serious sacrifices, and that we must openly and consciously make these sacrifices if we wanted to achieve our goal. . . .

The facts have proved that without this boldness and this confidence in the forces of the working class the party could not have achieved the victory of which we are now so justly proud.

▼ ▼ ▼

What are the results of the Five-Year Plan in four years in the sphere of *industry?* . . .

We did not have an iron and steel industry, the foundation for the industrialization of the country. Now we have this industry.

We did not have a tractor industry. Now we have one.

We did not have an automobile industry. Now we have one.

We did not have a machine-tool industry. Now we have one.

We did not have a big and up-to-date chemical industry. Now we have one.

We did not have a real and big industry for the production of modern agricultural machinery. Now we have one.

We did not have an aircraft industry. Now we have one.

In output of electric power we were last on the list. Now we rank among the first.

In the output of oil products and coal we were last on the list. Now we rank among the first. . . .

And as a result of all this the capitalist elements have been completely and irrevocably eliminated from industry, and socialist industry has become the sole form of industry in the U.S.S.R.

And as a result of all this our country has been converted from an agrarian into an industrial country; for the proportion of industrial output, as compared with agricultural output, has risen from 48 per cent of the total in the beginning of the Five-Year Plan period (1928) to 70 per cent at the end of the fourth year of the Five-Year Plan period (1932). . . .

Finally, as a result of all this the Soviet Union has been converted from a weak country, unprepared for defense, into a country mighty in defense, a country prepared for every contingency, a country capable of producing on a mass scale all modern weapons of defense and of equipping its army with them in the event of an attack from without. . . .

We are told: This is all very well; but it would have been far better to have abandoned the policy of industrialization, . . . and to have produced more cotton, cloth, shoes, clothing, and other articles of general use. The output of articles of general use has been smaller than is required, and this created certain difficulties.

But, then, we must know and take into account where such a policy of relegating the task of industrialization to the background would have led us. Of course, out of the 1,500,000,000 rubles in foreign currency that we spent on purchasing equipment for our heavy industries, we could have set apart a half for the purpose of importing raw cotton, hides, wool, rubber, etc. Then we would now have more cotton cloth, shoes and clothing. But we would not have a tractor industry or an automobile industry; we would not have anything like a big iron and steel industry; we would not have metal for the manufacture of machinery — and we would be unarmed, while we are surrounded by capitalist countries which are armed with modern technique. . . . Our position would be more or less analogous to the present position of China, which has no heavy industry and no war industry of her own and which is pecked at by everybody who cares to do so. . . .

▾▾▾

The Five-Year Plan in the sphere of agriculture was a Five-Year Plan of collectivization. What did the party proceed from in carrying out collectivization?

The party proceeded from the fact that in order to consolidate the dictatorship of the proletariat and to build up socialist society it was necessary, in addition to industrialization, to pass from small, individual peasant farming to large-scale collective agriculture equipped with tractors and modern agricultural machinery, as the only firm basis for the Soviet power in the rural districts.

The party proceeded from the fact that without collectivization it would be impossible to lead our country onto the highroad of building the economic foundations of socialism, impossible to free the vast masses of the laboring peasantry from poverty and ignorance. . . .

The party has succeeded, in a matter of three years, in organizing more than 200,000 collective farms and about 5,000 state farms specializing mainly in grain growing and livestock raising, and at the same time it has succeeded, in the course of four years, in enlarging the crop area by 21,000,000 hectares.[1]

The party has succeeded in getting more than 60 per cent of the peasant farms, which account for more than 70 per cent of the land cultivated by peasants, to unite into collective farms, which means that we have *fulfilled* the Five-Year Plan *threefold*. . . .

The party has succeeded in routing the kulaks as a class, although they have not yet been dealt the final blow; the laboring peasants have been emancipated from kulak bondage and exploitation, and a firm economic basis for the Soviet government, the basis of collective farming, has been established in the countryside.

The party has succeeded in converting the U.S.S.R. from a land of small peasant farming into a land where agriculture is run on the largest scale in the world. . . .

Do not all these facts testify to the superiority of the Soviet system of agriculture over the capitalist system? Do not these facts go to show that the collective farms are a more virile form of farming than individual capitalist farms? . . .

In putting into effect the Five-Year Plan for agriculture, the party pursued a policy of collectivization at an accelerated tempo. Was the party right in pursuing the policy of an accelerated

---

[1] In the metric system a *hectare* is slightly less than 2.5 acres.

tempo of collectivization? Yes, it was absolutely right, even though certain excesses were committed in the process.[2] In pursuing the policy of eliminating the kulaks as a class, and in destroying the kulak nests, the party could not stop half way. It was necessary to carry this work to completion. . . .

▾ ▾ ▾

What are the results of these successes as regards the improvement of the material conditions of the workers and peasants? . . .

In our country, in the U.S.S.R., the workers have long forgotten unemployment. Some three years ago we had about one and a half million unemployed. It is already two years now since unemployment has been completely abolished. . . . Look at the capitalist countries: what horrors are taking place there as a result of unemployment! There are now no less than thirty to forty million unemployed in those countries. . . .

Every day they try to get work, seek work, are prepared to accept almost any conditions of work but they are not given work, because they are "superfluous." And this is taking place at a time when vast quantities of goods and products are wasted to satisfy the caprices of the darlings of fate, the scions of capitalists and landlords. The unemployed are refused food because they have no money to pay for the food; they are refused shelter because they have no money to pay rent. How and where do they live? They live on the miserable crumbs from the rich man's table; by raking refuse cans, where they find decayed scraps of food; they live in the slums of big cities, and more often in hovels outside of the towns,

hastily put up by the unemployed out of packing cases and the bark of trees. . . .

The same thing must be said in regard to the peasants. They, too, have forgotten about the differentiation of the peasants into kulaks and poor peasants, about the exploitation of the poor peasants by the kulaks, about the ruin which, every year, caused hundreds of thousands and millions of poor peasants to go begging. . . .

[The Five-Year Plan] has undermined and smashed the kulaks as a class, thus liberating the poor peasants and a good half of the middle peasants from bondage to the kulaks. . . . It has thus eliminated the possibility of the differentiation of the peasantry into exploiters — kulaks — and exploited — poor peasants. It has raised the poor peasants and the lower stratum of the middle peasants to a position of security in the collective farms, and has thereby put a stop to the process of ruination and impoverishment of the peasantry. . . .

Now there are no more cases of hundreds of thousands and millions of peasants being ruined and forced to hang around the gates of factories and mills. That is what used to happen; but that was long ago. Now the peasant is in a position of security; he is a member of a collective farm which has at its disposal tractors, agricultural machinery, a seed fund, a reserve fund, etc., etc.

Such are the main results of the realization of the Five-Year Plan in industry and agriculture; in the improvement of the conditions of life of the working people and the development of the exchange of goods; in the consolidation of the Soviet power and the development of the class struggle against the remnants and survival of the dying classes.

---

[2]Stalin is understating the case more than a little. In fact, several million kulaks were executed or deported to Siberia because of their opposition to collectivization.

▼▼▼

Ultranationalism in Germany and Japan

Nationalism, the most important single cause of World War I, became even more potent in the 1920s and 1930s, leading to a second world war many times more costly and horrifying than the struggle between 1914 and 1918. In Italy and Germany extreme nationalism fueled right-wing, antidemocratic movements personified by Benito Mussolini, whose Fascists seized power in Italy in 1922, and Adolf Hitler, whose National Socialists took over Germany in 1933. In Japan ultranationalists never completely subverted the limited democracy established by the 1890 constitution, but in the 1930s their views inspired millions and became dogma to Japan's military and political leaders.

Germany, Italy, and Japan were similar in several respects. All three were recent creations: Italy gained national unity between 1859, when the Kingdom of Sardinia seized Lombardy, and 1870, when Rome and its environs joined the Kingdom of Italy; Germany became a unified nation-state in 1871; and a new Japan was created after the Meiji Restoration of 1868. All three had weak parliamentary governments and lacked democratic experience. All three resented their treatment after World War I: The Germans were humiliated by the Versailles Treaty, and the Italians and Japanese were insulted by the refusal of Great Britain and France to recognize all their territorial claims. Finally, all three faced severe postwar economic problems — problems that extreme nationalists claimed could be eliminated by expansion and conquest.

Ultranationalism in each state also had the same tragic result: It led all three into catastrophic wars. After conquering Manchuria in 1931, invading China in 1937, attacking the United States at Pearl Harbor in 1941, and expanding into Southeast Asia, Japan conceded defeat when atomic bombs devastated Hiroshima and Nagasaki in August 1945. Germany launched World War II in Europe with its attack on Poland in September 1939, but after conquering much of Western Europe and invading the Soviet Union in 1941, its armies were steadily pushed back until the leaders of a devastated land surrendered in May 1945. Italy entered World War II on the side of Germany in 1940, but its armies performed poorly, and only massive German support prevented its rapid collapse. Anti-Fascists captured Mussolini and shot him without trial on April 28, 1945, just a few days before Adolf Hitler committed suicide in his bunker under the rubble of what had been Berlin.

Hitler's Dreams
▼▼▼

92 ▼ *Adolf Hitler, MEIN KAMPF*

Born the son of an Austrian customs official and his German wife in 1889, Adolf Hitler moved to Vienna at the age of nineteen to seek a career as an artist or architect. His efforts failed, however, and he lived at the bottom of Viennese society, drifting from one low-paying job to another. In 1912 he moved to Munich, where his life fell into the same purposeless pattern. Enlistment in the German army in World War I rescued Hitler, giving him comradeship and a sense of direction he had lacked. After the war a shattered Hitler returned to Munich, where in 1919 he joined the small German Workers' Party, which in 1920 changed its name to the National Socialist German Workers' Party, or Nazis.

After becoming leader of the National Socialists, Hitler staged an abortive coup d'état against the government of the German state of Bavaria in 1923. For this he was sentenced to a five-year prison term (serving only nine months), during which he wrote the first volume of *Mein Kampf (My Struggle)*. To a remarkable degree this work, completed in 1925, provided the ideas that inspired his millions of followers and guided the National Socialists until their destruction in 1945.

QUESTIONS FOR ANALYSIS

1. What broad purpose does Hitler see in human existence?
2. How, in Hitler's view, are the Aryans and Jews dissimilar?
3. What is Hitler's view of political leadership?
4. What role do parliaments play in a "folkish" state, according to Hitler?
5. How does Hitler plan to reorient German foreign policy? What goals does he set for Germany, and how are they to be achieved?
6. Based on these excerpts, what can you infer about his objections to the ideologies of democracy, liberalism, and socialism?
7. How do Hitler's views of race compare to those of von Treitschke (source 67)?

NATION AND RACE

There are some truths that are so plain and obvious that for this very reason the everyday world does not see them or at least does not apprehend them. . . .

So humans invariably wander about the garden of nature, convinced that they know and understand everything, yet with few exceptions are blind to one of the fundamental principles Nature uses in her work: the intrinsic segregation of the species of every living thing on the earth. . . . Each beast mates with only one of its own species: the titmouse with titmouse, finch with finch, stork with stork, field mouse with field mouse, house mouse with house mouse, wolf with wolf. . . . This is only natural.

Any cross-breeding between two not completely equal beings will result in a product that is in between the level of the two parents. That means that the offspring will be superior to the parent who is at a biologically lower level of being but inferior to the parent at a higher level. This means the offspring will be overcome in the struggle for existence against those at the higher level. Such matings go against the will of Nature for the higher breeding of life.

A precondition for this lies not in the blending of beings of a higher and lower order, but rather the absolute victory of the stronger. The stronger must dominate and must not blend with the weaker orders and sacrifice their powers. Only born weaklings can find this cruel, but after all, they are only weaker and more narrow-minded types of men; unless this law dominated, then any conceivable higher evolution of living organisms would be unthinkable. . . .

Nature looks on this calmly and approvingly. The struggle for daily bread allows all those who are weak, sick, and indecisive to be defeated, while the struggle of the males for females gives to the strongest alone the right or at least the possibility to reproduce. Always this struggle is a means of advancing the health and power of resistance of the species, and thus a means to its higher evolution.

As little as nature approves the mating of higher and lower individuals, she approves even less the blending of higher races with lower ones; for indeed otherwise her previous work toward higher development perhaps over hundreds of thousands of years might be rendered useless with one blow. If this were not the case, progressive development would stop and even deterioration might set in. . . .

All the great civilizations of the past died out because contamination of their blood caused them to become decadent. . . . In other words, in order to protect a certain culture, the type of human who created the culture must be preserved. But such preservation is tied to the inalterable law of the necessity and the right of victory of the best and the strongest.

Whoever would live must fight. Whoever will not fight in this world of endless competition does not deserve to live. Whoever ignores or despises these laws of race kills the good fortune that he believes he can attain. He interferes with the victory path of the best race and with it, the precondition for all human progress. . . .

It is an idle undertaking to argue about which race or races were the original standard-bearers of human culture and were therefore the true founders of everything we conceive by the word humanity. It is much simpler to deal with the question as it pertains to the present, and here the answer is simple and clear. What we see before us today as human culture, all the yields of art, science, and technology, are almost exclusively the creative product of the Aryans.[1] Indeed this fact alone leads to the not unfounded conclusion that the Aryan alone is the founder of the higher type of humanity, and further that he represents the prototype of what we understand by the word: MAN. He is the Prometheus[2] from whose brow the bright spark of genius has forever burst forth, time and again rekindling the fire, which as knowledge has illuminated the night full of silent mysteries, and has permitted humans to ascend the path of mastery over the other beings of the earth. Eliminate him — and deep darkness will again descend on the earth after a few thousand years; human civilization will die out and the earth will become a desert. . . .

The Jew provides the greatest contrast to the Aryan. With no other people of the world has the instinct for self-preservation been so developed as by the so-called chosen race.[3] The best proof of this statement rests in the fact that this race still exists. Where can another people be found in the past 2,000 years that has undergone so few changes in its inner qualities, character, etc. as the Jews? What people has undergone upheavals as great as this one — and nonetheless has emerged unchanged from the greatest catastrophes of humanity? What an infinitely tenacious will to live and to preserve one's kind is revealed in this fact. . . .

---

[1]*Aryan,* strictly speaking, is a linguistic term referring to a branch of the Indo-European family of languages known as Indo-Iranian. It is also used to refer to a people who as early as 4000 B.C.E. began to migrate from their homeland in the steppes of western Asia to Iran, India, Mesopotamia, Asia Minor, and Europe. Their related family of languages, based on an even older language known as Proto-Indo-European, is believed to be the ancestor of all Indo-European languages, including Greek, Latin, Celtic, Persian, Sanskrit, and Balto-Slavonic, as well as their derivatives. In the nineteenth century, Aryan was used to refer to the racial group that spoke these languages. According to Hitler and the Nazis, the Aryans provided Europe's original racial stock and stood in contrast to other peoples such as the Jews, who spoke Semitic languages.

[2]In Greek mythology Prometheus was the titan (titans were offspring of Uranus, Heaven, and Gaea, Earth) who stole fire from the gods and gave it to humans, along with all other arts and civilization. He was also variously regarded as the creator of man (from clay), the first mortal man (along with his brother Epimetheus), and humanity's preserver when Zeus threatened to kill all human beings.

[3]A reference to the Jewish belief that God had chosen the Jews to enter into a special covenantal relationship in which God promised to be the God of the Hebrews and favor them in return for true worship and obedience.

Since the Jew . . . never had a civilization of his own, others have always provided the foundations of his intellectual labors. His intellect has always developed by the use of those cultural achievements he has found ready at hand around him. Never has it happened the other way around.

For though their drive for self-preservation is not smaller, but larger than that of other people, and though their mental capabilities may easily give the impression that their intellectual powers are equal to those of other races, the Jews lack the most basic characteristic of a truly cultured people, namely an idealistic spirit.

It is a remarkable fact that the herd instinct brings people together for mutual protection only so long as there is a common danger that makes mutual assistance necessary or unavoidable. The same pack of wolves that an instant ago combined to overcome their prey will soon after satisfying their hunger again become individual beasts. . . . It goes the same way with the Jews. His sense of self sacrifice is only apparent. It lasts only so long as it is strictly necessary. As soon as the common enemy departs, however, as soon as the danger is gone and the booty secured, the superficial harmony among the Jews ends, and original conditions return. Jews act together only when a common danger threatens them or a common prey attracts them. When these two things are lacking, then their characteristic of the crassest egoism returns as a force, and out of this once unified people emerges in a flash a swarm of rats fighting bloodily against one another.

If the Jews existed in the world by themselves, they would wallow in their filth and disasters; they would try to get the best of the other in a hate-filled struggle, and even exterminate one another, that is, if their absolute lack of a sense of self sacrifice, which is expressed in their venality, did not turn this drama into comedy also. . . .

That is why the Jewish state — which should be the living organism for the maintenance and improvement of the race — has absolutely no borders. For the territorial definition of a state always demands a certain idealism of spirit on the part of the race which forms the state and espe-

cially an acceptance of the idea of work. . . . If this attitude is lacking then the prerequisite for civilization is lacking.

▷ Hitler describes the process by which Jews in concert with communists have come close to subverting and controlling the peoples and nations of Europe.

Here he stops at nothing, and his vileness becomes so monstrous that no one should be surprised if among our people the hateful figure of the Jew is taken as the personification of the devil and the symbol of evil. . . .

How close they see their approaching victory can be seen in the frightful way that their dealings with members of other races develop.

The black-haired Jewish youth, with satanic joy on his face, lurks in wait for hours for the innocent girls he plans to defile with his blood, and steal the young girl from her people. With every means at hand he seeks to undermine the racial foundations of the people they would subjugate. . . . For a people which is racially pure and is conscious of its blood, will never be able to be subjugated by the Jews. The Jew in this world will forever only be the masters of bastardized people. . . .

Around those nations which have offered sturdy resistance to their internal attacks, they surround them with a web of enemies; thanks to their international influence, they incite them to war, and when necessary, will plant the flag of revolution, even on the battlefield.

In economics he shakes the foundations of the state long enough so that unprofitable business enterprises are shut down and come under his financial control. In politics he denies the state its means of self-preservation, destroys its means of self-maintenance and defense, annihilates faith in state leadership, insults its history and traditions, and drags everything that is truly great into the gutter.

Culturally, he pollutes art, literature and theater, makes a mockery of natural sensibilities, destroys every concept of beauty and nobility, the worthy and the good, and instead drags other men down to the sphere of its own lowly type of existence.

Religion is made an object of mockery, morality and ethics are described as old-fashioned, until finally the last props of a people for maintaining their existence in this world are destroyed.

PERSONALITY AND THE IDEAL OF THE FOLKISH[4] STATE

. . . The folkish state must care for the well-being of its citizens by recognizing in everything the worth of the person, and by doing so direct it to the highest level of its productive capability, thus guaranteeing for each the highest level of participation.

Accordingly, the folkish state must free the entire leadership, especially those in political leadership, from the parliamentary principle of majority rule by the multitude, so that the right of personality is guaranteed without any limitation. From this is derived the following realization. *The best state constitution and form is that which with unquestioned certainty raises the best minds from the national community to positions of leading authority and influence.* . . .

There are no majority decisions, rather only responsible individuals, and the word "advice" will once again have its original meaning. Each man will have advisers at his side, *but the decision will be made by one man.*

The principle that made the Prussian army in its time the most splendid instrument of the German people will have to become someday the foundation for the construction of our completed state: *authority of every leader downward and responsibility upward.* . . .

This principle of binding absolute responsibility with absolute authority will gradually bring forth an elite group of leaders which today in an era of irresponsible parliamentarianism is hardly thinkable.

THE DIRECTION AND POLITICS OF EASTERN EUROPE

The foreign policy of the folkish state has as its purpose to guarantee the existence on this planet of the race that it gathers within its borders. With this in mind it must create a natural and healthy ratio between the number and growth of the population and the extent and quality of the land and soil. The balance must be such that it accords with the vital needs of the people. What I call a *healthy* ratio is one in which the support of the people is assured by its own land and soil. Any other condition, even if it lasts centuries or a thousand years, is nevertheless an unhealthy one and will lead sooner or later to damage, if not the total destruction of the affected people. *Only a sufficiently large space on the earth can assure the independent existence of a people.* . . .

If the National Socialist Movement really is to be consecrated in history as fulfilling a great mission for the people, it must, spurred by knowledge and filled with pain over its true situation on this earth, boldly and with a clear sense of direction, take up the battle against the aimlessness and incompetence of our foreign policy. It must, without consideration of "traditions" or preconceived notions, find the courage to gather our people and their forces and advance them on the path from their present restricted living space to new land and soil. This will free the people from the dangers of disappearing from the earth altogether or becoming a slave people in the service of another.

The National Socialist movement must seek to eliminate the disproportion between our people's population and our territory — viewing this as a source of food as well as a basis for national power — and between our historical past and our present hopeless impotence. While doing so it must remain conscious of the fact that we as protectors of the highest humanity on earth are bound also by the highest duty that will be fulfilled only if we inspire the German people with the racial ideal, so that they will occupy themselves not just with the breeding of

---

[4]The word Hitler uses, *völkisch,* is an adjective derived from *Volk,* meaning "people" or "nation," which Hitler defined in a racial sense; thus a "folkish" state is one that expresses the characteristics of and furthers the interests of a particular race, in this case, the Aryans.

good dogs, horses, and cats but also show concern about the purity of *their own* blood.

Against everything else we National Socialists must hold unflinchingly to our goal of foreign policy, namely, *to secure for the German people the land on this earth to which they are entitled.* . . .

State boundaries are made by man and can be changed by man.

The fact that a nation has acquired a large amount of land is no mandate that this should be recognized forever. . . . And only in force lies the right of possession. If today the German people are imprisoned within an impossible territorial area and for that reason are face to face with a miserable future, this is not the commandment of fate, any more than a revolt against such a situation would be a violation of the laws of fate; . . . the soil on which we now live was not bestowed upon our ancestors by Heaven; rather, they had to conquer it by risking their lives. So with us, in the future we will win soil and with it the means of existence of the people not through some sort of folkish grace but only through the power of the triumphant sword.

But we National Socialists must go further: *The right to land and soil will become an obligation if without further territorial expansion a great people is threatened with its destruction.* And that is particularly true when the people in question is not some little nigger people, but the German mother of life, which has given cultural shape to the modern world. *Germany will either become a world power or will no longer exist.* To achieve world power an expansion in size is needed, which will give the state meaning in today's world and will give life to its citizens. . . .

And so we National Socialists consciously draw a line below the direction of our foreign policy before the war. We take up where we broke off six hundred years ago. We put a stop to the eternal pull of the Germans toward the south and western Europe and turn our gaze to the lands of the east. We put an end to the colonial and commercial policy of the prewar period and shift to the land-oriented policy of the future.

When today we speak of new territory and soil in Europe, we think primarily of *Russia* and her subservient border states.

The Nationalist Agenda in Japan

▼▼▼

93 ▼ *The Black Dragon Society, ANNIVERSARY STATEMENT*

During the Meiji period traditional Japanese pride in their independence and cultural distinctiveness was transformed into something recognizable as modern nationalism as Japan competed for territory and markets in Asia and sought recognition as one of the Great Powers. In the 1920s and 1930s, Japanese nationalism gained broader support and, as in Germany and Italy, came to be identified with antidemocratic and antisocialist movements. Its appeal grew in response to several developments, including resentment of the West for its treatment of Japan after World War I, fears of a united China under Chiang Kai-shek and the Nationalists, opposition to "dangerous" ideologies such as socialism and communism, anxieties about Western influence on Japan, and most important, the effects of the worldwide economic depression of the 1930s. With the onset of the Great Depression

Japanese exports declined by half, workers' incomes fell, and unemployment reached 3 million. The failure of the rice crop in northern Japan in 1931 reduced families to begging, eating bark and roots, and selling daughters to brothel keepers. Facing economic catastrophe, increasing numbers of Japanese came to support the ultranationalist claim that authoritarian government and military expansion would solve the nation's problems.

With strong support in the rural population and the army, ultranationalism became a major force between 1931 and 1936, when its disciples assassinated business leaders and politicians, including a prime minister, and plotted to overthrow the government. The most serious coup attempt took place in February 1936, when officers and troops of the First Division attacked and briefly occupied government buildings in downtown Tokyo. The government suppressed the rebellion and executed its leaders, but to many Japanese those executed were heroes not traitors. Constitutional government survived on paper, but when Japanese and Chinese troops clashed in the summer of 1937 near Beijing, the ensuing war between China and Japan put political authority firmly in the hands of militarists and nationalists.

The Black Dragon Society was one of the many nationalist organizations that flourished in Japan in the first half of the twentieth century. An offshoot of a secret society established in 1881 by former samurai (warrior aristocrats), the Black Dragon Society was founded in 1901. Its original goal was to promote war with Russia as a means of expanding Japan's influence on the Asian mainland. After the Russo-Japanese War of 1904–1905, which gave Japan a protectorate over Korea, the group advocated an aggressive foreign policy in Asia and denounced democracy, big business, Americanization, socialism, and party politics, all of which were viewed as threats to Japanese culture and their plans for military conquest. Although membership in the Black Dragon Society and similar organizations was small, their self-promotion, assassinations, and strong-arm tactics kept alive their brand of extreme nationalism, allowing it to flourish in the troubled atmosphere of the 1930s.

In 1930 the Black Dragon Society published a two-volume *Secret History of the Annexation of Korea,* in which it claimed a key role in inspiring early Japanese expansion. It concluded the second volume with the statement that follows.

QUESTIONS FOR ANALYSIS

1. What aspects of the Black Dragon Society's philosophy caused it to support interventions in Korea, China, and the Philippines?
2. In what ways, according to the authors of the document, has Japanese foreign policy been thwarted in the years since World War I?
3. According to the Society, how has Japan's domestic situation deteriorated?
4. According to the Society, what are the causes of Japan's problems, and what solutions does it offer?
5. What might explain the appeal of such ideas to the Japanese populace?

From the first, we members of the Amur [Black Dragon] Society have worked in accordance with the imperial mission for overseas expansion to solve our overpopulation; at the same time, we have sought to give support and encouragement to the peoples of East Asia. Thus we have sought the spread of humanity and righteousness throughout the world by having the imperial purpose extend to neighboring nations.

Earlier, in order to achieve these principles, we organized the Heavenly Blessing Heroes in Korea in 1894 and helped the Tong Hak rebellion there in order to speed the settlement of the dispute between Japan and China.[1] In 1899 we helped Aguinaldo in his struggle for independence for the Philippines.[2] In 1900 we worked with other comrades in helping Sun Yat-sen start the fires of revolution in South China. In 1901 we organized this Society and became exponents of the punishment of Russia, and thereafter we devoted ourselves to the annexation of Korea while continuing to support the revolutionary movement of China. . . .

During this period we have seen the fulfillment of our national power in the decisive victories in the two major wars against China and Russia,[3] in the annexation of Korea, the acquisition of Formosa [Taiwan] and Sakhalin, and the expulsion of Germany from the Shandong peninsula.[4] Japan's status among the empires of the world has risen until today she ranks as one of the three great powers, and from this eminence she can support other Asiatic nations. . . .

However, in viewing recent international affairs it would seem that the foundation established by the great Meiji emperor is undergoing rapid deterioration. The disposition of the gains of the war with Germany was left to foreign powers, and the government, disregarding the needs of national defense, submitted to unfair demands to limit our naval power.[5] Moreover, the failure of our China policy[6] made the Chinese more and more contemptuous of us, so much so that they have been brought to demand the surrender of our essential defense lines in Manchuria and Mongolia. Furthermore, in countries like the United States and Australia our immigrants have been deprived of rights which were acquired only after long years of struggle, and we now face a highhanded anti-Japanese expulsion movement which knows no bounds.[7] Men of purpose and of humanity who are at all concerned for their country cannot fail to be upset by the situation.

When we turn our attention to domestic affairs, we feel more than deep concern. There is a great slackening of discipline and order. Men's hearts are becoming corrupt. Look about you! Are not the various government measures and establishments a conglomeration of all sorts of evils and abuses? The laws are confusing, and evil grows apace. The people are overwhelmed by heavy taxes, the confusion in the business world

---

[1]The Tonghak, or Eastern Learning, movement was a late-nineteenth-century Korean religious movement that drew on Daoist, Buddhist, Confucian, and Catholic traditions. In 1894 members of the movement rebelled against the China-oriented government of Korea because of its corruption and indifference to the plight of the poor. Japanese and Chinese troops intervened, leading to the Sino-Japanese War of 1894–1895. The result was the recognition of Korea's independence by China.

[2]Emilio Aguinaldo (1869–1964) led an insurrection against the Spaniards in 1898 and established the Philippine Republic in January 1899. Following the Spanish American War, he resisted the U.S. takeover, but was defeated.

[3]Victory over China in the Sino-Japanese War and over Russia in the Russo-Japanese War (1904–1905).

[4]Japan received Taiwan (Formosa) after the Sino-Japanese War. Its authority over Korea and its claim to the southern half of Sakhalin Island were recognized after the Russo-Japanese War. Japan was granted former German concessions in China's Shandong province after World War I.

[5]The Washington Conference of 1921 set Japan's naval strength at 60 percent of that of the United States and that of Great Britain.

[6]The Twenty-One Demands, submitted by Japan to China in 1915, would have established extensive Japanese influence over the Chinese government. These demands were successfully resisted by China.

[7]Both Australia and the United States severely restricted Japanese (and Chinese) immigration in the 1920s.

complicates the livelihood of the people, the growth of dangerous thought threatens social order, and our national polity, which has endured for three thousand years, is in danger. This is a critical time for our national destiny; was there ever a more crucial day? What else can we call this time if it is not termed decisive?

And yet, in spite of this our government, instead of pursuing a farsighted policy, casts about for temporary measures. The opposition party simply struggles for political power without any notion of saving our country from this crisis. And even the press, which should devote itself to its duty of guiding and leading society, is the same. For the most part it swims with the current, bows to vulgar opinions, and is chiefly engrossed in money making. Alas! Our empire moves ever closer to rocks which lie before us. . . .

. . . Therefore we of the Amur Society have determined to widen the scope of our activity. Hereafter, besides our interest in foreign affairs, we will give unselfish criticism of internal politics and of social problems, and we will seek to guide public opinion into proper channels. . . . We . . . are resolved to reform the moral corruption of the people, restore social discipline, and ease the insecurity of the people's livelihood by relieving the crises in the financial world, restore national confidence, and increase the national strength, in order to carry out the imperial mission to awaken the countries of Asia. In order to clarify these principles, we here set forth our platform to all our fellow patriots.

▼▼▼

PLATFORM

1. Developing the great plan of the founders of the country, we will widen the great Way [Dao] of Eastern culture, work out a harmony of Eastern and Western cultures, and take the lead among Asian peoples.

2. We will bring to an end many evils, such as formalistic legalism; it restricts the freedom of the people, hampers common sense solutions, prevents efficiency in public and private affairs, and destroys the true meaning of constitutional government. Thereby we will show forth again the essence of the imperial principles.

3. We shall rebuild the present administrative systems. We will develop overseas expansion through the activation of our diplomacy, further the prosperity of the people by reforms in internal government, and solve problems of labor and management by the establishment of new social policies. Thereby we will strengthen the foundations of the empire.

4. We shall carry out the spirit of the Imperial Rescript[8] to Soldiers and Sailors and stimulate a martial spirit by working toward the goal of a nation in arms. Thereby we look toward the perfection of national defense.

5. We plan a fundamental reform of the present educational system, which is copied from those of Europe and America; we shall set up a basic study of a national education originating in our national polity. Thereby we anticipate the further development and heightening of the wisdom and virtue of the Yamato race.[9]

---

[8]Issued by the emperor in 1882, the rescript stated that supreme command of the armed forces rests in the hands of the emperor alone, thus strengthening the military's independence from civilian control.

[9]According to tradition, Japan's imperial line can be traced back to the state founded by a descendant of the Sun Goddess on the Yamato plain around 660 B.C.E.

Japanese Foreign Policy Priorities on the Eve of the China War

▼▼▼

94 ▼ *FUNDAMENTAL PRINCIPLES OF NATIONAL POLICY, 1936*

Despite the failure of the takeover of central Tokyo by nationalist soldiers and officers of the First Division in early 1936, the military retained a strong voice in government. Many politicians bent over backward in support of the military and its right-wing agenda in order to prevent renewed violence. The cabinet of Hirota Koti, in power from March 1936 to February 1937, increased military spending and passed stricter laws against communists and socialists.

In August 1936 the Hirota cabinet approved the following policy on foreign and domestic policy. It is an effort to strike a balance between the army's traditional focus on north China and Manchuria as a means of countering the Soviet Union's strength and the navy's new southward policy and its concerns with U.S. naval power. It also shows the degree to which militarism and expansionism had become the bedrock of Japanese politics on the eve of the war with China.

QUESTIONS FOR ANALYSIS

1. What view of Japan's role in Asian affairs is expressed in this statement?
2. What views of the Soviet Union and the Western powers does the document express?
3. According to the authors of the document, what steps must be taken to prepare Japan for the foreign policy challenges it will meet?
4. What specific statements in the document reveal the militarist priorities of the Hirota government?
5. How do the ideas expressed in this document compare to those of the Black Dragon Society's 1930 anniversary statement (source 93)?

(1) Japan must strive to eradicate the aggressive policies of the great powers, and share with East Asia the joy which is based on the true principle of co-existence and co-prosperity. This is the realization of the spirit of the Imperial Way which must be accepted as the consistent guiding principle in Japan's policy of foreign expansion.

(2) Japan must complete her national defense and armament to protect her national security and development. In this way, the position of the Empire as the stabilizing force in East Asia can be secured both in name and in fact.

(3) The policy toward the continent must be based on the following factors: in order to promote Manchukuo's[1] healthy development and to stabilize Japan-Manchukuo national defense, the threat from the north, the Soviet Union, must be eliminated;[2] in order to promote our economic

---

[1] The Japanese name for the puppet government of Manchuria established after the 1931 conquest.
[2] In the mid-1930s the Soviet Union had approximately

240,000 troops in its far eastern provinces, compared to 160,000 Japanese troops in Manchuria.

development, we must prepare against Great Britain and the United States and bring about close collaboration between Japan, Manchukuo, and China. In the execution of this policy, Japan must pay due attention to friendly relations with other powers.

(4) Japan plans to promote her racial and economic development in the South Seas, especially in the outerlying South Seas[3] areas. She plans to extend her strength by moderate and peaceful means and without rousing other powers. In this way, concurrently with the firm establishment of Manchukuo, Japan may expect full development and strengthening of her national power.

B. Utilizing the above fundamental principles as the axis, we must unify and coordinate our foreign and domestic policies, and reform our administration thoroughly to reflect the current conditions. The following are the basic outlines.

(1) Japan's national defense and armament must be completed in the following manner:

a. The Army's arms preparations must have as their goal, the ability to withstand the forces which can be deployed by the Soviet Union in the Far East. The Army must expand its Kwantung[4] and Chōsen (Korean) forces to the extent that they can deliver the first decisive blow against the Soviet Far Eastern Army at the outbreak of war.

b. The Navy's arms preparations must have as their goal, creation of forces sufficient to withstand an attack from the U.S. Navy to secure the control of the Western Pacific for Japan.

(2) Our foreign policy must be based on the principle of the smooth execution of the fundamental national policies. It must therefore be co-ordinated and reformed. In order to facilitate the smooth functioning of activities of diplomatic bureaus, the military must endeavor to give behind-the-scenes assistance, and must avoid overt activities.

(3) In order to conform to the above basic national policies, in effecting reform and improvement in political and administrative organizations, in establishing financial and economic policies, and in administering other agencies, appropriate actions must be taken on the following matters:

a. The domestic public opinion must be led and unified, so as to strengthen the nation's resolve in coping with the present national emergency.

b. Appropriate reforms in administrative agencies and economic organizations must be effected to bring about improvement in industries and important foreign trade necessary for executing national policies.

c. Appropriate measures must be taken to ensure stabilization of national life, strengthening of physical fitness, and development of sound national thought.

d. Appropriate plans must be undertaken to promote rapid growth in aviation and maritime transportation industries.

e. We must promote the establishment of a policy of self-sufficiency with regard to important natural resources and materials required for national defense and industries.

f. Concurrently with the reform of diplomatic bureaus, information and propaganda organizations must be well established to enhance vigorously diplomatic functions and cultural activities overseas.

---

[3]The southern Pacific.
[4]The Kwantung forces were Japan's army in Manchuria; the Chōsen army was in Korea.

▼▼▼

The Legacy of World War II

In the two decades after World War I weapons became more destructive, nationalism more impassioned, and leaders' ambitions more fantastic. As a result, the war that began in Asia in 1937 and in Europe in 1939 — World War II — became the most devastating and destructive war in history. Modern communication and transportation systems enabled generals to plan and execute massive campaigns such as the German invasion of the Soviet Union in 1941 and the Allies' Normandy invasion in 1944. The airplane, only a curiosity in World War I, became an instrument of destruction in World War II, making possible the German assault on English cities in 1940, the Japanese attack on Pearl Harbor in 1941, the around-the-clock bombing of Germany by Britain and the United States from 1943 to 1945, and the American fire-bombing of Tokyo in 1945.

Only the closing months of the war, however, fully revealed the destructive possibilities of modern technology and large bureaucratic states. As Allied armies liberated Europe in the winter and spring of 1945, they found in the Third Reich's concentration and extermination camps the horrifying results of the Nazi assault on political enemies, religious dissidents, prisoners of war, gypsies, Slavs, and especially Jews. Then on August 6 the United States dropped an atomic bomb on Hiroshima, Japan. It killed nearly 80,000 people, seriously injured twice that number, and obliterated three-fifths of the city. On August 9 the United States dropped a second atomic bomb on Nagasaki, intending to destroy the Mitsubishi shipyards. It missed its target but destroyed half the city and killed 75,000 people.

A half century later the names Hiroshima and Nagasaki still evoke nightmares in a world where thousands of nuclear warheads exist, and many nations have the capacity to manufacture nuclear weapons many times more powerful than those dropped on Japan. Similarly, the Holocaust, the Nazi attempt to exterminate the Jews, continues to haunt the imagination. Racism and ethnic hatreds are universally condemned, but they flourish in many parts of the world. Anti-Semitism has resurfaced in Central and Eastern Europe, the Serbs have bombed and starved Bosnian and Kosovar towns and cities in the name of ethnic cleansing, Tutsi and Hutus have slaughtered one another in central Africa, and racial tensions continue to plague the United States and dozens of other societies.

Was the Holocaust an aberration resulting from the unique prejudices of the Germans and the perverse views of a handful of their leaders? Or was something much more basic in human nature involved? These are just two of the many disturbing questions raised by the Nazi campaign to exterminate the Jews.

"Führer, You Order. We Obey"

▼▼▼

95 ▼ Rudolf Höss, MEMOIRS

On gaining power, the Nazis began to implement the anti-Jewish policies Hitler and the Nazis had promised in *Mein Kampf* and thousands of books, pamphlets, and speeches. Jewish shops were plundered while police looked the other way, Jewish physicians were excluded from hospitals, Jewish judges lost their posts, Jewish students were denied admission to universities, and Jewish veterans were stripped of their benefits. In 1935 the Nazis promulgated the Nuremberg Laws, which deprived Jews of citizenship and outlawed marriage between Jews and non-Jews. In November 1938 the regime organized nationwide violence against Jewish synagogues and shops in what came to be known as *Kristallnacht,* or "night of the broken glass."

After the war began in late 1939, conquests in Eastern Europe gave the Nazis new opportunities to address the "Jewish problem." In early 1941 they began to deport Jews from Germany and conquered territories to Poland and Czechoslovakia, where Jews were employed as slave laborers or placed in concentration camps. In June 1941 special units known as *Einsatzgruppe* ("special action forces") were organized to exterminate Jews in territories conquered on the eastern front. In eighteen months, they gunned down over 1 million Jews and smaller numbers of Gypsies and non-Jewish Slavs. Then in January 1942 at the Wannsee Conference outside Berlin, the Nazi leadership approved the Final Solution to the so-called Jewish problem. Their goal became the extermination of European Jewry, and to reach it they constructed special camps where their murderous work could be done efficiently and quickly.

When World War II ended, the Nazis had not achieved their goal of annihilating Europe's 11 million Jews. They did, however, slaughter close to 6 million, thus earning themselves a permanent place in the long history of man's inhumanity to man.

The following excerpt comes from the memoirs of Rudolf Höss, the commandant of the Auschwitz concentration camp in Poland between 1940 and 1943. Born in 1900, Höss abandoned plans to become a priest after serving in World War I and became involved in a number of right-wing political movements, including the Nazi Party, which he joined in the early 1920s. After serving a jail sentence for participating in the murder of a teacher suspected of "treason," Höss became a farmer and then in 1934, on the urging of Heinrich Himmler, a member of the Nazi SS, or *Schutzstaffel* (Guard Detachment). The SS under Himmler grew from a small security force to guard Hitler and other high-ranking Nazis into a powerful party organization involved in police work, state security, intelligence gathering, administration of conquered territories, and management of the concentration camps. After postings at the Dachau and Sachsenhausen camps, Höss was appointed commandant of Auschwitz, which began as a camp for Polish political prisoners but became a huge, sprawling complex where over a million Jews were gassed or shot and tens of thousands of prisoners served as slave laborers in nearby factories. In

1943 Höss became overseer of all the Third Reich's concentration camps, but he returned to Auschwitz in 1944 to administer the murder of 400,000 Hungarian Jews. After his capture in 1946, he was tried and convicted for crimes against humanity by the international military tribunal at Nuremberg. He was hanged on April 16, 1947, within sight of the villa where he and his family had lived while he served as commandant at Auschwitz.

While awaiting trial, Höss was encouraged to compose his memoirs to sharpen his recollection of events he experienced. In the following passage he discusses his views of the Jews and his reaction to the mass killings he planned and witnessed.

QUESTIONS FOR ANALYSIS

1. What does Höss claim to have been his attitude toward the Jews?
2. How do his statements about the Jews accord with his assertion that he was a fanatic National Socialist?
3. Does Höss make any distinction between the Russians and Jews that he had exterminated?
4. What was Höss's attitude toward the Final Solution? How does Höss characterize his role in the mass extermination of the Jews?
5. How did his involvement in the Holocaust affect him personally? How, according to Höss, did it affect other German participants?
6. What would you describe as the key components of Höss's personality? To what extent was his personality shaped by the Nazi philosophy to which he was dedicated?
7. What insight does this excerpt provide about the issue of how much the German people knew of and participated in the Holocaust?

Since I was a fanatic National Socialist, I was firmly convinced that our idea would take hold in all countries, modified by the various local customs, and would gradually become dominant. This would then break the dominance of international Jewry. Anti-Semitism was nothing new throughout the whole world. It always made its strongest appearance when the Jews had pushed themselves into positions of power and when their evil actions became known to the general public. . . . I believed that because our ideas were better and stronger, we would prevail in the long run. . . .

I want to emphasize here that I personally never hated the Jews. I considered them to be the enemy of our nation. However, that was precisely the reason to treat them the same way as the other prisoners. I never made a distinction concerning this. Besides, the feeling of hatred is not in me, but I know what hate is, and how it manifests itself. I have seen it and I have felt it.

The original order . . . to annihilate all the Jews stated, "All Jews without exception are to be destroyed." It was later changed by Himmler so that those able to work were to be used in the arms factories. This made Auschwitz the assembly point for the Jews to a degree never before known. . . .

When he gave me the order personally . . . to prepare a place for mass killings and then carry it out, I could never have imagined the scale, or what the consequences would be. Of course, this order was something extraordinary, something monstrous. However, the reasoning behind the order of this mass annihilation seemed correct to me. At the time I wasted no thoughts about it. I had received an order; I had to carry it out. I could not allow myself to form an opinion as to whether this mass extermination of the Jews was necessary or not. At the time it was beyond my frame of mind. Since the Führer himself had ordered "The Final Solution of the Jewish Question," there was no second guessing for an old National Socialist, much less an SS officer. "Führer, you order. We obey" was not just a phrase or a slogan. It was meant to be taken seriously.[1]

Since my arrest I have been told repeatedly that I could have refused to obey this order, and even that I could have shot Himmler dead. I do not believe that among the thousands of SS officers there was even one who would have had even a glimmer of such a thought. . . . Of course, many SS officers moaned and groaned about the many harsh orders. Even then, they carried out every order. . . . As leader of the SS, Himmler's person was sacred. His fundamental orders in the name of the Führer were holy. There was no reflection, no interpretation, no explanation about these orders. They were carried out ruthlessly, regardless of the final consequences, even if it meant giving your life for them. Quite a few did that during the war.

It was not in vain that the leadership training of the SS officers held up the Japanese as shining examples of those willing to sacrifice their lives for the state and for the emperor, who was also their god. SS education was not just a series of useless high school lectures. It went far deeper, and Himmler knew very well what he could demand of his SS. . . .

Whatever the Führer or Himmler ordered was always right. Even democratic England has its saying, "My country, right or wrong," and every patriotic Englishman follows it.

▼ ▼ ▼

Before the mass destruction of the Jews began, all the Russian politruks[2] and political commissars were killed in almost every camp during 1941 and 1942. According to the secret order given by Hitler, the Einsatzgruppe searched for and picked up the Russian politruks and commissars from all the POW camps. They transferred all they found to the nearest concentration camp for liquidation. . . . The first small transports were shot by firing squads of SS soldiers.

While I was on an official trip, my second in command, Camp Commander Fritzsch, experimented with gas for killings. He used a gas called Cyclon B, prussic acid,[3] which was often used as an insecticide in the camp to exterminate lice and vermin. There was always a supply on hand. When I returned Fritzsch reported to me about how he had used the gas. We used it again to kill the next transport.

The gassing was carried out in the basement of Block 11. I viewed the killings wearing a gas mask for protection. Death occurred in the crammed-full cells immediately after the gas was thrown in. Only a brief choking outcry and it was all over. . . .

At the time I really didn't waste any thoughts about the killing of the Russian POWs. It was ordered; I had to carry it out. But I must admit openly that the gassings had a calming effect on me, since in the near future the mass annihilation of the Jews was to begin. Up to this point it was not clear to me . . . how the killing of the expected masses was to be done. Perhaps by gas? But how, and what kind of gas? Now we had discovered the gas and the procedure. I was always horrified of death by firing squads, especially when I thought of the huge numbers of women and children who would have to be killed. I had had enough of hostage executions, and the mass

---

[1] All SS members swore the following oath: "I swear to you Adolf Hitler, as Führer and Chancellor of the Reich, loyalty and bravery. I vow to you and to the authorities appointed by you obedience onto death, so help me God."
[2] Communist Party members.

[3] Cyclon (or Zyclon) B is a blue crystalline substance; its active ingredient, hydrocyanic acid, sublimates into a gas when it contacts the air. It causes death by combining with the red blood cells and preventing them from carrying oxygen.

killings by firing squad order by Himmler and Heydrich.[4]

Now I was at ease. We were all saved from these bloodbaths, and the victims would be spared until the last moment. That is what I worried about the most when I thought of Eichmann's[5] accounts of the mowing down of the Jews with machine guns and pistols by the Einsatzgruppe. Horrible scenes were supposed to have occurred: people running away even after being shot, the killing of those who were only wounded, especially the women and children. Another thing on my mind was the many suicides among the ranks of the SS Special Action Squads who could no longer mentally endure wading in the bloodbath. Some of them went mad. Most of the members of the Special Action Squads drank a great deal to help get through this horrible work. According to [Captain] Höffle's accounts, the men of Globocnik's[6] extermination section drank tremendous quantities of alcohol.

In the spring of 1942 the first transports of Jews arrived from Upper Silesia. All of them were to be exterminated. They were led from the ramp across the meadow, later named section B-II of Birkenau,[7] to the farmhouse called Bunker I. Aumeier, Palitzsch, and a few other block leaders led them and spoke to them as one would in casual conversation, asking them about their occupations and their schooling in order to fool them. After arriving at the farmhouse they were told to undress. At first they went very quietly into the rooms where they were supposed to be disinfected. At that point some of them became suspicious and started talking about suffocation and extermination. Immediately a panic started. Those still standing outside were quickly driven

into the chambers, and the doors were bolted shut. In the next transport those who were nervous or upset were identified and watched closely at all times. As soon as unrest was noticed these troublemakers were inconspicuously led behind the farmhouse and killed with a small-caliber pistol, which could not be heard by the others. . . .

I also watched how some women who suspected or knew what was happening, even with the fear of death all over their faces, still managed enough strength to play with their children and to talk to them lovingly. Once a woman with four children, all holding each other by the hand to help the smallest ones over the rough ground, passed by me very slowly. She stepped very close to me and whispered, pointing to her four children, "How can you murder these beautiful, darling children? Don't you have any heart?"

Another time an old man hissed while passing me, "Germany will pay a bitter penance for the mass murder of the Jews." His eyes glowed with hatred as he spoke. In spite of this he went bravely into the gas chamber without worrying about the others. . . .

Occasionally some women would suddenly start screaming in a terrible way while undressing. They pulled out their hair and acted as if they had gone crazy. Quickly they were led behind the farmhouse and killed by a bullet in the back of the neck from a small-caliber pistol. . . . As the doors were being shut, I saw a woman trying to shove her children out the chamber, crying out, "Why don't you at least let my precious children live?" There were many heartbreaking scenes like this which affected all who were present.

In the spring of 1942 hundreds of people in the full bloom of life walked beneath the bud-

---

[4]Reinhard Heydrich (1904–1942) was Himmler's chief lieutenant in the SS. He organized the mass execution of Jews in Eastern Europe in 1941.

[5]Adolf Eichmann (1906–1962) was a Nazi bureaucrat originally involved with Jewish emigration. After the Wannsee Conference he was given responsibility for organizing the deportation of approximately 3 million Jews to the death camps. He fled to Argentina in 1946, but was captured by

Israeli agents who took him to Israel, where he was tried and executed in 1962.

[6]Odilio Globocnik was the officer responsible for organizing and training SS units in Eastern Europe.

[7]Birkenau was the German name for the town where a large addition to the Auschwitz complex was built in late 1941 and early 1942.

ding fruit trees of the farm into the gas chamber to their death, most of them without a hint of what was going to happen to them. To this day I can still see these pictures of the arrivals, the selections, and the procession to their death. . . .

The mass annihilation with all the accompanying circumstances did not fail to affect those who had to carry it out. They just did not watch what was happening. With very few exceptions all who performed this monstrous "work" had been ordered to this detail. All of us, including myself, were given enough to think about which left a deep impression. Many of the men often approached me during my inspection trips through the killing areas and poured out their depression and anxieties to me, hoping that I could give them some reassurance. During these conversations the question arose again and again, "Is what we have to do here necessary? Is it necessary that hundreds of thousands of women and children have to be annihilated?" And I, who countless times deep inside myself had asked the same question, had to put them off by reminding them that it was Hitler's order. I had to tell them that it was necessary to destroy all the Jews in order to forever free Germany and the future generations from our toughest enemy.

It goes without saying that the Hitler order was a firm fact for all of us, and also that it was the duty of the SS to carry it out. However, secret doubts tormented all of us. Under no circumstances could I reveal my secret doubts to anyone. I had to convince myself to be like a rock when faced with the necessity of carrying out this horribly severe order, and I had to show this in every way, in order to force all those under me to hang on mentally and emotionally. . . .

Hour upon hour I had to witness all that happened. I had to watch day and night, whether it was the dragging and burning of the bodies, the teeth being ripped out, the cutting of the hair,[8] I had to watch all this horror. For hours I had to

stand in the horrible, haunting stench while the mass graves were dug open, and the bodies were dragged out and burned. I also had to watch the procession of death itself through the peephole of the gas chamber because the doctors called my attention to it. I had to do all of this because I was the one to whom everyone looked, and because I had to show everybody that I was not only the one who gave the orders and issued the directives, but that I was also willing to be present at whatever task I ordered my men to perform. . . .

And yet, everyone in Auschwitz believed the Kommandant really had a good life. Yes, my family had it good in Auschwitz, every wish that my wife or my children had was fulfilled. The children could live free and easy. My wife had her flower paradise. The prisoners tried to give my wife every consideration and tried to do something nice for the children. By the same token no former prisoner can say that he was treated poorly in any way in our house. My wife would have loved to give a present to every prisoner who performed a service for us. The children constantly begged me for cigarettes for the prisoners. The children especially loved the gardeners. In our entire family there was a deep love for farming and especially for animals. Every Sunday I had to drive with them across all the fields, walk them through the stables, and we could never skip visiting the dog kennels. Their greatest love was for our two horses and our colt. The prisoners who worked in the household were always dragging in some animal the children kept in the garden. Turtles, martens, cats, or lizards; there was always something new and interesting in the garden. The children splashed around in the summertime in the small pool in the garden or the Sola River. Their greatest pleasure was when daddy went into the water with them. But he had only a little time to share all the joys of childhood.

Today I deeply regret that I didn't spend more time with my family. I always believed that I had

---

[8]Teeth extracted from the corpses were soaked in muriatic acid to remove muscle and bone before the gold fillings were extracted. Some of the gold was distributed to dentists who used it in fillings for SS men and their families; the rest was deposited in the Reichsbank. Hair was used to make felt and thread.

to be constantly on duty. Through this exaggerated sense of duty I always had made my life more difficult than it actually was. My wife often urged me, "Don't always think of your duty,

think of your family too." But what did my wife know about the things that depressed me? She never found out.[9]

---

[9]In an interview with a court-appointed psychiatrist during the Nuremberg trials in 1946, Höss stated that his wife actually did learn of his participation in the mass executions at

the camp, and that afterward, they became estranged and ceased having sexual relations.

"The Face of War Is the Face of Death"
▼▼▼

96 ▼ Henry L. Stimson, "THE DECISION TO USE THE ATOMIC BOMB"

President Truman, who as a senator from Missouri and as vice president under Roosevelt did not even know about the Manhattan Project, learned of the atomic bomb in a meeting with Secretary of War Henry L. Stimson on April 25, 1945, two weeks after President Roosevelt's death. His first response was to appoint a small committee, known as the Interim Committee, to advise him on the use of atomic weapons in the war and the immediate postwar era. Its members included Stimson and seven others: George Harrison, an insurance executive who was a special assistant to Stimson; James Byrnes, a presidential advisor and soon secretary of state; Ralph Bard, undersecretary of the navy; William Clayton, assistant secretary of state; Vannevar Bush, president of the Carnegie Institution in Washington; Karl Compton, president of the Massachusetts Institute of Technology; and James Conant, president of Harvard University. They were advised by a Scientific Panel, made up of four persons who had played leading roles in the Manhattan Project: Enrico Fermi of Columbia University; Arthur H. Compton of the University of Chicago; Ernest Lawrence of the University of California at Berkeley; and Robert Oppenheimer, director of the atomic energy research project at Los Alamos, New Mexico.

The chair of the Interim Committee and the author of the excerpt that follows was Stimson. Born in 1867 in New York City and a graduate of Harvard College and Yale Law School, Stimson had a distinguished career as a lawyer and public servant. Having served as secretary of war under President Taft and secretary of state under President Hoover, he was named secretary of war by the Democratic president Roosevelt in 1940, despite being a Republican. In 1947, after his retirement from public service and less than three years before his death in 1950, he published the article "The Decision to Use the Atomic Bomb" in *Harper's Magazine.* It focuses on the work of the Interim Committee and the reasons why Stimson advised President Truman to drop the bombs on Japan without warning. Excerpts from the article follow.

QUESTIONS FOR ANALYSIS

1. How did the background and specific purposes of the Manhattan Project affect decision making in 1945?
2. For those who supported the immediate use of the bombs, what specific goals did they hope to achieve?
3. How was the choice of Hiroshima and Nagasaki as targets related to these goals?
4. How seriously does it appear that views opposing the use of atomic weapons were considered by the Interim Committee and Stimson? Why did they ultimately reject such views?
5. What were Stimson's views of the nature of war? How did his views affect his decision to support the immediate use of the atomic bombs?

[GOALS OF THE MANHATTAN PROJECT]

The policy adopted and steadily pursued by President Roosevelt and his advisers was a simple one. It was to spare no effort in securing the earliest possible successful development of an atomic weapon. The reasons for this policy were equally simple. The original experimental achievement of atomic fission had occurred in Germany in 1938, and it was known that the Germans had continued their experiments. In 1941 and 1942 they were believed to be ahead of us, and it was vital that they should not be the first to bring atomic weapons into the field of battle. Furthermore, if we should be the first to develop the weapon, we should have a great new instrument for shortening the war and minimizing destruction. At no time, from 1941 to 1945, did I ever hear it suggested by the President, or by any other responsible member of government, that atomic energy should not be used in the war. All of us of course understood the terrible responsibility involved in our attempt to unlock the doors to such a devastating weapon; President Roosevelt particularly spoke to me many times of his own awareness of the catastrophic potentialities of our work. But we were at war, and the work must be done. . . .

[RECOMMENDATIONS OF THE INTERIM COMMITTEE AND THE SECRETARY OF WAR]

. . . The committee's work included the drafting of the statements which were published immediately after the first bombs were dropped, the drafting of a bill for the domestic control of atomic energy, and recommendations looking toward the international control of atomic energy. . . . At a meeting with the Interim Committee and the Scientific Panel on May 31, 1945 I urged all those present to feel free to express themselves on any phase of the subject, scientific or political.

On June 1, after its discussions with the Scientific Panel, the Interim Committee unanimously adopted the following recommendations:

(1) The bomb should be used against Japan as soon as possible.
(2) It should be used on a dual target — that is, a military installation or war plant surrounded by or adjacent to houses and other buildings most susceptible to damage, and
(3) It should be used without prior warning [of the nature of the weapon]. One member of the committee, Mr. Bard,[1] later changed his view and dissented from recommendation.

---

[1]Undersecretary of the navy and a member of the Interim Committee. He was the single member of the Interim Committee to oppose its recommendations.

In reaching these conclusions the Interim Committee carefully considered such alternatives as a detailed advance warning or a demonstration in some uninhabited area. Both of these suggestions were discarded as impractical. They were not regarded as likely to be effective in compelling a surrender of Japan, and both of them involved serious risks. Even the New Mexico test would not give final proof that any given bomb was certain to explode when dropped from an airplane. Quite apart from the generally unfamiliar nature of atomic explosives, there was the whole problem of exploding a bomb at a predetermined height in the air by a complicated mechanism which could not be tested in the static test of New Mexico. Nothing would have been more damaging to our effort to obtain surrender than a warning or a demonstration followed by a dud — and this was a real possibility. Furthermore, we had no bombs to waste. It was vital that a sufficient effect be quickly obtained with the few we had. . . .

The committee's function was, of course, entirely advisory. The ultimate responsibility for the recommendation to the President rested upon me, and I have no desire to veil it. The conclusions of the committee were similar to my own, although I reached mine independently. I felt that to extract a genuine surrender from the Emperor and his military advisers, they must be administered a tremendous shock which would carry convincing proof of our power to destroy the Empire. Such an effective shock would save many times the number of lives, both American and Japanese, that it would cost.

The facts upon which my reasoning was based and steps taken to carry it out now follow.

The principal political, social, and military objective of the United States in the summer of 1945 was the prompt and complete surrender of Japan. Only the complete destruction of her military power could open the way to lasting peace. . . .

In the middle of July 1945, the intelligence section of the War Department General Staff estimated Japanese military strength as follows: in the home islands, slightly under 2,000,000; in Korea, Manchuria, China proper, and Formosa, slightly over 2,000,000; in French Indo-China, Thailand, and Burma, over 200,000; in the East Indies area, including the Philippines, over 500,000; in the by-passed Pacific islands, over 100,000. The total strength of the Japanese Army was estimated at about 5,000,000 men. . . .

As we understood it in July, there was a very strong possibility that the Japanese government might determine upon resistance to the end, in all the areas of the Far East under its control. In such an event the Allies would be faced with the enormous task of destroying an armed force of five million men and five thousand suicide aircraft, belonging to a race which had already amply demonstrated its ability to fight literally to the death.

The strategic plans of our armed forces for the defeat of Japan, as they stood in July, had been prepared without reliance upon the atomic bomb, which had not yet been tested in New Mexico. We were planning an intensified sea and air blockade, and greatly intensified strategic air bombing, through the summer and early fall, to be followed on November 1 by an invasion of the southern island of Kyushu. This would be followed in turn by an invasion of the main island of Honshu in the spring of 1946. The total U.S. military and naval force involved in this grand design was of the order of 5,000,000 men; if all those indirectly concerned are included, it was larger still.

We estimated that if we should be forced to carry this plan to its conclusion, the major fighting would not end until the latter part of 1946, at the earliest. I was informed that such operations might be expected to cost over a million casualties to American forces alone. Additional large losses might be expected among our allies, and, of course, if our campaign were successful and if we could judge by previous experience, enemy casualties would be much larger than our own.

It was already clear in July that even before the invasion we should be able to inflict enormously severe damage on the Japanese homeland by the combined application of "conventional" sea and air power. The critical question was whether this kind of action would induce surrender. It therefore became necessary to consider very carefully the probable state of mind of the enemy, and to assess with accuracy the line of conduct which might end his will to resist.

▷   After Japan on July 28 rejected the Potsdam ultimatum, which gave their leaders the choice of immediate surrender or the "utter destruction of the Japanese homeland," plans went forward for using the atomic bombs.

Because of the importance of the atomic mission against Japan, the detailed plans were brought to me by the military staff for approval. With President Truman's warm support I struck off the list of suggested targets the city of Kyoto. Although it was a target of considerable military importance, it had been the ancient capital of Japan and was a shrine of Japanese art and culture. We determined that it should be spared. I approved four other targets including the cities of Hiroshima and Nagasaki.

Hiroshima was bombed on August 6, and Nagasaki on August 9. These two cities were active working parts of the Japanese war effort. One was an army center; the other was naval and industrial. Hiroshima was the headquarters of the Japanese Army defending southern Japan and was a major military storage and assembly point. Nagasaki was a major seaport and it con-

tained several large industrial plants of great wartime importance. We believed that our attacks had struck cities which must certainly be important to the Japanese military leaders, both Army and Navy, and we waited for a result. We waited one day.

FINAL REFLECTIONS

. . . As I look back over the five years of my service as Secretary of War, I see too many stern and heartrending decisions to be willing to pretend that war is anything else than what it is. The face of war is the face of death; death is an inevitable part of every order that a wartime leader gives. The decision to use the atomic bomb was a decision that brought death to over a hundred thousand Japanese. No explanation can change that fact and I do not wish to gloss it over. But this deliberate, premeditated destruction was our least abhorrent choice. The destruction of Hiroshima and Nagasaki put an end to the Japanese war. It stopped the fire raids and the strangling blockade; it ended the ghastly specter of a clash of great land armies.

In this last great action of the Second World War we were given final proof that war is death. . . . The bombs dropped on Hiroshima and Nagasaki ended a war. They also made it wholly clear that we must never have another war. This is the lesson men and leaders everywhere must learn, and I believe that when they learn it they will find a way to lasting peace. There is no other choice.

August 6, 1945

▼▼▼

97 ▼ *Iwao Nakamura and Atsuko Tsujioka, RECOLLECTIONS*

In 1951 Dr. Arata Osada, a professor of education at the University of Hiroshima, sponsored a project in which young Japanese from primary grades through the university level were asked to write down their memories of the August 6 bombing and its aftermath. Moved by their recollections, he arranged to have published a sample of their compositions in 1951. His stated purpose was to reveal the horrors of nuclear war and thereby encourage nuclear disarmament. An English translation appeared in 1980.

QUESTIONS FOR ANALYSIS

Readers are encouraged to formulate their own questions about the events and experiences described in these memoirs.

IWAO NAKAMURA

11th Grade Boy (5th Grade at the Time)

Today, as I begin to write an account of my experiences after five years and several months have passed, the wretched scenes of that time float up before my eyes like phantoms. And as these phantoms appear, I can actually hear the pathetic groans, the screams.

In an instant it became dark as night, Hiroshima on that day. Flames shooting up from wrecked houses as if to illuminate this darkness. Amidst this, children aimlessly wandering about, groaning with pain, their burned faces twitching and bloated like balloons. An old man, skin flaking off like the skin of a potato, trying to get away on weak, unsteady legs, praying as he went. A man frantically calling out the names of his wife and children, both hands to his forehead from which blood trickled down. Just the memory of it makes my blood run cold. This is the real face of war. . . .

I, who cannot forget, was in the fifth year of primary school when it happened. To escape the frequent air raids, I and my sisters had been evacuated to the home of our relatives in the country, but on August 2, I returned to my home at Naka Kakomachi (near the former Prefectural Office) during the summer vacation, to recover from the effects of a summer illness that had left me very weak. . . .

It was after eight on August 6 and the midsummer sun was beginning to scorch down on Hiroshima. An all-clear signal had sounded and with relief we sat down for breakfast a little later than usual. Usually by this time, my father had left the house for the office and I would be at the hospital for treatment.

I was just starting on my second bowl of rice. At that moment, a bluish-white ray of light like a magnesium flare hit me in the face, a terrific roar tore at my eardrums and it became so dark I could not see anything. I stood up, dropping my rice bowl and chopsticks. I do not know what happened next or how long I was unconscious. When I came to, I found myself trapped under what seemed like a heavy rock, but my head was free. It was still dark but I finally discovered that I was under a collapsed wall. It was all so sudden that I kept wondering if I was dreaming. I tried very hard to crawl free, but the heavy wall would not budge. A suffocating stench flooded the area and began to choke me. My breathing became short, my ears began to ring, and my heart was pounding as if it were about to burst. "I can't last much longer," I said to myself, and then a draft of cold air flowed past me and some light appeared. The taste of that fresh air is something I shall never forget. I breathed it in with all my might. This fresh air and the brighter surroundings gave me renewed vigor and I somehow managed to struggle out from under the wall. . . .

Nothing was left of the Hiroshima of a few minutes ago. The houses and buildings had been destroyed and the streets transformed into a black desert, with only the flames from burning buildings giving a lurid illumination to the dark sky over Hiroshima. Flames were already shooting out of the wreckage of the house next door. We couldn't see my two brothers. My mother was in tears as she called their names. My father went frantic as he dug among the collapsed walls and scattered tiles. It must have been by the mercy of God that we were able to rescue my brothers from under the wreckage before the flames reached them. They were not hurt, either. The five of us left our burning home and hurried toward Koi. Around us was a sea of flames. The street was filled with flames and smoke from the burning wreckage of houses and burning power poles which had toppled down blocked our way time after time, almost sending us into the depths of despair. It seems that everyone in the area had already made their escape, for we saw no one but sometimes we heard moans, a sound like a wild beast. . . . As we passed Nakajima Primary School area and approached Sumiyoshi Bridge, I saw a damaged water tank in which a number of people had their heads down, drinking. I was so thirsty and attracted by the sight of people that I left my parents' side without thinking, and approached the tank. But when I got near and was able to see into the tank, I gave an involuntary cry and backed away. What I saw reflected in the blood-stained water were the faces of monsters. They had leaned over the side of the tank and died in that position. From the burned shreds of their sailor uniforms, I knew they were schoolgirls, but they had no hair left and their burned faces were crimson with blood; they no longer appeared human. After we came out on the main road and cross Sumiyoshi Bridge, we finally came across some living human beings — but maybe it would be more correct to say that we met some people from Hell. They were naked and their skin, burned and bloody, was like red rust and their bodies were bloated up like balloons. . . . The houses on both sides of this street, which was several dozen yards wide, were in flames so that we could only move along a strip in the center about three or four yards wide. This narrow passage was covered with seriously burned and injured people, unable to walk, and with dead bodies, leaving hardly any space for us to get through. At places, we were forced to step over them callously, but we apologized in our hearts as

we did this. Among them were old people pleading for water, tiny children seeking help, students unconsciously calling for their parents, brothers, and sisters, and there was a mother prostrate on the ground, moaning with pain but with one arm still tightly embracing her dead baby. But how could we help them when we ourselves did not know our own fate?

When we reached the Koi First Aid Station, we learned that we were among the last to escape from the Sumiyoshi Bridge area. After my father had received some medical treatment, we hurried over Koi Hill to our relatives at Tomo Village in Asa County. When we were crossing the hill late that evening, we could see Hiroshima lying far below, now a mere smoldering desert. After offering a silent prayer for the victims, we descended the hill toward Tomo.

ATSUKO TSUJIOKA

Student, Hiroshima Women's Junior College

It happened instantaneously. I felt as if my back had been struck with a big hammer, and then as if I had been thrown into boiling oil. I was unconscious for a while. When I regained my senses, the whole area was covered with black smoke. . . . I lay on the ground with my arms pressed against my chest, and called for help, again and again: "Mother! Mother! Father!"

But, of course, neither Mother nor Father answered me. . . . I could hear the other girls shouting for their mothers in the hellish darkness, and I sensed that they were getting away. I got up and just ran after them desperately. Near Tsurumi Bridge, a red hot electric wire got wrapped around my ankles. I pulled free of it somehow, without thinking, and ran to the foot of the Tsurumi Bridge. By that time, there was white smoke everywhere. I had been working in a place called Tanaka-cho, about 600 yards from the blast center. I seemed to have been blown quite a bit north and had to take a completely different route to the bridge, which would have been straight ahead of me if I was where I should have been.

There was a large cistern at the foot of the bridge. In the tank were some mothers, one holding her naked, burned baby above her head, and another crying and trying to give her baby milk from her burned breast. Also in the tank were schoolchildren, with only their heads, and their hands clasped in prayer, above the surface of the water. They were sobbing for their parents, but everyone had been hurt, so there was no one to help them. People's hair was white with dust, and scorched; they did not look human. "Surely not me," I thought, and I looked down at my own hands. They were bloody and what looked like rags hung from my arms, and inside was freshlooking flesh, all red, white and black. I was shocked and reached for the handkerchief I carried in the pocket of my trousers, but there was no handkerchief or pocket. The lower part of the trousers had been burned away. I could feel my face swelling up, but there was nothing I could do about it. I and some friends decided to try to get back to our houses in the suburbs. Houses were blazing on both sides of the street as we walked along, and my back started hurting worse.

We heard people calling for help inside wrecked buildings, and then saw the same buildings go up in flames. A boy of about six, covered in blood, was jumping up and down in front of one of the burning houses, holding a cooking pot in his hands and yelling something we could not understand. . . . I wonder what happened to those people? And the ones trapped in the buildings. In our rush to get home quickly, the four of us were proceeding toward the center of the atomic explosion, in the opposite direction from everyone else. However, when we reached Inari-machi, we could not go any further because the bridge had been destroyed, so we headed for Futaba Hill, instead. My legs gave out near Futaba, and I almost crawled the last part of the way to the foot of the hill, saying, "Wait for me! Please wait for me!"

Luckily for us, we met some kind soldiers in white coats there, who took us to a place we could lie down and rest, and treated our wounds.

They dug around and told me that they had removed pieces of tile from the back of my head. They bandaged my head for me and tried to console us by saying, "Rest here now. Your teacher is bound to come and get you soon." . . .

That first night ended. There were cries for water from early morning. I was terribly thirsty. There was a puddle in the middle of the barracks. I realized that the water was filthy, but I scooped up some of it with my shoe and drank it. It looked like coffee with milk. . . . I found out that there was a river just behind the barracks and went out with my shoes and drank to my heart's content. After that, I went back and forth many times to get water for those lying near me, and for the injured soldiers. . . . Mercurochrome had been painted on my burns once, and they got black and sticky. I tried to dry them out in the sun. My friends and the other people were no longer able to move. The skin had peeled off of their burned arms, legs, and backs. I wanted to move them, but there was no place on their bodies that I could touch. Some people came around noon on the second day and gave us some rice balls. Our faces were burned and swollen so badly that we could hardly open our mouths, so we got very little of the rice into them. My eyes had swollen up by the third day, and I could not move around. I lay down in the barracks with my friends. I remember being in a kind of dream world, talking on and on with my delirious friends. . . .

Another time, I must have been dreaming: I thought that my father and sister were coming up the hill to get me. I was so glad that I forced my eyes open with my fingers to see, but it was dark and I could not see anything. People who came to the barracks would call out the names and addresses of the people they were looking for. My father and four or five of our neighbors had been searching for me since the bombing. They found me in a corner of the barracks at the foot of Futaba Hill, on the evening of the third day. They were able to find me because the wooden name tag my father had written for me was on my chest. The writing on the tag had been

418   The Global Community and Its Challenges

burned all the way through it, as if it had been etched.

"Atsuko! This is your father!"

I was so happy I couldn't speak. I only nodded my head. My eyes were swollen closed. I could not see my father, but I was saved.

I still have the scars from that day; on my head, face, arms, legs, and chest. There are reddish black scars on my arms and the face that I see in the mirror does not look as if it belongs to me. It always saddens me to think that I will never look the way I used to. I lost all hope at first. I was obsessed with the idea that I had become a freak and did not want to be seen by anyone. I cried constantly for my good friends and kind teachers who had died in such a terrible way.

My way of thinking became warped and pessimistic. Even my beautiful voice, that my friends had envied, had turned weak and hoarse. When I think of the way it was then, I feel as if I were being strangled. But I have been able to take comfort in the thought that physical beauty is not everything, that a beautiful spirit can do away with physical ugliness. This has given me new hope for the future. I am going to study hard and develop my mind and body, to become someone with culture and inner beauty.

Chapter 12

▼▼▼

Anticolonialism, Nationalism, and Revolution in Africa, Asia, and Latin America

During the nineteenth century the industrialized nations of Europe and the United States — "the West" — achieved unprecedented global dominance. For India and most of Africa and Southeast Asia, this meant colonial status and outright political control by Western nations. For China and many states in the Middle East and Latin America, it meant the subordination of their economic interests to those of the West and erosion of their political sovereignty. The great majority of people in Europe and the United States viewed these developments as just and inevitable. To them, their global primacy confirmed their intellectual and moral superiority to black-, yellow-, and brown-skinned people, whom the English writer Rudyard Kipling had depicted in his poem "The White Man's Burden" as "half devil and half child."

In the first half of the twentieth century, however, Africans, Asians, and Latin Americans challenged the West's ascendancy and self-proclaimed superiority. In areas ruled by the West as colonies, anticolonial movements gained followers and coalesced into organized parties that demanded more political power and ultimate independence. Anticolonialism was strongest in India, where opposition to more than a century of British rule escalated from polite requests by educated Indians for greater political responsibility to nationwide boycotts and mass demonstrations for independence. Despite French, British, and Dutch repression in Southeast Asia, dozens of political parties and secret organizations worked for the peaceful end or violent overthrow of colonial regimes. In Africa, although colonized only in the late 1800s and despite its ethnic and linguistic diversity, articulate and forceful proponents of Pan-Africanism, anticolonialism, and nationalism also emerged. In the Arab Middle East, where nationalist aspirations after World War I were dashed by the mandate system and the continuation of the British protectorate in Egypt, opponents of Anglo-French political control worked for the independence of Egypt, Iraq, Lebanon, and Syria.

While nationalism in colonial areas was directed against foreign rule, in those parts of Asia and Latin America where states were independent but nonetheless subservient to U.S. and European interests, it focused on overcoming economic dependency and political weakness. In Turkey this meant a sharp break from its past and implementation of an aggressive program of secularization and modernization under Mustafa Kemal Ataturk, the father of modern Turkey. In China it resulted in a struggle to rebuild the country and end foreign interference in the face of warlordism, civil war between Nationalists and Communists, and the Japanese invasions of Manchuria in 1931 and China itself in 1937. In Latin America it inspired leaders to pursue new plans for economic development after the Great Depression of the 1930s eroded world demand for the region's agricultural and mineral products. Such efforts intensified political struggles between entrenched elites and populist leaders who promised the masses social reforms.

When World War II ended in 1945, many Wetern leaders thought they could return to the world they had dominated before the war. In the immediate postwar years, the Dutch, French, and British all used force to maintain their empires but soon realized the futility of their efforts. Asian and African demands for independence proved irresistible, something for which developments in the first half of the twentieth century were largely responsible.

▼▼▼

African Society and Identity under Colonial Rule

Compared with the experience of India, the unfolding of colonialism in Africa resembles watching a film shown at high speed. Europeans arrived in force at the end of the nineteenth century, and after overcoming resistance and deciding among themselves who controlled what, they gave serious thought to the policies that would determine the future of their new acquisitions. Not long after these issues had been resolved, World War II was fought, and independence movements swept through Africa. In 1957, when the Gold Coast, a British colony, became the independent nation of Ghana, it sparked a chain of events that resulted in the establishment of dozens of new independent states within a decade and a half.

So brief was Africa's colonial experience, and so rapid was the Europeans' exit, that nationalism in Africa never became the broad popular movement that evolved in India during its long struggle against British rule. Furthermore, African nationalist movements were impeded by the indifference of chiefs, farmers, and petty traders who benefited from European rule, the paucity of Africans with formal education and political experience, the gap between educated city-dwellers and the rural masses, and rivalries among linguistic and ethnic groups. Nevertheless, Africans in the interwar years found ways to express their opposition to colonial rule. They demonstrated against labor conscription, new taxes, and government-mandated land confiscations. They organized political associations, published journals, wrote books and newspaper editorials, joined independent African Christian churches, attended international meetings, and sent representatives to European capitals to state their grievances. Despite many obstacles, voices of African nationalism multiplied before World War II, and a growing audience listened to what they had to say.

The results of colonialism in Africa went well beyond politics and the birth of nationalism. Colonialism also fostered population growth, encouraged urbanization, undermined traditional religions, altered gender relationships, introduced new sports and pastimes, and changed how people dressed and what languages they spoke. Most important, it forced Africans to consider new ways of looking at themselves and their place in the world. Inevitably many features of old Africa — traditional names, music, art, marriage customs, and systems of inheritance — were weakened or lost. Whether such changes were beneficial or harmful for Africa is still debated among Africans today. There was less debate among Africans who actually lived under colonialism. They, with few exceptions, found their colonial experience unsettling, dispiriting, and demeaning.

The Literature of Hope and Oppression
▼▼▼

98 ▼ *James Aggrey, PARABLE OF THE EAGLE,*
Léon G. Damas, LIMBO,
Léopold Sédar Senghor, PRAYER FOR PEACE,
and David Diop, VULTURES

Africans found colonialism dispiriting and repugnant because so much of it was predicated on the assumption of black inferiority. Colonialism's message, stated or unstated, was that Africans were incapable of governing themselves, or at least incapable of governing themselves effectively; nor were they capable of managing a modern economy or even creating a viable culture and social order. For all these tasks they needed Europeans, who justified their authority by asserting their moral and intellectual superiority. Furthermore, Africans were told that in order to succeed under colonialism — to become clerks or civil servants in the colonial administration or to become "assimilated" (an *evolué,* or "evolved one") in French Africa — they would have to shed their African identity and adopt the ideas, views, work habits, dress, and customs of Europeans. This was the price Africans would have to pay to overcome their backwardness.

When organized African nationalist movements finally began to take shape after World War II, many African political leaders denounced the corrosive effect of colonialism on African tradition and on the Africans' sense of identity. Well before then, however, African poets, novelists, and short story writers, as well as black authors living outside of Africa, had explored these issues with great power and insight. These authors were for the most part European educated, wrote mainly in English or French, and brought to their work a familiarity with contemporary European literary trends. Their themes and emotions, however, centered on what it meant to be black after centuries of enslavement and years of colonial rule. Many French-language writers came to be identified with the Paris-centered literary movement known as *Négritude,* which, beginning in the 1930s, affirmed the worth of African tradition, emphasized the spiritual unity of black people everywhere, and explored black people's unique historical experience. English-speaking writers tended to focus less on the commonalities of blacks' oppression and more on ways colonialism affected specific groups and individuals. Both groups expressed pride in Africa's spiritual, physical, and cultural heritage and mourned the wounds inflicted on it by slavery, colonialism, underdevelopment, and prejudice.

Four selections, each offering a different African perspective on the experience of colonialism, follow. "Parable of the Eagle" was written by James Aggrey, who was born in 1875 in the Gold Coast, a British colony. Educated in a Protestant mission school and a convert to Christianity, at age twenty-three he traveled to the United States to study for the ministry. He remained in the United States for twenty years, studying economics and agriculture, speaking out against racial prejudice, and working among poor African Americans in South Carolina. He returned to Africa in 1918 and died in 1927.

The author of the second work, "Limbo," is Léon G. Damas, one of several black writers of the 1930s and 1940s who was born outside of Africa but who nonetheless identified with Africa and wrote eloquently about the damage caused by colonialism. Born in 1912 in French Guyana, a colony in South America, Damas was educated on Martinique, a French Caribbean island, before beginning studies at the University of Paris. At Paris, Damas, with fellow students Léopold Senghor from Senegal and Aimé Césaire from Martinique, founded the literary journal *L'étudiant noir (The Black Student),* which many see as the beginning of the Négritude movement. Damas's poem "Limbo" was one of thirty-one poems published in the anthology *Pigments* in 1937. According to Christian tradition, *Limbo* refers to the abode of souls who are barred from Heaven because they have been unbaptized, hence a place of neglect and oblivion. After World War II, in which Damas fought for the French, he worked for the United Nations in Africa and then emigrated to the United States, where he taught black literature at Federal City University and Howard University in Washington, D.C.

The second poem, "Prayer for Peace," is the work of Léopold Sédar Senghor, the most famous French-speaking poet of Africa. Born in Senegal, Senghor was raised a Catholic and educated in Catholic schools. At age twenty-two he went to Paris, where he studied and taught literature and helped inspire the Négritude movement. After World War II, in which he fought for France and was taken prisoner by the Germans, he entered politics and was elected to the French Chamber of Deputies. When Senegal became an independent state in 1960, he was elected president, an office he held until he retired in 1981. His "Prayer for Peace" was the concluding poem of his collection *Hosties Noires,* which can be translated either as *Black Victims* or *Black Hosts.* It is set in January 1945, after France had been liberated and the final defeat of the Nazis was imminent. In the poem he enumerates the sins of colonialism but combines his condemnation with a plea for forgiveness and universal brotherhood. It is a powerful expression of the poet's ambivalence toward France, both the oppressor of Africa and a beacon of enlightenment.

The final poem, "Vultures," is by David Diop, who flourished as a poet at the end of the colonial period. Born in France to a Senegalese father and a Cameroonian mother, in his twenties he left medical school to study literature and write poetry. Acclaimed in French-speaking Africa for his denunciations of colonialism, he moved to Senegal in 1958 after French rule ended. He died in 1960 in a plane crash. "Vultures" was published in 1956 in the anthology *Coups de Pilon,* or *Hammer Blows.*

QUESTIONS FOR ANALYSIS

1. What specific features of colonialism does each author condemn? How are their views of colonialism similar? How are they different?
2. How do the four authors view Africans and African culture? In what ways do they find positive value in African practices and traditions?
3. What specific criticisms do the authors make of European values and characteristics? In what ways do they believe that African ways are superior to those of Europe?
4. To what degree do the four works offer a message of hope for Africa?

James Aggrey,
Parable of the Eagle

A certain man went through a forest seeking any bird of interest he might find. He caught a young eagle, brought it home and put it among his fowls and ducks and turkeys, and gave it chickens' food to eat even though it was an eagle, the king of birds.

Five years later a naturalist came to see him and, after passing through his garden, said: "That bird is an eagle, not a chicken."

"Yes," said its owner, "but I have trained it to be a chicken. It is no longer an eagle, it is a chicken, even though it measures fifteen feet from tip to tip of its wings."

"No," said the naturalist, "it is an eagle still: it has the heart of an eagle, and I will make it soar high up to the heavens."

"No," said the owner, "it is a chicken, and it will never fly."

They agreed to test it. The naturalist picked up the eagle, held it up, and said with great intensity: "Eagle, thou art an eagle; thou dost belong to the sky and not to this earth; stretch forth thy wings and fly."

The eagle turned this way and that, and then, looking down, saw the chickens eating their food, and down he jumped.

The owner said: "I told you it was a chicken."

"No," said the naturalist, "it is an eagle. Give it another chance tomorrow."

So the next day he took it to the top of the house and said: "Eagle, thou art an eagle; stretch forth thy wings and fly." But again the eagle, seeing the chickens feeding, jumped down and fed with them.

Then the owner said: "I told you it was a chicken."

"No," asserted the naturalist, "it is an eagle, and it still has the heart of an eagle; only give it one more chance, and I will make it fly tomorrow."

The next morning he rose early and took the eagle outside the city, away from the houses, to the foot of a high mountain. The sun was just rising, gilding the top of the mountain with gold, and every crag was glistening in the joy of that beautiful morning.

He picked up the eagle and said to it: "Eagle, thou art an eagle; thou dost belong to the sky and not to this earth; stretch forth thy wings and fly!"

The eagle looked around and trembled as if new life were coming to it; but it did not fly. The naturalist then made it look straight at the sun. Suddenly it stretched out its wings and, with the screech of an eagle, it mounted higher and higher and never returned. It was an eagle, though it had been kept and tamed as a chicken!

My people of Africa, we were created in the image of God, but men have made us think that we are chickens, and we still think we are; but we are eagles. Stretch forth your wings and fly! Don't be content with the food of chickens!

Léon G. Damas, Limbo

. . . Give me back my black dolls. I want to play
  with them,
Play the ordinary games that come naturally to
  me,
Stay in the shadow of their rules,
Get back my courage and my boldness,
Feel myself, what I was yesterday,
Without complexity.
Yesterday, when I was torn up by the roots.

Will they ever know the rancor eating at my
  heart,
My mistrustful eye open too late?
They have stolen the space that was mine
The customs, the days of my life
The singing, the rhythm, the strain,
The path, the water, the hut
The earth, gray, smoky
And wisdom, the words, the palavers,[1]
The ancients.
And the beat, the hands, the beating of the
  hands
And the stamping of feet on the ground.

Give them back to me, my black dolls,
My black dolls,
Black dolls
Black.

---

[1]Long, rambling, and informal discussions.

Léopold Sédar Senghor, Prayer for Peace

[For grand organ]

To Georges and Claude Pompidou

". . . Sicut et nos dimittimus debitoribus nostris"

Lord Jesus, at the end of this book, which I offer You as a ciborium[2] of sufferings

At the beginning of the Great Year, in the sunlight of Your peace on the snowy roofs of Paris

— Yet I know that my brothers' blood will redden once more the Yellow East, on the shores of the Pacific Ocean ravaged by storms and hatreds[3]

I know that this blood is the spring libation[4] with which the Great Publicans[5] have been fertilizing the Empire's lands for seventy years

Lord, at the foot of this cross — and it is no longer You who are the tree of sorrow, but above the Old and New Worlds, Crucified Africa

And her right arm stretches over my land, and her left side shades America

And her heart is beloved Haiti, Haiti[6] who dared to proclaim Man before the Tyrant

At the feet of my Africa crucified for four hundred years and yet still breathing

Let me recite to you Lord, her prayer of peace and pardon.

II

Lord God, forgive white Europe!

And it is true, Lord, that for four enlightened centuries, she has thrown the spit and baying of her watch-dogs on my lands

And Christians, renouncing Your light and the gentleness of Your heart

Lighted their campfires with my parchments, tortured my disciples, deported my doctors and my masters of science.

Their gunpowder crumbled in a flash our proud fortresses and the hills

And their cannon balls blasted through the loins of vast empires as a bright day, from the Western Horn to the Eastern horizon

And as though they were hunting grounds, they burned the intangible forests, dragging Ancestors and spirits by their peaceful beards.

And they made their sacred mystery the Sunday diversion of sleepwalking bourgeoisie[7]

Lord, forgive those who made guerrilla fighters of the Askia,[8] sergeants of my princes

Boys of my servants and wage-earners of my peasants, a race of proletarians of my people.

For you must forgive those who hunted my children as though they were wild elephants

And they disciplined them with whiplashes and made them the black hands of those whose hands were white.

For you must forget those who exported ten million of my sons in the leper camps of their ships

Who killed two hundred million of them.[9]

And they made a lonely old age for me in the forest of my nights and the savannah of my days.

Lord, the mirror of my eyes grows cloudy

And now the serpent of hate rears its head in my heart, that serpent I had thought dead . . .

---

[2]In the Catholic mass, a goblet-shaped vessel that holds a consecrated communion wafer.

[3]Senghor does not expect a quick end to the war against Japan, in which African soldiers were involved in combat, especially in Indochina.

[4]The ritual pouring of wine or oil on the ground as a way of sacrifice to a god.

[5]In the Roman Empire, tax collectors, notorious for their greed and extortion.

[6]In 1801 the overwhelmingly black population of the French sugar colony St. Domaigne rebelled against French rule and won their independence as Haiti.

[7]A reference to African religious art on display in European museums where it is viewed by half-awake middle-class visitors.

[8]The ruling house of the West African empire of Songhai in the 1500s.

[9]If Senghor is suggesting that the transatlantic slave trade resulted in 200 million deaths, this would be a sizable exaggeration. Perhaps he means that colonialism killed 200 million Africans in a figurative sense.

III

Kill it Lord, for I must continue my journey,
    and I want to pray especially for France.
Lord, among the white nations, place France at
    the Father's right hand.
Oh! I do know that she too is Europe, that she
    snatched my children from me like a cattle-
    stealing brigand from the North, to fertilize
    her fields of cane and cotton, for black sweat is
    manure.
That she too brought death and guns to my blue
    villages, that she set my people against one
    another like dogs fighting over a bone
That she treated those who resisted like bandits
    and spat on the heads harboring great plans.
Yes Lord, forgive France who speaks for the
    right way and treads the devious paths
Who invites me to her table and bids me bring
    my own bread, who gives with her right hand
    and takes back half with her left.
Yes Lord, forgive France who hates her
    occupiers[10] and yet imposes such grave
    occupation on me
Who opens triumphal ways to heroes and treats
    her Senegalese like mercenaries, making them
    the black watchdogs of the Empire
Who is the Republic and hands over countries
    to big business
And of my Mesopotamia, of my Congo, they
    have made a vast cemetery under the white
    sun.

IV

Oh! Lord, erase from my memory the France
    that is not France, that mask of meanness and
    of hate on France's face
That mask of meanness and of hate for which I
    have but hate — but I can surely hate Evil
For I have a great weakness for France.

Bless this shackled nation who has twice
    succeeded in freeing her hands and dared
    proclaim the accession of the poor to the royal
    throne
Who changed slaves of the day into men who
    were free, equal, brothers[11]
Bless this nation who brought me Your Good
    News,[12] Lord, and opened my heavy eyelids to
    the light of faith.
She opened my heart to the knowledge of the
    world, showing me the rainbow of the new
    faces that are my brothers.
I greet you my brothers: you Mohamed Ben
    Abdallah, you Razafymahatratra, and then
    you out there Pham-Manh-Tuong,[13] you from
    the pacific seas and you from the enchanted
    forests
I greet you all with a catholic heart.
Ah! I know well that more than one of Your
    messengers hunted my priests like game and
    made great carnage of pious images.
And yet we could have lived in harmony, for
    these very images were the Jacob's ladder[14]
    from the earth to Your heaven
The clear oil lamp that helps us wait for dawn,
    the stars that foreshadow the sun.
I know that many of Your missionaries blessed
    the arms of violence and made compacts with
    the bankers' gold
But there must always be traitors and fools.

V

Oh bless this nation, Lord, who seeks her own
    face under the mask and finds it hard to
    recognize
Who seeks You in the cold, in the hunger that
    gnaws at her bones and entrails
And the betrothed mourns her widowhood,
    and the young man sees his youth stolen
    away
And the wife laments the absent eye of her

---

[10]The Germans.
[11]A reference to the French Revolution.
[12]The Christian gospel.
[13]Refers to other peoples under French colonial rule — the
Arabs of North Africa, the Malagasy of Madagascar, and the
Vietnamese.
[14]The ladder from Earth to Heaven that Jacob saw in a
dream (Genesis 28:12).

husband, and the mother seeks the dream of
her child amidst the rubble.

Oh! bless this nation who breaks her bonds,
bless this nation at bay who defies the
ravenous pack of bullies and torturers.

And with her all the peoples of Europe, all the
peoples of Asia all the peoples of Africa and
all the peoples of America

Who sweat blood and sufferings. And in the
midst of these millions of waves, see the
surging heads of my people.

And grant that their warm hands embrace the
earth in a band of brotherly hands

UNDER THE RAINBOW OF YOUR PEACE.

Paris, January 1945

David Diop, Vultures

In that time
When civilization struck with insults

When holy water struck domesticated brows
The vultures built in the shadow of their claws
The bloody monument of the tutelary[15] era
In that time
Laughter gasped its last in the metallic hell of
roads
And the monotonous rhythm of Paternosters[16]
Covered the groans on plantations run for profit
O sour memory of extorted kisses
Promises mutilated by machine-gun blasts
Strange men who were not men
You knew all the books you did not know love
Or the hands that fertilize the womb of the
earth
The roots of our hands deep as revolt
Despite your hymns of pride among boneyards
Villages laid waste and Africa dismembered
Hope lived in us like a citadel
And from the mines of Swaziland to Europe's
sweatshops[17]
Spring will put on flesh under our steps of light.

---

[15]Of or relating to guardianship.
[16]Prayers, or more specifically, The Lord's Prayer.
[17]Diop, a Marxist, is drawing an analogy between the exploited factory workers of Europe and the miners in Swaziland, a tiny British protectorate in South Africa.

White Rule and African Families in South Africa
▼▼▼

99 ▼ *Charlotte Maxeke,*
SOCIAL CONDITIONS AMONG
BANTU WOMEN AND GIRLS

Few groups in Africa were affected more by colonialism than women. In the pre-
colonial African village, a division of labor between men and women had existed
in which women were responsible for planting, weeding, and harvesting in addition to food preparation and child care, while men cleared the land, built houses,
herded cattle, and sometimes helped with field work. Such arrangements broke
down in western Africa when cash-crop agriculture was introduced. Men took
over the farming of cotton and cocoa, leaving the responsibility for growing food
for domestic consumption exclusively to women. Worse disruption took place in
southern and eastern Africa, where men left their villages for wage-paying jobs
in mines or cities. This meant long absences of husbands from their families,

greater work and domestic responsibilities for women, and frequently the break-down of family life altogether.

All these changes troubled the South African woman Charlotte Maxeke, the founder of the African National Congress (ANC) Women's League, social worker, teacher, and leader in the African Methodist Episcopal Church. Born Charlotte Makgomo Manye in 1874, she received her primary and secondary education in South Africa; in her early twenties she toured England, Canada, and the United States with an African choir. She remained in the United States to study at Wilberforce College in Ohio, where she received her Bachelor of Science degree and met and married another South African, Reverend Marshall Maxeke. On her return to South Africa, she co-founded a secondary school with her husband and remained active in ANC and denominational affairs until her death in 1939.

In 1930 she presented her views on the plight of black women and families in a speech delivered to a rally attended by white and black Christian youth.

QUESTIONS FOR ANALYSIS

1. What, according to Maxeke, are the reasons for the Bantu exodus from the countryside to cities?
2. What special challenges and difficulties confront newly arrived blacks in urban areas?
3. How do the problems of men and women in such circumstances differ?
4. What seems to have been the effect of the changes Maxeke describes on children and young people?
5. What solutions does Maxeke propose to solve the problems confronting African women and their families?

There are many problems pressing in upon us Bantu,[1] to disturb the peaceful working of our homes. One of the chief is perhaps the stream of Native life into the towns. Men leave their homes, and go into big towns like Johannesburg, where they get a glimpse of a life such as they had never dreamed existed. At the end of their term of employment they receive the wages for which they have worked hard, and which should be used for the sustenance of their families, but the attractive luxuries of civilisation are in many instances too much for them, they waste their hard earned wages, and seem to forget completely the crying need of their family out in the veld.[2]

The wife finds that her husband has apparently forgotten her existence, and she therefore makes her hard and weary way to the town in search of him. When she gets there, and starts looking round for a house of some sort in which to accommodate herself and her children, she meets with the first rebuff. The Location Superintendent[3] informs her that she cannot rent accommodations unless she has a husband. Thus she is driven to the first step on the downward path, for if she would have a roof to cover her

---

[1] In this context, blacks of South Africa who spoke languages of the Bantu family and who traditionally had been farmers and herders.

[2] Afrikaans (the Dutch-based language spoken by Afrikaners) for the grasslands of southern and eastern Africa.

[3] A white official in charge of a black township; these townships, adjacent to white towns or cities, were areas where blacks were legally compelled to live.

children's heads a husband must be found, and so we get these poor women forced by circumstances to consort with men in order to provide shelter for their families. Thus we see that the authorities in enforcing the restrictions in regard to accommodation are often doing Bantu society a grievous harm, for they are forcing its wedded womanhood to the first steps on the downward path of sin and crime.

Many Bantu women live in the cities at a great price, the price of their children; for these women, even when they live with their husbands, are forced in most cases to go out and work, to bring sufficient income into the homes to keep their children alive. The children of these unfortunate people therefore run wild, and as there are not sufficient schools to house them, it is easy for them to live an aimless existence, learning crime of all sorts. . . .

If these circumstances obtain when husband and wife live together in the towns, imagine the case of the woman, whose husband has gone to town and left her, forgetting . . . all his responsibilities. Here we get young women, the flower of the youth of the Bantu, going up to towns in search of their husbands, and . . . living as the reputed wives of other men, because of the location requirements, or becoming housekeepers to men in the locations and towns, and eventually their nominal wives.

In Johannesburg, and other large towns, the male Natives are employed to do domestic work, . . . and a female domestic servant is a rarity. We thus have a very dangerous environment existing for any woman who goes into any kind of domestic service in these towns, and naturally immorality of various kinds ensues, as the inevitable outcome of this situation. Thus we see that the European is by his treatment of the Native . . . only pushing him further and further down in the social scale, forgetting that it was he and his kind who brought these conditions about in South Africa, forgetting his responsibilities to those who labour for him and to whom he introduced the benefits, and evils, of civilisation. . . .

Then we come to the *Land Question*. This is very acute in South Africa, especially from the Bantu point of view.[4] South Africa in terms of available land is shrinking daily owing to increased population, and to many other economic and climatic causes. Cattle diseases have crept into the country, ruining many a stock farmer, and thus Bantu wealth is gradually decaying. As a result there are more and more workers making their way to the towns and cities such as Johannesburg to earn a living. . . . The majority earn about £3 10s. per month, out of which they must pay 25s. for rent, and 10s. for tram fares, so I leave you to imagine what sort of existence they lead on the remainder.

Here again we come back to the same old problem . . . — that of the woman of the home being obliged to find work in order to supplement her husband's wages, with the children growing up undisciplined and uncared for. . . . We find that in this state of affairs, the woman in despair very often decides that she cannot leave her children uncared for, and she therefore gives up her employment in order to care for them, but is naturally forced into some form of home industry, which, as there is very little choice for her in this direction, more often than not takes the form of the brewing and selling of Skokiaan.[5] Thus the woman starts on a career of crime for herself and her children, a career which often takes her and her children right down the depths of immorality and misery. The woman, poor unfortunate victim of circumstances, goes to prison, and the children are left even more desolate than when their mother left them to earn her living. . . . About ten years ago, there was talk of industrial schools being started for such unfortunate children, but it was only talk, and we are today in the same position, aggravated by the increased num-

---

[4]A reference to the Natives Land Act of 1913.
[5]*Skokiaan* is Afrikaans for "Bantu beer," an alcoholic beverage brewed from sorghum.

bers steadily streaming in from the rural areas, all undergoing very similar experiences to those I have just outlined. . . .

Many of the Bantu feel and rightly too that the laws of the land are not made for Black and White alike. Take the question of permits for the right to look for work. . . . The poor unfortunate Native, fresh from the country does not know of these rules and regulations, naturally breaks them and is thrown into prison; or if he does happen to know the regulations and obtains a pass[6] for six days, and is obliged to renew it several times, as is of course very often the case, he will find that when he turns up for the third or fourth time for the renewal of his permit, he is put into prison, because he has been unsuccessful in obtaining work. And not only do the Bantu feel that the law for the White and the Black is not similar, but we even find some of them convinced that there are two Gods, one for the White and one for the Black. I had an instance of this in an old Native woman who had suffered much, and could not be convinced that the same God watched over and cared for us all, but felt that the God who gave the Europeans their life of comparative comfort and ease, could not possibly be the same God who allowed his poor Bantu to suffer so. As another instance of the inequalities existing in our social scheme, we have the fact of Natives not being allowed to travel on buses and trams in many towns, except those specially designed for them.

In connection with the difficulty experienced through men being employed almost exclusively in domestic work in the cities, I would mention that this is of course one of the chief reasons for young women, who should rightly be doing that work, going rapidly down in the social life of the community. The solution to the problem seems to me to be to get women into service, and to give them proper accommodation, where they know they are safe. Provide hostels, and clubrooms, and rest rooms for these domestic servants, where they may spend their leisure hours, and I think you will find the problem of the employment of female domestic servants will solve itself, and that a better and happier condition of life will come into being for the Bantu.

---

[6]To prevent too many unemployed blacks from living in towns, the government required every black to carry a "pass," which showed the name of his or her employer. Those looking for work were granted temporary passes.

Without a valid pass, blacks could be fined, arrested, deported to a rural reserve, or forced to accept a low-paying job for a white employer.

▼▼▼

Political and Religious Currents in the Middle East

The aftermath of World War I brought political disaster to the Middle East. The Turks, who had fought on Germany's side, were forced in 1920 to accept the humiliating Treaty of Sèvres, which stripped Turkey of its Arab territories, limited the Turkish army to 50,000 men, gave France, Britain, and Italy control of its finances, and proposed to cede parts of Turkey itself to Italy, Greece, and the new states of Kurdistan and Armenia. The sultan, overwhelmed by problems of lawlessness, army desertions, and inflation, not only accepted the treaty but also offered no resistance when the Greeks landed troops in western Anatolia in May 1919.

While the Turks felt despair, their former subjects, the Arabs, experienced bitter disappointment, even though they had been on the winning side in the war. Promised self-rule for joining the Anglo-French alliance and fighting against their Ottoman overlords, they learned in 1919 that the British and French had agreed in 1916 to divide Arab lands between themselves, and that this, rather than the promises of Arab independence, would determine the postwar settlement. In 1920 Iraq, Syria, Palestine, Lebanon, and Jordan all became British or French mandates, a status that differed from old-style colonialism in name only.

Arabs were also incensed by the continuation of the British protectorate in Egypt and by the British commitment to honor their promises made during the war to support the establishment of a national home in Palestine for the Jewish people. Farther east, another major Islamic state, Persia, under the decrepit rule of the Qajar Dynasty, also seemed on the verge of becoming a British protectorate.

Efforts to reverse the postwar settlements were most successful in Turkey and Iran. Under Mustafa Kemal, the Turks rallied to drive out the Greeks and smash the nascent Armenian state between 1919 and 1922. In 1922, the Turks abolished the sultanate, and in 1923 the European powers agreed to replace the Treaty of Sèvres with the Treaty of Lausanne, which recognized the integrity and independence of the new Turkish republic. Mustafa Kemal now had his opportunity to transform Turkey into a modern secular state. In Iran, which barely avoided becoming a British protectorate in 1919, Colonel Reza Khan (1878–1944) was named shah in 1925 and, like his hero, Kemal, sought to regenerate his country through economic development, educational reform, and Westernization.

Arab efforts to achieve independence and prevent Jewish immigration to Palestine were less successful. Of the twenty Arab states that stretched from Morocco in the west to Iraq in the east, only Saudi Arabia and Yemen were truly independent in the interwar years. Egypt and Iraq attained limited self-rule, but the presence of British troops and continuing British influence over foreign and military affairs was a source of friction and anger in both countries. The drive for independence was even more frustrating in French-controlled Lebanon and Syria. In the 1930s the French reneged on promises to relinquish their authority, and Lebanon remained a mandate until 1943 and Syria until 1945. Arabs throughout the Middle East were also angered by growing Jewish migration to Palestine, especially in the 1930s, when U.S. immigration restrictions and mounting anti-Semitism in Europe created a mass of new immigrants.

While confronting these immediate postwar diplomatic and political problems, the people and leaders of the region faced other fundamental issues. What could be done to end poverty and illiteracy? How could the teachings and expectations of Islam be reconciled with the realities and demands of modernization? Was modernization itself desirable, and, if so, how was it to be achieved? Was the goal of Arab nationalism the expulsion of the British and French and the stifling of Zionism or was it the attainment of a single united Arab state? Questions such as these were not new to the people of the Middle East. But in the face of the changes that swept through the region in the first half of the twentieth century, finding answers to them became more urgent and more difficult.

Secularism and Nationalism in Republican Turkey

▼▼▼

100 ▼ Mustafa Kemal, SPEECH TO THE CONGRESS OF THE PEOPLE'S REPUBLICAN PARTY

The archsymbol of secularism and nationalism in the Muslim world in the inter-war years was Mustafa Kemal (1881–1938), who first achieved prominence as a military hero during World War I and went on to serve as first president of the Turkish republic. Disgusted by the Ottoman sultan's acquiescence to the Greek occupation of the Turkish port of Smyrna (Izmir) in 1919, Kemal assumed leadership of a resistance movement that by 1923 had overthrown the sultan, defeated the Greeks, and won the annulment of the punitive Sèvres Treaty. Exercising broad powers as president of the new Turkish republic until his death in 1938. Kemal sought to transform Turkey into a modern secular nation-state. To accomplish this, he broke the power of Islam over education and the legal system, encouraged industrialization, accorded women full legal rights, mandated the use of a new Turkish alphabet, and ordered Turks to adopt Western-style dress. Directing all Turks to adopt hereditary family names, he took for himself the name *Ataturk,* or "Great Turk."

Having consolidated his authority, Kemal decided in 1927 to review his accomplishments and impress upon his subjects the need for continued support. He chose as the occasion the meeting of the People's Republican Party, which he had founded and was Turkey's only legal political party. Here he delivered an extraordinary speech. Having worked on it for three months (in the process exhausting dozens of secretaries), he delivered it over a period of six days.

In these excerpts, he discusses Turkey's past and future, explains his reasons for abolishing the caliphate, the ancient office by virtue of which Turkish sultans had been the theoretical rulers of all Muslims, and justifies his suppression of the Progressive Republican Party, which despite its name was a party of conservatives who opposed Turkey's modernization.

QUESTIONS FOR ANALYSIS

1. What, according to Kemal, were the "erroneous ideas" that had guided the Ottoman state in the past?
2. Why does Kemal argue that nation-states, not empires, are the most desirable form of political organization?
3. What is Kemal's view of the West?
4. What are his views of Islam?
5. What arguments does Kemal offer against the continuation of the caliphate?
6. How does Kemal justify his suppression of the Progressive Republicans? What, in his view, were the positive results of this step?

[NATIONALISM AND EMPIRE]

. . . Among the Ottoman rulers there were some who endeavored to form a gigantic empire by seizing Germany and Western Europe. One of these rulers hoped to unite the whole Islamic world in one body, to lead it and govern it. For this purpose he obtained control of Syria and Egypt and assumed the title of Caliph.[1] Another Sultan pursued the twofold aim, on the one hand of gaining the mastery over Europe, and on the other of subjecting the Islamic world to his authority and government. The continuous counterattacks from the West, the discontent and insurrections in the Muslim world, as well as the dissensions between the various elements which this policy had artificially brought together within certain limits, had the ultimate result of burying the Ottoman Empire, in the same way as many others, under the pall of history. . . .

To unite different nations under one common name, to give these different elements equal rights, subject them to the same conditions and thus to found a mighty State is a brilliant and attractive political ideal; but it is a misleading one. It is an unrealizable aim to attempt to unite in one tribe the various races existing on the earth, thereby abolishing all boundaries. Herein lies a truth which the centuries that have gone by and the men who have lived during these centuries have clearly shown in dark and sanguinary events.

There is nothing in history to show how the policy of Panislamism[2] could have succeeded or how it could have found a basis for its realization on this earth. As regards the result of the ambition to organize a State which should be governed by the idea of world-supremacy and include the whole of humanity without distinction of race, history does not afford examples of this. For us, there can be no question of the lust of conquest. . . .

In order that our nation should be able to live a happy, strenuous, and permanent life, it is necessary that the State should pursue an exclusively national policy and that this policy should be in perfect agreement with our internal organization and be based on it. When I speak of national policy, I mean it in this sense: To work within our national boundaries for the real happiness and welfare of the nation and the country by, above all, relying on our own strength in order to retain our existence. But not to lead the people to follow fictitious aims, of whatever nature, which could only bring them misfortune, and expect from the civilized world civilized human treatment, friendship based on mutuality. . . .

[THE ISSUE OF THE CALIPHATE]

I must call attention to the fact that Hodja Shukri, as well as the politicians who pushed forward his person and signature, had intended to substitute the sovereign bearing the title of Sultan or Padishah by a monarch with the title of Caliph.[3] The only difference was that, instead of speaking of a monarch of this or that country or nation, they now spoke of a monarch whose authority extended over a population of three hundred million souls belonging to manifold nations and dwelling in different continents of the world. Into the hands of this great monarch, whose authority was to extend over the whole of Islam, they placed as the only power that of the Turkish people, that is to say, only from 10 to 15 millions

---

[1] A reference to Selim I, who conquered Egypt and Syria in 1515–1516; it is doubtful that he actually considered himself caliph, that is, leader and protector of all Muslims.

[2] The program of uniting all Muslims under one government or ruler.

[3] These events took place in January 1923. After Sultan Mehmed V was deposed on November 1, 1922, his cousin was designated caliph. Because of their long rule and vast territories, Ottoman sultans by the nineteenth century were viewed by many Muslims as caliphs, that is, "successors" of the prophet Muhammad, with jurisdiction over all of Islam. Shukri was a *hodja* (or *hojja*), a Turkish religious leader; he hoped that the new Turkish state would continue to support the caliphate even after the sultanate was abolished. In 1924, however, Kemal abolished the caliphate.

of these three hundred million subjects. The monarch designated under the title of Caliph was to guide the affairs of these Muslim peoples and to secure the execution of the religious prescriptions which would best correspond to their worldly interests. He was to defend the rights of all Muslims and concentrate all the affairs of the Muslim world in his hands with effective authority. . . .

If the Caliph and Caliphate, as they maintained, were to be invested with a dignity embracing the whole of Islam, ought they not to have realized in all justice that a crushing burden would be imposed on Turkey, on her existence; her entire resources and all her forces would be placed at the disposal of the Caliph? . . .

I made statements everywhere, that were necessary to dispel the uncertainty and anxiety of the people concerning this question of the Caliphate. . . . I gave the people to understand that neither Turkey nor the handful of men she possesses could be placed at the disposal of the Caliph so that he might fulfill the mission attributed to him, namely, to found a State comprising the whole of Islam. The Turkish nation is incapable of undertaking such an irrational mission.

For centuries our nation was guided under the influence of these erroneous ideas. But what has been the result of it? Everywhere they have lost millions of men. "Do you know," I asked, "how many sons of Anatolia have perished in the scorching deserts of the Yemen? Do you know the losses we have suffered in holding Syria and Iraq and Egypt and in maintaining our position in Africa? And do you see what has come out of it? Do you know? . . .

"New Turkey, the people of New Turkey, have no reason to think of anything else but their own existence and their own welfare. She has nothing more to give away to others." . . .

[THE SUPPRESSION OF THE PROGRESSIVE REPUBLICANS]

As you know, it was at the time that the members of the opposition had founded a party under the name of "Republican Progressive Party" and published its program. . . .

Under the mask of respect for religious ideas and dogmas the new Party addressed itself to the people in the following words:

"We want the re-establishment of the Caliphate; we do not want new laws; we are satisfied with the religious law; we shall protect the Medressas, the Tekkes, the pious institutions, the Softahs, the Sheikhs[4] and their disciples. Be on our side; the party of Mustafa Kemal, having abolished the Caliphate, is breaking Islam into ruins; they will make you into unbelievers. . . ."

Read these sentences, Gentlemen, from a letter written by one of the adherents of this program: . . . "They are attacking the very principles which perpetuate the existence of the Muslim world. . . . The assimilation with the Occident means the destruction of our history, our civilisation. . . ." Gentlemen, facts and events have proved that the program of the Republican Progressive Party has been the work emanating from the brain of traitors. This Party became the refuge and the point of support for reactionary and rebellious elements. . . .

The Government and the Committee found themselves forced to take extraordinary measures. They caused the law regarding the restoration of order to be proclaimed, and the Independence Courts to take action. For a considerable time they kept eight or nine divisions of the army at war strength for the suppression of disorders, and put an end to the injurious organisation which bore the name "Republican Progressive Party."

---

[4]A *medressa* is an advanced school of Islamic learning; a *tekke* is a small teaching mosque usually built over the tomb of a saint; a *softah* is a student in an Islamic school; a *sheikh,* or *shaykh,* is a master of a religious order of Sufis, who adopted a mystical approach to Islam.

The result was, of course, the success of the Republic. . . .

Gentlemen, it was necessary to abolish the fez,[5] which sat on our heads as a sign of ignorance, of fanaticism, of hatred to progress and civilisation, and to adopt in its place the hat, the customary headdress of the whole civilised world, thus showing, among other things, that no difference existed in the manner of thought between the Turkish nation and the whole family of civilised mankind. We did that while the law for the Restoration of Order was still in force. If it had not been in force we should have done so all the same; but one can say with complete truth that the existence of this law made the thing much easier for us. As a matter of fact the application of the law for the Restoration of Order prevented the morale of the nation being poisoned to a great extent by reactionaries.

Gentlemen, while the law regarding the Restoration of Order was in force there took place also the closing of the Tekkes, of the convents, and of the mausoleums, as well as the abolition of all sects[6] and all kinds of titles such as Sheikh, Dervish, . . . Occultist, Magician, Mausoleum Guard, etc.[7]

One will be able to imagine how necessary the carrying through of these measures was, in order to prove that our nation as a whole was no primitive nation, filled with superstitions and prejudices.

Could a civilised nation tolerate a mass of people who let themselves be led by the nose by a herd of Sheikhs, Dedes, Seids, . . . Babas and Emirs,[8] who entrusted their destiny and their lives to chiromancers,[9] magicians, dice-throwers and amulet sellers? Ought one to conserve in the Turkish State, in the Turkish Republic, elements and institutions such as those which had for centuries given the nation the appearance of being other than it really was? Would one not therewith have committed the greatest, most irreparable error to the cause of progress and reawakening?

If we made use of the law for the Restoration of Order in this manner, it was in order to avoid such a historic error; to show the nation's brow pure and luminous, as it is; to prove that our people think neither in a fanatical nor a reactionary manner.

Gentlemen, at the same time the new laws were worked out and decreed which promise the most fruitful results for the nation on the social and economic plane, and in general in all the forms of the expression of human activity . . . the Citizens' Legal Code, which ensures the liberty of women and stabilises the existence of the family.

Accordingly we made use of all circumstances only from one point of view, which consisted therein: to raise the nation on to that step on which it is justified in standing in the civilised world, to stabilise the Turkish Republic more and more on steadfast foundations . . . and in addition to destroy the spirit of despotism for ever.

---

[5]The fez was a brimless hat popular among Turkish men during the nineteenth century; its lack of a brim allowed the wearer to touch his forehead to the ground while kneeling during prayer without removing the hat.

[6]Islamic religious orders.

[7]A *dervish,* or *darvish,* was a member of an Islamic sect famous for its whirling dances that symbolized the movement of the heavenly spheres; an *occultist* was a Sufi who achieved a state of withdrawal from the world; a *mausoleum guard* guarded the tomb of a saint or holy person.

[8]A *dede* was head of a Sufi order; *seids,* or *sayyids,* were descendants of the prophet Muhammad through his daughter Fatima; *baba* was a popular surname among Sufi preachers; in this context *emir* is an honorary Turkish title.

[9]People who told the future by reading palms.

A Call for Islamic Social and Political Action
▼▼▼

101 ▼ *The Muslim Brotherhood,*
TOWARD THE LIGHT

Although the commitment to modernization advocated by Mustafa Kemal had supporters throughout the Middle East, it also had staunch opponents. Many Muslims — from all classes of society and across all educational levels — were alarmed by the prospect of a secularized, Westernized future and sought instead to establish a true Islamic society guided by the Quran and conforming to Islamic law. In the interwar years their hopes were best represented by the Muslim Brotherhood, founded in 1929 by an Egyptian schoolteacher, Hasan al-Banna (1906–1949).

Born in a small town in the Nile Delta, Hasan al-Banna as a student in Cairo after World War I was deeply troubled by the factionalism, social conflict, poverty, and religious indifference he observed in Egypt. He concluded that British colonialism and the widespread acceptance of Western values had caused these ills and that a return to fundamental Islamic teachings would cure them. In 1927 he became a schoolteacher in the Sinai town of Ismailia, where he organized religious study groups and committed himself to Islamic renewal. In 1929 he founded the Muslim Brotherhood, an organization dedicated to the realization of Islamic government in Egypt and other Muslim lands.

In the 1930s the Brotherhood grew into a tightly knit, disciplined organization with a million members from all walks of life and a network of branches made up of numerous secret cells. It built mosques, schools, and small hospitals; sponsored youth programs, social clubs, and light industries; and publicized its religious message through preaching and publications. In the 1940s, with a greater commitment to political activism, it clashed with British authorities and the Egyptian government itself. Linked to the assassination of several officials, the Brotherhood was outlawed by the Egyptian government in 1949, and Hasan al-Banna himself was assassinated by government agents in the same year.

The Brotherhood regained legal status in Egypt in 1950 and since then has continued to be an important religious and political force in the Arab Middle East. It has branches in Sudan, Syria, and other Arab states, vast financial resources, and an estimated membership of 2 million. It has accomplished this despite attempts by the Egyptian government to suppress the organization on two occasions in the 1950s and 1960s after members of the Brotherhood were implicated in assassination plots and antigovernment conspiracies. The organization also has experienced bitter internal divisions between militants and moderates. In Egypt, the Brotherhood officially rejected violence in the 1980s in favor of advancing its program by winning elected office and increasing its commitment to social service activities. This moderate policy caused some of its members to defect to more militant groups. Organizations such as Islamic Jihad and Hamas, which are committed to the cause of Palestinian nationhood and oppose any compromise with Israel, are both offshoots of the Muslim Brotherhood.

The following excerpt is drawn from a pamphlet issued by the Brotherhood in 1936. Directed to King Faruk of Egypt and other Arab leaders, it summarizes the goals of the Brotherhood in its early years of existence.

QUESTIONS FOR ANALYSIS

1. How would you characterize the Brotherhood's views on the purpose and goals of government?
2. According to this document, what was the Brotherhood's conception of the ideal government official?
3. What does the document reveal about the Brotherhood's attitude toward the West? Are there aspects of Western culture the Brotherhood finds acceptable?
4. What role does the Brotherhood envision for women in Islamic society?
5. According to the Brotherhood, what are the goals of education? How are they to be achieved?
6. What policies does the Brotherhood propose to help the poor?
7. What is there in the statement that might help account for the widespread support of the Brotherhood among Middle Eastern Muslims?

After having studied the ideals which ought to inspire a renascent nation on the spiritual level, we wish to offer, in conclusion, some practical suggestions. We will list here only the chapter headings because we know very well that each suggestion will require profound study as well as the special attention of experts; we know also that the needs of the nation are enormous; we do not believe that the fulfilling of the needs and the aspirations of the country will be an easy thing; what is more, we do not think that these goals can be reached in one journey or two. We realize the obstacles which these problems must overcome. The task will require a great deal of patience, a great deal of ability, and a willing tenacity.

But one thing is certain: resolve will lead to success. A dedicated nation, working to accomplish the right, will certainly reach, with God's help, the goals toward which it strives.

The following are the chapter headings for a reform based upon the true spirit of Islam:

I. In the political, judicial, and administrative fields:

1st. To prohibit political parties and to direct the forces of the nation toward the formation of a united front;

2nd. To reform the law in such a way that it will be entirely in accordance with Islamic legal practice;

3rd. To build up the army, to increase the number of youth groups; to instill in youth the spirit of holy struggle, faith, and self-sacrifice;

4th. To strengthen the ties among Islamic countries and more particularly among Arab countries which is a necessary step toward serious examination of the question of the defunct Caliphate;[1]

5th. To propagate an Islamic spirit within the civil administration so that all officials will understand the need for applying the teachings of Islam;

---

[1]The office of caliph, or successor of Muhammad as head of the Muslim community, had been held by the Ottoman sultans but was abolished by Kemal in 1924.

6th. To supervise the personal conduct of officials because the private life and the administrative life of these officials forms an indivisible whole;

7th. To advance the hours of work in summer and in winter so that the accomplishment of religious obligations will be eased and to prevent all useless staying up late at night;

8th. To condemn corruption and influence peddling; to reward only competence and merit;

9th. Government will act in conformity to the law and to Islamic principles; the carrying out of ceremonies, receptions, and official meetings, as well as the administration of prisons and hospitals should not be contrary to Islamic teachings. The scheduling of government services ought to take account of the hours set aside for prayer.

10th. To train and to use Azharis, that is to say, the graduates of Al-Azhar University,[2] for military and civil roles;

II. In the fields of social and everyday practical life:

1st. The people should respect public mores: this ought to be the object of special attention — to strongly condemn attacks upon public mores and morality;

2nd. To find a solution for the problems of women, a solution that will allow her to progress and which will protect her while conforming to Islamic principles. This very important social question should not be ignored because it has become the subject of polemics and of more or less unsupported and exaggerated opinion;

3rd. To root out clandestine or public prostitution and to consider fornication as a reprehensible crime the authors of which should be punished;

4th. To prohibit all games of chance (gaming, lotteries, races, golf);

5th. To stop the use of alcohol and intoxicants — these obliterate the painful consequences of people's evil deeds;

6th. To . . . educate women, to provide quality education for female teachers, school pupils, students, and doctors;

7th. To prepare instructional programs for girls; to develop an educational program for girls different than the one for boys;

8th. Male students should not be mixed with female students — any relationship between unmarried men and women is considered to be wrong until it is approved;

9th. To encourage marriage and procreation — to develop legislation to safeguard the family and to solve marriage problems;

10th. To close dance halls; to forbid dancing;

11th. To censor theater productions and films; to be severe in approving films;

12th. To supervise and approve music;

13th. To approve programs, songs, and subjects before they are released, to use radio to encourage national education;

14th. To confiscate malicious articles and books as well as magazines displaying a grotesque character or spreading frivolity;

15th. To carefully organize vacation centers;

16th. To change the hours when public cafes are opened or closed, to watch

---

[2]An educational institution in Cairo specializing in Islamic studies.

the activities of those who habituate them — to direct these people towards wholesome pursuits, to prevent people from spending too much time in these cafes;

17th. To use the cafes as centers to teach reading and writing to illiterates, to seek help in this task from primary school teachers and students;

18th. To combat the bad practices which are prejudicial to the economy and to the morale of the nation, to direct the people toward good customs and praiseworthy projects such as marriage, orphanages, births, and festivals. . . .

19th. To bring to trial those who break the laws of Islam, who do not fast, who do not pray, and who insult religion;

20th. To transfer village primary schools to the mosque. . . .

21st. Religious teaching should constitute the essential subject matter to be taught in all educational establishments and faculties;

22nd. To memorize the Quran in state schools — this condition will be essential in order to obtain diplomas with a religious or philosophical specialty — in every school students should learn part of the Quran;

23rd. To develop a policy designed to raise the level of teaching. . . .

24th. Interested support for teaching the Arabic language in all grades — absolute priority to be given to Arabic over foreign languages;

25th. To study the history of Islam, the nation, and Muslim civilization;

26th. To study the best way to allow people to dress . . . in an identical manner;

27th. To combat foreign customs (in the realm of vocabulary, customs, dress, nursing) and to Egyptianize all of these (one finds these customs among the well-to-do members of society);

28th. To orient journalism toward wholesome things, to encourage writers and authors, who should study specifically Muslim and Oriental[3] subjects;

29th. To safeguard public health through every kind of publicity — increasing the number of hospitals, doctors, and out-patient clinics;

30th. To call particular attention to the problems of village life (administration, hygiene, water supply, education, recreation, morality).

III. The economic field:

1st. Organization of the zakat tax[4] according to Islamic precepts, using zakat proceeds for welfare projects such as aiding the indigent, the poor, orphans; the zakat should also be used to strengthen the army;

2nd. To prevent the practice of usury, to direct banks to implement this policy; the government should provide an example by giving up the interest fixed by banks for servicing a personal loan or an industrial loan, etc.;

3rd. To facilitate and to increase the number of economic enterprises and to employ the jobless, to employ for the nation's benefit the skills possessed by the foreigners in these enterprises;

4th. To protect workers against monopoly companies, to require these com-

---

[3]As opposed to Western studies.
[4]A fixed share of income or property that all Muslims must pay as a tax or as charity for the welfare of the needy.

panies to obey the law, the public should share in all profits;

5th. Aid for low-ranking employees and enlargement of their pay, lowering the income of high-ranking employees; . . .

7th. To encourage agricultural and industrial works, to improve the situation of the peasants and industrial workers;

8th. To give special attention to the technical and social needs of the workers, to raise their level of life and aid their class;

9th. Utilization of certain natural resources (unworked land, neglected mines, etc.). . . .

▼▼▼

Anticolonialism in India and Southeast Asia

During the late nineteenth century, when Indians were already in a full-scale debate about their relationship with Great Britain and some were demanding independence, many Southeast Asians were experiencing direct European political control for the first time. Nonetheless, in the first half of the twentieth century developments in both areas showed some marked similarities. Nationalism swept through the Indian population, and despite their many differences in religion, education, and caste status, millions of Indians came to agree that Great Britain should "quit India" and allow Indian self-rule. The British responded with minor concessions but mostly delaying tactics and armed repression. Nationalism also intensified in Southeast Asia, especially in Vietnam and the Dutch East Indies, where force was needed to suppress anticolonial movements in both areas in the 1920s and 1930s.

The reasons for this broad upsurge of anti-European sentiment included religious revivals of Hinduism in India, Buddhism in Burma, and Islam in Southeast Asia, all of which heightened people's awareness of their differences from the West; the emergence of Japan, which demonstrated that an Asian nation could become a great power; the carnage of World War I, which raised doubts about the Europeans' "superiority"; and the spread of Western education and political ideologies. Most telling, however, was anger over the disparity between the Europeans' stated good intentions about their colonies' futures and their actual record of economic exploitation, racial prejudice, and opposition to self-rule.

To this was added the extraordinary influence of charismatic leaders such as Mohandas Gandhi, who drew the Indian masses into the nationalist movement; Jawaharlal Nehru, who guided the Indian Congress Party in the 1930s and 1940s; Ho Chi Minh, who built a strong nationalist coalition in Vietnam in the face of French persecution; and Achmed Sukarno, who rallied Indonesian nationalists despite opposition from the Dutch.

World War II was the catalyst for the creation of independent nations throughout the region in the late 1940s and 1950s. But events and leaders of the first half of the twentieth century provided the foundation for the achievement of independence.

Gandhi's Vision for India
▼▼▼

102 ▼ Mohandas Gandhi, INDIAN HOME RULE

Mohandas Gandhi, the outstanding figure in modern Indian history, was born in 1869 in a village north of Bombay on the Arabian Sea. His father was a government official who presided over an extended family with strict Hindu practices. Gandhi studied law in England, and after failing to establish a legal practice in Bombay, he moved to South Africa in 1893 to serve the area's large Indian population.

In South Africa, he became incensed over the laws that discriminated against Indians, many of whom were indentured servants employed by whites or petty Indian merchants. During his struggle to improve the lot of South Africa's Indian population, Gandhi developed his theory of *satyagraha,* usually translated into English as "soul force." Satyagraha sought justice not through violence but through love, a willingness to suffer, and conversion of the oppressor. Central to his strategy was nonviolent resistance: Gandhi's followers disobeyed unjust laws and accepted the consequences — even beatings and imprisonment — to reach the hearts of the British and change their thinking.

Gandhi first wrote about his theories of satyagraha in 1908 after meeting with a group of Indians in England who favored force to oust the British. In response, he composed a pamphlet, "Hind Swaraj," or "Indian Home Rule," in which he explained his theory of nonresistance and his doubts about the benefits of modern civilization. Written in the form of a dialogue between a reader and an editor (Gandhi), "Indian Home Rule" was printed in hundreds of editions and still serves as the best summary of Gandhi's philosophy.

QUESTIONS FOR ANALYSIS

1. What does Gandhi see as the major deficiency of modern civilization?
2. How, according to Gandhi, has civilization specifically affected women?
3. Why does Gandhi have faith that Hindus and Muslims will be able to live in peace in India?
4. What, according to Gandhi, is true civilization, and what is India's role in preserving it?
5. What leads Gandhi to his conviction that love is stronger than force?
6. Why did Gandhi's attack on civilization gain him support among the Indian masses?
7. Compare Gandhi's view of progress with that of Condorcet (source 37). On what points do the two men disagree?

CHAPTER VI

Civilization

READER: Now you will have to explain what you mean by civilization. . . .

EDITOR: Let us first consider what state of things is described by the word "civilization." Its true test lies in the fact that people living in it make bodily welfare the object of life. We will take some examples: The people of Europe today live in better-built houses than they did a hundred years ago. This is considered an emblem of civilization, and this is also a matter to promote bodily happiness. Formerly, they wore skins, and used as their weapons spears. Now, they wear long trousers, and for embellishing their bodies they wear a variety of clothing, and, instead of spears, they carry with them revolvers containing five or more chambers. If people of a certain country, who have hitherto not been in the habit of wearing much clothing, boots, etc., adopt European clothing, they are supposed to have become civilized out of savagery. Formerly, in Europe, people plowed their lands mainly by manual labor. Now, one man can plow a vast tract by means of steam-engines, and can thus amass great wealth. This is called a sign of civilization. Formerly, the fewest men wrote books, that were most valuable. Now, anybody writes and prints anything he likes and poisons people's minds. Formerly, men traveled in wagons; now they fly through the air, in trains at the rate of four hundred and more miles per day. This is considered the height of civilization. It has been stated that, as men progress, they shall be able to travel in airships and reach any part of the world in a few hours. Men will not need the use of their hands and feet. They will press a button, and they will have their clothing by their side. They will press another button, and they will have their newspaper. A third, and a motor-car will be in waiting for them. They will have a variety of delicately dished up food. Everything will be done by machinery. Formerly, when people wanted to fight with one another, they measured between them their bodily strength; now it is possible to take away thousands of lives by one man working behind a gun from a hill. This is civilization. Formerly, men worked in the open air only so much as they liked. Now, thousands of workmen meet together and for the sake of maintenance work in factories or mines. Their condition is worse than that of beasts. They are obliged to work, at the risk of their lives, at most dangerous occupations, for the sake of millionaires. Formerly, men were made slaves under physical compulsion, now they are enslaved by temptation of money and of the luxuries that money can buy. There are now diseases of which people never dreamed before, and an army of doctors is engaged in finding out their cures, and so hospitals have increased. This is a test of civilization. Formerly, special messengers were required and much expense was incurred in order to send letters; today, anyone can abuse his fellow by means of a letter for one penny. True, at the same cost, one can send one's thanks also. Formerly, people had two or three meals consisting of homemade bread and vegetables; now, they require something to eat every two hours, so that they have hardly leisure for anything else. What more need I say? All this you can ascertain from several authoritative books. These are all true tests of civilization. And, if any one speaks to the contrary, know that he is ignorant. This civilization takes note neither of morality nor of religion. . . .

This civilization is irreligion, and it has taken such a hold on the people in Europe that those who are in it appear to be half mad. They lack real physical strength or courage. They keep up their energy by intoxication. They can hardly be happy in solitude. Women, who should be the queens of households, wander in the streets, or they slave away in factories. For the sake of a pittance, half a million women in England alone are laboring under trying circumstances in factories or similar institutions. This awful fact is one of the causes of the daily growing suffragette movement.

This civilization is such that one has only to be patient and it will be self-destroyed.

CHAPTER X

The Condition of India (Continued)
The Hindus and the Muslims

READER: But I am impatient to hear your answer to my question. Has the introduction of Islam not unmade the nation?

EDITOR: India cannot cease to be one nation because people belonging to different religions live in it. The introduction of foreigners does not necessarily destroy the nation, they merge in it. A country is one nation only when such a condition obtains in it. That country must have a faculty for assimilation. India has ever been such a country. In reality, there are as many religions as there are individuals, but those who are conscious of the spirit of nationality do not interfere with one another's religion. If they do, they are not fit to be considered a nation. If the Hindus believe that India should be peopled only by Hindus, they are living in dreamland. The Hindus, the Muslims, the Parsees[1] and the Christians who have made India their country are fellow-countrymen, and they will have to live in unity if only for their own interest. In no part of the world are one nationality and one religion synonymous terms; nor has it ever been so in India.

READER: But what about the inborn enmity between Hindus and Muslims?

EDITOR: That phrase has been invented by our mutual enemy.[2] When the Hindus and Muslims fought against one another, they certainly spoke in that strain. They have long since ceased to fight. How, then, can there be any inborn enmity? Pray remember this too, that we did not cease to fight only after British occupation. The Hindus flourished under Muslim sovereigns and Muslims under the Hindu. Each party recognized that mutual fighting was suicidal, and that neither party would abandon its religion by force of arms. Both parties, therefore, decided to live in peace. With the English advent the quarrels recommenced. . . .

Hindus and Muslims own the same ancestors, and the same blood runs through their veins. Do people become enemies because they change their religion? Is the God of the Muslim different from the God of the Hindu? Religions are different roads converging to the same point. What does it matter that we take different roads, so long as we reach the same goal? Wherein is the cause for quarreling?

CHAPTER XIII

What Is True Civilization?

READER: You have denounced railways, lawyers and doctors. I can see that you will discard all machinery. What, then, is civilization?

EDITOR: The answer to that question is not difficult. I believe that the civilization India has evolved is not to be beaten in the world. Nothing can equal the seeds sown by our ancestors. Rome went, Greece shared the same fate, the might of the Pharaohs was broken, Japan has become westernized, of China nothing can be said, but India is still, somehow or other, sound at the foundation. The people of Europe learn their lessons from the writings of the men of Greece or Rome, which exist no longer in their former glory. In trying to learn from them, the Europeans imagine that they will avoid the mistakes of Greece and Rome. Such is their pitiable condition. In the midst of all this, India remains immovable, and that is her glory. It is a charge against India that her people are so uncivilized, ignorant, and stolid, that it is not possible to induce them to adopt any changes. It is a charge really against our merit. What we have tested and found true on the anvil of experience, we dare not change. Many thrust their advice upon India, and she remains steady. This is her beauty; it is the sheet-anchor of our hope.

Civilization is that mode of conduct which points out to man the path of duty. Performance

---

[1]Followers of the Zoroastrian religion who fled India when Islamic armies conquered Persia in the seventh century C.E.

[2]The British.

of duty and observance of morality are convertible terms. To observe morality is to attain mastery over our mind and our passions. So doing, we know ourselves. The Gujarati[3] equivalent for civilization means "good conduct."

If this definition be correct, then India, as so many writers have shown, has nothing to learn from anybody else, and this is as it should be.

CHAPTER XVII

Passive Resistance

READER: Is there any historical evidence as to the success of what you have called soul-force or truth-force? No instance seems to have happened of any nation having risen through soul-force. I still think that the evil-doers will not cease doing evil without physical punishment.

EDITOR: . . . The force of love is the same as the force of the soul or truth. We have evidence of its working at every step. The universe would disappear without the existence of that force. But you ask for historical evidence. It is, therefore, necessary to know what history means. . . .

The fact that there are so many men still alive in the world shows that it is based not on the force of arms but on the force of truth or love. Therefore the greatest and most unimpeachable evidence of the success of this force is to be found in the fact that, in spite of the wars of the world, it still lives on.

Thousands, indeed, tens of thousands, depend for their existence on a very active working of this force. Little quarrels of millions of families in their daily lives disappear before the exercise of this force. Hundreds of nations live in peace. History does not and cannot take note of this fact. History is really a record of every interruption of the even working of the force of love or of the soul. . . . Soul-force, being natural, is not noted in history.

READER: According to what you say, it is plain that instances of the kind of passive resistance are

not to be found in history. It is necessary to understand this passive resistance more fully. It will be better, therefore, if you enlarge upon it.

EDITOR: Passive resistance is a method of securing rights by personal suffering; it is the reverse of resistance by arms. When I refuse to do a thing that is repugnant to my conscience, I use soul-force. For instance, the government of the day has passed a law which is applicable to me: I do not like it; if, by using violence, I force the government to repeal the law, I am employing what may be termed body-force. If I do not obey the law and accept the penalty for its breach, I use soul-force. It involves sacrifice of self.

Everybody admits that sacrifice of self is infinitely superior to sacrifice of others. Moreover, if this kind of force is used in a cause that is unjust, only the person using it suffers. He does not make others suffer for his mistakes. Men have before now done many things which were subsequently found to have been wrong. No man can claim to be absolutely in the right, or that a particular thing is wrong, because he thinks so, but it is wrong for him so long as that is his deliberate judgment. It is, therefore, meet [proper] that he should not do that which he knows to be wrong, and suffer the consequence whatever it may be. This is the key to the use of soul-force. . . .

READER: From what you say, I deduce that passive resistance is a splendid weapon of the weak but that, when they are strong, they may take up arms.

EDITOR: This is gross ignorance. Passive resistance, that is, soul-force, is matchless. It is superior to the force of arms. How, then, can it be considered only a weapon of the weak? Physical-force men are strangers to the courage that is requisite in a passive resister. Do you believe that a coward can ever disobey a law that he dislikes? Extremists are considered to be advocates of brute-force. Why do they, then, talk about obeying laws? I do not blame them. They can say nothing else. When they succeed in driving out the English, and they themselves become gover-

---

[3]An Indian dialect spoken in Gujarat, in northwest India.

nors, they will want you and me to obey their laws. And that is a fitting thing for their constitution. But a passive resister will say he will not obey a law that is against his conscience, even though he may be blown to pieces at the mouth of a cannon.

What do you think? Wherein is courage required — in blowing others to pieces from behind a cannon or with a smiling face to approach a cannon and to be blown to pieces? Who is the true warrior — he who keeps death always as a bosom-friend or he who controls the death of others? Believe me that a man devoid of courage and manhood can never be a passive resister.

This, however, I will admit: that even a man, weak in body, is capable of offering this resistance. One man can offer it just as well as millions. Both men and women can indulge in it. It does not require the training of an army; it needs no Jiu-jitsu. Control over the mind is alone necessary, and, when that is attained, man is free like the king of the forest, and his very glance withers the enemy.

Passive resistance is an all-sided sword; it can be used anyhow; it blesses him who uses it and him against whom it is used. Without drawing a drop of blood, it produces far-reaching results.

A Vietnamese Condemnation of French Rule
▼▼▼

103 ▼ *Nguyen Thai Hoc,* *LETTER TO THE FRENCH CHAMBER OF DEPUTIES*

After the French seized Vietnam's three southernmost provinces, a region known as Cochin China, in 1862, they extended their authority over Tongking (northern Vietnam) and Annam (central Vietnam) in the mid 1880s. Convinced of their civilizing mission, the French sought to undermine Vietnam's Confucian culture by creating a French-trained Vietnamese elite willing to cooperate with the colonial regime. Although some members of Vietnam's upper class resisted French rule (including the young emperor Duy-tan, whose plot to overthrow the French was uncovered in 1916), most at first sought some sort of compromise between Western culture and Confucianism.

Revolutionary nationalistic movements gained adherents in the 1920s, however, as more and more Vietnamese became incensed over continued economic exploitation and political repression, even though 90,000 Vietnamese troops and laborers had helped the French during World War I. The leading nationalist organization was the Viet Nam Quoc Dan Dang (Vietnamese Nationalist Party, or VNQDD), founded in 1927 by Nguyen Thai Hoc, a teacher from Hanoi. As a young man he sought to improve conditions in Vietnam through moderate reforms but became disillusioned with the French and turned to revolution. The VNQDD was modeled on Sun Yat-sen's Nationalist Party and was dedicated to achieving an independent and democratic-socialist Vietnam. In 1929, with the VNQDD membership at about 1,500, its leaders plotted an anti-French insurrection. The uprising, known as the Yen Bay Revolt, was crushed in 1930, and the VNQDD leaders were arrested and executed.

While awaiting his execution, Nguyen Thai Hoc wrote the following letter to France's parliament, the Chamber of Deputies. A defense of his actions and a denunciation of French colonialism, the letter was also released to the Vietnamese public.

QUESTIONS FOR ANALYSIS

1. In Nguyen Thai Hoc's view, what are French intentions in Vietnam and what has been the effect of French occupation?
2. How did Nguyen Thai Hoc evolve from a moderate reformer to a revolutionary?
3. If implemented, how would his suggestions to Governor General Varenne have improved the lot of the Vietnamese people?
4. What does the French response to the Yen Bay uprising reveal about the nature of French colonial rule?
5. What do you suppose Nguyen Thai Hoc hoped to accomplish by writing this letter?

Gentlemen:

I, the undersigned, Nguyen Thai Hoc, a Vietnamese citizen, twenty-six years old, chairman and founder of the Vietnamese Nationalist Party, at present arrested and imprisoned at the jail of Yen Bay, Tongking, Indochina, have the great honor to inform you of the following facts:

According to the tenets of justice, everyone has the right to defend his own country when it is invaded by foreigners, and according to the principles of humanity, everyone has the duty to save his compatriots when they are in difficulty or in danger. As for myself, I have assessed the fact that my country has been annexed by you French for more than sixty years. I realize that under your dictatorial yoke, my compatriots have experienced a very hard life, and my people will without doubt be completely annihilated, by the naked principle of natural selection. Therefore, my right and my duty have compelled me to seek every way to defend my country which has been invaded and occupied, and to save my people who are in great danger.

At the beginning, I had thought to cooperate with the French in Indochina in order to serve my compatriots, my country and my people, particularly in the areas of cultural and economic development. As regards economic development, in 1925 I sent a memorandum to Governor General Varenne,[1] describing to him all our aspirations concerning the protection of local industry and commerce in Indochina. I urged strongly in the same letter the creation of a Superior School of Industrial Development in Tongking. In 1926 I again addressed another letter to the then Governor General of Indochina in which I included some explicit suggestions to relieve the hardships of our poor people. In 1927, for a third time, I sent a letter to the Résident Supérieur[2] in Tongking, requesting permission to publish a weekly magazine with the aim of safeguarding and encouraging local industry and commerce. With regard to the cultural domain, I sent a letter to the Governor General in 1927, requesting (1) the privilege of opening tuition-free schools for the children of the lower classes, particularly children of workers and peasants; (2) freedom to open

---

[1]Alexandre Varenne was governor-general of Indochina from 1925 to 1929.

[2]The *résident supérieur* of Tongking was the chief French administrator for northern Vietnam.

popular publishing houses and libraries in industrial centers.

It is absolutely ridiculous that every suggestion has been rejected. My letters were without answer; my plans have not been considered; my requests have been ignored; even the articles that I sent to newspapers have been censored and rejected. From the experience of these rejections, I have come to the conclusion that the French have no sincere intention of helping my country or my people. I also concluded that we have to expel France. For this reason, in 1927, I began to organize a revolutionary party, which I named the Vietnamese Nationalist Party, with the aim of overthrowing the dictatorial and oppressive administration in our country. We aspire to create a Republic of Vietnam, composed of persons sincerely concerned with the happiness of the people. My party is a clandestine organization, and in February 1929, it was uncovered by the security police. Among the members of my party, a great number have been arrested. Fifty-two persons have been condemned to forced labor ranging from two to twenty years. Although many have been detained and many others unjustly condemned, my party has not ceased its activity. Under my guidance, the Party continues to operate and progress towards its aim.

During the Yen Bay uprising someone succeeded in killing some French officers. The authorities accused my party of having organized and perpetrated this revolt. They have accused me of having given the orders for the massacre. In truth, I have never given such orders, and I have presented before the Penal Court of Yen Bay all the evidence showing the inanity of this accusation. Even so, some of the members of my party completely ignorant of that event have been accused of participating in it. The French Indochinese government burned and destroyed their houses. They sent French troops to occupy their villages and stole their rice to divide it among the soldiers. Not just members of my party have been suffering from this injustice — we should rather call this cruelty than injustice — but also many simple peasants, interested only in their daily work in the rice fields, living miserable lives like buffaloes and horses, have been compromised in this reprisal. At the present time, in various areas there are tens of thousands of men, women, and children, persons of all ages, who have been massacred.[3] They died either of hunger or exposure because the French Indochinese government burned their homes. I therefore beseech you in tears to redress this injustice which otherwise will annihilate my people, which will stain French honor, and which will belittle all human values.

I have the honor to inform you that I am responsible for all events happening in my country under the leadership of my party from 1927 until the present. You only need to execute me. I beg your indulgence for all the others who at the present time are imprisoned in various jails.

---

[3]Many civilian deaths resulted from French actions following the revolt, but Nguyen Thai Hoc's estimate of 10,000 deaths is an exaggeration.

Latin America in an Era of Economic Challenge and Political Change

A popular slogan among Latin America's politicians, business leaders, and landowners in the late nineteenth century was "order and progress," and to an extent exceptional in the region's turbulent history, they achieved both. Around 1870 Latin America's economy entered a period of export-driven expansion that lasted until the 1920s. The region became a major supplier of wheat, beef, mutton, coffee, raw rubber, nitrates, copper, tin, bananas, and a host of other primary products to Europe and the United States, and with little industrialization itself, a major market for European and U.S. manufactured goods. Land prices soared, and English and U.S. capital flowed into Latin America in the form of investments in railroads, banks, food-processing facilities, and mining operations and as loans to governments for the construction of roads, bridges, and public buildings.

Latin America's economic boom took place in a climate of relative political stability. In Argentina, Chile, and Brazil this meant republican governments controlled by an oligarchy of landowning families, sometimes in alliance with businessmen in the import-export trade; in Mexico, Peru, Ecuador, and Venezuela it meant rule by a strongman or dictator (caudillo), who also represented the interests of landowners. Oligarchs and dictators alike sought economic growth by maintaining law and order, approving land confiscations from the Church and peasantry, and most important, keeping foreign business interests happy by keeping taxes and tariffs low.

Latin America during these years is often viewed as a classic example of *neocolonialism*. Although the region had achieved political independence from Spain and Portugal in the early 1800s, economic relationships reminiscent of the colonial era persisted. It was still dependent on the export of primary products, mainly foodstuffs and minerals, to industrialized Europe and the United States, and was still dependent on those same regions for manufactured goods and capital for investments. The main beneficiaries of such a system were Latin America's landowning elite, European and U.S. bondholders, and foreign businesses with investments in construction, railroads, shipping, and mining. Dependency on foreign markets, capital, and manufactured goods made Latin American governments vulnerable to diplomatic arm-twisting by their wealthier and more powerful economic "partners." In the Caribbean and Central America it also led to U.S. military intervention.

By the 1930s, the neocolonial economy and the political order it supported were both in shambles, confirming the fears of individuals such as the Peruvian statesman Francisco García Calderón, who in the 1910s had warned of the dangers of the region's economic dependence on the United States and Europe. The main cause of the breakdown was the worldwide economic depression of the 1930s. Demand for Latin America's agricultural products and raw materials plummeted, driving millions into unemployment and depriving the region of the foreign exchange needed to buy manufactured goods from abroad. Loans and investments from the United

States and Europe dried up after the international banking system and stock markets collapsed. Governments faced insolvency, and capital shortages crippled plans to end the economic slump through industrialization. Latin Americans increasingly resented European and especially U.S. ownership of tin and copper mines, oil fields, railroads, banks, processing plants, and prime agricultural land. Once welcomed as a means of attracting capital and encouraging growth, foreign ownership now was condemned as a form of imperialist plunder.

As the Great Depression spread economic misery across Latin America, one government after another fell in an epidemic of election swings, revolts, military coups, and countercoups. While most of these short-lived regimes had no lasting political impact, in Brazil and Mexico political changes in the 1930s had long-term consequences for the nations themselves and for Latin America as a whole. In Brazil they were connected with the career of Gétulio Vargas, who seized power in 1930 and dominated Brazilian politics until 1945 and again from 1951 to 1954. By the end of the 1930s his *Estado Nova* (New State), a mixture of dictatorship, repression, anticolonialism, economic planning, nationalism, industrialization, and government-sponsored programs for housing, improved wages, and medical care provided Latin America with an authoritarian model for entry into an era of mass politics. In Mexico, changes took place during the presidency of Lázaro Cárdenas, who between 1934 and 1940 sought to rekindle the spirit of Mexico's Revolution of 1911 through educational reform, land redistribution, and nationalization of foreign-owned businesses.

Economic Dependency and Its Dangers
▼▼▼

104 ▼ *Francisco García Calderón,*
LATIN AMERICA: ITS RISE AND PROGRESS

During the late nineteenth century the United States became deeply involved in Latin America. Until then the United States had few economic ties with the region in comparison to Great Britain and France, and the U.S. government pursued a foreign policy more concerned with keeping foreigners out of Latin American politics than with extending its own influence. The foundation of its Latin American policy was the Monroe Doctrine, announced by President James Monroe in 1823, which warned European powers that the United States would not tolerate any attempts to re-establish their authority over the newly independent states in the Western Hemisphere. U.S. interests in Latin America focused almost exclusively on Mexico, whose territories in Texas, California, and New Mexico became part of the United States by virtue of the Treaty of Guadalupe Hidalgo, negotiated after the U.S. victory over Mexico in the Mexican War of 1846–1848. Other schemes to annex Cuba, Nicaragua, and the Mexican provinces of Yucatán and Lower California (mainly advanced by politicians interested in increasing the number of slave states) proved impractical or failed to generate support.

U.S.–Latin American relations changed dramatically after 1880. As the United States developed into a major industrial power, it gradually replaced Great Britain as the region's main purchaser of exports and supplier of manufactured goods. By 1910, the United States purchased 30 percent of Latin America's exports and provided it with 25 percent of its imports. By then U.S. investments had increased to $1.6 billion, almost all of it "new money" invested since the end of the Civil War in 1865. As U.S. businesses expanded their operations in Latin America, successive administrations in Washington encouraged their efforts and pledged to protect their interests. In 1905 President Theodore Roosevelt announced the Roosevelt Corollary to the Monroe Doctrine, which stated that the United States reserved the right to intervene in the internal affairs of any state in the Western Hemisphere that was guilty of "chronic wrongdoing," a euphemism for a failure to pay its debts or maintain law and order. Roosevelt's successor, William Howard Taft, was even more explicit. He stated that his foreign policy would include "active intervention to secure our merchandise and our capitalists' opportunity for profitable investment." These were not idle words. Between 1898 and 1934, the United States annexed Puerto Rico and intervened militarily in Cuba, Mexico, Guatemala, Honduras, Nicaragua, Panama, Colombia, and the Dominican Republic.

Condemnation of Latin America's economic dependence on foreigners and denunciations of "Yankee imperialism" became commonplace with the onset of the Great Depression, but such criticisms began earlier. One of the first such critics was the Peruvian diplomat and author Francisco García Calderón. Born into a wealthy and politically prominent family in Lima in 1883, García Calderón entered the Peruvian foreign service soon after graduating from the University of San Marcos. A career diplomat with postings to London and Paris and ambassadorships to Belgium and Portugal, he authored numerous essays and books on Latin America and its place in the world. His most widely read book by far was *Latin America: Its Rise and Progress,* which ranged over the region's history and discussed a number of contemporary issues, including immigration, the state of the economy, and Latin America's foreign relations. First published in 1912, it remained in print until the 1920s, having gone through numerous editions in several languages.

QUESTIONS FOR ANALYSIS

1. According to García Calderón, how has U.S. foreign policy toward Latin America evolved since the time of the Monroe Doctrine?
2. How does he explain these changes?
3. According to García Calderón, what benefits have accrued to Latin America as a result of foreign investments? How has Latin America been hurt by such investments?
4. How does García Calderón characterize Latin Americans, and how do they differ from the "Anglo-Saxons" of the United States?
5. How have the Latin American states contributed to their own economic problems?
6. If one accepts the premises of García Calderón's arguments, what would the Latin American states have had to do to overcome the problems connected with foreign economic dependency?

To save themselves from Yankee imperialism the [Latin] American democracies would almost accept a German alliance, or the aid of Japanese arms; everywhere the Americans of the North are feared. In the Antilles and in Central America hostility against the Anglo-Saxon[1] invaders assumes the character of a Latin crusade. Do the United States deserve this hatred? Are they not, as their diplomatists preach, the elder brothers, generous and protecting? And is not protection their proper vocation in a continent rent by anarchy? . . .

The nation which was peopled by nine millions of men in 1820 now numbers eighty millions — an immense demographic power; in the space of ten years, from 1890 to 1900, this population increased by one-fifth. By virtue of its iron, wheat, oil, and cotton, and its victorious industrialism, the democracy aspires to a world-wide significance of destiny; the consciousness of its powers is creating fresh international duties. Yankee pride increases with the endless multiplication of wealth and population, and the patriotic sentiment has reached such an intensity that it has become transformed into imperialism. . . .

This . . . expansion is opposed to the primitive simplicity of the Monroe doctrine. In 1823 . . . President Monroe upheld the republican integrity of the ancient [former] Spanish colonies. The celebrated message declared that there were no free territories in America, thus condemning in advance any projected establishment of European colonies upon the unoccupied continent of America, and that the United States limited their political action to the New World, and renounced all intervention in the disputes of Europe. . . .

The Monroe doctrine has undergone an essential transformation; it has passed successively from the defensive to intervention and thence to the offensive. From a theory which condemned any change of political *régime* among the new democracies under European pressure, and which forbade all acquisitions of territory, or the transfer of power from a weak to a strong nation, there arose the Polk doctrine,[2] which, in 1845, decreed the annexation of Texas for fear of foreign intervention. . . . In 1895 Secretary of State Olney,[3] at the time of the trouble between England and Venezuela, declared that the United States were in fact sovereign in America. From Monroe to Olney the defensive doctrine has gradually changed to a moral tutelage. . . .

Interventions have become more frequent with the expansion of frontiers. The United States have recently intervened in the territory of Acre,[4] there to found a republic of rubber gatherers; at Panama, there to develop a province and construct a canal; in Cuba, under cover of the Platt amendment,[5] to maintain order in the interior; in San Domingo, to support the civilising revolution and overthrow the tyrants; in Venezuela, and in Central America, to enforce upon these nations, torn by intestine disorders, the political and financial tutelage of the imperial democracy. In Guatemala and Honduras the loans concluded with the monarchs of North American finance have reduced the people to a new slavery. Supervision of the customs and the dispatch of pacificatory [peace-keeping] squadrons to defend the interests of the Anglo-Saxon have enforced peace and tranquility: such are the means employed. The *New York American* announces that Mr. Pierpont Morgan[6] proposes to encompass the finances

---

[1]A loosely used term, Anglo-Saxon usually refers to people of English descent.

[2]President James Polk in 1845 announced that the United States would not tolerate any action by a European power designed to hinder any peoples in North America from "deciding their own destiny." By this Polk meant the right to be annexed by the United States.

[3]Richard Olney (1835–1917) served as secretary of state under President Grover Cleveland between 1895 and 1897.

[4]A state in western Brazil.

[5]The Platt Amendment refers to a series of provisions spon-

sored by Senator Orville Platt of Connecticut and approved by the U.S. Congress that was attached to Cuba's constitution in 1901. It limited Cuba's treaty-writing capacity, restricted its right to contract public debt, gave the United States the right to maintain naval bases, and provided for U.S. intervention in Cuba if an unstable government failed to protect "life, liberty, and property."

[6]John Pierpont Morgan (1837–1913), founder of the investment bank J. P. Morgan and Company, was one of the wealthiest and most powerful financiers in the United States in the late nineteenth and early twentieth centuries.

of Latin America by a vast network of Yankee banks. Chicago merchants and Wall Street financiers created the Meat Trust in the Argentine. The United States offer millions for the purpose of converting into Yankee loans the moneys raised in London during the last century by the Latin American states; they wish to obtain a monopoly of credit. It has even been announced, although the news hardly appears probable, that a North American syndicate wished to buy enormous belts of land in Guatemala. . . . The fortification of the Panama Canal, and the possible acquisition of the Galapagos Islands in the Pacific, are fresh manifestations of imperialistic progress.

▼ ▼ ▼

Unexploited wealth abounds in [Latin] America. Forests of rubber, as in the African Congo; mines of gold and diamonds, which recall the treasures of the Transvaal and the Klondike; rivers which flow over beds of auriferous [gold-bearing] sand . . . coffee, cocoa, and wheat, whose abundance is such that these products are enough to glut the markets of the world. But there is no national capital [for investment]. This contrast between the wealth of the soil and the poverty of the States gives rise to serious economic problems. . . .

Since the very beginnings of independence the Latin democracies, lacking financial reserves, have had need of European gold. . . . The necessities of the war with Spain and the always difficult task of building up a new society demanded the assistance of foreign gold; loans accumulated, and very soon various States were obliged to solicit the simultaneous reduction of the capital borrowed and the rate of interest paid. The lamentable history of these bankrupt democracies dates from this period.

For geographical reasons, and on account of its very inferiority, South America cannot dispense with the influence of the Anglo-Saxon North, with its exuberant wealth and its industries. South America has need of capital, of enterprising men, of bold explorers, and these the United States supply in abundance. The defence of the South should consist in avoiding the establishment of privileges or monopolies, whether in favor of North Americans or Europeans.

▼ ▼ ▼

The descendants of the prodigal Spanish conquerors, who knew nothing of labor or thrift, have incessantly resorted to fresh loans in order to fill the gaps in their budgets. Politicians knew of only one solution of the economic disorder — to borrow, so that little by little the Latin-American countries became actually the financial colonies of Europe.

Economic dependence has a necessary corollary — political servitude. French intervention in Mexico[7] was originally caused by the mass of unsatisfied financial claims; foreigners, the creditors of the State, were in favor of intervention. England and France, who began by seeking to ensure the recovery of certain debts, finally forced a monarch upon the debtor nation. The United States entertained the ambition of becoming the sole creditor of the American peoples: this remarkable privilege would have assured them of an incontestable hegemony over the whole continent.

In the history of Latin America loans symbolise political disorder, lack of foresight, and waste. . . . Old debts are liquidated by means of new, and budgetary deficits are balanced by means of foreign gold. . . .

The budgets of various States complicate still further a situation already difficult. They increase beyond all measure, without the slightest relation to the progress made by the nation. They are based upon taxes which are one of the causes of

---

[7]In 1861 Spain, Great Britain, and France sent troops to Mexico to force the Mexican government to pay its debts. After gaining assurances of future payments, Spain and Great Britain withdrew their troops, but Emperor Napoleon III of France went forward with a plan to establish a new Mexican government under French protection. The French-sponsored candidate for emperor of Mexico was Archduke Ferdinand Maximilian of Hapsburg, brother of Austrian emperor Franz Josef. Maximilian served as emperor from 1863 to 1865, when the threat of U.S. intervention convinced Napoleon III to abandon his Mexican project.

the national impoverishment, or upon a protectionist tariff which adds greatly to the cost of life. The politicians, thinking chiefly of appearances, neglect the development of the national resources for the immediate augmentation of the fiscal revenues; thanks to fresh taxes, the budgets increase. These resources are not employed in furthering profitable undertakings, such as building railroads or highways, or increasing the navigability of the rivers. The bureaucracy is increased in a like proportion, and the budgets, swelled in order to dupe the outside world, serve only to support a nest of parasites. In the economic life of these countries the State is a kind of beneficent providence which creates and preserves the fortune of individual persons, increases the common poverty by taxation, display, useless enterprises, the upkeep of military and civil officials, and the waste of money borrowed abroad. . . .

To sum up, the new continent, politically free, is economically a vassal. This dependence is inevitable; without European capital there would have been no railways, no ports, and no stable government in [Latin] America. But the disorder which prevails in the finances of the country changes into a real servitude what might otherwise have been a beneficial relation.

Economic Nationalism in Mexico
▼▼▼

105 ▼ Lázaro Cárdenas, SPEECH TO THE NATION

Following the overthrow of dictator Porfirio Díaz in 1911, instability and conflict among aspiring leaders marked the first decade of Mexico's revolution, and it was unclear whether the revolutionary movement would survive. In 1917, however, a constitutional convention drafted a new charter for the nation that confirmed the principles of free speech, religious toleration, universal suffrage, the separation of powers, and the inviolability of private property. It also committed the government to social reform and greater control over foreign corporations.

Little changed, however, until the presidency of Lázaro Cárdenas from 1934 to 1940. In a series of bold steps he confiscated millions of acres of land from large estates for redistribution to peasants, introduced free and compulsory elementary education, and sponsored legislation to provide medical and unemployment insurance. His most audacious step, however, was the nationalization of Mexico's oil industry. In 1936 a dispute between unions and the U.S. and British oil companies erupted into a strike, and in the ensuing legal battle, seventeen oil companies refused to accept the pro-union ruling of an arbitration board appointed by Cárdenas, even after the Mexican Supreme Court upheld the decision. In response, on the order of Cárdenas, the government seized the property of the oil companies. Cárdenas announced his decision on March 18, 1938, in a radio speech to the nation. In the following excerpt, Cárdenas, after recounting the events in the labor dispute, comments on the role of the oil companies in Mexico's economic and social development.

QUESTIONS FOR ANALYSIS

1. In the account of Cárdenas, which actions by the foreign oil companies forced him to nationalize the oil industry?

2. According to Cárdenas, what truth is there in the oil companies' claims that they have benefited Mexico?
3. According to Cárdenas, who is ultimately responsible for the actions of the oil companies?
4. Which political activities of the oil companies does Cárdenas condemn?
5. What hardships does Cárdenas anticipate for the Mexican people as a result of his decision?
6. In what ways is Cárdenas's speech an appeal to Mexican nationalism?

In each and every one of the various attempts of the Executive to arrive at a final solution of the conflict within conciliatory limits . . . the intransigence of the companies was clearly demonstrated.

Their attitude was therefore premeditated and their position deliberately taken, so that the Government, in defense of its own dignity, had to resort to application of the Expropriation Act, as there were no means less drastic or decision less severe that might bring about a solution of the problem. . . .

It has been repeated *ad nauseam* that the oil industry has brought additional capital for the development and progress of the country. This assertion is an exaggeration. For many years throughout the major period of their existence, oil companies have enjoyed great privileges for development and expansion, including customs and tax exemptions and innumerable prerogatives; it is these factors of special privilege, together with the prodigious productivity of the oil deposits granted them by the Nation often against public will and law, that represent almost the total amount of this so-called capital.

Potential wealth of the Nation; miserably underpaid native labor; tax exemptions; economic privileges; governmental tolerance — these are the factors of the boom of the Mexican oil industry.

Let us now examine the social contributions of the companies. In how many of the villages bordering on the oil fields is there a hospital, or school or social center, or a sanitary water supply, or an athletic field, or even an electric plant fed by the millions of cubic meters of natural gas allowed to go to waste?

What center of oil production, on the other hand, does not have its company police force for the protection of private, selfish, and often illegal interests? These organizations, whether authorized by the Government or not, are charged with innumerable outrages, abuses, and murders, always on behalf of the companies that employ them.

Who is not aware of the irritating discrimination governing construction of the company camps? Comfort for the foreign personnel; misery, drabness, and insalubrity for the Mexicans. Refrigeration and protection against tropical insects for the former; indifference and neglect, medical service and supplies always grudgingly provided, for the latter; lower wages and harder, more exhausting labor for our people.

The tolerance which the companies have abused was born, it is true, in the shadow of the ignorance, betrayals, and weakness of the country's rulers; but the mechanism was set in motion by investors lacking in the necessary moral resources to give something in exchange for the wealth they have been exploiting.

Another inevitable consequence of the presence of the oil companies, strongly characterized by their anti-social tendencies, and even more harmful than all those already mentioned, has been their persistent and improper intervention in national affairs.

The oil companies' support to strong rebel factions against the constituted government in the Huasteca region of Veracruz and in the Isthmus of Tehuantepec during the years 1917 to 1920 is no longer a matter for discussion by anyone. Nor is anyone ignorant of the fact that in later periods and even at the present time, the oil companies have almost openly encouraged the ambitions of elements discontented with the country's government, every time their interests were affected either by taxation or by the modification of their privileges or the withdrawal of the customary tolerance. They have had money, arms, and munitions for rebellion, money for the anti-patriotic press which defends them, money with which to enrich their unconditional defenders. But for the progress of the country, for establishing an economic equilibrium with their workers through a just compensation of labor, for maintaining hygienic conditions in the districts where they themselves operate, or for conserving the vast riches of the natural petroleum gases from destruction, they have neither money, nor financial possibilities, nor the desire to subtract the necessary funds from the volume of their profits.

Nor is there money with which to meet a responsibility imposed upon them by judicial verdict, for they rely on their pride and their economic power to shield them from the dignity and sovereignty of a Nation which has generously placed in their hands its vast natural resources and now finds itself unable to obtain the satisfaction of the most elementary obligations by ordinary legal means.

As a logical consequence of this brief analysis, it was therefore necessary to adopt a definite and legal measure to end this permanent state of affairs in which the country sees its industrial progress held back by those who hold in their hands the power to erect obstacles as well as the motive power of all activity and who, instead of using it to high and worthy purposes, abuse their

economic strength to the point of jeopardizing the very life of a Nation endeavoring to bring about the elevation of its people through its own laws, its own resources, and the free management of its own destinies.

With the only solution to this problem thus placed before it, I ask the entire Nation for moral and material support sufficient to carry out so justified, important, and indispensable a decision. . . .

It is necessary that all groups of the population be imbued with a full optimism and that each citizen, whether in agricultural, industrial, commercial, transportation, or other pursuits, develop a greater activity from this moment on, in order to create new resources which will reveal that the spirit of our people is capable of saving the nation's economy by the efforts of its own citizens.

And, finally, as the fear may arise among the interests now in bitter conflict in the field of international affairs[1] that a deviation of raw materials fundamentally necessary to the struggle in which the most powerful nations are engaged might result from the consummation of this act of national sovereignty and dignity, we wish to state that our petroleum operations will not depart a single inch from the moral solidarity maintained by Mexico with the democratic nations, whom we wish to assure that the expropriation now decreed has as its only purpose the elimination of obstacles erected by groups who do not understand the evolutionary needs of all peoples and who would themselves have no compunction in selling Mexican oil to the highest bidder, without taking into account the consequences of such action to the popular masses and the nations in conflict.

---

[1] World War II in Europe was still more than a year away, but the Japanese invasion of China was in full swing, Spain was in the midst of its civil war, and Hitler had just annexed Austria.

▼▼▼

China in an Era of Political Disintegration and Revolution

The overthrow of the Qing Dynasty following China's Revolution of 1911 resulted not in China's long-awaited national revival but four decades of diplomatic humiliation, invasion, civil war, and immense suffering for the Chinese people. In the aftermath of the revolution, Sun Yat-sen and his dreams of democracy were pushed aside by General Yuan Shikai, who ruled the Chinese "republic" as a dictator between 1912 and 1916 and was planning to have himself declared emperor when he died in 1916. After his death, China was carved up by dozens of generally unscrupulous and irresponsible warlords, military men whose local authority was based on their control of private armies and whose grip on China was not completely broken until after the Communists took power in 1949. With a weak national government, the Chinese endured continued Western domination of their coastal cities and could offer only feeble resistance when the Japanese conquered Manchuria in 1931 and invaded China itself in 1937. Massive flooding of the Yellow River and widespread famine in north China in the 1920s deepened the people's misery.

With Confucian certainties shattered and China falling into ruin, Chinese intellectuals of the 1920s and 1930s intensely debated their country's predicament. The 1920s in particular were years of intellectual experiment and inquiry, in which members of study groups, journalists, poets, writers of fiction, academics, and university students scrutinized what it meant to be Chinese and debated the country's future. Most of these intellectuals vehemently rejected traditional Chinese values, customs, philosophy, and education, arguing that only a sharp break from the past would enable China to stand up to Japan and the West. Most of them believed that China needed to model itself on the West, although what specific Western values and institutions should be borrowed was a matter of debate.

In politics, Chinese who despaired of warlord depredation, Western imperialism, and Japanese aggression had two options. Two revolutionary parties emerged — the Nationalist Party, or Guomindang (GMD), and the Chinese Communist Party (CCP), each with its own plan of how to unify, govern, and revive China. The Guomindang, led by Sun Yat-sen until his death in 1925, was theoretically dedicated to Sun's "three principles of the people" — democracy, nationalism, and livelihood. The party came to be identified with the educated, Western-oriented bourgeoisie of China's coastal cities and in practice, under General Chiang Kai-shek (1887–1975), concentrated less on social reform and democracy than on fighting the warlords in the 1920s and the Communists in the 1930s. The Chinese Communist Party, founded in 1921, was dedicated to Marxism-Leninism, with its leadership provided by intellectuals and its major support eventually coming from China's rural masses.

Aided by agents of the Soviet Union, the Guomindang and the Communists formed a coalition in 1923 to destroy the warlords. With their forces combined into the National Revolutionary Army, they launched the Northern Expedition against the warlords in 1926. The alliance disintegrated in 1927, when Chiang Kai-shek, buoyed by his early victories and generous financial support from Chinese businessmen, purged the Communists from the army and ordered Guomindang troops in Shanghai to kill Communist leaders who had gathered there. Communist troops and their leaders fled to the countryside, where under the leadership of Mao Zedong (1893–1976), they rebuilt the party into a formidable military and political force. After a long struggle against the Guomindang and the Japanese, who invaded China in 1937, the Communists gained control of China in 1949.

The Maoist Version of Marxism
▼▼▼

106 ▼ *Mao Zedong,*
REPORT ON AN INVESTIGATION OF THE PEASANT MOVEMENT IN HUNAN and STRATEGIC PROBLEMS OF CHINA'S REVOLUTIONARY WAR

Mao Zedong (1893–1976) was born into a well-to-do peasant family in Hunan Province and as a university student participated in the anti-Qing revolution of 1911. During the next several years, while serving as a library assistant at Beijing University, he embraced Marxism and helped organize the Chinese Communist Party, which was officially founded in 1921. Originally given the task of organizing urban labor unions, Mao came to believe that the peasants, whose capacity for class revolution was discounted by orthodox Marxist-Leninists, were the force to lead China to socialism. He summarized his ideas in his "Report on an Investigation of the Peasant Movement in Hunan," written in 1927.

After the break from the Guomindang, the Communists took their small army to the remote and hilly region on the Hunan-Jiangxi border, where in 1931 they proclaimed the Chinese Soviet Republic. In 1934 Chiang Kai-shek's troops surrounded the Communists' forces, but as they moved in for the kill, more than 100,000 Communist troops and officials broke out of the Guomindang encirclement and embarked on the Long March. This legendary trek lasted more than a year and covered 6,000 miles before a remnant found safety in the remote mountains around Yan'an in northern Shaanxi province. It was here that Mao, now the party's recognized leader, rebuilt his army and readied himself and his followers for what would be fourteen more years of struggle against the Japanese and the Guomindang.

Mao was a prolific writer who produced many hundreds of treatises, essays, and even works of poetry. The following excerpts are drawn from two of his most important writings. The first, his "Report on an Investigation of the Peasant Movement in Hunan," was written in 1927 after he visited Hunan Province to study the activities and accomplishments of peasant associations, groups of peasants who with the help of Communist organizers, had seized land, humiliated or killed landlords, and taken control of their communities. In it Mao seeks to convince other party members that the peasants are the main source of revolution in China. The second excerpt, from his "Strategic Problems of China's Revolutionary War," is based on a series of lectures presented at the Red Army College in late 1936. In it Mao assesses China's military situation and outlines his strategy for victory over the Guomindang through guerrilla warfare.

QUESTIONS FOR ANALYSIS

1. What specific developments in Hunan Province reinforced Mao's convictions about the peasantry as a revolutionary force?
2. What criticisms have been made of the Hunan peasant movement, and how does Mao attempt to counter these criticisms?
3. What can be learned from these two writings about Mao's views of the role of the Communist Party in China's revolutionary struggle?
4. According to Mao, what have been the sources of oppression of the Chinese people? Once these sources of oppression are removed what will China look like?
5. According to Mao, what are the four unique characteristics of China's revolutionary war, and how do they affect Mao's military strategy?
6. What are the characteristics of Mao's "active defense" as opposed to "passive defense"?
7. How do Mao's ideas about revolution resemble and differ from those of Marx (source 63)? How do they resemble and differ from those of Lenin (source 90)?

REPORT ON AN INVESTIGATION OF THE PEASANT MOVEMENT IN HUNAN

During my recent visit to Hunan[1] I made a first-hand investigation of conditions in the five counties of Hsiangtan, Hsianghsiang, Hengshan, Liling and Changsha. . . . All talk directed against the peasant movement must be speedily set right. All the wrong measures taken by the revolutionary authorities concerning the peasant movement must be speedily changed. Only thus can the future of the revolution be benefited. For the present upsurge of the peasant movement is a colossal event. In a very short time, in China's central, southern and northern provinces, several

hundred million peasants will rise like a mighty storm, like a hurricane, a force so swift and violent that no power, however great, will be able to hold it back. They will smash all the trammels that bind them and rush forward along the road to liberation. They will sweep all the imperialists, warlords, corrupt officials, local tyrants and evil gentry into their graves. Every revolutionary party and every revolutionary comrade will be put to the test, to be accepted or rejected as they decide. There are three alternatives. To march at their head and lead them? To trail behind them, gesticulating and criticizing? Or to stand in their way and oppose them? Every Chinese is free to choose, but events will force you to make the choice quickly. . . .

---

[1]Hunan, a province of 105,000 sqaure miles in southeast central China, had a population of approximately 28 million in 1936.

"Yes, peasant associations are necessary, but they are going rather too far." This is the opinion of the middle-of-the-roaders. But what is the actual situation? True, the peasants are in a sense "unruly" in the countryside. Supreme in authority, the peasant association allows the landlord no say and sweeps away his prestige. This amounts to striking the landlord down to the dust and keeping him there. . . . People swarm into the houses of local tyrants and evil gentry who are against the peasant association, slaughter their pigs and consume their grain. They even loll for a minute or two on the ivory-inlaid beds belonging to the young ladies in the households of the local tyrants and evil gentry. At the slightest provocation they make arrests, crown the arrested with tall paper-hats, and parade them through the villages, saying, "You dirty landlords, now you know who we are!" . . . This is what some people call "going too far," or "exceeding the proper limits in righting a wrong," or "really too much." Such talk may seem plausible, but in fact it is wrong. First, the local tyrants, evil gentry and lawless landlords have themselves driven the peasants to this. For ages they have used their power to tyrannize over the peasants and trample them underfoot; that is why the peasants have reacted so strongly. . . . Secondly, a revolution is not a dinner party, or writing an essay, or painting a picture, or doing embroidery; it cannot be so refined, so leisurely and gentle, so temperate, kind, courteous, restrained and magnanimous. A revolution is an insurrection, an act of violence by which one class overthrows another. A rural revolution is a revolution by which the peasantry overthrows the power of the feudal landlord class. Without using the greatest force, the peasants cannot possibly overthrow the deep-rooted authority of the landlords which has lasted for thousands of years. . . . To put it bluntly, it is necessary to create terror for a while in every rural area, or otherwise it would be impossible to suppress the activities of the counter-revolutionaries in the countryside or overthrow the authority of the gentry.

▼ ▼ ▼

A man in China is usually subjected to the domination of three systems of authority: (1) the state system, . . . ranging from the national, provincial and county government down to that of the township; (2) the clan system, . . . ranging from the central ancestral temple and its branch temples down to the head of the household; and (3) the supernatural system (religious authority), ranging from the King of Hell down to the town and village gods belonging to the nether world, and from the Emperor of Heaven down to all the various gods and spirits belonging to the celestial world. As for women, in addition to being dominated by these three systems of authority, they are also dominated by the men (the authority of the husband). These four authorities — political, clan, religious and masculine — are the embodiment of the whole feudal-patriarchal system and ideology, and are the four thick ropes binding the Chinese people, particularly the peasants. . . .

The political authority of the landlords is the backbone of all the other systems of authority. With that overturned, the clan authority, the religious authority and the authority of the husband all begin to totter. . . . In many places the peasant associations have taken over the temples of the gods as their offices. Everywhere they advocate the appropriation of temple property in order to start peasant schools and to defray the expenses of the associations, calling it "public revenue from superstition." In Liling County, prohibiting superstitious practices and smashing idols have become quite the vogue. . . .

In places where the power of the peasants is predominant, only the older peasants and the women still believe in the gods, the younger peasants no longer doing so. Since the latter control the associations, the overthrow of religious authority and the eradication of superstition are going on everywhere. As to the authority of the husband, this has always been weaker among the poor peasants because, out of economic necessity, their womenfolk have to do more manual labour than the women of the richer classes and therefore have more say and greater power of decision in family matters. With the increasing bankruptcy of the rural economy in recent years, the basis for men's domination over women has already been weakened. With the rise of the peasant movement, the women in many places have now begun to organize rural women's associations; the opportunity has come for them to lift up their heads, and the authority of the husband is getting shakier every day. In a word, the whole feudal-patriarchal system and ideology is tottering with the growth of the peasants' power.

STRATEGIC PROBLEMS OF CHINA'S REVOLUTIONARY WAR

What then are the characteristics of China's revolutionary war?

I think there are four.

The first is that China is a vast semi-colonial country which is unevenly developed both politically and economically. . . .

The unevenness of political and economic development in China — the coexistence of a frail capitalist economy and a preponderant semi-feudal economy; the coexistence of a few modern industrial and commercial cities and the boundless expanses of stagnant rural districts; the coexistence of several millions of industrial workers on the one hand and, on the other, hundreds of millions of peasants and handicraftsmen under the old regime; the coexistence of big warlords controlling the Central government and small warlords controlling the provinces; the coexistence of two kinds of reactionary armies, i.e., the so-called Central army under Chiang Kai-shek and the troops of miscellaneous brands under the warlords in the provinces; and the coexistence of a few railway and steamship lines and motor roads on the one hand and, on the other, the vast number of wheel-barrow paths and trails for pedestrians only, many of which are even difficult for them to negotiate. . . .

The second characteristic is the great strength of the enemy.

What is the situation of the Guomindang, the enemy of the Red Army? It is a party that has seized political power and has relatively stabilized it. It has gained the support of the principal counter-revolutionary countries in the world. It has remodeled its army, which has thus become different from any other army in Chinese history and on the whole similar to the armies of the modern states in the world; its army is supplied much more abundantly with arms and other equipment than the Red Army, and is greater in numerical strength than any army in Chinese history, even than the standing army of any country in the world. . . .

The third characteristic is that the Red Army is weak and small. . . .

Our political power is dispersed and isolated in mountainous or remote regions, and is deprived of any outside help. In economic and cultural conditions the revolutionary base areas are more backward than the Guomindang areas. The revolutionary bases embrace only rural districts and small towns. . . .

The fourth characteristic is the Communist Party's leadership and the agrarian revolution.

This characteristic is the inevitable result of the first one. It gives rise to the following two features. On the one hand, China's revolutionary war, though taking place in a period of reaction in China and throughout the capitalist world, can yet be victorious because it is led by the Communist Party and supported by the peasantry. Because we have secured the support of the peasantry, our base areas, though small, possess great political power and stand firmly opposed to the political power of the Guomindang which encompasses a vast area; in a military sense this creates colossal difficulties for the attacking Guomindang troops. The Red Army, though small, has great fighting capacity, because its men under the leadership of the Communist Party have sprung from the agrarian revolution and are fighting for their own interests, and because officers and men are politically united.

On the other hand, our situation contrasts sharply with that of the Guomindang. Opposed to the agrarian revolution, the Guomindang is deprived of the support of the peasantry. Despite the great size of its army it cannot arouse the bulk of the soldiers or many of the lower-rank officers, who used to be small producers, to risk their lives voluntarily for its sake. Officers and men are politically disunited and this reduces its fighting capacity. . . .

Military experts of new and rapidly developing imperialist countries like Germany and Japan positively boast of the advantages of strategic offensive and condemn strategic defensive. Such an idea is fundamentally unsuitable for China's revolutionary war. Such military experts point out that the great shortcoming of defense lies in the fact that, instead of gingering up [enlivening] the people, it demoralizes them. . . . Our case is different. Under the slogan of safeguarding the revolutionary base areas and safeguarding China, we can rally the greatest majority of the people to fight single-mindedly, because we are the victims of oppression and aggression. . . . Defensive battles in a just war can not only exercise a lulling influence on the politically alien elements but mobilize the backward sections of the masses to join in the war. . . .

In military terms, our warfare consists in the alternate adoption of the defensive and the offensive. It makes no difference to us whether our offensive is regarded as following the defensive or preceding it, because the turning-point comes when we smash the campaigns of "encirclement and annihilation." It remains a defensive until a campaign of "encirclement and annihilation" is smashed, and then it immediately begins as an offensive; they are but two phases of the same thing, as one campaign of "encirclement and annihilation" of the enemy is closely followed by another. Of the two phases, the defensive phase is more complicated and more important than the offensive phase. It involves numerous problems of how to smash the campaign of "encirclement and annihilation." The basic principle is for active defense and against passive defense.

In the civil war, when the Red Army surpasses the enemy in strength, there will no longer be any use for strategic defensive in general. Then our only directive will be strategic offensive. Such a change depends on an overall change in the relative strength of the enemy and ourselves. The only defensive measures that remain will be of a partial character.

A Story of a Revolutionary Heroine

▼▼▼

107 ▼ Cao Ming, "A NATIVE OF YAN'AN"

For dedicated revolutionaries literature has one overriding purpose — to further the revolutionary cause. This certainly applies to the Chinese Communist author Cao Ming, whose many short stories and novels made heroes of Mao's followers and villains of his opponents. Born in 1913 to a poor rural family, Cao Ming began her writing career with the publication of a short story in 1932. In the 1930s she wrote anti-Japanese propaganda after the invasion of Manchuria and became a member of the Communist Party in 1940. She spent the next eight years in Yan'an, where she worked with peasants and wrote stories that followed the party line. After the Communist victory in 1949 she held various government posts while continuing her writing.

One of Cao Ming's best-known short stories is "A Native of Yan'an," written in 1947, two years before the Communist victory. Its main character is an old, illiterate peasant woman, Granny Wu, whose self-sacrifice is held up as a model of dedication to the party. The story presents an idealized picture of Mao Zedong and his program while reviling his Guomindang enemies.

The story begins in 1937, when Granny Wu has a conversation with a courteous Red Army soldier who urges her to use her hands and mind to support the Communist cause. Only after speaking with her daughter-in-law does she realize that the officer was Mao Zedong himself.

QUESTIONS FOR ANALYSIS

1. What is the image of Mao portrayed in the short story?
2. How is Granny Wu's life transformed as a result of her conversation with Mao? What point is the author trying to make in this regard?
3. What is the background of the individuals who gather to discuss Mao's visit? What point is the author making here?
4. What are the views of the townspeople about the ideals and achievements of the Communists?
5. How do these views differ from those of the Guomindang?
6. What is revealed about the Guomindang from the behavior of their troops?

. . . "Ma, who have you been talking to for such a long time?" asked her daughter-in-law, when she came out of the house, putting down the winnower and shaking the flour off her body.

"I expect he's a cadre [a Communist Party official], I've been talking to him." She pointed to the group of people who had just left.

The younger woman shaded the sun from her eyes with her hands and looked carefully in the direction indicated by her mother-in-law. She exclaimed in surprise:

"Ma, that's him. Ma, that's him!"

Granny Wu was alarmed; she stood up slowly: "Who is he?"

"He is Chairman Mao, Ma, that's him. I heard him speak at the May Day celebration; I've also heard him speak at the mobilization meeting." . . .

"That's Chairman Mao!"

"There's no mistake, it's really him!"

The shopkeepers all ran out of the houses, trying hard to identify the tall shape as that of their beloved leader. A few intellectuals who had just come here from the south, eagerly joined the masses, and confirmed what the people were saying. One of them even said that once he had seen Chairman Mao have a long chat with the peasants in the fields. By now there were about ten people all watching with rapt attention the group that was getting further and further away. . . . His mighty figure grew as he went further away and his genius and solemn appearance seemed to become a tangible brilliance which shone with the sun. . . .

The old woman who had never been taken seriously before, now unexpectedly became the center of attention. Previously, she had thought that a woman's place was at home doing the housework, so she had been unwilling to attend mass meetings and even when propaganda teams arrived at her home, she received them coolly. However, after chatting with Chairman Mao and then being shown so much respect, she suddenly changed. Her conservative thinking became more enlightened, she began to display her hidden wisdom. She talked eloquently about the ordinary things she had heard in the past and they became part of her experience. Moreover, she felt that from now on she had enough courage to take on anything, however difficult. She sat placidly among the people, proudly enjoying their admiration and answering their questions.

"Immediately I felt that his eyes were different from other people's, they were grey, really exceptional! Ay, without such eyes, how could he see so clearly the suffering of the poor!"

The old woman straightened her back and continued with her description. It seemed as if she had become over ten years younger. "Moreover, I noticed that his forehead was rather broad, what an intelligent head! He can solve problems which have baffled hundreds and thousands of people. . . .

"Only the Communist Party works for us wholeheartedly. For generations we didn't have any land. Now, we've got land, cows, and sheep. Everybody can see that they don't have any privileges, they eat the same food as their soldiers, five cents a day for food, and they wear shabby clothes. It's said that their parents and children living in the Guomindang areas are being tortured every day by Chiang Kai-shek.

"Did you hear that during the 8,000 mile Long March,[1] Chairman Mao met an old woman who was about to freeze to death? He immediately took off his goat-fur-lined waist coat and put it on her. Have you ever seen anyone serving the people so wholeheartedly? . . ."

Now, the old woman's emotions swelled up like mountain torrents during the monsoon season, or as if thousands of galloping horses were charging inside her head and shaking her soul. While she talked she wiped away her tears of emotion.

"You are quite right!" Wang Xianggui, the blacksmith, cut in. "I was told that on the 8,000 mile Long March several cadres were so exhausted that they wanted to rest for three days and three nights. Chairman Mao said to them, 'Have a good rest! I'm going to tell you a story about victory.' After he finished his story, everyone was inspired with enthusiasm and didn't even want to rest for three hours, because they all wanted to march forward toward the final victory. I've also heard that when they were crossing the grasslands, they ate wild vegetables and leather soles. Some subordinates prepared some . . . wheat flour for him but he gave the flour to the comrades who were sick."

"Who isn't afraid when the word 'landlords' is mentioned. But the Communist Party has suppressed them. Without Chairman Mao and the Communist Party, we don't know how long we would still have to suffer!" sighed the primary school teacher, stroking his long beard.

"How the ruling class harmed us! My bound-feet were only unbound after the Red Army arrived.[2] If it wasn't for feudal oppression wouldn't we women be the same as men?" Her daughter-in-law began talking but before she could finish, the man from the south butted in:

"Things were plentiful in the south, but under the oppression of Chiang Kai-shek we were forbidden to fight against the Japanese so we came to the liberated area. Here we found freedom. Although the millet here is somewhat coarse, it is more delicious than the fish and meat over there. No wonder the French say: 'Without freedom one might as well die.'" . . .

Another student from Nanjing described Chiang Kai-shek with scorn:

"Chiang Kai-shek doesn't dare to go out without his armored car. In fact he has three armored cars, just as a wily hare has three burrows. Quite unlike Chairman Mao who can walk and chat to people in the streets." . . .

"Ah, when the whole country is liberated, may the people of the whole country be able to see Chairman Mao," remarked another peasant sympathetically.

The students laughed naively: "What the Communist Party stands for has been well known to people for a long time. Peasants in the countryside, workers and students in the cities are all longing for an early liberation."

They chatted with enthusiasm the whole morning and didn't disperse until they had poured out their innermost thoughts.

From that day on, Granny Wu responded enthusiastically to every call of the local govern-

---

[1]Cao Ming is exaggerating the length of the Long March, which was approximately 6,000, not 8,000, miles.

[2]When they took control of an area, the Communists ended the ancient custom of binding the feet of Chinese girls.

ment. She frequently set a good example for the men and young people in their work. . . .

▷ Ten years pass.

In March 1947, Chiang Kai-shek and Hu Zongnan's army invaded Yan'an. After destroying the enemy's main force, the people and the army voluntarily evacuated this empty town. At that time, Granny Wu had been ill in bed for two months. She refused to be persuaded by her son and daughter-in-law and was determined to stay in Yan'an.

"I want to see Hu Zongnan buried here with my own eyes."

The valleys, bridges, and fields were all mined. With the exception of the local people, no one dared to move about. Half an hour after the covering force had left, Chiang Kai-shek and Hu Zongnan's army became bold enough to rush into the town of Yan'an yelling and shouting.

When the enemy soldiers caught Granny Wu, they acted as if they had captured something valuable. They laughed contemptuously:

"We thought that there must be treasure hidden in Yan'an, but there's nothing but a skinny old granny!"

While the troops were laughing obscenely, one low-ranking officer squeezed forward, and after ordering the soldiers to make room, he asked:

"Are you a native here?"

"I am a Yan'aner!" answered Granny Wu, lifting up her head.

"In what direction did the main forces of the communist army retreat? How far have they gone?"

"Who knows how far they've gone. They left three days ago."

The officer stamped his foot and roared, "Three days ago? We've been tricked by the Communists. It's a pity our senior officers are as timid as mice; they kept shelling but were afraid to come in. . . . Well, in what direction did the covering force retreat?"

Weakly, Granny Wu pointed to the narrow mountain path, "They left a few hours ago. If you hurry up, you may catch up to them."

On hearing this, the low-ranking officer was about to report it to his superiors when Granny Wu stopped him:

"Officer, I see you're an honest man. To tell you the truth, they've laid a lot of mines there. If you want to chase them, it's better to take this narrow path. You should go through there quickly, the faster the better. When you get on to the main road, walk carefully by sticking to one side of the road. . . ."

The officer thanked the old woman and ordered his soldiers to watch her.

They sent a company of cavalrymen to chase the Communists at lightning speed along the path pointed out by the old woman.

Granny Wu seated herself on the millstone in front of her house groaning. While the hooves of the galloping horses were running along the narrow path, a terrible deafening explosion thundered through the whole valley. Forty to fifty dead soldiers and horses were thrown in every direction. Scarlet blood flowed down the hillside to the main road like tiny rivulets after the rain.

Granny Wu seemed to be suddenly recovered from her illness. She laughed loudly and vigorously, as if another bomb had exploded inside her body. She laughed as if her sides would split. However, she was immediately seized by numerous devilish hands. One of the soldiers aimed his gun at her, but was stopped by the low-ranking officer who walked up to her and asked in a muddle-headed way:

"Did you know that this meant death for you?"

"Yes, I knew." She stopped laughing.

"What did you do it for? I don't understand. Is there anything more precious than life?"

"What for? For him!" she answered solemnly.

"Who's he?" He felt somewhat perplexed.

"The benefactor who leads us!"

"He has fled! You'll die here in his stead!"

"No, he's forever with us, we'll never die, we'll win!"

"Why did you tell us to walk through that narrow path quickly?"

"Stupid! So that more of you will be killed!"

The low-ranking officer nodded his head and finally understood the strong willpower of the people of northwest China. After he had finished his questioning, he took up his pistol and fired three shots at Granny Wu's chest.

This old woman destroyed some of the enemy's strength with her patriotic honesty and wisdom. In her dizzy semiconsciousness before death the wave-like songs, now strident, now deep, of the northwestern people who were prepared to sacrifice everything to defeat the savage onslaught of the enemy, sounded once more.

Chapter 13

▼▼▼

The Global Community from the 1940s through the 1980s: An Era of Cold War and Decolonization

After World War I victors and vanquished alike failed to comprehend how many things the war had changed and dreamed that people and nations could return to patterns of life that had existed before the slaughter began in 1914. After World War II few people harbored such illusions. This war, they realized, had irrevocably altered human affairs, setting the stage for a new era in which change rather than continuity would predominate. Such expectations proved to be accurate. The four decades following the end of World War II were full of changes, creating conditions for humanity that in many ways were unprecedented.

Most notably, the postwar era saw a fundamental transformation in world political relationships. Before World War II seven or eight states could reasonably claim Great Power status; after the war only two states, the United States and the Soviet Union, could do so. Divided by ideology and fearful of each other's intent, these two superpowers became intense rivals, whose efforts to strengthen and extend their influence throughout the world dominated international politics until the very end of the twentieth century. Against the backdrop of this Cold War, another remarkable political transformation took place: Empires for all intents and purposes disappeared from the world scene. European empires in Asia, Africa, and Oceania were gradually dismantled in the 1950s and 1960s; the Soviet empire in Eastern Europe collapsed in the late 1980s; and the Soviet Union itself, basically a Russian-dominated imperial state, ceased to exist in 1991. As a result, approximately 120 new, sovereign states came into existence in the postwar era.

Major changes were not limited to the worlds of politics and diplomacy. Never before did human beings make so many revolutionary scientific, medical, and technological discoveries as they did between the 1940s and the 1980s. Human beings walked on the moon, designed and built powerful computers, transformed agriculture through the Green Revolution, developed vaccines for diseases such as polio, launched television satellites, and installed sophisticated telephone systems and computer networks that made possible instantaneous worldwide communication. Humans also learned to produce new weapons with destructive capacities so great that people routinely contemplated the obliteration of humanity if Soviet and U.S. nuclear arsenals were put to use in a third world war. Such fears were well-grounded. The atomic bomb the United States dropped on Hiroshima in 1945 was equal in strength to 12,500 tons of TNT and destroyed an entire city. By the 1970s the United States and the Soviet Union had thousands of nuclear weapons just one of which was equal in strength to *millions* of tons of TNT; such weapons could be delivered by guided missiles to targets across oceans or over the polar ice cap within minutes after launch.

Another notable change after World War II was the increase in interaction and interdependency among human beings around the world. Despite the very limited commercial and cultural contacts between the "free world" — the United States and its allies — and the communist world — the Soviet Union, its East European satellites, and China — migration, tourism, world trade, the speed of global communications, and cross-cultural influence all increased between the 1940s and the 1980s. International organizations such as the United Nations, international sporting events such as the Olympic Games and the soccer World Cup, worldwide coordination of activities such as postal services, disease control, whale hunting, and protection of the ozone layer all came to be taken for granted by the century's end.

Significant economic growth also took place in the postwar years. Record levels of population, international trade, industrial productivity, and energy production all were attained, and despite the worldwide economic slump of the 1970s and 1980s, the economically advanced countries of Europe and North America, along with Australia and New Zealand reached new levels of prosperity. Japan emerged from its defeat in World War II to become the world's second-greatest economic power after the United States. Previously peripheral regions such as the Middle East and states such as Nigeria and Venezuela assumed new economic importance as a result of the world's growing dependence on the petroleum that lay under their lands or off their coasts. Not all the world prospered, however. During the postwar years the number of people living in poverty also reached record levels, with most of them in Africa and South Asia and lesser numbers in Latin America and the Middle East.

These events and developments do not exhaust the list of significant changes that occurred between the mid 1940s and the mid 1980s. The growth of religious fundamentalism as a major political force; the demands by many groups, especially blacks, women, and homosexuals, for equal rights; the emergence of a worldwide environmental movement; and the first stirrings of modern China as a major economic force all could be added to the list.

Then beginning in the mid 1980s changes of even greater consequence began to occur. Communist China abandoned its dedication to radical egalitarianism and revolution in favor of new policies designed to foster economic growth. The Soviet Union entered a period of reform designed to reinvigorate an economic and political system whose flaws were openly admitted by its new leader, Mikhail Gorbachev. Reform brought collapse rather than revival to the USSR. By the early 1990s the Soviet Union no longer existed, former East European satellites had rejected communism, and the Cold War was over. Few people doubted that another new era of change was about to begin.

▼▼▼

The End of a European-Dominated World

Despite their enormous losses in World War I, European states maintained their preponderant role in world affairs in the 1920s and 1930s. Their colonial empires remained intact and even expanded in areas such as the Middle East, where the mandate system established at the Paris Peace Conference gave Great Britain control of Palestine and Iraq and France control of Syria and Lebanon. With the United States withdrawing from international commitments and the new communist regime in the Soviet Union shunned as an outcast, European states, especially Great Britain and France, and later, a resurgent Germany, dominated international diplomacy. Japan was the only non-European state that could boast of Great Power status.

The aftermath of World War II was far different. With their economies ruined and their people exhausted, European states lost their dominance of world affairs to the United States and the Soviet Union, the two states whose size, industrial might, and military strength had been largely responsible for the defeat of the Axis powers. The unlikely alliance between the democratic, capitalist United States and the totalitarian, communist Soviet Union began to break down, however, in the closing months of World War II and disintegrated completely after hostilities ended. The establishment of pro-Soviet regimes in Eastern and Central Europe and the Soviet Union's annexation of Latvia, Lithuania, Estonia, and parts of Poland confirmed the West's old fears about communist designs for world domination. At the same time, staunch Western opposition to Soviet expansion reinforced the Soviet leaders' convictions that capitalist nations were determined to destroy communism. Out of these mutual fears began the Cold War, the conflict between the Soviet Union and the United States that dominated world diplomacy until the late 1980s.

Another symptom of Europe's diminished international role after World War II was the disintegration of the European colonial empires. This dramatic political change had many causes, including the military and financial exhaustion of postwar Great Britain and France, the expansion and subsequent collapse of Japan's Asian empire, Soviet and U.S. opposition to colonialism, the upsurge of nationalism in the colonies, and the leadership of such men as Jawaharlal Nehru and Mohandas Gandhi in India, Achmed Sukarno in Indonesia, Kwame Nkrumah in Ghana, Ho Chi Minh in Vietnam, Jomo Kenyatta in Kenya, and others. By the mid 1960s just short of ninety former European colonies, most of them in Africa and Asia, had become independent.

In the second half of the twentieth century, Europeans, especially Western Europeans, enjoyed high incomes, excellent health care, and exceptional educational opportunities. European states continued to play an important role in world affairs. But the age of European world dominance had ended.

Cold War Origins: A U.S. Perspective
▼▼▼
108 ▼ *George Kennan, THE LONG TELEGRAM*

Historians have minutely examined the events and issues that led to the Cold War, and much has been written about which side, the Soviet Union or the United States, was more to blame for causing it. One thing is certain, however: 1946 was a pivotal year in Soviet–U.S. relations. Until then, despite wartime disagreements over military strategy and emerging differences about the postwar settlement in Europe, many statesmen and diplomats sought cooperation, not confrontation, between the two emerging superpowers. During 1946, however, attitudes hardened. Negotiations over nuclear arms control failed in June, and the Paris foreign ministers' conference over Eastern Europe ended in acrimony in August. By the end of the year moderates such as U.S. Secretary of Commerce Henry Wallace and the Soviet career diplomat Maksim Litvinov had both been removed from office. Leaders on both sides now saw little chance that further Soviet–U.S. conflict could be avoided.

Within the U.S. administration one document in particular articulated this bleak assessment of Soviet–U.S. relations in 1946. Written in February by the Moscow-based career diplomat George Kennan, what came to be known as the Long Telegram profoundly influenced U.S. policy toward the Soviet Union in the immediate postwar era and throughout the Cold War. Its author, born into a strict Protestant household in Milwaukee in 1904, entered the U.S. Foreign Service directly after graduating from Princeton in 1925. Having mastered Russian through studies at the University of Berlin, he served in Moscow, Berlin, and Prague before returning to Moscow in 1944 as a special advisor to the U.S. ambassador to the Soviet Union, Averell Harriman. In early February 1946 he received a directive from the State Department to analyze a recent speech by Joseph Stalin that Washington considered confrontational and hostile. Kennan, an advocate of a hard line against the Soviet Union, used the opportunity to compose what is arguably the best-known such dispatch in the history of the U.S. Foreign Service. The Long Telegram was read by State Department officials, cabled to U.S. embassies around the world, and made required reading for hundreds of military officers. In 1947 an edited version of the telegram was published as an article by "X" in the journal *Foreign Affairs.*

In 1947 Kennan was appointed head of the State Department's newly created policy planning staff with responsibility for long-range foreign policy planning. His opposition to the formation of the North Atlantic Treaty Organization, to increased military spending, and to U.S. involvement in the Korean War led to his resignation in 1951. Since then with the exception of brief ambassadorships to the Soviet Union in 1952 and to Yugoslavia between 1961 and 1963, he has devoted himself to research, writing, and university teaching on foreign policy and Soviet affairs.

QUESTIONS FOR ANALYSIS

1. What views of capitalism and socialism are articulated, according to Kennan, in official Soviet propaganda?
2. What does Kennan consider the most notable characteristics of the Russian past?
3. How, according to Kennan, has this past shaped the policies and views of the Soviet government since 1917?
4. In Kennan's view what role does communist ideology play in shaping the Soviet government's policies?
5. According to Kennan, what strengths and weaknesses does the Soviet Union bring to the anticipated conflict with the United States?
6. What, according to Kennan, are the implications of his analysis for U.S. foreign and domestic policies? What must be done to counter the Soviet threat?

PART 1: BASIC FEATURES OF POSTWAR SOVIET OUTLOOK, AS PUT FORWARD BY OFFICIAL PROPAGANDA MACHINE, ARE AS FOLLOWS

(a) USSR still lives in antagonistic "capitalist encirclement" with which in the long run there can be no permanent peaceful coexistence. . . .

(b) Capitalist world is beset with internal conflicts, inherent in nature of capitalist society. . . . Greatest of them is that between England and US.

(c) Internal conflicts of capitalism inevitably generate wars. Wars thus generated may be of two kinds: intra-capitalist wars between two capitalist states and wars of intervention against socialist world. Smart capitalists, vainly seeking escape from inner conflicts of capitalism, incline toward the latter.

(d) Intervention against USSR, while it would be disastrous to those who understood it, would cause renewed delay in progress of Soviet socialism and must therefore be forestalled at all costs.

(e) Conflicts between capitalist states, though likewise fraught with danger for USSR, nevertheless hold out great possibilities for advancement of socialist cause, particularly if USSR remains militarily powerful, ideologically monolithic and faithful to its present brilliant leadership. . . .

PART 2: BACKGROUND OF OUTLOOK

At bottom of Kremlin's neurotic view of world affairs is traditional and instinctive Russian sense of insecurity. Originally, this was insecurity of a peaceful agricultural people trying to live on vast exposed plain in neighborhood of fierce nomadic peoples. To this was added, as Russia came into contact with economically advanced West, fear of more competent, more powerful, more highly organized societies in that area. But this latter type of insecurity was one which afflicted Russian

rulers rather than Russian people; for Russian rulers have invariably sensed that their rule was relatively archaic in form, fragile and artificial in its psychological foundations, unable to stand comparison or contact with political systems of Western countries. For this reason they have always feared foreign penetration, feared direct contact between Western world and their own, feared what would happen if Russians learned truth about world without or if foreigners learned truth about world within. And they have learned to seek security only in patient but deadly struggle for total destruction of rival power, never in compacts and compromises with it.

It was no coincidence that Marxism, which had smouldered ineffectively for half a century in Western Europe, caught hold and blazed for the first time in Russia. Only in this land which had never known a friendly neighbor or indeed any tolerant equilibrium of separate powers, either internal or international, could a doctrine thrive which viewed economic conflicts of society as insoluble by peaceful means. After establishment of Bolshevist regime, Marxist dogma, rendered even more truculent and intolerant by Lenin's interpretation, became a perfect vehicle for sense of insecurity with which Bolsheviks, even more than previous Russian rulers, were afflicted. In this dogma, with its basic altruism of purpose, they found justification for their instinctive fear of outside world, for the dictatorship without which they did not know how to rule, for cruelties they did not dare not to inflict, for sacrifices they felt bound to demand. In the name of Marxism they sacrificed every single ethical value in their methods and tactics. Today they cannot dispense with it. It is fig leaf of their moral and intellectual respectability. Without it they would stand before history, at best, as only the last of that long succession of cruel and wasteful Russian rulers who have relentlessly forced country on to ever new heights of military power in order to guarantee external security of their internally weak regimes. . . . Thus Soviet leaders are driven [by] necessities of their own past and present position to put forward a dogma which [apparent omission] outside world as evil, hostile and menacing, but as bearing within itself germs of creeping disease and destined to be wracked with growing internal convulsions until it is given final coup de grace by rising power of socialism and yields to new and better world. . . .

PART 3: PROJECTION OF SOVIET OUTLOOK IN PRACTICAL POLICY ON OFFICIAL LEVEL

We have now seen nature and background of Soviet program. What may we expect by way of its practical implementation? . . .

On official plane we must look for following:

(a) Internal policy devoted to increasing in every way strength and prestige of Soviet state: intensive military-industrialization; maximum development of armed forces; great displays to impress outsiders; continued secretiveness about internal matters, designed to conceal weaknesses and to keep opponents in the dark.

(b) Wherever it is considered timely and promising, efforts will be made to advance official limits of Soviet power. . . .

(c) Russians will participate officially in international organizations where they see opportunity of extending Soviet power or of inhibiting or diluting power of others. . . .

(d) Toward colonial areas and backward or dependent peoples, Soviet policy . . . will be directed toward weakening of power and influence and contacts of advanced Western nations, on theory that insofar as this policy is successful, there will be created a vacuum which will favor Communist-Soviet penetration. . . .

(e) Russians will strive energetically to develop Soviet representation in, and official ties with, countries in which they sense strong possibilities of opposition to Western centers of power. This applies to such widely separated points as Germany, Argentina, Middle Eastern countries, etc.

(f) In international economic matters, Soviet policy will really be dominated by pursuit of autarchy[1] for Soviet Union and Soviet-dominated adjacent areas taken together. . . .

PART 4: FOLLOWING MAY BE SAID AS TO WHAT WE MAY EXPECT BY WAY OF IMPLEMENTATION OF BASIC SOVIET POLICIES ON UNOFFICIAL, OR SUBTERRANEAN PLANE. . . .

(a) To undermine general political and strategic potential of major Western Powers. Efforts will be made in such countries to disrupt national self-confidence, to hamstring measures of national defense, to increase social and industrial unrest, to stimulate all forms of disunity. All persons with grievances, whether economic or racial, will be urged to seek redress not in mediation and compromise, but in defiant, violent struggle for destruction of other elements of society. Here poor will be set against rich, black against white, young against old, newcomers against established residents, etc. . . .

(b) Where individual governments stand in path of Soviet purposes pressure will be brought for their removal from office. . . .

(d) In foreign countries Communists will, as a rule, work toward destruction of all forms of personal independence — economic, political or moral. Their system can handle only individuals who have been brought into complete dependence on higher power. Thus, persons who are financially independent — such as individual businessmen, estate owners, successful farmers, artisans — and all those who exercise local leadership or have local prestige — such as popular local clergymen or political figures — are anathema.

(e) Everything possible will be done to set major Western Powers against each other. Anti-British talk will be plugged among Americans,

---

[1]Economic self-sufficiency as a national policy; getting along without goods from other countries.

anti-American talk among British. Continentals, including Germans, will be taught to abhor both Anglo-Saxon powers.[2] . . .

PART 5: [PRACTICAL DEDUCTIONS FROM STANDPOINT OF US POLICY]

In summary, we have here a political force committed fanatically to the belief that with US there can be no permanent modus vivendi,[3] that it is desirable and necessary that the internal harmony of our society be disrupted, our traditional way of life be destroyed, the international authority of our state be broken, if Soviet power is to be secure. . . . In addition, it has an elaborate and far-flung apparatus for exertion of its influence in other countries, an apparatus of amazing flexibility and versatility, managed by people whose experience and skill in underground methods are presumably without parallel in history. Finally, it is seemingly inaccessible to considerations of reality in its basic reactions. . . . This is admittedly not a pleasant picture. Problem of how to cope with this force [is] undoubtedly greatest task our diplomacy has ever faced and probably greatest it will ever have to face. . . . But I would like to record my conviction that problem is within our power to solve — and that without recourse to any general military conflict. And in support of this conviction there are certain observations of a more encouraging nature I should like to make:

(1) Soviet power, unlike that of Hitlerite Germany, is neither schematic[4] nor adventuristic. It does not work by fixed plans. It does not take unnecessary risks. Impervious to logic of reason, and it is highly sensitive to logic of force. For this reason it can easily withdraw — and usually does — when strong resistance is encountered at any point. Thus, if the adversary has sufficient force and makes clear his readiness to use it, he rarely

has to do so. If situations are properly handled there need be no prestige-engaging showdowns.

(2) Gauged against Western world as a whole, Soviets are still by far the weaker force. Thus, their success will really depend on degree of cohesion, firmness and vigor which Western world can muster. . . .

(3) Success of Soviet system, as form of internal power, is not yet finally proven. . . .

(4) All Soviet propaganda beyond Soviet security sphere is basically negative and destructive. It should therefore be relatively easy to combat it by any intelligent and really constructive program.

For these reasons I think we may approach calmly and with good heart problem of how to deal with Russia. As to how this approach should be made, I only wish to advance, by way of conclusion, following comments:

(1) Our first step must be to apprehend, and recognize for what it is, the nature of the movement with which we are dealing. We must study it with same courage, detachment, objectivity, and same determination not to be emotionally provoked or unseated by it, with which doctor studies unruly and unreasonable individual.

(2) We must see that our public is educated to realities of Russian situation. . . .

(3) Much depends on health and vigor of our own society. World communism is like malignant parasite which feeds only on diseased tissue. This is point at which domestic and foreign policies meet. Every courageous and incisive measure to solve internal problems of our own society, to improve self-confidence, discipline, morale and community spirit of our own people, is a diplomatic victory over Moscow worth a thousand diplomatic notes and joint communiqués. . . .

(4) We must formulate and put forward for other nations a much more positive and construc-

---

[2]England and the United States.
[3]Latin for "manner of living"; hence, a temporary agreement in a dispute pending final settlement.

[4]In this context, having a definite outline or plan to follow.

tive picture of sort of world we would like to see than we have put forward in past. . . .

(5) Finally we must have courage and self-confidence to cling to our own methods and conceptions of human society. After all, the greatest danger that can befall us in coping with this problem of Soviet communism is that we shall allow ourselves to become like those with whom we are coping.

Cold War Origins: A Soviet Perspective
▼▼▼

109 ▼ *Nikolai Novikov,*
TELEGRAM, SEPTEMBER 27, 1946

According to some scholars there is a Soviet version of the Long Telegram: a cable sent to Moscow from Washington in September 1946 by the recently appointed Soviet ambassador to the United States, Nikolai Novikov. Trained in the early 1930s at Leningrad State University in Middle Eastern economics and languages, Novikov abandoned plans for an academic career when he was drafted into the foreign service because of his knowledge of the Middle East. In 1941 he was named ambassador to Egypt, where he also served as liaison to the Yugoslav and Greek governments in exile, both of which were located in Cairo. Early in 1945 he was named deputy chief of the Soviet mission in Washington, D.C.; in April he became Soviet ambassador to the United States. He resigned from the foreign service in 1947 and returned to the Soviet Union, where he lived in obscurity. He published a memoir of his foreign service career in 1989.

We have little information about the background of Novikov's telegram, which was unknown to scholars until a Soviet official revealed it to a group of Soviet and U.S. historians attending a meeting on the origins of the Cold War in Washington in 1990. According to Novikov's memoir, while he and the Soviet foreign minister Vyacheslav Molotov (1890–1986) were attending the Paris foreign ministers' conference in August 1946, Molotov requested that he write an analysis of U.S. foreign policy goals. Also according to Novikov, Molotov examined an early outline of the document in Paris and made several suggestions about improvements. This information lends credence to the theory that Molotov, who favored a hard line against the West, wanted Novikov's report to present a dark and perhaps exaggerated picture of U.S. foreign policy goals to strengthen his hand against rivals who favored caution and compromise.

We know that Molotov read Novikov's completed cable. The passages underlined in the following excerpt were passages that Molotov himself underlined on the original document. What happened next is unclear. Did Molotov show the telegram to Stalin and other high-ranking officials? Did Novikov's telegram contribute to the atmosphere of confrontation building in 1946? The answer to both questions is probably yes, but until historians gain access to Soviet archives, no one will know exactly how important Novikov's telegram was in the Cold War's murky beginnings.

QUESTIONS FOR ANALYSIS

1. What specific evidence does Novikov cite to prove his assertion that the goal of U.S. foreign policy is world domination?
2. In his view, how does the United States propose to achieve its goal?
3. What is his evaluation of U.S. strengths and weaknesses?
4. How does he view the prospects of Anglo-American cooperation? Is this something the Soviet Union should fear? Why or why not?
5. How does Novikov's analysis compare with Kennan's description in the *Long Telegram* (source 108) of the "Postwar Soviet Outlook, as Put Forward by Official Propaganda Machine"?
6. What insights does your answer to question 5 provide about the reasons Novikov's memorandum was written?

The enormous relative weight of the USSR in international affairs in general and in the European countries in particular, the independence of its foreign policy, and the economic and political assistance that it provides to neighboring countries, both allies and former enemies, has led to the growth of the political influence of the Soviet Union in these countries and to the further strengthening of democratic tendencies in them.

Such a situation in Eastern and Southeastern Europe cannot help but be regarded by the American imperialists as an obstacle in the path of the expansionist policy of the United States. . . .

One of the stages in the achievement of dominance over the world by the United States is its understanding with England concerning the partial division of the world on the basis of mutual concessions. The basic lines of the secret agreement between the United States and England regarding the division of the world consist, as shown by facts, in their agreement on the inclusion of Japan and China in the sphere of influence of the United States in the Far East, while the United States, for its part, has agreed not to hinder England either in resolving the Indian problem or in strengthening its influence in Siam and Indonesia. . . .

The American policy in China is striving for the complete economic and political submission of China to the control of American monopolistic capital. Following this policy, the American gov-

ernment does not shrink even from interference in the internal affairs of China. At the present time in China, there are more than 50,000 American soldiers. . . .

China is gradually being transformed into a bridgehead for the American armed forces. American air bases are located all over its territory. . . . The measures carried out in northern China by the American army show that it intends to stay there for a long time.

In Japan, despite the presence there of only a small contingent of American troops, control is in the hands of the Americans. . . .

Measures taken by the American occupational authorities in the area of domestic policy and intended to support reactionary classes and groups, which the United States plans to use in the struggle against the Soviet Union, also meet with a sympathetic attitude on the part of England. . . .

▾ ▾ ▾

Obvious indications of the U.S. effort to establish world dominance are also to be found in the increase in military potential in peacetime and in the establishment of a large number of naval and air bases both in the United States and beyond its borders.

In the summer of 1946, for the first time in the history of the country, Congress passed a law on the establishment of a peacetime army, not on a volunteer basis but on the basis of universal military service. The size of the army, which is supposed to amount to about one million persons as of July 1, 1947, was also increased significantly. The size of the navy at the conclusion of the war decreased quite insignificantly in comparison with war-time. At the present time, the American navy occupies first place in the world, leaving England's navy far behind, to say nothing of those of other countries.

Expenditures on the army and navy have risen colossally, amounting to 13 billion dollars according to the budget for 1946–47 (about 40 percent of the total budget of 36 billion dollars). This is more than ten times greater than corresponding expenditures in the budget for 1938, which did not amount to even one billion dollars. . . .

The establishment of American bases on islands that are often 10,000 to 12,000 kilometers from the territory of the United States and are on the other side of the Atlantic and Pacific oceans clearly indicates the offensive nature of the strategic concepts of the commands of the U.S. army and navy. This interpretation is also confirmed by the fact that the American navy is intensively studying the naval approaches to the boundaries of Europe. For this purpose, American naval vessels in the course of 1946 visited the ports of Norway, Denmark, Sweden, Turkey, and Greece. In addition, the American navy is constantly operating in the Mediterranean Sea.

All of these facts show clearly that a decisive role in the realization of plans for world dominance by the United States is played by its armed forces.

▼ ▼ ▼

In recent years American capital has penetrated very intensively into the economy of the Near Eastern countries, in particular into the oil industry. At present there are American oil concessions in all of the Near Eastern countries that have oil deposits (Iraq, Bahrain, Kuwait, Egypt,

and Saudi Arabia). American capital, which made its first appearance in the oil industry of the Near East only in 1927, now controls about 42 percent of all proven reserves in the Near East, excluding Iran. . . .

In expanding in the Near East, American capital has English capital as its greatest and most stubborn competitor. The fierce competition between them is the chief factor preventing England and the United States from reaching an understanding on the division of spheres of influence in the Near East, a division that can occur only at the expense of direct British interests in this region. . . .

The irregular nature of relations between England and the United States in the Near East is manifested in part also in the great activity of the American naval fleet in the eastern part of the Mediterranean Sea. Such activity cannot help but be in conflict with the basic interests of the British Empire. These actions on the part of the U.S. fleet undoubtedly are also linked with American oil and other economic interests in the Near East. . . .

. . . The strengthening of U.S. positions in the Near East and the establishment of conditions for basing the American navy at one or more points on the Mediterranean Sea will therefore signify the emergence of a new threat to the security of the southern regions of the Soviet Union.

The ruling circles of the United States obviously have a sympathetic attitude toward the idea of a military alliance with England, but at the present time the matter has not yet culminated in an official alliance. Churchill's speech in Fulton[1] calling for the conclusion of an Anglo-American military alliance for the purpose of establishing joint domination over the world was therefore not supported officially by Truman or Byrnes,[2] although Truman by his presence [during the "Iron Curtain" speech] did indirectly sanction Churchill's appeal.

---

[1]A reference to Winston Churchill's Iron Curtain Speech, delivered at Westminster College in Fulton, Missouri, in March 1946.

[2]James Byrnes (1879–1972), secretary of state from 1945 to 1947.

Even if the United States does not go so far as to conclude a military alliance with England just now, in practice they still maintain very close contact on military questions. The combined Anglo-American headquarters in Washington continues to exist, despite the fact that over a year has passed since the end of the war. . . .

▼▼▼

One of the most important elements in the general policy of the United States, which is directed toward limiting the international role of the USSR in the postwar world, is the <u>policy with regard to Germany.</u> In Germany, the United States is taking measures to strengthen reactionary forces for the purpose of opposing democratic reconstruction. Furthermore, it displays special insistence on accompanying this policy with completely inadequate measures for the demilitarization of Germany. . . . Instead, the United States is considering the possibility <u>of terminating the Allied occupation</u> of German territory before the main tasks of the occupation — the demilitarization and democratization of Germany — have been implemented. This would create the prerequisites for the revival of an imperialist Germany, which the United States plans to use in a future war on its side. One cannot help seeing that such a policy has a clearly outlined <u>anti-Soviet edge</u> and constitutes a serious danger to the cause of peace.

The numerous and extremely hostile statements by American government, political, and military figures with regard to the Soviet Union and its foreign policy are very characteristic of the current relationship between the ruling circles of the United States and the USSR. These statements are echoed in an even more unrestrained tone by the overwhelming majority of the American press organs. <u>Talk about a "third</u> <u>war,"</u> meaning a war against the Soviet Union, and even a direct call for this war — with the threat of using the atomic bomb — such is the content of the statements on relations with the Soviet Union by reactionaries at public meetings and in the press. . . .

The basic goal of this anti-Soviet campaign of American "public opinion" is to exert political pressure on the Soviet Union and compel it to make concessions. Another, no less important goal of the campaign is the attempt <u>to create an atmosphere of war psychosis</u> among the masses, who are weary of war, thus making it easier for the U.S. government to carry out measures for the maintenance of high military potential. . . .

Of course, all of these measures for maintaining a high military potential are not goals in themselves. They are only intended <u>to prepare the conditions for winning world supremacy</u> in a new war, the date for which, to be sure, cannot be determined now by anyone, but which is contemplated by the most bellicose circles of American imperialism.

Careful note should be taken of the fact that the preparation by the United States for a future war is being conducted with the prospect of <u>war against the Soviet Union,</u> which in the eyes of American imperialists is the main obstacle in the path of the United States to world domination. This is indicated by facts such as the tactical training of the American army for war with the Soviet Union as the future opponent, the siting of American strategic bases in regions from which it is possible to launch strikes on Soviet territory, intensified training and strengthening of Arctic regions as close approaches to the USSR, and attempts to prepare Germany and Japan to use those countries in a war against the USSR.

Great Britain Lets Go of India
▼▼▼

110 ▼ *DEBATE IN THE HOUSE OF COMMONS, MARCH 1947*

A turning point in the dismantling of Europe's Asian and African empires took place in August 1947 when the Indian people gained independence from Great Britain and the new states of India and Pakistan were created. After the greatest imperial power released its hold on the "jewel in the crown" of its empire, nationalist leaders throughout Asia and Africa demanded equal treatment and European politicians found it more difficult to justify continued colonial rule.

British and Indian leaders had debated the timing and framework of Indian independence for decades, but World War II brought the issue to a head. Many Indians, still embittered by the meager benefits they had received for their sacrifices in World War I, showed little enthusiasm for the British cause in World War II, especially after the British viceroy announced that India was at war with Germany in September 1939 without even consulting Indian leaders. In 1942, after Japan's lightning conquest of Southeast Asia, the British government sent Sir Stafford Cripps to Delhi to offer India dominion status after the war if India would support the war against Japan. Negotiations broke down, however, leading Gandhi to launch the "Quit India" movement, his last nationwide passive resistance campaign against British rule. Anti-British feeling intensified in 1943 when a disastrous famine took between 1 million and 3 million lives, and the pro-Japanese Indian National Army was organized by Subhas Bose and declared war on Great Britain.

A shift in postwar British politics also affected India's future. The 1945 elections initiated six years of rule by the Labour Party, which had less enthusiasm for the idea of empire than the Conservatives. In the face of mounting restiveness in India, Prime Minister Clement Attlee dispatched a three-person cabinet mission to India in early 1946 charged with preserving Indian unity in the face of Hindu-Muslim enmity and arranging for India's independence as soon as possible. Although the Hindus and Muslims could not reconcile their differences, on February 20, 1947, the Labour government went ahead and announced British rule would end in India no later than June 1948.

This led to an emotional two-day debate in Parliament in which Churchill's Conservatives and some Liberals argued that independence should be delayed. The Labour Party had a strong majority, however, and in March 1947 Parliament approved its plan. At midnight on August 14–15, 1947, predominantly Hindu India and predominantly Muslim Pakistan became independent states.

The following excerpts are from the parliamentary debates of March 4 and 5, 1947. All the speakers are opposing a proposal of Sir John Anderson, a Liberal representing the Scottish universities, that Great Britain should promise independence by June 1948 but withdraw the offer and require further negotiations if a suitable Hindu-Muslim agreement could not be achieved.

QUESTIONS FOR ANALYSIS

1. What were the points of disagreement among members of Parliament about the benefits and harm of British colonial rule in India?
2. Some speakers who believed British colonialism had benefited India still supported independence. Why?
3. The critics of British rule in India supported immediate independence. What was their line of argument?
4. According to the speakers, what military and economic realities make it impractical to continue British rule in India?
5. How do the speakers view developments in India as part of broader historical trends?
6. Most of the speakers were members of the Labour Party and thus sympathetic to socialism. What examples of socialist perspectives can you find in their speeches?

MR. CLEMENT DAVIES[1] (MONTGOMERY) It is an old adage now, that "the old order changeth, yielding place to new," but there has been a more rapid change from the old to the new in our time than ever before. We have witnessed great changes in each one of the five Continents, and for many of those changes this country and its people have been directly or indirectly responsible. . . . In all the lands where the British flag flies, we have taught the peoples the rule of law and the value of justice impartially administered. We have extended knowledge, and tried to inculcate understanding and toleration.

Our declared objects were twofold — first, the betterment of the conditions of the people and the improvement of their standard of life; and, second, to teach them the ways of good administration and gradually train them to undertake responsibility so that one day we could hand over to them the full burden of their own self-government. Our teachings and our methods have had widespread effect, and we should rejoice that so many peoples in the world today are awake, and aware of their own individualities, and have a desire to express their own personalities and their traditions, and to live their own

mode of life. . . . Our association with India during two centuries has been, on the whole — with mistakes, as we will admit — an honorable one. So far as we were able we brought peace to this great sub-continent; we have introduced not only a system of law and order, but also a system of administration of justice, fair and impartial, which has won their respect. . . . We have tried to inculcate into them the feeling that although they are composed of different races, with different languages, customs, and religions, they are really part of one great people of India.

The standard of life, pathetically low as it is, has improved so that during the last 30 years there has been an increase in the population of 100 million and they now number 400 million people. We have brought to them schools, universities, and teachers, and we have not only introduced the Indians into the Civil Service but have gradually handed over to them, in the Provinces and even in the Central Government, the administration and government of their own land and their own people. . . . Then in 1946, there was the offer of complete independence, with the right again, if they so chose, of contracting in and coming back within the British Commonwealth of Nations.[2]

---

[1]A London lawyer (1884–1962) who was a Liberal member of Parliament from 1929 until the time of his death.
[2]The British Commonwealth of Nations was founded by Parliament in 1931 through the Statute of Westminster. It is a free association of nations comprised of Great Britain

and a number of its former dependencies which have chosen to maintain ties of friendship and practical cooperation. Members acknowledge the British monarch as symbolic head of their association. Since 1946 it has been known as the Commonwealth of Nations.

I agree that these offers were made subject to the condition that the Indian peoples themselves would co-operate to form a Central Government and draw up not only their own Constitution, but the method of framing it. Unfortunately, the leaders of the two main parties in India have failed to agree upon the formation of even a Constituent Assembly, and have failed, therefore, to agree upon a form of Constitution. . . .

What are the possible courses that could be pursued? . . . The first of the courses would be to restore power into our own hands so that we might not only have the responsibility but the full means of exercising that responsibility. I believe that that is not only impossible but unthinkable at this present stage. . . . Secondly, can we continue, as we do at present, to wait until an agreement is reached for the formation of a Central Government with a full Constitution, capable of acting on behalf of the whole of India? The present state of affairs there and the deterioration which has already set in — and which has worsened — have shown us that we cannot long continue on that course.

The third course is the step taken by His Majesty's Government — the declaration made by the Government that we cannot and do not intend in the slightest degree to go back upon our word, that we do not intend to damp the hopes of the Indian peoples but rather to raise them, and that we cannot possibly go on indefinitely as we have been going on during these past months; that not only shall they have the power they now really possess but after June 1948, the full responsibility for government of their own peoples in India. . . .

MR. SORENSEN[3] (LEYTON, WEST) I have considerable sympathy with the hon. and gallant Member for Ayr Burghs (Sir T. Moore),[4] because, politically, he has been dead for some time and does not know it. His ideas were extraordinarily reminiscent of 50 years ago, and I do not propose, therefore, to deal with so unpleasant and decadent a subject. When he drew attention to the service we have rendered to India — and we have undoubtedly rendered service — he overlooked the fact that India has had an existence extending for some thousands of years before the British occupation, and that during that period she managed to run schools, establish a chain of rest houses, preserve an economy, and reach a high level of civilization, when the inhabitants of these islands were in a condition of barbarism and savagery. One has only to discuss such matters with a few representative Indians to realize that they can draw up a fairly powerful indictment of the evil we have taken to India as well as the good. . . .

Whatever may have been the origin of the various problems in India, or the degree of culpability which may be attached to this or that party or person, a situation now confronts us which demands decision. . . . That is why, in my estimation, the Government are perfectly right to fix a date for the transference of power. . . . Responsibility is ultimately an Indian matter. Acute problems have existed in India for centuries, and they have not been solved under our domination. Untouchability, the appalling subjugation of women, the division of the castes, the incipient or actual conflict between Muslim and Hindu — all those and many others exist.

I do not forget what is to me the most terrible of all India's problems, the appalling poverty. It has not been solved by us, although we have had our opportunity. On the contrary, in some respects we have increased that problem, because, despite the contributions that we have made to India's welfare, we have taken a great deal of wealth from India in order that we ourselves might enjoy a relatively higher standard of life. Can it be denied that we have benefited in the past substantially by the ignorant, sweated labor

---

[3]Reginald Sorensen (1884–1971) was a clergyman who served in Parliament as a member of the Labour Party from 1929 to 1931 and from 1939 to 1954.

[4]Lieutenant-Colonel Thomas Moore (1888–1971) was a Conservative member of Parliament from 1929 to 1962. He had just spoken against the government's plan for Indian independence.

of the Indian people? We have not solved those social problems. The Indians may not solve them either. There are many problems that the Western world cannot solve, but at least, those problems are India's responsibility. Indians are more likely, because they are intimate with their own problems, to know how to find their way through those labyrinths than we, who are, to the Indian but aliens and foreigners.

Here I submit a point which surely will receive the endorsement of most hon. Members of this House. It is that even a benevolent autocracy can be no substitute for democracy and liberty. . . .

I would therefore put two points to the House tonight. Are we really asked by hon. Members on the other side to engage in a gamble, first by continuing as we are and trying to control India indefinitely, with the probability that we should not succeed and that all over India there would be rebellion, chaos, and breakdown? Secondly, are we to try to reconquer India and in doing so, to impose upon ourselves an economic burden which we could not possibly afford? How many men would be required to keep India quiet if the great majority of the Indians were determined to defy our power? I guarantee that the number would not be fewer than a million men, with all the necessary resources and munitions of war. Are we to do this at a time when we are crying out for manpower in this country, when in the mines, the textile industry, and elsewhere we want every man we can possibly secure? There are already 1,500,000 men under arms. To talk about facing the possibility of governing and policing India and keeping India under proper supervision out of our own resources is not only nonsense, but would provide the last straw that breaks the camel's back. . . .

FLIGHT-LIEUTENANT CRAWLEY[5] (BUCKINGHAM) Right hon. and hon. Members opposite, who en-

visage our staying in India, must have some idea of what type of rule we should maintain. A fact about the Indian services which they seem to ignore is that they are largely Indianized. Can they really expect the Services, Indianized to the extent of 80 or 90 percent, to carry out their policy any longer? Is it not true that in any situation that is likely to arise in India now, if the British remain without a definite date being given for withdrawal, every single Indian member of the Services, will, in the mind of all politically conscious Indians become a political collaborator? We have seen that in Palestine where Arab hates Arab and Jew hates Jew if they think they are collaborating with the British.[6] How could we get the Indianized part of the Services to carry out a policy which, in the view of all political Indians, is anti-Indian? The only conceivable way in which we could stay even for seven years in India would be by instituting a type of rule which we in this country abhor more than any other — a purely dictatorial rule based upon all the things we detest most, such as an informative police, not for an emergency measure, but for a long period and imprisonment without trial. . . .

MR. HAROLD DAVIES[7] (LEEK) . . . I believe that India is the pivot of the Pacific Ocean area. All the peoples of Asia are on the move. Can we in this House, by wishful thinking, sweep aside this natural desire for independence, freedom, and nationalism that has grown in Asia from Karachi to Peking,[8] from Karachi to Indonesia and Indo-China? That is all part of that movement, and we must recognize it. I am not a Utopian. I know that the changeover will not be easy. But there is no hon. Member opposite who has given any concrete, practical alternative to the decision, which has been made by my right hon. friends. What alternative can we give?

---

[5]Aidan Crawley (1908–1992) was an educator and journalist who served in the Royal Air Force during World War II. He was a Labour member of Parliament from 1945 to 1951.

[6]The British were attempting to extricate themselves from Palestine, which they had received as a mandate after World War I and was the scene of bitter Arab-Jewish rivalry.

[7]Harold Davies (1904–1984) was an author and educator who served in Parliament as a member of the Labour Party from 1959 to 1964.

[8]Karachi, a port city on the Arabian Sea, was soon to become Pakistan's first capital city. *Peking* is a variant spelling of *Beijing.*

This little old country is tottering and wounded as a result of the wars inherent in the capitalist system. Can we, today, carry out vast commitments from one end of the world to another? Is it not time that we said to those for whom we have spoken so long, "The time has come when you shall have your independence. That time has come; the moment is here"? I should like to recall what Macaulay[9] said:

_____
[9]Thomas B. Macaulay (1800–1859) was an English essayist, historian, and statesman.

Many politicians of our times are in the habit of laying it down as a self-evident proposition, that no people ought to be free until they are fit to use their freedom. This maxim is worthy of the fool in the old story who resolved not to go into the water until he had learned to swim.

India must learn now to build up democracy. . . .

▼▼▼

Religion and Politics in the 1970s and 1980s

During much of the twentieth century, it would not have been unreasonable to conclude that religion was a dying force among the world's peoples. The Islamic Brotherhood's popularity in the Arab world during the 1930s and 1940s and the Hindu-Muslim strife accompanying Indian independence are examples of religion's continuing vigor, but in general organized religion was on the defensive. Avowedly atheist regimes in the Soviet Union and communist China sought to obliterate religious belief and practice altogether. In the West, mainline Protestant churches experienced declining membership and attendance, and the Roman Catholic Church found it increasingly difficult to attract young men to the priesthood. In Turkey, Iran, India, and Indonesia, governments embraced aggressively secularist policies as part of campaigns to modernize their economies, educational systems, and culture.

For all these reasons, when the people of Iran in 1979 rose up against the Western-oriented, secularist government of Shah Muhammad Reza Pahlavi and instituted an Islamic republic guided by religious values and laws, many considered it an aberration or a sign of a defect within Islam. It is now clear, however, that Iran's revolution was no aberration. It was one of many examples of religion's continuing vitality and growing political importance in the recent past.

The most striking sign of religious vigor in the late twentieth century was the phenomenon of religious fundamentalism. Fundamentalists, irrespective of their confessional allegiance, share two basic beliefs. First, they reject modernism, secularism, and any intellectual or religious doctrine that challenges or belittles religious truths passed down by tradition or set forth in sacred texts. Second, they believe that these religious truths should regulate and inspire all aspects of public and private life.

In the late twentieth century, fundamentalist movements gained strength in every major faith and in states at every level of economic development. The religious right in the United States flexed its political muscle at the local, state, and national levels during the 1980s and 1990s; conservative religious Jews in Israel increased their influence on foreign and domestic policy. Fundamentalism was strongest, however, in the Middle East, North Africa, India, and Southeast Asia, where affirmation of traditional religious values provided a way to strengthen cultural identity and limit the influence of foreign, Western-inspired values.

Most fundamentalists are conservative in that they oppose social, political, and cultural changes that threaten their beliefs and practices. But deeply religious individuals also have promoted progressive social and political movements in many parts of the world. A Baptist minister, Martin Luther King Jr., with broad support from the nation's clergy, led the civil rights movement in the United States. Religious people also played important roles in the struggle against apartheid in South Africa, in various movements on behalf of nuclear disarmament, and even in the events that led to the downfall of communism in Eastern Europe in the 1980s. In Latin America during the 1970s and 1980s, while poverty worsened and much of the region groaned under harsh authoritarian rule, Catholic clergy committed themselves to serving the poor, called for social justice and democracy, and denounced dictatorship. They did so at great risk. No fewer than 850 priests, nuns, and bishops were murdered by right-wing death squads or individual assassins in the 1970s and 1980s. Their martyrdom is convincing evidence of religion's enduring power in the late twentieth century.

Latin American Catholicism and the Theology of Liberation
▼▼▼

111 ▼ *FINAL DOCUMENT OF THE THIRD GENERAL CONFERENCE OF THE LATIN AMERICAN EPISCOPATE, 1979*

When some 600 bishops gathered in Puebla, Mexico, in 1979 for the Third General Conference of the Latin American Episcopate, they sensed that the Latin American Church, with 35 percent of the world's Catholics, was at a crossroads. In the 1960s reformist and even revolutionary currents had emerged among the clergy. This was in part a response to the liberal atmosphere in the broader church after the Second Vatican Council of 1962 and in part an expression of the conviction that the Church's indifference to social injustice distorted Christ's teachings and threatened to lose the masses to Marxism or religious apathy. During the 1960s bishops spoke out in favor of land reform; young priests went into urban slums to establish clinics, schools, and self-help organizations; and Catholic intellectuals developed a new "theology of liberation," which centered the Church's mission on ministering to the poor. Their efforts culminated in decisions made at the second conference of Latin American bishops in Medellin, Colombia, in 1968, by which bishops committed the Church to the task of liberating Latin America's poor from economic and social injustice.

This leftward shift generated a counterreaction in the 1970s. Conservative bishops denounced reformers as more Marxist than Christian, and many Catholics expressed reservations about the clergy's political activism. Conservatives hoped to regain control of the Church at the third Catholic bishops' conference in Puebla in 1979. Well-known liberation theologians were excluded, and conservative bishops drafted a policy statement that, if accepted, would have endorsed capitalism and rejected the clergy's involvement in politics. Remarks by Pope John Paul II, who addressed the opening of the conference, seemed to support the progressives, however, and after two weeks of discussion, the delegates approved a generally progressive statement from which the following excerpts are drawn.

After Puebla, the Latin American Church remained divided. Churchmen in Chile and Brazil continued to speak out against military regimes, and clergy in Central America were still in the forefront of the struggle for social change. Overall, however, conservatives made gains, especially in Argentina and Colombia. This trend was supported by an increasingly cautious Pope John Paul II, who named conservatives as bishops and approved the disciplining of Leonardo Boff, the Brazilian liberation theologian, in the mid 1980s. While the Catholic Church struggled to clarify its mission, more Latin Americans abandoned religion or joined one of the many pentecostal Protestant sects spreading through the region.

QUESTIONS FOR ANALYSIS

1. What is the document's overall assessment of the economic and political state of Latin America?
2. What can be gleaned from the document about the bishops' views of the underlying causes of Latin American poverty?
3. Why, according to the Puebla statement, should Latin American Catholics find widespread poverty intolerable?
4. What statements in the document seem to confirm the view that it was a compromise between progressives and conservatives?
5. Critics of the Puebla statement contend that it was essentially worthless because it lacked concrete proposals to deal with Latin America's problems. Do you agree with such criticisms?

Viewing it in the light of faith, we see the growing gap between rich and poor as a scandal and a contradiction to Christian existence. . . . The luxury of a few becomes an insult to the wretched poverty of the vast masses. . . . This is contrary to the plan of the Creator and to the honor that is due him. In this anxiety and sorrow the Church sees a situation of social sinfulness, all the more serious because it exists in countries that call themselves Catholic and are capable of changing the situation. . . .

This situation of pervasive extreme poverty takes on very concrete faces in real life. In these faces we ought to recognize the suffering features of Christ the Lord, who questions and challenges us. They include:

• the faces of young children, struck down by poverty before they are born, their chance for self-development blocked by irreparable mental and physical deficiencies; and of the vagrant children in our cities who are so often exploited, products of poverty and the moral disorganization of the family;

- the faces of young people, who are disoriented because they cannot find their place in society, and who are frustrated, particularly in marginal rural and urban areas, by the lack of opportunity to obtain training and work;
- the faces of the indigenous peoples, and frequently of the Afro-Americans as well; living marginalized lives in inhuman situations, they can be considered the poorest of the poor;
- the faces of the peasants; as a social group, they live in exile almost everywhere on our continent, deprived of land, caught in a situation of internal and external dependence, and subjected to systems of commercialization that exploit them;
- the faces of laborers, who frequently are ill-paid and who have difficulty in organizing themselves and defending their rights;
- the faces of the underemployed and the unemployed, who are dismissed because of the harsh exigencies of economic crises, and often because of development-models that subject workers and their families to cold economic calculations;
- the faces of marginalized and overcrowded urban dwellers, whose lack of material goods is matched by the ostentatious display of wealth by other segments of society;
- the faces of old people, who are growing more numerous every day, and who are frequently marginalized in a progress-oriented society that totally disregards people not engaged in production.

We share other anxieties of our people that stem from a lack of respect for their dignity as human beings, made in the image and likeness of God, and for their inalienable rights as children of God.

. . . Our mission to bring God to human beings, and human beings to God, also entails the task of fashioning a more fraternal society here. And the unjust social situation has not failed to produce tensions within the Church itself. On the one hand they are provoked by groups that stress the "spiritual" side of the Church's mission and resent active efforts at societal improvement. On the other hand they are provoked by people who want to make the Church's mission nothing more than an effort at human betterment.

There are other novel and disturbing phenomena. We refer to the partisan political activity of priests — not as individuals, as some had acted in the past . . . , but as organized pressure groups. And we also refer to the fact that some of them are applying social analyses with strong political connotations to pastoral work.

The Church's awareness of its evangelizing mission[1] has led it in the past ten years to publish numerous pastoral documents about social justice; to create [organizations] designed to express solidarity with the afflicted, to denounce outrages, and to defend human rights, . . . and to endure the persecution and at times death of its members in witness to its prophetic mission. Much remains to be done, of course, if the Church is to display greater oneness and solidarity. Fear of Marxism keeps many from facing up to the oppressive reality of liberal capitalism. One could say that some people, faced with the danger of one clearly sinful system, forgot to denounce and combat the established reality of another equally sinful system. We must give full attention to the latter system, without overlooking the violent and atheistic historical forms of Marxism. . . .

To this are added other anxieties that stem from abuses of power, which are typical of regimes based on force. There are the anxieties based on systematic or selective repression; it is accompanied by accusations, violations of privacy, improper pressures, tortures, and exiles. There are the anxieties produced in many families by the disappearance of their loved ones, about

---

[1]*Evangelization* means preaching Christianity with the view of bringing about conversion or rededication to the faith.

whom they cannot get any news. There is the total insecurity bound up with arrest and detention without judicial consent. There are the anxieties felt in the face of a system of justice that has been suborned or cowed. As the Supreme Pontiffs point out, the Church . . . must raise its voice to denounce and condemn these situations, particularly when the responsible officials or rulers call themselves Christians.

Then there are the anxieties raised by guerrilla violence, by terrorism, and by the kidnappings carried out by various brands of extremists. They, too, pose a threat to life together in society. . . .

The free-market economy, in its most rigid expression, is still the prevailing system on our continent. Legitimated by liberal ideologies, it has increased the gap between the rich and the poor by giving priority to capital over labor, economics over the social realm. Small groups in our nations, who are often tied in with foreign interests, have taken advantage of the opportunities provided by these older forms of the free market to profit for themselves while the interests of the vast majority of the people suffer.

Marxist ideologies have also spread among workers, students, teachers, and others, promising greater social justice. In practice their strategies have sacrificed many Christian, and hence human, values; or else they have fallen prey to utopian forms of unrealism. Finding their inspiration in policies that use force as a basic tool, they have only intensified the spiral of violence.

Islamic Law in the Modern World
▼▼▼

112 ▼ *Ruhollah Khomeini, ISLAMIC GOVERNMENT*

Ruhollah Khomeini, whose name is synonymous with Islamic fundamentalism and Iran's Islamic Revolution of 1979, was born in 1902 in Khumayn, an Iranian village some sixty miles southwest of Teheran. Following the example of his father and grandfather, he became a religious scholar, and by the late 1930s was director of the prestigious school of Islamic studies in Qum, a pilgrimage site and the spiritual center for Iran's Shia Muslims. In the late 1950s he became a vocal critic of Iran's reigning monarch, Shah Muhammad Reza Pahlavi, attacking him for his pro-U.S. policies, dictatorial rule, and efforts to diminish Islam's role in Iranian life. In 1963, the arrest and imprisonment of Khomeini led to nationwide antigovernment demonstrations and rioting, which were suppressed by army troops at the cost of thousands of lives. Released from prison and sent into exile in 1964, Khomeini continued to denounce the shah, whose secularism, heavy-handed rule, corrupt government, and ill-conceived economic policies continued to cause widespread discontent. In January 1978 rioting again broke out in Qum, this time sparked by the publication of articles in the state-controlled press accusing Khomeini of treason. In the following months millions of Iranians, spurred on by Khomeini and other religious leaders, took to the streets chanting "death to the shah." In early 1979 events moved quickly. In January the shah left the country; in February Khomeini returned from exile; and in March a national referendum approved the establishment of the Islamic Republic of Iran.

Iran's new government was a republic in name only. Although it had an elected parliament and president, it was dominated by Khomeini and a small circle of like-minded Islamic clerics. During the 1980s they purged the shah's supporters from government, suppressed political and religious opponents, instituted religious courts to enforce Islamic law, and used the army and schools as instruments of religious indoctrination. Although Khomeini had promised to address the problems of poverty and social inequality, his efforts foundered in the face of war with Iraq, inflation, and population growth at the rate of 4 percent a year. Nonetheless, by the time of his death in 1989 millions of Muslims in Iran and elsewhere venerated Khomeini as a heroic defender of their religion against the forces of secularism and imperialism, and his austere, uncompromising version of Islam had become a major force in world politics.

The following selection is an excerpt from *Islamic Government,* Khomeini's best-known work. The book was based on a series of lectures he delivered in 1970 while in exile to students at a religious school in the Iraqi city of Najaf. It is not a complete exposition of Islamic political philosophy; nor does it provide a detailed outline of what an Islamic state would be like. Khomeini's goal was to inspire his student listeners to work for the establishment of an Islamic state and to assume executive and judicial positions within it.

QUESTIONS FOR ANALYSIS

1. Whom does Khomeini identify as the enemies of Islam? What are these enemies' goals?
2. How, according to Khomeini, do the enemies of Islam distort Islamic doctrine and practice? How does he counter their arguments?
3. How does Khomeini characterize the relationship between Islam and modern science and technology?
4. What are the shortcomings of existing governments in the Islamic world according to Khomeini?
5. What benefits will accrue to society if Islamic laws are rigorously enforced?
6. What is the meaning of the term *jihad* as used by Khomieini in this treatise?
7. What similarities and differences do you see between Khomeini's ideas and those of previous Islamic reformers whose writings are included in this volume: 'Abdullah Wahhab (source 52), Usman dan Fodio (source 53), Sayyid Jamal ad-Din (source 75), The Muslim Brotherhood (source 101)?

[MISCONCEPTIONS ABOUT ISLAMIC LAW]

From the very beginning, the historical movement of Islam has had to contend with the Jews, for it was they who first established anti-Islamic propaganda. . . . Later they were joined by other groups, who were in certain respects more satanic than they. These new groups began their imperialist penetration of the Muslim countries about three hundred years ago, and they regarded it as necessary to work for the extirpation of Islam in order to attain their ultimate goals. . . .

For example, the servants of imperialism declared that Islam is not a comprehensive religion providing for every aspect of human life and has no laws or ordinances pertaining to society. It has no particular form of government. . . . It may have a few ethical principles, but it certainly has nothing to say about human life in general and the ordering of society. . . .

At a time when the West was a realm of darkness and obscurity — with its inhabitants living in a state of barbarism and America still peopled by half-savage redskins — and the two vast empires of Iran and Byzantium[1] were under the rule of tyranny, class privilege, and discrimination, and the powerful dominated all without any trace of law or popular government, God, Exalted and Almighty, by means of the Most Noble Messenger [Muhammad] (peace and blessings be upon him), sent laws that astound us with their magnitude. He instituted laws and practices for all human affairs and laid down injunctions for man extending from even before the embryo is formed until after he is placed in the tomb. . . . Islamic law is a progressive, evolving, and comprehensive system of law. All the voluminous books that have been compiled from the earliest times on different areas of law, such as judicial procedure, social transactions, penal law, retribution, international relations, regulations pertaining to peace and war, private and public law — taken together, these contain a mere sample of the laws and injunctions of Islam. There is not a single topic in human life for which Islam has not provided instruction and established a norm. . . .

The agents of imperialism sometimes write in their books and their newspapers that the legal provisions of Islam are too harsh. . . .

I am amazed at the way these people think. They kill people for possessing ten grams of heroin and say, "That is the law." . . . Inhuman laws like this are concocted in the name of a campaign against corruption, and they are not to be regarded as harsh. (I am not saying it is permissible to sell heroin, but this is not the appropriate punishment. The sale of heroin must indeed be prohibited, but the punishment must be in proportion to the crime.) When Islam, however, stipulates that the drinker of alcohol should receive eighty lashes, they consider it "too harsh." They can *execute* someone for possessing ten grams of heroin and the question of harshness does not even arise!

Many forms of corruption that have appeared in society derive from alcohol. The collisions that take place on our roads, and the murders and suicides, are very often caused by the consumption of alcohol. . . .

But when Islam wishes to prevent the consumption of alcohol . . . stipulating that the drinker should receive eighty lashes, or sexual vice, decreeing that the fornicator be given one hundred lashes (and the married man or woman be stoned), then they start wailing and lamenting: "What a harsh law that is, reflecting the harshness of the Arabs!" They are not aware that these penal provisions of Islam are intended to keep great nations from being destroyed by corruption. Sexual vice has now reached such proportions that it is destroying entire generations, corrupting our youth, and causing them to neglect all forms of work. They are all rushing to enjoy the various forms of vice that have become so freely available and so enthusiastically promoted. Why should it be regarded as harsh if Islam stipulates that an offender should be publicly flogged in order to protect the younger generation from corruption? . . .

[SCIENCE, MATERIALISM AND ISLAM]

So far, we have sketched the subversive and corrupting plan of imperialism. We must now take into consideration as well certain internal factors, notably the dazzling effect that the material progress of the imperialist countries has had on some members of our society. As the imperialist countries attained a high degree of wealth and affluence — the result both of scientific and technical progress and of their plunder of the nations of Asia and Africa — these individuals lost all self-confidence and imagined that the only way to achieve technical progress was to abandon their own laws and beliefs. When the moon land-

[1]During Muhammad's lifetime (570–632 C.E.) the region to the north of Arabia was dominated by two large empires, the Byzantine Empire, centered in Asia Minor, and the Sassanid Empire of Persia.

ings took place, for instance, they concluded that Muslims should jettison their laws! But what is the connection between going to the moon and the laws of Islam? Do they not see that countries having opposing laws and social systems compete with each other in technical and scientific progress and the conquest of space? Let them go all the way to Mars or beyond the Milky Way; they will still be deprived of true happiness, moral virtue, and spiritual advancement and be unable to solve their own social problems. For the solution of social problems and the relief of human misery require foundations in faith and morals; merely acquiring material power and wealth, conquering nature and space, have no effect in this regard. They must be supplemented by, and balanced with, the faith, the conviction, and the morality of Islam in order truly to serve humanity instead of endangering it. . . .

[THE TIMELESSNESS OF ISLAMIC LAW]

It is self-evident that the necessity for enactment of the law, which necessitated the formation of a government by the Prophet (upon whom be peace), was not confined or restricted to his time, but continues after his departure from this world. According to one of the noble verses of the Quran, the ordinances of Islam are not limited with respect to time or place; they are permanent and must be enacted until the end of time. They were not revealed merely for the time of the Prophet [Muhammad], only to be abandoned thereafter, with retribution and the penal code of Islam no longer to be enacted, or the taxes prescribed by Islam no longer collected, and the defense of the lands and people of Islam suspended. The claim that the laws of Islam may remain in abeyance or are restricted to a particular time or place is contrary to the essential credal bases of Islam. Since the enactment of laws, then, is necessary after the departure of the Prophet from this world, and indeed, will remain so until the end of time, the formation of a government and the establishment of executive and administra-

tive organs are also necessary. Without the formation of a government and the establishment of such organs to ensure that through enactment of the law, all activities of the individual take place in the framework of a just system, chaos and anarchy will prevail and social, intellectual, and moral corruption will arise. . . .

In this system of laws, all the needs of man have been met: his dealings with his neighbors, fellow citizens, and clan, as well as children and relatives; the concerns of private and marital life; regulations concerning war and peace and intercourse with other nations; penal and commercial law; and regulations pertaining to trade and agriculture. Islamic law contains provisions relating to the preliminaries of marriage and the form in which it should be contracted, and others relating to the development of the embryo in the womb and what food the parents should eat at the time of conception. It further stipulates the duties that are incumbent upon them while the infant is being suckled, and specifies how the child should be reared, and how the husband and the wife should relate to each other and to their children. Islam provides laws and instructions for all of these matters, aiming, as it does, to produce integrated and virtuous human beings. . . .

[THE FAULTS OF EXISTING GOVERNMENTS]

In order to attain the unity and freedom of the Muslim peoples, we must overthrow the oppressive governments installed by the imperialists and bring into existence an Islamic government of justice that will be in the service of the people. . . .

Through the political agents they have placed in power over the people, the imperialists have also imposed on us an unjust economic order, and thereby divided our people into two groups: oppressors and oppressed. Hundreds of millions of Muslims are hungry and deprived of all form of health care and education, while minorities comprised of the wealthy and powerful live a life of indulgence, licentiousness, and corruption, The hungry and deprived have constantly struggled to free themselves from the oppression of their plundering overlords, and their struggle continues to this day. But their way is blocked by the ruling minorities and the oppressive governmental structures they head. It is our duty to be a helper to the oppressed and an enemy of the oppressor. . . . The scholars of Islam have a duty to struggle against all attempts by the oppressors to establish a monopoly over the sources of wealth. . . . They must not allow the masses to remain hungry and deprived while plundering oppressors usurp the sources of wealth. . . .

We must end all this plundering and usurpation of wealth. The people as a whole have a responsibility in this respect, but the responsibility of the religious scholars is graver and more critical. We must take the lead over other Muslims in embarking on this sacred *jihad,*[2] this heavy undertaking; because of our rank and position, we must be in the forefront. If we do not have the power today to prevent these misdeeds from happening and to punish these embezzlers and traitors, these powerful thieves that rule over us, then we must work to gain that power. At the same time, to fulfill our minimum obligation, we must not fail to expound the truth and expose the thievery and mendacity of our rulers. When we come to power, we will not only put the country's political life, economy, and administration in order, we will also whip and chastise the thieves and the liars. . . .

Do you imagine all that bombastic propaganda being broadcast on the radio is true? Go see for yourself at first hand what state our people are living in. Not even one out of every two hundred villages has a clinic. No one is concerned about the poor and the hungry, and they do not allow the measures Islam has devised for the sake of the poor to be implemented. Islam has solved the problem of poverty and inscribed it at the very top of its program: "*Sadaqat*[3] is for the poor." Islam is aware that first, the conditions of the poor must be remedied, the conditions of the deprived must be remedied. But *they* do not allow the plans of Islam to be implemented.

Our wretched people subsist in conditions of poverty and hunger, while the taxes that the ruling class extorts from them are squandered. They buy Phantom jets[4] so that pilots from Israel and its agents can come and train in them in our country. So extensive is the influence of Israel in our country — Israel, which is in a state of war with the Muslims, so that those who support it are likewise in a state of war with the Muslims — and so great is the support the regime gives it, that Israeli soldiers come to our country for training! . . .

[A FINAL CHARGE TO HIS LISTENERS]

If you present Islam accurately and acquaint people with its world-view, doctrines, principles, ordinances, and social system, they will welcome it ardently (God knows, many people want it). I have witnessed that myself. A single word was enough once to cause a wave of enthusiasm among the people, because then, like now, they were all dissatisfied and unhappy with the state of affairs. They are living now in the shadow of the bayonet, and repression will let them say nothing. They want someone to stand up fearlessly and speak out. So, courageous sons of Islam, stand up! Address the people bravely; tell the truth about our situation to the masses in simple language; arouse them to enthusiastic activity, and turn the people in the street and the bazaar, our simplehearted workers and peasants, and our alert students into dedicated *mujahids.* The entire population will become *mujahids.* All

---

[2]*Jihad* means "to struggle, strive, or exert." A *mujahid* is a person who engages in jihad.
[3]Arabic for charity.

[4]Under the shah Iran purchased more than 200 F-4 Phantom jets, making it the second largest purchaser after Israel of these U.S.-produced planes.

segments of society are ready to struggle for the sake of freedom, independence, and the happiness of the nation, and their struggle needs religion. Give the people Islam, then, for Islam is the school of *jihad,* the religion of struggle; let them amend their characters and beliefs in accordance with Islam and transform themselves into a powerful force, so that they may overthrow the tyrannical regime imperialism has imposed on us and set up an Islamic government.

The Place of Hinduism in Modern India
▼▼▼

113 ▼ *Girilal Jain,*
EDITORIAL ON HUNDUISM AND ISLAM

India since independence has never been free of religious tensions. Even after Muslims were given their own state of Pakistan in 1947, religious pluralism characterized India's population: Today it is composed of approximately 83 percent Hindus, 11 percent Muslims, 2.6 percent Christians, slightly over 1 percent Sikhs, and smaller numbers of Jains, Parsis, and Buddhists. None of these groups has been completely satisfied with India's constitution, which states that India is a secular state with partiality toward no religious group. Many Hindus are convinced the government bends over backward to protect Muslims and Sikhs; Muslims and Sikhs, conversely, are equally certain that the government panders to Hindus. In the early 1980s religious tensions intensified as Muslims began to make converts among low-caste Hindus in the south, Sikhs agitated for an independent Punjab, and Hindus organized their own political party, the Bharatiya Janata (Indian People's Party), or BJP, whose goal was the "Hinduization" of India. Founded in 1982, the BJP increased its representation in parliament from two members in 1984 to 185 in 1996, fifty more than that of the Congress Party, which had enjoyed a parliamentary majority in all but four years since 1947.

An important spokesman for Hindu nationalism and the BJP before his death in 1993 was the journalist Girilal Jain, who was editor-in-chief of the New Delhi *Times of India* between 1978 and 1988. Born into a poor rural family in 1922 and educated at Delhi University, Jain was jailed by the British during the 1942 Quit India campaign. As a journalist he was best known for his impassioned support of Indira Gandhi, prime minister from 1966 to 1970 and 1980 to 1984. During the 1980s he was drawn to Hindu nationalism and the BJP.

The following editorials were written in 1990, when Hindu-Muslim tensions were peaking over the over the Babri mosque in the city of Ayodhya, built in the sixteenth century on the site of a Hindu temple believed to be the birthplace of the Hindu god-king Ram. Hindus demanded the destruction of the mosque, which was no longer used, so a temple in honor of Ram could be built. In December 1992, Hindus stormed the mosque and destroyed it, precipitating a government crisis and causing violence that took the lives of thousands. The government, with its commitment to religious pluralism and democracy, survived, but religious tensions remained high.

QUESTIONS FOR ANALYSIS

1. What are the reasons for Jain's disenchantment with India's government?
2. What does Jain mean when he says that the issues that concern the BJP have to do with "civilization," not religion?
3. How does Jain define the West? How does he view the West's role in Indian history?
4. Why, according to Jain, is the controversy over the Ayodhya mosque so significant for India's future?
5. In Jain's viewpoint, why have the Muslims been satisfied to go along with the secularist policies of the Indian state?
6. What is Jain's vision of India's future?

A specter haunts dominant sections of India's political and intellectual elites — the specter of a growing Hindu self-awareness and self-assertion. Till recently these elites had used the bogey of Hindu "communalism"[1] and revivalism as a convenient device to keep themselves in power and to "legitimize" their slavish imitation of the West. Unfortunately for them, the ghost has now materialized.

Millions of Hindus have stood up. It will not be easy to trick them back into acquiescing in an order which has been characterized not so much by its "appeasement of Muslims" as by its alienness, rootlessness and contempt for the land's unique cultural past. Secularism, a euphemism for irreligion and repudiation of the Hindu ethos, and socialism, a euphemism for denigration and humiliation of the business community to the benefit of ever expanding rapacious bureaucracy, . . . have been major planks of this order. Both have lost much of their old glitter and, therefore, capacity to dazzle and mislead. . . .

The Hindu fight is not at all with Muslims; the fight is between Hindus anxious to renew themselves in the spirit of their civilization, and the state, Indian in name and not in spirit and the political and intellectual class trapped in the debris the British managed to bury us under be-fore they left. The proponents of the Western ideology are using Muslims as auxiliaries and it is a pity Muslim "leaders" are allowing themselves to be so used. . . .

Secularist-versus-Hindu-Rashtra[2] controversy is, of course, not new. In fact, it has been with us since the twenties when some of our forebears began to search for a definition of nationalism which could transcend at once the Hindu-Muslim divide and the aggregationist approach whereby India was regarded as a Hindu-Muslim-Sikh-Christian land. But it has acquired an intensity it has not had since partition. . . .

India, to put the matter brusquely, has been a battleground between two civilizations (Hindu and Islamic) for well over a thousand years, and three (Hindu, Muslim and Western) for over two hundred years. None of them has ever won a decisive enough and durable enough victory to oblige the other two to assimilate themselves fully into it. So the battle continues. This stalemate lies at the root of the crisis of identity the intelligentsia has faced since the beginning of the freedom movement in the last quarter of the nineteenth century. . . .

The more resilient and upwardly mobile section of the intelligentsia must, by definition, seek to come to terms with the ruling power and

---

[1]*Communalism* is a system in which rival minority groups are devoted to their own interests rather than those of the whole society; in the context of Indian politics, the term refers to loyalties of religious communities.

[2]*Rashtra* is Hindi for state, or polity.

its mores, and the less successful part of it to look for its roots and seek comfort in its cultural past. This was so during the Muslim period; this was the case during the British Raj;[3] and this rule has not ceased to operate since independence.

Thus in the medieval period of our history there grew up a class of Hindus in and around centers of Muslim power who took to the Persian-Arabic culture and ways of the rulers; similarly under the more securely founded and far better organized and managed Raj there arose a vast number of Hindus who took to the English language, Western ideas, ideals, dress and eating habits; . . . they, their progeny and other recruits to their class have continued to dominate independent India.

They are the self-proclaimed secularists who have sought, and continue to seek, to remake India in the Western image. The image has, of course, been an eclectic one; if they have stuck to the institutional framework inherited from the British, they have been more than willing to take up not only the Soviet model of economic development,[4] but also the Soviet theories on a variety of issues such as the nationalities problem and the nature of imperialism and neo-colonialism.

Behind them has stood, and continues to stand, the awesome intellectual might of the West, which may or may not be anti-India, depending on the exigencies of its interests, but which has to be antipathetic to Hinduism. . . .

Some secularists may be genuinely pro-Muslim. . . . because they find high Islamic culture and the ornate Urdu language attractive. But, by and large, that is not the motivating force in their lives. They are driven, above all, by the fear of what they call regression into their own past which they hate and dread. Most of the exponents of this viewpoint have come and con-

tinue to come understandably from the Left, understandably because no other group of Indians can possibly be so alienated from the country's cultural past as the followers of Lenin, Stalin and Mao, who have spared little effort to turn their own countries into cultural wastelands. . . .

The state in independent India has, it is true, sought, broadly speaking, to be neutral in the matter of religion. But this is a surface view of the reality. The Indian state has been far from neutral in civilizational terms. It has been an agency, and a powerful agency, for the spread of Western values and mores. It has willfully sought to replicate Western institutions, the Soviet Union too being essentially part of Western civilization. It could not be otherwise in view of the orientation and aspirations of the dominant elite of which Nehru[5] remains the guiding spirit.

Muslims have found such a state acceptable principally on three counts. First, it has agreed to leave them alone in respect of their personal law (the Sharia). . . . Secondly, it has allowed them to expand their traditional . . . educational system in madrasahs[6] attached to mosques. Above all, it has helped them avoid the necessity to come to terms with Hindu civilization in a predominantly Hindu India. This last count is the crux of the matter. . . .

In the past up to the sixteenth century, great temples have been built in our country by rulers to mark the rise of a new dynasty or to mark a triumph. . . . In the present case, the proposal to build the Rama temple[7] has also to help produce an "army" which can in the first instance achieve the victory the construction can proclaim.

The raising of such an "army" in our democracy, however flawed, involves not only a body of disciplined cadres, which is available in the shape of the RSS,[8] a political organization, which too is

---

[3]*Raj* is Hindi for reign or rule; often used to refer to the British colonial administration.

[4]In 1951 the government adopted a series of five-year plans for the nation's economic development in imitation of the Five-Year Plans initiated by Stalin in 1928. The plans featured central planning and state ownership of major enterprises.

[5]Jawaharlal Nehru (1889–1964), India's first prime minister, was a major target of Jain because of his commitment to socialism and secularism.

[6]Madrasahs were advanced schools of learning devoted to Islamic studies.

[7]This refers to the controversy about the Babri mosque in Ayodhya; see source introduction.

[8]RSS stands for Rashtriya Swayamsevak Sangh, a militant Hindu organization founded in 1925 and dedicated to the strengthening of Hindu culture.

available in the Bharatiya Janata Party, but also an aroused citizenry. . . . The Vishwa Hindu Parishad[9] and its allies have fullfilled this need in a manner which is truly spectacular.

The BJP-VHP-RSS leaders have rendered the country another great service. They have brought Hindu interests, if not the Hindu ethos, into the public domain where they legitimately belong. . . .

The Nehru order is as much in the throes of death as its progenitor, the Marxist-Leninist-Stalinist order. A new order is waiting to be conceived and born. It needs a mother as well as a mid-wife.

---

[9]The Vishwa Hindu Parishad (VHP), or World Hindu Society, was founded in 1964. It is dedicated to demolishing mosques built on Hindu holy sites.

▼▼▼

Third World Women between Tradition and Change

During the twentieth century, political leaders of industrialized nations, revolutionaries such as Lenin and Mao, and nationalist heroes as different as Ataturk and Gandhi all supported the ideal of women's equality with men. The United Nations Charter of 1945 commits the organization to the same ideal, and the UN Universal Declaration of Human Rights of 1948 reaffirms the goal of ending all forms of gender-based discrimination. Beginning in the 1960s powerful feminist movements with agendas ranging from equal educational access to legalized abortion took root in the Western industrialized nations and to a lesser degree in Asia, Latin America, and Africa.

Despite this broad support for gender equality, progress for women worldwide was uneven in the 1970s and 1980s. In developed industrial societies, women undoubtedly made great strides. Large numbers of women entered professions such as law, medicine, and university teaching; contraception and abortions were legalized in most nations; laws forbidding gender-based discrimination were passed. Nonetheless, even in developed countries women still earned less than men for doing the same job, were underrepresented in managerial positions, and played a less significant role in politics than did men. Furthermore, movements for gender equality met strong opposition from individuals and groups who were convinced that women's liberation would threaten the family, undermine morality, and leave women unhappy and unfulfilled.

In less economically developed parts of the world, attainment of gender equality faced even more obstacles. Feminist movements were hindered by the small pool of educated women and by the gap between middle-class, urban women and the millions of women in urban slums or rural villages whose lives were a daily struggle against poverty. Religious fundamentalists in the Islamic world and elsewhere also sought to keep women in traditional roles. Even in China and India, both of which adopted strong antidiscrimination laws, it proved difficult to modify, let alone eradicate, centuries-old educational patterns, work stereotypes, marriage customs, and attitudes. More so than in almost any other area of modern life, tradition has held its own against those movements and ideologies that have sought to liberate Third World women from the burdens of patriarchy and inequality.

An African Perspective on Female Circumcision
▼▼▼

114 ▼ *Association of African Women for Research and Development, A STATEMENT ON GENITAL MUTILATION*

Female circumcision is a general term describing a variety of ritual procedures ranging from the drawing of blood, to clitoridectomy (the removal of the clitoris), to infibulation (the removal of the clitoris, the labia minora, and most of the labia majora, the remaining sides of which are joined together to leave a small opening). The operation, which in different societies takes place anytime from shortly after birth to the onset of puberty, is usually performed by midwives or village women without benefit of anesthesia or antibiotics. No accurate statistics on the prevalence of the practice exist. It is most common in sub-Saharan Africa, especially in the Sudan region, but it is also practiced in New Guinea, Australia, Malaysia, Brazil, Mexico, Peru, India, Egypt, and the southern and eastern parts of the Arabian Peninsula. Presumably instituted to encourage chastity by dulling a woman's sexual desire, the practice has come under harsh criticism both from within the societies in which it exists and from outsiders, especially from the West. Efforts to suppress the practice have had, however, little effect among peoples who consider the custom part of their ethnic and religious heritage and a necessary rite of passage into womanhood.

Denunciations of female circumcision by Westerners and Western-inspired campaigns to end the practice have frequently backfired, especially in Africa, where the custom is most deeply rooted. The following statement, issued in 1980 by the Association of African Women for Research and Development (AAWORD), which was founded in 1977 in Dakar, Senegal, reveals that even Africans who oppose the practice resent Western interference.

QUESTIONS FOR ANALYSIS

1. What is the basis of the authors' assertion that critics of female circumcision are guilty of "latent racism"?
2. How have Western criticisms of female circumcision hindered the efforts of African critics to limit the practice?
3. In the view of the authors, what would be an appropriate Western approach to the issue of female circumcision?
4. How might an ardent Western critic of female circumcision in Africa counter the arguments contained in the AAWORD statement?

In the last few years, Western public opinion has been shocked to find out that in the middle of the 20th century thousands of women and children have been "savagely mutilated" because of "barbarous customs from another age." The good conscience of Western society has once again been shaken. Something must be done to help these people, to show public disapproval of such acts.

There have been press conferences, documentary films, headlines in the newspapers, information days, open letters, action groups — all this to mobilize public opinion and put pressure on governments of the countries where genital mutilation is still practiced. . . .

. . . In trying to reach their own public, the new crusaders have fallen back on sensationalism, and have become insensitive to the dignity of the very women they want to "save." They are totally unconscious of the latent racism which such a campaign evokes in countries where ethnocentric prejudice is so deep-rooted. And in their conviction that this is a "just cause," they have forgotten that these women from a different race and a different culture are also *human beings,* and that solidarity can only exist alongside self-affirmation and mutual respect.

This campaign has aroused three kinds of reaction in Africa:

1. the highly conservative, which stresses the right of cultural difference and the defence of traditional values and practices whose supposed aim is to protect and elevate women; this view denies Westerners the right to interfere in problems related to culture;
2. which, while condemning genital mutilation for health reasons, considers it premature to open the issue to public debate;
3. which concentrates on the aggressive nature of the campaign and considers that the fanaticism of the new crusaders only serves to draw attention away from the fundamental problems of the economic exploitation and oppression of developing countries, which contribute to the continuation of such practices.

Although all these reactions rightly criticize the campaign against genital mutilation as imperialist and paternalist, they remain passive and defensive. As is the case with many other issues, we refuse here to confront our cultural heritage and to criticize it constructively. We seem to prefer to draw a veil of modesty over certain traditional practices, whatever the consequences may be. However, it is time that Africans realized they must take a position on all problems which concern their society, and to take steps to end any practice which debases human beings.

AAWORD, whose aim is to carry out research which leads to the liberation of African people and women in particular, *firmly condemns* genital mutilation and all other practices — traditional or modern — which oppress women and justify exploiting them economically or socially, as a serious violation of the fundamental rights of women. . . .

However, as far as AAWORD is concerned, the fight against genital mutilation, although necessary, should not take on such proportions that the wood cannot be seen for the trees. Young girls and women who are mutilated in Africa are usually among those who cannot even satisfy their basic needs and who have to struggle daily for survival. This is due to the exploitation of developing countries, manifested especially through the impoverishment of the poorest social classes. In the context of the present world economic crisis, tradition, with all of its constraints, becomes more than ever a form of security for the peoples of the Third World, and especially for the "wretched of the earth." For these people, the modern world, which is primarily Western and bourgeois, can only represent aggression at all levels — political, economic, social and cultural. It is unable to propose viable alternatives for them.

Moreover, to fight against genital mutilation without placing it in the context of ignorance, obscurantism, exploitation, poverty, etc., without questioning the structures and social relations which perpetuate this situation, is like "refusing to see the sun in the middle of the day." This, however, is precisely the approach taken by many Westerners, and is highly suspect, especially since Westerners necessarily profit from the exploitation of the peoples and women of Africa, whether directly or indirectly.

Feminists from developed countries — at least those who are sincerely concerned about this situation rather than those who use it only for their personal prestige — should understand this other aspect of the problem. They must accept that it is a problem for *African women,* and that no change is possible without the conscious participation of African women. They must avoid ill-timed inter-ference, maternalism, ethnocentrism and misuse of power. These are attitudes which can only widen the gap between the Western feminist movement and that of the Third World. . . .

On the question of such traditional practices as genital mutilation, African women must no longer equivocate or react only to Western interference. They must speak out in favour of the total eradication of all these practices, and they must lead information and education campaigns to this end within their own countries and on a continental level.

The Impact of the Indian Dowry System
▼▼▼

115 ▼ EDITORIAL AGAINST DOWRY

Although some improvement in the status of Hindu women took place under British rule, major steps toward gender equality were taken only after Indian independence in 1947. Women received the right to vote, hold political office, own property, and divorce their husbands; in addition, the government outlawed child marriage and polygamy, and eased restrictions against intercaste marriages. In 1961, the government also outlawed dowries, the gifts of property a new bride's family was expected to make to the husband or the husband's family. It was hoped that such a step would lessen the financial burdens of families with daughters and encourage men from higher castes to marry women from lower castes.

As the following editorial shows, however, the practice of dowries continued, often with tragic results for young married women. This anonymous editorial was originally published in 1979 in *Manushi,* an Indian magazine for women.

QUESTIONS FOR ANALYSIS

1. According to the author of this editorial, is the giving and taking of dowries the result of recent developments or of long-standing Indian traditions?
2. According to the author, why have efforts to end the practice of dowries failed?
3. What does the author see as the solution to the problem?
4. According to the author, to what degree do dowry murders fit into a general pattern of mistreatment of women in Indian society?

Most people are not even aware that the giving and taking of dowry is a legal offense. Since the Prohibition of Dowry Act was passed in 1961, the custom has flowered and flourished, invad-ing castes and communities among whom it was hitherto unknown — sprouting new forms and varieties. It is percolating downwards and becoming so widespread even among the working classes that it is no longer possible to consider it a problem of the middle class alone.

With the entire bourgeois mass media oriented towards viciously promoting the religion of mindless consumerism, demands for dowry are becoming more and more "modernized." Marriages are made and broken for such items as cars, scooters, TVs, refrigerators and washing machines, wedding receptions in five-star hotels or an air ticket plus the promise of a job for the son-in-law in a foreign country.

In India, we have a glorious heritage of systematic violence on women in the family itself, sati[1] and female infanticide being the two better-known forms. Today, we do not kill girl-babies at birth. We let them die through systematic neglect — the mortality rate among female children is 30–60% higher than among male children. Today, we do not wait till a woman is widowed before we burn her to death. We burn her in the lifetime of her husband so that he can get a new bride with a fatter dowry.

"Woman burnt to death. A case of suicide has been registered. The police are enquiring into the matter." For years, such three-line news items have appeared almost every day in the newspapers and gone unnoticed. It is only lately that dowry deaths are being given detailed coverage. It is not by accident that fuller reporting of such cases has coincided with a spurt of protest demonstrations.

We, as women, have too long been silent spectators, often willing participants in the degrading drama of matrimony — when girls are advertised, displayed, bargained over, and disposed of with the pious injunction: "Daughter, we are sending you to your husband's home. You are not to leave it till your corpse emerges from its doors." It is significant that in all the cases of dowry murders recently reported, the girls had on previous occasions left the in-laws' houses where they were being tortured and felt insecure.

Their parents had insisted on their going back and "adjusting" there.

Death may be slow in coming — a long process of killing the girl's spirit by harassment, taunts, torture. It may be only too quick — fiery and sudden. Dousing the woman with kerosene and setting her on fire seems to have become the most popular way of murdering a daughter-in-law because with police connivance it is the easiest to make out as a case of suicide or accident.

And for every one reported murder, hundreds go unreported, especially in rural areas where it is almost impossible to get redress unless one is rich and influential. . . .

Why is it that gifts have to be given with the daughter? Hindu scriptures proclaim that the girl herself is the most precious of gifts "presented" by her father to her husband. Thus the money transaction between families is bound up with the marriage transaction whereby the girl becomes a piece of transferrable property. So little is a woman worth that a man has literally to be paid to take her off her father's hands. The dramatic increase in dowry-giving in the post-independence period reflects the declining value of women in our society. Their only worth is as reproducers who provide "legitimate" heirs for their husbands' property.

Most people opposing dowry feel that the problem can be solved by giving girls an equal share in their fathers' property. This was one of the reasons why daughters were given near-equal rights in the Hindu Succession Act, 1956. And yet the law has been reduced to a farce because in most cases, daughters are pressured to, or even willingly sign away their rights in favor of their brothers. In any case, it is the woman's husband who usually controls any property she inherits. So the property transaction remains between men, women acting only as vehicles for this transaction.

This will continue to be so as long as the ma-

---

[1]Sati is the custom in which a Hindu widow is willingly cremated on the funeral pyre of her dead husband as a sign of devotion to him.

jority of women remain economically dependent on men and as long as this dependence is reinforced by our social values and institutions so that even those women who earn seldom have the right to control their own income. . . .

. . . We appeal, therefore, to all the women's organizations to undertake a broad-based united action on this issue and launch an intensive, concerted campaign instead of the isolated, sporadic protests which have so far been organized, and which can have only a short-term, limited impact.

Perhaps even more urgent is the need to begin the movement from our own homes. Are we sure that none of us who participated so vociferously in these demonstrations will take dowry from our parents or give it to our daughters in however veiled a form? That we will rather say "No" to marriage than live a life of humiliations and compromises? Do we have the courage to boycott marriages where dowry is given? Even the marriage of a brother or sister or of a dear friend? Will we socially ostracize such people, no matter how close they are to us? All the protest demonstrations will be only so much hot air unless we are prepared to create pressures against dowry beginning from our own homes.

"I Mistakenly Blamed Her"
▼▼▼

116 ▼ Wu Jinbo,
LETTER TO THE EDITOR OF CHINESE WOMEN

On taking power in 1949, the communists under Mao Zedong immediately set about implementing their long-standing commitment to ending the oppression of women in China. China's new constitution and the Marriage Law, both adopted in 1950, guaranteed women's equality with men and gave women the right to choose their own marriage partners and demand a divorce. Foot binding was outlawed, and girls were given access to schools. During the Great Leap Forward of 1958–1959 women entered the workforce in large numbers, and during the Great Cultural Revolution of 1970–1976 millions of young women were freed from parental control and encouraged to roam the countryside denouncing "bourgeois" elements in China's population. Further changes in women's status occurred after 1978 when the government rejected Maoist egalitarianism in favor of economic development. As part of its plan to raise China's standard of living, in 1979 the government adopted its "one-child" policy, which put enormous pressure on women to give birth to boys, traditionally preferred to girls, especially in rural areas. Since it was widely believed that mothers determined the gender of their children, mothers who gave birth to daughters were often abused or rejected by their husbands. Female infanticide, which had been widely practiced in traditional China but had declined in the 1950s, 1960s, and 1970s, as well as gender-based abortions, increased dramatically. These increases occurred despite government campaigns to discourage both practices and the decision to allow rural families to have two children rather than one.

As a source of tension and conflict within countless Chinese families, the "one-child" policy was a frequent topic of discussion in state-sponsored publications and unofficial magazines and newspapers. The following letter, supposedly written by Wu Jinbo, a young husband from Benxi, a steel-producing city in northeast China, appeared in the government-sponsored magazine *Zhongguo funü (Chinese Women)* in 1982. The husband, distraught over the birth of a daughter, sees the error of his ways after being enlightened by senior workers at his steel plant and by an agent from his local family planning office.

QUESTIONS FOR ANALYSIS

1. How does Wu explain his behavior after the birth of his daughter?
2. What kinds of protections did the new mother have after Wu began to abuse her?
3. What lessons does Wu's letter try to teach?
4. What does the story of Wu tell us about the nature of "ideal marriage" in the 1980s according to official doctrine?

Comrade Editor:

My name is Wu Jinbo. I am a bricklayer for the Steel and Mining Construction Company in the city of Benxi. My wife, Jing Lijie, works at the Water Company. Because I had the feudal notion of "respecting men and looking down on women," and furthermore did not understand basic biological facts, I believed it was my wife's fault that she gave birth to a daughter. I cursed her and beat her, and I even proposed divorce. Fortunately the leadership and comrades in the pertinent agencies educated me and forced me to recognize my mistake, and now I have made up with my wife.

Originally my wife and I played together as children, and as we grew older, fell in love. We cared for each other a great deal and lived very happily together. We hoped that we could have a son as soon as possible.

Because of my desire to have a son, when my wife became pregnant last February, I asked someone to consult a "sex prediction chart." In addition a child who had just learned to talk wished me luck, and I engaged in several other superstitious activities. All of these indicated that my wife would bear a son. My wife even dreamed that she gave birth to a son. So I be-

lieved that it was almost certain that we would have a son, and I was extremely happy. Every day I made her special food, and I did not let her do any work. I even went to Shenyang especially to buy 700 eggs for her to eat during the first month after delivery.

The day my wife was to give birth I waited at the hospital, and did not eat a thing, looking forward to the good news. Finally a nurse came and told me, "It's a girl." At that moment my head throbbed, and I almost fainted. Finally I reeled out of the hospital.

From the time my wife gave birth to a daughter, I felt increasingly disgusted with her. I didn't like to return home after work. Either I would stay at my unit and play poker or checkers, or I would hang out on the street. I really did not want to see mother or daughter. I was even prepared to take the eggs I had bought for my wife and sell them. As soon as the baby was a month old I made my wife do heavy tasks, and even kicked her out sometimes. Once I swore at her and she talked back. I was so furious that I took a water ladle and beat her on the head until her nose started bleeding. She couldn't stand it and went to stay at her work unit. The baby was starving and wouldn't stop crying. I grabbed a belt, went to her unit, and whipped her with the belt. She was so angry that she went to court and filed a complaint against me.

Those days were terrible. When I'd get home from work the baby would be crying, the fire in the stove would be dead, and we didn't have much to eat. Plus, every other day the court would subpoena me. I resolved to get a divorce.

I never would have imagined that the leaders of my work unit would brave a snowstorm to come visit me. They talked to me and pointed out that a husband and wife are not only partners in daily life, but also comrades in revolution. They must love each other, help each other, study together, and encourage each other to work well. They also brought a copy of the Constitution and the Marriage Law for me to study. The Constitution stipulates: "With respect to their economic, social, cultural, and family position, women are equal to men and have the same rights." "Marriage, the family, mothers, and children will receive the protection of the government." Through their education and criticism, I finally understood the true meaning of being husband and wife. In the past I had treated my wife as inferior to me. I regarded her as simply a tool to produce a son for me. When she failed to do that I hated her and beat her. This was not only immoral but also illegal.

After listening to the head of the family planning office, Mr. Ma, talk about the scientific aspects of childbirth, and seeing the educational film strips "Produce a Better Child," "Cultivating Intelligence," and "Children's Family Education," I came to realize that whether a baby is male or female actually depends largely on the father's sperm. Now I understand how ignorant it was of me to blame my wife.

To restore our relationship, I admitted my mistake to her. Every day after work I help her with housework, and share with her the job of taking care of our child. I am also willing to publicize my experience in order to help others who discriminate against daughters, and who curse and beat their wives for having borne a daughter, to come to a better understanding of the issue.

Wu Jinbo

Chapter 14

▼▼▼

The Recent Past: The Mid 1980s to the Twenty-first Century

The twentieth century's last decade had a promising start. After forty years of international tension, ideological conflict, and the threat of nuclear holocaust, the Cold War ended, and according to the U.S. president George H. W. Bush (1989–1993) a "new world order" had dawned. No one claimed to know exactly what the new order would be like. All but the most cynical, however, hoped that the end of communist totalitarianism and Cold War conflict marked the beginning of a more peaceful and promising era for humanity. Such dreams may yet be realized, but the post–Cold War era has been anything but peaceful and harmonious. Only a few years into the twenty-first century, it is painfully clear that a world without a Cold War does not mean a world without conflict, danger, fanaticism, and fear.

The final years of the 1980s and the 1990s did have their share of impressive, even inspiring, achievements. In November and December of 1989 thousands of Berliners took up sledgehammers, crowbars, and chisels to destroy the Berlin Wall, the ten-foot-high barrier dividing East and West Berlin where hundreds of people since 1961 had been shot down attempting to flee the Soviet zone. In 1994 the inauguration of Nelson Mandela, a black man, as president of South Africa definitively ended that nation's apartheid era, one of the century's cruelest manifestations of racial bigotry, and inspired hope that human beings elsewhere could resolve conflicts and end injustices. In Eastern Europe parliamentary governments replaced communist police states, and in Africa and Latin America, lands of dictators in the 1970s and 1980s, dozens of new democracies were instituted. In part because of the economic boom that encompassed much of the world between 1992 and 1998, human beings in the 1990s lived longer and educated more of their children than ever before. Worldwide population growth slowed, with the mean number of births per woman in Asia, Africa, and Latin America decreasing to half of what it had been two decades earlier. Scientific and technological advances continued. The mapping of the human genetic code and developments in computer technology and global communications reconfirmed the awesome power of human intelligence.

Other developments in the 1990s were less encouraging. Festering conflicts between Protestants and Catholics in Northern Ireland and between Palestinians and Israelis in the Middle East seemed on the verge of solution only to have painstakingly achieved compromises blasted away by renewed violence. Wars continued to be fought, and nuclear war and nuclear accidents were still possibilities. In the early 2000s, the United States, Russia, France, Great Britain, and China collectively had 30,000 nuclear weapons in their arsenals, and Israel, India, and Pakistan had an undetermined number. In 2001 the Bush administration committed billions of dollars to continue work on a "star wars" defensive shield against nuclear attack; in 2002 conflict between India and Pakistan over Kashmir raised the specter of nuclear war between these two bitter rivals; and in 2003 North Korea resumed its efforts to develop nuclear weapons, and the United States and Great Britain invaded Iraq and overthrew its dictator, Saddam Hussein, in part because of their claim that his regime was well on its way to producing nuclear warheads.

Ethnic hatreds continued. In Bosnia and Kosovo in southeastern Europe, Rwanda in central Africa, and East Timor in the East Indies, they led to mass murder and unspeakable atrocities. In Rwanda in 1994 Hutus slaughtered 800,000 Tutsis in just two months. Religious militancy became an increasingly poisonous force in many parts of the world. In Israel in 1995 Prime Minister Itzhak Shamir, who sought peace in the Middle East through compromise, was gunned down by a Jewish student convinced that God had given the Land of Israel to the Jewish people and no other. In India in 1998 the Bharatiya Janata Party (BJP), many of whose leaders preach a doctrine of unremitting hostility to India's Muslim minority, replaced the Congress as India's dominant party. In the Middle East and Islamic states across the globe, increasing numbers of Islamic radicals sought the Islamization of society, and some within their ranks went further and endorsed jihad, or holy war, against Israel and the United States, which they viewed as the archenemy of Islam and the personification of godless materialism. Jihad often meant terrorism — suicide bombings, airline hijackings, attacks on nightclubs and hotels, kidnappings, hostage taking, and most notorious, the flying of planes into the World Trade Center and the Pentagon on September 11, 2001.

Facing problems that lacked the clarity and straightforwardness of Cold War conflicts, the international community had difficulty knowing how to respond. In 1990 and 1991, when Iraq's invasion of Kuwait threatened the flow of oil to the industrialized world, the United States forged a broad coalition of allies that defeated the armies of Saddam Hussein in the first Persian Gulf War. But when faced with other crises — ethnic cleansing in Bosnia, famine and AIDS in Africa, mass murder in Rwanda — the response was slow, tentative, and, in the case of Rwanda, so slight as to be useless. International conferences sponsored by the United Nations on the environment (Rio de Janeiro, 1992), human rights (Vienna, 1993), population growth (Cairo, 1994), women's rights (Beijing, 1995), global warming (Kyoto, 1997), and economic development (Johannesburg, 2003) revealed wide disagreements on fundamental issues, especially between developed and developing countries. Prospects of global cooperation were further dimmed in the early 2000s when the United States declined to sign the Kyoto Treaty on global warming, withdrew its support of conventions on the use of landmines and biological weapons, and invaded Iraq in 2003 with the support of only one major ally, Great Britain.

Optimism in the early twenty-first century was also tempered by uncertainty over the implications of globalization. Although the 1990s were marked by vigorous debate about the definition and significance of globalization, it was generally agreed that with the demise of communism, the apparent triumph of free-market capitalism, the Internet revolution, and the increasing domination of national economies by global financial markets and multinational corporations, the world had entered a new stage of global interrelatedness and interdependence. To some, such changes promise economic development, growing prosperity, and greater harmony and understanding among the world's peoples. To others, they portend deepening poverty, environmental irresponsibility, political impotence, and an abandonment of humanity's sense of moral responsibility. Which, if either, scenario is correct will be revealed by future events, ideas, and actions — all of which will become part of the human record.

Another New Era: The Failure of Communism and the End of the Cold War

In the mid twentieth century global political relationships entered an era of moral and ideological absolutes. On one side was the communist world composed of the Soviet Union, its Eastern European satellites, and China. Characterized by authoritarian, one-party governments and centralized economic planning, these states proclaimed their commitment to the worldwide triumph of Marxism and the demise of capitalism. On the other side was the "free world" — a bloc of nations led by the United States with the goal of defending capitalism and spreading liberal democracy. For more than forty years these two blocs organized themselves into formidable military alliances, built up huge nuclear arsenals, supported giant intelligence establishments, and competed for support among nonaligned nations. For both sides the dualisms of the Cold War — communism versus capitalism, the United States versus the Soviet Union, NATO versus the Warsaw Pact — gave clarity, direction, and meaning to international politics.

In reality, the conflict between the free and the communist worlds was never completely about ideology. From the very start of the Cold War, the United States and its allies propped up dictators when it served their purposes of containing communism. Furthermore, cracks and fissures began to appear in both coalitions as early as the 1950s. Anti-Soviet revolts took place in Eastern Europe in 1956 and 1968, and diplomatic relations between China and the Soviet Union cooled in the mid 1960s. Also in the 1960s, the prospering, stable democracies of Western Europe, inspired by the independent course of France's leader, Charles de Gaulle, no longer unquestioningly accepted U.S. policies concerning military deployment in Europe and U.S. involvement in Vietnam.

There were times when the Cold War appeared on the verge of ending, but on each occasion old tensions returned. In the mid 1950s talk of peaceful coexistence gave way to renewed acrimony after the downing of a U.S. spy plane over Soviet territory in 1960, the building of the Berlin Wall in 1961, and the Cuban missile crisis of 1962. U.S.–Soviet relations improved once more in the 1970s when the two powers signed treaties on arms limitation and access to Berlin. Relations again deteriorated, however, after the Soviet invasion of Afghanistan in 1979 and the resulting U.S. boycott of the 1980 Moscow Olympics. In 1980 President Ronald Reagan branded the Soviet Union an "evil empire"; sent U.S. troops to Grenada to overthrow a Marxist government; provided arms to forces trying to overthrow communist regimes in Afghanistan, Nicaragua, and Angola; and sponsored a rapid arms build-up in the United States. Soviet suspicions of the United States deepened, and U.S. leaders showed no sign that they expected anything other than continuing Soviet–U.S. conflict.

By 1991, however, the Cold War was over. In one state after another in Soviet-controlled Eastern Europe, communist regimes either collapsed or were voted out of power and replaced by constitutional democracies. Within the Soviet Union, reforms initiated by Premier Mikhail Gorbachev in 1985 began with policies of *glasnost* (openness) and *perestroika* (restructuring) as a means to rejuvenate Soviet society. But his efforts to save communism by democratization and economic liberalization set in motion forces he could not control, and by the end of 1991, communist rule and the Soviet Union itself had ceased to exist.

Meanwhile changes no less profound were taking place in communist China. After the death of Mao Zedong in 1976, China, under the leadership of Deng Xiaoping, de-emphasized ideology and egalitarianism in favor of pragmatism and economic development. Deng approved the opening of small private businesses, fostered a market economy in agriculture, opened China to foreign investment, supported scientific and technological education, and encouraged Chinese exports of manufactured goods. The results were spectacular, with annual economic growth rates of 12 percent in the early 1990s. China remained authoritarian and officially communist, but with its commitment to "market socialism," it was far different from the isolated, ideology-driven China of previous decades.

China's New Course
▼▼▼
117 ▼ *Deng Xiaoping, SPEECHES AND WRITINGS*

Of all the events that took place in the closing decades of the twentieth century, China's full entry into the global economy and its decision to commit itself to economic development may in the long run prove to be the most significant. Since its emergence as a unified empire in the third century B.C.E., China for many centuries was the world's most successful state in terms of size, wealth, technological sophistication, and the continuity of its political institutions. This was easy to forget in the nineteenth and twentieth centuries, when China became a pawn of the Western powers and a victim of political disintegration, military defeat, and deepening poverty. In the 1980s, however, China's leaders set a new course for their country, which, if successful, might well restore China to its preeminence in Asia, if not its primacy among the world's powers.

The man responsible for launching China on its new path was Deng Xiaoping. Born into the family of a well-off landowner in 1904, Deng studied in China and then in France after World War I. Having run out of funds, he worked in a French factory before returning to China by way of the Soviet Union, where he studied in 1925–1926. On his return to China he joined the Communist Party and became one of Mao's most loyal followers in the struggle against the Japanese and the Guomindang.

After 1949 Deng became a member of the politburo and party secretary general, with responsibilities for overseeing economic development in southwest China. He supported the strategy of developing China's economy by following the Stalinist model of agricultural collectivization, centralized planning, and investment in heavy industry. This was scrapped in 1958 when Mao instituted the Great Leap Forward. In a little more than two years, some 24,000 People's Communes were established, each containing approximately 30,000 people who performed industrial and agricultural work, received political indoctrination, and participated in various social experiments. The Great Leap Forward was an economic disaster, and in its wake, Deng and other moderates were responsible for dismantling the communes and reintroducing centralized planning.

This made Deng a prime candidate for vilification after Mao launched the Great Cultural Revolution in 1966. Designed to revive revolutionary fervor and rescue China from materialism and Soviet-style bureaucratization, the revolution unleashed the energies of millions of young people who were urged to rise up and smash "bourgeois" elements throughout society. Deng fell from power, was paraded through the streets in a dunce cap, and put to work in a mess hall and a tractor repair shop. As the intensity of the Cultural Revolution faded, Deng was reinstated as a party official, and after Mao's death he led the moderates in their struggle with the radical faction led by Mao's widow, Jiang Qing. Deng's faction won, and in December 1978, the Central Committee of the Chinese Communist Party officially abandoned Mao's emphasis on ideology and class struggle in favor of a moderate, pragmatic policy designed to achieve the Four Modernizations in agriculture, industry, science and technology, and the military.

To encourage economic growth, the government fostered free markets, competition, and private incentives. Although Deng claimed that China had entered its "second revolution," it was an economic revolution only. Reformers who demanded the "Fifth Modernization" — democracy — were arrested and silenced in 1979. When millions of Chinese demonstrated for democracy in the spring of 1989, the government crushed the demonstration in Beijing with soldiers and tanks, thus assuring the continuation of the party dictatorship. After 1989 Deng withdrew from public life and died in early 1997. The following excerpts are from speeches and interviews given by Deng between 1983 and 1986.

QUESTIONS FOR ANALYSIS

1. According to Deng, what had been the shortcomings of China's economic development planning under Mao Zedong?
2. According to Deng, how is China's new economic policy truly Marxist and truly socialist?
3. How does Deng view China's role in the world? What implications will China's new economic priorities have for its foreign policy?
4. What is Deng's rationale for opposing democracy in China?
5. What similarities and differences do you see between Deng's economic program for China and Stalin's plans for the Soviet Union in the late 1920s and 1930s (see source 91)?

MAOISM'S FLAWS

After the founding of the People's Republic, in the rural areas we initiated agrarian reform and launched a movement for the co-operative transformation of agriculture,[1] while in the cities we conducted the socialist transformation of capitalist industry and commerce.[2] We were successful in both. However, from 1957 on, China was plagued by "Left" ideology, which gradually became dominant. During the Great Leap Forward in 1958, people rushed headlong into mass action to establish people's communes. They placed lopsided emphasis on making the communes large in size and collective in nature, urging everyone to "eat from the same big pot," and by so doing brought disaster upon the nation. We won't even mention the "cultural revolution." . . . During the 20 years from 1958 to 1978 the income of peasants and workers rose only a little, and consequently their standard of living remained very low. The development of the productive forces was sluggish during those years. In 1978 per capita GNP was less than $250. . . .

Comrade Mao Zedong was a great leader, and it was under his leadership that the Chinese revolution triumphed. But he made the grave mistake of neglecting the development of the productive forces. I do not mean he didn't want to develop them. The point is, not all of the methods he used were correct. For instance, the people's communes were established in defiance of the laws governing socio-economic development. The most important lesson we have learned, among a great many others, is that we must be clear about what socialism is and how to build it.

The fundamental principle of Marxism is that the productive forces must be developed. The goal for Marxists is to realize communism, which must be built on the basis of highly developed productive forces. What is a communist society? It is a society in which there is vast material wealth and in which the principle of from each according to his ability, to each according to his needs is applied. . . .

Our experience in the 20 years from 1958 to 1978 teaches us that poverty is not socialism, that socialism means eliminating poverty. Unless you are developing the productive forces and raising people's living standards, you cannot say that you are building socialism.

After the Third Plenary Session[3] we proceeded to explore ways of building socialism in China. Finally we decided to develop the productive forces and gradually expand the economy. The first goal we set was to achieve comparative prosperity by the end of the century. . . . So taking population increase into consideration, we planned to quadruple our GNP, which meant that per capita GNP would grow from $250 to $800 or $1,000. We shall lead a much better life when we reach this level, although it is still much lower than that of the developed countries. That is why we call it comparative prosperity. When we attain that level, China's GNP will have reached $1,000 billion, representing increased national strength. And the most populous nation in the world will have shaken off poverty and be able to make a greater contribution to mankind. With a GNP of $1,000 billion as a springboard, within 30 or 50 more years — 50, to be more accurate — China may reach its second goal, to approach the level of the developed countries. How are we to go about achieving these goals? . . . We began our reform in the countryside. The main point of the rural reform has been to bring the peasants' initiative into full play by introducing the responsibility system and discarding the system whereby everybody ate

---

[1]Following the communist victory in 1949 large rural estates were confiscated from landlords and redistributed to the peasantry. But in the early 1950s agriculture became collectivized under state control and peasants essentially became agricultural laborers who turned their crops over to the government in return for wages.

[2]During the 1950s private businesses involved in manufac-

turing and finance were phased out of existence and became state enterprises.

[3]The Third Plenary Session of Eleventh Central Committee of the Chinese Communist Party, held in December 1978, approved the Four Modernizations Program favored by Deng.

from the same big pot. Why did we start in the countryside? Because that is where 80 per cent of China's population lives. If we didn't raise living standards in the countryside, the society would be unstable. Industry, commerce and other sectors of the economy cannot develop on the basis of the poverty of 80 per cent of the population. After three years of practice the rural reform has proved successful. I can say with assurance it is a good policy. The countryside has assumed a new look. The living standards of 90 per cent of the rural population have been raised. . . .

After our success in rural reform we embarked on urban reform. Urban reform is more complicated and risky. This is especially true in China, because we have no experience in this regard. Also, China has traditionally been a very closed society, so that people lack information about what's going on elsewhere.

Although some problems have arisen in the process, we are confident that we can handle them. . . . We are sure it will be successful.

It is our hope that businessmen and economists in other countries will appreciate that to help China develop will benefit the world. China's foreign trade volume makes up a very small portion of the world's total. If we succeed in quadrupling the GNP, the volume of our foreign trade will increase considerably, promoting China's economic relations with other countries and expanding its market. Therefore, judged from the perspective of world politics and economics, China's development will benefit world peace and the world economy. . . .

TRUE SOCIALISM

Our modernization programme is a socialist programme, not anything else. All our policies for carrying out reform, opening to the outside world and invigorating the domestic economy are designed to develop the socialist economy.

We allow the development of individual economy, of joint ventures with both Chinese and foreign investment and of enterprises wholly owned by foreign businessmen, but socialist public ownership will always remain predominant. The aim of socialism is to make all our people prosperous, not to create polarization. If our policies led to polarization, it would mean that we had failed; if a new bourgeoisie emerged, it would mean that we had strayed from the right path. In encouraging some regions to become prosperous first, we intend that they should help the economically backward ones to develop. Similarly, in encouraging some people to become prosperous first, we intend that they should help others who are still in poverty to become better off, so that there will be common prosperity rather than polarization. A limit should be placed on the wealth of people who become prosperous first, through the income tax, for example. In addition, we should encourage them to contribute money to run schools and build roads, although we definitely shouldn't set quotas for them. We should encourage these people to make donations, but it's better not to give such donations too much publicity.

In short, predominance of public ownership and common prosperity are the two fundamental socialist principles that we must adhere to. We shall firmly put them into practice. And ultimately we shall move on to communism.

SPECIAL ECONOMIC ZONES

In establishing special economic zones[4] and implementing an open policy, we must make it clear that our guideline is just that — to open and not to close.

I was impressed by the prosperity of the Shenzhen[5] Special Economic Zone during my stay there. The pace of construction in Shenzhen is rapid. It is particularly fast in Shekou, because

---

[4]The Special Economic Zones were restricted areas where foreign firms could set up businesses and house foreign personnel.

[5]A district next to Hong Kong.

the authorities there are permitted to make their own spending decisions up to a limit of U.S. $5 million. Their slogan is "time is money, efficiency is life." In Shenzhen, it doesn't take long to erect a tall building; the workers complete a storey in a couple of days. The construction workers there are from inland cities. Their high efficiency is due to the "contracted responsibility system," under which they are paid according to their performance, and to a fair system of rewards and penalties.

A special economic zone is a medium for introducing technology, management and knowledge. It is also a window for our foreign policy. Through the special economic zone we can import foreign technology, obtain knowledge and learn management, which is also a kind of knowledge. . . . Public order in Shenzhen is reportedly better than before, and people who slipped off to Hongkong have begun to return. One reason is that there are more job opportunities and people's incomes and living standards are rising, all of which proves that cultural and ideological progress is based on material progress.

CHINA'S FOREIGN RELATIONS

While invigorating the domestic economy, we have also formulated a policy of opening to the outside world. Reviewing our history, we have concluded that one of the most important reasons for China's long years of stagnation and backwardness was its policy of closing the country to outside contact. Our experience shows that China cannot rebuild itself with its doors closed to the outside and that it cannot develop in isolation from the rest of the world. It goes without saying that a large country like China cannot depend on others for its development; it must depend mainly on itself, on its own efforts. Nevertheless, while holding to self-reliance, we should open our country to the outside world to obtain such aid as foreign investment capital and technology. . . .

CHINA'S POLITICAL FUTURE

The recent student unrest[6] is not going to lead to any major disturbances. But because of its nature it must be taken very seriously. Firm measures must be taken against any student who creates trouble at Tiananmen Square. . . . In the beginning, we mainly used persuasion, which is as it should be in dealing with student demonstrators. But if any of them disturb public order or violate the law, they must be dealt with unhesitatingly. Persuasion includes application of the law. When a disturbance breaks out in a place, it's because the leaders there didn't take a firm, clear-cut stand. This is not a problem that has arisen in just one or two places or in just the last couple of years; it is the result of failure over the past several years to take a firm, clear-cut stand against bourgeois liberalization. It is essential to adhere firmly to the Four Cardinal Principles;[7] otherwise bourgeois liberalization will spread unchecked — and that has been the root cause of the problem. . . .

In developing our democracy, we cannot simply copy bourgeois democracy, or introduce the system of a balance of three powers. I have often criticized people in power in the United States, saying that actually they have three governments. Of course, the American bourgeoisie uses this system in dealing with other countries, but when it comes to internal affairs, the three branches often pull in different directions, and that makes trouble. We cannot adopt such a system. . . .

Without leadership by the Communist Party and without socialism, there is no future for China. This truth has been demonstrated in the

---

[6]Deng made these remarks in December 1986, when student demonstrations and speechmaking on behalf of the Pro-Democracy Movement had been going on in Tiananmen Square in Beijing for several years.

[7]Issued by Deng in 1979, the Four Cardinal Principles were (1) the socialist path, (2) the dictatorship of the proletariat, (3) party leadership, and (4) Marxism-Leninism-Mao Zedong thought.

past, and it will be demonstrated again in future. When we succeed in raising China's per capita GNP to $4,000 and everyone is prosperous, that will better demonstrate the superiority of socialism over capitalism, it will point the way for three quarters of the world's population and it will provide further proof of the correctness of Marxism. Therefore, we must confidently keep to the socialist road and uphold the Four Cardinal Principles.

We cannot do without dictatorship. We must not only affirm the need for it but exercise it when necessary. Of course, we must be cautious about resorting to dictatorial means and make as few arrests as possible. But if some people attempt to provoke bloodshed, what are we going to do about it? We should first expose their plot and then do our best to avoid shedding blood, even if that means some of our own people get

hurt. However, ringleaders who have violated the law must be sentenced according to law. Unless we are prepared to do that, it will be impossible to put an end to disturbances. If we take no action and back down, we shall only have more trouble down the road.

The struggle against bourgeois liberalization is also indispensable. We should not be afraid that it will damage our reputation abroad. China must take its own road and build socialism with Chinese characteristics — that is the only way China can have a future. We must show foreigners that China's political situation is stable. If our country were plunged into disorder and our nation reduced to a heap of loose sand, how could we ever prosper? The reason the imperialists were able to bully us in the past was precisely that we were a heap of loose sand.

A Plan to Save Communism in the Soviet Union
▼▼▼
118 ▼ *Mikhail Gorbachev, PERESTROIKA*

Throughout the 1970s and early 1980s the Soviet Union was one of the world's two superpowers, with an enormous army, a huge industrial establishment, an impressive record of technological achievement, and a seemingly unshakable authoritarian government. No one saw any reason why it would not continue as the United States's great rival in world affairs. In reality, industrial and agricultural production were stagnating, the people's morale was plummeting, and the fossilized bureaucracy was mired in old policies and theories that no longer worked. Against this background Mikhail Gorbachev became general secretary of the Communist Party in March 1985 and began the task of rejuvenating Soviet communism by introducing policies based on *glasnost,* or openness, and *perestroika,* or restructuring.

Gorbachev, who was fifty-four years old when he took power, was born of peasant parents and had studied law and agricultural economics. After filling a variety of positions in the Communist Party, he became a member of the politburo in 1979. After serving as Soviet leader for two years, he published a book, *Perestroika* (1987), from which the following excerpt is taken. In it he describes his goals for Soviet communism. To his sorrow and the world's shock he fell from power in 1991, with his reforms having led not to communism's reform but its demise and not to the Soviet Union's revival but its dismemberment.

QUESTIONS FOR ANALYSIS

1. What developments in the Soviet Union led Gorbachev to the conclusion that Soviet society and government were in need of reform?
2. In Gorbachev's analysis, what caused Soviet society to "lose its momentum"?
3. In Gorbachev's view, how will the "individual" in Soviet society be affected by his reforms?
4. To what extent is perestroika democratic?
5. What similarities and differences do you see between Gorbachev's statements about perestroika and Deng's comments about the needs of China (source 117)?

Russia, where a great Revolution took place seventy years ago, is an ancient country with a unique history filled with searchings, accomplishments, and tragic events. It has given the world many discoveries and outstanding personalities.

However, the Soviet Union is a young state without analogues in history or in the modern world. Over the past seven decades — a short span in the history of human civilization — our country has traveled a path equal to centuries. One of the mightiest powers in the world rose up to replace the backward semi-colonial and semi-feudal Russian Empire. . . .

At some stage — this became particularly clear in the latter half of the seventies — something happened that was at first sight inexplicable. The country began to lose momentum. Economic failures became more frequent. Difficulties began to accumulate and deteriorate, and unresolved problems to multiply. Elements of what we call stagnation and other phenomena alien to socialism began to appear in the life of society. A kind of "braking mechanism" affecting social and economic development formed. And all this happened at a time when scientific and technological revolution opened up new prospects for economic and social progress. . . .

Analyzing the situation, we first discovered a slowing economic growth. In the last fifteen years the national income growth rates had de-

clined by more than a half and by the beginning of the eighties had fallen to a level close to economic stagnation. A country that was once quickly closing on the world's advanced nations began to lose one position after another. . . .

It became typical of many of our economic executives to think not of how to build up the national assets, but of how to put more material, labor, and working time into an item to sell it at a higher price. Consequently, for all our "gross output," there was a shortage of goods. We spent, in fact we are still spending, far more on raw materials, energy, and other resources per unit of output than other developed nations. Our country's wealth in terms of natural and manpower resources has spoilt, one may even say corrupted, us. . . .

The presentation of a "problem-free" reality backfired: a breach had formed between word and deed, which bred public passivity and disbelief in the slogans being proclaimed. It was only natural that this situation resulted in a credibility gap: everything that was proclaimed from the rostrums and printed in newspapers and textbooks was put in question. Decay began in public morals; the great feeling of solidarity with each other that was forged during the heroic times of the Revolution, the first five-year plans, the Great Patriotic War,[1] and postwar rehabilitation was weakening; alcoholism, drug addiction, and crime were growing; and the penetration of

---

[1]World War II.

the stereotypes of mass culture alien to us, which bred vulgarity and low tastes and brought about ideological barrenness, increased.

Political flirtation and mass distribution of awards, titles, and bonuses often replaced genuine concern for the people, for their living and working conditions, for a favorable social atmosphere. An atmosphere emerged of "everything goes," and fewer and fewer demands were made on discipline and responsibility. Attempts were made to cover it all up with pompous campaigns and undertakings and celebrations of numerous anniversaries centrally and locally. The world of day-to-day realities and the world of feigned prosperity were diverging more and more. . . .

An unbiased and honest approach led us to the only logical conclusion that the country was verging on crisis. This conclusion was announced at the April 1985 Plenary Meeting of the Central Committee,[2] which inaugurated the new strategy of perestroika and formulated its basic principles. . . .

By saying all this I want to make the reader understand that the energy for revolutionary change has been accumulating amid our people and in the Party for some time. And the ideas of perestroika have been prompted not just by pragmatic interests and considerations but also by our troubled conscience, by the indomitable commitment to ideals which we inherited from the Revolution and as a result of a theoretical quest which gave us a better knowledge of society and reinforced our determination to go ahead.

Today our main job is to lift the individual spiritually, respecting his inner world and giving him moral strength. We are seeking to make the whole intellectual potential of society and all the potentialities of culture work to mold a socially active person, spiritually rich, just, and conscientious. An individual must know and feel that his contribution is needed, that his dignity is not being infringed upon, that he is being treated with trust and respect. When an individual sees all this, he is capable of accomplishing much.

Of course, perestroika somehow affects everybody; it jolts many out of their customary state of calm and satisfaction at the existing way of life. Here I think it is appropriate to draw your attention to one specific feature of socialism. I have in mind the high degree of social protection in our society. On the one hand, it is, doubtless, a benefit and a major achievement of ours. On the other, it makes some people spongers.

There is virtually no unemployment. The state has assumed concern for ensuring employment. Even a person dismissed for laziness or a breach of labor discipline must be given another job. Also, wage-leveling has become a regular feature of our everyday life: even if a person is a bad worker, he gets enough to live fairly comfortably. The children of an outright parasite will not be left to the mercy of fate. We have enormous sums of money concentrated in the social funds from which people receive financial assistance. The same funds provide subsidies for the upkeep of kindergartens, orphanages, Young Pioneer[3] houses, and other institutions related to children's creativity and sport. Health care is free, and so is education. People are protected from the vicissitudes of life, and we are proud of this.

But we also see that dishonest people try to exploit these advantages of socialism; they know only their rights, but they do not want to know their duties: they work poorly, shirk, and drink hard. There are quite a few people who have adapted the existing laws and practices to their own selfish interests. They give little to society, but nevertheless managed to get from it all that is possible and what even seems impossible; they have lived on unearned incomes.

The policy of restructuring puts everything in its place. We are fully restoring the principle of socialism. "From each according to his ability, to each according to his work," and we seek to af-

---

[2]The Central Committee of the Communist Party, the body that sets broad policy for the Soviet government.

[3]A youth organization sponsored by the Soviet regime.

firm social justice for all, equal rights for all, one law for all, one kind of discipline for all, and high responsibilities for each. Perestroika raises the level of social responsibility and expectation. . . .

It is essential to learn to adjust policy in keeping with the way it is received by the masses, and to ensure feedback, absorbing the ideas, opinions, and advice coming from the people. The masses suggest a lot of useful and interesting things which are not always clearly perceived "from the top." That is why we must prevent at all costs an arrogant attitude to what people are saying. In the final account the most important thing for the success of perestroika is the people's attitude to it.

Thus, not only theory but the reality of the processes under way made us embark on the program for all-round democratic changes in public life which we presented at the January 1987 Plenary Meeting of the CPSU[4] Central Committee.

The Plenary Meeting encouraged extensive efforts to strengthen the democratic basis of Soviet society, to develop self-government and extend glasnost, that is openness, in the entire management network. We see now how stimulating that impulse was for the nation. Democratic changes have been taking place at every work collective, at every state and public organization, and within the Party. More glasnost, genuine control from "below," and greater initiative and enterprise at work are now part and parcel of our life. . . .

The adoption of fundamental principles for a radical change in economic management was a big step forward in the program of perestroika. Now perestroika concerns virtually every main aspect of public life. . . .

Perestroika means overcoming the stagnation process, breaking down the braking mechanism, creating a dependable and effective mechanism for the acceleration of social and economic progress and giving it greater dynamism.

Perestroika means mass initiative. It is the comprehensive development of democracy, so-

cialist self-government, encouragement of initiative and creative endeavor, improved order and discipline, more glasnost, criticism, and self-criticism in all spheres of our society. It is utmost respect for the individual and consideration for personal dignity.

Perestroika is the all-round intensification of the Soviet economy, the revival and development of the principles of democratic centralism in running the national economy, the universal introduction of economic methods, the renunciation of management by injunction and by administrative methods, and the overall encouragement of innovation and socialist enterprise.

Perestroika means a resolute shift to scientific methods, an ability to provide a solid scientific basis for every new initiative. It means the combination of the achievements of the scientific and technological revolution with a planned economy.

Perestroika means priority development of the social sphere aimed at ever better satisfaction of the Soviet people's requirements for good living and working conditions, for good rest and recreation, education, and health care. It means unceasing concern for cultural and spiritual wealth, for the culture of every individual and society as a whole.

Perestroika means the elimination from society of the distortions of socialist ethics, the consistent implementation of the principles of social justice. It means the unity of words and deeds, rights and duties. It is the elevation of honest, highly-qualified labor, the overcoming of leveling tendencies in pay and consumerism.

I stress once again: perestroika is not some kind of illumination or revelation. To restructure our life means to understand the objective necessity for renovation and acceleration. And that necessity emerged in the heart of our society. The essence of perestroika lies in the fact that it *unites socialism with democracy* and revives the Leninist

---

[4]Communist Party of the Soviet Union.

concept of socialist construction both in theory and in practice. Such is the essence of perestroika, which accounts for its genuine revolutionary spirit and its all-embracing scope.

The goal is worth the effort. And we are sure that our effort will be a worthy contribution to humanity's social progress.

▼▼▼

Terrorism in a Global Age

On the morning of September 11, 2001, four U.S. commercial airliners — two from Logan Airport in Boston, and one each from Dulles International Airport in Washington, D.C., and Newark International Airport in New Jersey — were hijacked shortly after departures by members of al-Quaida, a terrorist organization founded in the 1980s by the Saudi Arabian millionaire Osama bin Laden. One of the four jets was commandeered by passengers and crashed in a field in southwestern Pennsylvania with no survivors, but the other three found their targets. One was flown to Washington, D.C., where it crashed into the Pentagon, the symbol of U.S. military might; the other two were flown to New York City where they smashed into the twin towers of the World Trade Center, the symbol of U.S. capitalism. The results were devastating. The twin towers were destroyed, more than 3,000 people were killed, and fighting terrorism became the priority of governments around the world.

Terrorism can be defined as acts of violence — assassinations, bombings, kidnappings, hijackings, and the use of chemical or biological weapons — carried out by individuals or groups against a more powerful opponent, usually a government or its citizenry. The goal of such acts is to discredit, destabilize, and demoralize the opponent through fear and intimidation, thereby forcing a change in policies or practices to bring them in line with the terrorists' political or religious views. Terrorists tend to be individuals who are totally dedicated to a political or religious cause, one they consider so noble and righteous that it justifies mass killings and extreme self-sacrifice, even to the point of their own deaths. Although terrorists are vilified as murderers and cowards by those who are their targets, they are considered idealists and heroes by those who share their views.

Terrorism has a long history. Standard histories of the subject begin with the first century C.E., when Roman authorities financed dissidents and malcontents to murder enemies in subject territories or neighboring states, and members of a small Jewish sect assassinated officials and prominent individuals in and around Jerusalem to bring about the end of Roman rule in Palestine. Terrorism's history includes the Persian religious sect known as the Assassins, whose members used terror in their campaign to end the rule of the Seljuk Turks in Southwest Asia;

Catholics who sought to discredit England's Protestant government by plotting to blow up the houses of parliament with thirty-six barrels of gunpowder in 1605; and European anarchists and radical socialists who assassinated some fifty prominent politicians from the late 1800s through the early 1900s, including Tsar Alexander II of Russia, President William McKinley of the United States, President Sadi Carnot of France, King Umberto of Italy, and Prime Minister Antonio Canovas of Spain. The assassination of Austrian-Hungarian Archduke Franz-Ferdinand in July 1914 by a member of the Serbian sect called "Union or Death" led directly to the outbreak of World War I one month later.

With the onset of World War I terrorism declined but revived with a vengeance after World War II. Beginning in the late 1940s, terrorist acts have taken place in every part of the world and have been carried out by groups espousing many different causes: anticolonialists in Africa and Asia; left-wing radicals in Europe; Arabs bent on the destruction of Israel; abortion foes in the United States; religious extremists in India, Northern Ireland, Indonesia, and Africa; enemies of apartheid in South Africa; and Chechen separatists in Russia, to name but a few. They also include obscure religious sects such Aum Shinrikyo, whose members killed twelve and injured thousands when they released saran gas in the Tokyo subway system in 1995, alienated individuals such as Theodore Kaczynski, the American opponent of technology whose letter bombs killed three and injured twenty-three before his arrest in 1997, and self-professed patriots like Timothy McVeigh, who sought to strike a blow against the "tyranny" of the U.S. government when his truck bomb destroyed the federal building in Oklahoma City and killed 168 in 1995.

Although a worldwide phenomenon, terrorism in recent decades has been identified in particular with the Middle East, a region where many terrorist acts have taken place and is a major source of recruitment, organizational effort, and financing for terrorist activities in other parts of the world. Depending on one's perspective, views of Middle Eastern terrorism differ. Many Westerners equate terrorism with Islamic fundamentalism and Arab nationalism, but to many Muslims this is a false perception. To them, those viewed as terrorists in the West are religious and political heroes, responding in kind to acts of violence perpetrated by the true terrorists, the leaders and agents of Israel and the United States.

Terrorist bombing, hijackings, kidnappings, and assassinations related to political and religious conflict in the Middle East took more than a thousand lives from the 1970s through the 1990s, but it was the attack on the World Trade Center and the Pentagon on September 11, 2001, that caused a seismic shift in world politics and made the prevention of terrorism the twenty-first century's first great challenge. The two sources in this section seek to provide insight into the beliefs and values of those who were responsible for that attack.

The Worldview of Osama bin Laden
▼▼▼

119 ▼ *DECLARATION OF JIHAD AGAINST AMERICANS OCCUPYING THE LAND OF THE TWO HOLY MOSQUES*

Osama bin Laden, the founder of al-Qaeda, was born in 1957 in Saudi Arabia, the son of Muhammad bin Laden, an illiterate Yemeni dockworker who became the billionaire owner of a construction company, and a cultured Syrian woman who was Muhammad's tenth or eleventh wife. Raised according to the strict doctrines of Wahhabi Islam, the young Osama led a privileged existence of private schooling, vacations in Scandinavia, and English lessons in Oxford. At age seventeen, he enrolled as a civil engineering student at King Abdul Aziz University in Jeddah, Saudi Arabia, rather than a Western university. Here he developed an interest in Islamic theology and forged friendships with a number of Islamic radicals. In 1980 he left for the Pakistani-Afghan border to aid Afghan holy warriors, or mujahideen, who were fighting against Soviet troops who had invaded Afghanistan in late 1979 to prop up the pro-Soviet regime. Using his inheritance (perhaps as much as $300 million), he organized an office to provide money and weapons for the thousands of Muslim volunteers who flocked to Afghanistan to fight for their faith; from the mid 1980s onward he became an active fighter himself. Out of these contacts and activities al-Qaeda, meaning "the base" in Arabic, began to take shape under bin Laden's direction.

On his return to Saudi Arabia, bin Laden became an outspoken critic of the Saudi regime for its corruption, failure to implement shariah, or Islamic law, and its acceptance of a U.S. military presence during and after the first Persian Gulf War. In 1991 he fled to Sudan, where for five years he extended and expanded al-Qaeda to include perhaps as many as several thousand agents with cells ranging from Indonesia and the Philippines to the United States. Between 1992 and 1995 al-Qaeda was linked to attacks on U.S. troops in Yemen and Somalia, the bombing of an American-operated Saudi National Guard training center in Riyadh, and unsuccessful plots to assassinate Pope John Paul II, President Bill Clinton, and Egyptian President Hosni Mubarak. Under U.S. pressure the Sudanese government expelled bin Laden and his operation in 1996, forcing al-Qaeda to establish a new base in Afghanistan, which was coming under the control of the radical Islamic group known as the Taliban. Between 1996 and 2000 al-Qaeda was responsible for numerous acts of terrorism, including the car bombing of an apartment building in Dhahran, Saudi Arabia, that killed nineteen U.S. soldiers; the simultaneous bombings of U.S. embassies in Tanzania and Kenya that killed 234 and injured several thousand; and the attack on the USS *Cole* in Aden, Yemen, that killed 17 U.S. sailors and wounded 39. After the attacks of September 11, 2001, the United States invaded Afghanistan, ended Taliban rule, and smashed al-Qaeda headquarters and training camps. Bin Laden eluded capture, however, presumably moving to the mountainous region straddling the Pakistani-Afghan border. Al-Qaeda also survived, still dedicated to its holy war against the United States.

Bin Laden has published little, and as leader of a secret terrorist organization has given few interviews or public speeches. One exception is the speech he delivered to his followers in eastern Afghanistan in August 1996 in which he "declared war" on the United States. Printed in Arabic-language newspapers and audiotaped for worldwide distribution, bin Laden's speech describes his motives and priorities.

QUESTIONS FOR ANALYSIS

1. How does bin Laden perceive the Muslims' place in the world? Who are their main enemies?
2. Why does bin Laden oppose the existing government of Saudi Arabia?
3. What are the goals of the "Zionist-Crusaders alliance" according to bin Laden?
4. What lessons can be learned, according to bin Laden, by the U.S. response to terrorist attacks and military setbacks in Beirut, Aden, and Somalia?
5. Why is bin Laden convinced that Muslims will triumph in their struggle with the United States?
6. What do you perceive as bin Laden's ultimate political and religious goals?

Praise be to Allah, we seek His help and ask for his pardon. We take refuge in Allah from our wrongs and bad deeds. Whoever has been guided by Allah will not be misled, and who ever has been misled, he will never be guided. I bear witness that there is no God except Allah, no associates with Him and I bear witness that Muhammad is His slave and messenger. . . .

It should not be hidden from you that the community of Islam has suffered from aggression, iniquity and injustice imposed on them by the Zionist-Crusaders alliance and their collaborators; to the extent that the Muslims' blood became the cheapest and their wealth as loot in the hands of the enemies. Their blood was spilled in Palestine and Iraq. The horrifying pictures of the massacre of Qana[1] in Lebanon are still fresh in our memory. Massacres in Tajikistan, Burma, Kashmir, Assam, the Philippines, Fatani, Ogadin, Somalia, Eritrea, Chechnya and in Bosnia Herzegovina[2] took place, massacres that send shivers in the body and shake the conscience. All of this and the world watched and listened, and not only didn't respond to these atrocities, but also with a conspiracy between the USA and its allies and under the cover of the iniquitous United Nations the dispossessed people were even prevented from obtaining arms to defend themselves.

The people of Islam awakened and realized that they are the main target for the aggression of the Zionist-Crusaders alliance. All false claims

[1]In April 1996 the Israelis launched a two-week bombardment of territory in southern Lebanon where the terrorist group Hezbollah was located. On April 18, 100 civilians were killed when the Israelis shelled the battalion headquarters of a UN peacekeeping force where some 800 Lebanese had taken refuge. The Israelis blamed "technical and procedural errors," an explanation questioned by an official UN report.

[2]This is a rather wide-ranging list. The massacres in Assam, a province of northeastern India, were carried out by an Assam separatist group in 1990 and claimed several dozen victims, not all of whom were Muslims. Attacks on Burmese Muslims in the early 1990s were carried out by Buddhists.

and propaganda about "Human Rights" were hammered down and exposed by the massacres that took place against the Muslims in every part of the world. The latest and the greatest of these aggressions experienced by the Muslims since the death of the Prophet is the occupation of the land of the two Holy Places,[3] the foundation of the house of Islam, the place of the revelation, the source of the message and the place of the noble Kabah, the Qiblah of all Muslims,[4] by the armies of the American Crusaders and their allies.

Today we work . . . to lift the iniquity that had been imposed on the Umma [the Muslim community] by the Zionist-Crusaders alliance, particularly after they have occupied the blessed land of Jerusalem, route of the journey of the Prophet,[5] . . . and the land of the two Holy Places. . . . We wish to study the means by which we could return the situation [in Saudi Arabia] to its normal path and to return to the people their own rights, particularly after the large damages and the great aggression on the life and the religion of the people. An injustice that had affected every section and group of the people: the civilians, military and security men, government officials and merchants, the young and the old people as well as school and university students. Hundreds of thousands of the unemployed graduates were also affected.

Injustice had affected the people in industry and agriculture. It affected the people of the rural and urban areas. And almost everybody complains about something. The situation at the land of the two Holy Places became like a huge volcano at the verge of eruption that would destroy the Kuffar[6] and the corruption and its sources. . . .

People are fully concerned about their everyday living; everybody talks about the deterioration of the economy, inflation, ever increasing debts and jails full of prisoners. Government employees with limited income talk about debts of ten thousands and hundred thousands of Saudi Riyals. They complain that the value of the Riyal is greatly and continuously deteriorating among most of the main currencies. Great merchants and contractors speak about hundreds and thousands of million Riyals owed to them by the government. . . .

Through its course of actions the regime has torn off its legitimacy:

(1) Suspension of the Islamic Sharia law and exchanging it with man-made civil law. . . .

(2) The inability of the regime to protect the country and allowing the enemy of the Umma, the American crusader forces, to occupy the land for the longest of years. . . . As a result of the policy imposed on the country, especially in the oil industry where production is restricted or expanded and prices are fixed to suit the American economy, ignoring the economy of the country. Expensive deals were imposed on the country to purchase arms. People are asking what then is the justification for the very existence of the regime?

Quick efforts were made by individuals and by different groups in society to contain the situation and to prevent the danger. They advised the government both privately and openly; they sent letters and poems, reports after reports, reminders after reminders, they explored every avenue and enlisted every influential man in their

---

[3]Mecca, the birthplace of Muhammad, and the site of the Kabah, Islam's holiest shrine, and Medina, the city to which Muhammad and his followers fled in 622 C.E.
[4]The Kabah is the cube-shaped shrine in Mecca; the Qiblah is the direction pointing to the Kabah toward which Muslims must pray.

[5]Muhammad's miraculous "night journey" took him and the angel Gabriel from Mecca to Jerusalem, from which they ascended into heaven then returned to Mecca the following morning. They rode a horselike creature or *Buraq*.
[6]Those who do not believe in God.

movement of reform and correction. They wrote in a style of passion, diplomacy and wisdom asking for corrective measures . . . from the "great wrongdoings and corruption" that had engulfed even the basic principles of the religion and the legitimate rights of the people.

But to our deepest regret the regime refused to listen to the people. . . .

Under such circumstances, to push the enemy out of the country is a prime duty. No other duty after Belief is more important. . . . Also to remind the Muslims not to be engaged in an internal war among themselves, as that will have consequences, namely:

1. Consumption of the Muslims' human resources as casualties and fatalities . . .

2. Exhaustion of the economic and financial resources

3. Destruction of the country's infrastructures

4. Disruption of society

5. Destruction of the oil industries. . . .

6. Division of the land of the two Holy Places, and annexing of the northern part of it by Israel. Dividing the land of the two Holy Places is an essential demand of the Zionist-Crusaders alliance. . .

The regime is fully responsible for what has been incurred by the country and the nation; however, the occupying American enemy is the principle and the main cause of the situation. Therefore efforts should be concentrated on de-stroying, fighting and killing the enemy until, by the Grace of Allah, it is completely defeat-ed. . . .

▼▼▼

It is incredible that our country is the world's largest buyer of arms from the USA and the area's biggest commercial partner of the Americans who are assisting their Zionist brothers in occu-pying Palestine and in evicting and killing the Muslims there, by providing arms, men and fi-nancial support. To deny these occupiers . . . the enormous revenues from their trade with our country is a very important help for our Jihad against them. . . .

We expect the women of the land of the two Holy Places and other countries to carry out their role in boycotting the American goods. If eco-nomic boycott is intertwined with the military operations of the Mujahideen [holy warriors], then defeating the enemy will be even nearer, by the Permission of Allah. . . .

▼▼▼

A few days ago the news agencies had reported that the Defense Secretary[7] of the Crusading Americans had said that "the explosions at Riyadh and Al Khobar[8] had taught him one les-son: that is, not to withdraw when attacked by coward terrorists."

We say to the Defense Secretary that his talk can induce a grieving mother to laughter! . . . Where was this false courage of yours when the explosion in Beirut took place in 1983? You were turned into scattered bits and pieces at that time;

---

[7]William Perry, secretary of defense between 1994 and 1997.
[8]In November 1995 a car bomb in Riyadh at a Saudi National Guard training center killed five Americans; the bombing of Khobar Towers, a U.S. Air Force housing com-plex in Dhahran, Saudi Arabia, killed nineteen Americans.

241 marine soldiers were killed.[9] And where was this courage of yours when two explosions made you to leave Aden in less than twenty-four hours![10]

But your most disgraceful case was in Somalia;[11] where . . . you moved an . . . international force, including twenty-eight thousand American soldiers. . . . However, when tens of your soldiers were killed in minor battles and one American pilot was dragged in the streets of Mogadishu you left the area carrying disappointment, humiliation, defeat and your dead with you. Clinton appeared in front of the whole world threatening and promising revenge, but these threats were merely a preparation for withdrawal. You have been disgraced by Allah and you withdrew; the extent of your impotence and weaknesses became very clear. . . .

Since the sons of the land of the two Holy Places feel and strongly believe that fighting against the nonbelievers in every part of the world is absolutely essential; then they would be even more enthusiastic, more powerful and larger in number upon fighting on their own land, the place of their births, defending the greatest of their sanctities, the noble Kabah (the Qiblah of all Muslims). They know that the Muslims of the world will assist and help them to victory. To liberate their Holy Places is the greatest of issues concerning all Muslims; it is the duty of every Muslim in this world. I say to you William [Perry] that: These youths love death as you love life. They inherit dignity, pride, courage, generosity, truthfulness and sacrifice from father to father. They are most . . . steadfast at war. They inherit these values from their ancestors. . . .

These youths believe in what has been told by Allah and His messenger about the greatness of the reward for the Mujahideen martyrs. . . .

Those youths know that their reward in fighting you, the USA, is double their reward in fighting someone else. . . . They have no intention except to enter paradise by killing you. . . .

Those youths will not ask you for explanations, they will tell you . . . there is nothing between us that needs to be explained, there is only killing and neck smiting.

In the heat of battle they do not care, and cure the insanity of the enemy by their 'insane' courage. Terrorizing you, while you are carrying arms on our land, is a legitimate and morally required duty. It is a legitimate right well known to all humans and other creatures. Your example and our example is like a snake which entered into a house of a man and got killed by him. The coward is the man who lets you walk, while carrying arms, freely on his land and provides you with peace and security.

Those youths are different from your soldiers. Your problem will be how to convince your troops to fight, while our problem will be how to restrain our youths to wait for their turn in fighting. . . .

The youths hold you responsible for all of the killings and evictions of the Muslims and the violation of the sanctities, carried out by your Zionist brothers in Lebanon; you openly supplied them with arms and finance. More than 600,000 Iraqi children have died due to lack of food and medicine and as a result of the unjustifiable aggression imposed on Iraq and its nation.[12]

---

[9]President Reagan ordered the withdrawal of marine peacekeepers after a bomb killed 241 marines and navy seamen in October 1983 in Beirut.
[10]The Pentagon withdrew 100 army personnel after the U.S. embassy was bombed in Aden in 1993.
[11]President Clinton ordered the withdrawal of U.S. peacekeepers from Somalia by March 1994 after a clash with Somali warlords in Mogadishu in October 1993 resulted in the deaths of eighteen army rangers.
[12]The alleged victims of economic sanctions imposed on Iraq after the first Persian Gulf War.

The children of Iraq are our children. You, the USA, together with the Saudi regime are responsible for the shedding of the blood of these innocent children. Due to all of that, whatever treaty you have with our country is now null and void. . . .

It is a duty now on every tribe on the Arab Peninsula to fight in the cause of Allah and to cleanse the land from those occupiers. Allah knows that their blood is permitted to be spilled and their wealth is a booty; their wealth is a booty to those who kill them. . . . Our youths knew that the humiliation suffered by the Muslims as a result of the occupation of their Holy Places cannot be removed except by explosions and Jihad.

The Final Step toward Martyrdom
▼▼▼

120 ▾ *Mohammed Atta, THE LAST NIGHT*

Mohammed Atta was born in a Cairo suburb on September 1, 1968, and died on September 11, 2001, when he flew a hijacked American Airlines passenger jet into one of the towers of the World Trade Center in lower Manhattan. The son of a lawyer, Atta graduated with a degree in architecture from Cairo University. He then moved to Germany, where he registered as a student at the Technical University of Hamburg and was employed part-time at a Hamburg consulting firm. Devoted to Islam, he made a pilgrimage to Mecca in 1995, and on his return to Hamburg began an Islamic prayer group. In July 2000 Atta attended a flight school, Huffman Aviation International, in Venice, Florida, and in December went to the Miami area to practice on a Boeing 707 simulator. In 2001 he briefly visited Germany and Spain, then returned to Florida, where he took additional flying lessons. On the morning of September 11 he and another conspirator drove from their motel in South Portland, Maine, to Portland International Airport, flew to Boston, and boarded American Airlines Flight 11.

It was later discovered that Atta had left behind a bag containing airline uniforms, flight manuals, and a four-page document in Arabic, copies of which were also found in the effects of two of the other terrorists. The document is a list of instructions for the terrorists to review on the night of September 10. Excerpts from these instructions follow.

QUESTIONS FOR ANALYSIS

1. How, according to Atta, should the participants prepare themselves for what lies ahead of them?
2. Is Atta totally confident about the success of the mission? What might go wrong, and what can be done to prevent failure?
3. What rewards can the participants expect from their anticipated martyrdom?

4. What feelings does Atta express about the victims of their actions?
5. On the basis of this document, what conclusions can be drawn about Atta's, and by extension, the other participants' motives?

1. Make an oath to die and renew your intentions. Shave excess hair from the body and wear cologne. Shower.[1]

2. Make sure you know all aspects of the plan well, and expect the response, or a reaction, from the enemy.

3. Read al-Tawba and Anfal[2] and reflect on their meanings and remember all of the things that God has promised for the martyrs.

4. Remind your soul to listen and obey and remember that you will face decisive situations that might prevent you from 100 percent obedience, so tame your soul, purify it, convince it, make it understand, and incite it.

5. Pray during the night and be persistent in asking God to give you victory, control and conquest, and that he may make your task easier and not expose us.

6. Remember God frequently, and the best way to do it is to read the Holy Quran. . . . It is enough for us that it are [*sic*] the words of the Creator of the Earth and the planets, the One that you will meet [on the Day of Judgment].

7. Purify your soul from all unclean things. Completely forget something called "this world." The time for play is over and the serious time is upon us. How much time have we wasted

in our lives? Shouldn't we take advantage of these last hours to offer good deeds and obedience?

8. You should feel complete tranquility, because the time between you and your marriage [in heaven] is very short [soon to come]. Afterward begins the happy life, where God is satisfied with you, and eternal bliss "in the company of the prophets, the companions, the martyrs and the good people, who are all good company." Ask God for his mercy and be optimistic. . . .

9. Keep in mind that, if you fall into hardship, how will you act and how will you remain steadfast and remember that you will return to God and remember that anything that happens to you could never be avoided, and what did not happen to you could never have happened to you. . . .

10. Remember the words of Almighty God [lines from the Quran]: "You were looking to the battle before you engaged in it, and now you see it with your own two eyes." Remember: "How many small groups beat big groups by the will of God." And his words: "If God gives you victory, no one can beat you. And if he betrays you, who can give you victory without Him? So the faithful put their trust in God.". . .

12. Bless your body with some verses of the Quran [done by reading verses into one's hands and then rubbing the hands over whatever is to be blessed], the luggage, clothes, the knife, your

[1]These are ritual acts of self-purification to prepare oneself for martyrdom and salvation.
[2]The ninth and eighth chapters (surahs) of the Quran, some-

times referred to as the "war chapters"; they describe the need for holy war against Islam's persecutors.

personal effects, your ID, your passport, and all of your papers.

13. Check your weapon before you leave and long before you leave. (You must make your knife sharp and you must not discomfort your animal during the slaughter.) . . .

THE SECOND STEP

When the taxi takes you to (M) [this initial probably stands for *matar,* airport in Arabic] remember God constantly while in the car. . . .

When you have reached (M) and have left the taxi, say a supplication of place ["O Lord, I ask you for the best of this place, and ask you to protect me from its evils"], and everywhere you go say that prayer and smile and be calm, for God is with the believers. And the angels protect you without you feeling anything. Say this supplication: "God is more dear than all of his creation." And say: "O Lord, protect me from them as you wish." And say: "O Lord, take your anger out on them [the enemy] and we ask you to protect us from their evils." And say: "O Lord, block their vision from in front of them, so that they may not see." And say: "God is all we need, he is the best to rely upon.". . .

All of their equipment and gates and technology will not prevent, nor harm, except by God's will. The believers do not fear such things. The only ones that fear it are the allies of Satan, who are the brothers of the devil. . . . "This is only the Devil scaring his allies" who are fascinated with Western civilization, and have drunk the love [of the West] like they drink water . . . and have become afraid of their weak equipment "so fear them not, and fear Me, if you are believers.". . .

You must remember your brothers with all respect. No one should notice that you are making the supplication, "There is no God but God," because if you say it 1,000 times no one will be able to tell whether you are quiet or remember God. And among its miracles is what the proph-

et, peace be upon him, said: Whoever says, "There is no God but God," with all his heart, goes to heaven. The prophet, peace be upon him, said: "If you put all the worlds and universes on one side of the balance, and 'No God but God' on the other, 'No God but God' will weigh more heavily." You can repeat these words confidently, and this is just one of the strengths of these words. . . .

Also, do not seem confused or show signs of nervous tension. Be happy, optimistic, calm because you are heading for a deed that God loves and will accept [as a good deed]. It will be the day, God willing, you spend with the women of paradise. . . .

THE THIRD PHASE

When you ride the (T) [probably for *tayyara,* airplane in Arabic], before your foot steps in it, and before you enter it, you make a prayer and supplications. Remember that this is a battle for the sake of God. . . . When the (T) moves, even slightly, toward (Q) [unknown reference], say the supplication of travel. Because you are traveling to Almighty God, so be attentive on this trip. . . .

And then it takes off. This is the moment that both groups come together. So remember God, as he said in his Book: "Oh Lord, pour your patience upon us and make our feet steadfast and give us victory over the infidels.". . . Pray for yourself and all of your brothers that they may be victorious and hit their targets and [unclear] and ask God to grant you martyrdom facing the enemy, not running away from it, and for him to grant you patience and the feeling that anything that happens to you is for him.

Then every one of you should prepare to carry out his role in a way that would satisfy God. You should clench your teeth, as the pious early generations did.

When the confrontation begins, strike like champions who do not want to go back to this world. Shout, "Allahu Akbar" ["God is great"], because this strikes fear in the hearts of the non-believers. . . . Know that the gardens of paradise are waiting for you in all their beauty, and the women of paradise are waiting, calling out, "Come hither, friend of God." They have dressed in their most beautiful clothing.

If God decrees that any of you are to slaughter, you should dedicate the slaughter to your fathers . . . because you have obligations toward them. . . . If you slaughter, do not cause the discomfort of those you are killing, because this is one of the practices of the prophet, peace be upon him. . . .

Do not seek revenge for yourself. Strike for God's sake. . . . This means that before you do anything, make sure that your soul is prepared to do everything for God only.

Then implement the way of the prophet in taking prisoners. Take prisoners and kill them. As Almighty God said: "No prophet should have prisoners until he has soaked the land with blood. You want the bounties of this world [in exchange for prisoners] and God wants the other world [for you], and God is all-powerful, all-wise."

If everything goes well, every one of you should pat the other on the shoulder in confidence. . . . Remind your brothers that this act is for Almighty God. Do not confuse your brothers or distract them. He should give them glad tidings and make them calm, and remind them [of God] and encourage them. How beautiful it is for one to read God's words, such as: "'And those who prefer the afterlife over this world should fight for the sake of God." And his words: "Do not suppose that those who are killed for the sake of God are dead; they are alive. . . ." And others. Or they should sing songs to boost their morale, as the pious first generations did in the throes of battle, to bring calm, tranquility, and joy to the hearts of his brothers.

. . . When the hour of reality approaches, the zero hour . . . wholeheartedly welcome death for the sake of God. Always be remembering God. Either end your life while praying, seconds before the target, or make your last words: "There is no God but God, Muhammad is his messenger."

Afterward, we will all meet in the highest heaven, God willing. . . .

And may the peace of the God be upon the prophet.

▼▼▼

Globalization, Free Trade, and World Economic Development

Globalization became the buzzword of the 1990s, producing in little more than a decade a mountain of scholarship and commentary that sought to describe and de-mystify a concept that at best was poorly understood and often vaguely defined. Historians contributed to the discussion by pointing out that *globalization* — if the term is understood as the process by which different regions of the world come to mutually affect each other economically, politically, or culturally — is nothing new. Recent developments are the culmination of trends that began thousands of years ago and intensified in the last 500 years as a result of the European discovery of the

Americas, the increase in world trade, Europe's imperial expansion, the Industrial Revolution, and a long list of technological innovations ranging from the development of the caravel by European ship designers in the 1400s to the invention of the telephone and telegraph in the nineteenth century. Developments in the twentieth century further accelerated the process of globalization, especially in the 1990s, when the end of the Cold War signaled the triumph of free-market capitalism, and the Internet revolution made it possible for human beings around the globe to instantaneously find information, exchange ideas, transfer capital, make deals, and share cultures seven days a week, twenty-four hours a day.

Debates about the meaning and significance of globalization have been intense. Mainly a topic for politicians and academics throughout most of the 1990s, globalization grabbed international headlines in the fall of 1999 when tens of thousands of opponents of globalization disrupted a meeting of the executive council of the World Trade Organization (WTO) being held in Seattle. Subsequent well-publicized demonstrations against globalization took place at meetings of the WTO, the World Bank, the International Monetary Fund (IMF), the Group of Eight industrialized nations, and the World Economic Forum, an annual meeting of senior politicians and business leaders held in Davos, Switzerland. Antiglobalist protestors have an agenda with dozens of items ranging from specific policies of the World Bank and WTO to exploited labor, job loss, environmental degradation, the ethos of corporate greed, gender inequality, genetically engineered food, Third World poverty, the rights of indigenous people, the plight of small farmers, and much else. More so than any other topic, however, free trade has been at the center of the globalization debate.

Free trade as a means of encouraging economic growth has been advocated (and opposed) by economists ever since the Scottish moral philosopher Adam Smith made his famous defense of laissez faire in his *Wealth of Nations* of 1776 (see source 39). In the twentieth century free trade was embraced by the economists, business leaders, and politicians who met at the Bretton Woods Conference in New Hampshire in July 1944 to lay the foundation for the postwar international economy. Convinced that protectionism, universally practiced in the first half of the twentieth century, had hindered growth, inflated prices, sharpened national rivalries through trade wars, and contributed to the Great Depression, the delegates sought to create an institutional framework that would achieve economic growth by unleashing capitalism's full potential through free trade. They created the International Monetary Fund, which promotes monetary cooperation and exchange; the World Bank, which makes loans for economic development; and the General Agreement on Tariffs and Trade (GATT), which until it was replaced by the World Trade Organization in 1995 provided rules for settling trade disputes and negotiating reductions in tariffs and trade barriers.

Although tariffs decreased in the 1960s and 1970s as a result of a series of negotiations or "rounds" sponsored by GATT, free trade went out of favor in the 1970s and early 1980s when many states returned to protectionism in response to the worldwide economic slump. Beginning in the 1980s, however, with the backing of multinational corporations eager to tap into new markets and with the support of newly elected U.S. and European politicians dedicated to free-market principles, free trade made a comeback. In 1994 the eighth round of GATT-sponsored tariff discussions, the Uruguay Round, resulted in tariff reductions on a broad range of goods and services, including agricultural products. More important, it established the World Trade Organization, which from its headquarters in Geneva, Switzerland, was given authority to investigate grievances, settle disputes, and enforce rules. Also in 1994, Mexico, the United States, and Canada signed the North American Free Trade Agreement (NAFTA), which created a free-trade zone in North America.

Free trade was once more ascendant, and its supporters were confident that a new era of capitalist expansion was at hand. But free trade still had many opponents, and disagreements about its benefits and liabilities continue to be the focus of the larger debate about the future of globalization.

The first two selections in this section give a sense of the arguments made by the opponents and advocates of free trade. The third source presents a body of data on demographic and economic trends in states from different parts of the world and at different levels of economic development over the past twenty-five years. Such information provides a context for evaluating the strengths and weaknesses of arguments in the free-trade debate. More broadly, it provides insight into the economic record of the recent past and may inform our vision of what that record might include in the future.

The Dangers of NAFTA, GATT, and Free Trade

▼▼▼

121 ▼ *Ralph Nader,* *FREE TRADE AND THE DECLINE OF DEMOCRACY*

During the nationwide debate preceding the congressional vote on the North American Free Trade Agreement in December 1993, opponents denounced the treaty's economic, political, and environmental implications. A leading critic was Ralph Nader, a lawyer from Connecticut who in the 1960s emerged as a prominent consumer advocate when he published a book, *Unsafe at Any Speed,* about the dangers of flawed automobile design. In the 1970s and 1980s Nader rallied support for a wide range of consumer and environmental causes, and helped found organizations such as the Center for Study of Responsive Law, the Public Interest Research Group, Congress Watch, and the Tax Reform Group. In 2000 he ran for president on the Green Party ticket, receiving 3 percent of the popular vote. The following article was published in 1993 in an anthology, *The Case Against "Free Trade."*

QUESTIONS FOR ANALYSIS

1. According to Nader, why are multinational corporations so supportive of NAFTA and the new GATT proposals?
2. What will be the economic implications of NAFTA for the U.S. economy, according to Nader?
3. What, in Nader's view, are the potential political dangers of free trade?
4. Why is Nader convinced that there are "no winners" in free trade?
5. What is Nader's alternative to an international economy based on free trade?

Citizens beware. An unprecedented corporate power grab is underway in global negotiations over International trade.

Operating under the deceptive banner of "free" trade, multinational corporations are working hard to expand their control over the international economy and to undo vital health, safety, and environmental protections won by citizen movements across the globe in recent decades.

The megacorporations are not expecting these victories to be gained in town halls, state offices, the U.S. Capitol, or even at the United Nations. They are looking to circumvent the democratic process altogether, in a bold and brazen drive to achieve an autocratic far-reaching agenda through two trade agreements, the U.S.-Mexico-Canada free trade deal (formally known as NAFTA, the North American Free Trade Agreement) and an expansion of the General Agreement on Tariffs and Trade (GATT), called the Uruguay Round.

The Fortune 200's GATT and NAFTA agenda would make the air you breathe dirtier and the water you drink more polluted. It would cost jobs, depress wage levels, and make workplaces less safe. It would destroy family farms and undermine consumer protections such as those ensuring that the food you eat is not compromised by unsanitary conditions or higher levels of pesticides and preservatives.

And that's only for the industrialized countries. The large global companies have an even more ambitious set of goals for the Third World. They hope to use GATT and NAFTA to capitalize on the poverty of Third World countries and exploit their generally low environmental, safety,

and wage standards. At the same time, these corporations plan to displace locally owned businesses and solidify their control over developing countries' economies and natural resources. . . .

U.S. corporations long ago learned how to pit states against each other in "a race to the bottom" — to profit from the lower wages, pollution standards, and taxes. Now, through their NAFTA and GATT campaigns, multinational corporations are directing their efforts to the international arena, where desperately poor countries are willing and able to offer standards at 19th century American levels and below.

It's an old game: when fifty years ago the textile workers of Massachusetts demanded higher wages and safer working conditions, the industry moved its factories to the Carolinas and Georgia. If California considers enacting environmental standards in order to make it safer for people to breathe, business threatens to shut down and move to another state.

The trade agreements are crafted to enable corporations to play this game at the global level, to pit country against country in a race to see who can set the lowest wage levels, the lowest environmental standards, the lowest consumer safety standards. . . .

Enactment of the free trade deals virtually ensures that any local, state, or even national effort in the United States to demand that corporations pay their fair share of taxes, provide a decent standard of living to their employees, or limit their pollution of the air, water, and land will be met with the refrain, "You can't burden us like that. If you do, we won't be able to compete. We'll have to close down and move to a country that offers us a more hospitable business climate." This sort of threat is extremely powerful — communities already devastated by plant closures and a declining manufacturing base are desperate not to lose more jobs, and they know all too well from experience that threats of this sort are often carried out.

Want a small-scale preview of the post-GATT and NAFTA free trade world? Check out the U.S.-Mexico border region, where hundreds of U.S. companies have opened up shop during the last two decades in a special free trade zone made up of factories known as *maquiladoras*. . . . Here are some examples of conditions that prevail in the U.S.-Mexico border region:

- In Brownsville, Texas, just across the border from Matamoros, a *maquiladora* town, babies are being born without brains in record numbers; public health officials in the area believe there is a link between anencephaly (the name of this horrendous birth defect) and exposure of pregnant women to certain toxic chemicals dumped in streams and on the ground in the *maquiladoras* across the border. Imagine the effect on fetal health in Matamoros itself.
- U.S. companies in Mexico dump xylene, an industrial solvent, at levels up to 50,000 times what is allowed in the United States, and some companies dump methylene chloride at levels up to 215,000 times the U.S. standards, according to test results of a U.S. Environmental Protection Agency certified laboratory. . . .
- Working conditions inside the *maquiladora* plants are deplorable. The National Safe Workplace Institute reports that "most experts are in agreement that *maquila* workers suffer much higher levels of injuries than U.S. workers," and notes that "an alarming number of mentally retarded infants have been

born to mothers who worked in *maquila* plants during pregnancies."

In many instances, large corporations are already forcing U.S. workers and communities to compete against this Dickensian[1] industrialization — but the situation will become much worse with NAFTA and Uruguay Round expansion of GATT. . . .

Worst of all, the corporate-induced race to the bottom is a game that no country or community can win. There is always some place in the world that is a little worse off, where the living conditions are a little bit more wretched. . . .

. . . "Non-tariff trade barriers," in fact, has become a code phrase to undermine all sorts of citizen-protection standards and regulations. Literally, the term means any measure that is not a tariff and that inhibits trade — for instance restrictions on trade in food containing too much pesticide residue or products that don't meet safety standards. Corporate interests focus on a safety, health, or environmental regulation that they don't like, develop an argument about how it violates the rules of a trade agreement, and then demand that the regulation be revoked. . . .

. . . Already, a Dutch and several U.S. states' recycling programs, the U.S. asbestos ban, the U.S. Delaney clause prohibiting carcinogenic additives to food, a Canadian reforestation program, U.S., Indonesian, and other countries' restrictions on exports of unprocessed logs . . . , the gas guzzler tax, driftnet fishing and whaling restrictions, U.S. laws designed to protect dolphins, smoking and smokeless tobacco restrictions, and a European ban on beef tainted with growth hormones have either been attacked as non-tariff barriers under existing free trade agreements or threatened with future challenges under the Uruguay Round when it is completed. . . .

U.S. citizen groups already have enough problems dealing in Washington with corporate lobbyists and indentured politicians without being

---

[1] Many of the novels of the famous English writer Charles Dickens (1812–1879) focused on the bleakness of early factory life.

told that decisions are going to be made in other countries, by other officials, and by other lobbies that have no accountability or disclosure requirements in the country. . . .

To compound the autocracy, disputes about non-tariff trade barriers are decided not by elected officials or their appointees, but by secretive panels of foreign trade bureaucrats. Only national government representatives are allowed to participate in the trade agreement dispute resolution; citizen organizations are locked out.

. . . As the world prepares to enter the twenty-first century, GATT and NAFTA would lead the planet in exactly the wrong direction. . . . No one denies the usefulness of international trade and commerce. But societies need to focus their attention on fostering community-oriented production. Such smaller-scale operations are more flexible and adaptable to local needs and environmentally sustainable production methods, and more susceptible to democratic controls. They are less likely to threaten to migrate, and they may perceive their interests as more overlapping with general community interests.

Similarly, allocating power to lower level governmental bodies tends to increase citizen power. Concentrating power in international organizations, as the trade pacts do, tends to remove critical decisions from citizen influence — it's a lot easier to get ahold of your city council representative than international trade bureaucrats.

Free Trade *Is* the Answer

▼▼▼

122 ▼ Gary Burtless, Robert Z. Lawrence, Robert E. Litan, and Robert Shapiro, GLOBAPHOBIA. CONFRONTING FEARS ABOUT OPEN TRADE

The following defense of free trade was published in 1998 by four economists connected with the Brookings Institution in Washington, D.C. Founded in 1916 and named after a St. Louis businessman who was an early benefactor of the organization, the Brookings Institution maintains a program of research and publication on public policy issues in the areas of foreign relations, economics, and governance. With financial backing from dozens of large corporations and private philanthropists, it supports the work of approximately 100 scholars. Centrist and nonpartisan, its goal is to improve the performance of U.S. institutions and the quality of public policy by linking scholarship and decision-making.

QUESTIONS FOR ANALYSIS

1. What is the focus of the authors' arguments? Are there issues raised by Nader they ignore?
2. Conversely, do they make points that Nader failed to mention in his commentary?
3. List and briefly explain the benefits that according to the authors result from free trade.

4. The authors concede that some individuals will experience pain as a result of free trade. How and in what way will this occur?
5. In your view, who has made the stronger argument, Nader or the Brookings Institution scholars?

We have written this book to demonstrate that the fear of globalization — or "globaphobia" — rests on very weak foundations. . . .

First, the United States globalized rapidly during the golden years before 1973, when productivity and wages were growing briskly and inequality was shrinking, demonstrating that living standards can advance at a healthy rate while the United States increases its links with the rest of the world. . . .

Second, even though globalization harms some American workers, the protectionist remedies suggested by some trade critics are, at best, short-term palliatives and, at worst, harmful to the interests of the broad class of workers that they are designed to help. Sheltering U.S. firms from imports may grant some workers a short reprieve from wage cuts or downsizing. But protection dulls the incentives of workers and firms to innovate and stay abreast of market developments. As a result, its benefits for individual workers and firms are often temporary. Indeed, protection invites foreign exporters to leap trade barriers by building plants in this country — as foreign manufacturers of automobiles, automobile parts, film, and other products have done. We are not criticizing this result: the United States has a strong national interest in attracting foreign investors, who typically bring technologies and management practices that ultimately yield higher wages and living standards for U.S. workers. But the movement to the United States of foreign companies and their plants simply underscores how erecting barriers to imports is often fools' gold for those who believe that protection will permanently shelter jobs or the profits of employers.

Third, erecting new barriers to imports also has an unseen boomerang effect in depressing exports. . . . While higher barriers to imports can

temporarily improve the trade balance, this improvement would cause the value of the dollar on world exchange markets to rise, undercutting the competitive position of U.S. exports and curtailing job opportunities for Americans in export industries. Moreover, by increasing the costs of input (whether imported or domestic) that producers use to generate goods and services, protection further damages the competitive position of U.S. exporters. This is especially true in high-tech industries, where many American firms rely on foreign-made parts or capital equipment. The dangers of protection are further compounded to the extent it provokes retaliation by other countries. In that event, some Americans who work in exporting industries would lose their jobs, both directly and because higher barriers abroad would induce some of our exporting firms to move their plants (and jobs) overseas. In short, protection is not a zero-sum policy for the United States: it is a *negative sum* policy.

Fourth, globaphobia distracts policymakers and voters from implementing policies that would directly address the major causes of the stagnation or deterioration in the wages of less-skilled Americans. *The most significant problem faced by underpaid workers in the United States is not foreign competition. It is the mismatch between the skills that employers increasingly demand and the skills that many young adults bring to the labor market.* For the next generation of workers, the problem can be addressed by improvements in schooling and public and private training. The more difficult challenge is faced by today's unskilled adults, who find themselves unable to respond to the help wanted ads in daily newspapers, which often call for highly technical skills. It is easy to blame foreign imports for low wages, but doing so will not equip these workers with the new skills that employers need. The role of government is to help those who want to help themselves; most important, by maintaining a high-pressure economy that continues to generate new jobs, and secondarily, by facilitating training and providing effective inducements to displaced workers to find new jobs as rapidly as possible.

Fifth, Americans in fact have a vested interest in negotiating additional reductions of overseas barriers that limit the market for U.S. goods and services. These barriers typically harm the very industries in which America leads the world, including agriculture, financial services, pharmaceuticals, aircraft, and telecommunications. . . .

Sixth, it cannot be stressed too heavily that open trade benefits consumers. Each barrier to trade raises prices not only on the affected imports but also on the domestically produced goods or services with which they compete. Those who would nonetheless have the United States erect barriers to foreign goods — whether in the name of "fair trade," "national security," or some other claimed objective — must face the fact that they are asking the government to tax consumers in order to achieve these goals. And Americans must decide how willing they are to pay that tax. By contrast, lowering barriers to foreign goods delivers the equivalent of a tax cut to American consumers, while encouraging U.S. firms to innovate. The net result is higher living standards for Americans at home.

Finally, to ensure support for free trade, political leaders must abandon the argument traditionally used to advance the cause of trade liberalization: that it will generate *more* jobs. Proponents of freer trade should instead stick with the truth. Total employment depends on the overall macroeconomic environment (the willingness and capacity of Americans to buy goods and services) not on the trade balance. . . . We trade with foreigners for the same reasons that we trade among ourselves: to get better deals. Lower trade barriers in other countries mean *better* jobs for Americans. Firms in industries that are major exporters pay anywhere from 5 to 15 percent more than the average national wage. The "price"

for gaining those trade opportunities — reducing our own trade barriers — is one that Americans should be glad to pay.

In spite of the enormous benefits of openness to trade and capital flows from the rest of the world and notwithstanding the additional benefits that Americans would derive from further liberalization, it is important to recognize that open borders create losers as well as winners. Openness exposes workers and company owners to the risk of major losses when new foreign competitors enter the U.S. market. Workers can lose their jobs. This has certainly occurred in a wide range of industries exposed to intense foreign competition — autos, steel, textiles, apparel, and footwear. . . . In some cases, workers are forced to accept permanent reductions in pay, either in the jobs they continue to hold in a trade-affected industry or in new jobs they must take after suffering displacement. Other workers, including mainly the unskilled and semiskilled, may be forced to accept small pay reductions as an indirect effect of liberalization. Indeed, the job losses of thousands of similar workers in traded goods industries may tend to push down the wages of *all* workers — even those in the service sector — in a particular skill category.

We acknowledge that these losses occur. . . . Nonetheless, we believe the nation has both a political and a moral responsibility to offer better compensation to the workers who suffer sizable losses as a result of trade liberalization. . . . Decent compensation for the workers who suffer losses is easily affordable in view of the substantial benefits the country enjoys as a result of open trade. Liberal trade, like technological progress, mainly creates winners, not losers. Among the big winners are the stockholders, executives, and workers of exporting firms such as Boeing, Microsoft, and General Electric, as well as Hollywood (whose movies and television shows are seen around the world). There are many millions of more modest winners as well, including the workers, retirees, and nonworking poor, who benefit from lower prices and a far wider and better selection of products.

One problem in making the case for open borders is that few of the winners recognize the extent of the gains they enjoy as a result of free trade. The losses suffered by displaced workers in the auto, apparel, or shoemaking industries are vividly portrayed on the nightly news, but few Americans realize that cars, clothes, and shoes are cheaper, better made, or more varied as a result of their country's openness to the rest of the world. Workers who make products sold outside the United States often fail to recognize how much their jobs and wages depend on America's willingness to import as well as its capacity to export.

People contributing to a pension fund seldom realize that their returns . . . are boosted by the fund's ability to invest overseas, and almost no borrower understands that the cost of a mortgage or car loan is lower because of America's attractiveness to foreigners as a place to invest their money. All of these benefits help improve the standard of living of typical Americans, and they can be directly or indirectly traced to our openness. They are nearly invisible to most citizens, however; certainly far less visible than the painful losses suffered by workers who lose their jobs when a factory is shut down.

The Wealth and Poverty of Nations

▼▼▼

123 ▼ *World Bank,* *WORLD DEVELOPMENT INDICATORS, 2003*

The tables in this source provide insight into world economic relationships, the meaning of poverty, and the nature and size of the gap between developed and developing nations. These statistics were compiled by the World Bank, also known as the International Bank for Reconstruction and Development, one of many international organizations concerned with alleviating world poverty by encouraging economic development. Founded at the Bretton Woods Conference in 1944, the World Bank soon became affiliated with the newly established United Nations. Using funds subscribed by UN members, it advances loans to nations and private businesses for projects that further economic development. Although most loans at first went for postwar reconstruction projects, since the 1950s the bank mainly has supported loans for projects in developing areas. Since 1978 it has published annually its *World Development Report,* with commentary on development strategy and statistics on economic, demographic, fiscal, and educational trends. Since 2001 most of the statistical data have been published in a separate volume, *World Development Indicators.*

As is true with all historical evidence, the following data must be evaluated and interpreted. Take, for example, the category of "'Gross National Product per Capita," a number calculated by dividing a country's population into the Gross National Product (or Gross National Income), the value of all goods and services the economy produces. Such information gives a broad idea of a country's overall standard of living, but cannot be viewed as an accurate gauge of the prevalence of poverty. For this we would need further information about how a country's wealth is distributed. One would expect, for example, that in two countries with roughly similar GNPs per capita, Latvia (which is not included in the following tables) and Brazil, the incidence of poverty would be higher in Brazil, where people in the upper 20 percent income bracket receive 65 percent of all income, than in Latvia, where people in the upper 20 percent income bracket receive only 40 percent of all income. Similarly, data on the number of students attending postsecondary educational institutions tell us nothing about graduation rates or the quality of schools these students are attending. Even with these caveats, the information provided by the World Bank can reveal a great deal about how we as human beings live and where we may be heading.

QUESTIONS FOR ANALYSIS

1. What are the major population trends revealed in the tables?
2. To what extent do the tables reveal uneven development among the world's major regions?
3. Does the information in the tables suggest that the gap between rich and poor nations is getting larger or smaller?
4. For those nations that have not achieved significant economic progress, what insights do the tables provide into reasons for their lack of success?
5. What information do the tables provide on the relationship of economic growth and environmental quality?
6. On the basis of the information in the tables would it appear that things are getting better or worse for humankind?

World Bank Statistics

| | Population in Millions | | Percentage Urban Population | | Life Expectancy at Birth | | | | Mortality Rate under Age 5 per 1,000 Live Births | | Gross National Product per Capita (U.S. Dollars) | | |
| | | | | | | | Female | Male | | | | | |
	1976	2001	1980	2001	1960	1975	2001	2001	1980	2001	1976	1990	2001
Ethiopia	28.7	66.0	10	16	34	48	43	41	213	172	100	120	100
Mozambique	9.5	18.1	13	33	38	44	43	41	230	197	170	80	210
Mali	5.8	11.1	18	31	35	38	43	40	295	231	100	270	210
Uganda	11.9	22.8	9	15	43	50	43	43	180	124	240	220	280
Nigeria	77.1	129.9	27	44	34.	41	47	45	196	183	380	290	290
India	620.4	1033.4	23	28	42	50	64	62	173	93	150	350	460
Haiti	4.7	8.1	24	36	43	50	55	50	195	123	200	370	480
Indonesia	135.2	213.6	22	42	40	48	68	65	125	45	240	570	680
China	835.8	1271.9	20	37	51	62	72	69	64	39	410	270	890
Egypt	31.8	65.2	44	43	45	52	70	67	175	41	280	600	1530
Guatemala	6.5	11.7	37	40	44	51	68	62	139	58	630	900	1670
Iran	34.3	64.7	50	65	44	51	70	68	130	42	1930	na	1750
Colombia	24.2	43.0	63	75	55	61	75	69	56	23	630	1260	1910
Thailand	43	61.2	17	20	49	58	71	67	58	28	380	1420	1970
Turkey	41.2	66.2	44	66	49	57	72	67	133	43	990	1630	2540
Brazil	110	172.6	67	82	56	61	72	64	92	36	1140	2680	3060
Chile	10.5	15.4	81	86	56	63	76	70	39	12	1050	1940	4350
Mexico	62.0	99.4	66	75	56	63	76	60	74	29	1090	2490	5540
Korea, Republic of	26.0	47.6	57	61	53	61	77	70	18	5	670	5400	9400
Israel	3.6	6.4	89	92	68	71	81	77	19	6	3920	10,920	16,710
Canada	23.2	31.0	76	79	71	72	82	76	13	7	7510	20,470	21,340
United Kingdom	56.1	59.9	89	90	70	72	80	75	14	7	4020	16,100	24,230
Singapore	2.3	4.1	100	100	63	70	80	75	13	4	2700	11,160	24,740
United States	215.1	284.0	74	77	70	71	85	78	15	8	7890	21,790	34,870
Japan	112.8	127.1	76	79	67	73	85	78	10	5	4910	25,430	35,990
Switzerland	6.4	7.2	57	67	71	72	83	77	11	6	8890	32,680	36,970

na = not available

(continued)

World Bank Statistics *(continued)*

	Personal Computers per 1,000 People		Adult Illiteracy Rate % Ages 15 and Above				Carbon Dioxide Emissions			Access to Fresh Water % Population			
			Male		Female		Total Million Metric Tons		Per Capita Metric Tons	Urban		Rural	
	1997	2001	1990	2001	1990	2001	1980	1999	1999	1980	2000	1980	2000
Ethiopia	na	1.1	63	52	80	68	1.8	5.5	0.1	80	81	17	12
Mozambique	1.6	3.5	51	39	82	70	3.2	1.3	0.1	na	81	na	41
Mali	0.6	1.2	71	63	90	83	0.4	0.5	0.0	65	74	52	61
Uganda	1.4	3.1	31	22	57	42	0.6	1.4	0.1	81	80	40	47
Nigeria	5.1	6.8	41	27	62	42	68.1	40.4	0.3	83	80	40	47
India	2.1	5.8	38	31	64	54	347.3	1077.0	1.1	88	95	61	79
Haiti	na	na	57	47	63	51	0.8	1.4	0.2	59	48	50	45
Indonesia	8.0	11.0	13	8	27	17	94.6	235.6	1.1	92	90	62	69
China	6.0	19.0	13	7	31	21	1478.8	2824	2.3	99	94	60	66
Egypt	7.3	15.5	40	33	66	55	45.2	123.6	2.0	97	99	92	96
Guatemala	3.0	12.8	31	23	47	38	4.5	9.7	0.9	88	98	69	88
Iran	4.0	69.7	28	16	46	30	116.1	301.4	1.2	92	90	62	69
Colombia	33.4	42.1	11	8	12	8	39.8	63.6	1.5	98	99	84	70
Thailand	19.8	27.8	5	3	11	6	40	199.7	3.3	87	95	89	81
Turkey	20.7	40.7	11	6	34	23	76.3	198.5	3.1	83	81	72	86
Brazil	26	62.9	17	13	19	13	183.4	300.7	1.8	93	95	54	53
Chile	54.1	106.5	6	4	6	4	27.5	62.5	4.2	98	99	49	58
Mexico	37.3	68.7	9	7	16	11	252.5	378.5	3.9	90	95	52	69
Korea, Republic of	150.7	265.0	2	1	7	3	124.9	208.7	9.4	na	97	na	71
Israel	186.1	245.9	5	3	12	7	21.1	61.1	10.0	na	na	na	na
Canada	270.6	459.9	*	*	*	*	420.9	238.6	14.4	100	100	99	99
United Kingdom	242.4	366.2	*	*	*	*	580.3	539.3	9.2	100	100	100	100
Singapore	399.5	508.3	6	4	17	11	30.1	54.3	13.7	100	100	100	na
United States	406.7	625	*	*	*	*	4626.8	5495.4	19.7	100	100	100	100
Japan	202.4	348.8	*	*	*	*	3920.4	1155.2	9.1	100	100	100	100
Switzerland	394.9	540.2	*	*	*	*	40.9	40.6	5.7	100	100	100	100

na = not available; * = less than 3 percent

World Bank Statistics (continued)

	% of Relevant Age Group Enrolled in Postsecondary Education	
	1980	**2000**
Ethiopia	*	2
Mozambique	*	1
Mali	1	2
Uganda	1	3
Nigeria	0	3
India	5	10
Haiti	1	na
Indonesia	4	15
China	2	7
Egypt	16	39
Guatemala	17	na
Iran	*	10
Colombia	9	23
Thailand	15	35
Turkey	5	15
Brazil	11	17
Chile	12	38
Mexico	14	21
Korea, Republic of	na	na
Israel	29	53
Canada	57	60
United Kingdom	19	60
Singapore	8	na
United States	56	73
Japan	31	48
Switzerland	18	42

na = not available; * = less than 3 percent

Sources

Prologue

(1) From Cecil Jane, ed. and trans., *Selected Documents Illustrating the Four Voyages of Columbus,* 2 vols. (London: Hakluyt Society, 1930–1933), 1:2–18. Reprinted with permission of David Higham Associates. (2) Anonymous, Woodcut of 1511.

Part One ▼ The 1400s through the 1600s: A New Era of Human Interconnectedness

Chapter 1

Source 1: From *Self and Society and Ming Thought,* edited by Theodore de Bary (New York: Columbia University Press, 1970), pp. 352–361. Copyright © 1970 Columbia University Press. Reprinted with the permission of the publisher. **Source 2:** David J. Lu, *Japan: A Documentary History* (Armonk, NY: M. E. Sharpe, 1997), pp. 258–261. Reprinted by permission of the author. **Source 3:** From "The Merchant Network in 16th Century China," by Timothy Brook, *Journal of the Economic and Social History of the Orient,* XXIV, May 1981. Reprinted with permission of Brill Academic Publishers, The Netherlands. **Source 4:** Reprinted with the permission of The Free Press, a Division of Simon & Schuster Adult Publishing Group, from *Chinese Civilization and Society: A Sourcebook* by Patricia Buckley Ebrey. Copyright © 1993 by Patricia Buckley Ebrey. All rights reserved. **Source 5:** Ryusaka Tasunoda, William Theodore de Bary, Donald Keene, and others, *Sources of Japanese Tradition* (New York: Columbia University Press, 1958), pp. 117–200. **Source 6:** David John Lu, *Sources of Japanese History* (New York: McGraw-Hill, 1974), vol. 1, pp. 207–209. **Source 7:** From *China in the Sixteenth Century* by Matthew Ricci, translated by Louis J. Gallagher, S.J. Copyright © 1942, 1953 and renewed 1970 by Louis J. Gallagher, S.J. Used by permission of Random House, Inc. **Source 8:** *Records of the Relations between Siam and Foreign Countries in the Seventeenth Century* (Bangkok: Council of the Vajiranana National Library, 1916), vol. 2, pp. 10–14, 17–18.

Chapter 2

Source 9: Ogier Ghiselin de Busbecq, *The Life and Letters of Ogier Ghiselin de Busbecq* (London: Kegan Paul, 1881), pp. 113–120 (passim), 153–155, 218–220, 254. **Source 10:** From Fr. Paul Simon, *A Chronicle of the Carmelites in Persia and the Papal Mission of the XVIIIth and XVIII Centuries* (London: Eyre and Spottiswoode, 1939), I, 158–161. **Source 11:** David Price, trans., *Memoirs of the Emperor Jahanguir Written by Himself* (London: Oriental Translation Society, 1928), pp. 8–12, 13–20, 33–36, 51–53, 65–66. **Source 12:** John J. Saunders, ed., *The Muslim World on the Eve of Europe's Expansion* (Englewood Cliffs, NJ: Prentice-Hall, 1966), pp. 41–43. **Source 13:** Abul Fazl, *The Ain-i-Akari,* ed. and trans. by H. S. Jarrett (Calcutta, India: Baptist Mission Press, 1868–1894), vol. 3, pp. 8, 114–119, 159–160, 225–232, 279, 284, 285–286, 291–292. **Source 14:** From Judith E. Tucker, *In The House of the Law: Gender and Islamic Law in Ottoman Syria and Palestine.* Copyright © 1998 The Regents of the University of California. Reprinted with permission.

Chapter 3

Source 15: William Hazlitt, ed. and trans., *The Table Talk of Martin Luther* (London: H. G. Bohn, 1857), pp. 25–27, 117, 198, 205–206, 219, 294, 298, 300, 357, 359. **Source 16:** From Hans J. Schroeder, *Canons and Decrees of the Council of Trent* (St. Louis, MO: B. Herder, 1941), pp. 42–43, 273, 276–278, 175–176, 152–153, 253–254, 215–216. **Source 17:** (1) Hans Beham, *An Allegory of the Monastic Orders,* Albertina Museum, Vienna. (2) Anonymous, *A Mirror for the Blind,* by permission of the British Library. (3 and 4) Lucas Cranach, *Two Kinds of Preaching: Evangelical and Papal,* Bildarchiv Preussischer Kulturbesitz / Art Resource, NY. **Source 18:** Gomes Eannes de Azurara, *The Chronicle of the Discovery and Conquest of Guinea,* trans. Charles Raymond Beazely and Edgar Prestage, 2 vols. (London: Hakluyt Society, 1896), vol. 1, pp. 27–29, 83–85. **Source 19:** King Ferdinand and Queen Isabella, "Agreements with Columbus of April 17 and April 30, 1492," in J. B. Thatcher, *Christopher Columbus, His Life and Work,* 3 vols. (New York and London: Putnam's Sons, 1903), vol. 2, pp. 442–451. **Source 20:** Richard Hakluyt, "A Discourse of Western Planting," in Charles Deane and Leonard Woods, eds., *Documentary History of the State of Maine* (Collections of the Maine Historical Society, 2nd series, vol. 2, 1877). **Source 21:** From *Della Famiglia,* Guido Guarino, trans. and editor, 1971, pp. 120–124, 216–219. Reprinted by permission of Bucknell University Press. **Source 22:** (1) Erhard Schön, *No More Precious Treasure Is on the Earth Than a Gentle Wife Who Longs for Honor,* Courtesy of Schlossmuseum Gotha, Gotha, Germany. (2) Hans Sebold Beham, *A Nuremberg Couple Wooing,* Germanisches Nationalmuseum, Nürnberg. **Source 23:** From *Women Writers of the Renaissance and Reformation,* edited by Katharina M. Wilson, 1987, The University of Georgia Press, pp. 382–383. Reprinted with permission of The University of Georgia Press. **Source 24:** Excerpts from *Discoveries and Opinions of Galileo* by Galileo Galilei. Copyright © 1957 by Stillman Drake. Used by permission of Doubleday, a division of Random House, Inc. **Source 25:** James Spedding, R. L. Ellis, and Douglas Heath, eds., *The Works of Francis Bacon* (New York: Hurd and Houghton, 1864), vol. 10, pp. 67–69, 72–75, 131–132, 140–142.

Chapter 4

Source 26: From John Parry and Robert Keith, *New Iberian World,* Vol. 1, Times Books, 1984, pp. 246–249. **Source 27:** (1) A Benin Wall Plaque, Multiple Figures, Edo Peoples, Benin Kingdom, Nigeria, Photograph by Franko Khoury, mid 16th–17th century, copper alloy, H x W x D: 45.6 x 35 x 8.9 cm. Purchased with funds provided by the Smithsonian Collection Acquisition Program, National Museum of African Art, 82-5-3, Smithsonian Institution. (2) A Benin-Portuguese Saltcellar, Courtesy of the Trustees of the British Museum. **Source 28:** Basil Davidson, trans., *The African Past* (London: Curis Brown, Ltd., 1964). **Source 29:** George McCall Theal, ed. and trans. *Records of South-Eastern Africa* (London: F. W. Clowes for the Government of the Cape Colony, 1898), vol. 7, pp. 293–300. **Source 30:** The selections here from Book Twelve are translated from the Nahuatl by James Lockhart and appear in the book he edited, *We People Here: Nahuatl Accounts of the Conquest of Mexico,* University of California Press, 1993. Reprinted with permission of the author. **Source 31:** From David Pieterzen DeVries, *Voyages from Holland to America* (New York: Billin and Brothers, 1853), pp. 114–117. **Source 32:** From *The Spanish Tradition in America* by Charles Gibson, pp. 123–127. Copyright © 1968 by Charles Gibson. Reprinted by permission of HarperCollins Publishers, Inc. **Source 33:** From John Parry and Robert Keith, *New Iberian World,* Vol. 3, Times Books, 1984, p. 443. **Source 34:** Antonio Vazquez de Espinosa, *Compendium and Description of the West Indies* (Washington, DC: Smithsonian Institution, 1942), pp. 621–625, 629, 631–634.

Part Two ▼ A World in Transition, from the Mid Seventeenth Century to the Early Nineteenth Century

Chapter 5

Source 35: (1 and 2) Sébastien Le Clerc, *The Royal Academy and Its Protectors* and *A Dissection at the Jardin des Plantes.* Courtesy of The Bancroft Library, University of California at Berkeley. **Source 36:** From *Les Philosophes* by Norman L. Torrey, Copyright © 1960 by Norman L. Torrey. Used by permission of G. P. Putnam's Sons, a division of Penguin Group (USA) Inc. **Source 37:** Marquis de Condorcet, *Esquisse d'un tableau historique des progrès de l'esprit humain,* in *Oeuvres de Condorcet,* vol. 6 (Paris: Firmin Didot Frères, 1847), pp. 186–187, 223–225, 229–321, 237–244, 250–251, 255–256, 263–266, 272–276. **Source 38:** Jean-Baptiste Colbert, *Lettres, instructions et mémoires de Colbert* (Paris: Imprimerie Nationale, 1870), vol. 6, pp. 262–266; vol. 7, pp. 233–256. **Source 39:** Adam Smith, *An Inquiry into the Nature and Causes of the Wealth of Nations* (Hartford, CT: Cooke and Hale, 1818), vol. 7, pp. 10–12, 40, 43, 299–304, 316, 317, 319, 330, 331. **Source 40:** Marthe Blinoff, *Life and Thought in Old Russia* (University Park: Pennsylvania State University Press, 1961), pp. 49–50; Eugene Schuyler, *Peter the Great,* vol. 2, pp. 176–177; L. Jay Oliva, *Peter the Great* (Englewood Cliffs, NJ: Prentice-Hall, 1970), p. 50; George Vernadsky et al., *A Source Book for Russian History from Early Times to 1917,* vol. 2 (New Haven and London: Yale University Press, 1972), pp. 347, 329, 357. **Source 41:** From *On the Corruption of Morals in Russia* from M. M. Shcherbatov, A. Lenten, trans. and ed. Copyright © 1969 Cambridge University Press. Reprinted with the permission of Cambridge University Press. **Source 42:** *The Statutes: Revised Edition* (London: Eyre and Spottiswoode, 1871), vol. 1, pp. 10–12. **Source 43:** J. B. Buchez and P.-C. Roux, *Histoire parlementaire de la revolution française* (Paris: Librarie Paulin, 1834), vol. 1, pp. 335–354, trans. by J. Overfield. **Source 44:** "Declaration of the Rights of Man and of the Citizen," in J. B. Buchez and P.-C. Roux, *Histoire parlementaire de la revolution française* (Paris: Librarie Paulin, 1834), vol. 11, pp. 404–406. **Source 45:** (1) *The Present,* Bibliothèque nationale de France. (2) *The Past,* Bibliothèque nationale de France. (3) *I Really Knew We Would Have Our Turn,* Musée Carnavalet / Réunion des Musées Nationaux / Art Resource, NY. (4) *A Tenant Farmer in Drudgery,* Bibliothèque nationale de France. (5) *The Press,* Bibliothèque nationale de France. (6) *The Present,* Bibliothèque nationale de France. **Source 46:** Thomas Paine, *The Political Writings of Thomas Paine* (New York: Solomon King, 1830), vol. 1, pp. 21, 22, 25, 28, 29, 31, 33–35, 40–47. **Source 47:** From Simón Bolívar, *Selected Writings,* ed., Harold A. Bierck, Jr., trans. by Lewis Bertrand, 1951, pp. 103–122.

Chapter 6

Source 48: Paul Edwards, ed. and trans., *Equiano's Travels* (Oxford Heinemann Educational Books, 1967), pp. 25–42. **Source 49:** Thomas Phillips, "A Journal of a Voyage Made in the Hannibal of London in 1694," in Elizabeth Donnan, ed., *Documents Illustrative of the History of the Slave Trade to America* (Washington, DC: Carnegie Institute, 1930), pp. 399–410. **Source 50:** From Wright, Walter L., Jr., *The Book of Counsel for Viziers and Governors,* pp. 88–89, 95, 96, 102–106, 111, 112, 126. Copyright © 1935 by Princeton University Press. Reprinted by permission of Princeton University Press. **Source 51:** Robert Clive in a letter to William Pitt, in John Malcolm, *The Life of Robert, Lord Clive* (London: John Murray, 1836), vol. 2, pp. 119–125. **Source 52:** J. O'Kinealy, "Translation of an Arabic Pamphlet on the History and Doctrines of the Wahhabis, Written by 'Abdullah, Grandson of 'Abdul Wahhab, the Founder of the Wahhabis," Journal of the Asiatic Society of Bengal, vol. 43 (1874), pp. 68–82. **Source 53:** Usman dan Fodio, "The Book of Differences," from M. Hiskett, "Kitab al-farq: A Work on the Habe Kingdoms Attributed to Uthmann dan Fodio," in *Bulletin of the School of Oriental and African Studies,* vol. 23 (1960); "Concerning the Government of Our Country," from Tanbih al-ikhwan, translation in Thomas Hodgkin, *Nigerian Perpectives* (Oxford: Oxford

University Press, 1975), pp. 244, 245; "Light of Intellectuals," from Nur al-albab, in Hodgkin, pp. 254–255; "Dispatch to the Folk of the Sudan, from A. D. H. Bivar, "The Whatiqat ahl al-Sudan: A Manifesto of the Fulani Jihad," in *The Journal of African History,* vol. 2 (1961).

Chapter 7

Source 54: From *Emperor of China* by Jonathan D. Spence, pp. 29–30, 32–34, 40, 50, 51, 67, 75, 79–82. Copyright © 1974 by Jonathan D. Spence. Used by permission of Alfred A. Knopf, a division of Random House, Inc. **Source 55:** Sir Henry Dundas in a letter to Lord George Macartney, Cheng Pei-kai, and Michael Lestz, in *The Search for Modern China: A Documentary Collection* (New York: Norton & Co., 1999), pp. 92–98. **Source 56:** Emperor Qianlong, "Edict on Trade with Great Britain," in J. O. P. Brand, *Annals and Memoirs of the Court of Peking* (Boston: Houghton Mifflin, 1914), pp. 325–331. **Source 57:** Mitsui Takafusa, "Some Observations on Merchants," from "Some Observations on Merchants, a translation of Mitsui Takafusa's Choni Koken Roku," ed. and trans. E. S. Crawcour in *Transactions of the Asiatic Society of Japan,* Third series, vol. 8 (Tokyo, 1961), pp. 39–41, 49, 56, 57, 77, 78, 82, 103, 121. Reprinted by permission of The Asiatic Society of Japan. **Source 58:** Excerpts from Donald Keene, *The Japanese Discovery of Europe, 1720–1830,* Revised Edition. Copyright © 1952 and 1969 by Donald Keene. Used with the permission of Stanford University Press, www.sup.org. **Source 59:** Robert McNab, *Historical Records of New Zealand* (Wellington, New Zealand: Government Printing Office, 1908), vol. 1, pp. 417–421. **Source 60:** *House of Common Parliamentary Papers* (London: Her Majesty's Printing Office, 1839), enclosures no. 2 in "Copies of Extracts of Dispatches Relative to the Massacre of Various Aborigines of Australia in the Year 1838 and Respecting the Trial of Their Murderers," pp. 6–13.

Part Three ▾ The World in the Age of Western Dominance: 1800–1914

Chapter 8

Source 61: "Report from the Committee on the Bill to Regulate the Labour of Children in the Mills and the Factories of the United Kingdom," *British Sessional Papers,* vol. 15 (London, 1832), pp. 195, 196; "Second Report of the Commission of Inquiry into the Employment of Children in Factories," *British Sessional Papers,* vol. 21, pt. D-3 (London, 1833), pp. 26–28; "First Report of the Commission of Inquiry into the Employment of Children in Mines," *British Sessional Papers,* vol. 16 (London, 1842), pp. 149, 230, 258, 263–264. **Source 62:** Samuel Smiles, *Self-Help* (New York: Harper, 1897), pp. 21–23, 298–299, 302, 305; *Thrift* (London: John Murray, 1875), pp. 30–40. **Source 63:** Karl Marx and Friedrich Engels, *The Manifesto of the*

Communist Party, authorized English trans. by Samuel Moore (London: W. Reeves, 1888). **Source 64:** Charles Darwin, "On the Origin of Species and The Descent of Man" in Charles Darwin, *The Origin of Species* (New York: Appleton and Company, 1896), pp. 75–78; and Charles Darwin, *The Descent of Man* (New York: Appleton and Company, 1896), pp. 62–63, 164–165, 613, 616–617. **Source 65:** Gerda Lerner, ed., *The Female Experience: An American Documentation* (Indianapolis, IN: Bobbs Merrill, 1977), pp. 343–347. **Source 66:** Mrs. Humphry Ward, "An Appeal against Women's Suffrage," in *Nineteenth Century* (June 1899). **Source 67:** From Louis Snyder, *Documents of German History,* pp. 259–262. Copyright © 1958 by Rutgers, the State University. Reprinted by permission of Rutgers University Press. **Source 68:** From Theodor Herzl, *The Jews' State,* trans. and edited by Henk Overberg, 1977, pp. 123, 129, 130, 134, 135, 139, 140, 144–146, 148, 149, 196. Reprinted with permission of Jason Aronson, Inc. **Source 69:** Ralph Austen, ed., *Modern Imperialism* (Lexington, MA: D. C. Heath, 1969), pp. 70–73. Copyright © 1969. Used by permission. **Source 70:** (1–3) Mrs. Ernest (Mary Frances) Ames, *An ABC for Baby Patriots* (London: Dean & Son, 1899), pp. "N," "I," "W." Courtesy of de Grummond Children's Literature Collection, University of Southern Mississippi. (4) From *The Kipling Reader* (London: Macmillan, 1908), illus. by J. MacFarlane. By permission of the Houghton Library, Harvard University. (5) Lipton Teas ad from *Illustrated London News,* vol. XVI, no. 3058, November 27, 1897. Courtesy of The Illustrated London News Picture Library. (6–7) "On the Swoop," from *Punch,* 1894, Punch Cartoon Library & Archive and "Britannia and Her Suitors," from *Punch,* 1901.

Chapter 9

Source 71: Edward Hertslet, ed., *The Map of Africa by Treaty,* 2nd ed. (Her Majesty's Stationery Office, 1896), vol. 1, pp. 467–468. **Source 72:** From C. W. Newbury, *British Policy Towards West Africa: Select Documents 1875–1914* (Oxford: Clarendon Press, 1971), pp. 94–95. **Source 73:** Margery Perham, ed., *Ten Africans.* Copyright © 1936 by Faber & Faber. **Source 74:** E. A. Van Dyck, *Report upon the Capitulations of the Ottoman Empire since the Year 1150* (Washington, DC: United States Government Printing Office, 1881, 1882), Part 1, pp. 106–108. **Source 75:** Edward G. Brown, *The Persian Revolution of 1905.* Copyright © 1966 by Frank Cass & Co. Used with permission. **Source 76:** "Announcement to the Arabs" by Sylvia G. Haim, *Arab Nationalism: An Anthology* (Berkeley: University of California Press, 1962), 83–88. Selection and translation of text are made by her and copyrighted by her. **Source 77:** Rammohun Roy, *The English Works of Raja Rammohun Roy* (Allahabad, India: Panini Office, 1906), pp. 471–474. **Source 78:** "The Azamgarh Proclamation," in Charles Ball, *The History of the Indian Mutiny* (London: London Printing and Publishing, 1858–1859), vol. 2, pp. 630–632.

Chapter 10

Source 79: Dun J. Li, *China in Transition 1517–1911,* 1st edition. © 1969. Reprinted with permission of Wadsworth, a division of Thomson Learning: www.thomsonrights.com. Fax: 800-730-2215. **Source 80:** Dun J. Li, *China in Transition 1517–1911,* 1st edition. © 1969. Reprinted with permission of Wadsworth, a division of Thomson Learning: www.thomsonrights.com. Fax: 800-730-2215. **Source 81:** Reprinted from *Prescriptions for Saving China: Selected Writings of Sun Yat-sen,* edited by Julie Lee Wei, Ramon H. Myers, and Donald G. Gillin, with the permission of the publisher, Hoover Institution Press. Translation copyright 1994 by the Board of Trustees of the Leland Stanford Junior University. **Source 82:** From Charles Terry, unpublished master's thesis published in *Sources of Japanese Tradition* by Tsunodo, de Bary, and Keene, pp. 609–615. Copyright © 1951 Columbia University Press. Reprinted with the permission of the publisher. **Source 83:** David John Lu, *Sources of Japanese History* (New York: McGraw-Hill, 1974), vol. 2, pp. 42–45. **Source 84:** (1) *One of Commodore Perry's Black Ships,* Kurofune-Kan [Black Ship Museum], Kashiwazaki, Japan. Photograph courtesy of the International Society for Educational Information (ISEI). (2) *Commander Henry Adams,* Anonymous, 1853, Japan. "Visit of American Ships in Shimoda Harbor, Kaei VI (1853) with Commodore Perry, Officers and Men, etc." Handscroll in colors on paper. Gift of Mrs. Walter F. Dillingham (Given in Memory of Alice Perry Grew), 1960. HAA 2732.1. Courtesy of Honolulu Academy of Arts. (3) Kobayashi Kyochika, Fukuchi Gen'ichiro. The Metropolitan Museum of Art, Gift of Lincoln Kirstein, 1962 (JP3420). (4) Kanagaki Robun, *Hiking through the West,* Courtesy of the Library of Congress. (5) Honda Kinkichiro, *Monkey Show Dressing Room,* courtesy of the Library of Congress. (6) Kobayashi Kyochika, *Hands Dance, Feet Stomp, Call Out Hurrah!* (New York: John Weatherhill, 1986). Courtesy of the Library of Congress. **Source 85:** From Chomchai Prachom, *Chulalongkorn The Great,* Tokyo: Centre for East Asian Cultural Studies, 1965, pp. 52–56, 90–95. Reprinted with permission of The Toyo Bunko. **Source 86:** Letter to Emperor Tu Doc and Last Message to his Administration from *We The Vietnamese* by Francois Sully and Donald Kirk. Copyright © 1971 by Praeger Publishers Inc. Reprinted by permission of Henry Holt and Company, LLC.

Part Four ▼ Global Community and Its Challenges in the Twentieth and Twenty-First Centuries

Chapter 11

Source 87: (1) B. Hennerberg, *The Departure,* in *World War I and European Society: A Sourcebook,* by Marilyn Shevin-Coetzee and Frans Coetzee (Lexington, MA: D. C. Heath, 1995), p. 6. Copyright © 1995, Used by permission of D. C. Heath & Co. (2) Advertisement card from Golden Dawn Cigarettes, courtesy of Imperial War Museum, London. (3) Australian recruitment poster, courtesy of Imperial War Museum, London. (4) Septimus Scott, *These Women Are Doing Their Bit,* Courtesy of the Trustees of the British Museum. **Source 88:** H. S. Clapham, *Mud and Khaki: Memoirs of an Incomplete Soldier,* Hutchinson & Co., 1930, pp. 141–153. **Source 89:** Comments of the German Delegation to the Paris Peace Conference on the Conditions of Peace, from *International Conciliation,* October 1919 (no. 143), pp. 1208, 1210–1213, 1215–1222. **Source 90:** V. L. Lenin, *Collected Works,* vol. 5, (London: Lawrence and Wishart, 1973), pp. 352–353, 375–376, 399–401, 413–414, 425, 454, 463–467. **Source 91:** Joseph Stalin, "The Tasks of Business Executives" (Speech at the First All-Union Conference of Managers of Soviet Industry, February 1931), in *Problems of Leninism* (Moscow, 1940), pp. 359–360, 365–366. **Source 92:** Adolf Hitler, *Mein Kampf* (Munich: F. Eher Nachfolger, 1927), trans. by J. Overfield. **Source 93:** From *Sources of Japanese Tradition,* Vol. 2, by de Bary and Keene. Copyright © 1964 Columbia University Press. Reprinted with the permission of the publisher. **Source 94:** From *Japan: A Documentary History. Volume II: The Late Tokugawa Period to the Present,* ed. David J. Lu (Armonk, NY: M. E. Sharpe, 1997), pp. 418–420. Translation Copyright © 1997 by David J. Lu. Reprinted with permission of M. E. Sharpe, Inc. **Source 95:** From Rudolph Höss, *Death Dealer: The Memoirs of the SS Kommandant at Auschwitz* edited by Steven Paskuly. (Amherst, NY: Prometheus Books). Copyright (c) 1992. Reprinted with permission. **Source 96:** From "The Decision to Use the Atomic Bomb," by Harry L. Stimson. Copyright © 1947 by *Harper's Magazine.* All rights reserved. Reproduced from the February 1947 issue by special permission. **Source 97:** Iwao Nakamura and Atsuko Tsujioka, "Recollections from Arata Osada," in *Children of Hiroshima* (London: Taylor and Francis, 1981), pp. 173–175, 265–269.

Chapter 12

Source 98: (1) James Aggrey, "Parable of the Eagle," in Edward W. Smith, *Aggrey of Africa.* Copyright © 1929 by SCM Press. Used by permission. (2) From Léon G. Damas, *Pigments* (Paris: Presence Africaine, 1962). (3) From *The Collected Poetry of Leopold Sedhar Senghor,* Melvin Dixon, ed. and trans., 1991. Reprinted with permission of the University of Virginia Press. (4) From *Hammer Blows and Other Writings,* by David Diop. Copyright © 1973 Indiana University Press. Reprinted with permission. **Source 99:** Thomas Karis and Gwendolen M. Carter, eds., From *Protest to Challenge. A Documentary History of South Africa, 1882–1964,* Vol. 1 (Stanford, Calif.: Hoover Institution Press, 1972), 344–346. **Source 100:** Mustafa Kemal, *A Speech Delivered by Ghazi Mustapha Kemal* (Leipzig: F. F. Koehler, 1929), pp. 376–379, 589–594, 717, 721–722. **Source 101:** From Hasan al-Banna, "Towards the Light," in Robert Langdon, *The Emergence of the Middle East,* Van Nostrand, 1970. **Source 102:** Mohandas Gandhi, *Indian Home Rule* (Madras, India: Ganesh & Co., 1922), pp. 30–35, 47–50, 63, 64, 85, 68, 90, 91. Copyright © 1922. Used by permission of Ganesh & Co. **Source 103:** Harry Benda and John Larkin, *The World of Southeast Asia* (New York: Harper & Row, 1967), pp. 182–185. Copyright © 1967 by Harper & Row, Publishers. Reprinted by permission of the authors. **Source 104:** From Francisco Garcia Calderón, *Latin America: Its Rise and Progress,* Bernard Miall, trans., 1924, pp. 298, 301–303, 306, 311, 378–382. Reprinted with permission of A&C Black Publishers Limited. **Source 105:** Benjamin Keen, ed. and trans., *Readings in Latin American Civilization* (Boston: Houghton Mifflin, 1955), pp. 362–364. **Source 106:** Mao Zedong, *Selected Works* (New York: International Publishers, 1954). Reprinted by permission. **Source 107:** From *Masterpieces of Chinese Fiction,* by Lu Xun et al., 1983, pp. 482–493. Reprinted with permission of Foreign Languages Press.

Chapter 13

Source 108: George Kennan, "The Long Telegram," in Kenneth Jensen, ed. *Origins of the Cold War,* Kovikov, Kennan, and Roberts, "Long Telegrams of 1946," 1991. Reprinted with permission of Endowment of the U.S. Institute of Peace. **Source 109:** Nikolai Novikov, "Telegram, September 27, 1946," in Kenneth Jensen, ed. *Origins of the Cold War,* Kovikov, Kennan, and Roberts, "Long Telegrams of 1946," 1991. Reprinted with permission of Endowment of the U.S. Institute of Peace. **Source 110:** *Parliamentary Debates,* 5th ser., vol. 434 (London: His Majesty's Printing Office, 1947). **Source 111:** *Final Document of the Third General Conference of the Latin American Episcopate,* copyright © 1979 United States Conference of Catholic Bishops, Inc., Washington, DC. Used with permission. All rights reserved. **Source 112:** From Ruhallah Khomeini, *Islam and Revolution. Writings and Declarations of Imanm Kholeini,* Hamid Algar, ed. and trans., 1981, pp. 27–31, 33–36, 49–50, 120–121, 131–132. Reprinted with permission of Mizan Press/Islamic Publications International. **Source

113:** Girilal Jain, "On Hindu Rashtra," from Koenrad Elst, *Ayodhya and After* (New Delhi: Crescent Printing Works, 1991), pp. 364–367, 369–371, 373–375. Reprinted by permission of the author. **Source 114:** From *Third World, Second Sex,* by Miranda Davies, ed., 1983, pp. 217–220. Reprinted with permission of Zed Books, Ltd. **Source 115:** From *In Search of Answers: Indian Voices from Manushi,* by Madhu Kishwar and Ruth Vanitar, 1984. Reprinted with permission of Zed Books, Ltd. **Source 116:** Excerpts from Emily Honig and Gail Hershatter, *Personal Voices, Chinese Women in the 1980s,* pp. 204–205. Copyright © 1988 by the Board of Trustees of the Leland Stanford Jr. University. Reprinted with permission.

Chapter 14

Source 117: Deng Xiaoping, *Fundamental Issues in Present-Day China* (Beijing: Foreign Languages Press, 1987), 42–44, 69–72, 101–102, 105–109, 162–163. Pergamon Press. **Source 118:** From *Perestroika* by Mikhail Gorbachev. Copyright © 1987 by Mikhail Gorbachev. Reprinted by permission of HarperCollins Publishers, Inc. **Source 119:** "Declaration of Jihad against Americans Occupying the Land of the Two Holy Mosques," from http://azzam.com/html/articlesdeclaration.htm. **Source 120:** The original letter was translated by Capital Communications Group, Inc., Washington, DC. Reprinted with permission. **Source 121:** From *The Case Against Free Trade: GATT, NAFTA, and the Globalization of Corporate Power* by Ralph Nader *et al.,* published by North Atlantic Books. Copyright © 1993 by Earth Island Press. Reprinted by permission of the publisher. **Source 122:** From Gary Burtless, Robert Z. Lawrence, Robert E. Litan, and Robert Shapiro, *Globaphobia. Confronting Fears About Open Trade,* Washington DC, The Brookings Institution, Progressive Policy Institute, and Twentieth Century Fund, 1988, pp. 6–11. Reprinted with permission of The Brookings Institution. **Source 123:** From *World Development Indicators 2003* by World Bank. Copyright 2003 by World Bank. Reproduced with permission of World Bank via Copyright Clearance Center.

37156100326344

The human record